REASSESSING PALEOLITHIC SUBSISTENCE

The Neandertal and Modern Human Foragers of Saint-Césaire

EUGÈNE MORIN

Trent University, Canada

CAMBRIDGE
UNIVERSITY PRESS

CAMBRIDGE
UNIVERSITY PRESS

University Printing House, Cambridge CB2 8BS, United Kingdom

One Liberty Plaza, 20th Floor, New York, NY 10006, USA

477 Williamstown Road, Port Melbourne, VIC 3207, Australia

314-321, 3rd Floor, Plot 3, Splendor Forum, Jasola District Centre, New Delhi - 110025, India

103 Penang Road, #05-06/07, Visioncrest Commercial, Singapore 238467

Cambridge University Press is part of the University of Cambridge.

It furthers the University's mission by disseminating knowledge in the pursuit of education, learning and research at the highest international levels of excellence.

www.cambridge.org
Information on this title: www.cambridge.org/9781009125062

© Eugène Morin 2012

First published 2012
First paperback edition 2022

A catalogue record for this publication is available from the British Library

Library of Congress Cataloging in Publication data
Morin, Eugène, 1974–
Reassessing paleolithic subsistence : the Neandertal and modern human foragers of Saint-Césaire / Eugène Morin.
   p. cm.
Includes bibliographical references and index.
ISBN 978-1-107-02327-7 (hardback)
1. Paleolithic period – France – Saint-Césaire Rockshelter.   2. Neanderthals – France – Saint-Césaire Rockshelter.   3. Animal remains (Archaeology) – France – Saint-Césaire Rockshelter.
4. Hunting and gathering societies – France – Saint-Césaire Rockshelter.
5. Hunting, Prehistoric – France – Saint-Césaire Rockshelter.
6. Saint-Césaire Rockshelter (France)   I. Title.
GN772.22.F7M655   2012
569.9'8609364–dc23   2011040838

ISBN 978-1-107-02327-7 Hardback
ISBN 978-1-009-12506-2 Paperback

REASSESSING PALEOLITHIC SUBSISTENCE

The contribution of Neandertals to the biological and cultural emergence of early modern humans remains highly debated in anthropology. Particularly controversial is the long-held view that Neandertals in western Europe were replaced 30,000 to 40,000 years ago by early modern humans expanding out of Africa. This book contributes to this debate by exploring the diets and foraging patterns of both Neandertals and early modern humans. Eugène Morin examines the faunal remains from Saint-Césaire in France, which contain an exceptionally long and detailed chronological sequence, as well as genetic, anatomical, and archaeological evidence, to shed new light on the problem of modern human origins.

Eugène Morin is an Assistant Professor in the Department of Anthropology at Trent University in Canada. He has published articles in *Journal of Archaeological Science, Geoarchaeology,* and *PNAS* and serves on the editorial board of *Ethnobiology Letters.*

A Laure, Lucas, Charles, et Louis
pour leur amour, leur patience, et leur soutien

CONTENTS

Contents

LIST OF FIGURES

LIST OF TABLES

LIST OF APPENDICES

PROLOGUE

In 1999, I met with François Lévêque, then the Conservateur en Chef Honoraire du Patrimoine for the Poitou-Charentes area, in Poitiers, France, to discuss the possibility of studying Paleolithic materials from Saint-Césaire. Located in western France, this rockshelter has been the focus of relentless attention since 1979, when Lévêque's team unexpectedly discovered Neandertal skeletal remains associated with Upper Paleolithic artifacts within one of its layers. Despite this attention and the publication in 1993 of a monograph concentrating on the site, a decade later little anthropological information was available on the Saint-Césaire faunal assemblages, except for the EJOP occupation. During our meeting, it was decided that I would conduct an economically oriented analysis of the faunas from this site. Two years later, in 2001, I left Ann Arbor, Michigan, for the Université de Bordeaux I (Talence, France) to initiate the study of the sequence. The first days were particularly long and stressful. Shortly after, however, I made several new friends. Suddenly, the days became bright and much too short! Two stays, totaling sixteen months, were needed to complete the investigation of the selected occupations.

The data that I accumulated during my stays in Talence formed the basis of a dissertation, which I defended in 2004. My dissertation looked at foraging strategies across the Middle to Upper Paleolithic transition in western France. In the years that followed, I began to enlarge the scope of my analysis by including materials from other sites and other regions of Europe in the hope of publishing a monograph. In the early months of 2008, I read a thought-provoking paper published in 2006 by Jim O'Connell contrasting the diet breadth of late Neandertals and early modern humans. After reading it, I decided to reframe my analysis to test the productive ideas presented in that paper. The following twelve chapters summarize these efforts.

Generally, collecting large amounts of information involves much cooperation and help. This book is no exception. I first want to thank Bob Whallon, my advisor while at Michigan, for his support and inspiration. This book owes much to him.

My gratitude also goes to Norman Clermont, now retired from the Université de Montréal, who guided me through the early literature on human evolution. Norman's influence on this work is more profound than the preceding would suggest, however, as he introduced me, during my undergraduate years, to the exigencies of scientific thinking and data analysis. For this, I can never thank him enough.

I would also like to express my appreciation to John Speth, who spent countless hours discussing faunal problems with me. Many of the methods and ideas presented in this monograph were suggested or influenced by him.

The analysis of the Saint-Césaire materials was realized within the framework of human behavioral ecology. This approach has much to offer to anthropologists because it can be used to make constructive predictions on change in foraging patterns. I am indebted to Cédric Beauval, Jack Broughton, Michael Cannon, Jean-Christophe Castel, David Cochard, Luc-Alain Giraldeau, Donald Grayson, Keith Hunley, Emily Jones, Lee Lyman, Natalie Munro, Filipa Naughton, John Speth, and Aaron Stutz for critical comments made on the various chapters that build on this approach. These comments contributed significantly to improve the final manuscript.

The examination of the data was enriched by several discussions. Among many others, I would especially like to acknowledge the input from the following people: Ofer Bar-Yosef, Cédric Beauval, Anna Belfer-Cohen, Jean-Guillaume Bordes, Jean-Philip Brugal, Jean-Christophe Castel, Sandrine Costamagno, Catherine Cretin, Françoise Delpech, Sylvain Ducasse, Jean-George Ferrié, Federica Fontana, Jean-Luc Guadelli, John Hoffecker, Liora Horwitz, Jacques Jaubert, François Lacrampe-Cuyaubère, Mathieu Langlais, Véronique Laroulandie, Françoise Lavaud-Girard, Olivier Le Gall, Lluis Lloveras Roca, Jean-Baptise Mallye, Tiina Manne, Jean-Claude Marquet, Bruno Maureille, Liliane Meignen, Alexandre Michel, André Morala, Suzanne Münzel, Margherita Mussi, Marco Peresani, Damien Pesesse, Rivka Rabinovich, William Rendu, Hélène Rougier, Alfred Sanchis Serra, Britt Starkovich, Antonio Tagliacozzo, Ursula Thun-Hohenstein, Paola Villa, and João Zilhão. These discussions were most appreciated and often permitted to improve the text. David Cochard created Figure 4.1, whereas François Lacrampe-Cuyaubère provided help for some of the figures presented in Chapters 9 through 11. The Saint-Césaire photos (Figures 4.2–4.7, 5.1, as well as the left photo in Figure 4.9) were all taken by François Lévêque.

The subjects treated in this book sometimes required the help of specialists from other disciplines. I am indebted to Frank Miller (Canadian Wildlife Service), Serge Couturier (Ministère des Ressources Naturelles et de la Faune, Québec), Eigil Reimers (University of Oslo), and Jim Schaefer (Trent University) for sharing information on caribou and reindeer biology. Caroline Pond from the Open University (England) kindly provided unpublished data on fat composition in various species. Francisco Palomares from the Estación Biológica de Doñana (Spain) shed light on various environmental factors that could have affected rabbit behavior in the past. Similarly, María Fernanda Sánchez Goñi, Stéphanie Desprat – both associated with the Centre National de la Recherche Scientifique (Bordeaux, France) – and Filipa Naughton (Departamento de Geologia Marinha, Laboratório Nacional de Energia e Geologia, Lisbon, Portugal) offered valuable assistance while I was analyzing paleoclimatic data. This book has also benefited from suggestions made by Michael Cannon, James Conolly, Aaron Stutz, and, more particularly, Robert Whallon with respect to statistical analyses.

Funding for this research was provided by the National Science Foundation, the Social Sciences and Humanities Research Council of Canada, and the Fonds de Recherche sur la Société et la Culture (province of Québec). A postdoctoral fellowship funded by the Centre Interuniversitaire d'Études sur les Lettres, les Arts et les Traditions (CELAT, Université Laval) allowed me to make progress on the manuscript. In France, the financial and logistical support received from the Service Régional de l'Archéologie, Poitou-Charente, via Jean-François Baratin and his successor, Jacques Buisson-Catil, deserves special mention here. The faunal assemblages from Saint-Césaire were mostly unwashed and unlabeled when I received them. I would like to acknowledge the immense work by Nicolay Sirakov (son) and Tsenka Tsanova who prepared this material for study. Thanks also to Dominique Commelin, the librarian for the Economies, Sociétés et Environnements Préhistoriques (ESEP) research unit in Aix-en-Provence, for sending several papers published in poorly diffused journals. Jean-Claude Dubreuil and Françoise Coutton hosted me during my summer stays in France. Their support has been invaluable. Lastly, my extended appreciation goes to my former student Elspeth Ready for her thorough editorial work. Her patience, professionalism, and linguistic skills have been most appreciated.

Finally, in addition to my family, this book is dedicated to the memory of François Lévêque, who passed away while I was completing this book. His assistance, kindness, and amiability will never be forgotten.

1

THE RESEARCH PROBLEM

IN THE ANTHROPOLOGY OF HUMAN ORIGINS, FEW SUBJECTS HAVE STIMULATED AS much research or generated as much controversy as the Neandertals. Most debates have centered on the problem of their affiliation and interaction with early modern humans during the Middle to Upper Paleolithic transition, a period dated roughly between 40 and 30 thousand years ago (kilo-years ago or ka) in western Europe. Important cultural changes are recorded during this episode. Most notable are the emergence of art, personal ornaments, and elaborated bone technology; the diffusion of laminar (blade) and lamellar (bladelet) reduction sequences; the diversification of stone tool types; and the transfers of raw materials over large (>100 km) distances.

Today, it is universally accepted that Neandertals were the only human population present in western Europe during the Mousterian. The faunal evidence indicates that Neandertals primarily hunted large ungulates, with an emphasis on prime-aged individuals (Burke 2000, 2004; Grayson and Delpech 2003; Steele 2004; Morin 2008). The Mousterian Neandertals produced various Levallois-based industries, although several other concepts of core preparation, including blade reduction sequences, are also documented (Delagnes *et al.* 2007). In contrast, an overwhelming body of data indicates that modern humans were the only occupants of western Europe *after* the Middle to Upper Paleolithic transition, with the possible exception of Iberia, where Neandertal skeletal features are said to have persisted until *ca.* 30 ka (Hublin *et al.* 1995; Churchill and Smith 2000).

Although there is wide agreement on the taxonomy of the human occupants of western Europe before and after the Middle to Upper Paleolithic transition, there is little consensus on the nature of the biological and cultural changes associated with the transition itself. This book reexamines this transition, the study of which has produced contradictory, if intriguing, hypotheses about our relationship to Neandertals. Of special concern in this book is the issue of whether Neandertals and early modern humans differed appreciably in terms of foraging patterns.

Two models, based primarily on biological evidence, have arisen since the 1980s as solutions to the problem of modern human origins. The first, the *recent out-of-Africa model* or, more simply, the *replacement model*, asserts that modern humans emerged in Africa at least by 160 ka and spread into Eurasia to replace Neandertals and the other archaic *sapiens* (Stringer and Andrews 1988; Mellars 1996; Klein 2008). Authors supporting this model generally consider Neandertals to differ biologically and culturally from early modern humans, many viewing them as different species. A selective advantage favoring modern humans over Neandertals is usually put forward as one of the main causal mechanisms that permitted the replacement of the archaic *sapiens* populations.

Replacement scenarios differ from most other archaeological hypotheses because they imply the coexistence of two human species or semi-species, a situation that has no close analogue today. Because Neandertals and early modern humans are extinct populations, hypotheses about their interaction in the Late Pleistocene must be based on indirect evidence, such as human skeletal remains, ancient DNA, lithic assemblages, and archaeofaunas. As a result, linking the static archaeological remains with current observable phenomena is critical to our understanding of the Middle to Upper Paleolithic transition.

The second model, known as the *multiregional model*, posits that Neandertals were connected with early modern humans through gene flow and that they contributed to the gene pool of subsequent populations (Thorne and Wolpoff 1981; Wolpoff 1999). Partisans of this model also assert that Neandertals were a small *Homo sapiens* population found at the periphery of the human distribution. In response to local evolutionary pressures, Neandertals are argued to have developed characteristics that distinguished them from other, more centrally located populations with which they exchanged genes.

These two polarized hypotheses about Neandertal and modern human relationships have generated considerable debate and research. Numerous tests of the models just described, including several studies that favor intermediate positions (e.g., Eswaran *et al.* 2005; Trinkaus 2007), have been published in an attempt to shed light on the origins of modern humans in Eurasia. These tests are mostly based on human fossils or genetic evidence (e.g., White *et al.* 2003; Noonan *et al.* 2006). However, many of these tests are unsatisfactory because they do not incorporate the full range of archaeological, skeletal, and genetic data.

Little comparable effort has been made in archaeology, although some have attempted to explain the Middle to Upper Paleolithic transition from the perspective of changes in technology, social organization, ecology, cognitive abilities, or a combination of these (Binford 1982; White 1982; Whallon 1989; Otte 1990; Bar-Yosef 1994; Lieberman and Shea 1994; Mellars 1996; d'Errico *et al.* 1998; Gamble 1999; Conard and Bolus 2003; Klein 2003; Kuhn and Stiner 2006; O'Connell 2006; Zilhão 2007; Stiner and Kuhn 2009). An important issue in several archaeological analyses of the transition concerns similarities in material production. A number of partisans of the replacement model have emphasized processes of emulation and acculturation to explain the similar sets of artifacts found in Neandertal and modern human assemblages (e.g., Demars and Hublin 1989; Mellars 1996). However, this issue remains highly controversial (d'Errico *et al.* 1998; Zilhão *et al.* 2010). This last debate highlights the fact that there is little agreement on what differentiated these groups from a behavioral viewpoint. This includes their dietary patterns.

FRAMING THE PROBLEM: DID NEANDERTALS AND EARLY MODERN HUMANS DIFFER IN TERMS OF FORAGING BEHAVIORS?

It is fair to say that despite recent advances in the interpretation of human behavioral and demographic change in the Late Pleistocene, little progress has been made recently toward a cogent explanation of the Middle to Upper Paleolithic transition. This atmosphere has provided fertile ground for the production of post hoc accommodative arguments. In general, a failure to address basic contradictions in results obtained from sister disciplines (e.g., molecular anthropology versus archaeology) seems to explain this lack of success. To remedy this problem, a reevaluation of our interpretive models concerning the evolution of Neandertals and early modern humans is in order.

This book is a step in this direction. The present study examines the replacement model, which argues for a recent demic expansion of modern humans out of Africa. In this book, *demic expansion* is defined as a group of interbreeding individuals that expands numerically and geographically. More specifically, the next chapters investigate O'Connell's (2006) proposition that modern humans responded to competition by broadening their diet, in contrast to Neandertals. According to O'Connell (2006), this strategy allowed modern humans to sustain higher population densities than could be maintained by the archaic *sapiens*, which would have provided the former groups with a demographic advantage during the expansion process. Because O'Connell's model makes unambiguous predictions about diet breadth, it should be possible to test the faunal implications of his proposition using materials derived from the archaeological record. For simplicity, O'Connell's model is referred to hereafter as the *early Upper Paleolithic intensification hypothesis*, or simply, the *intensification hypothesis*.

The faunal predictions examined in the present analysis build on earlier (e.g., Binford 1978; Speth 1983; O'Connell *et al.* 1988) and more recent (Barlow and Metcalfe 1996; Bird 1997; Broughton 1999; Stiner and Munro 2002; Cannon 2003; Grayson and Delpech 2003; Jones 2004a; Nagaoka 2005; O'Connell 2006; Speth and Clark 2006; Bliege Bird and Bird 2008; Wolverton 2008) archaeologically-oriented studies of resource exploitation by human foragers. The dietary implications of O'Connell's (2006) model are scrutinized here from the standpoint of foraging theory, the strength of which is found in the existence of universals of predator-prey dynamics and a large body of observations on decision making in the context of resource use (MacArthur and Pianka 1966; Charnov 1976; Stephens and Krebs 1986; Danchin *et al.* 2005; Stephens *et al.* 2007). One important quality of this approach is that it can be used to formulate testable theories of human foraging behavior (Winterhalder and Smith 2000; Bird and O'Connell 2006).

A critical implication of the intensification hypothesis is that Neandertals and early modern humans differed in terms of diet breadth. To test this hypothesis, the exceptionally long and detailed sequence of Saint-Césaire, a stratified site in central western France, was selected. This site is well-suited to this task because it contains eight faunal assemblages spanning a significant portion of the Middle to Upper Paleolithic transition. Evidence for changes in diet breadth in the Saint-Césaire assemblages might bring support for O'Connell's hypothesis. However, interpreting diet breadth in the archaeological record is not a straightforward task because several factors, including climate change, technological innovation, seasonality, group composition, and occupation intensity, may affect its interpretation (Hill *et al.* 1987; Grayson and Cannon 1999; Zeanah 2004). Therefore, these factors must be controlled for. Lastly, it is worth stressing that even though the test is applied to a site from western Europe, the same approach is potentially applicable to other regions as well.

ORGANIZATION OF THE BOOK

Before proceeding to the analysis of the Saint-Césaire faunas, it is useful to set the replacement and multiregional models in their historical context, as viewed from the angles of genetics, paleoanthropology, and archaeology. This historical outlook paves the way to a discussion of the theoretical underpinnings of the intensification hypothesis and to how this proposition can be meaningfully applied to the faunal record of Saint-Césaire. These aspects of the research problem are discussed in Chapters 2 and 3.

The focal points of Chapters 4 through 7 consist of a presentation of archaeological research at Saint-Césaire and of a description of the faunal samples. This includes an overview of the site's stratigraphy and chronology, as well as an in-depth analysis of the taphonomic processes that modified the composition of the faunal samples. These chapters also address the issue of the respective contribution of humans and carnivores to the faunal accumulations and the problem of occupational mixing. Lastly, these chapters investigate seasonality patterns in the assemblages, a factor that can affect the interpretation of diet breadth. The methods employed for that purpose, some of which are new, are used to identify the modal seasons of prey procurement throughout the sequence.

The last set of chapters (8–12) begins with an investigation of transport decisions at Saint-Césaire and is followed by a confrontation of the dietary predictions of the intensification hypothesis with the faunal assemblages. The results from this test lay the ground for an extensive literature review, which is carried out in Chapter 10, of the evidence for dietary change in coeval sequences from Europe and Southwest Asia. In contrast, Chapter 11 switches from a spatial to a temporal perspective and examines factors that appear to have mediated variations in diet breadth in western France throughout the Late Pleistocene. In the final chapter, the conclusions that emerged from these analyses of foraging patterns are evaluated in light of current debates about biological and cultural changes during the Middle to Upper Paleolithic transition.

2

HUMAN ORIGINS AND THE PROBLEM OF NEANDERTALS

THE "NEANDERTAL PROBLEM" HAS LONG FASCINATED BOTH THE SCIENTIFIC community and the public. To satisfy this insatiable interest, excellent historical reviews of ideas about modern human evolution have appeared over the years, the most comprehensive ones being those of Grayson (1983) and Trinkaus and Shipman (1993). Because the goal of this book is not to provide a detailed historiographic analysis of the Neandertal problem but rather to test key ideas about dietary change across the Middle to Upper Paleolithic transition, only a cursory examination of the development of this research is provided. The reader is invited to consult the foregoing references for additional information. Specifically, this chapter provides a discussion on the historical development of the demic expansion model and synthesizes recent information collected by anthropologists and geneticists about the nature of the presumed interactions between Neandertals and early modern humans. This review highlights contradictions between the models and the data that lay the ground for the formulation of an archaeological test of the demic expansion hypothesis. This test is presented at the end of this chapter.

TWENTIETH-CENTURY THOUGHT AND THE EMERGENCE
OF THE REPLACEMENT MODEL

The idea that Neandertals were replaced as a result of a dispersal event can be traced back at least to the beginning of the twentieth century and the work of scholars such as Boule (1908, 1923), Sollas (1911), Verneau (1913), Peyrony (1933, 1934), Garrod (1938), and Breuil and Lantier (1951). Despite differences in interpretation, propositions made by these scholars were similar in relying heavily on diffusion and migration to explain the demise of Neandertals. These concepts were then widely, and often abusively, used in anthropology (Trigger 1989). As noted by Trigger (1989), the belief that cultural behavior was biologically determined, combined with disenchantment about the benefits of industrial development, generated overall skepticism about human creativeness during the early twentieth century. The assumption was that humans are innately resistant to change and that independent evolution of particular cultural features was unlikely in the past. In this framework, Paleolithic "cultures" were perceived as relatively stable constructs. Consequently, industrial sequences were generally interpreted as reflecting the replacement of one "culture" by another at a more "advanced" stage of development (e.g., Sollas 1911; Breuil and Lantier 1951). A brief example taken from one of the most respected Paleolithic experts of his times, Denis Peyrony, will illustrate the view that permeated many of these early studies.

Peyrony (1933, 1934) attributed changes during the Middle to Upper Paleolithic transition to two episodes of migration. For him, the Châtelperronian (*ca.* 39–36 ka), the earliest Upper Paleolithic industry in France, coincided with a westward expansion of oriental modern humans who replaced the local Mousterian Neandertals. In contrast, Peyrony (1934) saw both similarities and differences between the Châtelperronian and the Aurignacian, which he interpreted as reflecting "contacts" between a recently arrived *Homo sapiens* population and a novel population of migrants from the same species. Indeed, his observations led him to wonder "whether the men from La Ferrassie (the 'Châtelperronians') had contacts with the first Cro-Magnons (the 'Aurignacians') who arrived in the Vézère valley, and whether these contacts could not have been a cause for the relatively rapid transformation of the toolkit" (Peyrony 1934:42; translation by the author). Although this short excerpt does not do justice to the diversity of views that were expressed during that period (some, such as Hrdlička [1927] and Weidenreich [1947], were more favorable to a gradual evolution of Neandertals into modern humans), Peyrony's view of the early Upper Paleolithic was typical in that it downplayed local processes of change.

In the 1950s and 1960s, scholars became increasingly discontented with diffusion and migration as explanatory mechanisms for change (Trigger 1989). The postulates that cultural behavior is determined by biology and that specific innovations rarely emerged more than once in prehistory were severely criticized and challenged. Under the impulse of the *new physical anthropology* of Sherwood Washburn (1951) and the *new archaeology* of Lewis Binford (1962), the focus shifted from the documentation of "culture" diffusion and population replacement to systemic explanations based on quantitative methods, deductive reasoning, and evolutionary thinking (Bettinger 1991; Trinkaus and Shipman 1993). In Paleolithic research, these new perspectives prefaced the emergence of gradualist views of modern human evolution (Brace 1964; Brose and Wolpoff 1971) and of more sophisticated versions of the replacement model (Stringer 1974; Howells 1976). This last camp included an influential archaeologist: François Bordes.

Bordes, Peyrony's pupil, spent a considerable portion of his career working on Neandertal stone tool productions. His views on biological and cultural evolution in the Late Pleistocene are laid out in a volume that he edited after a symposium on human origins held in Paris (Bordes 1972a, 1972b). Although he rejected the hyper-diffusionism of Breuil and Garrod, approaches that he attributed to a lack of empirical data and to an inappropriate use of historical analogies, Bordes did not completely dismiss population replacement as a cause of change. Bordes firmly believed that two distinct biological populations, the Neandertals and the Pre-*sapiens* (ancestral modern humans), occupied France throughout the Mousterian, a view also held by a few biological anthropologists (e.g., Vallois 1949). With respect to the early Upper Paleolithic, Bordes assumed that the Pre-*sapiens* were the makers of the Châtelperronian and that a *foreign* population of modern humans was the author of the Aurignacian.

Bordes (1961:808) described the Aurignacians as "oriental" modern humans who migrated to France with a "well-developed culture" that allowed them to replace the "occidental" modern humans associated with the Châtelperronian. Bordes thought that the purported "inter-stratifications" of Châtelperronian and Aurignacian industries at

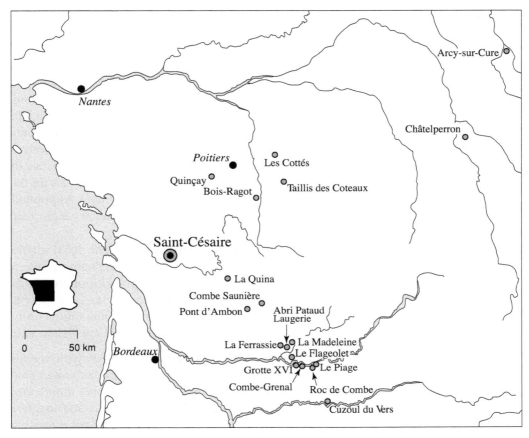

FIGURE 2.1. Location of Saint-Césaire and some other important sites cited in the text.

Le Piage, Roc de Combe, and El Pendo brought support to his replacement model (Bordes and Labrot 1967; Champagne and Espitalié 1967; Bordes 1984). These inter-stratifications, including those recently reported at the Châtelperron type-site (Gravina *et al*. 2005), are now known to be based on incorrect observations and redeposited materials (d'Errico *et al*. 1998; Bordes 2002; Zilhão *et al*. 2007). However, it was a discovery made in 1979 in Charente-Maritimes, France, that first cast strong doubts on Bordes's proposition.

SAINT-CÉSAIRE AND THE UPPER PALEOLITHIC NEANDERTALS

In the seventies, modern humans were nearly universally considered the sole makers of Upper Paleolithic industries in Europe, including the Châtelperronian. Indeed, few scholars believed that Neandertals contributed to innovations such as the production of personal ornaments or the emergence of bone tool technology, which were regarded as hallmarks of the Aurignacian expansion (Trinkaus and Shipman 1993). This view was, in part, discredited in July 1979 when a Neandertal skeleton was uncovered associated with a number of Châtelperronian objects in a site locally known as "la Roche à Pierrot" near the city of Saint-Césaire (Figure 2.1) in western France (Lévêque and Vandermeersch

1980). This association, unanticipated at the time of the discovery, profoundly modified the then-prevailing views about the advent of the early Upper Paleolithic.

The Saint-Césaire discovery caused a paradigm shift by changing the identity of the Châtelperronians from modern humans to Neandertals, which constituted a fatal blow to the Pre-*sapiens* hypothesis (Trinkaus and Shipman 1993). The implication of this new identity was far-reaching: Neandertals *did* contribute to the Upper Paleolithic. For many, this finding forced a reappraisal of Neandertal cognitive abilities and made claims for behavioral differences between archaic *sapiens* and early modern humans less compelling. Some supporters of the replacement model took a different perspective on the problem and argued for a Neandertal "acculturation" to explain similarities in cultural behavior between the Châtelperronian and the Early Aurignacian, not unlike Peyrony had done sixty years earlier (Demars and Hublin 1989; Mellars 1996). As pointed out earlier, this interpretation is highly debated (d'Errico *et al.* 1998; Mellars *et al.* 1999; Conard and Bolus 2003).

Wolpoff and his collaborators (Thorne and Wolpoff 1981; Wolpoff et *al.* 1984) saw in the Saint-Césaire finding evidence for the local evolution of Neandertals into modern humans. This view became known as the multiregional model, a proposition that finds its roots in the gradualist models of Weidenreich (1947) and Brace (1964). Gene flow is presented in the multiregional model as the principal mechanism that maintained unity between African and Eurasian populations throughout the Middle and Late Pleistocene:

> Multiregional Model posits that humans evolved as an interconnected polytypic species from a single origin in Africa some 2 myr ago. The small population effects during initial colonizations as humans expanded out of Africa helped establish regional differences, some of which were subsequently maintained through isolation-by-distance and adaptive variation. Advantageous changes spread widely because of genic exchanges across the interconnected network of populations. (Wolpoff 1999:543)

The multiregional model attributes the maintenance of regional differences between the interconnected human populations to a "center-and-edge" effect (Thorne 1981). According to this hypothesis, early modern human groups from Africa – a region then located at the center of the human range – were associated with patterns of gene flow, drift, and local selection that differed from those encountered by populations at the periphery. Indeed, because the center of a range usually provides optimal habitat conditions, more variation can be tolerated. Central populations will therefore tend to be larger and in more frequent contact with each other, conditions that promote gene flow and counter genetic drift. In contrast, at the periphery, less-than-ideal ecological conditions increase selective pressures on variation. In addition, the presumably small population sizes of colonizer groups at the fringes of the range are conducive to partial isolation, which favors the loss of variation and the emergence of novel adaptive features as new habitat conditions are encountered. As a result, the multiregional model predicts that skeletal homogeneity will be greater in peripheral than in central populations. Data from central Europe, and more particularly southeastern Asia and Australia, were argued to be in agreement with these views (Smith 1982; Wolpoff et *al.* 1984; Hawks *et al.* 2000).

At the same time that these propositions were being made, a new player – human genetics – came to the forefront of the debates on modern human origins. Brown (1980) performed one of the first genetic analyses focusing on this problem. He argued that variation in the mitochondrial DNA (mtDNA, an organelle in the cell membrane that contains a short sequence of DNA) of living humans indicates that modern populations went through a severe "population constriction" around 180 to 360 ka, a scenario that became known as the *garden of Eden* hypothesis. Following Brown's lead, Cann and her associates proposed, in 1987, a second model of modern human origins. These authors stated that current mtDNA diversity reflects a severe bottleneck in population size around 200 ka and concluded that this phenomenon was accompanied by the replacement of archaic populations by a newly emerged and rapidly expanding African population: anatomically modern *Homo sapiens* (Cann *et al.* 1987:35–36). This model, dubbed the *mitochondrial Eve hypothesis*, was claimed to provide strong support for the replacement model.

In the Near East, the early dates (≈100 ka) that were then being published for some Mousterian assemblages containing modern human skeletons were received with a good deal of skepticism by supporters of the multiregional model because they were not consistent with a gradual model of *Homo sapiens* emergence (Valladas *et al.* 1988). Building on these and the molecular findings, Stringer and Andrews (1988) gave new impetus to the replacement model by positing that modern humans arose early in Africa and later spread to Eurasia where they supplanted the local populations. Importantly, these authors argued that the replacement process occurred without significant interbreeding. Several empirical predictions were derived from these propositions:

> The model of a recent African origin . . . predicts different patterns of variation comparing African populations and those from elsewhere. Variation should be greatest within African populations (based on their earlier divergence, and assuming predominantly neutral genetic change), and they should be sharply distinguished in gene frequencies from non-African populations. Transitional fossils would not occur outside the African area of origin, and population replacement would represent the mode of establishment of *Homo sapiens* in other areas. The earliest record of *Homo sapiens* fossils should occur in the continent of origin of the species (Africa), and the youngest records at the peripheries of the radiation. Population relationships in Europe, Asia, and Australasia would approximate those of the Holocene only in the later Pleistocene. (Stringer and Andrews 1988:1264)

The approximately 160,000-year-old early modern human remains found in 1997 at Herto in the Middle Awash in Ethiopia (White *et al.* 2003) are important in this respect because they were said to corroborate this view (Stringer 2003).

The *assimilation model*, a variant of the earlier *hybridization model* (Bräuer 1981), incorporates elements from the replacement and multiregional positions in suggesting that the demic expansion of modern humans into Eurasia was accompanied by admixture with archaic *sapiens* (Smith *et al.* 1989; Eswaran *et al.* 2005; Trinkaus 2005, 2007). In general, the assimilation model is similar to the replacement model, with which it differs only relative to the extent of gene flow inferred to have taken place (virtually none in the replacement model, some in the hybridization model). The discovery of "hybrid" specimens in Romania (Trinkaus *et al.* 2003; Soficaru *et al.* 2006, 2007; Rougier *et al.* 2007) and at Lagar Velho in Portugal (Duarte *et al.* 1999), as well as molecular evidence for gene flow between archaic *sapiens* and early modern humans (e.g., Garrigan *et al.* 2005b; Evans *et al.* 2006; Garrigan and Hammer 2006; Hayakawa *et al.* 2006; Green *et al.* 2010), have been presented in support of this model.

CURRENT ISSUES IN THE MODERN HUMAN ORIGINS DEBATE

As we have seen, before the rise of the *new archaeology*, major changes in the archaeological record of western Europe – for instance, between the Châtelperronian and the Aurignacian or the Gravettian and the Solutrean – were generally perceived as evidence for large-scale migrations and physical replacement of local populations. In the sixties, many of these hypotheses were substituted by models emphasizing local continuity. However, the assumption that the Aurignacian constitutes a migration and replacement event has been, and still is, widely accepted. Critics of this position have been few (Clark 1992; Straus 1997). However, new interpretations of the data are sometimes at odds with this hypothesis. These conflicting interpretations are considered in this section.

Early Modern Human Fossils in Europe

Although most scholars consider the Aurignacian to be the first industry produced by early modern humans in western Europe, this assumption is not shared by all (e.g., Bar-Yosef 2002). Likewise, some doubts have recently been raised concerning the association of Neandertals with the Châtelperronian (Bar-Yosef and Bordes 2010).

At the moment, human remains attributed with some degree of certainty to the Early Aurignacian are limited to a few cranial fragments and isolated teeth that are not easily diagnosed (Churchill and Smith 2000; Henry-Gambier *et al*. 2004; Bailey and Hublin 2005; Bailey *et al*. 2009; Ramirez Rozzi *et al*. 2009). With a date of ≈35 ka, the modern human specimens (a mandible as well as a complete cranium from a second individual) from Peştera cu Oase in Romania may be considered coeval with the Early Aurignacian. Unfortunately, these specimens have no associated artifacts (Trinkaus *et al*. 2003; Rougier *et al*. 2007). Concerning the cranium, Rougier and colleagues (2007:1170) noted that "Oase 2 is 'modern' in its abundance of derived modern human features, but it remains 'nonmodern' in its complex constellation of archaic and modern features." Another early specimen, sometimes attributed to modern humans, consists of a 35,000- to 37,000-year-old maxilla from Kent's Cavern in England (Jacobi *et al*. 2006). However, the taxonomic affinities of this maxilla are uncertain because some scholars question, given its fragmentary nature, whether it is possible to attribute it to a specific morphotype (Higham *et al*. 2006).

Scarce information is available for the later Aurignacian. The human fossil assemblage from Mladeč, Czech Republic, dated at ≈31 ka, and therefore, postdating the Early Aurignacian, provides evidence for anatomically modern morphology in the later Aurignacian (Wild *et al*. 2005). However, some authors see archaic characteristics in this assemblage as possibly indicative of a Neandertal ancestry, a claim that is debated (Bräuer *et al*. 2004). In Romania, human remains from Peştera Muierii, dated to ≈30 ka, as well as a slightly later (≈29 ka) cranium from Cioclovina, have been argued to indicate admixture between Neandertals and early modern humans (Soficaru *et al*. 2006, 2007). In France, modern human specimens from La Crouzade are also attributed to this period (Henry-Gambier and Sacchi 2008).

In this chronological framework, the 32- to 33-ka age obtained for the Vindija G_1 remains (a right mandible fragment and a parietal fragment) from Croatia is intriguing, given the geographic origin of the specimens. This is because if one accepts the demic

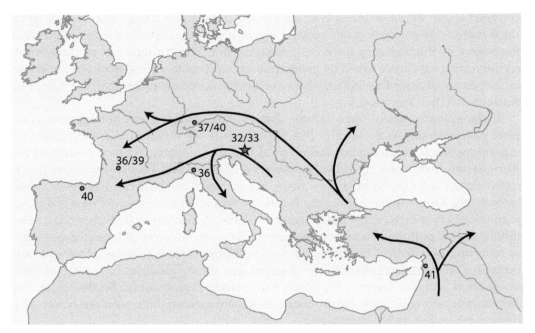

FIGURE 2.2. Hypothetical migration route followed by expanding modern human populations according to the replacement model. The star corresponds to Vindija.

expansion model, one would expect to find late Neandertals in western rather than central Europe (Figure 2.2). This pattern has been interpreted by Higham *et al.* (2006:555) as either reflecting the low number of dated human remains for the Aurignacian or "a result of semi-independence of the spread of the Aurignacian (a cultural process) and the westward dispersal of early modern humans (a biological population process)." However, as pointed out by Conard and Bolus (2003), this young date may simply reflect the low accuracy of the radiocarbon method for this time period.

As this brief overview suggests, the identity of the first European Aurignacians is unclear. It should be noted that this taxonomic ambiguity also holds for the early Upper Paleolithic of the Levant (Arensburg and Belfer-Cohen 1998; Belfer-Cohen and Hovers 2010). Overall, because they appear to show mixed archaic and modern human characters, the fossil remains discussed in this section may be viewed as support for the assimilation model or the multiregional model but seem to argue against strict replacement hypotheses (Trinkaus 2007). Consequently, few paleoanthropologists today adhere to the view that the emergence of modern humans in Europe occurred without some degree of gene flow with the archaic *sapiens* populations. However, there is much disagreement about the extent of gene flow between these populations, some viewing it as insignificant (e.g., Bailey and Hublin 2005), whereas others argue for more substantial genetic interactions (e.g., Eswaran *et al.* 2005).

Geographic Origin of the Aurignacian

A further problem concerns the origin of the Aurignacian. In most demic expansion scenarios, this industry is presented as a modern human cultural manifestation that emerged somewhere outside of western Europe. Yet despite almost a century of work since Breuil's proposition of an oriental origin for the Aurignacian, attempts to find the source of this industry have been unsuccessful. The Aurignacian of the Levant, an interesting candidate given its geographic connection to Africa, does not appear to qualify as a source for this industry because it is considered younger than the European Aurignacian (Bar-Yosef 2002).

Replacement scenarios often assume that the Aurignacian was a homogeneous cultural phenomenon. At the root of this hypothesis is the notion that a single, rapidly expanding, modern human population produced this industry. Yet recent work on the Aurignacian uncovered considerably more variation within Europe than was previously recognized (Teyssandier *et al.* 2010). For instance, comparisons have been made between the lithic assemblages of the Aquitaine area in southwestern France and those immediately to the east in the Mediterranean region. According to Bon (2002:184), these differences are profound enough to warrant considering the Aurignacian of these regions as reflecting two distinct traditions. In eastern Europe, recent analyses of several purportedly "Aurignacian" assemblages showed that these industries have, in fact, little in common with the western European Aurignacian (Tsanova and Bordes 2003). For Teyssandier and colleagues (2010), these results are incompatible with the notion of a homogeneous European Aurignacian.

The fragmented cultural picture emerging from these lithic studies, a pattern equally true of the Protoaurignacian (Discamps *et al.* 2010), cannot be easily reconciled with the Aurignacian expansion hypothesis. Some of these discrepancies prompted Bar-Yosef (2002:372) to reject the idea that the Aurignacian was the "first culture of the Cro-Magnons." The problem then is that, if it was not the Aurignacian, which industry should we view as signaling the early modern human expansion into western Europe? At the moment, no unambiguous signature of such an expansion can be found in this area, mostly because lithic industries show considerable regional variation during the early Upper Paleolithic.

Early Modern Human versus Neandertal Behaviors

Early European modern humans are often portrayed as possessing modern behavioral capacities, usually based on the assumption that art and ornaments are valid proxies for such capacities (e.g., Mellars 1996; Bar-Yosef 2002; Klein 2008). Yet other authors have pointed out that these complex behaviors are also documented in some *Mousterian* Neandertal groups (Soressi and d'Errico 2007; Zilhão *et al.* 2010; Peresani *et al.* 2011). This finding raises the issue of within- and between-group behavioral variation, two scales of analysis that have rarely been contrasted in studies investigating the Middle to Upper Paleolithic transition. For instance, did all Neandertal and early modern human groups use symbols? Closer to our research problem, is there evidence for variation in diet breadth within the same populations? As emphasized by these questions, for progress to be made on the modern human origin debate, behavioral variation must be investigated *both within and between hominin taxa*. Indeed, behavioral variations may not always covary with identified human phenotypes (Belfer-Cohen and Hovers 2010).

These issues are not limited to western Europe. In the Levant, the evidence suggests that Neandertals competed successfully with modern humans over a minimum period of

30,000 years, sometimes even expanding within their geographic range. If this is correct, how can we explain that Neandertals were suddenly replaced? It has been suggested that the acquisition of more efficient tools or a mutation allowing the emergence of language conferred a decisive advantage to modern humans (e.g., Milo and Quiatt 1993; Klein 2003). For others, the decisive advantage came from the fact that Neandertal sites lacked internal organization (Farizy 1994). These propositions are, however, highly speculative and poorly supported (Speth 2004a). Mellars (1998) has suggested that climatic changes would have driven the modern human expansion. Although possible, this proposition does not explain why these changes would have favored modern humans and not Neandertals, nor does it explain why it happened at that moment and not during prior or later climatic oscillations. Testing some of these propositions might contribute to a better understanding of behavioral variation during the transition.

Genetic Evidence for a Population Expansion

Over the past twenty years, the field of molecular biology has recorded a florescence of theoretical advances and technological breakthroughs, including techniques such as polymerase chain reaction (PCR) or high-throughput sequencing (O'Rourke 2007). These and other techniques generated vast amounts of genetic data that could be used to interpret biological variation from an evolutionary standpoint (Relethford 2001; Tishkoff and Gonder 2007). The spectacular results obtained by human geneticists during this period have been extremely influential in the debate on modern human origins. This influence has been, to some extent, disproportionate because claims were sometimes based on inaccurate models or affected by sample contamination (Wall and Kim 2007). Despite these shortcomings, there is little doubt that there is much to learn from this innovative approach to human evolution.

Molecular studies concerned with modern human emergence generally approach genetic diversity from two perspectives: they sample either living humans or fossil specimens. The vast majority of the early DNA studies, which were largely based on patterns of mitochondrial genetic variation in current humans, concluded that archaic *sapiens* populations were replaced by expanding modern humans without interbreeding (e.g., Cann *et al.* 1987). Do the more recent molecular analyses confirm these claims?

This question is important because the mitochondrial genome, which is found outside of the nucleus of the cell, differs in several important respects from the nuclear genome. Although the autosomes (non–sex chromosomes in the nucleus) are biparentally transmitted and subject to recombination, the mitochondrial genome is passed down, without recombination, exclusively through the maternal line (for a further discussion of these differences, including those relating to the sexual chromosomes, see Rubicz *et al.* 2007). Consequently, the mitochondrial genome only documents variation in female lineages. In addition to nonrecombination and strict maternal inheritance, the mitochondrial genome is very small, representing only 0.00006% of the total human genome (Tishkoff and Gonder 2007). Thus, because the mtDNA genome provides a very limited window into genetic variation, some authors were quick to point out that the early mtDNA studies might have erroneously rejected interbreeding (Nordborg 1998; Wall 2000). These authors emphasized that several unlinked (independent) loci of the genome are needed to test the admixture hypotheses.

Newer genetic analyses have addressed these problems by investigating variation at multiple (often in the hundreds or more) unlinked loci in the much larger nuclear genome. In general, these studies support the idea that humanity's most recent common ancestors came from sub-Saharan Africa (Tishkoff and Gonder 2007). This claim is mainly based on two sets of observations: the greater genetic diversity documented in this region and evidence that non-African regions are largely subsets of the variation found within sub-Saharan Africa (e.g., Yu *et al.* 2002a; International Human Genome Sequencing Consortium 2010). These observations have generally been interpreted as reflecting an out-of-Africa expansion estimated to have occurred some 100 to 50 ka (e.g., Underhill *et al.* 2000; Shi *et al.* 2009). This demic expansion shows serial founder effects, meaning that each new founder population seems to be a subsample drawn from the previous founder population, the genetic diversity of which decreases with increasing distance from Africa (Ramachandran *et al.* 2005; DeGiorgio *et al.* 2009; Hunley *et al.* 2009; Shi *et al.* 2009; Xing *et al.* 2010). However, because telltale signs of low levels of admixture possibly persist only at a relatively small number of loci, it has proven difficult to reject interbreeding as one of the potential sources of current genetic variation (Weaver and Roseman 2008).

Yet a small but increasing number of analyses of sequence patterns in the noncoding portions of the genomes of living humans have documented gene flow between archaic and early modern human populations (e.g., Garrigan *et al.* 2005a, 2005b). Similar evidence has been observed at genetic loci under strong selection, including the *MAPT* (Hardy *et al.* 2005), *dystrophin* (Zietkiewicz *et al.* 2003), *CD209/CD209L* (Barreiro *et al.* 2005), and *microcephalin* (Evans *et al.* 2006) loci. In fact, as much as 5% of the loci under selection appear to bear signs of admixture, which attests to ancient diffusions ("introgressions") of favorable alleles from archaic to modern *sapiens* populations (Plagnol and Wall 2006). Studies of the *microcephalin* locus, a gene that seems to influence brain size during development (Evans *et al.* 2005), is illustrative of these recent findings.

By concentrating on the diversity and geographic distribution of combinations of alleles that are located close together on the same chromosome, called haplotypes, inferences can be drawn regarding the evolution of past populations. Analyses of genetic variation at the *microcephalin* gene recorded in 89 individuals from across the globe yielded 86 haplotypes distributed over two distinct lineages (Evans *et al.* 2006). One of these lineages, characterized by the D allele, is present in 70% of the sampled chromosomes. Its prevalence is particularly high in Eurasia but low in sub-Saharan Africa (Evans *et al.* 2005). The estimated age of this lineage ($\approx$37 ka) is recent. In contrast, the less frequent (30%) lineage, called the "non-D" lineage, is considerably older ($\approx$990 ka). These patterns imply recent strong positive selection for the D allele (Figure 2.3). Moreover, several mutually exclusive mutations differentiate these two lineages, which indicate that they became isolated well before the emergence of early modern humans ($\approx$1.7 million years ago). As pointed out by Evans and colleagues (2006), the long isolation of the two lineages, the explosive spread of the D allele in Eurasia, and its low frequency in sub-Saharan Africa are not compatible with a simple out-of-Africa model. Instead, these patterns suggest a recent introgression of the D allele *from* archaic *sapiens to* early modern humans.

Results obtained from ancient DNA (aDNA) analyses largely support these conclusions. Whereas early aDNA studies found little indication for admixture during the

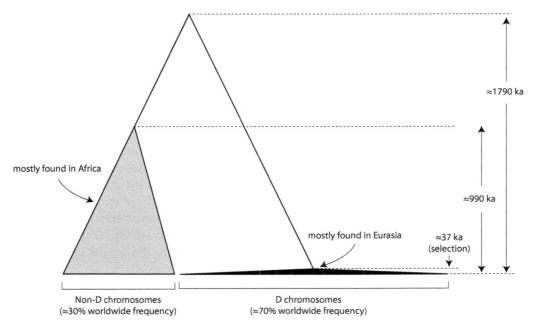

mostly found in Africa

≈1790 ka

≈990 ka

mostly found in Eurasia

≈37 ka
(selection)

Non-D chromosomes
(≈30% worldwide frequency)

D chromosomes
(≈70% worldwide frequency)

FIGURE 2.3. The genealogy of the *microcephalin* gene (modified from Evans *et al.* 2006:18179, fig. 2a). The lineage with the non-D chromosomes, represented by a large light gray triangle, is shown on the left side of the genealogy, and the lineage with the D allele chromosomes is represented by a flattened black triangle on the right side of the genealogy. The width of the triangles symbolizes the current frequency of the allele. As shown in this figure, the D allele spread very recently to high frequency in the population probably through strong positive selection.

expansion process (e.g., Krings *et al.* 1997, 2000; Serre *et al.* 2004; Noonan *et al.* 2006), the recent sequencing of the Neandertal nuclear genome suggests, to the contrary, low levels (1–4%) of gene flow between archaic *sapiens* and modern humans (Green *et al.* 2010). These authors infer that this gene flow occurred *before* the expansion, possibly when those populations were competing with each other in the Near East.

In general, five conclusions emerge from the molecular studies:

1. In living humans, genetic diversity is greatest among sub-Saharan Africans. Other regions appear to be subsets of the variations found in sub-Saharan Africa.
2. The combination of these patterns suggests that an out-of-Africa demic expansion occurred in the past. Estimates for this expansion range between approximately 100 and 50 ka. These recent dates are explained by the overall low genetic diversity observed in humans compared with other primates.
3. Colonization of major world regions during the demic expansion appears to have occurred though a process of serial founder effects, with each newly formed population containing a subset of the genetic diversity of its parental population. Studies have shown that within-region genetic diversity decreases with increasing distance from Africa.
4. Most early mtDNA, autosomal DNA, and aDNA studies concluded that Neandertals fall outside of the diversity observed among living humans.

5. However, recent studies of autosomal DNA, X-chromosomal, and aDNA find evidence that a nontrivial portion of the genomes of living people derive from archaic *sapiens*. Some of these studies even suggest that admixture introduced novel beneficial alleles into the human genome.

As emphasized earlier, these conclusions are not always consistent with the Paleolithic record, primarily because of a lack of an unequivocal archaeological signal reflecting the alleged expansion. Thus far, we have examined issues pertinent to the modern human origins debate. From the early invasion theories to the emergence of aDNA studies, the demic expansion hypothesis has proven to be unusually resilient. However, contradictions persist, and many of the core assumptions embedded in the replacement model require critical reexamination. Because they can shed light on some of these contradictions, the following section examines dietary predictions derived from the demic expansion hypothesis by O'Connell (2006). These predictions, which form the core of the present study, are applied in the subsequent chapters to the faunal sequence of Saint-Césaire.

FORMULATION OF A TEST APPLICABLE TO ARCHAEOLOGICAL REMAINS

Evolution is competitive. Variants that can more efficiently harvest resources for reproduction should become more prevalent through time. The nature and distribution of resources are thus primary conditioning factors that determine adaptations. Any comprehensive theory of hominid evolution and contemporary human social behavior will rest heavily upon a theory of resource acquisition. (Kaplan and Hill 1992:168)

Testing a hypothesis usually requires the derivation, through deduction, of the logical implications of a proposition. From these implications, predictions may then be generated and tested with empirical data. If the test is correctly designed, the results may confirm or refute the hypothesis under scrutiny or lead to a new cycle of testing. In the present study, several models of resource acquisition derived from foraging theory are used to determine whether early modern humans exploited a broader and costlier diet than Neandertals during the Middle to Upper Paleolithic transition, as suggested by O'Connell (2006). The next section focuses on how this proposition can be tested with archaeological data.

The Demic Expansion Hypothesis and Its Ecological Implications

The replacement of archaic *sapiens* populations in demic expansion models is often perceived to have occurred through the cumulative effects of the budding off of small modern human groups at the edge of an expanding wave front (Eswaran 2002; Eswaran *et al.* 2005). Because both Neandertals and early modern humans appear to have focused on high-ranked prey taxa (Burke 2000, 2004; Speth and Tchernov 2001; Grayson and Delpech 2002, 2008; Bar-Oz and Adler 2005; Stiner 2005; Adler *et al.* 2006; O'Connell 2006; Morin 2008), the demic expansion is likely to have led to direct or indirect competition for animal resources (see also Stringer and Gamble 1993 for a similar conclusion). Obviously, this raises important questions about how these populations adapted to increased resource competition. However, few studies have tackled this problem, with one significant exception.

In a recent article, O'Connell (2006) presents an elegant explanatory model for the replacement process. Drawing on archaeological examples for linguistic, and presumably population, expansions in Australia and western North America, O'Connell argues that early modern humans adjusted to competition in the early Upper Paleolithic by broadening their diet, a strategy that would have allowed them to occupy a wider range of habitats, occasionally at higher densities, than Neandertals. Significantly, O'Connell (2006:55) asserts that the replacement process was not the outcome of an inherent "superiority" of modern human groups but rather was made possible because the migrants "were prepared to operate a more expensive subsistence economy, one that succeeded only because they arrived in numbers large enough to prevent the resident Neanderthals from continuing to do as they had for tens of thousands of years before."

The question then is this: If, as claimed in this model, both populations were comparable in terms of cognitive and behavioral abilities, what prevented Neandertals from adopting the modern human strategy? According to O'Connell, the answer to this question lies in fitness-related opportunity costs associated with different subsistence options. The model postulates that Neandertal women, like females in general, were concerned with maximizing daily foraging returns, their fitness goal being to optimize trade-offs between numbers of births and offspring survival. Given these goals, O'Connell theorizes that options for diet broadening would have been limited for Neandertal women living in cool temperate environments, because only a few economically unattractive resources would have been available to them.

In this model, male strategies committed to the maximization of mating opportunities and alliance building were an additional factor determining the narrow diets of Neandertals. Indeed, O'Connell (2006) notes that among the Hadza, such goals often channel males toward prestige-enhancing activities – such as large-game hunting – which effectively turn them away from less prestigious ones (e.g., small game exploitation), however beneficial these activities might be to their mates and offspring. Yet this model does not specify why modern humans, males and females, would have differed from Neandertals in their foraging goals. Moreover, it should be pointed out that O'Connell's model departs from the standard prey choice model by assuming that modern humans added prey types to their diet that would have lowered the overall net return rate. In contrast, a strict prey choice model approach predicts that the diet of Neandertals and early modern humans should have been identical where their range overlapped.

In sum, O'Connell's model posits that modern humans outcompeted Neandertals through dietary intensification. Particularly, the model builds on the notion that the use of a wider range of resources fueled the replacement process by allowing modern humans to maintain higher densities than Neandertals. The subsistence implications of these propositions are straightforward: assemblages accumulated by Neandertals should reflect relatively narrow diets dominated by high-ranked resources, whereas assemblages deposited by modern humans should evidence shifts toward broader diets and sustained exploitation of low-ranked resources. Importantly, O'Connell (2006:54) specifies that his model may be tested by contrasting several lines of evidence, including changes in patterns of skeletal representation, in the age structure of high-ranked prey types, and in the intensity of resource processing. These lines of evidence, which are examined in detail in Chapter 3, will guide the test of the intensification hypothesis.

Assumptions Underlying the Archaeological Test

The current majority view is that Neandertals produced the Châtelperronian, whereas modern humans are considered to be the makers of the Aurignacian (e.g., Mellars 1996; Conard and Bolus 2003; Bailey *et al.* 2009; but see Bar-Yosef and Bordes 2010 for a critique of these assumptions). Moreover, these industries are often interpreted as representing distinct temporal stages of the inferred modern human expansion. For simplicity, these assumptions are adopted here when testing the predictions derived from the intensification hypothesis.

The possibility that diet broadening was not associated primarily with a greater use of animals but rather with an intensification of plant exploitation must also be considered, given that these resources often play a central role in studies of dietary change (Binford 1968; Flannery 1969; Hawkes *et al.* 1982; Pate 1986; Barlow and Metcalfe 1996; Munro 2004; Winterhalder and Kennett 2006). However, ethnographic analogues (e.g., mid- and high-latitude foragers of North America and Eurasia) and paleoenvironmental reconstructions (e.g., Barron *et al.* 2003; Guiot and Cheddadi 2004; Sánchez Goñi *et al.* 2008) militate against this possibility in the present case because they indicate that plants would have been largely unavailable during the long cold season. Further support for the limited dietary contribution of plants is found in isotopic analyses, which demonstrate that Neandertals and early modern humans subsisted mostly on animal foods (Richards *et al.* 2000, 2001; Bocherens *et al.* 2005; Balter and Simon 2006; Beauval *et al.* 2006; Lee-Thorp and Sponheimer 2006; Lee-Thorp 2008; Richards *et al.* 2009). Therefore, because plants appear to have contributed little to the diet, the analysis of the faunal record should provide valuable insights into shifts in subsistence strategies during the Middle to Upper Paleolithic transition.

Four models from foraging theory – the prey choice model, the patch choice model, the marginal value theorem, and the central place forager prey choice model – provide the theoretical backbone for examining the archaeological implications of the intensification model. These models are described in the following chapter.

3

FORAGING THEORY AND THE ARCHAEOLOGICAL RECORD

At the "Man the Hunter" conference, Birdsell wondered why it was that hunters-gatherers do not concentrate on resources such as mice, which in terms of sheer biomass are more abundant than deer (Lee and DeVore 1968:95). The answer should now be clear: the return rate of harvesting such a tiny, burrowing animal is so low that there are many far more efficient resources to be used even if they are less abundant. (Kelly 1995:87)

FORAGING THEORY, AN EMERGING FIELD WHEN THE "MAN THE HUNTER" CONFERENCE was held, provided the answer to Birdsell's question. At the core of foraging theory is the notion that feeding behavior has evolved by natural selection, a process that operates at the individual level (Ydenberg et al. 2007). The feeding process is therefore perceived as an adaptive system involving rational agents who must make decisions about food acquisition that may affect their survival and reproduction (Giraldeau 2005). This approach assumes that the maximization of reproductive fitness guides foraging decisions, the idea being that more efficient energy acquisition leaves more time for activities (e.g., child care, socializing) that may enhance fitness (Schoener 1971; Pyke et al. 1977; Bird and O'Connell 2006). Because this concept is difficult to measure empirically, evolutionary biologists and anthropologists generally use foraging efficiency – defined as the net rate of energy intake over the long term – as a correlate of reproductive fitness (Emlen 1966; Stephens and Krebs 1986; Winterhalder and Kennett 2006). Although convenient, it should be noted that the net rate of energy intake is only one among several possible correlates of fitness (e.g., risk minimization).

In anthropology, applications of foraging theory generally derive testable hypotheses from mathematical models to assess adaptive problems (Winterhalder and Smith 2000). What is being analyzed in these models is how an individual with a goal (e.g., maximizing the net return rate or the net delivery rate of energy) chooses between different behavioral options (e.g., to pursue the encountered prey or search for another one), taking into account a certain number of constraints (e.g., maximum load size) defining the foraging context (Giraldeau 2005). To compare the costs and benefits of the various behavioral options, these models rely on a currency. This currency may be measured in terms of amount of energy or any other unit (e.g., number of mates or children) that is considered relevant. Ultimately, this currency is no more than a proxy for reproductive fitness.

The process of model selection is a critical step in this approach because a model applied in a context in which one or more of its assumptions are violated may not constitute a valid test of the implications generated from it (Stephens and Krebs 1986). In this case, model selection depends on the evaluation of which model's assumptions and constraints best fit the archaeological situation. The use of these models allows the researcher to evaluate how alternative behavioral strategies affect the fitness of individuals and to examine why the theory fails when the predictions are not upheld. For example, the confrontation of a model with the empirical world may allow the identification of a new constraint (e.g., danger of predation when handling a prey) or an alternative currency (e.g., fat energy) that better explains the data (Keegan 1986; Nonacs 2001; Sih and Christensen 2001). In contrast, the archaeologist studying subsistence decisions rarely tests the foraging models being applied, because of the intractability of many constituent parameters (e.g., prey density) in the past. Instead, these models are viewed as robust enough to inform the analysis of the cumulative effects of foraging behavior in the archaeological record.

Methodologically, a "resource type" or "prey type" in foraging theory generally refers to any category of food or material, be it a Linnaean species of plant or animal, an anatomical part, a sex class, or an age group (Stephens and Krebs 1986; Grayson 1989; Smith 1991). What really matters in this respect is that prey types are discontinuous and composed of identical items with constant profitability and identifiability (Giraldeau 2005). A similar reasoning applies to forager "types." For instance, research has shown that the range of exploited resources may diverge, sometimes considerably, between children and adults and between males and child-raising females, a phenomenon probably fueled by differences in physiology, reproductive goals, and mobility constraints (Simms 1987; Kelly 1995; Kaplan *et al.* 2000; Zeanah 2004). Following the logic of foraging theory, these groups are probably best perceived as distinct forager types, so that each group is composed of individuals with similar foraging characteristics and maximizing goals. The fact that individuals within these groups appear to forage according to theoretical expectations, once their respective goals and constraints are taken into account, is consistent with this position (Hill *et al.* 1987; Hawkes *et al.* 1995; Bird and Bliege Bird 2000; Lupo 2007).

Given its potential for solving important evolutionary questions, foraging theory has attracted the attention of many biologists and anthropologists. Because species vary widely in their adaptations, a single, general, and for that reason, simple model cannot explain all the diversity in foraging strategies. Generally, multiple factors are crucial in mediating the resource acquisition behaviors of different forager types. These factors may include patch sampling (visiting a concentration of food to derive or update expected return rates) and the forager's response to variance in capture rate (for instance, foragers tend to be risk-prone when their energy budget is negative), danger of predation (often leads to time-minimizing strategies during consumption), nutritional constraints on food intake (e.g., the presence of a toxin), costs of transport (for foragers that do not consume prey on encounter), and competition from congeners (Stephens and Krebs 1986; Nonacs 2001; Giraldeau 2005; Ydenberg 2007). The recognition of these additional factors has stimulated the development of several foraging models over the years (e.g., Orians and Pearson 1979; Schoener 1979; Barlow and Metcalfe 1996; Cannon 2003).

The following section reviews the foraging theory models that are most frequently used in anthropology and identify how they can be used to test the early Upper

Paleolithic intensification hypothesis. The prey choice model is a natural starting point for this discussion.

THE PREY CHOICE MODEL

The *prey choice model* (also known as the *diet-breadth model*) makes predictions about prey selection in a homogeneous environment (MacArthur and Pianka 1966). Simply put, this model seeks to predict whether a forager should pursue an encountered prey or continue searching with the hope of locating a more valuable (higher-ranked) one (Winterhalder and Kennett 2006). To solve this problem, the model builds on a number of assumptions. Particularly, the prey choice model postulates that resources are encountered randomly and sequentially in the environment according to a Poisson distribution and that they are searched for simultaneously (MacArthur and Pianka 1966). In this approach, the process of prey capture is conceptualized as consisting of two mutually exclusive components that exhaust all foraging time: searching and handling. The model further assumes that foragers build on past experiences and have complete information about the abundance, profitability, mean return rate, and costs associated with the acquisition of prey types (Kaplan and Hill 1992).

At the heart of the prey choice model is the assumption that resources vary in food value, which implies that they can be ranked relative to each other on the basis of their respective "profitability" or "utility." Differences in profitability or utility between alternative prey types are usually measured using their net postencounter return rate, which is the amount of energy provided by a prey type minus that expended while handling it, per unit of time spent handling it (Stephens and Krebs 1986). Typically, *handling* in foraging theory includes the activities of pursuing, capturing, processing, and consuming a prey item. Because encounters are assumed to occur at random and one at a time, prey rank can be determined based exclusively on postencounter return rates, *irrespective of search costs*, these applying equally to the entire set of resources captured during a foraging bout (Smith 1991). For the same reasons, prey types are ranked independently of their abundance because changes in encounter rates do not affect prey rank in this approach (Schoener 1971). Of course, although variation in encounter rates does not affect the postencounter food value of a prey, it may affect the diet of foragers. For instance, low-ranked resources may dominate a diet if high-ranked resources are rare in the environment.

A critical prediction of the prey choice model is that prey types producing the highest net gains of energy per unit of time (those with the highest utility) are *always* pursued on encounter, whereas less rewarding resources may – or may not – be exploited, depending on the availability of higher-ranked resources (Pulliam 1974). Low-return resources falling outside of the optimal diet are never taken, however abundant they might be, because they have a high *opportunity cost*: the time and energy the forager spends searching and handling them cannot be spent engaging in more profitable activities (Stephens and Krebs 1986; Hames 1992; Winterhalder and Kennett 2006). For example, a hunter who has little problem finding deer should always ignore acorns, a small-sized resource with high processing costs (Thomas 2008), even when the latter are profusely abundant. Doing so is efficient, according to this view, because processing acorns reduces the time that can be spent exploiting deer, a resource with a much higher return rate, or engaging in essential and/or fitness-enhancing activities (e.g., child care, socializing).

Prey types in the prey choice model are added to the diet sequentially in order of decreasing rank, that is, starting with the most profitable resource, followed by the second most profitable resource, and so on. The most profitable combination of prey types under particular conditions of resource abundance constitutes the "optimal diet." In periods of food abundance, the diet is dominated by a relatively small number of highly profitable prey types. However, when encounter rates with these prey types decline below a certain threshold, the forager is constrained to expand his diet by including less profitable prey types (Pulliam 1974). War stories relating famine outbreaks in besieged cities – the siege of Paris in 1590 being a good example – are replete with details about how hunger forced people to eat increasingly lower-ranked resources (e.g., rats), as food became scarcer. But what determines the breadth of the diet? Should a forager concentrate exclusively on the single most profitable prey and ignore all the other ones? Or should the focus be on the three most profitable prey types? This problem can be solved using foraging theory: a resource will be added to the forager's diet if it contributes to an increase in the overall long-term net return rate. If it does not, that is, if the net energy contributed by that resource is less on average than the forager's overall net return rate for the environment, the resource will be passed over (Stephens and Krebs 1986; Kaplan and Hill 1992).

The prey choice model assumes that prey types are encountered randomly in the environment. However, this assumption is commonly violated in real-world cases because many habitats consist of localized, spatially bounded, concentrations of prey or "patches." The prey choice model may be a poor predictor of foraging behavior in patchy environments because search time cannot be "detached" from individual prey types and be assigned to the entire set of prey types (Smith 1991). For instance, Atlantic mackerel (*Scomber scombrus*) are found in oceans but do not occur in forests. Therefore, in this example, the ocean represents a distinct patch from the forest because both vary predictably in encounter rates with that type of prey.

A simple solution to the problem of patchiness is to limit the application of the prey choice model to some specified fraction of total foraging time during which encounter with resources is approximately random. These conditions may be fulfilled when foraging *within* a patch or when foraging time is subdivided according to hunting types (e.g., lake fishing), or any other comparable analytical unit that respects the "fine-grained" (random encounter) assumption of the prey choice model (Smith 1991; Lupo 2007). In sum, the prey choice model can be applied to patchy environments when used in its restricted form, assuming that the selected foraging time unit consists of prey types that can be encountered more or less randomly. To avoid confusion with the model that will follow, this variant of the prey choice model will be referred to hereafter as the *within-patch prey choice* model.

THE PATCH CHOICE MODEL

Initially presented as a complement to the prey choice model, the *patch choice model* predicts patch selection in heterogeneous environments (MacArthur and Pianka 1966). Therefore, unlike the within-patch prey choice model, the patch choice model was designed expressly to tackle foraging behavior in patchy environments. The latter model assumes that patches are encountered at some distance from each other and, as a consequence, that foragers must travel through unproductive areas while moving between them (Stephens and Krebs 1986). Foraging time in this approach consists of two mutually exclusive activities: traveling and patch exploitation. A patch may be identified at various scales, from single bones to biotopes (Grayson 1989; Ritchie 1998; Broughton 1999). This methodological flexibility is particularly valuable given the many dimensions along which human decision making operates when it comes to food procurement strategies (Binford 1978; Speth 1983; O'Connell *et al.* 1988; Barlow and Metcalfe 1996; O'Connell 2000; Lyman 2003; Burger *et al.* 2005; Speth and Clark 2006; Lupo 2007; Morin 2007).

In a manner analogous to the prey choice model, the patch choice model infers that patches can be ranked and used according to their respective profitability, assuming that they are encountered randomly and sequentially (MacArthur and Pianka 1966). The many parallels that exist between the two models explain why they give rise to many of the same predictions. However, the patch choice model is usually more complex because a patch is rarely completely depleted of its resources by a forager, in contrast to many prey items that are consumed whole (Winterhalder and Kennett 2006). Moreover, patch selection is also contingent on the response of resources to exploitation and on returns expected from other patches. These issues are the focus of the next model.

THE MARGINAL VALUE THEOREM

Whereas the previous model seeks to explain the mechanisms of patch selection, the *marginal value theorem* makes predictions about how long a forager should stay in a patch before moving on to exploit another (Charnov 1976). For this reason, the marginal value theorem is generally considered a natural extension of the patch choice model. Central to the marginal value theorem is the notion that patch depletion is rarely linear and frequently follows a negatively accelerating or diminishing-returns curve. This depletion pattern implies that the marginal capture rate in a patch falls as the forager exploits it, or phrased otherwise, that as time passes, more and more efforts are incurred in capturing less and less energy (Ydenberg 2007). Although not all patches behave according to a diminishing-returns function (Stephens and Krebs 1986; Erwin 1989; Kaplan and Hill 1992), resources exploited by humans frequently follow this depletion pattern (Sahlins 1972; Kelly 1995; Burger *et al.* 2005).

Because it is a patch-based approach, the marginal value theorem shares basic features with the patch choice model – namely, the assumptions that patches are encountered randomly and sequentially and that traveling involves passing through areas devoid of food resources worth exploiting. However, the marginal value theorem differs from the patch choice model by its focus on time allocation rather than patch selection. This model posits that a forager will attempt to balance the benefits of continuing to deplete a patch against expected gains from other patches and travel costs (Charnov 1976). Specifically, this model assumes that exploitation of a patch ceases when the marginal return rate for the next unit of foraging time equals the average return rate for the entire set of patches in the habitat, including travel costs (Charnov *et al.* 1976). In simple terms, this means that leaving a patch too early is not the most advantageous strategy because the patch still provides a higher immediate return rate – even after taking travel costs into account – than could be obtained by moving to exploit another patch in the habitat, whereas leaving too late produces lower returns than could be obtained from another, less depleted patch. Key elements in the solution to this foraging dilemma are the expected gain for the patch, its depletion pattern, the average return rate for all of the patches, their depletion patterns, and the distance separating these patches (Kaplan and Hill 1992). Because all these factors can vary, the maximizing solution will vary as well.

A major feature of the marginal value theorem is its emphasis on the interdependency between residence time in a patch and expected return rates for all other patches – information that the forager is assumed to possess (Charnov 1976). In this model, time allocation in a patch type may change because of variations in the return rates for other patch types in the habitat, *even if the gain function* (the curve that mathematically represents the relationship between net energy gain and patch residence time) *of the first patch type remained constant* during the interval (Stephens and Krebs 1986). Importantly, the model further stipulates that the marginal return rate at the point of departure is the same for all exploited patches. From an archaeological viewpoint, this means that strong patterning is expected in the level of exploitation for a given prey type, holding all else equal. This strong patterning is expected because in the absence of change in the gain function of the patches and in the average distance between them, the return rate, and consequently the optimal solution, remains constant. In these conditions, the forager should *always leave the patch at the same point on the gain function curve* – that is, the one that maximizes the net return rate. Inversely, a significant change in the spacing of the patches or in their gain function should be manifested in the archaeological record by a change in the level of patch exploitation. The simplicity of this prediction makes the marginal value theorem a powerful tool for documenting resource depression.

A somewhat counterintuitive prediction of the marginal value theorem is that patch residence time is short when food is abundant (see Giraldeau 2005 for a theoretical exception to this rule). Conversely, if food becomes scarce, the forager is expected to increase patch residence time. A simple example illustrates these predictions. If peaches abound in an orchard made up of closely spaced trees, a "predator" is far more likely to collect peaches with the lowest costs – those on low branches – and to move quickly from one tree to the next, than to systematically and painfully collect all peaches from the first encountered tree. This result is expected because travel time is very short, a few seconds, between each patch (in this case, trees), and because peaches on low branches are much less costly to acquire than those farther up in the tree. However, if the same trees are separated by hundreds of meters, the person gains less from moving to another patch because, due to the higher travel costs, it will take longer for the immediate returns gained from staying in the patch to fall below those to be obtained by leaving. The degree of exploitation for each tree is expected to be consistently low in the first situation and consistently higher in the second.

Given its clear predictions with respect to patch exploitation, the marginal value theorem may be a productive source of insights into human foraging behavior under conditions of food stress. This approach is particularly informative when it comes to the analysis of carcass exploitation because these "patches" contain discontinuous components (e.g., skin, meat, marrow, bone grease) that vary widely in their net return rates (Binford 1978; Burger *et al.* 2005; Nagaoka 2005; Morin 2007; see Gende *et al.* 2001 for a similar application in biology). Specifically, the model predicts that as foraging efficiency declines, patch residence time should increase, which is expected to result in more complete use of vertebrate carcasses.

CENTRAL PLACE FORAGING MODELS

The marginal value theorem was designed to predict the behavior of foragers who consume prey at the point of capture. However, certain foragers preferentially deliver prey or material back to a nest, a den, a colony, or other "central places" (Ydenberg 2007). This strategy, which incurs travel and transport costs during round-trip excursions, may aim at feeding offspring, sharing food with conspecifics, accumulating surpluses in anticipation of difficult times, or reducing the danger of being captured while feeding (Giraldeau 2005). To elucidate how these costs mediate behavior, a family of *central place foraging models* was developed at the end of the 1970s (Orians and Pearson 1979; Schoener 1979). Given that these models deal with patch time allocation, they are best viewed as logical extensions of the marginal value theorem. Central place foraging models generally assume that the goal of the forager is to *maximize the net resource delivery rate* to the central place (Orians and Pearson 1979). The problem, as defined in these models, consists of determining how the type and quantity of resources that are loaded for transport varies with distance from the central place. Because hunter-gatherer groups share the tendency of radiating back and forth from a home base, these models are relevant to humans (Kelly 1995).

Early central place foraging models centered on taxa that carry loads that are small relative to their body size, such as nesting birds and chipmunks. For this reason, load mass was not considered to be a critical factor in these models (Wetterer 1989). However, load mass may be substantial for foragers like humans, hyenas, wolves, wild dogs, foxes, beavers, owls, eagles, and leaf-cutter ants (*Atta* sp.) who occasionally or frequently capture resources that are large relative to their body mass. Constraints on transport oblige these taxa to field-process the resource into more manageable units. This specific problem has received the attention of biologists (Jenkins 1980; Rudolph and Loudon 1986; Wetterer 1989; Rands *et al.* 2000; Guerra and Ades 2002) and, more particularly, anthropologists (Jones and Madsen 1989; Metcalfe and Barlow 1992; Barlow and Metcalfe 1996; Bettinger *et al.* 1997; Bird and Bliege Bird 1997; Cannon 2000, 2003; Zeanah 2004; Nagaoka 2005, 2006; Bird and O'Connell 2006; Lupo 2006).

Coming from an archaeological perspective, Cannon (2001a, 2003) has created a central place forager prey choice model that explores how a human agent should choose between patches that comprise prey types that have different postencounter rates and that are encountered at varying distances from the central place. In simple words, this model asks the question of which prey, and which part of that prey, should be brought back to camp by a delivery rate maximizer, taking into account that there is a maximum load size that can be transported. It should be pointed out that Cannon's model differs from Orians and Pearson's (1979) models for single prey and multiple prey loaders in its focus on the impact of field-processing costs on the transport decisions of large prey types.

The central place forager prey choice model shares some features with the standard prey choice model, which has been widely applied in archaeology (Nagaoka 2006). For instance, both models assume that prey types are ranked in decreasing order of profitability and that a decline in the relative abundance of high-return prey types is indicative of a decrease in foraging efficiency, all else being equal. However, the central place forager prey choice model departs in a fundamental way from the standard prey choice model (and also from the earlier central place foraging models in this respect) because it assumes nonrandom encounters with prey taxa. Instead, the model stipulates that the forager leaves camp with a specific prey type in mind, even though he or she may return with another. Ethnographic work shows that this is often a reasonable assumption (e.g., Binford 1978; Smith 1991).

Whereas prey ranks in the standard prey choice model are strictly based on estimates of postencounter return rates, the central place forager prey choice model also takes into consideration for the determination of these ranks *the average time it takes to encounter the prey taxon and to increase, if necessary, the utility of the load(s) through postcapture processing* (Cannon 2001a, 2003). The implication here is that a large taxon may be high-ranked when abundant near the camp but low-ranked if only encountered in distant patches. Therefore, according to this model, prey abundance, postencounter return rates, and field-processing costs must be considered along with search and transport time to identify the strategy that will maximize the net delivery rate in a given context.

In the central place forager prey choice model, each prey type is associated with a "processing function" (Cannon 2001a, 2003). This element of the model, mathematically represented by a diminishing-returns curve, describes the relationship between processing time and load utility. Metcalfe and Barlow (1992; Barlow and Metcalfe 1996) and Bettinger *et al.* (1997) have shown that to maximize the net delivery rate, central place foragers handling large prey must balance field-processing costs against transport costs. The options are either to make more trips with bulk resources or to reduce the number of trips by spending time culling low-utility parts, which allows for more energy to be transported per kilogram of load. The central place forager prey choice model incorporates these findings and asserts that rate-maximizing individuals handling large prey types should show greater selectivity and transport an increasingly narrow set of highly valued parts as distance from the central place increases. The increase in search and transport time explains why in this approach large prey taxa found in distant patches are low-ranked relative to the same prey taxa found near the camp.

In the central place forager prey choice model, a large taxon is usually more profitable than a smaller one, holding search and transport time equal. The fact that search and transport time may not be equal among various prey types leads to a number of predictions. If the abundance of a large prey that was initially common declines dramatically, as may occur due to resource depression or climate change, average search and transport time for that large prey type may increase up to a point at which pursuing a smaller prey that is abundant near the home base becomes more profitable. In this context, the forager is expected to primarily target that small prey type instead.

This situation has two archaeological implications for the study of central place foragers. First, the switch in prey ranks should result in an increase in the taxonomic abundance of the small taxon relative to the large taxon, a prediction that this model shares, in this specific context, with the diet-breadth model. Second, the analysis of skeletal representation for the large taxon should reveal an increase in mean utility reflecting the greater search and transport costs. But what happens if search and transport time begin to rise significantly for the small taxon as well? The model for central place foragers predicts that the forager will, at a certain point, increase the delivery rate by focusing on the large taxon in the *distant patch*. The archaeological implication, this time, is that the taxonomic abundance of the large taxon will *increase* or *"rebound"* relative to the small taxon. This last prediction is important because it cannot be made with the prey choice model without invoking a change in prey ranks caused by an increase in search and transport costs. This approach is not totally adequate because prey ranks in the standard prey choice model are normally independent of these factors.

Like the previous models, the central place forager prey choice model makes a number of assumptions about the foraging context. Before turning to the issue of which of these assumptions are most appropriate for the present test, a few points need to be addressed relative to the archaeological implementation of these models.

PROBLEMS IN ARCHAEOLOGICAL APPLICATIONS

The Body Size Rule

Applications of foraging models to anthropological test cases have been relatively successful overall, particularly with respect to qualitative predictions (Winterhalder 1981; Hames and Vickers 1982; Hawkes *et al.* 1982; Hill *et al.* 1987; Smith 1991; Zeleznik and Bennett 1991; Kaplan and Hill 1992; Alvard 1993, 1995; Winterhalder and Smith 2000; Bird and O'Connell 2006; Koster 2008a). However, some of these studies also note that the fit with quantitative predictions has been less than satisfactory (Hill *et al.* 1987; Smith 1991; Kaplan and Hill 1992), a problem that has also been observed in biology (Stephens and Krebs 1986; Sih and Christensen 2001; Giraldeau 2005). Although important, the problem of quantification is less consequential in archaeology because studies have generally focused on qualitative predictions.

More controversial in archaeology has been the use of prey body size as a proxy for the net return rates of prey types because this measure does not always predict resource rank accurately (Smith 1991; Stiner and Munro 2002; Lupo and Schmitt 2005; Stiner 2005; Ugan 2005; Jones 2006; Stiner *et al.* 2008; Bird *et al.* 2009). This proxy assumes that the relationship between body size and profitability is curvilinear, with very small (e.g., snails) and very large (e.g., elephants, whales) prey types showing proportionally higher handling costs than taxa of intermediate sizes (Bayham 1979; Broughton 1994). Between these two extremes, the rule of thumb has been that the larger the prey, the higher the profitability (Bayham 1979; Simms 1987).

A well-described problem with using body size as a proxy of energy gain is that hunting techniques affect net return rates. For instance, the adoption of shotguns, snowmobiles, or dogs can improve the encounter rate with certain resources or decrease pursuit time, and, as a result, alter diet breadth (Winterhalder 1981; Hames and Vickers 1982; Simms 1987; Smith 1991; Alvard 1993; Koster 2008a). Likewise, communal and mass-collecting techniques (e.g., rabbit drives, bird net-hunting) may increase the profitability of a previously low-ranked resource, making it more rewarding than resources of larger individual body size (Madsen and Schmitt 1998; Jones 2006). Concerning this last claim, recent studies indicate, however, that the boost in payoffs afforded by mass collecting is limited to a smaller range of behavioral contexts than has been suggested and may even disappear when the time spent preparing and performing these activities is fully taken into account (Lupo and Schmitt 2002; Ugan 2005). Nonetheless, it is clear from these studies that hunting techniques, particularly mass collecting, can, in certain circumstances, weaken the body size rule.

The body size rule has also been criticized for its reliance on Linnaean taxonomy, which may not always be the most appropriate unit of analysis for assessing prey rank (Kaplan and Hill 1992; Stiner *et al.* 1999, 2008; Bird and O'Connell 2006). For instance, studies have shown that the profitability of a prey taxon may vary appreciably over the course of a year (Winterhalder 1981; Speth 1983; Hill *et al.* 1984, 1987; Smith 1991; Speth and Clark 2006). These variations are often due to changes in behavior (e.g., the prey type becomes more reclusive) and/or in physiological condition (e.g., the prey type becomes very lean).

This issue is exemplified by agouti (*Dasyprocta punctata*) hunts in Nicaragua. Koster (2008a) calculated return rate estimates of 3,560, 6,503, and nearly 100,000 kcal/h for this species, depending on whether the animal was, respectively, dug from a burrow, dislodged from a tree trunk, or chased into water. Surely, averaging return rates in this case, as is typically done by archaeologists, inaccurately portrays the profitability of agouti hunts. However, because ethnographic return rates are typically based on small samples and cover a short period of time, mean or modal values may provide profitability estimates that are, despite their artificial nature, still useful for ascertaining long-term change in foraging efficiency. Contextual and seasonal information may also help identify which values are most relevant in a given archaeological situation.

Another weakness of the body size rule is that it is oblivious to taxonomic differences in antipredator behavior, an essential component of prey adaptation (Caro 2005). Research suggests that sessile and slow-moving taxa that use armor or quills as a shield (e.g., mussels, crabs, tortoises, porcupines, pangolins), an efficient strategy for deterring most predators, are generally associated with lower pursuit costs, higher success of capture, and higher return rates for human foragers than taxa with similar body weights (e.g., rabbits and ptarmigans) that escape at great speed (Stiner et al. 1999, 2008; Munro 2004; Stiner 2005; Bird et al. 2009). These differences in antipredator behavior may cause prey rank inversions, which occur when a small-bodied species is shown to be more profitable than a larger one, in contradiction to the body size rule. This issue highlights the importance of understanding how mobility is patterned across species.

Maximal velocity, the top speed attained by a fleeing animal, may provide information about the susceptibility of a prey taxon to predation, the assumption being that the faster the prey, the lower the probability of capture (Djawdan and Garland 1988; Iriarte-Díaz 2002). In anthropology, this assumption finds empirical support in ethnographic reports indicating that prey velocity reduces capture rates (Bird *et al.* 2009). The problem then is to assess how maximal velocity varies taxonomically and, importantly, whether it scales with body size. The worldwide data collected by Garland and his collaborators on the relationship between maximal running velocity in terrestrial mammals and body mass are particularly useful in this regard (Garland 1983; Djawdan and Garland 1988; Garland *et al.* 1988; Garland and Janis 1993). These data are presented by taxon ($n = 147$) in Table 3.1 and were analyzed using Pearson's *r*.

TABLE 3.1. *Data on maximal running speed (km/hr) and body mass (in kg) in terrestrial mammals*

Mammal	Weight	Speed	Ref.	Mammal	Weight	Speed	Ref.
Artiodactyla				*Bettongia penicillata*	1.13	24.2	G88
Hippopotamus amphibius	3800	25	G83	*Potorus tridactylus*	0.998	21.4	G88
Giraffa camelopardalis	1075	60	GJ	*Isoodon obesulus*	0.718	14.4	G88
Bison bison	865	56	GJ	*Myrmecobius fasciatus*	0.48	33	G88
Bos sauveli	800	29	G83	*Dasyuroides byrnei*	0.12	18.6	G88
Syncerus caffer	620	57	GJ	*Monodelphis brevicaudata*	0.0745	11.4	G88
Camelus dromedarius	550	32	GJ	*Antechinus flavipes*	0.052	13.2	G88
Taurotragus oryx	511	70	GJ	*Antechinus stuartii*	0.0315	15.1	G88
Alces alces	384	56	GJ	*Antechinomys laniger*	0.025	13.8	G88
Cervus elaphus	300	72	GJ	*Sminthopsis macroura*	0.02	13.4	G88
Connochaetes gnu	300	90	G83	*Sminthopsis crassicaudata*	0.017	10.9	G88
Hippotragus equinus	226.5	56	GJ	*Cercartetus concinnus*	0.015	5.6	G88
Connochaetes taurinus	216	80	GJ	Perissodactyla			
Alcelaphus buselaphus	136	80	GJ	*Ceratotherium simum*	2000	25	GJ
Damaliscus lunatus	130	70	GJ	*Diceros bicornis*	1200	45	GJ
Oreamnos americanus	113.5	33	GJ	*Equus ferus caballus*	350	70	GJ
Rangifer tarandus	100	80	GJ	*Equus zebra*	300	64	G83
Lama guanicoe	95	56	GJ	*Tapirus bairdii*	250	40	GJ
Ovis canadensis nelsoni	85	48	GJ	*Equus quagga (burchelli)*	235	70	GJ
Phacochoerus aethiopicus	85	55	G83	*Equus hemionus*	200	70	GJ
Odocoileus hemionus	74	61	GJ	Primates			
Capra caucasia	70	45	G83	*Gorilla gorilla*	127	32	G83
Ovis ammon	65	60	G83	*Homo sapiens*	70	40	G83
Gazella granti	62.5	81	GJ	*Presbytis*	13	37	G83
Odocoileus virginianus	57	64	GJ	Proboscidea			
Dama dama	55	65	GJ	*Loxodonta africana*	6000	35	G83
Aepyceros melampus	53.25	47	GJ	*Elephas maximus*	4000	26	G83
Antilocapra americana	50	100	GJ	Rodentia			
Capreolus capreolus	50	60	G83	*Erethizon dorsatum*	9	3.2	G88
Rupicapra rupicapra	50	40	G83	*Marmota monax*	4	16	G88
Antilope cervicapra	37.5	105	GJ	*Uromys caudimaculatus*	1.18	16.6	G88
Saiga tatarica	35	80	G83	*Sciurus niger*	1.078	24	G88
Antidorcas marsupialis	34	97	G83	*Spermophilopsis leptodactylus*	0.6	36	G88
Capra aegagrus	30	45	G83	*Spermophilus undulatus*	0.6	20	G88
Gazella subgutturosa	30	97	G83	*Sciurus carolinensis*	0.5	30	G88
Procapra gutturosa	30	80	G83	*Spermophilus citellus*	0.5	18	G88
Gazella thomsonii	20.5	81	GJ	*Scirus vulgaris and persicus*	0.4	20	G88
Madoqua kirkii	5	42	GJ	*Spermophilus beldingi*	0.3	13	G88
Carnivora				*Rattus*	0.25	9.7	G83
Ursus maritimus	265	40	GJ	*Spermophilus saturatus*	0.222	22.2	G88
Ursus arctos (horribilis)	251.3	48	GJ	*Tamiasciurus hudsonicus*	0.22	14.6	G88
Panthera tigris	161	56	GJ	*Spermophilus tridecemlineatus*	0.125	12.2	G88
Panthera leo	155.8	59	GJ	*Spermophilus tereticaudus*	0.1126	15.2	G88
Ursus americanus	93.4	48	GJ	*Dipodomys deserti*	0.112	29.9	G88
Acinonyx jubatus	58.8	110	GJ	*Mesocricetus brandti*	0.11	9	G88
Panthera pardus	52.4	60	GJ	*Neotoma lepida*	0.1052	19.2	G88
Crocuta crocuta	52	65	GJ	*Tamias striatus*	0.1	17.1	G88
Canis lupus	35.3	64	GJ	*Ammospermophilus leucurus*	0.0762	18.7	G88
Hyaena hyaena	26.8	50	GJ	*Pseudomys nanus*	0.061	14.4	G88

(continued)

TABLE 3.1 *(continued)*

Mammal	Weight	Speed	Ref.	Mammal	Weight	Speed	Ref.
Canis familiaris	25	67	G83	*Zymomys argurus*	0.0605	12.4	G88
Lycaon pictus	20	70	Gj	*Dipodomys microps*	0.056	21	G88
Canis latrans	13.3	65	GJ	*Notomys cervinus*	0.0525	15.7	G88
Meles meles	11.6	30	GJ	*Tamias amoenus*	0.051	19.4	G88
Canis aureus	8.8	56	GJ	*Microtus pennsylvanicus*	0.05	11	G88
Canis mesomelas/adustus	7	60	G83	*Pseudomys australis*	0.05	16.4	G88
Procyon lotor	7	24	GJ	*Heteromys desmarestianus*	0.05	12.5	G88
Vulpes vulpes (fulva)	4.8	72	GJ	*Dipodomys ordii*	0.05	15.3	DG
Nasua narica	4.4	27	GJ	*Lyomis pictus*	0.042	17.2	G88
Urocyon cinereoargenteus	3.7	64	GJ	*Chaetodipus baileyi*	0.0397	14.9	G88
Mephitis mephitis	2.5	16	GJ	*Dipodomys merriami*	0.035	32	G88
Edentata				*Pitymys pinetorum*	0.03	6.8	G88
Bradypus tridactylus	4	1.6	G83	*Zapus trinotatus*	0.0285	14.3	G88
Soricomorpha				*Tamias minimus*	0.028	17.4	G88
Talpa europaea	0.1	4	G83	*Perognathus parvus*	0.026	14.6	DG
Scalopus aquaticus	0.1	2.4	G83	*Napeozapus insignis*	0.025	8.6	G83
Blarina brevicauda	0.016	3.6	G83	*Peromyscus leucopus*	0.025	11	G88
Lagomorpha				*Notomys alexis*	0.0245	14.9	G88
Lepus arcticus	4.6	64	G83	*Peromyscus maniculatus*	0.0227	15.9	G88
Lepus alleni	4.4	72	G83	*Peromyscus eremicus*	0.0186	14.2	G88
Lepus europeus	4	72	G83	*Pseudomys hermannsberg.*	0.018	12.6	G88
Lepus townsendii	3.5	56	G83	*Zapus hudsonicus*	0.018	8.9	G83
Lepus californicus	2	64	G83	*Peromyscus truei*	0.0178	14.4	G88
Oryctolagus cuniculus	1.9	56	G83	*Peromyscus crinitus*	0.0163	12.5	DG
Lepus americanus	1.5	50	G83	*Onychomys torridus*	0.016	11	G88
Sylvilagus	1.5	40	G83	*Chaetodipus fallax*	0.016	14.2	G88
Marsupialia				*Mus musculus*	0.016	13.1	G88
Macropus	50	65	G88	*Leggadina forresti*	0.0155	12.6	G88
Didelphis marsupialis	5	7.4	G83	*Microdipodops megacephalus*	0.011	14.2	G88
Macropus eugenii	4	40	G88				

Species names have sometimes been revised for consistency with current nomenclature (as in Wilson and Reeder 2005). Data are from the listed references.

Abbreviations: G83 = Garland 1983; G88 = Garland *et al.* 1988; DG = Djawdan and Garland 1988; GJ = Garland and Janis 1993.

Figure 3.1 is a bivariate plot of these data after $\log_{10}$-transform to straighten the relationships. Two linear patterns can be readily identified in this diagram: maximal running speed scales positively with body mass up to ≈150 kg, but negatively at larger sizes. Both patterns of increase ($r = .74$, $p \leq .0001$; 123 taxa <150 kg) and decrease ($r = -.69$, $p \leq .0001$; 25 taxa >150 kg) are highly significant. The coefficients of determination indicate that body mass alone would explain 55% and 48%, respectively, of the variation in maximal velocity within these body size categories. If we exclude two conspicuous outliers from these data, consisting of small species (porcupine and pale-throated sloth, see Figure 3.1) that build on predator avoidance strategies alternative to running (quills and camouflage), the pattern of increase is even stronger ($r = .83$, $p \leq .0001$).

The effect of phylogeny on these trends needs also to be explored because this factor frequently mediates body size patterns (Peters 1983; Garland and Janis 1993; Caro 2005).

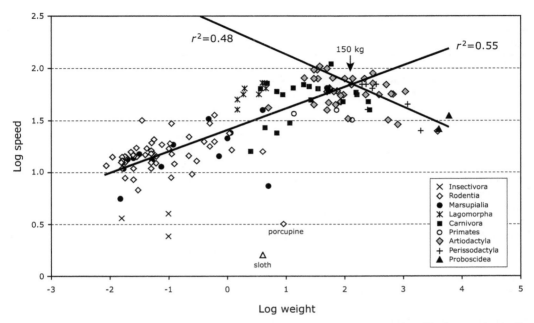

FIGURE 3.1. Bivariate plot showing the relation between maximal running speed and body mass in small (≤150 kg) versus large (>150 kg) terrestrial mammals. Species to the left of the arrow are smaller than 150 kg, those to the right are larger than 150 kg. Data from Table 3.1.

It should be noted that because partitioning the data according to evolutionary lineage reduces sample sizes appreciably, conspicuous outliers were sometimes excluded from the correlations. At the level of the order and for taxa <150 kg, each major monophyletic group shows an intra-lineage positive relationship between speed and body mass, with the notable exception of artiodactyls, which shows a weak, but nonsignificant, inversion of the trend (Artiodactyla: $r = -.36, p < .09$, *Madoqua kirkii* excluded; Carnivora: $r = .53$, $p < .03$; Marsupialia: $r = .66, p < .01$; Lagomorpha: $r = .78, p < .03$; Rodentia: $r = .44, p \leq$ .001, *Erethizon dorsatum* excluded). In species >150 kg, maximal velocity decreases with increasing size within all concerned lineages (Artiodactyla: $r = -.70, p < .01$; Carnivora: $r = -.93, p < .10$; Perissodactyla: $r = -.79, p < .04$), although the trend cannot be fully evaluated in carnivores because of the small sample size ($n = 4$). In general, these results are consistent with those obtained when all lineages are aggregated, with the exception of artiodactyls <150 kg.

In addition to the trends themselves, substantial information can be gained from the outliers because these consist of taxa that may either be easier or more difficult to catch relative to prey of comparable size. These outliers – generously defined here as any species that deviate at least by one standard deviation from the main trends – are presented as standardized residuals in Table 3.2. Taxa that are slower than expected on the basis of their body size include fossorial species (moles, marmot, northern short-tailed shrew), some carnivores (skunk, brown bear), marsupials (opossum species), several ungulates (mountain goat, onager, moose, hippopotamus), and the very slow porcupine and pale-throated sloth, which were mentioned earlier in the chapter. Although these species should, on average, be more profitable than those that deviate less from the

TABLE 3.2. *Standardized residuals for the relationship between maximal running velocity and body mass*

"Slow" taxa			"Fast" taxa		
Small (<150 kg)					
Cercartetus concinnus	pygmy possums	−1.083	*Lepus americanus*	snowshoe hare	1.025
Mephitis mephitis	skunk	−1.094	*Lepus arcticus*	arctic hare	1.052
Rattus	rat	−1.136	*Antidorcas marsupialis*	springbok	1.056
Oreamnos americanus	mountain goat	−1.203	*Dipodomys deserti*	desert kangaroo rat	1.062
Marmota monax	marmot	−1.259	*Acinonyx jubatus*	cheetah	1.078
Gorilla gorilla	gorilla	−1.295	*Gazella subgutturosa*	goitered gazelle	1.1
Blarina brevicauda	short-tailed shrew	−1.857	*Urocyon cinereoargent.*	gray fox	1.128
Talpa europaea	European mole	−2.322	*Oryctolagus cuniculus*	European rabbit	1.135
Didelphis marsupialis	common opossum	−2.65	*Antilope cervicapra*	blackbuck	1.157
Scalopus aquaticus	eastern mole	−3.192	*Vulpes vulpes*	red fox	1.237
Erethizon dorsatum	common porcupine	−4.284	*Lepus alleni*	antelope jackrabbit	1.268
Bradypus tridactylus	pale-throated sloth	−5.179	*Lepus europeus*	European hare	1.301
			Lepus californicus	black-t. jackrabbit	1.344
			Dipodomys merriami	Merriam's kang. rat	1.587
Large (>150 kg)					
Ursus arctos	brown bear	−1.038	*Elephas maximus*	Asian elephant	1.126
Alces alces	moose	−1.275	*Panthera leo*	African lion	1.165
Hippopotamus amph.	hippopotamus	−1.386	*Diceros bicornis*	black rhinoceros	1.287
Ceratotherium simum	white rhinoceros	−1.401	*Hippotragus equinus*	Roan antelope	1.299
Equus hemionus	onager	−1.614	*Loxodonta africana*	African elephant	1.596
			Connochaetes gnou	black wildebeest	1.765

trend, the fact that some of these taxa also display behaviors that increase pursuit time (e.g., hiding in multi-entrance burrows) mean that their lower speed may not always translate into increased rates of capture.

On the basis of the residuals, taxa that are faster than expected given their body mass include kangaroo rats, leporids, some carnivores (foxes, cheetah, lion), Antilopinae (gazelles and antelopes), and some large ungulates (wildebeest, black rhinoceros, elephants). These species should generally be less profitable to the hunter than slower, similar-sized species. Because pursuit costs are likely to be substantial for several of these fast and difficult-to-catch species, the introduction of snares, scopes, shotguns, and other capture-enhancing devices is expected to have a proportionally greater effect on their profitability than on their slower counterparts.

The ramifications of these patterns may be significant for our understanding of pursuit decisions in human foragers. For nonartiodactyl mammals smaller than 150 kg, the decision to pursue a prey type should, all else being equal, be a trade-off between an increase in food mass and a decreased probability of capture. Given these opposing forces, the body size rule is probably vulnerable to rank inversions within that size range, particularly toward its smaller end. To illustrate this problem, should an antelope jackrabbit be conferred a higher rank than a cottontail rabbit, knowing that the former contains three times as much food but is also almost twice as fast as the latter? Additional research is needed to elucidate how these two factors play out across small body sizes. Geographically, this type of foraging dilemma should predominate in regions such as Central America, South America, and Australia where large species are rare (Fritz and Loison 2006). Preliminary data for Australia appear to be consistent with these generalizations because they show that speed is often as, if not more, important than body size for predicting the return rates of small prey taxa that differ widely in antipredator behaviors (Bird *et al.* 2009).

The problem is different for artiodactyls in general and nonartiodactyl mammals larger than 150 kg. In opposition to the trend seen in small species, speed patterns *strengthen* the body size rule in large species because maximum speed tends to decrease at the high end of the body size continuum. Therefore, the body size rule should, in theory, be a stronger index of profitability in that size range. However, as pointed out by other authors (Simms 1987; Broughton 1994; Byers and Ugan 2005), the picture is not so simple. The ethnographic literature suggests that traditional weapons are progressively less effective at killing large prey (particularly those larger than approximately 700 kg) as they increase in size. As we will see, this last problem is also probably an effect of scaling.

We have known since Galileo that the ability of muscles to support load is inversely related to body size (Biewener 1989, 2005). For this reason, large animals must have proportionally larger muscles than small animals to support their own weight, which explains why the former tend to be stockier (Peters 1983). This allometric constraint on body proportions seems to influence procurement of large prey in several ways. Through heightened protection of vital organs and tissues, relatively and absolutely larger muscles may reduce or delay death, the outcome being that the probability of capturing an injured and/or poisoned prey may decrease with growing body size. The remarkable strength of large animals can also cause damage to equipment (e.g., nets, projectiles) or injuries, costs that the hunter may not be willing to pay. The combined effect of these patterns is that animals in the high end of the body size spectrum tend to be associated with long pursuit time and low success rates. These costs, which increase with body size, must therefore be balanced against gains in energetic yield.

Taking all of these factors into account, it can be concluded that the body size rule should work best in mammals at intermediate prey sizes, for instance in the 50- to 700-kg size range, in which both types of trade-offs (increasing speed in small animals and increasing strength in large animals) are minimized. For birds and reptiles, the information is scant but suggests that these groups differ from mammals in speed and strength patterns (Lima 1993; Caro 2005; Bird *et al.* 2009). For example, escape speed may be less variable in birds, and more variable in reptiles, than in mammals, which would respectively strengthen and weaken the body size rule for these groups. Concerning reptiles, because escape behaviors appear to be more variable within this group, it may be wisest at the moment to exclude them from abundance ratios.

So far, the discussion has hinged on how patterns in flight speed and structural aspects of body proportions may affect profitability within and across body size categories. However, environmental variation in community structure may also be critical for understanding the mixed success of the body size rule. Specifically, the *distribution* of prey body sizes within a faunal community may be particularly significant because it may reduce or enhance overlap in return rates. For instance, it seems reasonable to expect a faunal community consisting of species with a wide range of well-graded body sizes (an example is the Canadian boreal forest) to show fewer rank inversions than one characterized by a narrow range of similarly sized species, as is the case, for instance, in the tropical forest of Central America. If this hypothesis is correct, body size should be a more accurate index of profitability in Canada than in Central America. This variation will evidently be conditioned by environmental clines in animal body size.

An abundant literature attests to the macroecologists' and biogeographers' renewed interest in Bergmann's rule, a generalization about environmental variation in animal body size named after the German naturalist Christian Bergmann, who first formulated it in 1847 (Blackburn and Gaston 1996; Blackburn *et al.* 1999; Ashton *et al.* 2000; Ashton 2002, 2004; Cardillo 2002; Ashton and Feldman 2003; Freckleton *et al.* 2003; Meiri and Dayan 2003; Blackburn and Hawkins 2004; Olifiers *et al.* 2004; Millien *et al.* 2006; Olalla-Tárraga *et al.* 2006; Rodríguez *et al.* 2006, 2008; Adams and Church 2007; Olalla-Tárraga and Rodríguez 2007; Meiri and Thomas 2007; Meiri *et al.* 2007; Gaston *et al.* 2008; Ramirez *et al.* 2008).

The interspecific form of Bergmann's rule stipulates that in endotherms ("warm-blooded" animals), closely related species tend to increase in body size with latitude/elevation and/or with decreasing ambient temperature. Likewise, the more intensely studied intraspecific form of Bergmann's rule holds that individuals living in the cooler portion of the geographic range of a species are generally larger than individuals occupying the warmer portion of the range (Millien *et al.* 2006). Initially, these size gradients were interpreted as a by-product of the thermal adaptation of endotherms to temperature variation, the rationale being that large body size maximizes heat conservation in cool habitats through a lower surface-to-volume ratio (Blackburn *et al.* 1999). The same mechanism would also favor heat dissipation in warm environments (Ashton and Feldman 2003).

The multiplication in the number of wildlife studies over the past thirty years have allowed in-depth testing of the validity of the body size clines inferred by Bergmann. These analyses have corroborated the tendency of mammals to conform to both the intra- and interspecific variants of Bergmann's rule, although there is much debate about the mechanism(s) that underlie these patterns (Fleming 1973; Ashton *et al.* 2000; Ashton 2002; Freckleton *et al.* 2003; Meiri and Dayan 2003; Blackburn and Hawkins 2004; Rodríguez *et al.* 2006, 2008). However, conformance to Bergmann's rule appears to be nonlinear in mammals and would primarily characterize cool areas with mean annual temperature below approximately 10 to 13°C, body size gradients being weaker, and sometimes reversed, in warmer regions (Rodríguez *et al.* 2006, 2008). Support for both forms of Bergmann's rule are also reported in birds (Blackburn and Gaston 1996; Cardillo 2002; Meiri and Dayan 2003; Ramirez *et al.* 2008; Teplitsky *et al.* 2008). According to Ramirez *et al.* (2008), avian body size clines should be stronger during the winter, when some species retreat to the temperate zone, than in the summer. As a final note, it should be pointed out that despite the generality of Bergmann's rule in endotherms, some species and clades (e.g., mustelids, heteromyids) do not conform to it or follow an inverse relationship (Meiri and Dayan 2003).

Ectotherms ("cold-blooded" animals) were largely omitted from early descriptions of Bergmann's rule because the causal mechanism envisioned by Bergmann – allometric variation in thermal adaptation – cannot, as initially defined, be extended to them (Ashton *et al.* 2000; Ashton and Feldman 2003). However, because Bergmann's thermal hypothesis is contested, some researchers have examined body size gradients in ectotherms as well. Results on this issue have largely been equivocal. In general, the evidence for Bergmannian trends in amphibians and reptiles is weak, with the possible exception of chelonians (turtles), which may be consistent with the intraspecific, but not the interspecific, form of the rule (Lindsey 1966; Ashton and Feldman 2003; Olalla-Tárraga *et al.* 2006; Adams and Church 2007; Olalla-Tárraga and Rodríguez 2007). In freshwater fishes, Bergmann's rule seems to apply at the interspecific, but not at the intraspecific, level (Lindsey 1966; Belk and Houston 2002).

As the foregoing examples make clear, Bergmann's rule is first and foremost an empirical generalization about environmental variation in body size (Ashton *et al.* 2000). However, the causes of these gradients remain controversial (Gaston *et al.* 2008). In addition to the thermal hypothesis, the mechanisms that are most frequently cited include starvation resistance (larger species cope better with seasonal fluctuations than smaller species because of their lower metabolic rate), interference competition (presumed to be less of a limiting factor to growth in cool areas), and phenotypic plasticity (Millien *et al.* 2006; Meiri *et al.* 2007; Teplitsky *et al.* 2008). Of more direct concern here are the foraging implications of environmental clines in body size with regard to the range of prey available to hunters-gatherers operating in diverse ecological settings.

A corollary of Bergmann's rule is that human foragers occupying cool environments would have access to prey species of larger size and, presumably to a wider range of prey sizes, than those in warm climates. Because both of these characteristics appear to minimize violations of the body size rule (by reducing overlap in the profitability of different species), the strength of the correlation between profitability and body size should increase with latitude and decrease with mean annual temperature because these parameters are correlated with body size clines.

To test these predictions, foraging and experimental studies providing net return rates and body masses for at least five captured prey types were compiled, along with latitude and temperature data (Table 3.3). Only case studies with a preponderance of endotherms and/or fish – groups that conform to the interspecific form of Bergmann's rule – were considered, with the exception of the Martu from Australia (prey set dominated by terrestrial ectotherms), which were included to increase sample size. It should be noted that the data are not perfect because the samples are small, include non-Bergmannian species, and are hindered by spatial autocorrelation (three case studies are not entirely independent in a statistical sense as they comprise some of the same species). Despite these caveats, the results are still useful because they encompass a wide range of environments and foraging contexts. Lastly, correlation analyses were performed using Spearman's rho.

As predicted, the strength of the correlation coefficients between prey body size and profitability increases with latitude ($r_s = .71$, $p < .09$) and decreases with mean annual temperature ($r_s = -.93$, $p < .03$), although only the latter trend is statistically significant. Excluding the Martu from the analysis has little impact on the results (latitude: $r_s = .77$, $p < .09$; temperature: $r_s = -.89$, $p < 0.05$). To ascertain whether Bergmannian gradients underlie these trends, the mean, standard deviation, and range of body weights were computed for each prey set and compared with the strength of the body size-profitability correlations. For all three variables, a strong, positive, and statistically significant correlation was found (strength of correlation vs. mean weight: $r_s = .93$, $p < .03$; strength of correlation vs. standard deviation: $r_s = .89$, $p < .03$; strength of correlation vs. range of weights: $r_s = .89$, $p < .03$).

TABLE 3.3. *Data on the relationship between body mass and postencounter return rates combined with information on latitude, mean annual temperature, and body mass characteristics of the faunas*

Group	r_s, p value	Latitude	Mean temperature	Mean, SD, and range of prey mass (kg)	Number of prey types and sources
Martu, Australia	0.24, <.53	22	28.8	4.2, 7.4, 22.0	8 prey types. Bird *et al.* 2009:11, table 2.
Mayangna, Miskito, Nicaragua	0.32, <.44	14	27	11.8, 13.8, 37.7	7 prey types[a]. Koster 2008a:940, table 2.; Koster 2008b:214, table 1
Aché, Paraguay	0.41, <.31	24.2	21	14.0, 12.4, 27.5	7 prey types. Hawkes *et al.* 1982:382, table 1; Hill *et al.* 1987:20, table 2.
Piro, Peru	0.65, <.07	11	26	32.6, 54.0, 168.5	9 prey types[b], tapir and capybara included. Alvard 1993:371, table 2 and p. 372.
Actualistic, Great Basin, US	**0.81, <.04**	39.5	9.3	16.9, 30.6, 79.4	8 prey types[c]. Simms 1987:45, tables 3 and 4.
Inujjuamiut, Québec, Canada	**0.81, <.0001**	58	−6.7	72.6, 121.3, 498.4	25 prey types[d]. Smith 1991, Jones 2004a:311, table 2 and p. 312.
Cree, Ontario, Canada	0.90, <.08	53	−0.4	57.4, 115.8, 263.4	5 prey types[e]. Winterhalder 1981:79, table 4.2 and p. 82–83, table 4.4.

Values that are significant are in bold. The list of groups is expanded and modified from Broughton (1999:124). When a range of return rates was provided, the midpoint was selected. Mean annual temperature data from the following sources: Hill *et al.* 1984, http://www.rimfrost.no; http://www.bom.gov.au/index.shtml, http://www.climate.weatheroffice.ec.gc.ca. Mean, range, and standard deviation calculated using the body mass for all of the prey types considered in the correlation coefficient.

[a] Includes giant anteater. Profitability data averaged for pacas and agoutis. Body size sums biomass data from Arang Dak and Suma Pipi divided by the total number of kills.

[b] Body size estimated by dividing "harvest" mass by numbers of kills. Following Alvard, profitability for tapir and capybara are 282,750 and 61,425 cal/hr, respectively. Body size for these two taxa were estimated to be 170 and 50 kg, respectively.

[c] To facilitate comparison, body size data from Garland (1983) were used instead of Simms's "edible weight" data. Deer and bighorn sheep combined in Simms's analysis. Body size for ducks, pocket gophers, and large ground squirrels were estimated to be 1, 0.6, and 0.4 kg, respectively.

[d] Body size data in correlation coefficients are based on "kcal/individual (edible portion)." Live weight data (from Smith 1991:181, table 1) was used for the computation of mass characteristics. "Ocean fish" and "ice netting" were excluded due to a lack of data.

[e] Body size based on "early winter group size" divided by the number of individuals. All seasons averaged. Moose and caribou are combined in Winterhalder's analysis. Net fishing was excluded due to a lack of data.

Overall, in this sample, the strength of the body size rule increases in communities that comprise several large-sized prey taxa with a wide range of body weight, conditions that tend to prevail in cool habitats. These correlations are important because body size distributions can be reconstructed archaeologically, even for communities that include extinct species, using modern analogues or bone size as a proxy for body mass. Therefore, it should be possible to determine a priori whether the body size rule is likely to be a robust measure of profitability in specific archaeological situations.

But do the results described invalidate the use of the body size rule in warm environments? Not necessarily. To avert the problem of rank inversions, a fruitful strategy in archaeology may be to design abundance indices (discussed subsequently) composed of taxa with similar antipredator strategies, principally with respect to maximal speed. Ideally, taxa in these indices would contrast as much as possible in terms of body size (e.g., small vs. large birds; small vs. large ungulates; solitary leporids vs. ungulates; small vs. large monkeys) and would exclude on the "small" side of the equation species that are prone to be mass-collected. Such a strategy, implicit in the work of Broughton (1999), can be productive because it strengthens the relationship between return rates and body size within the selected subsets. However, this approach also has the drawback of producing several competing body size scales, which may make them individually liable to sample size problems.

Summarizing these findings, it can be concluded that the strength of the body size rule will be contingent on the following characteristics: i) the prey species (maximum speed, muscle mass, behavior or contexts that favors mass collecting); ii) the prey set as a whole (i.e., dominated by endotherms and fish, by reptiles and amphibians or a combination thereof), and iii) the environment (e.g., mean annual temperature, latitude, elevation). Thus, depending on the context, some modifications may be necessary to ensure that the body size rule remains a valid proxy of return rates. These modifications may, for instance, require the elimination of taxa from the faunal set, which, on the basis of external evidence, are likely to cause rank inversions. Commonly, these taxa are small, energy-rich, resources that are easily collected and processed (e.g., tortoises). It is important to emphasize here that comparisons of low- and high-return species through the use of abundance indices should be based on prey taxa with clear differences in ranking. Comparisons involving animals with small differences in profitability (e.g., rabbits vs. hares) are prone to error because of possible inaccuracies in return rate estimates.

Abundance Indices

Developed by Bayham (1979), "abundance indices" are simple ratios that portray the representation of high- versus low-ranked resources. Mathematically, these ratios typically take the following form: $\sum$ large taxa/($\sum$ small taxa + $\sum$ large taxa). All other factors being equal, a temporal decrease in these ratios is generally interpreted to mean that smaller, presumably lower-return (but see discussion above), taxa are being increasingly exploited. As a result of their simplicity and potential explanatory power, abundance indices figure prominently in archaeological studies of dietary patterns (Lupo 2007).

Because no method is perfect, several problems have been raised concerning the interpretation of these indices (Grayson and Cannon 1999; Cannon 2000; Broughton 2002; Lupo and Schmidt 2005). One difficulty is that abundance ratios may foster erroneous conclusions when the representation of two taxa in the index fluctuates in opposite directions and/or at distinct rates (Grayson and Cannon 1999; Cannon 2000; Ugan and Bright 2001). For instance, a decrease in the abundance of a high-ranked taxon might have been compensated by a concomitant increase in the abundance of another high-ranked taxon. In this case, an abundance ratio that only includes the former may misrepresent real change in foraging efficiency.

Furthermore, we have seen that a temporal increase in the abundance of a high-ranked prey type, in lieu of a decline, may be observed when falling foraging efficiency in near patches prompts foragers to exploit more distant, and previously underutilized, patches (Hames and Vickers 1982; Broughton 1999; Cannon 2000, 2001a, 2003). However, this last problem may primarily concern semi- or fully sedentary foragers because mobile groups are expected to move camps to avoid escalating transport costs (Kelly 1995). These and other issues (see Grayson and Cannon 1999) highlight the importance of combining abundance indices with other lines of evidence to inform arguments about past variations in foraging patterns.

Currency and Foraging Goals in Humans

Several studies have shown that human male foragers sometimes ignore resources that would otherwise increase their overall return rate, or conversely, include resources that decrease it (Hill *et al.* 1987; Alvard 1993; Bird and O'Connell 2006). Both observations violate the predictions of the prey choice model. The main problem seems to be that males tend to behave as if plants, as a set, were ranked lower than animals (Kaplan and Hill 1992). In general, the fit with theoretical predictions is much more satisfactory when both classes of resources are considered separately. Without revisiting this problem in detail, it is nonetheless useful to highlight a few points.

Two hypotheses have been put forward to explain the male bias toward animal procurement. One view, espoused by Hill and his collaborators (1987; Hill 1988; Hurtado and Hill 1990; Kaplan and Hill 1992), questions the legitimacy of the currency (net energy intake) underlying most anthropological studies of foraging practices. These authors argue that fats and proteins (the most abundant macronutrients in soft animal tissue) may, in fact, have a higher nutritional value than equivalent amounts of energy derived from carbohydrates (dominant in many vegetables). This issue is germane to studies focusing on game hunters, given that the proportion of body fat often fluctuates dramatically across seasons in animals, particularly in those occupying mid to high latitudes (Pond 1998). One difficulty with this hypothesis is that females may not rank plants as low as males do, which may be an indication that they are less sensitive to macronutrient composition than males. However, constraints on foraging stemming from child rearing may largely account for this sexual difference by channeling females toward the procurement of low-risk resources such as plants and small game (Hurtado and Hill 1990; Bliege Bird and Bird 2008).

The second view, not exclusive of the first, holds that males favor big-game hunting because large animals are shared across broader social arenas than small game and plants. Noting that large game are normally associated with high variance in encounter and capture rates, the model asserts that public sharing of these resources increases political and mating opportunities by signaling the quality of the hunter (Hawkes and O'Connell 1992; Hawkes *et al.* 2001, 2010; Smith *et al.* 2003).

Yet foragers of the Australian desert do not entirely fit the expectations of the "showoff" hypothesis. Although male hunters from this region are, in agreement with the model, generally variance-prone in their pursuit decisions, they appear, in certain contexts, to be variance-averse, which contradicts it (Bliege Bird and Bird 2008; Bird *et al.* 2009). For instance, when hunting in perentie monitor (*Varanus giganteus*) and sand monitor (*Varanus gouldii*) patches, males almost systematically pass on hill kangaroos (*Macropus robustus*) and bustards (*Ardeotis australis*), prey taxa with moderately low capture rates (30%), to exploit the much smaller, but more reliable, reptiles encountered in the same patches (Bird *et al.* 2009:18). Importantly, these resources are passed over despite the fact that pursuing them would increase the mean overall return rate. This violation of the model calls for more research on foraging goals and on individual response to variation in capture rate.

OPERATIONALIZING THE TEST OF THE INTENSIFICATION HYPOTHESIS

Taking into account the foregoing reservations, the implications of the early Upper Paleolithic intensification hypothesis can be investigated in the archaeological record through the analysis of foraging decisions. For reasons outlined later, Saint-Césaire, an archaeological sequence documenting the Middle to Upper Paleolithic transition in Western France, was selected for this purpose. The following paragraphs summarize the foraging predictions that will be used to test the intensification hypothesis at this site. The presentation of these predictions is, however, preceded by a discussion focusing on climatic variation because this factor can seriously confound the interpretation of dietary change in the context of the Middle to Upper Paleolithic transition.

A Problem of Equifinality: Climate as a Cause of Diet Widening

Climate can have a significant impact on diet breadth by modifying encounter rates with prey taxa (Grayson and Cannon 1999). This issue is important because climatic oscillations during the early Upper Paleolithic have been documented (Barron *et al.* 2003; d'Errico and Sánchez Goñi 2003; Sánchez Goñi *et al.* 2008; Naughton *et al.* 2009). These oscillations possibly affected foraging decisions because they likely altered the density and distribution of high-ranked prey taxa. Two faunal studies (Grayson *et al.* 2001; Morin 2008) have tackled this problem in western France.

Grayson and colleagues (2001) examined variation in species abundance at Grotte XVI, a cave in southwestern France containing an archaeological sequence that starts with the Mousterian and continues through the Magdalenian. To investigate taxonomic diversity, these authors focused on evenness, a statistic that measures the degree to which a faunal assemblage consists of species that are all equally represented or, on the contrary, is dominated by one or a few taxa. Grayson and his collaborators noted a temporal increase in reindeer (*Rangifer tarandus*) dominance during the Upper Paleolithic. They attributed this temporal increase to abiotic factors that were favorable to reindeer – namely, decreased summer temperatures – as they reported a good match between patterns of reindeer dominance and Guiot's (1990) estimated July temperatures, the latter based on pollen sequences from eastern France.

At a much shorter, but finer, temporal scale, Morin (2008) compared patterns of evenness between micromammals (<500 g) and large (predominantly ungulates >80 kg) mammals across the Middle to Upper Paleolithic transition at Saint-Césaire, using the former species as a climatic control. Micromammals are particularly helpful in that respect because they tend to be sensitive to subtle variations in ecological conditions and were generally deposited by nonhuman predators during the Late Pleistocene

(Chaline 1970; Marquet 1993; Tchernov 1998). The analysis of the Saint-Césaire micro-mammals paid special attention to taxonomic diversity in light of the current latitudinal trend for the number of mammal species to decrease as one moves away from the equator (Badgley and Fox 2000; Lomolino *et al.* 2006).

The micromammal assemblages examined by Morin (2008) showed an abrupt decline of species diversity during the Middle to Upper Paleolithic transition (Figure 3.2). Because this change was not correlated with sample size and corresponded with a sharp increase in the relative abundance of the cold-adapted narrow-skulled vole (*Microtus gregalis*), these results were argued to signal the onset of a relatively severe climatic deterioration. Similar shifts in the taxonomic abundance of reindeer corroborated this interpretation.

The climatic deterioration identified during the transition between the Middle and the Upper Paleolithic was inferred to have significantly decreased environmental carrying capacity for humans (Morin 2008). This decreased carrying capacity was attributed to the combination of three factors: i) a marked reduction of large ungulate diversity, a variable that seems to negatively impact human density (Burch 1972; Keeley 1988); ii) the highly cyclical nature of *Rangifer*, on which humans became increasingly dependent (Meldgaard 1986; Minc 1986; Syroechkovskii 1995); and iii) the *tendency* of *Rangifer* populations to crash synchronously at the regional level (Gunn 2003). These arguments are presented in greater detail in Morin (2008).

This decline in carrying capacity, hereafter referred to as the *climatic deterioration hypothesis*, is critical, given that it alone might have fueled a diet breadth expansion in the early Upper Paleolithic. Indeed, reduced abundances of favorite prey taxa possibly led the local populations to widen their food base, which should be signaled by an increase in the relative abundance of low-ranked resources in faunal assemblages. Because the intensification hypothesis has similar archaeological implications – although the causal mechanism is population competition rather than climatic change – distinguishing these two hypotheses at Saint-Césaire may be difficult. A closer look at these hypotheses suggests ways to partially circumvent this problem of equifinality.

Diet broadening is not the only possible outcome in a situation of decreased environmental carrying capacity. For instance, despite climatic deterioration, early Upper Paleolithic foragers in France might have continued to ignore low-ranked taxa, as they did throughout the Mousterian, in favor of increasingly difficult-to-find large ungulates. Although not the most efficient strategy in terms of energy acquisition, this last option might have been preferred because it can enhance the prestige of male hunters and facilitate access to mates (Hawkes and Bliege Bird 2002; Smith *et al.* 2003; O'Connell 2006). In contrast, the intensification hypothesis explicitly argues that resource intensification allowed modern humans to displace Neandertals, a population characterized by a narrow diet. Therefore, a lack of evidence for a diet breadth expansion in the early Upper Paleolithic would clearly conflict with the intensification hypothesis. These nuances mean that it should be possible to refute, but much more difficult to validate, the intensification model in the climatic context of the Middle to Upper Paleolithic transition.

The sections that follow will focus mostly on the faunal implications of the intensification hypothesis, omitting, for the moment, the equifinality issues raised by the climatic

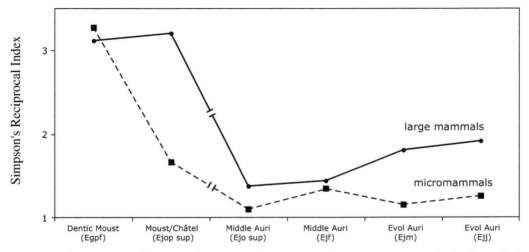

FIGURE 3.2. Large mammal versus micromammal species diversity, as measured by the Reciprocal of Simpson's Index, in the Saint-Césaire levels (modified from Morin 2008). The EJOP inf and EJO inf assemblages were excluded because of small sample sizes.

deterioration hypothesis. This problem will be taken up again when interpreting the data.

FAUNAL IMPLICATIONS WITH RESPECT TO PREY CHOICE

As pointed out earlier, the intensification and climatic deterioration hypotheses are in agreement in proposing that there was a reduced access to favorite prey taxa during the early Upper Paleolithic. The central place forager prey choice model (Cannon 2001a, 2003) was selected to evaluate the faunal implications of this argument. This model was chosen because animal resources were likely transported to, rather than captured at, Saint-Césaire, which was then a rockshelter or a small cave. The diversity and quantity of material recovered, the presence of numerous hearths, and the currency analysis presented in Chapter 8 also suggest that the site functioned as a central place. However, before proceeding further, it should be noted that one prediction of the central place forager prey choice model is unlikely to apply in many Paleolithic contexts.

Following Broughton (1999), the central place forager prey choice model predicts that in contexts of severe resource depression, foragers will exploit high-ranked prey taxa in distant patches when low-ranked prey taxa become rare near the central place (Cannon 2000, 2001a). This situation should lead to a resurgence of large taxa in the faunal assemblages (Broughton 1999). This prediction seems accurate for groups with *low* residential mobility, as would be the case of groups relying extensively on farming and/or storage (Keeley 1988). However, this assumption does not seem appropriate at Saint-Césaire, given that its occupants were probably "mapping onto" resources (*sensu* Binford 1980) and frequently moving their residential camps. Mobile groups do not typically make long logistical forays to distant patches, as assumed by the central place forager prey choice model, but instead tend to move camp closer to these patches, in a manner reminiscent of the marginal value theorem. If correct, this means that a resurgence of high-ranked taxa at Saint-Césaire should always signal an increase in

TABLE 3.4. *Scientific and common names of the species identified at Saint-Césaire and at other Late Pleistocene sites in the study region*

Scientific name	Common name	Scientific name	Common name
Artiodactyla		Rodentia	
Rangifer tarandus	reindeer, caribou	*Microtus gregalis*	narrow-skulled vole
Bos primigenius	aurochs	*Microtus arvalis*	common vole
Bison priscus	steppe bison	*Citellus superciliosus*	ground squirrel
Cervus elaphus	red deer	*Chionomys nivalis*	snow vole
Megaloceros giganteus	giant deer	*Arvicola terrestris*	water vole
Capreolus capreolus	roe deer	*Pitymys subterraneus*	pine vole
Sus scrofa	wild boar	*Microtus agrestis*	field vole
		Eliomys quercinus	garden dormouse
Perissodactyla		*Microtus oeconomus*	root vole
Equus ferus caballus	horse	*Microtus malei*	Male vole
Coelodonta antiquitatis	woolly rhino	*Dicrostonyx torquatus*	collared lemming
Equus hydruntinus	European ass	*Rattus rattus*	rat
Proboscidea		Aves	
Mammuthus primigenius	mammoth	*Anser* sp.	goose
		Anas acuta	pintail
Carnivora		*Anas crecca*	teal
Crocuta crocuta spelaea	cave hyena	*Aquila chrysaetos*	golden eagle
Canis lupus	wolf	*Lagopus* sp.	ptarmigan/willow grouse
Alopex lagopus	arctic fox	*Alle alle*	little auk
Vulpes vulpes	red fox	*Pluvialis* sp.	plover
Lynx lynx	Eurasian lynx	*Corvus corax*	raven
Mustela putorius	polecat	*Pyrrhocorax graculus*	alpine chough
Mustela nivalis	weasel	*Bubo scandiacus*	snowy owl
Martes martes	pine marten		
Meles meles	badger	Fish	
Panthera leo spelaea	cave lion	*Salmo trutta*	trout
Ursus spelaeus	cave bear	*Salmo salar*	salmon
		Alosa alosa	allis shad
Lagomorpha		*Anguilla anguilla*	European eel
Lepus timidus	hare	*Esox lucius*	pike
Oryctolagus cuniculus	rabbit	*Leuciscus cephalus*	European chub
		Leuciscus leuciscus	common dace
Insectivora		*Leuciscus idus*	ide
Talpa europaea	common mole	*Alburnus alburnus*	bleak

foraging efficiency, all else being equal. It is this slightly modified version of the central place forager prey choice model that is applied here.

Table 3.4 lists species that are recurrently identified in natural and archaeological contexts dated to the Middle to Upper Paleolithic transition in the study area (Delpech 1983; Guadelli *et al.* 1988; Le Gall 1992, 2000; Laroulandie 2004a). On the basis of this list, three analytical patches (dry land, wetland, and freshwater) – two focused on hunting, one on fishing – were created to test – or more accurately, to attempt to refute – the intensification hypothesis. These patches, which are compatible with, but not required by, the central place forager prey choice model (Cannon 2003), are kept separate here because they simplify the analysis of foraging decisions.

In this study, the dry land patch includes birds from several orders (Galliformes, Passeriformes, Strigiformes), and all carnivores (except the polecat), leporids, and ungulates (except the giant deer). The wetland patch comprises the polecat, waterfowl (Anseriformes), and the giant deer. Lastly, fish taxa obviously belong to the freshwater patch. Undoubtedly, these patches are very coarsely defined. Moreover, they are not closed units, which implies that some species were certainly occasionally encountered in other patches as well. Despite these shortcomings, these patches probably retain some analytical validity.

Body weight was used here to rank species in terms of net return rates within each of these patches. Very large animals, such as the woolly rhinoceros and the mammoth, as well as very small ones (micromammals), are not considered here because of ambiguities regarding their profitability and a lack of information concerning their mode of accumulation in Paleolithic sites. Taxa rarely identified in the study area (e.g., ibex *Capra ibex*, chamois *Rupicapra rupicapra*, porcupine *Hystrix cristata*) were also ignored. Following ichthyologic practice, maximal recorded weights (specifically, "rod caught records" in Britain, Maitland 2000), instead of mean weights, were used to describe fish body mass, growth being continuous in this group. Lastly, because small slow taxa (e.g., tortoises) often violate the body size rule (Stiner and Munro 2002), only fast small-sized taxa (i.e., leporids, birds, small carnivores, fish) were considered in the calculation of abundance ratios.

Figure 3.3 ranks species within each patch on the basis of their estimated mean body weight. According to the intensification hypothesis, if early modern humans did harvest a broader and costlier range of resources, taxa that have a low rank on these scales should be more abundant in assemblages that they deposited. In the dry land patch, low-ranked taxa that might have increased relative to reindeer, horse, bison, and other large species include red fox and other small carnivores, leporids, snowy owl, willow grouse, and alpine chough. In the wetland patch, the alleged broader diet of modern humans might have included the fast small-sized waterfowl, in addition to the high-ranked giant deer. Therefore, the analysis of the relative abundance of these two prey categories (fast small-sized versus large-sized taxa) provides us with a direct test of the intensification hypothesis in these patches. This analysis is presented in Chapter 9. Concerning the freshwater patch, the fact that fish was largely ignored during the Mousterian (Le Gall 1992) means that the exploitation of this patch by modern humans might signal a diet breadth expansion. To assess whether this was the case, the abundance of fish taxa is compared with the abundance of large ungulates in the dry land patch in Chapter 9.

As pointed out earlier, mass collecting might have affected the ranking of certain prey types. For instance, Jones (2004b, 2006) emphasized that mass-collected rabbits might have yielded much higher return rates than singly procured ones. This issue is not of concern at Saint-Césaire, given that the leporid sample seems dominated by *Lepus*, a taxon consisting of species with solitary habits (MacDonald and Barrett 2001).

A more important problem may impinge on the prey choice analysis. Small taxa, particularly carnivores, might have been accumulated at Saint-Césaire by nonhuman agents or procured for raw materials (e.g., fur, canines, long bone tubes, etc.) rather than for alimentary purposes. Despite this complication, it is important not to exclude small carnivores from the analysis because these animals were sometimes used as "starvation food" by ethnographic groups who collected them for fur (Binford 1978). Therefore, small carnivores may afford critical information on change in diet breadth. The study of fracture patterns, surface modification, skeletal representation, and mark frequencies should help evaluate whether carnivores were consumed in the selected assemblages.

We will see in the currency analysis (Chapter 8) that fat procurement appears to have been a major foraging goal of the Saint-Césaire occupants. Consequently, an attempt was made to rank species according to a second scale based, this time, on body fat weight. The production of this second scale proved more complex than anticipated because fat content is difficult to estimate and is unequally reported across taxonomic groups (Pond 1998). Furthermore, individual and seasonal variation in body fat can be very substantial, particularly in cold-adapted species (Dauphiné 1976; Franzmann *et al.* 1978; Pond *et al.* 1995). Because of a lack of data for many small taxa, no fat weight scale could be implemented for fish. Instead, body weight was used as a gauge of profitability in these species. In the other taxa, fat weight was obtained by multiplying estimated body mass by the proportion of fat calculated for individuals of the same, or closely related, species (Table 3.5). The vast majority of the fat percentages were derived from published and unpublished dissection values kindly provided by Caroline Pond and her colleagues (Pond and Mattacks 1985a, 1985b; Pond *et al.* 1993, 1995; pers. comm., 2009). However, before interpreting the results of these efforts, a few points must be raised about the limitations of the fat weight data.

A first difficulty is that for obvious logistical reasons, Pond's extensive data set was not collected during a single season or for a single sex. The implication is that some species might be represented by a greater proportion of individuals in prime condition than others. Moreover, the fat percentages are not always from wild animals, which possibly induces noise in the patterns. Another difficulty with these data is that the sampled individuals may not always be fully representative, especially when relying on a single animal or a substitute species. Lastly, because Pond's fat data exclude intramuscular and intraskeletal fat, the values probably slightly underestimate fat utility. In contrast, Emerson's data, which were used to derive values for bison, include these fat sources but omit other deposits (mesenteric fat, omental fat, and subcutaneous fat from the skull) examined by Pond and her colleagues. These differences mean that their protocols are not entirely comparable. It is assumed here that these methodological divergences, which affect only one taxon, cancel each other out for the most part. Future work will certainly improve the accuracy of these values.

The fat weight data were used to rank taxa in the dry land and wetland patches (Table 3.5, Figure 3.4). In general, the body fat scale and body weight scale rank prey species in a similar manner, particularly in the dry land patch (dry land: $r_s = .96$, $p < .0001$; wet land: $r_s = .77$, $p < .09$). Both scales point to the preeminence of bison and giant deer in their respective patches. Yet despite the similarity of the rankings – a result that was not unexpected given that fat is also included in the calculation of body weight – some large taxa show sensible shifts in rank position. In the dry land patch, horse, a relatively lean species, ranks much lower (-5 ranks) in the body fat scale than in the body weight scale. Conversely, reindeer ($+4$ ranks) and the cave lion ($+3$ ranks) improve their rank on the body fat scale. Changes are less dramatic at the lower end of the continuum: the arctic fox increases its position ($+2$ ranks) in the fat weight scale, whereas the hare (-3 ranks) moves in the opposite direction. In comparison, changes are minor in the wetland patch.

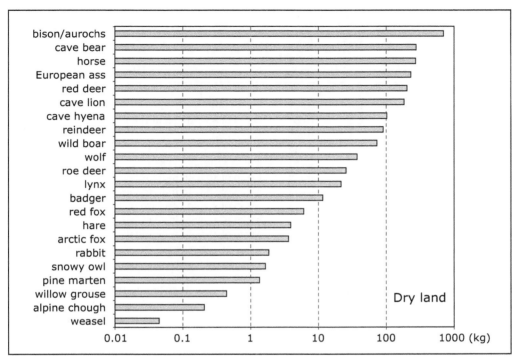

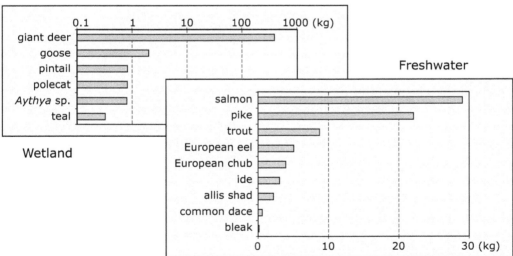

FIGURE 3.3. Body weight of prey taxa for the dry land, wetland, and freshwater patches. Note that the abscissa is on a log10 scale in the dry land and wetland diagrams. For species that still occur in Europe today, the data are from MacDonald and Barrett 2001, except for horse (data from Groves 1994) and birds (data from http://www.oiseaux.net). Midpoints were used when a single range was given or when values or ranges were provided separately for males and females. For extinct species (cave hyena, cave lion, European ass, cave bear, giant deer), body masses are based on estimations provided by Pushkina and Raia (2008:773). As specified in the text, rod-caught record values were used to determine fish weight, as provided by Maitland (2000).

TABLE 3.5. *Body mass and fat weight for species assigned to the dry land and wetland patches*

Patch type	Fatness (in %)	Body mass (in kg)	Fat weight (in kg)	Notes and references relative to fat data
Dry land				
weasel	3.20	0.04	0.001	1 wild individual, P85a
alpine chough	0.90	0.2	0.002	Mean of 8 wild *Corvus corone*, P85b
willow grouse	2.00	0.4	0.008	Estimated
pine marten	3.20	1.3	0.042	1 wild *Mustela nivalis*, P85a
snowy owl	5.10	1.6	0.082	2 wild *Strix aluco*, P85b
rabbit	6.49	1.8	0.117	Mean of 10 wild individuals, P85a
arctic fox	17.00	3.6	0.612	Mean of 28 wild individuals, P95a
hare	1.35	3.9	0.053	Mean of 5 wild *Lepus europaeus*, P85a
red fox	2.23	6.0	0.133	Mean of 12 wild individuals, P95a
badger	9.59	11.6	1.112	Mean of 16 wild individuals, P85a
lynx	9.07	21.5	1.950	Mean of 7 domestic *Felis catus*, P85a. One very obese cat excluded.
roe deer	4.97	25.5	1.267	Mean of 3 zoo *Axis axis*, P85a
wolf	5.27	37.0	1.950	Mean of 3 zoo individuals, P85a
wild boar	12.84	72.7	9.33	Mean of 4 domestic individuals, P85a
reindeer	19.10	90.0	17.190	Mean of the lowest (12.7%) and highest (25.5%) values for 23 wild individuals, P93
cave hyena	6.70	102.0	6.834	1 zoo *Acinonyx jubatus*, P85a
cave lion	13.25	183.0	24.248	1 zoo *Panthera leo*, P85a
red deer	4.97	202.5	10.064	Mean of 3 zoo *Axis axis*, P85a
European ass	6.71	230.0	15.433	1 domestic *Equus asinus*, P85a
horse	2.77	270.2	7.485	mean of 2 domestic individuals, P85a
cave bear	16.00	275.0	44.000	mean of 6 zoo *Ursus arctos*, P85a
bison/auroch	8.43	700.0	59.010	mean of 3 wild *Bison bison* adults, E90
Wetland				
teal	2.47	0.3	0.007	mean of 4 wild *Anas platyrhynchos*, P85b
Aythya sp.	0.40	0.8	0.003	1 wild *Aythya ferina*, P85b
pintail	2.47	0.8	0.020	mean of 4 wild *Anas platyrhynchos*, P85b
polecat	13.98	0.8	0.111	mean of 10 laboratory individuals, P85a
goose	1.10	2.0	0.022	1 wild *Anser anser* individual, P85b
giant deer	19.10	388.0	74.108	mean of the lowest (12.7%) and highest (25.5%) values for 23 wild *Rangifer tarandus*, P93

Data and references for body mass are the same as in Figure 3.3. Fat weight was obtained by multiplying the proportion of fat by body mass. When relevant, the species identified in the "notes and references" column indicates which taxon was used as a substitute. Juveniles were excluded except for *Anser anser* because the only sampled individual for this species was a juvenile.
Abbreviations and sources: E90 = Emerson 1990:513; P85a = Pond and Mattacks 1985a:188, fig. 2 and pers. comm.; P85b = Pond and Mattacks 1985b:196–197, tab. 1; P93 = Pond *et al.* 1993:22; P95 = Pond *et al.* 1995:598.

Overall, the body weight and the body fat scales are in general agreement with respect to the ranking of taxa. According to both scales, small carnivores, leporids, and birds would have been low-ranked prey types in the dry land and wetland patches. The study of their abundance relative to high-ranked taxa should therefore constitute an appropriate test of the intensification hypothesis. Predictions about skeletal part transport, processing intensity, and the selection of individuals within species can also be generated based on this hypothesis.

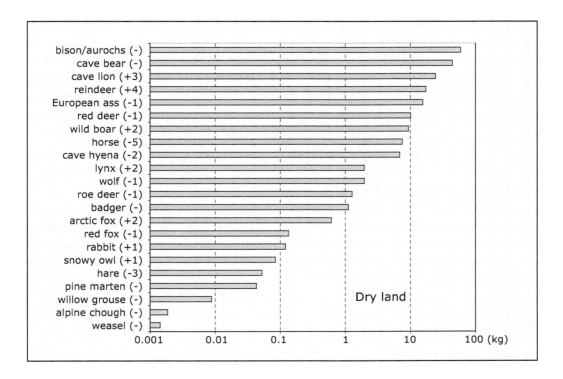

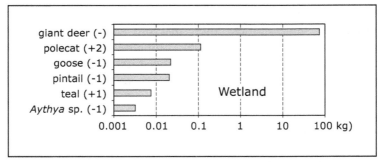

FIGURE 3.4. Bar graph showing body fat for prey taxa belonging to the dry land and wetland patches. The abscissa in both diagrams is on a log10 scale. Numbers in parentheses indicate change in rank position relative to the body weight scale. Data are from Table 3.5.

Prey Choice at the Individual Level

The discussion has so far focused on species. However, age classes within a species can also be viewed as distinct prey types when they differ significantly and predictably in profitability. For instance, many archaeological studies assume that juveniles were lower-ranked than prime adults as a result of their lower and leaner body mass (e.g., Broughton 1999; Munro 2004; Speth 2004b; Jones 2006; Speth and Clark 2006). The same argument is sometimes extended to old adults, given that they also tend to be lighter and leaner compared with prime adults.

One prediction that can be generated using the intensification hypothesis is that the broader diet of early modern humans possibly entailed an increased use of juveniles and old adults. This prediction is accurate insofar as these age classes did not overlap in profitability with prime adults. Is this assumption warranted for *Rangifer*, a high-ranked taxon for which there is sufficient age data at Saint-Césaire? The analysis of developmental trends in reindeer and caribou populations helps to clarify this issue. Bison and horse are here excluded from the discussion because of sample size issues.

In reindeer, sexual dimorphism is manifest, with males weighing 120 to 150 kg on average, compared with 75 to 100 kg in females, for a ratio of about 1.50 to 1.60 (Reimers 1983, 1984; MacDonald and Barrett 2001). Obviously, weight also varies as a function of season and age. During the winter, reindeer males may lose up to 54% of their prerut weight, which brings them closer in body mass to females during that period (Reimers 1984; Finstad and Pritchard 2000).

At birth, weight differences in *Rangifer* are minor (<0.5 kg) and favor males (Eloranta and Nieminen 1986; Boulet *et al.* 2007; Bergerud *et al.* 2008). As they get older, male calves become heavier, 7 to 15% on average, than female calves (Petersson and Danell 1993). This trend accelerates in yearlings. In caribou, yearling males add weight at a much faster rate than females until a plateau is reached when they are about 6.5 years old (Finstad and Pritchard 2000; Miller 2003). In opposition, weight gain in females slows down after their second year, and their maximum weight is reached at a much younger age than males, that is, when they are approximately 4.5 years old (Dauphiné 1976; Miller 2003). Size overlap between yearling males and adult females is not uncommon but is rare between calves and adults (Reimers 1983).

The problem of overlap is reduced when the focus is placed on body fat. According to Dauphiné (1976), healthy adult females are generally fatter than yearling males in caribou. The same author noted that old caribou (those approximately 10 years old or older) tend to be emaciated compared with prime adults. Assuming that these patterns are representative of Pleistocene reindeer, it is reasonable to conclude that juveniles and old adults were generally lower-ranked than prime adults.

LOW-RANKED AGE CLASSES AND THE OPTIMAL DIET. Variation in the representation of reindeer juveniles and old adults may permit insights into changes in diet breadth at Saint-Césaire. However, a number of factors can limit the usefulness of this approach. The following paragraphs examine some of these limitations.

A first complication with the "age class" argument is that it rarely takes into account how juveniles and old adults in a species ranked *relative to age classes in the other species forming the optimal diet*. This point is relevant because in a high-ranked species such as reindeer or bison, juveniles and old adults might have only rarely fallen outside of the optimal diet. Lower-ranked individuals in these taxa were, perhaps, only ignored during unusually productive episodes, when several animals were killed at once (e.g., as in a bison "drive") or during the colonization of rich habitats devoid of human occupation. In other words, fluctuations in the archaeological representation of these age classes might have simply tracked long-term shifts in the *availability* of juveniles and old adults rather than change in diet breadth.

The situation is more complicated for species of intermediate rank (e.g., roe deer in Pleistocene France) because juveniles and old adults may at times have fallen within, and at other times outside, of the optimal diet, depending on the range of prey types present in the environment, the season and method of procurement, the exact age of the animal ("young" and "old" juveniles may be ranked differently), the contingencies of the hunt, and other factors (e.g., the subsistence security of the group). Ultimately, the problem hinges on how different age classes affected the forager's net return rate.

SINGLE VERSUS MULTIPLE KILLS. Another difficulty with the interpretation of age structure relates to the formulation of archaeological predictions in contexts of multiple kills, an issue that deserves serious consideration given the gregarious habits of many large ungulates.

When several individuals of different ages are brought down together at some distance from the camp – for instance, a female and her calf – decisions must be made about which parts from which individuals should be transported. If the encounter rate with this prey "type" (the combined female and calf in this case) declines over time, the average distance that separates the point of capture and the residential site should increase.

In this situation, field-processing models such as those of Barlow and Metcalfe (1996) predict that, to increase load utility, juvenile parts will be culled at a greater rate than prime adult parts, assuming that prime adults are larger and fatter, and consequently more desirable than juveniles. At the residential site, this pattern should result in a *decrease* in juvenile representation for these multiple kills. From the point of view of the central place foraging prey choice model, this prediction conflicts with that for single kills, given that juvenile exploitation is expected to increase with declining abundance of prime adults near the residential camp (Cannon 2001a). Because kills made by hunters likely involved both single and multiple animals, it is not clear how these conflicting predictions can be reconciled when evaluating the archaeological record.

HUNTING PRESSURE. In high-ranked species, availability may have largely influenced the archaeological representation of juveniles and old adults. Among the factors known to condition the relative abundance of these age classes in natural habitats, human harvest pressure has probably received the most attention in archaeology (e.g., Klein and Cruz-Uribe 1983; Lyman 1987; Broughton 1999; Stiner *et al.* 1999; Munro 2004; Jones 2006; Wolverton 2008). Was ungulate age structure influenced by human-induced harvest pressure in the study region?

A known effect of harvest pressure on sessile and sedentary prey is to diminish average life span through the reduction of the number of individuals reaching old age (Mills 2007). In this context, sustained predation depresses the prey population below the carrying capacity of the environment. The corollary is that intraspecific competition for food is decreased, which, when population size is maintained at acceptable levels, stimulates recruitment and juvenile survival, especially if predation targets individuals with low reproductive value (Reynolds and Peres 2005; Mills 2007). Archaeologically, the observable effect of these cascading changes is a shift of the age structure toward juvenile-dominated, and old adult-depleted, mortality profiles (Wolverton 2008). Thus, a temporal increase in juvenile representation, *along with a decrease in old adult representation*, may be indicative of shifts in human-induced harvest pressure, keeping other factors, such as differential preservation and carnivore ravaging, constant.

This argument may not hold for all species. For instance, harvest pressure by humans often have a lesser impact on large migratory species because these taxa periodically escape predation by moving out of the predator's range (Tambling and Du Toit 2005). Migration is adaptive for these taxa because it enables them to maintain higher population densities than sedentary populations occupying the same habitat (Fryxell *et al.* 1988).

In *Rangifer*, population age structure seems to depend principally on weather conditions (particularly at the highest latitudes), carnivore predation (mostly affecting juveniles and old adults), and density-dependence (mediated by forage conditions), rather than on the intensity of human hunting (Skogland 1986; Mahoney and Schaefer 2002; Miller 2003; Post and Forchhammer 2004; but see Bergerud 1996). Therefore, in contrast to other situations described in the anthropological literature (e.g., Alvard 1995; Broughton 1999; Wolverton 2008), human-induced harvest pressure might have been too light and too sporadic to have significantly affected reindeer age structure in the study region, although stronger effects cannot be excluded if herds consisted of fully sedentary reindeer.

CARNIVORE PREDATION. There is a consensus in the wildlife literature that the responses of nonhuman predators to changes in prey density are complex and variable and that these responses can feedback on the demography of their prey (Sinclair *et al.* 2006). For instance, juvenile and old adult survival may be enhanced when prey density increases faster than carnivore density as is the case in caribou herds that demographically expand in areas in which alternative prey are rare (Valkenburg *et al.* 2003).

Conversely, where carnivore density is high relative to prey density, prey populations may experience mortality that is inversely density-dependent (depensatory mortality). This type of mortality occurs when the predation rate rises as prey density declines in one or more prey species (e.g., caribou and wolves; Dale *et al.* 1994). One effect of depensatory mortality is that it can maintain the affected prey at low density in a "predator pit" (Mills 2007). To provide an example, the range expansion of moose in North America during the twentieth century is said to have negatively affected juvenile survival in many woodland caribou populations by providing an alternate prey and fueling an increase in wolf densities (Seip 1991, 1992).

This issue is relevant in the present case because the cave hyena is poorly represented after the Middle to Upper Paleolithic transition in western Europe (Fosse 1995; Discamps 2008; Turner 2009). Lower densities of large carnivores might have increased the relative abundance of juvenile and old adult ungulates in the landscape. Therefore, higher representations of these age classes in late Aurignacian prey assemblages may simply reflect elevated encounter rates with these prey types, regardless of change in diet breadth. However, it should be emphasized that this argument is hypothetical because we lack data on the abundance patterns of large carnivores in the early Upper Paleolithic in general.

In sum, interpreting age structure in the archaeological record is probably more complex than has hitherto been believed. At Saint-Césaire, reindeer juveniles and old adults appear to have belonged to the optimal diet the majority of the time. For this reason, no attempt is made here to test the intensification hypothesis using patterns of age representation in this species. Data on reindeer age structure are nonetheless presented because they inform us on the foraging context at Saint-Césaire.

Selection of Marrow and Bone Grease Elements

At a finer scale of analysis than the species or the individual, the carcass can be conceived of as a patch composed of elements varying in marrow utility. From this viewpoint, marrow procurement becomes a problem of time allocation, an issue central to the marginal value theorem. What is being evaluated in this case are the variations in encounter rates with whole bones at the residential site, the analytical patch consisting of the total pool of delivered elements. The analysis of marrow cracking is more straightforward than the study of species exploitation, first of all, because transport costs incurred in the field are largely irrelevant to the process of selection, and, secondly, because the currency analysis is facilitated, marrow being almost pure fat.

One possible implication of the intensification hypothesis is that early modern humans exploited a wider range of marrow elements than Neandertals. This broader diet could have more frequently involved bones with marginal amounts of unsaturated marrow fat such as the mandible, scapula, calcaneum, talus (astragalus), innominates, and the phalanges (Morin 2007). Therefore, comparing the processing intensity of low-utility elements in Neandertal and modern human occupations may shed light on their respective foraging strategies.

However, marrow is not the only source of intraskeletal fat. Bone grease is compositionally identical to marrow, but differs from it in terms of mode of procurement. Whereas marrow occupies relatively large hollow spaces from which it can easily be dislodged, bone grease is encased in tiny pore spaces in spongy bone (for this reason, *spongy marrow* or *trabecular marrow* constitute more accurate terms to designate this product, yet the traditional usage is followed here for the sake of clarity). Bone grease can be obtained by pounding bones with a hammerstone on an anvil and by boiling the fragments in a water-filled container or simply by heating the fragments.

The handling costs associated with this extraction method are substantial given the small amount of fat that is typically collected at the end (Binford 1978; Saint-Germain 1997; Church and Lyman 2003). Consequently, bone grease is generally perceived as a low-ranked resource relative to marrow (Burger *et al.* 2005; Munro and Bar-Oz 2005). Because there is little evidence for bone grease rendering in the Middle Paleolithic (Stiner 2003; Manne *et al.* 2005; but see Costamagno 2010), the emergence of this activity might have been one of the manifestations of the broader diet of early modern humans in Europe (O'Connell 2006).

Why Saint-Césaire?

Three criteria guided the selection of the archaeological materials employed for testing the intensification hypothesis. First, the site had to be characterized by a well-dated high-resolution sequence documenting the Middle to Upper Paleolithic transition. Second, large and well-preserved samples were indispensable for monitoring temporal variation in decision making. Third, detailed information about the archaeological context of the assemblages had to be available to address taphonomic issues concerning the nature of the faunal accumulations.

Sites located in western France are most pertinent for testing the intensification hypothesis because this region has produced many of the best-known Neandertal and some of the earliest modern human remains of western Europe. Unfortunately, the majority of these skeletons were uncovered in the early days of the discipline, under conditions that were imperfect by modern archaeological standards. Thus, despite the considerable interest in this period, few sites spanning the Middle to Upper Paleolithic transition have been carefully excavated (Harrold 1981; Bordes 1984).

Saint-Césaire is a notable exception. This site presents a long sequence of occupation, including assemblages attributed – in some cases, reattributed – to the late Mousterian, Châtelperronian, Middle Aurignacian, and Evolved Aurignacian (see Chapter 4 for a discussion of recent changes in the cultural attribution of the Saint-Césaire levels). Faunal samples from this site are relatively large and well preserved. Importantly, the sediment was dry-sieved with a fine mesh, and all visible bones and flakes were collected, cataloged, and bagged, thus obviating the thorny issue of incomplete recovery and recording pervasive in old excavations (Turner 1989; Marean and Kim 1998; Bartram and Marean 1999; Grayson and Delpech 2008). Despite a relatively short hiatus corresponding to the Protoaurignacian and Early Aurignacian, Saint-Césaire provides a natural laboratory for comparing foraging strategies of Neandertals and early modern humans during the emergence of the Upper Paleolithic.

SUMMARY OF THE PREDICTIONS

The early Upper Paleolithic intensification hypothesis asserts that early modern humans exploited a broader and costlier diet than archaic *sapiens*. This strategy of dietary intensification was inferred to have conferred modern humans a decisive demographic advantage when competing with the local populations (O'Connell 2006). The main archaeological implication of this model is that, in Europe, faunas accumulated by early modern humans should indicate greater use of low-ranked resources compared to those deposited by Neandertals. Resources that might have been more frequently utilized by the newcomers include fast small-sized species and bones that contain marginal amounts of unsaturated marrow. The exploitation of previously ignored resources, such as fish and bone grease, would also be compatible with the intensification hypothesis. The analysis of Saint-Césaire should show whether its faunal samples conform to the foraging implications of this hypothesis.

However, evidence for a significant deterioration of climatic conditions in France during the early Upper Paleolithic complicates the test of the intensification hypothesis. This complication arises from the similar faunal implications of the two hypotheses because they both raise the possibility or assume that decreased encounter rates with high-ranked species led to diet widening. For this reason, validating one or the other hypotheses might not be possible in the present case. Yet because the exploitation of a broader range of low-ranked resources by modern humans is a necessary condition of the intensification hypothesis, but not of the climatic deterioration hypothesis, it should be possible to refute the former model.

Theoretical complications and a lack of fine-grained data precluded the formulation of predictions about age structure. Issues that were raised include the contentious argument that juveniles and old adults of high-ranked taxa would have fallen outside of the optimal diet and the difficulty of predicting transport decisions when prey items are killed singly versus in mass. Additional factors that can confound the analysis of age structure in migratory prey species, such as human harvest pressure and carnivore predation, were also discussed. Despite these interpretive problems, shifts in reindeer age structure are explored at Saint-Césaire because they can yield valuable information on the Neandertal and modern human foraging environment.

For a variety of reasons, some of the predictions laid out in this chapter may not find confirmation in the Saint-Césaire faunal assemblages. However, if all of them fail to show evidence for the use of a broader and costlier range of resources in the early Upper Paleolithic, one must seriously consider the possibility that early modern humans and Neandertals did not differ in terms of foraging strategies. Such a result would be inconsistent with the intensification model.

4

SAINT-CÉSAIRE

THE SAINT-CÉSAIRE SITE, LOCALLY KNOWN AS LA ROCHE-À-PIERROT, TAKES ITS NAME
from a village located 10 km northeast of the city of Saintes in Charente-Maritimes,
France. Located in a small valley (Figure 4.1), the site consists of a collapsed rockshelter
or cave at the base of a 5 to 6 m high Upper Turonian limestone cliff formerly exploited as
a quarry. In the 1970s, the quarry galleries were used to grow mushrooms. It was during
the construction of an access road to one of these galleries that the site was discovered
and partially destroyed (Figure 4.2).

Given the apparent importance of the site, a salvage program was quickly initiated
by the *Service Régional d'Archéologie* for the Poitou-Charente area (Lévêque 1993a). Early
work at the site confirmed its rich potential. As a result, a long-term study program was
implemented. Excavations were carried out during twelve consecutive seasons, from
1976 to 1987, under the direction of F. Lévêque (Figure 4.3). A few additional test pits
were dug in 1993 in the slope deposits (Backer 1994). Before its collapse, the rockshelter
or cave would have faced north-northwest in the direction of the Coran, a stream feeding
the Charente River.

The excavation methods employed at Saint-Césaire have been described by Lévêque
(2002). The site was dug using a grid system composed of 1-m-square units. Except
for a few test pits, squares were divided into four quadrants (subsquares). Excavation proceeded by *décapages*, the minimal stratigraphic unit for the site, defined as a
50×50 cm horizontal slice usually 5 to 10 cm thick. Stratigraphic layers normally consist of several superimposed décapages (Figure 4.4). Knives were used as excavation
tools.

Artifacts that were considered particularly informative, mostly stone tools and taxonomically identifiable faunal remains, were piece-plotted (assigned three-dimensional
coordinates) in situ, while the rest of the material was collected by décapage. Sediments
were dry-sieved using 5- and 2-mm mesh screens (Lévêque 2002). All visible bones,
including long bone shafts, were collected during the excavations, preventing a recovery bias against long bones (Turner 1989; Marean and Kim 1998; Bartram and Marean
1999). A life-size cast of a portion of the excavated surface, with the archaeological
vestiges still in situ, was made for both the EGPF (Denticulate Mousterian) and EJOP
(Mousterian/Châtelperronian) occupations.

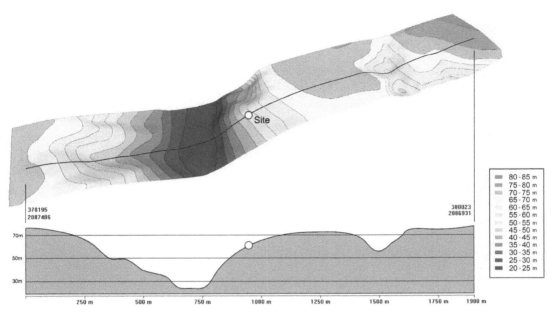

FIGURE 4.1. Cross-sectional view of the valley where Saint-Césaire is located. Illustration by David Cochard.

FIGURE 4.2. Saint-Césaire in 1976, shortly after its discovery. Photograph by François Lévêque.

FIGURE 4.3. View of the Saint-Césaire excavations from the access road. Photograph by François Lévêque.

FIGURE 4.4. Excavation of the very rich Denticulate Mousterian EGPF level. The picture shows how the matrix from this level contrasts with that of the overlying *décapages*, which are seen in the upper part of the picture. Photograph by François Lévêque.

FIGURE 4.5. The archaeological sequence at Saint-Césaire. Levels EGF, EGP, EGPF, and EJOP inf are attributed to the Denticulate Mousterian, EJOP sup to the Mousterian/Châtelperronian, EJO inf to an undiagnostic low-density occupation, EJO sup and EJF to the Middle Aurignacian, and EJM and EJJ to the Evolved Aurignacian. Photograph by François Lévêque.

THE SITE STRATIGRAPHY

The cultural and litho-stratigraphy of Saint-Césaire has been presented in several studies (Lévêque and Miskovsky 1983; Lévêque 1987, 1989, 1997; Lévêque *et al.* 1993; Miskovsky and Lévêque 1993). Only the assemblages relevant to this study – the eight uppermost faunal assemblages in the sequence, which include Denticulate Mousterian to Evolved Aurignacian (levels EGPF to EJJ, Figure 4.5) occupations – are detailed here. The other Mousterian levels have not yet been studied and will be the focus of a subsequent publication. The following description of the sedimentary sequence, based on an east-west (frontal) cut in rows 3/4, is a summary of a description provided by Miskovsky

TABLE 4.1. *Changes in the cultural attributions of the occupations at Saint-Césaire*

Stratigraphic label	Cultural affiliation (Lévêque 1993b)	Cultural affiliation (J.-G. Bordes, pers. comm., 2011)
EJJ	Evolved Aurignacian	Evolved Aurignacian
EJM	Evolved Aurignacian	Evolved Aurignacian
EJF	Early Aurignacian	**Middle Aurignacian**
EJO sup	Protoaurignacian	**Middle Aurignacian**
EJO inf	low density	Low density
EJOP sup	Châtelperronian	**Mousterian/Châtelperronian**
EJOP inf	Châtelperronian	**Denticulate Mousterian**
EGPF	Denticulate Mousterian	Denticulate Mousterian

New changes to the cultural sequence are shown in bold. The data are from Bordes (pers. comm., 2011).

and Lévêque (1993). However, it should be noted that recent and ongoing analyses of the lithic assemblages suggest significant changes to the oft-cited cultural stratigraphy of Saint-Césaire. These changes are summarized in Table 4.1.

The Saint-Césaire sequence consists of three major stratigraphic groups resting on the limestone bedrock (Table 4.2). The lowermost group, called the red group (*ensemble rouge*), is sterile. The intermediate gray group (*ensemble gris*) is, on average, 1.20 m thick and contains the majority of the Mousterian occupations identified at Saint-Césaire (Figure 4.6). Specifically, this group encompasses: two occupations attributed to the Mousterian of Acheulean Tradition, three low-density layers, and three Denticulate Mousterian occupations. Only the uppermost layer of this group, the very rich Denticulate Mousterian EGPF occupation (Thiébault 2005), is considered in the present analysis.

The upper yellow group (*ensemble jaune*), which is approximately 1.60 m thick, appears to be separated from the underlying gray group by an erosional unconformity (Miskovsky and Lévêque 1993). At the bottom of the yellow group is EJOP inf (for *inférieur*), a small occupation layer moderately rich in cultural remains. Initially attributed to the Châtelperronian, this occupation has recently been formally reassigned to the Denticulate Mousterian (Soressi 2010; J.-G. Bordes, pers. comm., 2011). The Neandertal skeleton discussed in Chapter 2 was discovered in the overlying EJOP sup (for *supérieur*) level (Lévêque and Vandermeersch 1980; Vandermeersch 1984; Crèvecoeur 2002). Lévêque (1993b) and Guilbaud (1993) considered this occupation as belonging to the Châtelperronian, noting that the presence of several artifacts (e.g., sidescrapers, Levallois cores) common in Mousterian contexts gives an "archaic" look to the assemblage. However, the ongoing study of the lithic sample suggests that the Châtelperronian may be, in fact, a minor component of this level (J.-G. Bordes, pers. comm., 2011). As a result of this ambiguity, EJOP sup is conservatively referred to here as "Mousterian/Châtelperronian." This layer is also important because it contains evidence of hearth construction and maintenance and rare traces of wood charcoal (Lévêque 1987; Backer 1993, 1994).

On top of EJOP sup is the low-density EJO inf layer, which contains few diagnostic artifacts. This low-density layer is found below the EJO sup occupation, a level that comprises, among other things, bone tools and tooth pendants (Morin and Liolios 2008). This occupation, which was previously attributed to the Protoaurignacian, is now believed

TABLE 4.2. *Summary of the Saint-Césaire stratigraphy*

Unit	Level	Cultural attribution	TL Dates	Level characteristics
	Humus (1)	Post-Paleolithic		Humus
	Eboulis (2)	?		Characterized by large limestone slabs.
	EJJ (3)	Evolved Aurignacian		Yellow clayey-sandy sediment with small limestone elements. Small reindeer-dominated sample.
	EJM (4)	Evolved Aurignacian		Yellow-brown clayey sediment with limestone elements that are generally bigger than in EJJ. Moderate-sized occupation dominated by reindeer.
	EJF (5)	Middle Aurignacian		Yellow clayey sediment containing medium to large clasts. Characterized by several hearths and dark soil color. Rich Middle Aurignacian assemblage dominated by reindeer.
Upper group (yellow)	EJO sup (6)	Middle Aurignacian	30.8 ± 3.3 34.0 ± 3.9	Yellow-orange sediment with small limestone clasts. Small assemblage dominated by reindeer.
	EJO inf (7)	Low-density		Yellow-orange sediment of fine texture. Almost devoid of blocks and artifacts.
	EJOP sup (8)	Mousterian/ Châtelperronian	36.6 ± 5.0 38.2 ± 5.3 33.7 ± 5.4 36.6 ± 4.9 37.4 ± 5.2 35.6 ± 4.6	Pale yellow-orange clayey-sandy sediment with numerous angular limestone blocks. Relatively rich Mousterian/Châtelperronian assemblage dominated by bison, reindeer, and horse remains. It is in this level that the Neandertal skeleton was found.
	EJOP inf (9)	Denticulate Mousterian		Pale yellow-orange clayey-sandy layer with only rare limestone fragments. Fauna dominated by bison, reindeer, and horse.
	EGPF (10)	Denticulate Mousterian	41.4 ± 4.2 (average of 9 dates)	Pale gray level with hearths. Extremely rich assemblage. Faunal sample dominated by bison, horse, and reindeer remains.
	EGP (11)	Denticulate Mousterian	39.7 ± 3.9 36.8 ± 3.7	Pale gray sediment, sometimes indurated, with limestone fragments. Small assemblage.
	EGF (12)	Denticulate Mousterian	42.4 ± 4.3	Gray sediment with evidence of burning. Small assemblage.
Lower group (gray)	EGC sup (13)	Few artifacts		Light gray sediment. Small assemblage.
	EGC (14)	Mousterian of Acheulean Tradition		Light gray sediment characterized by several patches of burning. Small assemblage.
	EGC inf (15)	Few artifacts		Light gray sediment. Very small assemblage. Probably Mousterian.
	EGB sup (16)	Mousterian of Acheulean Tradition		Gray-tan sandy sediment. Small assemblage.
	EGB inf (17)	Few artifacts		Gray-tan to reddish sandy sediment. Very small assemblage. Probably Mousterian.
Basal group (red)	ER	Sterile		Interface with the bedrock. Red sandy-clayey matrix with flint nodules and limestone elements.

Thermoluminescence dates are in thousands of years and are taken from Mercier *et al.* 1993.

FIGURE 4.6. The lower archaeological sequence of Saint-Césaire. Photograph by François Lévêque.

to be of Middle Aurignacian age (J.-G. Bordes, pers. comm., 2011). This shift in cultural attribution is consequential because it suggests the existence of an occupation hiatus (2–3 ka?) between the EJOP sup and EJO sup occupations. Above EJO sup, the EJF level is a rich occupation characterized by the presence of numerous hearths and a high concentration of relatively complete animal bones in a zone called the "charnier" ("charnel" or bone midden, Figure 4.7). Formerly described as an Early Aurignacian occupation, EJF has, like EJO sup, recently been reassigned to the Middle Aurignacian (J.-G. Bordes, pers. comm., 2011). No changes have been made to the cultural denomination of the two uppermost levels of the site, EJM and EJJ. These occupations date to the Evolved Aurignacian.

MORPHOLOGY OF THE DEPOSIT

A north-northeast dip has been observed in the Saint-Césaire deposit. The excavation grid is therefore slightly offset from the natural slope of the site. In general, the archaeological levels become thinner as distance from the cliff increases, to a point where they merge into a single unit. The slope becomes steeper as one moves away from the cliff. In the upper part of the sequence, the Aurignacian layers are slanted and are thicker near the cliff. The slope of the underlying EJOP sup occupation is more horizontal. The Mousterian levels, at the bottom of the sequence, are nearly horizontal over a distance of 10 m.

FIGURE 4.7. A section of the "charnier" (bone midden) uncovered during the excavation of the Middle Aurignacian EJF level. Photograph by François Lévêque.

Today the cliff that delimits the southeastern side of the site is relatively vertical. However, a sagittal view of the piece-plotted artifacts suggests that Saint-Césaire was a rockshelter or a shallow cave in prehistoric times because the levels immediately adjacent to the cliff dip toward it, a pattern often associated with the presence of an overhang (Figure 4.8). This morphology possibly results from the preferential accumulation of sediments near the prehistoric dripline.

CHRONOLOGY OF THE OCCUPATIONS

The Saint-Césaire chronology is relatively well understood because several occupations have been dated by thermoluminescence (TL). Dates were obtained for three of the four uppermost Mousterian occupations (Table 4.2). All three occupations cluster around 40,000 B.P. If this apparent synchronicity is not an artifact of the method, these dates indicate a moderately rapid sedimentation rate. The Mousterian/Châtelperronian EJOP sup level is slightly younger and is dated to *ca.* 36,300 B.P. TL dates of 30,800 ± 3,300 and 34,000 B.P. ± 3,900 were obtained for the Middle Aurignacian EJO sup occupation. In general, these dates are coherent with other equivalent assemblages, although the TL dates appear a bit young. Efforts are currently being made to obtain accelerator mass spectrometry radiocarbon dates for the site using new approaches because previous attempts have failed due to a lack of preserved collagen (Mercier *et al.* 1993).

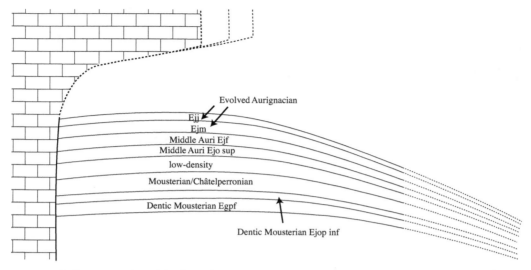

FIGURE 4.8. Reconstruction of the Saint-Césaire sagittal stratigraphy based on a three-dimensional analysis of piece-plotted artifacts. The broken line indicates the area of the deposit in which layers tend to merge.

HUMAN REMAINS

In July 1979, the remains of a Neandertal skeleton were found in the EJOP sup layer. These remains were consolidated in place, removed in block (Figure 4.9), and excavated in lab conditions by D. Gambier under the supervision of B. Vandermeersch. Most of the human bones (save for some isolated hand bones) were distributed over a surface of 70 cm in diameter and compressed within a few centimeters (Vandermeersch 1984). The skeleton is incomplete. The feet and the left half of the cranium, as well as some teeth, among other skeletal elements, were missing. Aspects of these remains have been studied by Lévêque and Vandermeersch (1980), Vandermeersch (1984, 1993), Lalueza *et al.* (1996), Del Prête and Vandermeersch (2001), Vandermeersch and Mann (2001), Trinkaus *et al.* (1998), and Zollikofer *et al.* (2002).

Vandermeersch (1993) suggested that the skeleton was buried intentionally. The fact that many parts of the human skeleton were found in anatomical position, which is in striking contrast with the scattering of the faunal remains (Morin *et al.* 2005), supports this claim. Importantly, the human skeleton is not the only individual represented in EJOP sup; teeth from at least two additional individuals are reported (Vandermeersch and Mann 2001). Lastly, an additional human bone, a proximal phalanx, was identified during the analysis reported here. This specimen belongs to the Middle Aurignacian EJF occupation and was found within the "charnier" zone.

Trinkaus *et al.* (1998) have highlighted the hyperarctic body proportions of the Saint-Césaire Neandertal skeleton. The femur indicates locomotor patterns comparable to those known for modern humans. Crèvecoeur (2002) studied the human hand bones found in this layer and showed that the Saint-Césaire specimens cluster metrically with Neandertals. The stable isotope composition of the skeleton was also studied to examine Neandertal diet. In agreement with other isotopic analyses of Neandertals (Richards and Trinkaus 2009), the results for the Saint-Césaire individual suggest that most of his or

FIGURE 4.9. The Saint-Césaire 1 Neandertal. The left picture shows the skeleton during excavation of the Mousterian/Châtelperronian (EJOP sup) layer, and the right picture shows a cast of the consolidated block. Left photograph taken by François Lévêque.

her dietary proteins were obtained from large ungulates (Drucker *et al.* 1999; Balter *et al.* 2001; Bocherens and Drucker 2003, Bocherens *et al.* 2005; Balter and Simon 2006).

PALEOECOLOGICAL SETTING

Several analyses of pollen from Saint-Césaire have been published (Leroi-Gourhan 1984; Leroyer 1988; Leroyer and Leroi-Gourhan 1993). The goal of these studies is to compare Saint-Césaire with other similarly dated sequences to interpret past climatic changes. However, the reliability of pollen sequences derived from caves and rockshelters are now in question because they rely on controversial assumptions about site formation processes (Sánchez Goñi 1994; Woodward and Goldberg 2001). For instance, postdepositional disturbance may explain why several pollen samples collected around the human hand in the EJOP sup occupation from Saint-Césaire yielded wildly conflicting results (Leroyer and Leroi-Gourhan 1993). Fortunately, other approaches to the study of paleoclimates are available, including those based on the study of faunal remains.

The faunal material from Saint-Césaire has been studied from a paleontological perspective by Lavaud-Girard (1987, 1993). According to her, the increased representation of reindeer and the lower percentages of horse (probably *E. ferus [caballus] germanicus*) and bovines in the Aurignacian levels are indicative of colder climatic conditions relative to the earlier occupations. Lavaud-Girard argued that climatic conditions were

---

milder at Saint-Césaire than at the site of Quinçay located 150 km to the northeast. She attributed the milder conditions at Saint-Césaire to its proximity to the Atlantic coast. Ferrié (2001) studied the Denticulate Mousterian EGPF faunal assemblage. His work, which included some additional material from the earlier and smaller Mousterian assemblages, showed that bovines, horse, and reindeer are well represented in the lower part of the Saint-Césaire sequence.

Marquet (1988, 1993) conducted an analysis of the Saint-Césaire microfauna (mammals <500 g). He found that the common vole (*Microtus arvalis*) is more frequent in the Denticulate Mousterian EGPF and the Mousterian/Châtelperronian EJOP occupations than in the Aurignacian levels, where the cold-adapted narrow-skulled vole (*Microtus gregalis*) strongly dominates the samples. These results suggested to Marquet that the Aurignacian was relatively cold and dry. Within the Aurignacian sequence, the Middle Aurignacian EJF was interpreted to have been somewhat dryer and the Evolved Aurignacian (levels EJM and EJJ) more humid. The results reported in this book are consistent with these observations.

5

THE FAUNA

THE ARCHAEOLOGICAL MODEL PRESENTED IN CHAPTER 3 AIMS TO EXAMINE CHANGES
in diet breadth during the Middle to Upper Paleolithic transition. This chapter provides basic data on taxonomic composition and skeletal representation in eight stratified
assemblages from Saint-Césaire that are directly relevant to the research problem. Information is also provided on the samples and methods that will be used to examine dietary
changes in these assemblages. These data, which focus on the three most abundant taxa
at Saint-Césaire (reindeer, bison, and horse), are analyzed in the following chapters.

SAMPLES AND METHODS

Eight occupations from Saint-Césaire were included in the faunal analysis. However,
some modifications of the samples were required to account for changes in the interpretation of the stratigraphy. The EJOP layer was dug as a single unit in the first years
of excavation. However, new stratigraphic observations in 1980 led to the division of
this level into a lower (EJOP inf) and an upper (EJOP sup) unit (Figure 5.1). Likewise,
the EJO level was split into two stratigraphic units (EJO inf and EJO sup) during the
same year. Therefore, the décapages dug in these layers *before* 1980 are not analytically
comparable with those excavated *after* this field season.

Décapages labeled "EJOP" that were stratigraphically above décapages labeled "EJOP
sup" were reattributed to EJOP sup, given that no reversal of stratigraphy is documented
at the site. This situation applies to 15% of the EJOP décapages. EJOP décapages capping
EJOP inf décapages were left unchanged, because it is not possible to know whether they
belong to EJOP inf, EJOP sup, or both layers. However, some décapages were reattributed
to more specific units with the help of François Lévêque, the excavator of the site, using
field notes and stratigraphic descriptions. Changes were made only in contexts in which
the stratigraphic information was absolutely clear and unambiguous. Approximately
5% of the EJOP décapages have been reattributed to more precise stratigraphic units
based on this method. The remaining EJOP décapages (80% of the total) were studied
according to their initial attribution.

Only 1% of the EJO décapages were reattributed to either EJO inf or EJO sup following a similar procedure. Concerning the other levels, square G4 was deleted from the
Middle Aurignacian EJF and the Evolved Aurignacian EJM samples as a result of stratigraphic problems. In addition, forty-two décapages (approximately 2.5% of the total)
were excluded from the analysis because of a lack of data concerning provenance or

FIGURE 5.1. Textural differences that motivated the decision to split the EJOP (lower photograph) and EJO (upper photograph) layers into upper and lower units. Photograph by François Lévêque.

contradictory stratigraphic information. Lastly, décapages that include materials from two or more layers were ignored in this study.

Certain stratigraphic units were not detected in some squares, principally in rows 6 through 9 where the layers are thin. In addition, heavy machinery truncated columns B and C, particularly in the most recent levels. Unidentified bones were not analyzed in these squares because an unknown portion of the décapages is missing. However, taxonomically identifiable bones recovered in these squares were examined to increase sample sizes. The very rich Denticulate Mousterian EGPF level has not yet been entirely analyzed, and only a subsample is considered here. This subsample, consisting of the uppermost décapages from all squares, is estimated to represent 15% of the faunal material of EGPF.

Estimating Abundance in the Faunal Samples

Two different protocols were used in the analysis of the faunal material, depending on whether the bone was identified to a particular taxon or not. By convention, NISP (*Number of Identified SPecimens*) refers to a specific bone, tooth, antler/horn, or fragment thereof, identified taxonomically to at least the genus level. However, foxes, leporids,

TABLE 5.1. *Body size classes adopted in this study*

Size class				
Size 1	Size 2	Size 3	Size 4	Size 5
roe deer	reindeer	horse	aurochs/bison	mammoth
wolf	European ass	cave lion	woolly rhinoceros	
fox	hyena	red deer	giant deer	
badger	wild boar	cave bear		

Birds, leporids, fishes, and rodents are excluded from this table.

birds, and fishes are exceptions to this rule, because it was not always possible to identify them as precisely as the other taxa. Non-refitted fragments identified to taxon were counted as single items in NISP calculations. However, mammoth teeth and reindeer antlers were sometimes severely fragmented. To avoid overestimating the abundance of these highly diagnostic parts, fragments smaller than 2 cm were omitted from NISP counts.

Fragments of bovine parts were often hard to distinguish from homologous fragmented parts of horse, red deer, and giant deer because the skeletal elements of these taxa tend to overlap in size and morphology. Following Costamagno (1999), remains that were affected by this problem were simply attributed to the *ungulate 3–4* size class (abbreviated as UNG3–4). However, because red deer and giant deer are poorly represented at Saint-Césaire, most UNG3–4 specimens likely belong to horse or bovines. Most of the other size classes (Table 5.1) were defined empirically, on the basis of both mean animal body size and skeletal size, rather than body size alone.

To further address issues of taxonomic identification and classification, a second category of remains, the *Number of Specimens of Uncertain Taxonomic Status* (NSUTS) is introduced here. This category includes fragments for which identification is limited to skeletal part, and, sometimes, body size class, without precise information regarding taxonomic status (e.g., UNG3–4 humerus, mammal tibia). Less precise skeletal identification – for instance, "long bone shaft" or "burned spongy fragment" – are not included in this category and are simply referred to as *indeterminate* specimens.

The *Minimum Number of Individuals* (MNI) allows determination of the minimum number of distinct individuals represented in a sample (Grayson 1984; Lyman 2008). The MNE is the *Minimum Number of Elements* necessary to account for the specimens observed (Binford 1984). For example, 13 left and 14 right complete distal tibiae give an MNE of 27 for this part. Because foragers often butcher carcasses, especially those of large animals, according to body units, MNE can be useful for investigating foraging decisions. However, as we will see, the relevance and accuracy of these metrics may vary depending on the archaeological context.

Many authors have shown that NISP and MNI suffer from various shortcomings (Grayson 1984; Klein and Cruz-Uribe 1984; Marshall and Pilgram 1993; Brugal *et al.* 1994; Grayson and Frey 2004; Lyman 2008). Problems with NISP are related to specimen interdependence, variation in the number of bones between taxa, the overrepresentation of easily identified elements and taxa, and susceptibility to fragmentation (Todd and Rapson 1988; Bartram 1993; Marshall and Pilgram 1993). The difficulties with MNI are different. Foremost among these are the nonlinear increase of MNI with increasing sample size and sample aggregation, and variation in MNI estimates between analysts (Grayson 1984; Klein and Cruz-Uribe 1984). For the most part, the same problems plague the use of MNE (Lyman 2008).

Assessing the degree of specimen interdependence in a site may help determine the method(s) that is (are) most appropriate for the problem under study. Because many basic statistical tests (e.g., chi-square) assume that tabulated specimens are independent of every other specimen included in the tabulation, specimen interdependence is a critical problem in faunal analysis (Grayson 1984). Although no simple solution exists to this problem, some general observations help to disentangle the issue.

As stressed by Thomas (1971) and Binford (1978), skeletal elements initially derived from a single carcass are likely to be gradually dissociated and dispersed as a result of culling, snacking, caching, sharing, exchange, bone tool making, and other activities. Consequently, the reliability of NISP for estimating abundance is expected to increase along the processing sequence, which begins with the complete animal carcass. Following this logic, shelter sites such as Saint-Césaire should contain proportionally more specimens from distinct carcasses and, therefore, be less affected by the problem of specimen interdependence than kill sites. Stated otherwise, because of the cumulative effects of activities that increased body part dispersion, NISP is probably a more reliable method for estimating taxonomic abundance at this site than MNI or MNE. The relatively low percentage of green-bone refits at Saint-Césaire supports this view (Morin *et al.* 2005). However, because the problem of specimen interdependence cannot be entirely controlled for at Saint-Césaire, NISP counts were used along with MNE counts to get a more complete picture of taxonomic representation in the assemblages.

The analytical units that are used to describe skeletal part frequencies in the Saint-Césaire assemblages are NISP and the percentage of *Minimal Animal Units* (%MAU), an analytical unit derived from MNE (Lyman 1994). MAU values are calculated by dividing the MNE of an element by the number of times this element is represented in a living individual. These values are then standardized (%MAU) by dividing them by the greatest MAU value in the assemblage (Binford 1978). This procedure is carried out for each taxon represented in an occupation. In the tables, MNE values are sometimes summed by taxon and presented as TMNE (*Total Minimum Number of Elements*). TMNE provides the minimum value for the sum of all elements present in a site for a given taxon. Because they provide much higher values than MNIs, TMNE counts offset some of the sample-size effects that plague the use of the former measure (Grayson 1984).

MNE counts were calculated for each skeletal element using the most common landmark (Todd and Rapson 1988) or zone (Morlan 1994), taking left and right sides of paired elements (e.g., long bones) into consideration. The procedure is comparable to the one followed by Bunn and Kroll (1986), except that here age, sex, and size were *not* taken into account. This decision is justified by the fact that consideration of age, sex, and size inflates the representation of diagnostic parts such as teeth and epiphyses, compared with less diagnostic parts such as ribs and long bone shafts. For reindeer, landmarks used by Enloe (1991) were adopted with minor modifications, whereas the terminology supplied by Barone (1999) has been followed for bovines and horses. Antlers were excluded from most counts because they tend to be highly fragmented and were possibly procured for reasons other than subsistence. For long bones, MNE counts were calculated for both proximal and distal ends, as well as for the shaft.

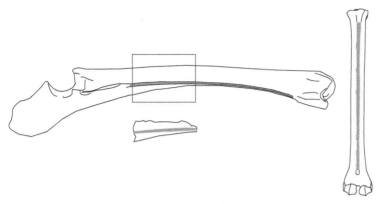

FIGURE 5.2. Features on the reindeer radio-ulna and metatarsal used for calculating the MNE in this study. A hypothetical radio-ulna fragment is shown below the complete radio-ulna. The shaded area represents the section of the groove that is actually measured.

In Paleolithic assemblages, extensive fragmentation may make the derivation of MNE values difficult for elements that lack landmarks diagnostic of bone portion. Castel (1999) developed a simple method to cope with this problem for the reindeer metatarsal shaft. He measured the length of the anterior groove on all metatarsal fragments and divided the sum of the measurements by the total groove length of a known complete specimen. The result is a minimum number of complete metatarsal shafts, based on length measurement. Castel (1999:25–27) extended this principle to the metacarpal and again used the length of the anterior groove for estimating abundance. Importantly, side, sex, age, and size are not taken into consideration in calculating length values. Both of these methods were adopted here to estimate metacarpal and metatarsal MNEs.

A similar approach was implemented to derive MNE counts for the shaft of the reindeer radio-ulna. Like the metapodials, length values were calculated using the (lateral) groove (Figure 5.2). However, some "standard" bones are necessary to calculate length MNEs. The mean length of the anterior groove on two relatively complete metacarpals from Saint-Césaire is 120 mm. For the metatarsal, the anterior groove on a complete specimen is estimated, on the basis of a modern individual comparable in size to those found in the archaeological assemblages, to be 180 mm long. The total length of the radio-ulnar groove on a nearly complete specimen from Saint-Césaire is 180 mm. These values were used to compute MNE in the assemblages.

Refitting

An extensive refitting program was carried out at Saint-Césaire to evaluate the degree of interlayer mixing in the sequence and to investigate the problem of specimen interdependence. Results of these efforts have been published (Morin *et al.* 2005). The main results of this refitting program are provided here because they have implications for the interpretation of taxonomic composition and skeletal part representation.

Because of the large quantity of material included in this analysis, it was logistically impossible to attempt to refit all bone fragments. It was therefore decided to focus on specific classes of bones. Spongy fragments were excluded from this program because

TABLE 5.2. *Protocol adopted in refitting the faunal remains from Saint-Césaire*

Skeletal element	Reindeer	Bison and horse	Other taxa
Long bones	Refitting across all levels[a]	Refitting across all levels	Refitting across all levels
Short bones	Intra-layer refitting only	Intra-layer refitting only	Refitting across all levels
Teeth	Intra-layer refitting only	Intra-layer refitting only	Refitting across all levels
Antlers/horns	Intra-décapage refitting only	Intra-layer refitting only	Refitting across all levels
Ribs	Intra-décapage refitting only	Refitting across all levels	Refitting across all levels

Short bones include carpals, tarsals, sesamoids, patellas, phalanges, and vertebrae.
[a] Except for the metatarsal, which was limited to intra-décapage refitting.

they are difficult to refit. The first step of the refitting procedure was limited to within-décapage refitting of ribs and UNG3–4 shaft fragments (Morin *et al.* 2005). Concerning long bones, refitting concentrated specifically on the shaft fragments from large ungulates because they appeared to have suffered greater postdepositional damage than those from smaller taxa (see Chapter 6).

The second step of the refitting program was the refitting of specimens that could be identified to taxon (Table 5.2). All taxa were examined. In contrast to the first part of the program, refitting was, in this case, performed systematically across all décapages and levels. However, because reindeer metatarsal and rib fragments were very abundant, only intra-décapage refitting was carried out for these elements.

Analysis of the Specimens

Analysis of the indeterminate portion of the material was limited to counts of burned and unburned specimens and the study of their spatial and vertical distribution. Maximum length and width were measured on most specimens identified to taxon, because they may inform on patterns of fragmentation. Furthermore, an attempt was made to assign all unidentified long bones to specific size class categories. Shaft fragments were coded according to shaft circumference (<1/2; >1/2; complete; Bunn and Kroll 1986), side, and shaft length (<1/4, 1/4–1/2, 1/2–3/4; >3/4 relative to a complete bone of that element and taxon; Villa and Mahieu 1991). Long bones were also analyzed using five regions: proximal epiphysis, proximal shaft, midshaft, distal shaft, and distal epiphysis. However, in most tables, counts are simply provided by element or according to three portions – that is, the shaft versus each of the epiphyses.

Evidence of burning, striations, calcite coating, longitudinal cracks, sheeting, exfoliation, and marks of human and carnivore activities was examined on each taxonomically identified specimen. *Sheeting* refers to bones that have broken down into one or more sheets according to fracture planes that tend to be parallel to the cortical surface (usually midshafts of large ungulates, Figure 5.3), whereas *exfoliation* (Figure 5.4) describes the loss of the first millimeters of cortical bone. This last type of damage can be observed on most categories of bones but is particularly common on the bones of fetuses or very young individuals.

The coding system advocated by Behrensmeyer (1978), in which bone surfaces are classified with respect to degree of weathering, was not used here because this type of damage differs from that encountered at Saint-Césaire (typically exfoliation and cracking). This may be because karstic environments are protected from the sun and provide

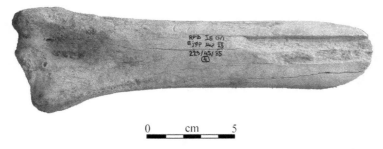

FIGURE 5.3. Bison metatarsal from Saint-Césaire showing evidence of sheeting.

damp conditions that likely slow down the process of bone weathering. The observation made by Tappen (1994) that weathering is infrequent on bones from wet tropical environments, contexts in which bones are also often protected from the sun, indirectly supports this interpretation.

To assess specimen preservation at the site, bone surfaces were classified according to four categories. These categories represent arbitrary divisions along a continuum (Figure 5.5). An *intact* surface is one for which virtually no surface damage is recorded. For instance, skeletal features and muscle attachments are undamaged. A bone with a *slightly damaged* surface shows only superficial damage. The bone surface is locally eroded or damaged, but morphological features are visible, as are cut and gnaw marks (when initially present). Sometimes, only a portion of the bone surface shows damage, but the rest of the bone surface is intact. *Damaged* bones have significantly altered surfaces. Muscle attachments and other skeletal features are faint. Marks, when present, are difficult to detect. Shallow marks may be completely eroded. Specimens with an *extensively damaged* surface are basically useless for studying any type of marks; the cortical surface of the bone is considerably damaged.

Several methods for classifying bone fractures have been proposed in the past three decades (reviewed in Lyman 1994:315–324). At Saint-Césaire, two systems were used in concert to describe fracture patterns. Fracture morphologies were described following the terminology of Villa and Mahieu (1991), which allows comparison with several

FIGURE 5.4. An exfoliated long bone from Saint-Césaire. The bar corresponds to 1 cm.

a)   b)

c)   d)

FIGURE 5.5. Classes of bone surface preservation: (a) a reindeer tibia shaft fragment with an *intact* surface. The cutmarks (left) and the muscle attachment (the vertical line on the right) are easily discernible on the picture; (b) a bison metatarsal shaft fragment with a *slightly damaged* surface. Even though the surface is partially exfoliated, the cutmarks (on the left) are still visible on the bone; (c) an UNG3–4 long bone fragment with a *damaged* surface. Many cracks run through the surface of the bone, and anatomical details are faint; (d) a reindeer tibia fragment with an *extensively damaged* surface. The bone surface was considerably damaged by root growth. No anatomical features (except for a foramen) or marks are preserved. All specimens are from Saint-Césaire. The black bars correspond to 1 cm.

published faunal assemblages. In contrast, the second coding system only takes into account unambiguous dry-bone and green-bone fractures.

In this study, dry-bone fractures, which may include some breaks produced during the excavation and subsequent handling of the specimens, consist of more or less transverse breaks with an irregular section. These fractures are sometimes darker or lighter in color than the rest of the bone. Green-bone fractures, often characterized by a spiral shape, smooth cross-section, and a uniform color (Haynes 1983), were also recorded (Morin *et al.* 2005). Following Villa (2004), fracture edges were studied for the information they may provide on site formation processes. Edges were described as *fresh* when angles were sharp. *Slightly abraded* edges have angles that show slight smoothing as a result of abrasion or other processes. When smoothing is pronounced, edges are considered *abraded*. Finally, *very abraded* edges are almost perfectly rounded or damaged and frequently present a shiny aspect.

TABLE 5.3. *Surface and volume analyzed by level at Saint-Césaire*

Layer	Cultural attribution	Surface studied (m²)	Volume studied (m³)
EJJ	Evolved Aurignacian	21.50	5.1
EJM	Evolved Aurignacian	17.25	3.1
EJF	Middle Aurignacian	31.00	9.3
EJO sup	Middle Aurignacian	17.50	2.9
EJO inf	Low-density	17.50	2.2
EJO	Inf or sup	16.50	3.0
EJOP sup	Mousterian/Châtelperronian	28.75	7.1
EJOP inf	Denticulate Mousterian	29.50	5.7
EJOP	Inf or sup	16.50	3.5
EGPF sample	Denticulate Mousterian	16.75	2.2
Total		212.75	44.1

Rows B and C are excluded from these counts.

Carnivore gnaw marks at Saint-Césaire were studied using the typology proposed by Binford (1981). The extent of carnivore marks on the bone cortical surface was also recorded because it was hypothesized that bones covered with gnaw marks might be more common in carnivore dens than in anthropic assemblages ravaged by carnivores. *Marginal gnawing* indicates that carnivore marks are uncommon on the specimen. Zones of gnawing that are *limited to one section* refer to specimens with marks restricted to one part of the bone, covering less than half of the bone surface. When marks are widespread on the specimen, the bone is said to be *covered* with gnaw marks.

To assess the incidence of marrow-cracking in the assemblages, frequencies and types of percussion marks were computed following the terminology presented by Capaldo and Blumenschine (1994). A conservative approach was adopted in recording cutmarks. Dubious cutmarks were not counted. All identified bones were studied using a 10× magnifying hand lens (Blumenschine *et al.* 1996).

Statistical Methods

In this study, differences in means between samples are assessed after arcsine-transformation of the data using the test statistic (denoted here as t_s) provided by Sokal and Rohlf (1969:607–610). Changes in skeletal representation are explored using Spearman's rho, a nonparametric test examining rank-order correlations. Tests are considered significant when $p \leq .05$. Other methods used in the analysis of the faunal samples are described when relevant.

PRESENTATION OF THE FAUNAL SAMPLES

The surface studied for each level ranges between 17 and 31 m² (Table 5.3), resulting in large samples for most occupations (Table 5.4, Figure 5.6). The total sample consists of approximately 1,650 décapages and slightly more than 132,500 bones, the vast majority of which are indeterminate fragments smaller than 2 cm. All bones were counted and studied.

With one exception (the low-density EJO inf layer), all the occupations from Saint-Césaire have pre-refit NISP counts greater than 420 specimens (excluding the mixed EJOP

TABLE 5.4. *Density of faunal remains and taxonomically identified specimens per level, excluding birds and microfaunal remains*

Layer	Total bone counts	Pre-refit NISP counts	Volume (m³)	Density total bones/m³	Pre-refit NISP/m³
Evol Auri (Ejj)	4231	473	5.1	830	93
Evol Auri (Ejm)	8033	1210	3.1	2591	390
Middle Auri (Ejf)	40075	4533	9.3	4309	487
Middle Auri (Ejo sup)	5610	522	2.9	1934	180
Low dens (Ejo inf)	801 *(147)*	103 *(18)*	2.2	364 *(67)*	47 *(8)*
EJO	4505	335	3.0	1502	112
Moust/Chât (Ejop sup)	28872	1154	7.1	4066	163
Dentic Moust (Ejop inf)	9510	422	5.7	1668	74
EJOP	9791	569	3.5	2797	163
Dentic Moust (Egpf)	21084	970	2.2	9584	441
Total/Average	132512	10291	44.1	3005	233

Italic numbers are counts after excluding the three unusually "rich" squares I4, I5, and J5. These squares are shown separately because they inflate abundance appreciably in this otherwise low-density level. Density is probably exaggerated for the Denticulate Mousterian EGPF, as the sample included in this study favors rich décapages.

Abbreviations for this and subsequent tables: Evol = Evolved; Auri = Aurignacian; low dens = low-density; Chât = Châtelperronian; Dent or Dentic = Denticulate; Moust = Mousterian.

and EJO samples). Refitting reduced the total NISP sample by 11.4% for a post-refit total of 9,114 identified specimens (Table 5.5). The highest NISP counts are found, in decreasing order, in the Middle Aurignacian EJF, Evolved Aurignacian EJM, Mousterian/ Châtelperronian EJOP sup, and Denticulate Mousterian EGPF occupations. The low-density, Denticulate Mousterian EJOP inf, and Middle Aurignacian EJO sup occupations have smaller assemblages compared with the other levels. One should note that only

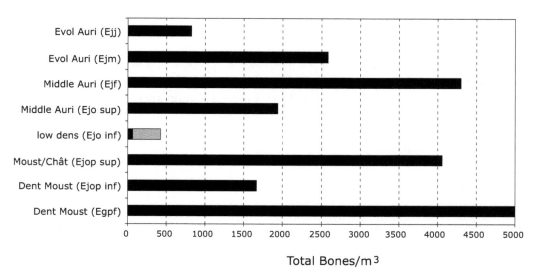

FIGURE 5.6. Density of bones (NISP/m³) by level at Saint-Césaire. Data from TABLE 5.4. The gray bar includes the unusually rich I4, I5, and J5 squares. Density of bones in the Denticulate Mousterian EGPF occupation is estimated because the study of this level is not yet completed.

TABLE 5.5. *Pre-refit and post-refit NISP counts for the levels of Saint-Césaire*

Layer	Pre-refit NISP n	Post-refit NISP n
Evolved Aurignacian (Ejj)	473	426
Evolved Aurignacian (Ejm)	1210	1083
Middle Aurignacian (Ejf)	4533	4102
Middle Aurignacian (Ejo sup)	522	480
Low density (Ejo inf)	103	83
EJO	335	292
Mousterian/Châtelperronian (Ejop sup)	1154	966
Denticulate Mousterian (Ejop inf)	422	331
EJOP	569	484
Denticulate Mousterian (Egpf)	970	867
Total	10291	9114

Birds and microfauna excluded. Pre-refit counts include all refitted fragments.

post-refit NISP counts are used in the analysis of the assemblages, because they minimize the problem of differential fragmentation and specimen interdependence and thus portray species and body part representation more accurately.

Data from the EJOP sample, including materials from both EJOP inf and EJOP sup, are sometimes provided in the tables as complementary information. The same is true for the EJO sample. It should be emphasized that MNI and MNE counts have a limited analytical value in these mixed samples, because they are strongly influenced by the way the samples were aggregated (Grayson 1984). As a result, MNI and MNE counts are not provided for the mixed samples. Microfauna and bird remains, which probably accumulated naturally at Saint-Césaire (see below), are presented in separate tables.

TAXONOMIC COMPOSITION OF THE ASSEMBLAGES

Ungulates are extremely abundant in all the Saint-Césaire assemblages, representing between 91.7 and 99.5% of NISP (Table 5.6). Among these, three taxa predominate: reindeer, large bovines, and horse (Table 5.7). In contrast, carnivores and other ungulates, such as red deer, mammoth, and rhinoceros, are poorly documented (Table 5.8). These last species are essentially represented by teeth, ribs, and some long bones. Importantly, hyena, bear, and wolf – well-known bone accumulators during the European Pleistocene – are rare at Saint-Césaire.

Looking at broad patterns in taxonomic composition, two faunal "sets" can be recognized in the Saint-Césaire sequence (Figure 5.7). The lowermost set, from the Denticulate Mousterian through to the Mousterian/Châtelperronian, comprises assemblages with similar percentages of bovines, reindeer, and horse. The former two taxa tend to be slightly more abundant than horse remains in these levels, except in the Denticulate Mousterian EGPF, which is dominated by horse and bovines. The relative abundance of horse decreases almost steadily across this part of the sequence.

In marked contrast, the upper faunal set – which includes all the Aurignacian levels – indicates a heavy focus on reindeer, a taxon that appears to decrease slightly in abundance after a peak in the Middle Aurignacian EJO sup occupation. Taxa other than

TABLE 5.6. *Percentages of ungulates, carnivores, and other taxa in the assemblages from Saint-Césaire*

Layer	Ungulates %	Carnivores %	Other %	Total NISP n
Evol Auri (Ejj)	98.8	1.2	0.0	329 (426)
Evol Auri (Ejm)	99.3	0.7	0.0	833 (1083)
Middle Auri (Ejf)	98.7	1.2	0.1	3459 (4102)
Middle Auri (Ejo sup)	96.6	3.1	0.2	417 (480)
Low dens (Ejo inf)	91.7	6.7	1.7	60 (83)
EJO	97.5	2.5	0.0	244 (292)
Moust/Châtel (Ejop sup)	96.2	3.3	0.5	824 (966)
Dentic Moust (Ejop inf)	99.0	1.0	0.0	286 (331)
EJOP	97.7	1.5	0.8	391 (484)
Dentic Moust (Egpf)	99.5	0.5	0.0	867 (867)
Total	98.4	1.5	0.2	7710 (9114)

Counts based on total post-refit NISP excluding antlers (total NISP including antlers are shown in parentheses). Birds and microfauna excluded.

reindeer and horse, including bovines, are poorly represented in these occupations. The EJO inf assemblage, stratigraphically located between the two faunal sets, is intermediate in composition. However, interpretation of the sample available from this level is limited because of its small size.

A similar picture is obtained when taxonomic composition is investigated using TMNEs, which correspond to the sum of the MNEs for all elements by species. TMNE counts indicate that the Denticulate Mousterian EGPF and Mousterian/Châtelperronian occupations have a mixed composition of reindeer, bovines, and horse (Table 5.9). Reindeer is very abundant in the Aurignacian occupations, where it accounts for between 66 and 76% of the skeletal elements. MNI values (Appendix 1) are globally consistent with this picture.

TABLE 5.7. *Relative abundance (in NISP) of reindeer, bison, horse, and some major taxonomic groups in the occupations from Saint-Césaire*

Layer	Reindeer %	Bison %	Horse %	Other ungulates %	Carnivores %	Other %	Total %
Evol Auri (Ejj)	68.7	11.8	17.3	0.9	1.2	0.0	99.9
Evol Auri (Ejm)	72.0	9.4	13.6	4.3	0.7	0.0	100.0
Mid Auri (Ejf)	81.6	4.7	11.1	1.2	1.2	0.1	99.9
Mid Auri (Ejo sup)	83.7	4.6	5.3	3.1	3.1	0.2	100.0
Low dens (Ejo inf)	33.3	23.3	21.7	13.3	6.7	1.7	100.0
EJO	66.4	15.2	13.1	2.8	2.5	0.0	100.0
M/Châtel (Ejop sup)	19.7	47.4	17.0	12.0	3.3	0.5	99.9
D Moust (Ejop inf)	32.9	35.7	26.2	4.0	1.0	0.0	99.8
EJOP	33.0	35.0	20.2	9.5	1.5	0.8	100.0
D Moust (Egpf)	24.7	37.9	34.0	2.8	0.5	0.0	99.9
Total	62.0	17.0	15.7	3.6	1.5	0.2	100.0

Counts based on total NISP excluding antlers. Birds and microfauna excluded.

TABLE 5.8. *NISP counts by species for mammal and fish remains from Saint-Césaire*

	Dent Moust (Egpf)		EJOP		Dent Moust (Ejop inf)		Moust/ Châtel (Ejop sup)		EJO		Low dens (Ejo inf)	
	n	%	n	%	n	%	n	%	n	%	n	%
Artiodactyla												
reindeer	214	24.7	129	33.0	94	32.9	162	19.7	162	66.4	20	33.3
bison	329	37.9	137	35.0	102	35.7	391	47.4	37	15.2	14	23.3
red deer	9	1.0	11	2.8	7	2.4	41	5.0	2	0.8	1	1.7
giant deer	7	0.8	2	0.5	1	0.3	.	.	1	0.4	.	.
roe deer	.	.	.	.	.	.	4	0.5	.	.	.	.
wild boar	.	.	2	0.5	1	0.3	4	0.5	1	0.4	.	.
Perissodactyla												
horse	295	34.0	79	20.2	75	26.2	140	17.0	32	13.1	13	21.7
wooly rhino	2	0.2	7	1.8	1	0.3	28	3.4	3	1.2	6	10.0
European ass	.	.	1	0.3	.	.	2	0.2	.	.	.	.
Proboscidea												
mammoth	7	0.8	14	3.6	2	0.7	21	2.5	.	.	1	1.7
Carnivora												
spotted hyena	2	0.2	1	0.3	.	.	3	0.4	1	0.4	1	1.7
wolf	1	0.1	.	.	2	0.7	2	0.2	2	0.8	.	.
arctic fox	.	.	.	.	.	.	2	0.2	.	.	1	1.7
unspec. fox	1	0.1	4	1.0	1	0.3	17	2.1	3	1.2	2	3.3
bear			1	0.3					.	.	.	.
polecat	.	.	.	.	.	.	1	0.1	.	.	.	.
pine marten	.	.	.	.	.	.	.	.	.	.	.	.
lynx	.	.	.	.	.	.	.	.	.	.	.	.
badger	.	.	.	.	.	.	.	.	.	.	.	.
cave lion	.	.	.	.	.	.	2	0.2	.	.	.	.
Leporidae												
hare	.	.	.	.	.	.	.	.	.	.	.	.
unspec. lepor.	.	.	3	0.8	.	.	1	0.1	.	.	1	1.7
Fish												
cyprinid	.	.	.	.	.	.	1	0.1	.	.	.	.
brown trout	.	.	.	.	.	.	2	0.2	.	.	.	.
Total NISP	867	99.8	391	100.1	286	99.8	824	99.8	244	99.9	60	100.1
Total + antlers	867		484		331		966		292		83	

Bison or Aurochs?

In European Paleolithic assemblages, it is often difficult to attribute specimens exclusively to bison (*Bison priscus*) or aurochs (*Bos primigenius*) because these two species overlap extensively in skeletal characteristics. Horns and cranial features are generally considered the most reliable criteria for distinguishing between these species (Brugal 1983; Slott-Moller 1988). Unfortunately, as at most Paleolithic sites, these body parts are poorly represented and highly fragmented at Saint-Césaire. Several dental and postcranial features may also be used to differentiate these taxa (Prat n.d.; Brugal 1983; Delpech 1983; Guadelli 1987, 1999; Slott-Moller 1988, 1990), but these criteria, some of which are described subsequently, are rarely perfectly dichotomous and are better used for characterizing populations rather than individuals (Brugal 1983).

TABLE 5.8. *NISP counts by species for mammal and fish remains from Saint-Césaire (continued)*

	Middle Auri (Ejo sup)		Middle Auri (Ejf)		Evol Auri (Ejm)		Evol Auri (Ejj)		Total	
	NISP	%	NISP	%	NISP	%	NISP	%	NISP	%
Artiodactyla										
reindeer	349	83.7	2823	81.6	600	72.0	226	68.7	4779	62.0
bison	19	4.6	164	4.7	78	9.4	39	11.8	1310	17.0
red deer	2	0.5	10	0.3	2	0.2	2	0.6	87	1.1
giant deer	.	.	7	0.2	.	.	.	.	18	0.2
roe deer	.	.	.	.	.	.	.	.	4	0.0
wild boar	.	.	1	0.0	.	.	.	.	9	0.1
Perissodactyla										
horse	22	5.3	385	11.1	113	13.6	57	17.3	1211	15.7
wooly rhino	3	0.7	8	0.2	1	0.1	.	.	59	0.8
European ass	.	.	.	.	.	.	.	.	3	0.0
Proboscidea										
mammoth	8	1.9	16	0.5	33	4.0	1	0.3	103	1.3
Carnivora										
spotted hyena	.	.	1	0.0	.	.	1	0.3	10	0.1
wolf	3	0.7	9	0.3	1	0.1	1	0.3	21	0.3
arctic fox	1	0.2	3	0.1	.	.	.	.	7	0.1
unspec. fox	6	1.4	23	0.7	4	0.5	2	0.6	63	0.8
bear	.	.	.	.	.	.	.	.	1	0.0
polecat	1	0.2	1	0.0	.	.	.	.	3	0.0
pine marten	2	0.5	.	.	.	.	.	.	2	0.0
lynx	.	.	1	0.0	.	.	.	.	1	0.0
badger	.	.	1	0.0	1	0.1	.	.	2	0.0
cave lion	.	.	2	0.1	.	.	.	.	4	0.0
Leporidae										
hare	1	0.2	.	.	.	.	.	.	1	0.0
unspec. lepor.	.	.	4	0.1	.	.	.	.	9	0.1
Fish										
cyprinid	.	.	.	.	.	.	.	.	1	0.0
brown trout	.	.	.	.	.	.	.	.	2	0.0
Total NISP	417	99.9	3459	99.9	833	100.0	329	99.9	7710	99.6
Total + antlers	480		4102		1083		426		9114	

Antlers counted separately
Abbreviations for this and subsequent tables: unspec. = unspecified; lepor. = leporids

In the Mousterian/Châtelperronian (EJOP sup) occupation, a level in which bovines are abundant, teeth were used to determine the respective proportions of bison and aurochs in the sample. According to Slott-Moller (1990:46 and p. 44, fig. 43), the longitudinal depression separating the two lobes of the M_1 and M_2 in lingual view is U-shaped in bison and more V-shaped in aurochs. In the assemblage, 12 out of 13 M_1/M_2 are clearly U-shaped and therefore more in line with bison. One specimen is intermediate in shape. In the EJOP sample, which comprises materials from both EJOP inf and EJOP sup, all three molars studied are U-shaped. Slott-Moller (1990:46 and p. 45, fig. 44) also emphasized that the width of the ectostylid (measured at mid-length) tends to be greater in bison than in aurochs, with a cutoff point around 4 mm. In the EJOP sup occupation of

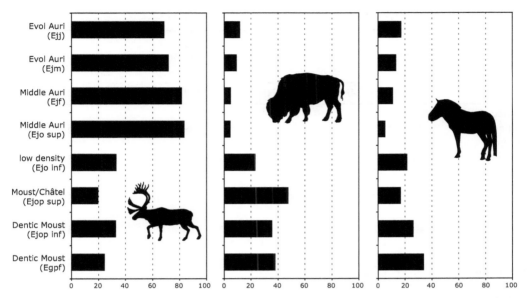

FIGURE 5.7. Percentages of reindeer, bison, and horse remains by level at Saint-Césaire. Data from TABLE 5.8.

Saint-Césaire, the ectostylids of the M_1/M_2 measure between 3.2 and 5.0 mm. Although most specimens have width greater than 4 mm, some of the molars fall in the upper range of the aurochs distribution.

Upper teeth were also included in the analysis of bovine teeth from the EJOP sup occupation. In aurochs, upper molars are frequently, but not always, characterized by a small "islet" (*îlot*) of enamel visible on the occlusal surface between the two lobes of the tooth, a feature said to be rare in bison (Slott-Moller 1990:38 and p. 40, fig. 31). In the EJOP sup sample, only 1 out of 22 M^1/M^2 shows the presence of an enamel islet. Combined with the previous observations, these data suggests that bison was by far the dominant, if not the only, bovine species represented in this occupation.

Ferrié (2001) studied a sample of bovine remains, mostly teeth, from the Denticulate Mousterian EGPF level. Using the criteria presented earlier and several others, a detailed analysis of the material led him to attribute the majority of the bovine specimens to bison. According to Guadelli (1987, 1999), the petrous bone can also be used for discriminating aurochs from bison. Guadelli's unpublished study of the Saint-Césaire petrous bones supports the foregoing conclusions, because he attributed all the specimens – the majority of which come from the EGPS, EGPF, and EJOP sup layers – in his sample ($n = 14$) to bison. Thus, cranial and postcranial data converge in their assignment of the majority of bovine remains from Saint-Césaire to bison. As a result, the latter taxon will be used in the remainder of this book when referring to large bovines. However, Lavaud-Girard (1987, 1993) noted that some M_3 from the EJOP level have a pinched, elongated, and vestibularly offset third lobe, features that are argued to be more characteristic of aurochs (but see Slott-Moller 1990). If Lavaud-Girard's interpretation is correct, this might suggest the presence of a small number of aurochs specimens in the assemblage.

TABLE 5.9. *MNE counts by species for mammal and fish remains from Saint-Césaire*

	Dent Moust (Egpf)		EJOP		Dent Moust (Ejop inf)		Moust/ Châtel (Ejop sup)		EJO		Low dens (Ejo inf)	
	MNE	%	MNE	%	MNE	%	MNE	%	MNE	%	MNE	%
Artiodactyla												
reindeer	56	31.6	48	37.8	29	31.9	60	24.5	39	52.0	9	29.0
bison	60	33.9	44	34.6	35	38.5	97	39.6	15	20.0	8	25.8
red deer	5	2.8	6	4.7	3	3.3	15	6.1	2	2.7	1	3.2
giant deer	3	1.7	1	0.8	1	1.1	.	.	1	1.3	.	.
roe deer	.	.	.	.	.	.	4	1.6	.	.	.	.
wild boar	.	.	1	0.8	1	1.1	3	1.2	1	1.3	.	.
Perissodactyla												
horse	46	26.0	13	10.2	17	18.7	30	12.2	10	13.3	5	16.1
wooly rhino	2	1.1	5	3.9	1	1.1	8	3.3	2	2.7	2	6.4
European ass	.	.	1	0.8	.	.	2	0.8	.	.	.	.
Proboscidea												
mammoth	1	0.6	1	0.8	1	1.1	1	0.4	.	.	1	3.2
Carnivora												
spotted hyena	2	1.1	1	0.8	.	.	3	1.2	1	1.3	1	3.2
wolf	1	0.6	.	.	2	2.2	2	0.8	2	2.7	.	.
arctic fox	.	.	.	.	.	.	2	0.8	.	.	1	3.2
unspec. fox	1	0.6	4	3.1	1	1.1	12	4.9	2	2.7	2	6.4
bear	.	.	1	0.8	.	.	.	.	.	.	.	.
polecat	.	.	.	.	.	.	1	0.4	.	.	.	.
pine marten	.	.	.	.	.	.	.	.	.	.	.	.
lynx	.	.	.	.	.	.	.	.	.	.	.	.
badger	.	.	.	.	.	.	.	.	.	.	.	.
cave lion	.	.	.	.	.	.	2	0.8	.	.	.	.
Leporidae												
hare	.	.	.	.	.	.	.	.	.	.	.	.
unspec. lepor.	.	.	1	0.8	.	.	1	0.4	.	.	1	3.2
Fish												
cyprinid	.	.	.	.	.	.	1	0.4	.	.	.	.
brown trout	.	.	.	.	.	.	1	0.4	.	.	.	.
Total MNE	177	100.0	127	99.9	91	100.1	245	99.8	75	100.0	31	99.7
Total + antlers	177		141		93		257		80		35	

Other Faunal Remains

Fox is the most common carnivore at Saint-Césaire. Because bones of arctic fox (*Alopex lagopus*) overlap in shape and dimensions with those of the red fox (*Vulpes vulpes*), a precise distinction of these taxa is not always possible. Using observations made by Poplin (1976), Cédric Beauval (2003) attributed remains from the Mousterian/Châtelperronian (one M^1 and one M_2), low-density EJO inf (one P_2), and Middle Aurignacian EJO sup (one M^1) and EJF (one radius, one M_1, and one P_2) levels to the arctic fox. The presence of the red fox is also suspected in the Mousterian/Châtelperronian and Middle Aurignacian EJF layers, although no specimen could be unequivocally assigned to this taxon.

TABLE 5.9. *MNE counts by species for mammal and fish remains from Saint-Césaire (continued)*

	Middle Auri (Ejo sup)		Middle Auri (Ejf)		Evol Auri (Ejm)		Evol Auri (Ejj)		Total	
	MNE	%	MNE	%	MNE	%	MNE	%	MNE	%
Artiodactyla										
reindeer	95	74.2	594	76.0	157	68.9	70	66.0	1157	58.1
bison	9	7.0	47	6.0	24	10.5	15	14.1	354	17.8
red deer	1	0.8	8	1.0	1	0.4	1	0.9	43	2.2
giant deer	.	.	1	0.1	.	.	.	.	7	0.3
roe deer	.	.	.	.	.	.	.	.	4	0.2
wild boar	.	.	1	0.1	.	.	.	.	7	0.3
Perissodactyla										
horse	7	5.5	89	11.4	40	17.5	15	14.1	272	13.7
wooly rhino	2	1.6	3	0.4	1	0.4	.	.	26	1.3
European ass	.	.	.	.	.	.	.	.	3	0.1
Proboscidea										
mammoth	1	0.8	1	0.1	1	0.4	1	0.9	9	0.4
Carnivora										
spotted hyena	.	.	1	0.1	.	.	1	0.9	10	0.5
wolf	2	1.6	7	0.9	1	0.4	1	0.9	18	0.9
arctic fox	1	0.8	2	0.3	.	.	.	.	6	0.3
unspec. fox	6	4.7	19	2.4	2	0.9	2	1.9	51	2.6
bear	.	.	.	.	.	.	.	.	1	0.0
polecat	1	0.8	1	0.1	.	.	.	.	3	0.1
pine marten	2	1.6	.	.	.	.	.	.	2	0.1
lynx	.	.	1	0.1	.	.	.	.	1	0.0
badger	.	.	1	0.1	1	0.4	.	.	2	0.1
cave lion	.	.	2	0.3	.	.	.	.	4	0.2
Leporidae										
hare	1	0.8	.	.	.	.	.	.	1	0.0
unspec. lepor.	.	.	4	0.5	.	.	.	.	7	0.3
Fish										
cyprinid	.	.	.	.	.	.	.	.	1	0.0
brown trout	.	.	.	.	.	.	.	.	1	0.0
Total MNE	128	100.2	782	99.9	228	99.8	106	99.7	1990	99.5
Total + antlers	132		829		238		108		2090	

Antlers counted separately.

A few remains of leporids, one positively identified as a hare, are also documented in the assemblages. Rabbits were not identified, although they may be present. Among the small burrowing animals, it should be noted that moles are uncommon in the samples but are more frequent in the EJOP sup assemblage (MNI = 6). Most of the mole remains were identified when screening soil samples for rodents.

Birds are sporadically present in the accumulations. Véronique Laroulandie (2004b) provided some taxonomic and taphonomic observations bearing on these remains. She identified several species from the order Anseriformes and a small number of raptors (Table 5.10). Bird remains that were identified to the species level in the assemblages include the pintail (*Anas acuta*), common teal (*Anas crecca*), raven (*Corvus corax*), eagle (*Aquila chrysaetos*), and little Auk (*Alle alle*).

TABLE 5.10. *NISP counts for the bird remains by species and level at Saint-Césaire*

	Dentic Moust (Egpf)	EJOP	Dentic Moust (Ejop inf)	Moust/ Châtel (Ejop sup)	EJO	Middle Auri (Ejo sup)	Middle Auri (Ejf)	Evol Auri (Ejm)	Total Total
Anseriformes									
Anser sp.	.	1	.	.	.	.	.	.	1
cf. *Anser*	.	.	.	.	.	.	1	.	1
Anas acuta	.	.	.	.	.	6	.	.	6
Anas cf. *acuta*	.	.	.	1	.	.	.	.	1
Anas crecca	.	.	.	.	.	.	1	.	1
Anas sp.	.	.	.	.	.	1	.	.	1
Aythya sp.	.	.	.	.	.	2	.	.	2
unspecified	.	.	.	1	1	3	2 (1*)	.	7
Accipitriformes									.
Aquila chrysaetos	1	.	.	.	.	.	.	.	1
unspec. vulture	.	.	1	.	.	.	3	1	5
unspecified	.	.	.	.	1	.	.	.	1
Galliformes									
Lagopus sp.	.	.	.	.	1	.	1	.	2
Charadriiformes									
Alle alle	.	.	.	.	.	3	.	.	3
Pluvialis sp.	.	.	.	.	.	1	4 (1*)	.	5
unspec. charadriidae	.	.	.	1	.	.	.	2*	3
unspec. charadriiform	.	.	2	.	.	.	1	2 (1*)	5
Strigiformes									
unspecified	.	.	.	.	.	1	1	.	2
Passeriformes									
Corvus corax	.	.	.	.	.	.	1*	.	1
unspecified	.	1	.	.	.	.	1	.	2
Total birds	1	2	3	3	3	17	16	5	50

Star denotes juveniles.

Three fish bones were identified in the EJOP sup layer. According to Olivier Le Gall (Centre National de la Recherche Scientifique, Université de Bordeaux I), these remains possibly correspond to as many individuals, based on size and morphology. The fact that these bones have the exact same three-dimensional coordinates suggests a single depositional event. Some amphibian bones ($n = 9$) were also identified in the Mousterian/Châtelperronian and Middle Aurignacian EJO sup occupations by Lavaud-Girard (1993) and Marquet (pers. comm., 2003). These last specimens were not included in this study because of sampling biases and because they presumably result from natural deaths in burrows, postdepositional contamination, carnivore/raptor predation, or a combination of these.

Micromammal (<500 g) species are poorly represented in the assemblages (Table 5.11). These low numbers are most certainly the result of recovery biases because micromammal remains were relatively abundant in the soil samples (Marquet, pers. comm., 2003; and personal observation). With respect to taxonomic composition, the narrow-skulled vole dominates the Saint-Césaire sequence, especially in the Aurignacian occupations (Marquet 1993). The common vole and the water vole, however, are also moderately abundant in the lower part of the sequence.

TABLE 5.11. *MNI counts for microfaunal remains by species and level at Saint-Césaire*

	Dentic Moust (Egpf)		Dentic Moust (Ejop inf)		Moust/ Châtel (Ejop sup)		Low density (Ejo inf)		Middle Auri (Ejo sup)		Middle Auri (Ejf)		Evolved Auri (Ejm)		Evolved Auri (Ejj)	
	n	%	n	%	n	%	n	%	n	%	n	%	n	%	n	%
Narrow-skulled vole	5	55.5	1	50.0	29	76.3	38	100	80	95.2	59	84.3	93	93.0	97	89.0
Common vole	2	22.2	.	.	4	10.5	.	.	1	1.2	1	1.4	.	.	7	6.4
Ground squirrel	.	.	.	.	.	.	.	.	.	.	1	1.4	1	1.0	1	0.9
Snow vole	1	1.11	.	.	.	.	.	.	.	.	.	.	.	.	.	.
Water vole	1	1.11	1	50.0	5	13.2	.	.	3	3.6	8	11.4	4	4.0	1	0.9
Pine vole	.	.	.	.	.	.	.	.	.	.	.	.	.	.	1	0.9
Field vole	.	.	.	.	.	.	.	.	.	.	.	.	.	.	.	.
Garden dormouse	.	.	.	.	.	.	.	.	.	.	.	.	1	1.0	.	.
Root/Male vole	.	.	.	.	.	.	.	.	.	.	.	.	1	1.0	1	0.9
Collared lemming	.	.	.	.	.	.	.	.	.	.	.	.	.	.	1	0.9
Rattus sp.	.	.	.	.	.	.	.	.	.	.	1	1.4	.	.	.	.
Total	9	99.9	2	100	38	100	38	100	84	100	70	99.9	100	100	109	99.9

Data from Marquet 1993 and unpublished results.

Overall, foxes, leporids, and birds are relatively infrequent at Saint-Césaire. They may indicate procurement unrelated to diet or, as is probably the case for the micro-mammals, background accumulation. However, because this interpretation cannot be corroborated by empirical data, foxes, leporids, and birds are considered in the test of the intensification hypothesis, keeping in mind that their origin at Saint-Césaire is nebulous.

SKELETAL PART REPRESENTATION AT SAINT-CÉSAIRE

This section describes trends in skeletal part representation for reindeer, bison, and horse, the three most common species in the Saint-Césaire levels, and presents information on burning and cutmark distribution. The low-density EJO inf occupation is excluded from this discussion because of sample size constraints. MNE values, from which the %MAU values are derived, are provided by taxon (reindeer, bison, and horse) and level in Appendix 2. It should be noted that the faunal patterns reported here for the EJOP sup assemblage differ appreciably from those published by Patou-Mathis (1993). These differences are, for the most part, due to the inclusion in the present analysis of shaft fragments and other elements that were only collected by décapage. These specimens, previously unstudied, represent the bulk of the identified material.

An important point needs to be stressed concerning the interpretation of body part representation at Saint-Césaire. Burning is not random in the assemblages and primarily affects the carpals, tarsals, innominates, vertebrae, and long bone epiphyses. Therefore, burning possibly reduced the abundance of these parts in the assemblages, an issue investigated in Chapter 6.

1. DENTICULATE MOUSTERIAN (EGPF). The head and tibia are the best represented bison parts in the EGPF assemblage, based on %MAU (Figure 5.8). For horse, the most abundant elements are the head, humerus, tibia, and metacarpal (Figure 5.9). Long

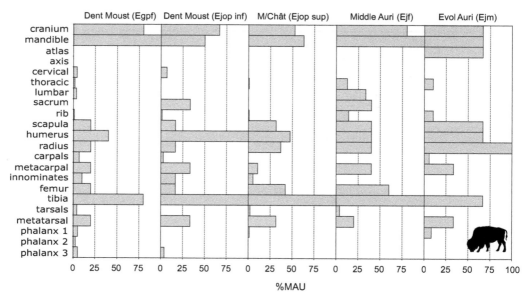

FIGURE 5.8. Bison body part representation in five assemblages from Saint-Césaire. Data from Appendix 2.

bones, especially those of the hind leg, dominate the reindeer sample (Figure 5.10). In all three species, phalanges, ribs, innominates, carpals, and tarsals are infrequent, as are segments of the axial skeleton. Importantly, long bone epiphyses are generally rare compared with shafts (Figure 5.11 to Figure 5.13). This last pattern is consistent across long bone elements and species.

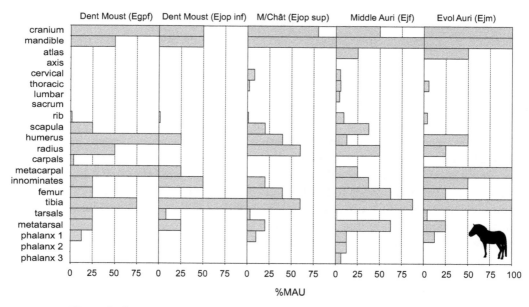

FIGURE 5.9. Horse body part representation in five assemblages from Saint-Césaire. Data from Appendix 2.

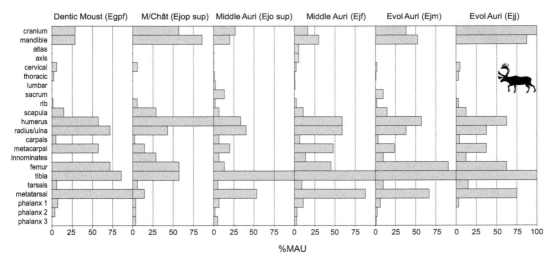

FIGURE 5.10. Reindeer body part representation in six assemblages from Saint-Césaire. Data from Appendix 2.

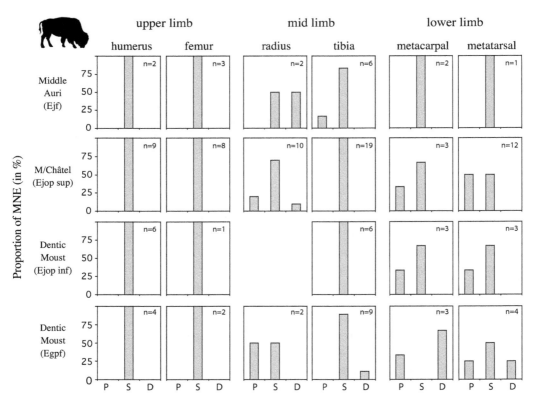

FIGURE 5.11. Relative abundances of proximal, shaft, and distal portions of bison long bones in four assemblages from Saint-Césaire. Data from Appendix 2. Percentages are calculated by dividing the MNE for each anatomical region (proximal, shaft, and distal portions) of an element by the sum of the MNE values for all three anatomical regions combined. An empty box indicates lack of data. Abbreviations: P = proximal, S = shaft, D = distal.

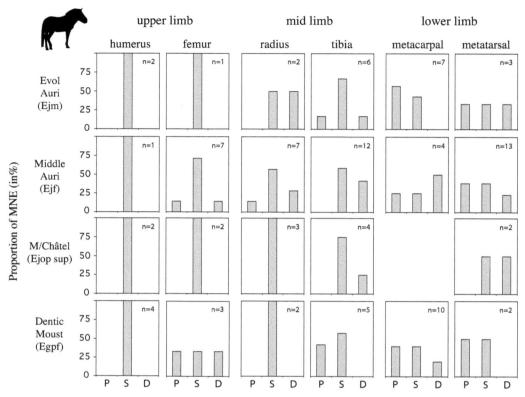

FIGURE 5.12. Relative abundances of proximal, shaft, and distal portions of horse long bones in four assemblages from Saint-Césaire. Data from Appendix 2. Percentages are calculated by dividing the MNE for each anatomical region (proximal, shaft, and distal portions) of an element by the sum of the MNE values for all three anatomical regions combined. An empty box indicates lack of data. Abbreviations: P = proximal, S = shaft, D = distal.

Burning affects several specimens ($n = 59$) in the EGPF occupation (Table 5.12, all species and NSUTS combined). The cranium shows a moderately high incidence (25.0%, $n = 88$) of exposure to fire. In contrast, the percentage of burned teeth (3.8%, $n = 132$) is low. Burning was rarely identified on the other classes of specimens, including long bones. However, we will see that several lines of evidence (e.g., the high incidence of burned spongy fragments in the indeterminate sample) suggest that burning significantly reduced the abundance of long bone epiphyses in this layer.

In the sample, cutmarks are fairly common on reindeer (49/163 or 30.1%, Table 5.13) and horse (9/36 or 25.0%, Table 5.14) long bones. This value is much lower in bison (7/84 or 8.3%, Table 5.15). The percentage of long bones that are cut-marked is significantly lower in bison than in horse ($t_s = 2.32$, $p < .05$) or reindeer ($t_s = 4.30$, $p < .0001$), but the latter taxa are not significantly different from each other (reindeer vs. horse: $t_s = 0.62$, $p < .54$). In general, higher percentages of cutmarks are recorded on long bones than on the axial skeleton. However, as emphasized in Chapter 6, differences in the relative frequencies of cutmarks should be interpreted with caution, given that the degree of surface preservation and fragmentation vary within and between the assemblages.

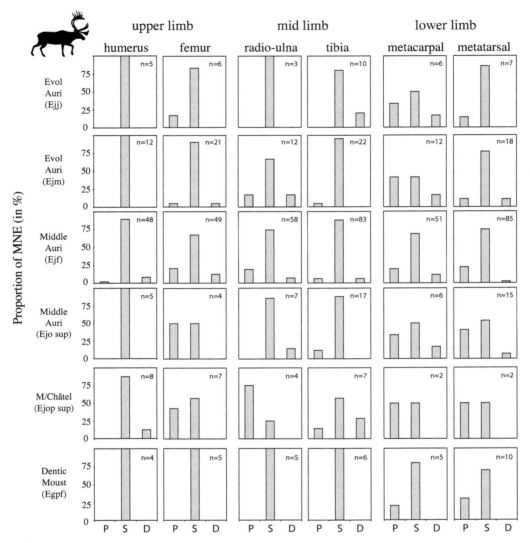

FIGURE 5.13. Relative abundances of proximal, shaft, and distal portions of reindeer long bones by level in six assemblages from Saint-Césaire. Data from Appendix 2. Percentages are calculated by dividing the MNE for each anatomical region (proximal, shaft, and distal portions) of an element by the sum of the MNE values for all three anatomical regions combined. An empty box indicates lack of data. Abbreviations: P = proximal, S = shaft, D = distal.

2. DENTICULATE MOUSTERIAN (EJOP INF). Bison is the most abundant species in this small assemblage. The humerus and tibia are well represented in this taxon, as are the cranium and mandible. Elements of the vertebral column are lacking, except for cervical vertebrae and the sacrum. The head and tibia are the most frequent elements in horse. No clear pattern emerges from the very small reindeer sample associated with this occupation. However, for all three species, shafts are more abundant than epiphyses. Only a few (n = 17) burned specimens were identified at least to body size class. Burned teeth, usually crown fragments, are moderately frequent (9.1%, n = 142). In general, cutmarks are more common on long bones than on the axial skeleton.

TABLE 5.12. *Percentage of burning in the occupations from Saint-Césaire*

NISP+NSUTS

	Burned	n	%burned		Burned	n	%burned
EJO				Evol Auri (Ejj)			
radio-ulna	1	13	7.7	mandible/maxill.	1	23	4.3
innominates	1	1	100.0	vertebrae	2	12	16.7
calcaneum	1	1	100.0	ribs	2	107	1.9
metatarsal	1	58	1.7	radio-ulna	2	28	7.1
				metacarpal	1	13	7.7
Mid Auri (Ejo sup)				innominates	2	5	40.0
petrous bone	1	3	33.3	femur	1	16	6.3
vertebrae	6	25	24.0	tibia	1	38	2.6
radio-ulna	2	24	8.3	tarsals	1	8	12.5
carpals	3	6	50.0	phalanges	1	8	12.5
femur	1	11	9.1				
tibia	1	49	2.0	Evolved Auri (Ejm)			
talus	3	6	50.0	cranium	2	20	10.0
metatarsal	2	104	1.9	tooth	1	140	0.7
sesamoid	1	5	20.0	vertebrae	8	29	27.6
				ribs	4	350	1.1
EJOP				humerus	1	32	3.1
ribs	1	125	0.8	radius	5	72	6.9
talus	2	2	100.0	femur	2	28	7.1
tooth	9	163	5.5	malleolus	1	1	100.0
				tarsals	7	12	58.3
M/Chât (Ejop sup)				metatarsal	4	166	2.4
mandible/maxill.	1	47	2.1				
tooth	22	564	3.9	Mid Auri (Ejf)			
rib	4	372	1.1	cranium	6	100	6.0
				tooth	28	333	8.4
Dent Moust (Ejop inf)				vertebrae	68	165	41.2
tibia	1	59	1.7	ribs	33	1688	1.9
metatarsal	2	42	4.8	humerus	6	124	4.8
cranium	1	13	7.7	radio-ulna	23	304	7.6
tooth	13	142	9.1	carpals	5	30	16.7
				innominates	12	42	28.6
Dent Moust (Egpf)				femur	11	134	8.2
horn	1	28	3.6	patella	1	6	16.7
cranium	22	88	25.0	tibia	25	425	5.9
mandible/maxill.	5	132	3.8	malleolus	4	5	80.0
tooth	27	526	5.1	tarsals	24	47	51.1
scapula	1	27	3.7	metatarsal	10	856	1.2
innominates	1	8	12.5	metapodial	1	76	1.3
fibula	1	3	33.3	phalanges	4	86	4.6
malleolus	1	4	25.0	vestigial phalanges	1	8	12.5

Only the elements showing evidence of burning are included. Samples consist of both NISP and NSUTS (number of specimens of uncertain taxonomic status) to maximize sample size.

TABLE 5.13. *Distribution of cutmarks on reindeer bones by body part and level at Saint-Césaire*

	Dentic Moust (Egpf) n	Dentic Moust (Ejop inf) n	Moust/ Châtel (Ejop sup) n	EJOP n	Middle Auri (Ejo sup) n	Middle Auri (Ejf) n	Evolved Auri (Ejm) n	Evolved Auri (Ejj) n	Total n	Total %
Cranium	0/1	.	.	.	0/3	0/25	0/5	0/3	0/37	0.0
Vertebrae	0/4	0/2	0/1	0/4	0/5	0/26	0/3	2/3	2/48	4.2
Ribs	0/8	0/7	1/40	0/11	2/53	10/427	2/47	0/15	15/608	2.5
Scapula	0/2	0/3	0/2	.	0/1	3/20	1/9	0/1	4/38	10.5
Humerus	3/10	1/2	3/10	0/1	1/9	25/108	9/26	1/9	43/175	24.6
Radio-ulna	6/19	0/5	1/7	1/11	0/22	34/272	3/63	0/13	45/412	10.9
Carpals	0/2	.	0/1	0/3	0/6	0/30	0/4	0/2	0/48	0.0
Metacarpal	7/13	2/9	0/3	2/5	1/12	34/124	2/20	3/11	51/197	25.9
Innominate	.	.	0/2	0/3	0/1	0/23	0/5	0/2	0/36	0.0
Femur	3/9	3/5	0/8	0/3	1/11	22/114	4/24	2/12	35/186	18.8
Tibia	16/36	4/15	0/16	5/10	8/47	102/392	12/81	8/32	155/629	24.6
Tarsals	0/1	1/2	0/2	0/5	0/5	2/41	0/11	0/7	3/74	4.0
Metatarsal	14/76	1/30	0/19	0/28	3/102	24/841	6/160	1/68	49/1324	3.7
Phalanges	0/3	0/1	0/4	1/5	0/18	3/75	0/12	0/2	4/120	3.3
Total	49/184	12/81	5/115	9/89	16/295	259/2518	39/470	17/180	406/3932	10.3

Number of specimens with at least one cutmark versus total NISP. Antler and teeth excluded. Cranium includes mandibular bone.

3. MOUSTERIAN/CHÂTELPERRONIAN (EJOP SUP). Bison dominates this moderately large assemblage, followed by reindeer and horse. The most abundant of these species is described first. Long bones and the head are the most frequent parts in bison. The abundance of long bone elements decreases distally in the forelimb, whereas the tibia is the most common bone of the hindlimb. Elements of the axial skeleton are rare or absent, a pattern also true of carpals, tarsals, and phalanges. Long bone epiphyses are poorly represented.

For reindeer, the most common parts are the head and long bones, particularly the humerus, femur, and tibia. The sample for this species contains few carpals, tarsals, phalanges, and elements of the axial skeleton. The horse sample is dominated by the head, humerus, and tibia. A small number of cervical and thoracic vertebra fragments document the transport of the neck and back in this species. Carpals, tarsals, and phalanges also show poor representation.

A small sample of burned specimens ($n = 26$) was identified at least to body size class in the EJOP sup assemblage. Most are tooth fragments. Cutmarks on bison specimens are most common on the tibia, humerus, and femur and are infrequent on metapodials and elements of the axial skeleton. Cutmarks are less abundant on reindeer and horse.

4. EJOP (8–9). It is possible to crosscheck some of the patterns observed in the Mousterian/Châtelperronian layer by looking at the EJOP sample, which comprises material from both EJOP inf and EJOP sup. The tibia is the best represented element in the bison assemblage. The head and humerus are next in abundance. No element of the spine was identified. Carpals and tarsals are poorly represented. For reindeer, the highest %MAU values are associated with the head, radio-ulna, tibia, and metatarsal. The horse sample is too small to provide reliable information on skeletal part abundance.

TABLE 5.14. *Distribution of cutmarks on horse bones by body part and level at Saint-Césaire*

	Dentic Moust (Egpf) n	Dentic Moust (Ejop inf) n	Moust/ Châtel (Ejop sup) n	EJOP n	Middle Auri n	Middle Auri (Ejf) n	Evolved Auri (Ejm) n	Evolved Auri (Ejj) n	Total n	Total %
Cranium	0/12	0/1	0/1	.	0/1	0/10	.	0/2	0/27	0.0
Vertebrae	0/1	.	2/5	0/1	0/1	1/9	0/5	0/2	3/24	12.5
Ribs	0/9	0/3	1/17	0/7	0/12	2/174	0/34	0/12	3/268	1.1
Scapula	0/1	.	0/1	0/1	0/1	1/5	.	0/3	1/12	8.3
Humerus	4/8	2/2	1/2	0/2	.	1/7	0/3	0/1	8/25	32.0
Radio-ulna	2/5	.	1/5	.	.	1/13	0/3	0/2	4/28	14.3
Carpals	0/1	.	.	.	.	.	.	.	0/1	0.0
Metacarpal	2/8	0/1	.	.	.	1/7	0/5	0/1	3/22	13.6
Innominates	0/2	0/2	1/1	0/1	0/1	1/13	0/4	1/1	3/25	12.0
Femur	0/4	.	1/4	0/1	.	0/13	0/4	0/1	1/27	3.7
Tibia	1/8	2/7	0/5	1/3	0/1	1/16	0/7	0/1	5/48	10.4
Tarsals	0/3	0/2	0/1	.	.	0/1	0/1	.	0/8	0.0
Metatarsal	0/3	0/2	1/2	.	.	0/12	1/4	.	2/23	8.7
Phalanges	0/1	.	0/2	.	.	1/7	0/1	0/1	1/12	8.3
Total	9/66	4/20	8/46	1/16	0/17	10/287	1/71	1/27	34/550	6.2

Number of specimens with at least one cutmark versus total NISP. Teeth excluded. Cranium includes mandibular bone.

TABLE 5.15. *Distribution of cutmarks on bison bones by body part and level at Saint-Césaire*

	Dentic Moust (Egpf) n	Dentic Moust (Ejop inf) n	Moust/ Châtel (Ejop sup) n	EJOP n	Middle Auri n	Middle Auri (Ejf) n	Evolved Auri (Ejm) n	Evolved Auri (Ejj) n	Total n	Total %
Horncore	0/28	.	0/1	0/1	.	.	.	.	0/30	0.0
Cranium	0/17	0/2	0/4	0/2	.	.	0/1	0/2	0/28	0.0
Vertebrae	1/4	0/3	1/3	.	0/1	0/22	0/4	0/2	2/39	5.1
Ribs	1/15	1/8	0/25	0/13	0/5	0/86	2/42	0/7	4/201	2.0
Scapula	1/7	0/2	0/15	0/4	0/1	0/7	0/3	0/2	1/41	2.4
Humerus	4/6	3/10	7/21	0/9	.	1/2	0/2	0/3	15/53	28.3
Radio-ulna	0/7	0/1	1/20	0/2	0/1	1/4	0/5	.	2/40	5.0
Carpals	0/4	0/1	.	0/2	.	.	0/1	.	0/8	0.0
Metacarpal	0/3	1/3	0/7	0/1	.	0/3	0/1	0/1	1/19	5.3
Innominates	0/2	0/1	1/1	.	.	.	.	.	1/4	25.0
Femur	0/6	1/3	6/18	2/6	.	0/4	.	0/1	9/38	23.7
Tibia	2/47	3/27	21/73	5/22	0/1	0/11	0/8	0/3	31/192	16.1
Tarsals	0/1	.	0/3	0/2	.	0/1	.	0/1	0/8	0.0
Metatarsal	1/15	0/6	4/37	0/7	0/2	0/1	0/2	2/6	7/76	9.2
Phalanges	0/7	0/1	0/3	0/5	.	.	0/1	0/1	0/18	0.0
Total	10/169	9/68	41/231	7/76	0/11	2/141	2/70	2/29	73/795	9.2

Number of specimens with at least one cutmark versus total NISP. Teeth excluded. Cranium includes mandibular bone.

FIGURE 5.14. A refitted portion of a bison vertebral column from the Middle Aurignacian EJF occupation.

Except for a few tooth fragments, few burned specimens could be identified in EJOP. Interestingly, the only two tali identified are burned. We will see that this bone is frequently burned in the Aurignacian levels. In the bison assemblage, cutmarks are most commonly found on the tibia. The small size of the reindeer and horse samples precludes interpretation of cutmark frequencies.

5. MIDDLE AURIGNACIAN (EJO SUP). This reindeer-dominated assemblage shows many of the general characteristics observed in the previous samples. Because of the small sample sizes for bison and horse, the discussion focuses exclusively on reindeer.

The tibia and metatarsal are well represented in the reindeer sample. Elements of the forelimb, especially the humerus and radio-ulna, are also common. In contrast, the cervical vertebrae, ribs, scapula, innominates, carpals, tarsals, and phalanges are rare or absent.

Many more burned specimens could be identified in this sample in comparison to the previous assemblages. Vertebrae are frequently burned (24.0%, $n = 25$). Carpals (50.0%, $n = 6$) and tali (50.0%, $n = 6$) are also frequently burned, although the sample is small in both cases. Six burned long bone fragments could be identified. Four of them are from epiphyses. Lastly, cutmarks on reindeer specimens are preferentially located on long bones and are infrequent on the cranium, vertebrae, phalanges, and ribs.

6. MIDDLE AURIGNACIAN (EJF). This level contains a large reindeer assemblage. The tibia and metatarsal are the most abundant elements of this species, followed by the humerus, radius, and femur. The metacarpal is poorly represented compared with other long bones. As in the previous layers, elements of the axial skeleton – the spine in particular – are underrepresented. Head parts are present at relatively low frequencies. Ribs, carpals, tarsals, innominates, and phalanges are also uncommon. The vertebral fragments are often burned. Conversely, burning was rarely identified on ribs, heads, and phalanges. The abundance of phalanges decreases distally.

In the horse sample, the most common elements are the tibia, mandible, femur, and metatarsal. The vertebral column is underrepresented, an observation that also applies to the humeri, carpals, tarsals, and phalanges. The bison sample is relatively small, which limits interpretation. The tibia and mandible are the most frequent parts in this taxon, along with the cranium and femur. Few carpals, tarsals, and phalanges were identified. However, a partially complete portion of a vertebral column, consisting of the last five lumbar vertebrae and the sacrum, was refitted in the lab (Figure 5.14).

These elements were distributed over a relatively small area in the "charnier" zone (see Figure 4.7).

A fairly large number of burned bones ($n = 262$) have been identified in this level. Most belong to reindeer (Morin 2010). As in the Middle Aurignacian EJO sup level, the percentages of burned vertebrae (41.2%, $n = 165$), carpals (16.7%, $n = 30$), and tarsals (51.1%, $n = 47$), are high in the assemblage. The innominates (28.6%, $n = 42$) and lateral malleolus (80.0%, $n = 5$) are also frequently burned. Long bones show a low incidence of burning (4.0%, $n = 1919$). However, most of the burned specimens are epiphyses (60.5%, $n = 76$). Burning is rarely observed on crania, antlers, ribs, and phalanges.

For reindeer, cutmarks are mostly concentrated on the humerus, tibia, femur, and scapula. Few cutmarks were identified on the metatarsal. Cutmarks are not infrequent, however, on the metacarpal. A small number of cutmarks was noted on the cranium, vertebrae, ribs, phalanges, carpals, and tarsals. In the horse assemblage, cutmarks are more common on long bones than on the remaining skeleton.

7. THE EVOLVED AURIGNACIAN (EJM). Reindeer also dominates this fairly large assemblage. The skeletal profile of reindeer in EJM is comparable to that described for the previous reindeer samples. Elements of the hindlimb, especially the femur and tibia, are common. The forelimb is also well represented, as are the cranium and mandible. The high frequencies of these parts stand in sharp contrast to the low frequencies of vertebrae, carpals, tarsals, and phalanges in the assemblage. Again, the abundance of phalanges decreases distally.

The horse sample is fairly small. The head, metacarpal, and tibia are the best represented parts of this taxon. Carpals, tarsals, phalanges, and elements of the axial skeleton show low representation. Little can be said about the skeletal profile of bison in the EJM assemblage, given the small size of the sample.

Many vertebrae (27.6%, $n = 29$) and tarsals (58.3%, $n = 12$) are burned in the assemblage. These high values are in good agreement with those reported for the Middle Aurignacian layers. However, no burned carpals were identified. Long bones are infrequently burned (4.0%, $n = 298$), but five of the twelve burned fragments are from epiphyses. The cranium, ribs, and phalanges are rarely affected by burning, if at all.

Cutmarks are common in the reindeer sample and are most frequent, in decreasing order, on the humerus, femur, tibia, and metacarpal. Cutmarks are rare on the axial skeleton in general. This is true of the radio-ulna, metatarsal, and phalanges as well. Very few cutmarks were recorded on the horse and bison remains.

8. THE EVOLVED AURIGNACIAN (EJJ). The cranium and the long bones are the most common elements in the EJJ reindeer sample. Vertebrae are rare or absent. Likewise, carpals, tarsals, and phalanges are poorly represented. Burning is most frequent on the innominates (40.0%, $n = 5$) and vertebrae (16.7%, $n = 12$). One tarsal and one phalanx are burned. As observed in the other levels, the head and ribs seldom show burning. Of the five burned long bone fragments, three are from epiphyses. The horse and bison samples from this level are too small to yield reliable information. Most cutmarks tend to be located on long bones.

This chapter has provided some basic information on taxonomic composition and skeletal representation in the Saint-Césaire occupations. The next two chapters focus on the taphonomy and seasonality of the assemblages.

6

TAPHONOMY

TAPHONOMY IS THE STUDY OF PROCESSES THAT AFFECT THE DECAY, ACCUMULATION, preservation, and analysis of faunal remains. These processes, which include postdepositional disturbance of layers by burrowing animals, human construction, freeze-thaw cycles, water transport, trampling, and scavenging of faunal debris by carnivores, as well as the incomplete recovery of remains by the archaeologist, are critical because they can modify the composition and distribution of faunal assemblages, particularly if they result in the destruction of specimens (Lyman 1994).

At Saint-Césaire, significant differences in specimen abundance and taxonomic composition were observed between some of the occupations. Conversely, skeletal part representation shows only minor changes throughout the sequence. What is the significance of these patterns, and do they tell us anything meaningful about the behavior of the various occupants of the site? In this chapter, the faunal assemblages from Saint-Césaire – and the agents that accumulated them – are scrutinized from a taphonomic perspective to answer these questions. Specifically, issues that are explored include occupation mixing, recovery methods, differential fragmentation and preservation, and the impact of burning and differential identification on anatomical and taxonomic composition. Because an excess of information may detract from the flow of the arguments, tables containing raw data are sometimes presented in appendices.

THE CHRONOLOGICAL GRAIN AT SAINT-CÉSAIRE

When confronted with small assemblages, combining several levels is sometimes necessary to increase sample size. However, this approach tends to suppress variation. To avoid this problem, layers were generally examined individually in this study. Post-depositional mixing can also reduce variation within a sequence by combining objects from distinct layers. For this reason, evaluating the chronological and spatial integrity of the assemblages under scrutiny is essential. This issue is especially relevant for Saint-Césaire, where concerns had been raised concerning the integrity of the stratigraphic sequence (Bordes 1981a; Sonneville-Bordes 1989). To address these concerns, a study of bone refits within and between layers was carried out. The analysis of the refits, combined with data on specimen distribution, body part representation, and taxonomic composition, showed that occupation mixing was limited at Saint-Césaire (Morin *et al.* 2005). The results from this study are briefly summarized in this section.

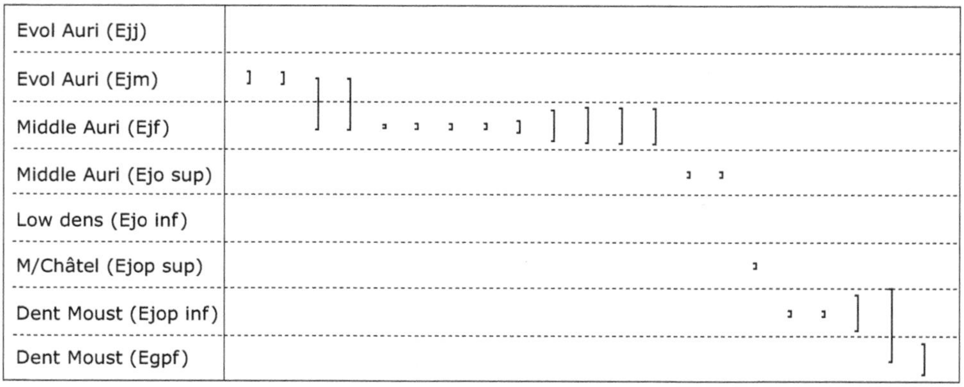

Evol Auri (Ejj)	
Evol Auri (Ejm)	
Middle Auri (Ejf)	
Middle Auri (Ejo sup)	
Low dens (Ejo inf)	
M/Châtel (Ejop sup)	
Dent Moust (Ejop inf)	
Dent Moust (Egpf)	

FIGURE 6.1. Vertical distribution of all refits on green-bone fractures from Saint-Césaire.

During the study of the Saint-Césaire faunal samples, 2,068 specimens were refitted (this value only considers refits from the NISP sample). Refitted specimens were distributed into 847 refit sets, for an average of 2.4 specimens per set. Only 10 out of 847 (1.2%) refit sets attest to translocation of artifacts across layers. Three refit sets indicate movement across more than one layer. All three of these cases involve the relatively thin EJO layers. A single refit set cuts across three layers. Importantly, fragments documenting occupation mixing were all separated by less than 20 cm in vertical distance, with one exception (refit set #25: 25–40 cm, Morin *et al.* 2005). However, most of these refits are on dry-bone (postdepositional) fractures, some of which were perhaps produced as recently as during the excavation of the site.

In contrast, refits on green-bone fractures link specimens that became disassociated during, or shortly after, the site occupation. For this reason, green-bone refits are more useful than dry-bone refits when addressing issues of occupation mixing. In this sample, only three refit sets out of eighteen (16.7%) are indicative of level disturbance (Figure 6.1). Overall, the low percentages of inter-layer refits recorded in the dry-bone and green-bone refit samples suggest that occupation mixing is a minor problem at Saint-Césaire, at least when examined between sedimentary units. These results do not preclude, of course, the accumulation of numerous, and possibly somewhat distinct, occupations within single layers, a problem raised in Chapter 4 with respect to the EJOP sup occupation.

RECOVERY METHODS

Several faunal studies have stressed the impact of recovery methods on body part representation (Klein 1989; Turner 1989; Marean and Kim 1998; Bartram and Marean 1999; Outram 2001; Stiner 2002; Pickering *et al.* 2003). A key point in these debates concerns the effects of discarded shaft fragments on the interpretation of anatomical profiles. This issue follows several decades of discussions on how recovery methods affect taxonomic composition, especially with regard to the representation of small species (e.g., Struever 1968; Thomas 1969; Payne 1972; Cossette 2000).

As emphasized earlier, sediments were dry-sieved at Saint-Césaire using 5- and 2-mm mesh screens. This resulted in relatively thorough recovery of the faunal material. However, this mesh size was probably too large for many microfaunal remains.

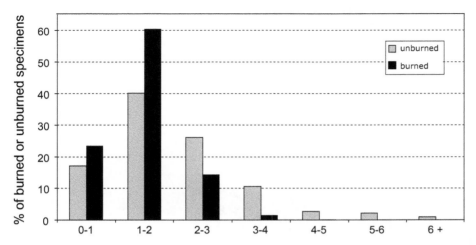

FIGURE 6.2. Comparison of the distributions of burned and unburned bones by size classes at Saint-Césaire. Data from Appendix 3. See text for a description of the sample.

Therefore, their abundance is probably underestimated in the samples. Except for a handful of specimens on exhibit in a museum in the village of Saint-Césaire, all the specimens from the selected layers and samples were studied.

Given the thoroughness of the recovery methods, it is no surprise to find that small fragments are very abundant in the assemblages. In a sample of 12 décapages that includes most layers from Saint-Césaire, 57.3% of the unburned bones are smaller than 2 cm (Figure 6.2). Within the same fragment size category, the percentage (84.0%) of burned bones is significantly higher ($t_s = 8.97$, $p < .0001$). Burned bones are not only smaller on average than unburned ones but also show a narrower range of sizes. Regardless of whether the fragments are burned, few specimens in the faunal assemblages are larger than 6 cm. This high degree of fragmentation is not unusual in Paleolithic assemblages (Villa *et al.* 2004).

In general, it can be concluded that biases due to recovery and sampling methods are minimal at Saint-Césaire, at least with respect to the macrofauna. However, because some sections of the site were destroyed before the excavations, it is not possible to ascertain at the moment how much of the initial samples are missing.

SPECIMEN FRAGMENTATION

The Saint-Césaire specimens vary in degree of fragmentation, as the samples include whole elements along with completely shattered specimens (Figure 6.3). This variation is important because fragmentation can influence specimen and mark identification. Therefore, comparisons of skeletal profiles and mark frequencies between levels may not be fully reliable if levels are differentially fragmented. To examine fragmentation patterns across the Saint-Césaire stratigraphy, mean fragment length was calculated for three abundant reindeer elements: the tibia, metatarsal, and rib. Shaft fragments are particularly useful in this regard because they are mechanically resistant and were rarely modified into tools during the Middle to Upper Paleolithic transition. Data were also collected for reindeer mandibles, as isolated teeth are common in the samples (Figure 6.4).

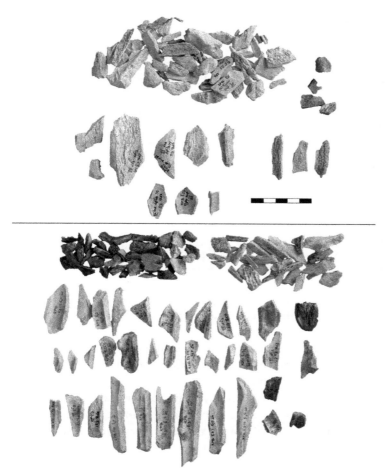

FIGURE 6.3. Samples of fragmented faunal remains from Saint-Césaire. The upper sample is from the Mousterian/Châtelperronian EJOP sup layer, and the lower sample is from the Middle Aurignacian EJF layer.

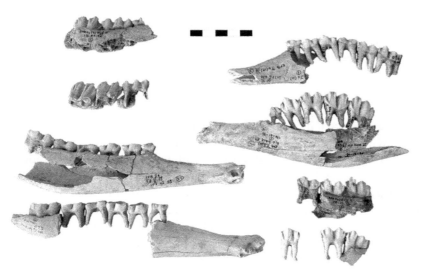

FIGURE 6.4. Examples of reindeer mandibles from the Middle Aurignacian EJF layer.

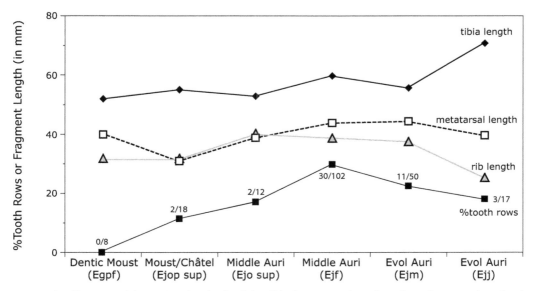

FIGURE 6.5. Patterns of fragmentation in the Saint-Césaire occupations, based on the mean length of reindeer tibia, metatarsal, and rib fragments, and the percentage of reindeer mandibular tooth rows. Data for the first three elements are presented in Appendix 4, while data for tooth rows are presented in the figure. Percentages of mandibular tooth rows were calculated by dividing the number of mandibles possessing two or more teeth by the total NISP for mandibular teeth (incisors and canines excluded).

In this case, the degree of fragmentation was evaluated on the basis of the number of tooth rows relative to the total NISP of mandibular teeth, defined as a mandibular specimen possessing a minimum of two articulated teeth.

These four proxies show similar patterns of fragmentation across the Saint-Césaire sequence (Figure 6.5). The values suggest that reindeer specimens in the lowermost layers are slightly more fragmented than those from the Aurignacian levels. However, these proxies are not easily compared because they vary sensibly in sample sizes and, in some cases, in measurement methods as well (e.g., length in mm vs. percentages). To circumvent these methodological difficulties, assemblages were ranked relative to one another on the basis of the values in Figure 6.5. The most fragmented assemblage was conferred a value of "1," whereas that of the least fragmented assemblage received a value of "6." This ranking routine was repeated for each of the four proxies (i.e., mean length of tibia, metatarsal, and rib fragments; percentage of mandibular tooth rows). The rank positions were then averaged for each assemblage to produce a single set of synthetic values that can be compared across levels.

The averaged rank values, presented in Figure 6.6, suggest that skeletal elements are slightly more fragmented in the Denticulate Mousterian EGPF and the Mousterian/ Châtelperronian assemblages than in the upper levels, excluding, perhaps, the Evolved Aurignacian EJJ occupation. On the basis of the limited information available (Appendix 4), the Denticulate Mousterian EJOP inf sample also appears to be more fragmented than most of the Aurignacian assemblages. In the sequence, fragmentation is lowest in the Middle Aurignacian EJF and Evolved Aurignacian EJM assemblages.

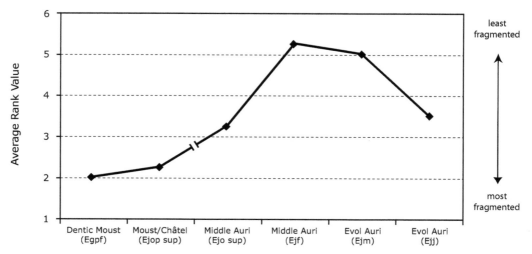

FIGURE 6.6. Variation in average fragmentation across the Saint-Césaire sequence, as estimated by averaging the four proxies (mean length of reindeer tibia, metatarsal, and rib fragments, and the percentage of tooth rows) presented in Figure 6.5. To derive the values, assemblages were ranked from "1" (most fragmented) to "6" (least fragmented). The rank values were then averaged for each assemblage. For example, the Middle Aurignacian EJF assemblage ranked fifth on all but one of the four proxies. Consequently, this assemblage received a score of "5.25" (i.e., 5.25 = [5 + 6 + 5 + 5]/4).

As emphasized above, differential fragmentation may affect mark identification at Saint-Césaire. Indeed, holding taxon and element constant, the relative abundance of cutmarks increases quasi-linearly with fragment size at Saint-Césaire (Figure 6.7). In fact, this pattern is likely to be universal in fragmented assemblages. Therefore, because specimen fragmentation is apparently less severe in the Middle Aurignacian EJF and Evolved Aurignacian EJM assemblages, percentages of cutmarks are expected to be higher in these than in the other more fragmented assemblages from Saint-Césaire.

PATTERNS OF PRESERVATION

All types of skeletal parts are represented in the Saint-Césaire assemblages, and no obvious preservation bias was perceived during the study of the material, with the exception of deciduous teeth, some of which (particularly those from artiodactyls) tend to be more fragmented than permanent teeth. Refitting helped alleviate this problem. It was also noted that bone surfaces from very young individuals were not as well preserved as those of adults.

Despite some variation in the degree of fragmentation, a visual inspection of the material suggests relatively good preservation of the fauna. The list of identified specimens includes several fragile elements, for instance, fetal bones ($n = 39$), hyoid bones ($n = 12$), sternum and costal cartilage ($n = 9$), and antlers ($n = 1406$). However, qualitative evaluations such as these can be highly subjective. Therefore, quantitative data are needed to validate or falsify these impressions.

Several methods have been developed over the years in an attempt to precisely measure bone density, or, to be more accurate, bone porosity, because the mineral density of

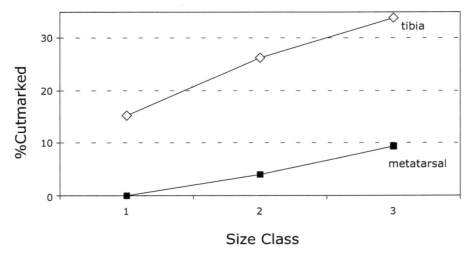

FIGURE 6.7. Percentages of cut-marked tibia and metatarsal specimens of reindeer for three size classes (the latter based on maximum fragment length). For the tibia, the size classes are 0–40 (21/137), 40–80 (106/404), and 80–120 mm (25/74). For the metatarsal, the size classes are 0–30 (0/339), 30–60 (30/757), and 60–90 mm (15/159). Values in parentheses are the number of specimens with at least one cutmark relative to the total number of specimens in the size class.

bone does not appear to change much across most skeletal elements (Boskey 2006). Correlations between bone density and specimen abundance are often considered evidence of differential preservation. However, these correlations are difficult to interpret, given that cultural activities, such as grease rendering or the use of bone as fuel, may also produce correlations with bone density (Grayson 1989; Lyman 1994; Rogers 2000; Lam and Pearson 2005; Morin 2010). A solution to this problem may be to look at evidence for mineral change in the assemblages (e.g., Schiegl *et al.* 2003). Unfortunately, no such studies were undertaken during the Saint-Césaire excavations. The strategy adopted here is a conservative one: rather than using all skeletal elements for interpreting body part representation, the discussion is limited, for the most part, to elements or bone portions with similar density values (see Chapter 8).

However, preservation may also affect mark identification, even on the densest elements. Thus, it is important to determine whether specimen preservation shows spatial and/or stratigraphic variations at Saint-Césaire. Concerning this issue, the position of the remains with respect to the slope and the surface of the deposit emerge as key factors for understanding changes in specimen preservation in the assemblages. Because the excavation grid was set off from the natural slope of the deposit (Figure 6.8), the impact of topography on bone surface preservation was investigated by comparing rows 2 through 9, rather than lines D to J where the slope is slight. This decision had little impact on the results because the patterns found in rows 2 to 9 were always repeated in lines D to J. The use of diagonals was avoided, this approach being very impractical within a square system. Coding for bone surface preservation was restricted to a sample of 4,639 specimens, mostly long bones. It is worth mentioning that calcite-encrusted specimens ($n = 10$) are virtually absent in the assemblages.

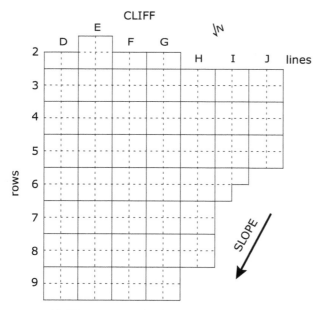

FIGURE 6.8. The square grid at Saint-Césaire. Lines B and C, which were truncated by roadwork, are not shown in this figure.

Most specimens from Saint-Césaire fall in the middle of the preservation spectrum, with few bones having a "poorly preserved" or an "intact" surface (Table 6.1). Generally, surfaces tend to show a lower degree of preservation in the Mousterian/Châtelperronian and the Evolved Aurignacian EJM and EJJ assemblages. This variation in surface preservation seems primarily conditioned by the spatial distribution of the remains. This is because, at Saint-Césaire, the degree of bone surface preservation decreases as one moves away from the cliff (Figure 6.9). To increase sample size, the Evolved Aurignacian levels

TABLE 6.1. *Bone surface preservation by level in bone samples dominated by long bone fragments*

Layers	Poorly preserved		Damaged		Slightly damaged		Intact		Total	
	n	%	n	%	n	%	n	%	n	%
Evol Auri (Ejj)	23	8.4	173	63.1	76	27.7	2	0.7	274	99.9
Evol Auri (Ejm)	49	8.3	367	62.5	170	29.0	1	0.2	587	100.0
Middle Auri (Ejf)	35	2.1	729	43.0	913	53.8	19	1.1	1696	100.0
Middle Auri (Ejo sup)	7	1.9	167	46.3	186	51.5	1	0.3	361	100.0
low dens (Ejo inf)	1	2.1	29	61.7	17	36.2	0	0.0	47	100.0
M/Chât (Ejop sup)	38	6.7	317	55.9	206	36.3	6	1.1	567	100.0
Dent Moust (Ejop inf)	11	5.0	86	39.4	115	52.8	6	2.8	218	100.0
Dent Moust (Egpf)	7	1.5	186	39.9	269	57.7	4	0.9	466	100.0
Total	171	4.1	2054	48.7	1953	46.3	39	0.9	4216	100.0

The bone samples correspond to taxonomically identified specimens that were coded for surface preservation. These samples include the majority of the identified specimens, excluding teeth and antlers. In the very rich Middle Aurignacian EJF level, the sample also excludes all reindeer ribs and metatarsals and varying proportions of other classes of long bones.

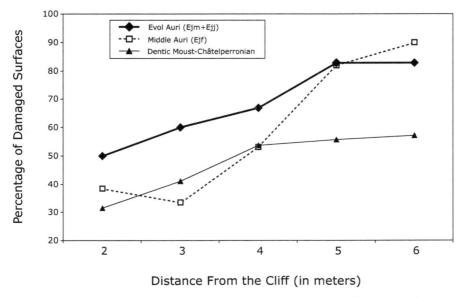

FIGURE 6.9. Percentages of bones that have either a damaged or poorly preserved surface by level and distance from the cliff. The data are from Appendix 5. The Denticulate Mousterian EGPF, EJOP inf, and Mousterian/Châtelperronian (EJOP sup) layers are combined in this figure, as are the two Evolved Aurignacian layers.

EJM and EJJ occupations were combined in this last analysis, as were the Denticulate Mousterian EGPF, EJOP inf, and Mousterian/Châtelperronian occupations.

The relationship between bone surface preservation and the relative abundance of marks at Saint-Césaire was investigated using cutmark data. Despite the use of a hand lens, a quasi-linear decrease in cutmark frequencies was observed, assuming equidistance between the categories, with decreasing surface preservation (Figure 6.10). This finding suggests that numerous marks have been obliterated from the bone surfaces.

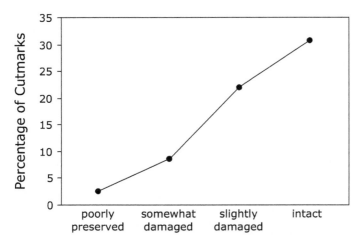

FIGURE 6.10. Relationship between percentages of cutmarks and quality of bone surface preservation. The data are from Appendix 6 (line for "total").

TABLE 6.2. *Incidence of root marks by level and as a function of distance from the cliff at Saint-Césaire*

		Distance Away from the Cliff in Meters						
		2	3	4	5	6	7	Total
Evolved Aurignacian (Ejj)	root	2	23	17	39	32	0	113
	total	8	51	25	100	89	1	274
	%root	25.0	45.1	68.0	39.0	36.0	0.0	41.2
Evolved Aurignacian (Ejm)	root	4	48	113	48	26	5	244
	total	28	97	332	75	45	7	584
	%root	14.3	49.5	34.0	64.0	57.8	71.4	41.8
Middle Aurignacian (Ejf)	root	37	48	59	24	21	22	211
	total	662	444	234	50	49	30	1469
	%root	5.6	10.8	25.2	48.0	42.9	73.3	14.4
Middle Aurignacian (Ejo sup)	root	2	2	1	3	4	0	12
	total	183	119	35	6	15	0	358
	%root	1.1	1.7	2.9	50.0	26.7	0.0	3.4
Moust/Châtel (Ejop sup)	root	1	0	6	2	5	49	63
	total	25	37	160	128	40	166	556
	%root	4.0	0.0	3.8	1.6	12.5	29.5	11.3
Dentic Moust (Ejop inf)	root	0	0	2	0	3	1	6
	total	57	37	28	20	35	12	189
	%root	0.0	0.0	7.1	0.0	8.6	8.3	3.2
Dentic Moust (Egpf)	root	0	7	5	3	9	3	27
	total	61	136	104	75	70	19	465
	%root	0.0	5.1	4.8	4.0	12.9	15.8	5.8
Total	root	46	128	203	120	100	80	676
	total	1024	921	918	454	343	235	3895
	%root	4.5	13.9	22.1	26.4	29.2	34.0	17.4

If we consider Figure 6.10, the percentage of cutmarks at Saint-Césaire can be estimated to have initially been close to 31%, which is more than a 100% increase compared with the mean (15.1%) that combines all surface categories. This pattern remains when both species and element are held constant, even though the resulting samples are sometimes very small, especially for the poorly represented categories (Appendices 7 and 8). In general, the data indicate that the Mousterian/Châtelperronian and the two Evolved Aurignacian levels are less likely to show well-preserved surfaces. This is in large part because taxonomically identified specimens in these assemblages tend to be concentrated on the slope (Figure 6.11), where preservation is poorer.

Root etching seems to be the best candidate for explaining variation in surface preservation at Saint-Césaire. In the sequence, root marks are most frequent in the Evolved Aurignacian EJM and EJJ assemblages (Table 6.2). As for bone surface preservation, the data suggest that the abundance of root marks decreases more or less steadily with increasing depth and/or distance from the slope (Figure 6.12). These patterns in root mark distribution possibly reflect the progressive retreat of the cliff with the accumulation of the deposit and the concomitant colonization of the surface by plants. However, other scenarios (e.g., denser vegetation on the slope during the Holocene) might also explain these patterns.

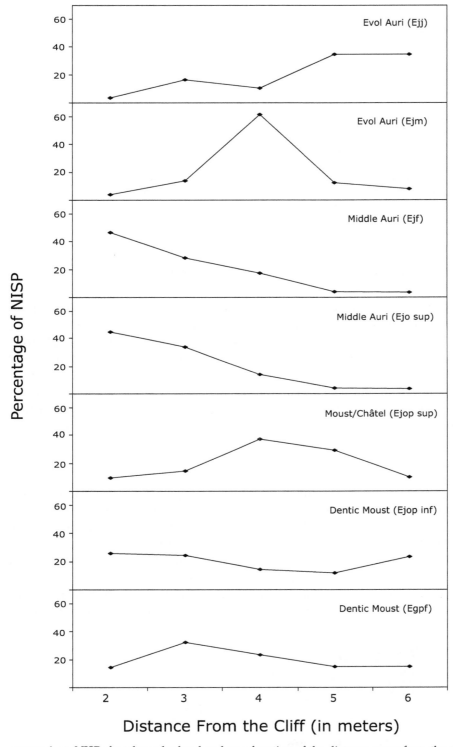

FIGURE 6.11. NISP abundance by level and as a function of the distance away from the cliff. The data are from Appendix 9.

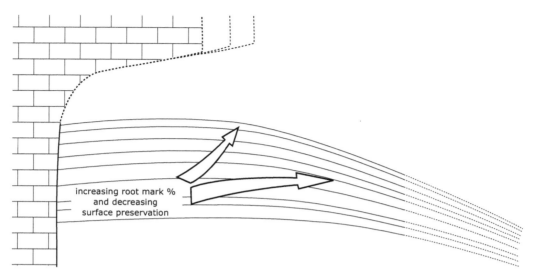

FIGURE 6.12. Schematic representation of the distribution of root etching at Saint-Césaire.

The implications of these spatial patterns are threefold. First, because bone surfaces show poorer preservation near the surface of the deposit, the relative abundance of marks is likely to be underestimated in the uppermost assemblages. A second implication is that the relative abundance of marks is expected to be lower in the Mousterian/ Châtelperronian and the two Evolved Aurignacian assemblages because many of the identified remains from these levels come from the slope, where conditions were less favorable to the preservation of marks. A third implication is that mark frequencies may be depressed at Saint-Césaire compared to sites with better faunal preservation.

Types of Damage

Sheeting (Figure 6.13), a type of damage described in Chapter 5, is rare at Saint-Césaire, being recorded on only 2.2% of the long bones. Furthermore, refitting reduced the difficulties in identification caused by sheeting, given that many specimens could be taxonomically identified after being pieced back together. As with root etching, sheeting increases with distance from the cliff (Table 6.3). It is possible that this pattern is related to root etching, given that 17.9% of the bones bearing root marks also show evidence of sheeting. This percentage is statistically higher than that for long bones lacking such marks (2.2%; $t_s = 4.26$, $p < .0001$). This result suggests that root etching and sheeting are

FIGURE 6.13. Subrectangular shaft splinters on a UNG3–4 long bone resulting from sheeting.

TABLE 6.3. *Percentages of long bones with evidence of sheeting, exfoliation, and cracks as a function of distance from the cliff at Saint-Césaire*

		\multicolumn{9}{c}{Distance Away from the Cliff in Meters}
		1	2	3	4	5	6	7	8	Total
Sheeting	with sheeting	0	5	3	12	11	13	13	4	61
	total bones	124	700	562	494	336	258	206	61	2741
	% sheeting	0.0	0.7	0.5	2.4	3.3	5.0	6.3	6.6	2.2
Exfoliation	exfoliated	14	65	51	44	26	18	17	6	241
	total bones	124	700	562	494	336	258	206	61	2741
	% exfoliated	11.3	9.3	9.1	8.9	7.7	7.0	8.3	9.8	8.8
Cracks	with cracks	12	49	51	77	34	30	31	8	292
	total bones	124	700	562	494	336	258	206	61	2741
	% with cracks	9.7	7.0	9.1	15.6	10.1	11.6	15.0	13.1	10.7

All occupations are combined.

causally related, although the relationship may be indirect. Unfortunately, the sample of bones indicative of sheeting is too small to evaluate whether this type of damage also varies across levels.

Exfoliation of the first millimeters of the bone's outer surface is not unusual in the assemblages (Table 6.3). It should be noted that this type of damage is more frequently found on fetal and juvenile bones. It could be expected that cutmarks would be identified less frequently on specimens affected by exfoliation. However, this does not seem to be the case at Saint-Césaire because cutmarks are as common ($t_s = 0.21$, $p < .84$) on exfoliated (9.3%) as on non-exfoliated (9.6%) bones. No spatial pattern is observed in the distribution of this type of damage. Lastly, edge abrasion is limited in the occupations and very homogeneous, given that 98% of the bones have slightly abraded edges.

AGENTS OF ACCUMULATION

The recovery of large samples of stone tools, plus evidence of bone tool manufacture and hearth maintenance, confirm the largely anthropogenic origin of the Saint-Césaire occupations (Backer 1993, 1994; Guilbaud 1993; Lévêque et al. 1993; Thiébault 2005; Soressi 2010). But did humans produce all of the faunal accumulations or only some of them? Did carnivores, or other animals, contribute to the faunal samples? The taphonomic analysis of the assemblages provides some answers to these questions.

Using the material identified by Lavaud-Girard, Patou-Mathis (1993) conducted a study of the Mousterian/Châtelperronian (EJOP sup) occupation and concluded that humans accumulated the vast majority of the faunal remains. However, her study did not include the very large numbers of remains that were not piece-plotted but instead collected by décapage, which raises the issue of the representativity of the data. In the samples considered in the present study, the percentages of specimens with cutmarks (Figure 6.14) are relatively high (4.6–15.8%, Table 6.4). These values, which are consistent with anthropogenic accumulations, are particularly significant, given that roots and other natural agents might have obliterated as many as half of the initial marks (see discussion earlier in the chapter).

TABLE 6.4. *Percentages of bones with anthropic modifications in the Saint-Césaire occupations*

Layers	Cutmarks			Burned Bones			Retouchers			Percussion Notches		
	Cut	NISP₁	%	Burned bones	Total sample	%	Retouchers	Total NISP	%	Notch	NISP[a]	%
Evol Auri Ejj	20	258	7.8	1240	4066	30.5	2	426	0.5	11	258	4.3
Evol Auri Ejm	42	673	6.2	2119	7613	27.8	.	1083	0.0	31	673	4.6
Mid Auri Ejf	269	3013	8.9	13524	38296	35.3	10	4102	0.2	154	3013	5.1
Mid Auri Ejo sup	16	345	4.6	1178	5453	21.6	.	480	0.0	15	345	4.3
low density	4	44	9.1	85	751	11.3	.	83	0.0	1	44	2.3
Moust/Châtel	63	514	12.3	7544	28004	26.9	18	966	1.9	25	514	4.9
D Moust Ejop inf	27	196	13.8	3497	9241	37.8	5	331	1.5	14	196	7.1
D Moust Egpf	79	500	15.8	7148	20436	35.0	.	867	0.0	19	500	3.8
Total	520	5543	9.4	39757	113860	34.9	35	8338	0.4	270	5543	4.9

Although percussion notches can be produced by carnivores, they are included in this table because the carnivore imprint on the assemblages is marginal (see the text for a fuller discussion).

[a] Excluding burned specimens, teeth, and antlers.

Abbreviations: *cut* = the total of specimens with at least one cutmark; notch = the total of specimens with at least one percussion notch.

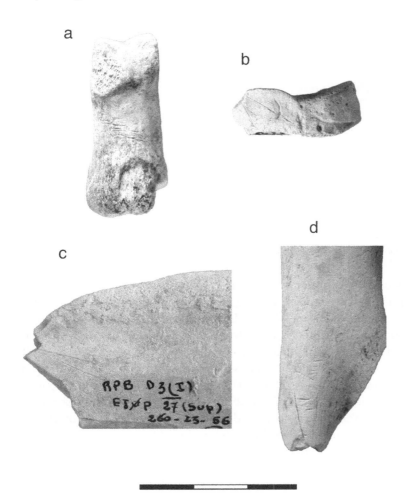

FIGURE 6.14. Cutmarks on a (a) reindeer second phalanx, (b) reindeer greater cuneiform, (c) bison metatarsal, (d) reindeer humerus. The black lines are 1 cm long.

Burning is a relatively robust signature of human agency that is documented on approximately 35% of the faunal remains from Saint-Césaire. Burned specimens are common in all of the occupations (range: 11.3–37.8%), although they are less frequent in the small EJO inf sample (Table 6.4). These high percentages of burning are not exceptional in France and characterize several Middle Paleolithic (Chase 1999; Villa *et al.* 2002) and Upper Paleolithic sites (Castel 1999; Costamagno *et al.* 1999; Villa *et al.* 2002; Airvaux *et al.* 2003; Normand *et al.* 2007).

Most burned bones at Saint-Césaire are black or brown in color, suggesting moderate fire temperature. Bones with white, blue, green, and gray colors, possibly indicative of higher fire temperature (Shipman *et al.* 1984; Stiner *et al.* 1995; Costamagno *et al.* 1999), were rarely encountered. It should be pointed out that this observation applies to both the NISP and indeterminate samples. This point is important because proportions of burning colors may differ between these samples, given that, because of intense fragmentation, high-fired bones are less likely to be identified than low-fired ones.

FIGURE 6.15. Long bone shaft fragments from Saint-Césaire showing percussion notches. The uppermost specimen is a percussion flake refitted with a UNG 3–4 shaft fragment. The lowermost specimen, probably from a reindeer, shows two overlapping percussion flakes still attached to a shaft fragment.

Although less diagnostic than cutmarks or burning, percussion notches (Figure 6.15) are useful in taphonomic analysis because they tend to be more common in anthropic than in natural assemblages (Blumenschine 1995). In addition, experiments suggest that percussion notches produced by humans can, despite considerable overlap in measurements, be statistically distinguished from those made by carnivores (Capaldo and Blumenschine 1994). However, it remains unclear whether these models can be applied to the large hyena (Ballesio 1979; Brugal *et al.* 1997) of the European Paleolithic. At Saint-Césaire, percussion notches are not particularly abundant, because they only occur on 2.3 to 7.1% of the specimens. Yet the very low incidence of carnivore-inflicted marks on the specimens (discussed later) suggests that humans produced the vast majority of the percussion notches recorded in the samples.

Retouchers

A century ago, Henri-Martin (1907) observed unusual marks on long bone fragments and phalanges from the Mousterian site of La Quina (southwestern France). These objects, called *compresseurs* by Henri-Martin, were said to be similar to other finds reported at the end of the nineteenth century at the Grotte des Fées and Pair-non-Pair, two sites also located in southwestern France (Patou-Mathis and Schwab 2002). These finds were interpreted as flint-knapping objects used for retouching and resharpening the edges of stone tools (Henri-Martin 1907; Chase 1990; Armand and Delagnes 1998). At present, these objects are referred to in French publications as *retouchoirs* (retouchers) and have been identified at a growing number of sites, from Spain to Russia (Patou-Mathis and Schwab 2002) and possibly in Africa (Henshilwood and Marean 2003). In Europe, retouchers are common in both the Middle and Upper Paleolithic.

Retouchers deserve close attention because some authors have interpreted them as carnivore-ravaged bones (Binford 1981). The marks described by Henri-Martin (1907) consist of small concentrations of linear depressions on the bone's cortical surface that are more or less perpendicular to the long axis of the specimen (Figure 6.16). Typically, these concentrations of marks are located near the end of a long bone fragment (Figure 6.17). Experimental studies show that these marks are consistent with those produced during

Taphonomy

FIGURE 6.16. Concentration of retouch marks on a retoucher from Saint-Césaire.

FIGURE 6.17. Retouchers from Saint-Césaire. The upper specimen is a femur from a large artiodactyl, the middle specimen is a red deer metacarpal, whereas the lower specimen is an unidentified long bone from a large ungulate. Cutmarks are present on the upper and lower specimens.

109

stone tool retouching (Armand and Delagnes 1998). Unambiguous carnivore marks are generally absent from the surfaces and edges of these specimens. In addition, the fact that scrape marks and cutmarks frequently overlap with retouch marks on these objects strengthens the argument about their human origin. In the present study, retouchers were analyzed along with the other faunal remains, given that they are assumed to have been opportunistically used tools.

Retouchers are relatively rare in the Saint-Césaire occupations (Table 6.4). Importantly, none of these objects show marks typically associated with carnivore ravaging, such as grooves, scooping, deep punctures, or evidence of digestion. Furthermore, unlike carnivore-inflicted marks, retouching marks are never found on the edges or the inner face (medullary face for long bones) of the specimens.

More decisive is the observation that the retouchers from Saint-Césaire show high percentages of cutmarks (26.3%) and percussion marks (10.5%). The same marks are rare or absent on the unambiguously ravaged specimens from the same site (cutmarks = 0%; percussion marks = 2.5%). These differences are significant or nearly significant (cut-marks: $t_s = 5.11, p < .0001$; percussion notches: $t_s = 1.85, p < .07$). Furthermore, cutmarks and retouching marks often overlap on the same fragments. These data invalidate the carnivore-ravaging hypothesis put forward by Binford (1981) to explain the origin of these objects. The high incidence of scrape marks and cutmarks on retouchers possibly reflects the removal of the periosteum and adhering tissues on fresh bones before the use of the specimens for stone tool retouching.

Carnivores

As discussed in Chapter 5, carnivores never account for more than 3% of the remains at Saint-Césaire, with the exception of the small EJO inf sample (6.7%). In fact, the percentages of carnivores at Saint-Césaire are lower than the lowest value documented by Fosse (1997) in a sample of European carnivore assemblages ($n = 27$). This includes den assemblages with very low carnivore NISP, such as Bois-Roche, layer 2 (8.6%, Villa *et al.* 2004), and Camiac (9.1%, Guadelli 1987; Guadelli *et al.* 1988). Furthermore, large bone-accumulating species (hyena, wolf, cave bear) are very marginally represented (32/9114 or 0.4%) at Saint-Césaire, the carnivore guild at the site being dominated by fox. However, the fact that some coprolite fragments were found by the author in soil samples signals the presence of active carnivores during the formation of the site.

Gnaw marks (Figure 6.18) and digested bones (Figure 6.19) are rare at Saint-Césaire, providing persuasive evidence that carnivores contributed minimally to the assemblages (Table 6.5). The low occurrence (range: 0.1–2.4%) of ravaged bones at Saint-Césaire is more than an order of magnitude lower than at the hyena den of Bois Roche (between 74 and 87% of the remains depending on the calculation method, Villa *et al.* 2004). Only four identified specimens from Saint-Césaire are digested. Although they are very rare, bones with gnaw marks are usually more frequent at Saint-Césaire than digested remains and preferentially affect bison, horse, and reindeer specimens (Table 6.6). Grooves are the most common type of gnaw marks, followed by pits.

According to Binford (1981), bone cylinders are more abundant in hyena dens than in assemblages deposited by humans. However, the difference between these two classes

FIGURE 6.18. Specimens from Saint-Césaire showing evidence of carnivore ravaging. The upper specimen is a thoroughly gnawed bison metatarsal from the Middle Aurignacian EJF layer. The lower left specimen, also from the Middle Aurignacian EJF layer, is a bison rib with puncture marks. Grooves are found on the lower right specimen, a horse scapula head found in the Evolved Aurignacian EJJ layer.

of sites appears to be less clear-cut than previously thought because small specimens (<2 cm) were rarely collected in earlier excavations of hyena dens (Villa *et al.* 2004). At Saint-Césaire, the percentage of cylinders varies little between the assemblages and is very low overall (17/2745 or 0.6%). This value is statistically ($t_s = 7.46$, $p < .0001$) much lower than that of the hyena den of Bois Roche, layer 2 (29/360 or 8%, Villa *et al.* 2004:724). These last authors also consider fragment length to be a useful criterion for discriminating assemblages made by carnivores from those produced by humans.

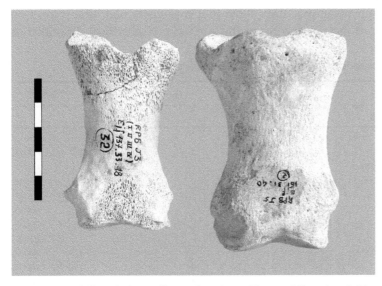

FIGURE 6.19. A first phalanx of horse showing evidence of digestion (left) compared with an undamaged specimen (right) from Saint-Césaire. Both specimens come from the Middle Aurignacian EJF layer.

TABLE 6.5. *Incidence of gnawing and digestion marks by level at Saint-Césaire*

Layer	Gnawed or digested n	Total NISP n	% of gnawed or digested %
Evolved Aurignacian (Ejj)	1	426	0.2
Evolved Aurignacian (Ejm)	1	1083	0.1
Middle Aurignacian (Ejf)	23 (2)	4102	0.6
Middle Aurignacian (Ejo sup)	4	480	0.8
Low density (Ejo inf)	2	83	2.4
Moust/Châtel (Ejop sup)	16 (2)	966	1.7
Dentic Mousterian (Ejop inf)	3	331	0.9
Dentic Mousterian (Egpf)	1	867	0.1
Total	51	9114	0.6

Numbers of digested bones are shown in italics.

However, sites might not be fully comparable in this respect due to differences in post-depositional breakage. Despite this caveat, the assemblages from Saint-Césaire clearly cluster with anthropogenic assemblages (Table 6.7).

Age profiles have been used to distinguish human from carnivore assemblages in Paleolithic contexts (e.g., Stiner 1994; Fosse 1995). Information bearing on carnivore age profiles is very limited at Saint-Césaire. Only two immature individuals, both represented by deciduous teeth, were identified. One of these teeth belongs to a hyena (found in EJOP) and the second to a wolf (found in the Middle Aurignacian EJO sup assemblage). Most of the other individuals are young adults, based on dental use-wear and stage of epiphyseal fusion. One atrophied phalanx may signal the presence of a senile hyena. The low incidence of very young individuals in the carnivore samples is not consistent with a den site.

In sum, taphonomic and taxonomic data show that carnivores had little impact on the Saint-Césaire faunas. In fact, carnivores at the site are probably best described as

TABLE 6.6. *Incidence of carnivore damage by species in the Saint-Césaire assemblages*

Species	Grooves n	Grooves %	Pits n	Pits %	Digested n	Digested %	Total n	Total %
Reindeer	14	77.8	4	22.2	.	.	18	100.0
Horse	9	61.4	4	28.6	1	7.1	14	100.0
Bison	12	100.0	.	.	.	.	12	100.0
Red deer	2	66.7	1	33.3	.	.	3	100.0
Rhinoceros	1	50.0	.	.	1	50.0	2	100.0
Fox	.	.	2	100.0	.	.	2	100.0
UNG3–4	.	.	1	100.0	.	.	1	100.0
Leporid	.	.	1	100.0	.	.	1	100.0
Hare	1	100.0	.	.	.	.	1	100.0
Lynx	.	.	.	.	1	100.0	1	100.0
Wild boar	.	.	.	.	1	100.0	1	100.0
Total	39	69.6	13	23.2	4	7.1	56	100.0

TABLE 6.7. *Mean fragment lengths of bison and horse long bones for a series of assemblages*

	Bison long bones		Horse long bones	
	n	Mean length	*n*	Mean length
Saint-Césaire				
Evolved Aurignacian (Ejj)	13	88.1	7	76.2
Evolved Aurignacian (Ejm)	18	96.0	27	91.6
Middle Aurignacian (Ejf)	25	102.0	67	78.5
Mousterian/Châtel (Ejop sup)	178	85.6	18	84.5
Denticulate Mousterian (Ejop inf)	53	88.1	13	88.7
Denticulate Mousterian (Egpf)	87	80.5	38	89.9
Combe Saunière				
Level IV	44	76.4	134	74.9
Jonzac				
Level 22	81	83.0	.	.
Bois Roche				
Layer 2	**173**	**148.7**	**43**	**156.0**

Values for sites other than Saint-Césaire are from Villa *et al.* (2004:717, table 10). Data for the carnivore assemblage of Bois Roche, layer 2 are shown in bold.

sporadic visitors that occasionally left their imprint on the assemblages. This interpretation does not preclude, however, the possibility that humans brought some of the carnivore remains into the site, an issue addressed in Chapter 9.

THE IMPACT OF IDENTIFICATION FILTERS ON THE ASSEMBLAGES

The probability of identifying certain elements may vary between assemblages due to differences in fragmentation, skeletal part representation, or taxonomic composition. This issue requires attention because it can affect the study of foraging patterns. Although the problem of differential identification has been recognized for decades (e.g., Lyman and O'Brien 1987; Marean and Kim 1998; Bartram and Marean 1999; Pickering and Egeland 2006), its methodological implications remain poorly explored. This section addresses this problem directly by factoring into the analysis the potential effects of differential identification on our understanding of the Saint-Césaire assemblages.

Differential Identification of Skeletal Elements

A comparison of the NISP and NSUTS (number of specimens of uncertain taxonomic status, see Chapter 4) samples has been carried out to investigate the issue of analytical representation at Saint-Césaire. What is examined here is the assumption that faunal patterns are sampled accurately by NISP counts. In theory, an assemblage with few broken elements will be dominated by taxonomically identified specimens (i.e., NISP), whereas a slightly more fragmented one should contain appreciable proportions of unidentified – and particularly anatomically but not taxonomically identified – remains (i.e., NSUTS, Figure 6.20). However, with further fragmentation, the proportion of

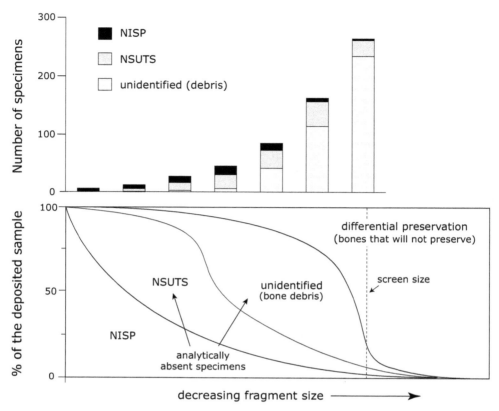

FIGURE 6.20. Hypothetical model showing the relationship between identifiability and degree of fragmentation in deposited versus excavated assemblages.

unidentified remains is expected to increase dramatically at the expense of NSUTS and NISP.

The changes in proportions of NISP, NSUTS, and indeterminate specimens induced by increasing fragmentation would not be a source of concern to faunal analysts if they did not affect the taxonomic or anatomical profiles of assemblages. However, this assumes that classes of elements are comparably identifiable, which seems unlikely for most vertebrate species. For instance, a poorly diagnostic skeletal element is likely to be rare in the NISP sample, somewhat more common in the NSUTS sample, and abundant in the indeterminate sample. Conversely, a highly diagnostic element should be frequent in the NISP sample and less well represented in the NSUTS sample.

This problem is illustrated in Figure 6.21. In most vertebrate species, tooth representation is expected to increase with fragmentation because of the decreasing identifiability of other comparatively more fragile and less diagnostic elements. In other words, teeth should dominate highly fragmented assemblages because they are highly diagnostic, even when fragmented. Therefore, two assemblages that were initially identical may produce analytically distinct anatomical profiles as a result of differential fragmentation. The impact of fragmentation on skeletal part representation will primarily be a function of the distance that separates the assemblages along the fragmentation spectrum.

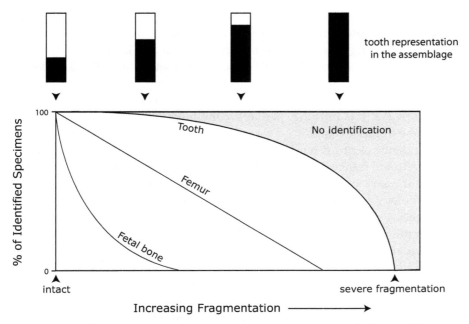

FIGURE 6.21. Inferred relationship between tooth representation and degree of fragmentation in an assemblage that comprises tooth, femur, and fetal bone specimens.

To assess this issue at Saint-Césaire, skeletal profiles in the NISP and NSUTS samples are compared in Figure 6.22. All of the occupations are combined in this figure to increase sample size. If differential identification is a minor problem at Saint-Césaire, the line in Figure 6.22 is expected to be straight and vertical, and the values for each class of skeletal elements should plot near the "0" value. Clearly, this is not the case. Antler and long bones are better represented in the NISP than in the NSUTS sample. On the contrary, rib, mandible/maxillary, cranial, tooth, and vertebra fragments are all proportionally more common in the NSUTS than in the NISP sample. Does this mean that the taxonomically identified sample is a skewed reflection of body part representation in the assemblages?

In fact, several classes of elements that are overrepresented in the NSUTS sample consist of fragile and/or poorly diagnostic portions ignored in the calculation of MNI and MNE values. For instance, the scapula is mostly represented by blade and border fragments in the NSUTS sample. However, because the glenoid cavity region provided the MNE values in the majority of the samples, the underrepresentation of the blade and border portions should have only minor effects on scapula representation. Likewise, there is little doubt that taxonomically identified teeth and petrous bones provide reliable estimates of head abundance in the assemblages that largely compensate for the overrepresentation of alveolar bone, calvaria, and tooth fragments in the NSUTS sample. However, the ease with which teeth can be identified, as well as their resilience to postdepositional processes, probably skews anatomical profiles by increasing head representation relative to other parts (Klein and Cruz-Uribe 1984).

Vertebrae are notably difficult to identify to the species level due to complex morphology, high individual variability, significant overlap in species variation, and the frequent dissociation of the processes and neural arch from the vertebral body. For the same reasons, they are also difficult to refit. However, focusing on the NSUTS sample may counteract some of these problems, as vertebral bodies are easily identified anatomically. Numerically speaking, vertebrae are not abundant in any of the samples from Saint-Césaire, representing no more than 2.8% of all of the material identified at least to the skeletal element. Therefore, the scarcity of vertebrae at Saint-Césaire does not appear to be explained by analytical underrepresentation. A more likely reason for their low occurrence at Saint-Césaire is burning, perhaps, combined with other processes (e.g., transport), as will be discussed later.

The initial abundance of ribs is harder to assess. In the assemblages, ribs were often broken parasagittally and transversely into short sections, a phenomenon that prevented the identification of many specimens. Moreover, given that there is considerable variation in rib morphology within and between individuals, and much overlap between closely related species of roughly similar size, taxonomic identification is considered more tentative for this part than for others. For these reasons, this class of elements may be significantly underrepresented in the NISP sample.

The problem is somewhat different for reindeer antlers. This part is easily identified, even when severely fragmented. Moreover, several antler fragments show evidence of tool making in the Upper Paleolithic occupations from Saint-Césaire (Morin and Liolios 2008). Both factors might inflate the relative abundance of reindeer heads. To reduce this potential bias, antlers were excluded from the analysis of body part representation.

Long bone shafts are abundant in the samples. In contrast, epiphyses are very poorly represented, a phenomenon outlined in Chapter 5. The relative absence of epiphyses in the assemblages does not seem, at first glance, to be attributable to analytical underrepresentation, given that these bone portions are statistically *less* common in the NSUTS than in the NISP sample (6.0 vs. 14.3%, $t_s = 2.97$, $p \leq .005$). At a lower level of identification, the indeterminate portion of the samples contains a large quantity of unidentified long bone fragments. However, the vast majority of them (estimated to be well over 95%) are unburned shaft splinters. Therefore, the indeterminate long bone sample cannot account for the very low incidence of long bone epiphyses at Saint-Césaire. There remains the alternative that epiphyses are characterized by extreme analytical underrepresentation, being so fragmented that most specimens went unidentified even as long bone fragments. In fact, the presence of many burned spongy remains in the indeterminate sample is consistent with this alternative. Unfortunately, it is not possible to quantify their abundance accurately. The possibility that epiphyses were systematically burned at Saint-Césaire is discussed in a later section of this chapter.

In general, the evidence suggests that vertebrae, ribs, and long bone epiphyses are significantly underrepresented in the NISP sample, which may affect the interpretation of these parts. For long bones, MNE counts based on shaft portions probably largely circumvent this problem. We also saw that counts are probably less accurate for ribs because of their high degree of fragmentation. An additional problem is that ethnographic data suggest that rib slabs are frequently broken off above the articulatory heads during carcass processing (Binford 1978; Bartram 1993; Oliver 1993). As a result, MNE counts based on the head portion of the ribs may constitute poor estimates of the original abundance of rib slabs in the assemblages and instead be indicative of the number of thoracic vertebral segments that were transported to the site.

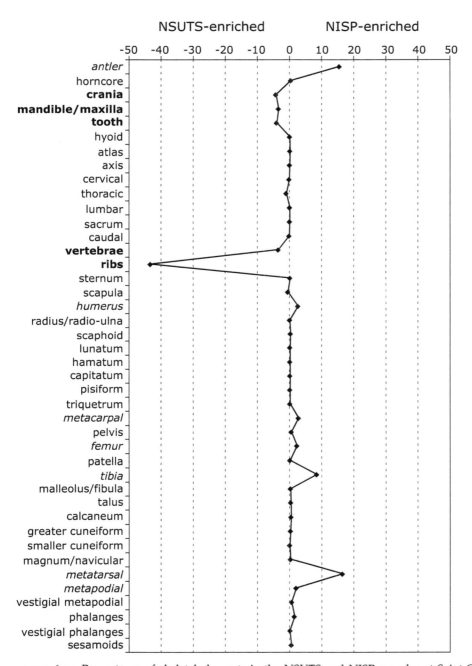

FIGURE 6.22. Percentages of skeletal elements in the NSUTS and NISP samples at Saint-Césaire. All of the occupations are combined. Values in bold are elements that are overrepresented in the NSUTS sample, whereas values in italics are elements that are overrepresented in the NISP sample. The data are from Appendix 10.

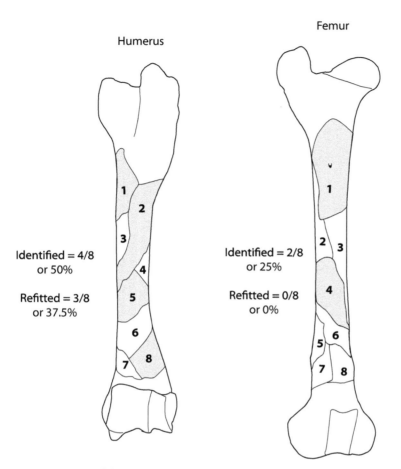

FIGURE 6.23. Model showing the relationship between differential identification and percentages of refits for two reindeer bones. In this example, no fragment could be refitted for the femur because fewer fragments were identified in comparison to the humerus.

Differential Identification of Long Bone Shafts

At Saint-Césaire, the relative abundance of long bones was largely estimated on the basis of shaft fragments. However, as Bouchud (1962, 1966) and, more recently, Marean and Kim (1998) have emphasized, unlike epiphyses, shaft fragments are not equally identifiable. For instance, when extensively fragmented, the femur shaft seems more difficult to identify in many artiodactyls than the other types of long bone shafts. It should be possible to verify these assertions by conducting blind tests using experimentally fragmented skeletal elements, but this is beyond the scope of this study. An alternative is to look at refit data.

All else being equal, highly diagnostic elements should be associated with a higher probability of refitting than elements that are difficult to identify. This follows from the fact that a greater proportion of (initially) contiguous fragments is expected to be present in the refitting sample for these elements (Figure 6.23). Controlling for fragment size is critical here because a fragile element is more likely to become fragmented and

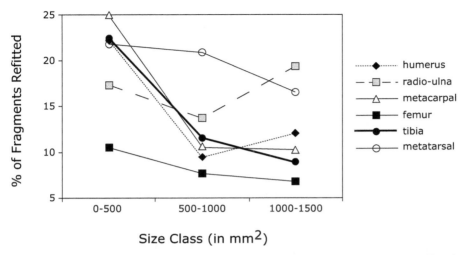

FIGURE 6.24. Percentages of refitted reindeer long bones by size class (in mm²). The data are from Appendix 11.

therefore be harder to identify, than a robust one. Because the type and number of diagnostic landmarks usually vary between taxa, refit percentages are most useful when analyzed by species. Despite some morphological variation, homologous elements in closely related taxa (e.g., red deer and reindeer) are expected to show similar biases with respect to identification.

At Saint-Césaire, percentages of refitted fragments were calculated for reindeer long bones. The degree of fragmentation was controlled, to some degree, by assigning each fragment to one of three size classes on the basis of the surface area of the fragment. These surface areas were estimated by multiplying the maximum length of the specimen by its maximum width.

When refit percentages are used irrespective of size classes, the reindeer data indicate a statistically significant overrepresentation of the metatarsal and radio-ulna relative to the femur, tibia, and humerus (femur/radio-ulna: $t_s = 2.37, p < .02$; femur/metatarsal: $t_s = 4.10, p < .0001$; humerus/radio-ulna: $t_s = 2.14, p < .04$; humerus/metatarsal: $t_s = 3.79$, $p \leq .0002$; tibia/radio-ulna: $t_s = 2.75, p \leq 0.01$; tibia/metatarsal: $t_s = 6.07, p < .0001$; based on the total for each element, as in Appendix 11). Figure 6.24 presents the same data, this time broken down by size classes. This figure indicates that the femur is consistently underrepresented relative to the other long bones, whereas the metatarsal shows the opposite trend. The metacarpal, tibia, and radio-ulna tend to have intermediate values. In sum, these data suggest that NISP counts probably underestimate femur abundance in the reindeer samples. Conversely, the metatarsal might be overrepresented relative to the other long bones.

Refit data are also available for bison. In this case, the sample is small and cannot be partitioned according to size class. Moreover, raw percentages for bison are not perfectly comparable with those of reindeer due to methodological differences in the refitting protocol for these two taxa (Morin *et al.* 2005). As for reindeer, the bison femur comprises proportionally fewer refits than the radius, humerus, and tibia (Table 6.8), although none of these differences are statistically significant (results not shown). Interestingly, the

TABLE 6.8. *Percentages of refitted long bone fragments for bison at Saint-Césaire*

	Bison long bones		
	Refit	*n*	%refitted
Tibia	168	309	54.4
Radius	24	45	53.3
Humerus	39	77	50.6
Femur	27	56	48.2
Metatarsal	38	103	36.9
Metacarpal	8	25	32.0
Total	304	615	49.4

All of the assemblages are included. Percentages of refits were calculated by subtracting the number of specimens refitted from the pre-refit NISP counts.

bison metatarsal is rarely refitted, in opposition to reindeer. This result makes intuitive sense because the metatarsal is smooth and relatively featureless in bison and lacks the highly diagnostic anterior groove of the reindeer metatarsal. In fact, bison metatarsals may be underrepresented in the NISP samples, given that the percentage of refitted specimens is statistically lower for this element than the percentage of refitted tibiae ($t_s = 3.10, p < .002$). The bison metacarpal may also be underrepresented relative to the other skeletal elements, although the sample is too small for statistical assessment. These results suggest that a low abundance of bison metapodials and, perhaps, femurs in an epiphysis-depleted assemblage may partly be an artifact of their lower identifiability.

Effects of Counting Methods on Head Representation

One of the main conclusions of this chapter is that certain classes of elements are likely to be under- or overrepresented in fragmented assemblages as a result of differential identification. What needs to be examined at this point is whether counting methods also influence the representation of parts affected by differential identification. The discussion focuses on teeth because there is a consensus that this element is generally easier to identify than most other skeletal parts.

In vertebrate assemblages composed of *whole* elements from distantly related species (e.g., horse and bison), the *level of identification* or *identifiability*, defined as the relationship between the number of specimens present in a sample and the number of those specimens that are identified taxonomically, is expected to vary little between classes of elements. In these assemblages, most classes of elements should be comparably identifiable. Vertebrae, ribs, sternebrae, and sesamoids may be exceptions to this generalization, these skeletal parts being more difficult to identify taxonomically than other types of elements even when complete.

In contrast, the level of identification is not constant across classes of elements in *fragmented* assemblages; it is predicted to be closer to 100% for teeth but much lower for most other parts, a phenomenon that induces overrepresentation of heads (Figure 6.25, left panel). Given that MNE does not increase linearly with NISP but instead follows a power function (Grayson 1984; Lyman 2008), the overrepresentation of heads is expected to be magnified in small MNE samples. This situation arises because teeth are likely

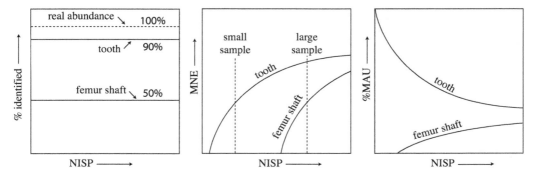

FIGURE 6.25. Hypothetical model illustrating the relationship between identification, skeletal representation, and sample size in fragmented assemblages. The left panel shows the percentages of identified
specimens for various elements (as in the previous models of skeletal element identification, the values
are fictive). The middle and right panels indicate how the representation of different elements may
change with increasing sample size when abundance is based on MNE counts. Head representation
decreases with increasing sample size as a result of the flattening of the MNE curve for teeth and the
identification of a wider range of parts in the larger samples.

to be identified *before other classes of elements* (Figure 6.25, middle panel). As sample
size increases, the slope of the MNE curve for teeth becomes more flattened than the
MNE curves for the other elements that begin to be identified. This means that when
one uses MNE counts the problem of head overrepresentation should decrease with
increasing sample size (Figure 6.25, right panel). Although the head is also likely to be
overrepresented in NISP counts, overrepresentation in this case should be independent
of sample size, as shown in the left panel of Figure 6.25.

The upper diagram in Figure 6.26 displays cranium and mandible representation
(based on %MAU values) for reindeer, horse, and bison assemblages at Saint-Césaire
versus the size of their associated NISP samples. This figure examines whether head
representation decreases with increasing sample size at Saint-Césaire, as inferred earlier.
On the basis of the plotted data, the relationship between these variables seems roughly
linear and negative: the larger the reindeer, bison, or horse assemblage (as measured by
NISP), the lower the representation of mandibles and crania (as measured by %MAU).
The statistical significance of this relationship was tested using Pearson's r because the
Spearman's rank-order correlation produced a high number of *ex aequos*. The results
($r = -.44$, $p < 0.02$) appear to confirm that the use of MNE inflates head representation
in small samples.

However, these patterns might simply mean that heads were more frequently transported in layers with small assemblages. It is possible to evaluate this proposition using
%NISP (instead of %MAU) as an estimate of head abundance, given that this quantitative unit is known to vary independently of sample size (Grayson 1984; Lyman 2008). If
the MNE patterns were caused by differential transport, the %NISP values for reindeer,
bison, and horse mandibles and crania should increase in the smallest samples, as was
the case for the %MAU values. The distribution of the %NISP values in the lower diagram of Figure 6.26 does not indicate an inflated representation of mandibles and crania
in the smaller samples. This interpretation is corroborated by a statistical analysis of the
data ($r = -.23$, $p < .21$). These results strongly indicate that the MNE method artificially

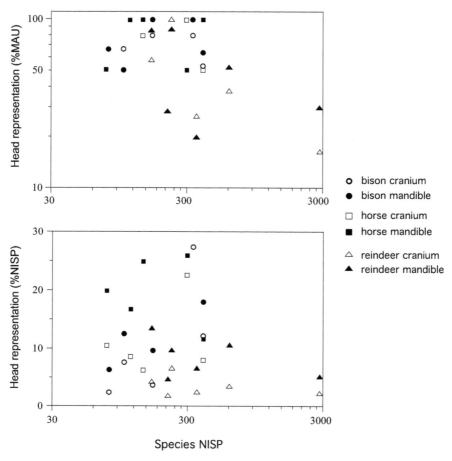

FIGURE 6.26. Relationship between the size (in NISP) of several reindeer, horse, and bison assemblages and cranium and mandible representation at Saint-Césaire, based on %MAU (upper panel) and %NISP (lower panel) values. The data are from Appendix 2. Note that some axes are in log10.

increases head representation in small faunal samples at Saint-Césaire. Because this problem emanates from the MNE measure itself, these conclusions are likely to apply across a wide range of fragmented assemblages.

Scalar Effects in Species Identification

After reviewing problems of identification at the level of the skeletal element, the discussion now turns to the issue of the differential identification of *taxa*. Compared with Africa, where many closely related species overlap in body size (Klein and Cruz-Uribe 1984), the identification of taxa is facilitated here because species in France are generally well separated on the body-size axis (Grayson and Delpech 2003). Despite this favorable context, scalar effects in fragmentation patterns may reduce the identification of certain species at Saint-Césaire. However, there is some disagreement in the archaeological literature about which method is most appropriate for assessing this problem.

TABLE 6.9. *Percentages of NISP versus total specimen counts by level at Saint-Césaire, excluding birds and microfauna*

Layer	NISP *n*	Total specimens *n*	NISP/Total %
Evol Auri (Ejj)	426	4182	10.2
Evol Auri (Ejm)	1083	7906	13.7
Middle Auri (Ejf)	4102	39636	10.3
Middle Auri (Ejo sup)	480	5567	8.6
Low density (Ejo inf)	83	781	10.6
Moust/Chât (Ejop sup)	**966**	**28665**	**3.4**
Dentic Moust (Ejop inf)	**331**	**9409**	**3.5**
Dentic Moust (Egpf)	**867**	**20975**	**4.1**
Total	8338	117121	7.1

Assemblages dominated by large ungulates are shown in bold. NISP are post-refit counts. The low-density EJO inf assemblage comprises roughly equal percentages of medium-sized (reindeer) and large-sized taxa (bison and horse).

The comparison of NISP/MNE ratios (Klein and Cruz-Uribe 1984) is probably the most popular measure for studying the differential identification of taxa. However, as pointed out by Grayson (1984), this approach is not entirely satisfactory because NISP increases linearly in an assemblage, whereas MNE does not. Therefore, large samples can be expected to have higher NISP/MNE ratios than smaller samples, irrespective of change in the level of taxonomic identification. An alternative approach is to compare percentages of taxonomically identified remains between assemblages. In the present case, these percentages were simply calculated by dividing the total NISP for a layer by the entire sample of faunal remains in that layer. In general, inter-level comparisons should be easier to interpret when assemblages have roughly similar anatomical profiles and are dominated by a small set of taxa, as is the case at Saint-Césaire.

Table 6.9 indicates that the percentages of taxonomically identified specimens are consistently lower at Saint-Césaire in occupations dominated by large ungulates (the Denticulate Mousterian EGPF, EJOP inf and Mousterian/Châtelperronian occupations) than in those dominated by reindeer (the Aurignacian occupations). Differences between reindeer-dominated and large ungulate-dominated assemblages are all highly significant (at the 0.0001 level, results not shown). Because patterns of body part representation are roughly comparable between the levels, it seems reasonable to hold differential fragmentation responsible for the lower identification of large ungulates relative to reindeer at Saint-Césaire. Costamagno (1999:412) reported a similar pattern of underidentification of large ungulates in her study of Magdalenian assemblages from southwestern France.

This issue can be explored further by focusing on long bones. Table 6.10 shows that despite some variation, the percentage of taxonomically identified long bones (calculated relative to total NISP) is broadly constant across the layers, the very small EJO inf sample excluded. These values suggest similar patterns of long bone representation across the layers. However, the percentage of *unidentified* long bones in the indeterminate samples is approximately two to three times lower in the large-ungulate-dominated than in the reindeer-dominated assemblages. In other words, despite similar anatomical

TABLE 6.10. *Percentages of long bones in the NISP and indeterminate samples*

	NISP			Unidentified		
layer	Identified long bones	Total NISP	%long bone NISP	Unidentified long bones	Total unidentified	%unid. long bones
Evol Auri Ejj	180	426	42.3	877	3641	24.1
Evol Auri Ejm	468	1083	43.2	1636	6530	25.1
Mid Auri Ejf	2053	4102	50.0	7857	34202	23.0
Mid Auri Ejo sup	228	480	47.5	821	4973	16.5
low dens	13	83	15.7	58	668	8.7
Moust/Châtel	**356**	**966**	**36.9**	**1738**	**27045**	**6.4**
Dent Moust Ejop inf	**164**	**331**	**49.5**	**858**	**8911**	**9.6**
Dent Moust Egpf	**323**	**867**	**37.3**	**1711**	**19569**	**8.7**
Total	3785	8338	45.4	15556	105539	14.7

Assemblages dominated by large ungulates are shown in bold. NISP are post-refit counts. The unidentified sample excludes NSUTS. The low-density EJO inf assemblage comprises roughly equal percentages of medium-sized (reindeer) and large-sized taxa (bison and horse).
Abbreviation: unid. = unidentified.

profiles (based on the NISP samples), the reindeer-dominated assemblages of Saint-Césaire comprise much higher proportions of unidentified long bone fragments and far fewer indeterminate remains than those dominated by larger ungulates. This result may indicate that, for large ungulates, long bone marrow-cracking produces higher percentages of undiagnostic fragments than is the case for smaller ungulates such as reindeer (Morin 2010).

Postdepositional damage may also decrease the identifiability of large ungulate long bones. Particularly, the presence of cracks on long bones may be used to test Klein's (1989) proposition that postdepositional breakage is more prevalent, in general, in large than in small ungulates. Controlling for spatial variation as much as possible, the incidence of cracks on long bones in the best-preserved rows of Saint-Césaire is much higher for horse and bison than for reindeer (Table 6.11). The differences between the larger ungulates and reindeer are statistically significant, whereas the difference between horse and bison is not (reindeer vs. horse: $t_s = 6.75$, $p < .0001$; reindeer vs. bison: $t_s = 6.14$, $p < .0001$, bison vs. horse: $t_s = 0.83$, $p < .41$, mean of meter 2 and 3). These data imply that horse and bison long bones are more likely to crack and break, presumably as a result

TABLE 6.11. *Incidence of cracks on long bones for three different species in the best-preserved lines of Saint-Césaire*

	Distance from the Cliff					
	2 m away			3 m away		
	With cracks	Total bones	% with cracks	With cracks	Total bones	% with cracks
Reindeer	27	1180	2.3	22	702	3.1
Horse	9	39	23.1	12	35	34.3
Bison	9	35	25.7	11	53	20.8

TABLE 6.12. *Percentages of burned specimens in the assemblages as a function of the level of identification*

	NISP			NSUTS			Unidentified fragments		
	Burned	NISP	%burned	Burned	NSUTS	%burned	Burned	Indet.	%burned
Evol Auri Ejj	10	426	2.3	4	116	3.4	1226	3641	33.7
Evol Auri Ejm	22	1083	2.0	13	293	4.4	2084	6530	31.9
Mid Auri Ejf	150	4102	3.7	114	1340	8.5	13260	34202	38.8
Mid Auri Ejo sup	17	480	3.5	3	114	2.6	1158	4973	23.3
Low density	0	83	0.0	0	30	0.0	85	668	12.7
Moust/Châtel	2	966	0.2	25	661	3.8	7517	27045	27.8
D Moust Ejop inf	13	331	3.9	4	168	2.4	3480	8911	39.1
D Moust Egpf	16	867	1.8	45	539	8.3	7087	19569	36.2
Total	230	8338	2.8	208	3261	6.4	35897	105539	34.0

Unidentified specimens exclude specimens from the NSUTS sample.
Abbreviations: indet. = indeterminate.

of scaling effects, and therefore be more difficult to identify, than those of reindeer. This effect might be associated with the greater gradient of moisture found in large animal bones relative to those of small animals (D. Fisher, pers. comm., 2003).

In general, these data suggest that bison and horse elements, particularly long bones, are underidentified at Saint-Césaire compared with those of reindeer. In a broader perspective, the lower identification of long bones may partly account for the high representation of head parts observed in many fragmented assemblages dominated by large ungulate taxa (Klein 1989).

BURNING

In the archaeozoological literature, burning is often assumed to have negligible or random effects on body part representation. However, this assumption may not be warranted in many assemblages, especially in western Europe (Morin 2010). The present study follows the lead of others (Castel 1999; Costamagno *et al.* 1999) in stressing the substantial impact that burning can have on anatomical profiles.

We saw in Chapter 5 that burning principally affects long bones, malleoli, innominates, vertebrae, carpals, and tarsals in the assemblages. To illustrate these patterns, the relative abundance of burned parts in the reindeer samples from the Middle Aurignacian EJO sup, EJF, and Evolved Aurignacian levels are compared in Figures 6.27 and 6.28. Unfortunately, the other, often smaller, assemblages could not be included in these figures as a result of small samples of burned specimens. Examples of two frequently burned elements in the Aurignacian occupations, cubo-naviculars and tali, are shown in Figure 6.29.

At Saint-Césaire, the frequency of burning increases as the level of identification decreases (Table 6.12). In addition, the data indicate that the anatomical profile of burned specimens changes with the level of identification. For instance, compared with NISP, the NSUTS sample comprises greater percentages of burned skull (mostly tooth), vertebra, and rib fragments but lower percentages of burned epiphyses, carpals, tarsals, and

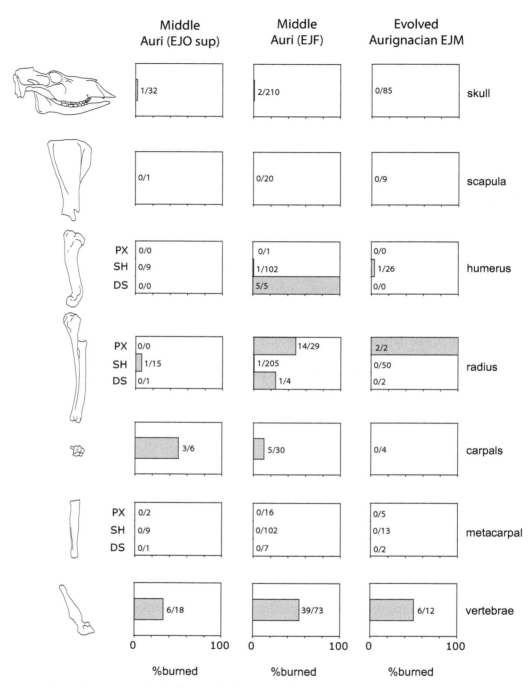

FIGURE 6.27. Percentages of skull, scapula, foreleg, and vertebra specimens that are burned in the reindeer samples from the Middle Aurignacian EJO sup, EJF, and Evolved Aurignacian EJM levels. The data are from Appendix 2. Because of the lower identifiability of vertebrae, values for this class of elements include NSUTS specimens that were assigned to the same body size class as reindeer (i.e., UNG2).

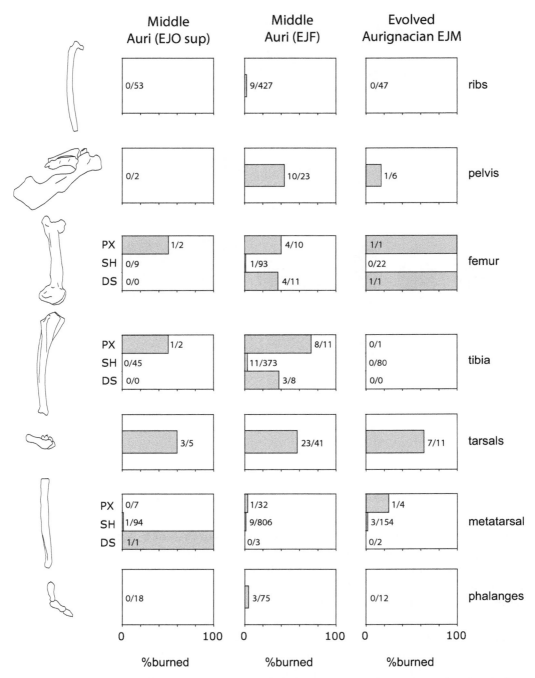

FIGURE 6.28. Percentages of rib, pelvis, hindleg, and phalanx specimens that are burned in the reindeer assemblages from the Middle Aurignacian EJO sup, EJF, and Evolved Aurignacian EJM levels. The data are from Appendix 2. All of the first, second, and third phalanges are combined.

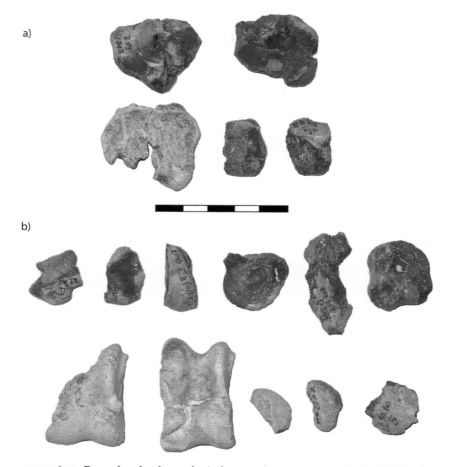

FIGURE 6.29. Burned and unburned reindeer specimens recovered in the Middle Aurignacian EJF layer from Saint-Césaire: (a) cubonaviculars (the lower left specimen is not burned); (b) tali (or astragali, the three lower left specimens are not burned). Note that the burned specimens are entirely carbonized.

pelves (Table 6.13). The differences between these categories of identification are statistically significant, as shown by the chi-square test ($\chi^2 = 244.4$, $p < .0001$, skulls, vertebrae, ribs, long bones, pelves, carpals, and tarsals only; all long bones combined). The indeterminate sample also differs from the NISP and NSUTS samples because it contains an abundance of burned spongy fragments, presumably largely derived from long bone epiphyses. In sum, few burned specimens were taxonomically identified in the assemblages, despite the presence of thousands of burned fragments. This means that the *NISP sample may provide little information on burning patterns because the burned fragments are likely to be unidentifiable, especially when the species are large.*

As outlined in Chapter 5, long bone epiphyses are consistently underrepresented in the assemblages. Table 6.14 strongly suggests that burning caused this pattern. Indeed, the data in this table indicate that long bone epiphyses are frequently burned at Saint-Césaire, in contrast to shafts. The significant decrease in the frequency of burning with increasing distance from the articulations corroborates this pattern

TABLE 6.13. *Variation in body part representation of burned specimens in the NISP and NSUTS samples*

Body part	NISP		NSUTS	
	n burned	% of total burned sample	*n* burned	% of total burned sample
Antler	1	0.4	–	–
Skull	36	15.2	107	49.1
Vertebrae	12	5.1	73	33.5
Rib	11	4.6	33	15.1
Scapula	–	–	1	0.5
Humerus	7	3.0	–	–
Radius	33	13.9	–	–
Carpals	8	3.4	–	–
Metacarpal	1	0.4	–	–
Pelvis	15	6.3	1	0.5
Femur	14	5.9	1	0.5
Patella	1	0.4	–	–
Tibia	27	11.4	1	0.5
Malleolus	6	2.5	–	–
Tarsals	38	16.0	–	–
Metatarsal	19	8.0	–	–
Metapodial	1	0.4	–	–
Phalanges	4	1.7	1	0.5
Vestigial phalanges	1	0.4	–	–
Fibula	1	0.4	–	–
Sesamoids	1	0.4	–	–
Total	237	100.0	218	100.0

All of the occupations and taxa are combined.

(epiphyseal vs. near-epiphyseal fragments $t_s = 5.12$, $p < .0001$; near-epiphyseal vs. mid-shaft fragments: $t_s = 11.01$, $p < .0001$; based on the totals in Table 6.14). The very low abundance of burned epiphyses in the NISP samples for the Denticulate Mousterian EGPF, EJOP inf, and Mousterian/Châtelperronian layers probably reflects the difficulty of identifying small burned fragments in these large-ungulate-dominated assemblages.

Additional data support the hypothesis that burning depressed the representation of long bone epiphyses at Saint-Césaire. The abundance of long bone portions (as measured by MNE) in the occupations is inversely correlated with the incidence of burning (Figure 6.30). This inverse relationship cannot be explained by the analytical absence of burned shafts, given that the sample of unidentified shafts shows relatively low percentages of fire damage in the levels (Table 6.15). All these patterns attest to the selective burning of long bone extremities in the Saint-Césaire occupations.

From these data, it can be concluded that burning is not randomly distributed within the assemblages. Parts that are most frequently burned include innominates, long bone epiphyses, malleoli, vertebrae, carpals, and tarsals. These findings suggest that the vertebral column and long bone epiphyses were frequently burned at Saint-Césaire, the latter possibly with attached carpals or tarsals. Obviously, the practice of burning certain categories of parts reduces the suite of elements for which reliable estimates of

TABLE 6.14. *Percentages of burned diaphyses and epiphyses at Saint-Césaire, based on NISP*

	Epiphyses only			Epiphyses and near-epiphyseal shafts			Shafts		
	Burned	Total	%burned	Burned	Total	%burned	Burned	Total	%burned
Evol Auri Ejj	3	4	75.0	3	12	25.0	2	168	1.2
Evol Auri Ejm	2	9	22.2	5	35	14.3	7	430	1.6
Mid Auri Ejf	40	82	48.8	46	190	24.2	30	1852	1.6
Mid Auri Ejo sup	4	9	44.4	4	21	19.0	2	205	1.0
Low density	0	1	0.0	0	4	0.0	0	9	0.0
Moust/Châtel	0	9	0.0	0	48	0.0	0	297	0.0
D Moust Ejop inf	1	3	33.3	1	15	6.7	2	149	1.3
D Moust Egpf	0	6	0.0	0	24	0.0	0	297	0.0
Total	50	123	40.6	59	349	16.9	43	3407	1.3

All of the taxa are combined.

abundance can be made. Counts for the other parts of the skeleton, including long bone shafts, are probably representative of initial abundances, with the possible exception of ribs. Concerning these points, it is important to note that without an in-depth study of the NSUTS and indeterminate samples, several of the patterns outlined here could have mistakenly been attributed to the action of other density-mediated processes, such as differential preservation or carnivore ravaging (Morin 2010). This is because identification filters can mute the archaeological signatures of burning in an assemblage. Importantly, selective recovery, which is likely biased against the collection of burned specimens, can be expected to have similar effects.

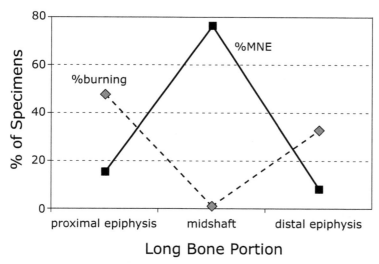

FIGURE 6.30. Percentages of burned proximal epiphyses, midshafts, and distal epiphyses versus the abundance (MNE counts) of the same bone portions at Saint-Césaire. Data for %burning are 31/65 (proximal), 43/3407 (shaft), and 19/58 (distal) and are based on NISP. %MNE are derived from the pooling of the MNE values for reindeer, horse, and bison long bones (the data are taken from Appendix 12). Complete long bones were excluded.

TABLE 6.15. *Percentages of burned long bones of size-2 ungulates (UNG2) and size 3–4 ungulates (UNG3–4) in the Saint-Césaire occupations*

	Unidentified UNG2 shafts			Unidentified UNG 3–4 shafts			Total unidentified shafts		
	Burned	Total	%	Burned	Total	%	Burned	Total	%
Evol Auri Ejj	96	716	13.4	7	161	4.3	103	877	11.7
Evol Auri Ejm	220	1483	14.8	18	153	11.8	238	1636	14.5
Mid Auri Ejf	1318	7385	17.8	93	472	19.7	1411	7857	18.0
Mid Auri Ejo sup	37	755	4.9	5	66	7.6	42	821	5.1
Low density	1	9	11.1	0	49	0.0	1	58	1.7
Moust/Châtel	6	330	1.8	5	1408	0.4	11	1738	0.6
D Moust Ejop inf	11	308	3.6	11	550	2.0	22	858	2.6
D Moust Egpf	14	538	2.6	74	1173	6.3	88	1711	5.1
Total	1703	11524	14.8	213	4032	5.3	1916	15556	12.3

CONCLUSIONS ON TAPHONOMY

Various taphonomic filters have shaped body part representation and taxonomic composition in the faunal assemblages from Saint-Césaire. This situation may limit the possibility of reconstructing Neandertal and modern human subsistence strategies accurately. However, in most cases, these biases are predicted to be roughly constant throughout the sequence (e.g., the underrepresentation of large ungulates relative to reindeer) or to have a limited impact on skeletal part representation and taxonomic composition (e.g., the underrepresentation of scapula blade fragments). However, cutmark frequencies in the assemblages are not always fully comparable because of differences in bone surface preservation. Therefore, variation in cutmark percentages at Saint-Césaire must be interpreted with caution. Likewise, differential fragmentation may affect patterns of skeletal representation between layers. Chapter 9 presents some of the methods that were used to control for this problem.

Burning is a more serious problem. This phenomenon appears to have decreased the abundance of vertebrae, innominates, malleoli, carpals, and tarsals in the assemblages. Therefore, it might be necessary to eliminate these parts from the analysis of skeletal part representation. One of the most robust patterns uncovered at Saint-Césaire is the systematic burning of long bone epiphyses. However, shafts were rarely burned and a considerable amount of time was devoted to identifying and refitting them. Therefore, using shaft counts should provide broadly accurate approximations of the initial abundance of long bone elements at Saint-Césaire, taking into account that some shaft portions (femur in reindeer, metapodials and femur in bison) may be less frequently identified than more diagnostic ones.

7

SEASONALITY

ARCHAEOLOGICAL APPLICATIONS OF FORAGING MODELS COMMONLY FOCUS ON THE composition of faunal samples to interpret long-term fluctuations in the abundance of high-ranked resources. However, a shift in site function (e.g., from a butchering station to a home base) or in the intensity (e.g., from week- to season-long sojourns, including adult males/females only or whole groups) and/or period (e.g., from winter to fall) of occupation of a site can produce changes in the range of prey species represented in a faunal sequence even in contexts in which foraging strategies varied little over time. This problem, which can confound the analysis of diet breadth, is particularly acute when faunal samples are examined from the viewpoint of a single or small number of sites, as is frequently the case in archaeology (Grayson and Cannon 1999). The issue here is one of sampling; what kinds of foraging activities took place at the site? Did these activities vary significantly in nature and frequency throughout the archaeological sequence? Although these questions are difficult to address with Paleolithic faunas, the analysis of seasonality data may shed light on patterns of site use at Saint-Césaire.

In this chapter, a number of methods based on fetal development, the annual antler cycle, bone fusion, and dental eruption and wear are used to assess whether seasonality patterns changed appreciably between the occupations of Saint-Césaire. These data are provided, when applicable, for reindeer, bison, and horse. The next pages also include a discussion of the biology of these taxa. Birth synchrony is emphasized because the timing of births in prey species strongly influences interpretations of seasonality in archaeological contexts. Despite the limited data at hand, the information provided in this chapter should help interpret variations in diet breadth at Saint-Césaire.

BIOLOGY OF THE MAIN UNGULATE SPECIES AT SAINT-CÉSAIRE

Reindeer

Most biologists recognize two distinct ecotypes of *Rangifer* (reindeer/caribou): the *woodland* and *tundra* forms (Banfield 1951). However, genetic studies have shown that caribou populations do not always cluster according to this traditional taxonomy (Miller 2003). Moreover, gene flow may be significant between migratory and sedentary caribou bands (Boulet *et al.* 2007). In general, woodland caribou and wild reindeer living in forested areas tend to migrate over small distances, with those living in mountainous areas making migrations that are predominantly vertical. The barren-ground caribou and tundra reindeer typically migrate over greater distances, traveling as much as 300 to 600 km (Kelsall 1968). However, as noted by Spiess (1979) and Miller (2003), considerable variation can be found in the migratory patterns of both ecotypes.

Ethological studies show that the distribution and aggregation of caribou/reindeer is relatively unpredictable from one year to the next, depending on prevailing environmental conditions (Kelsall 1968; Parker 1972; Miller 2003). In the winter months, snow cover and ice conditions, both above and below the snowpack, can affect food accessibility (Aanes *et al.* 2003). Other factors that may also influence the wintertime distribution of *Rangifer* include the presence of large carnivores on the winter range and the frequency of wildfires on the summer range.

Rangifer individuals tend to be dispersed in winter. In spring, the animals aggregate to form large herds and move to the calving grounds. One can roughly predict the path and timing of these springtime migrations (Burch 1972). However, archaeologists have tended to neglect the routine occurrence of mid-summer migrations in this species. Most, if not all, populations make a mid-summer southward migration, followed by a dispersal of the herd in August, before the better-known fall migration (Kelsall 1968; Parker 1972; Miller 1974). Thus, in late summer, reindeer and caribou may be more difficult to find (Parker 1972; Helle 1980).

Importantly, within a single herd of *Rangifer*, not all animals will participate in the springtime migration. Pregnant females tend to lead this migration, whereas the non-breeding portion of the population often lingers behind. It is common for adult males to stay longer in the winter range, moving northward much more slowly than parturient females and juveniles. Sometimes adult males do not participate in the springtime migration at all (Parker 1972; Helle 1980). Sexual segregation can also be observed in the early summer (Parker 1972).

Bison and Horse

North America has two subspecies of bison: the wood bison (*Bison bison athabascae*),[1] that approached extinction in the twentieth century, and the plains bison (*Bison bison bison*). Less is known about the European bison or wisent (*Bison bonasus*), confined today to the Bialowieza forest, which stretches across Poland and Belarus and to a number of reserves in Caucasia. These European populations are generally much smaller than the large North American herds and are mostly kept in semi- or full captivity (Krasinska *et al.* 1987; Pucek *et al.* 2003). Genetic studies suggest that the European bison represents a distinct species relative to the plains and wood bison, although this position remains controversial (Prusak *et al.* 2004). According to Brugal (1983, 1999), the Late Pleistocene form of bison found in France is *Bison priscus*, which may have evolved anagenetically from *Bison schoetensacki*. It is uncertain, however, whether *Bison priscus* was more closely related to the current European bison or to the wood bison, which is now restricted to North America.

---

[1] There is debate on the taxonomic status of the wood and plains bison. Although some have argued that these populations are not different subspecies but simple ecotypes (Geist 1991), the traditional terminology is used here because the issue is unsettled (Mitchell and Gates 2002).

Behavioral information on the wild horse (*Equus ferus caballus*) is limited compared with what is available for its domesticated variant. Today all feral horse populations living in North American reserves are derived from domestic horse and pony stock (Berger 1986). Przewalski's horse (or Takhi, *Equus ferus przewalskii*) is the only surviving wild horse (Groves 2002). Although it has recently been successfully reintroduced into Mongolia, Przewalski's horse is currently mostly confined to zoos and small reserves (Bouman *et al*. 1994; King and Gurnell 2005, 2007). This sub-species can be distinguished genetically from the closely related domestic horse (Lau *et al*. 2009).

Data on migratory patterns for bison and horse are scarce. Both species would have been easier to find and kill in summer and fall, a period during which animals gain weight, prepare for the rut, and initiate the shift to the winter range. However, migratory shifts for wood and plains bison are not as predictable as for reindeer. At the end of the summer, bison aggregate in preparation for the rut (Berger and Cunningham 1994). Horses, whose basic social unit is the harem, rarely gather in large groups (Slade and Godfrey 1982). Moreover, the horse is a relatively sedentary species relative to reindeer (King and Gurnell 2005). Therefore, local abundances of horse might have fluctuated less across seasons relative to bison or reindeer.

SYNCHRONY OF BIRTHING IN REINDEER, BISON, AND HORSE

Archaeological predictions about seasons of ungulate procurement normally assume birth synchrony and a single calving period per year. These assumptions are strongly supported for *Rangifer*. Calving occurs once a year in late spring and seems to be tightly related to photoperiod and plant phenology (Post *et al*. 2003; Pösö 2005). The peak of the calving season in a given population varies little from year to year, almost always falling within the same week. Occasionally, this period extends to two weeks and, rarely, to three weeks. However, variation in the peak calving period may occur within a population over time, particularly if weather and/or grazing conditions change. Favorable conditions promote an earlier initiation of calving and thus an earlier peak period. Unfavorable conditions cause a delay in the onset of calving and thus a later peak in calving (Reimers 1979, 2002).

In *Rangifer*, the peak of the calving season takes place between early May and the end of June and varies primarily as a function of location, overall condition of the herd, and latitude. Skoog (1968) and Parker (1972) have noted that 90 to 95% of the births occur within a two-week period in the Nelchina (Alaska) and Kaminuriak (west of Hudson Bay, Canada) barren-ground caribou herds. Kelsall (1968:177) reported that 75% of the calf crop was born over a single week in the Beverly barren-ground caribou herd of northwestern Canada. According to Syroechkovskii (1995:127), 90% of the calves in Taimyr (Siberia) are born within a 10-day period at the end of June. The same author indicates that calving takes place somewhat earlier (mid-May to end of May) in Yakutia, the Trans-Baikal region, and the Chukchi Peninsula. The calving season is also very restricted for three wild reindeer populations of southern Norway, with 90% of calves born within a 10-day period between early May and the end of the same month, depending on the herd (Holthe 1975).

A popular explanation for this tight clustering of births is that it represents an adaptation to winter predation in highly seasonal environments (Miller 2003). Calves born in early spring are able to grow stronger by building fat reserves in the warmer months of the year and are more successfully socialized into their mother's social unit compared with those born later in the calving season. These factors increase survival rates. Because birthing is highly synchronous in reindeer, some developmental features, especially fetal bones, can be used to identify seasons of procurement.

Birthing times are more difficult to predict in bison. Typically, calving in plains bison begins in mid-March or early April but appears to occur two weeks later in northern populations (Reynolds *et al.* 1982). After synthesizing data from three national reserves in North America, Berger and Cunningham (1994) concluded that 80% of births are spread over a 23- to 69-day period in spring. Although most births are completed by the end of June, some calves are delivered in October and November and sometimes even later (Reynolds *et al.* 1982). Even within the same population, the calving period may be delayed up to a month depending on the year (Meagher 1973). From an archaeological point of view, these are calves born "out-of-phase."

There are few data on the birthing schedule of bison from northern latitudes. In wood bison, which are mostly restricted to Canada, calves tend to be born in May through early June (Mitchell and Gates 2002). Calving in European bison herds occurs mostly in May and June, although some individuals give birth as late as October (Pucek *et al.* 2003). Berger and Cunningham (1994) have emphasized that healthy females "adjust" gestation to give birth in synchrony. However, undernourished females do not and may give birth much later. For these reasons, archaeological predictions about seasons of procurement for bison are unlikely to be as precise as those for reindeer, especially when dealing with nutritionally stressed populations. This is because the birth season for bison can last from two to three months, with as much as 10% of the estimates falling outside of this range.

Przewalski's horse differs from the domestic horse by having 66 instead of 64 chromosomes (Ryder 1994; Lau *et al.* 2009). Despite these genetic differences, the domestic horse and Przewalski's horse produce fertile hybrids and are very similar in reproductive physiology and general behavior (Berger 1986; Asa 2002). Importantly, they share a common gestation period and foal at the same time of year. In captivity, 75% of pregnant Przewalski mares give birth between April and July (Montfort *et al.* 1994). Berger (1986) noted that in a feral horse population from Nevada, 75% of births occurred in April and May and 85% from April through June. As for bison, births in some populations of feral horses may occur much later, for instance in November and December, or even in February (Berger 1986). However, Nevada's climate is far more temperate than that of Late Pleistocene France, which experienced greater seasonal fluctuations. Consequently, out-of-phase births are expected to have been less common in Late Pleistocene France because of increased selective pressure for birth synchrony.

Seasonality Patterns in Pleistocene Assemblages from France

Despite several decades of research, the question of how many reindeer subspecies roamed Paleolithic France remains unsettled. Nor do we know the number of migrations made within a year, the distance covered during these migrations, or whether the migrations were horizontal or altitudinal. However, recent and ongoing isotopic studies may soon shed light on these issues (e.g., Britton 2009). Although our knowledge of many details of the migratory habits of Pleistocene reindeer is limited, high birth synchrony can safely be assumed, given the very tight clustering of births observed in virtually all *Rangifer* populations.

Spiess (1979:77) suggested mid-May as the peak of the calving season for reindeer in Pleistocene France. Ethological data on Eurasian herds (Holthe 1975; Syroechkovskii 1995) suggest that this proposition is probably not too far off the mark. However, current wild reindeer populations are found farther north than the Pleistocene herds of southwestern France, and differences in photoperiod might have resulted in a slightly earlier onset of the calving season in the latter region.

Seasonality data provided by Spiess (1979), Gordon (1988), Castel (1999), Costamagno (1999), and Fontana (2000) may indicate that most of the Upper Paleolithic sites sampled in France document winter/spring procurement of reindeer. However, some of these studies were based on the analysis of cementum annuli, the preservation of which has been shown to be frequently affected by problems of collagen leaching and recrystallization (Stutz 2002). These problems are important because they may yield erroneous estimates of season of death. Therefore, except for a small number of recent studies (e.g., Rendu 2007) that address taphonomic issues of collagen leaching and recrystallization, cementum studies that were performed using the standard approach should be examined with extreme caution.

As noted earlier, several seasonality studies point to winter/spring procurement of reindeer. However, there are several exceptions to this generalization. A cementum annuli study led Rendu (2007) to conclude that during the Aurignacian at Isturitz in the Pyrenees, reindeer were obtained in the summer. Using the standard approach to the analysis of cementum annuli, Martin (2004) found evidence of reindeer procurement during the warm season in the Badegoulian and Magdalenian layers at Les Peyrugues and the Abri Gandil in the Quercy region. Lastly, Enloe and David (1997) argued that Verberie and Pincevent, two Magdalenian open-air sites located in the Paris basin, were occupied during the fall season, as suggested by crown height measurements.

Several studies document the seasons of bison procurement in Paleolithic assemblages from France. A standard analysis of cementum annuli of three bison teeth from the Mousterian site of Pech de l'Azé I suggested to Armand *et al.* (2001) that deaths occurred in late fall/early winter and late winter/early spring. A larger sample from the same site indicated to Rendu (2007) that bison were procured between spring and fall, depending on the level. At La Quina, also a Mousterian site, bison kills were attributed to the end of the warm season (Rendu 2007). A sample of d_4 from Mauran, a late Mousterian open-air site located in Haute-Garonne, has been interpreted as indicating a summer to early fall occupation (David and Enloe 1993). This interpretation is corroborated by a cementum annuli study of twenty teeth from the same assemblage, which points to a late summer to early fall occupation (Rendu 2007). Concerning the Upper Paleolithic, David and Poulain (2002) suggested that bison fetal bones in the Aurignacian level VII of Arcy-sur-Cure reflect winter procurement.

Much of the information on seasons of horse procurement in Pleistocene France derives from the work of Olsen (1989) and Burke (1995; Burke and Castanet 1995). According to these authors, during the Magdalenian, horses were mostly obtained in the summer and winter, with more data pointing to the importance of the former season. In contrast, horse procurement was infrequent in fall and spring. Few data are available for periods earlier than the Magdalenian. During the Aurignacian occupation at Solutré, horse appear to have been primarily procured in spring/summer, with few individuals acquired in late summer/fall (Olsen 1989). A cementum annuli study of horse teeth from the Aurignacian of Isturitz suggests summer kills (Rendu 2007). The presence of fetal bones and dental data indicate early- to mid-winter deaths in the Aurignacian of Arcy-sur-Cure (David and Poulain 2002).

METHODS USED AT SAINT-CÉSAIRE FOR DERIVING SEASONALITY DATA

At Saint-Césaire, several methods were employed to assess seasonality patterns. These methods focus on dental remains, the development cycle of antlers, patterns of bone fusion, and fetal growth. Although invasive methods such as cementum analysis can provide insights into seasonal modes of exploitation of large ungulates, these approaches were avoided to preserve the integrity of the specimens. The methods used in the analysis of the Saint-Césaire assemblages are reviewed in this section.

Dental Remains

In the assemblages, age estimates for teeth were generated using three methods: crown height measurements, patterns of wear, and tooth eruption sequences. All three methods were used to predict seasons of procurement whenever possible.

A common problem with aging methods based on tooth eruption and wear is that individual variation may be significant, especially with increasing ontogenic age. This is the case for reindeer (Miller 1974; Pike-Tay *et al.* 2000). Skogland (1988) and Kojola and colleagues (1998) argued that the quality of standing crops of terrestrial lichens in winter ranges significantly influences dental wear in this species. Poor crops, often due to overgrazing, would increase particle ingestion and, ultimately, tooth wear. However, although individual variation may be significant in adults, it is usually lesser in juveniles, particularly for individuals in their first, and to a lesser extent, second year.

As reviewed by Miller (1974), most studies are in general agreement about the sequence and timing of tooth eruption in reindeer, especially concerning the emergence of the M_1 (between 3 to 5 months) and M_2 (between 10 and 13 months). Because the range of variation in eruption is relatively small for these teeth, their stages of development can be considered reliable indicators of season of death. However, variation in the timing of the eruption of the M_3 may be up to a year, which makes this tooth unsuitable for seasonality studies.

Ten arbitrary age classes based on variations in tooth wear were created using the photographs of aged mandibles provided by Miller (1974). These classes are listed in Table 7.1. The first six age classes (classes I–VI) of this table correspond to age increments smaller than or equal to 6 months. These age classes were used to determine seasons of reindeer procurement at Saint-Césaire. Because there are many rapid and dramatic changes in reindeer dentition during the first six months of life, age classes II and III cover shorter time intervals than subsequent ones. The pooling of males and females in this classification does not significantly affect the results, given that both sexes show comparable levels of wear in these age classes (Miller 1974).

TABLE 7.1. *Arbitrary age classes used in the analysis of the reindeer teeth from Saint-Césaire*

Number	Age class	Correspondence with Miller's plates: cutoff points
I	Fetus to neonate	fetus *to* p. 38: left column, 1st mandible from the top
II	0.25–3 months	p. 38: left column, 1st mandible from the top *to* p. 38: left column, 4th mandible from the top
III	3–5 months	p. 38: left column, 4th mandible from the top *to* p. 38: left column, 5th mandible from the top
IV	5–12 months	p. 38: left column, 5th mandible from the top *to* p. 39: left column, 2nd mandible from the top
V	12–17 months	p. 39: left column, 2nd mandible from the top *to* p. 39: right column, 8th (last) mandible from the top
VI	17–24 months	p. 39: right column, 8th (last) mandible from the top *to* p. 41: right column, 6th mandible from the top
VII	24–36 months	p. 41: right column, 6th mandible from the top *to* p. 43: right column, 6th mandible from the top
VIII	36–72 months	p. 43: right column, 6th mandible from the top *to* p. 45: right column, 5th mandible from the top
IX	72–123 months	p. 45: right column, 5th mandible from the top *to* p. 47: right column, 9th mandible from the top
X	123 months and over	wear greater than p. 47: right column, 9th mandible from the top

The classification is based on data from Miller (1974).

To test for consistency, crown heights were also measured on deciduous teeth. Specifically, measurements were made on the protoconid, that is, on the buccal side of the mesial lobe, of all d_3 (dP$_3$) and d_4 (dP$_4$) identified in the Saint-Césaire assemblages. Pooling of these teeth for analysis was often necessary because of the small sample size but was limited, as much as possible, to specimens attributed to distinct individuals. Pooling d_3 and d_4 is not unreasonable, given that crown heights on adjacent teeth are highly correlated in *Rangifer* (Pike-Tay *et al.* 2000).

Protoconid height values for Saint-Césaire were compared with values for the Magdalenian assemblages of Pincevent and Verberie, two open-air sites that each reflect a single autumnal season of procurement (David and Enloe 1993; Enloe 1997). The Gravettian couche V from the rockshelter of Le Flageolet (Enloe 1993) is also considered in these comparisons because this location is similar to Saint-Césaire in terms of topography. However, this type of comparison should be used with great caution because it can lead to self-reinforcing cycles of season determination (Whittaker and Enloe 2000). To avoid circularity, in the concluding section of this chapter, the interpretations are confronted with the reference data presented in Table 7.1, which are based on modern individuals of well-controlled[2] ages.

[2] F. L. Miller (pers. comm., 2003) pointed out that none of the 999 caribou (943 from the Kaminuriak population and 56 from the Beverly population) in the sample used by Pike-Tay (1995) were animals "tagged at birth" (see also Dauphiné 1976:14). Rather, the "age composition of the Kaminuriak Population was estimated from tooth eruption and replacement, by linear dental measurements, and by microscopic examination of annuli in the cementum of mandibular teeth, prepared histologically" (Miller 1974:6). Miller believes, however, that precise and accurate age estimates were generated for animals between 1 and 39 months old by comparing information on season of capture, sex, antler development, body size, tooth eruption, dental wear patterns, and counts of cementum annuli. His position is that age estimates resulting

Equine breeders and biologists commonly use incisors for aging horses (e.g., Garrott 1991). Unfortunately, horse incisors are rarely numerous in Paleolithic assemblages. To solve this problem, Levine (1979) devised an aging system based on premolars and molars, which are usually far more abundant than incisors in archaeological samples. Her observations show that seasons of horse procurement can be determined with some accuracy for the mandible, given that deciduous cheek teeth are replaced over a relatively short period of time by the permanent dentition. Moreover, unlike the deciduous teeth of artiodactyls, those of horses appear fairly resistant to damage. The timing of dental changes described by Levine for juveniles is in general agreement with observations made by Guadelli (1998), although these two authors differ regarding the level of accuracy that they suggest can be achieved with these methods. Guadelli's system often provides broader age intervals, particularly for adults. Both studies were used for interpreting the samples of horse teeth from Saint-Césaire.

Aging methods have also been developed for bison. In the field, biologists generally inspect wear patterns on incisors to estimate age (e.g., Fuller 1959). However, possibly because incisors detach easily from the bodies of dead animals (Berger and Cunningham 1994:61), these teeth generally occur in low numbers in archaeological assemblages. Consequently, archaeologists normally focus on cheek teeth for assessing seasons of procurement for bison as well as horse.

Studies by Frison and Reher (1970, Reher and Frison 1980) and Gifford-Gonzalez (1991) have shown that, as a result of a slow eruption sequence, determining seasons of procurement for bison is relatively difficult. In addition, the aging methods proposed in these studies, which are all based on the same reference collection, have been criticized for their small comparative sample, the lack of information on how the age classes were derived, and the moderate fit obtained between age and crown height (Whittaker and Enloe 2000). Furthermore, little is known about variation in dental wear in bison, although soil types, amount of ingested silica, and extent of vegetal cover are believed to be important contributing factors (Wasilewski 1967; Haynes 1984). Despite these shortcomings, the system developed by Reher and Frison (1980) for individuals under two years of age was used, keeping in mind that the results are probably less precise than those for reindeer and horse.

Antler Development and Cycle

Unlike other cervids, antlers are grown and shed by both sexes in reindeer. The annual cycle of antler development and casting is primarily regulated by alkaline phosphatase, a hormone that varies in level as a function of age and sex (Bubenik *et al.* 2000). Other hormones such as estradiol and IGF-1 (insulin-like growth factor 1) are also involved in the process (Blake *et al.* 1998). It has been hypothesized that antlers give females a selective advantage over bulls during the winter season and enhance the fitness of pregnant versus barren females after parturition by increasing their rank. However, these hypotheses remain controversial (Barrette and Vandal 1990; Kumpula *et al.* 1992;

from the foregoing process are exact for all caribou between 1 and 24 months of age and for most animals between 25 and 39 months old. However, Miller cautions that ages assigned to older caribou should have at least a ± 1 year associated with each age estimate to better reflect the probable limitations (lack of consistency) of the composite approach and the histological examination of dental cementum.

Schaefer and Mahoney 2001; Holand *et al.* 2004). The following is a summary of data provided by various authors on the details of the annual antler cycle (Kelsall 1968; Espmark 1971; Bergerud 1976; Gagnon and Barrette 1992; Reimers 1993; Whitten 1995).

For most individuals, antler growth begins in winter or spring and is completed just before or during the autumn rut. Large bulls start growing their antlers in late March/early April and lose them at the end of the rut between late October and the end of December. Younger bulls usually shed their antlers by February/March, although they sometimes retain antlers as late as April or May. Antlers are cast by most parturient and pregnant females just before, during, or slightly after parturition in late May to mid-June. However, a few pregnant females drop their antlers as early as April or May. Barren females can shed their antlers anytime from April to a few days or weeks *before* the peak of the calving season. New growth is usually initiated a few days after the antlers are cast. Calves lose their small antlers at approximately the same time as barren females. However, these schedules may vary temporally and regionally because healthy populations are more likely to lose their antlers a little earlier than less healthy ones (Gagnon and Barrette 1992; Schaefer and Mahoney 2001).

Prime bulls usually begin antler growth in March, but growth may be delayed until April if the animal is in poor condition. Bulls begin stripping velvet from their antlers after late August and continue to do so through September. They then carry their hard polished antlers until the end of the rut, typically in October–November. Vigorous breeders may become "spent" before the rut is completely over and cast their antlers immediately. Most other breeding bulls cast their antlers soon after the rut is over, sometime from late November into December. Young males from one to four years old may retain their hard antlers from October through March and sometimes into April before shedding them and starting to grow a new pair. Young males carrying the previous year's antlers into May or even June can occasionally be seen among the cows and young females on the calving grounds.

In brief, breeding females are growing antlers in velvet or carrying hard antlers for almost the entire year (Figure 7.1). They are usually without antlers for only a couple of weeks, depending on their nutritional state. The period during which adult males lack antlers is much longer, up to three months. It is important to note that individuals rarely shed both antlers simultaneously; antlers drop one at a time, hours, days or even weeks apart (Bergerud 1976).

Bouchud (1966, 1975) examined thousands of prehistoric antlers with the goal of identifying herd structure, seasons of occupations, and the type (woodland versus barrenground) of reindeer present. Although innovative for its time, Bouchud's method of sexing and aging antlers was flawed, one of the reasons being that it downplayed sexual and developmental variation (Spiess 1979). Another problem with Bouchud's method is that it assumed that all reindeer bear antlers, a view now known to be incorrect. Although females without antlers are rare in barren-ground caribou, they are common in woodland caribou (Reimers 1993; Whitten 1995). For instance, Bergerud (1976) reported that between 28 and 93% of females in woodland caribou populations of Newfoundland lack antlers.

The Newfoundland case is not an isolated phenomenon. Syroechkovskii (1995) pointed out that in several regions of Eurasia (Altai, Yakutia, Siberia), as many as 25 to 33% of the females lack antlers. Moreover, the proportion of antlerless females may

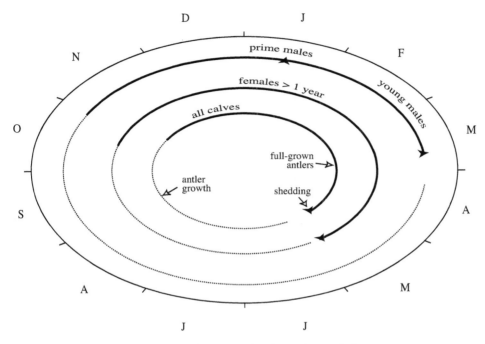

FIGURE 7.1. A simplified summary of the annual antler cycle in reindeer.

also vary through time within a single herd, depending on health condition, snow cover, and population density (Espmark 1971; Reimers 1993; Schaefer and Mahoney 2001). For these reasons, the proportion of male and female antlers recovered in archaeological assemblages cannot be used as indicators of sex ratios or herd structure (see also Weinstock 2000). In contrast, antlers are seldom absent in males, and little variation is recorded between subspecies (Bergerud 1976; Whitten 1995).

The time required for antlers to deteriorate on the ground after shedding has important implications for the interpretation of seasonality patterns. One reason for this is that the viscosity and elasticity of newly shed antlers makes them an ideal medium for tools because they resist longitudinal compression and impact far better than dry antlers (Liolios 1999). For this reason, dry or damaged antlers are unlikely to have been utilized extensively by Upper Paleolithic groups, except, perhaps, as drying racks. Unfortunately, we will see that data relevant to these issues are relatively limited.

Rodents, carnivores (especially foxes), and ungulates (including reindeer) are known to gnaw on shed antlers (Bergerud *et al.* 2008). According to Reimers (1993:1323), shed antlers do not seem to last long among some reindeer populations in Norway: "the fact that reindeer frequently chew on cast antlers during summer . . . and that almost all animals killed during winter in Snøhetta and Hardangervidda had antlers that were heavily gnawed . . . may indicate that minerals are part of the food-limitation complex." According to Bergerud *et al.* (2008) and F. Miller (pers. comm., 2004), gnawing would be more frequent on the tips of the antlers, perhaps because tines often stick up when the antlers are lying on the ground. Moreover, on unshed antlers, tines are more accessible for other caribou/reindeer to gnaw on as well. The relatively large size of the antler base may also dissuade small animals from chewing on it.

However, not all authors agree on the amount of time required for antlers to deteriorate once shed. Spiess (1979) observed some well-preserved specimens in the Canadian Arctic that were four years old. In the same region, F. Miller (pers. comm., 2004) also observed caribou antlers around his camps that had been on the ground for 10 to 20 years but had suffered minimal deterioration and were still suitable for making tools. Miller suspects that the topographic and environmental conditions of a site determine the rate of antler deterioration. For instance, antlers that fall on wet ground seem to deteriorate more rapidly than those that fall on dry ground.

In the large sample (total NISP = 1404) of reindeer antlers from Saint-Césaire, specimens that bear gnaw marks are extremely rare ($n = 3$), suggesting that antlers were collected during the shedding season or removed from animals shortly after death. However, given the variation in the amount of time antlers take to deteriorate, this inference is not particularly strong. Yet it might not be unreasonable to assume that *most* antlers were collected shortly after casting or after the death of the animal because antlers are present in substantial quantities *and* are rarely damaged at Saint-Césaire. This proposition is strengthened when we consider the southerly location of France, which probably enjoyed longer summers in the Late Pleistocene than does the Canadian Arctic today, conditions that would probably have hastened the deterioration of fallen antlers.

Knowing the sex and ontogenic age of antler specimens can shed light on seasons of reindeer procurement because males and females, and juveniles and adults, shed their antlers at different periods of the year. Høymork and Reimers (2002) explored different methods for determining sex in reindeer using antler measurements. These data, which were collected in a study of a semi-domesticated herd from central Norway, are important because they fill a methodological gap in faunal analysis. Although most measurements established in the study (e.g., antler height) cannot be applied to fragmented antlers, one measurement is easily obtained on prehistoric material: the circumference of the burr (i.e., the base of the antler). Høymork and Reimers (2002:81) pointed out that calf antlers cannot be sexed but can be separated without difficulty from those of older individuals because they "have small and distinctive straight, tine-less antlers, which are not easily confused with adults." These are generally referred to as "spike" antlers (*daguets*). It is important to note, however, that some calves do not grow antlers (Bergerud 1976) and that some yearlings, especially females, may also carry spike antlers (F. Miller, pers. comm., 2004).

The results obtained by Høymork and Reimers (2002) indicate that antlers from males older than 2.5 years are generally larger than those of females. They also note that male antlers peak in size at around 6 or 7 years of age and then tend to regress somewhat with age. However, antlers of old males never regress to the point where they could be confused with those of females (Reimers, pers. comm., 2003). Thus, it should be possible to use antler measurements to isolate males older than 2.5 or, with greater confidence, 3.5 years, from all females. On the basis of figure 2 in Høymork and Reimers (2002:78), non-spike antlers with a burr circumference smaller than 80 mm would mostly belong to females. Their study also shows that very few females have a burr circumference larger than 120 mm. Consequently, antlers with a greater circumference would almost certainly belong to males. In summary, the analysis conducted by Høymork and Reimers has three important archaeological implications: i) calf antlers are easy to identify both morphologically and metrically, ii) non-spike burr circumferences smaller than 80 mm

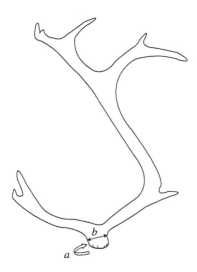

FIGURE 7.2. Measurements taken on the reindeer antlers of Saint-Césaire. Measurement *a* is the burr circumference measured directly on the bony corona, whereas measurement *b* is the anteroposterior diameter of the beam taken 1 cm above the bony corona.

are probably from females, and iii) those that are larger than 120 mm are almost certainly from males.

These threshold values are limited by the fact that they are derived from a single modern herd that may not be representative of prehistoric reindeer populations. A comparison of the measurements derived from the Norwegian calf sample with those taken on the Saint-Césaire spike antlers should clarify this issue. Høymork and Reimers (2002:79) observed mean burr circumferences of 52 and 56 mm for female and male calves, respectively. The mean (54 mm) of these values is larger than the mean for Saint-Césaire (48.5 mm on 10 individuals). This suggests that the calf antlers from Saint-Césaire are somewhat smaller than those from the reference sample. To remove this discrepancy, the threshold values used at Saint-Césaire were scaled down by 11.3%, based on the difference in the mean values of the two samples. Consequently, in the present analysis, non-spike burr circumferences smaller than 71.9 mm (instead of 80 mm) will be considered to derive from females, whereas those that are larger than 107.8 mm (instead of 120 mm) will be assumed to be from males. This scaling routine was not performed in the initial analysis of the data (Morin 2004).

Using these criteria, the numerous antler burrs ($n = 168$) from Saint-Césaire were measured to produce probabilistic statements regarding the sex of the antlers. Combined with data about the type (shed or unshed) of antlers present, these estimations may yield information on the timing of the occupations. In small assemblages, sample size was increased using the following equation, which predicts the circumference of incomplete burrs:

$$b = 0.981 + 0.282 \times a \qquad (1)$$

where b is the burr circumference and a is the anteroposterior diameter of the beam. Measurement a (Figure 7.2) is taken directly on the bony corona (*cercle de pierrures*), whereas measurement b is taken on the beam, 1 cm above the bony corona. Concerning

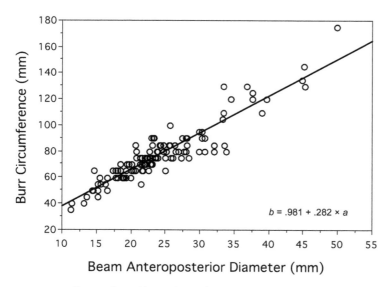

FIGURE 7.3. Regression of burr circumference versus anteroposterior diameter for the reindeer antlers of Saint-Césaire.

this last measurement, when the brow tine (*andouiller d'oeil*) merges with the burr, the point of lowest diameter, often the bony corona, was measured.

The regression shown in Figure 7.3 explains 85.1% of the variation in burr circumference. The data for all of the occupations indicate that no antler with a burr circumference larger than 71.9 mm has an anteroposterior diameter smaller than 20 mm. Furthermore, no antler with a beam circumference larger than 107.8 mm has an anteroposterior diameter smaller than 32 mm. Therefore, in the archaeological assemblages, non-spike antlers with an anteroposterior diameter smaller than 20 mm were attributed to females, whereas values larger than 32 mm were attributed to adult males.

Bone Fusion

Hufthammer (1995) published a summary of bone fusion in reindeer. Her results suggest that the scapula head may be a useful seasonal indicator because the *tuber scapulae* was fused by six months of age on all the specimens she studied, but unfused on a two month-old individual. A loose *tuber scapulae* would thus indicate procurement during summer or late fall. However, it is possible that the fusion of this part varies depending on the nutritional condition of the individual. Bone fusion is too variable in other parts for determining season of death.

Barone (1999) provided information on bone fusion in domestic horse and cattle, which are used here as proxies for wild horse and steppe bison because of a lack of data on the wild forms. Barone reported that many cranial parts fuse at an early age and with limited variation in these species. However, horse and bison crania tend to be severely fragmented in archaeological sites. For this reason, these parts are of limited value for assessing seasonality patterns. More useful is the age at which the horse radius fuses with the ulna (3–5 months). On the basis of this information, an unfused radio-ulna

TABLE 7.2. *Equations used to estimate the ontogenic age (in days) of fetal horse bones*

Part	Source of data	Regression	r^2
Humerus	Habermehl 1975	$y = -9.9036 + 25.6397 \times (\mathrm{SQRT}(x))$	.99
Radius	Guffy *et al.* 1970; Habermehl 1975	$y = 6.77872 + 21.9387 \times (\mathrm{SQRT}(x))$	.99
Metacarpal	Guffy *et al.* 1970; Habermehl 1975	$y = 32.0941 + 20.6867 \times (\mathrm{SQRT}(x))$	.98
Femur	Habermehl 1975	$y = -6.7754 + 22.5592 \times (\mathrm{SQRT}(x))$	.99
Tibia	Guffy *et al.* 1970; Habermehl 1975	$y = 7.91166 + 21.9623 \times (\mathrm{SQRT}(x))$	.98
Metatarsal	Guffy *et al.* 1970; Habermehl 1975	$y = 29.5154 + 19.4317 \times (\mathrm{SQRT}(x))$	.99

The regressions were calculated based on data provided by Guffy *et al.* (1970) and Habermehl (1975, as cited by Prummel 1989). These data are presented in Appendices 13 and 14.
Symbols: y = fetal age in days after conception; x = diaphyseal length in mm; SQRT = square root; r^2 = coefficient of determination.

would signal death sometime in spring to fall. Patterns of bone fusion are too variable in other parts to allow the identification of seasons of procurement.

Fetal Bones

Bones grow very rapidly at the fetal stage. Consequently, season of procurement can be estimated with some accuracy by measuring the diaphyseal length of fetal bones in species characterized by high birth synchrony. In ungulates, the confidence intervals associated with the age predictions may be as short as a few weeks to as long as a few months, depending on the species. However, fetal bones may not preserve well and are sometimes difficult to identify to the species level. The descriptions provided by Prummel (1987a; 1987b; 1988; 1989) facilitated the identification of the fetal remains from Saint-Césaire.

The approximate age of reindeer fetal bones can be estimated on the basis of the linear regression presented by Spiess (1979). However, the accuracy of this equation is limited by the small sample size used to derive it. The equations of Bünger-Marek (1972; as cited in Prummel 1989) for fetal cattle are probably good approximations of bison fetal growth because the two species are interfertile (Mitchell and Gates 2002). For horse, raw data from Habermehl (1975, as cited in Prummel 1989) and data read from the graphs of Guffy *et al.* (1970) were used to generate a number of equations (Table 7.2 and Appendices 13 and 14). These equations use the square root of the diaphyseal length to predict age in days. A substantial amount of variation in these data, between 98.5 and 99.4%, is explained by the regressions (Figure 7.4). Moreover, the fit between the two sources of data is very good, which increases the reliability of the results.

Incorporating Variation in Birth Synchrony in Fetal Age Estimates

Seasonality studies relying on fetal age estimates assume birth synchrony. Dispersion in the distribution of births within a given year and inter-annual variation in the onset of the calving season are rarely taken into account in these age estimates. Both sources of variation are assessed in this section.

In the present analysis, the developmental age predictions for bison fetal bones are presented along with an 80% confidence interval of 60 days. To compensate for uncertainties regarding the peak date of the calving period in Late Pleistocene France, a conservative birth interval is used here. This interval was computed by adding 10 days – an arbitrary figure – to the mean number of days (49.6, Berger and Cunningham 1994:117) necessary to account for 80% of the births in various North American populations of bison.[3] August 1 is considered the peak day of conception, and the mean gestation length is assumed to be approximately 285 days (range: 276.6–292.5 days in a 4-year period, Berger and Cunningham 1994:117). More inclusive confidence intervals (e.g., 90% or 95%) could not be calculated with the available data.

The birthing period in a feral horse population of Nevada is slightly more extended than in bison, with 75% of the births generally occurring within a period of 60 days (Berger 1986:104). However, the calving season might have been slightly shorter in the more seasonal environment of Late Pleistocene France. Taking these observations into account, the 80% confidence interval proposed for horse is 70 days. Conception in the study area was set as beginning on June 15, whereas the mean gestation length is considered to be about 345 days (Berger 1986; Montfort *et al.* 1994).

As discussed earlier, births are highly synchronous in reindeer. In addition, the onset of the calving season is comparable between populations living at the same latitude. As a result, a more inclusive confidence interval can be calculated for this species. The 90% confidence interval proposed here covers 20 days. The mean gestation length is estimated to be approximately 228 days (Miller 1982; Geist 1998), and the peak breeding date is set as being October 1.

SEASONS OF PROCUREMENT IN THE ASSEMBLAGES

With these methods in hand, it is now possible to establish seasonality patterns at Saint-Césaire. Seasonality data are provided for each occupation, including the mixed EJOP and EJO samples.

1. THE DENTICULATE MOUSTERIAN EGPF ASSEMBLAGE. An isolated d$_3$ of bison has been attributed to a fetus or a very young calf in this assemblage. The crown wear patterns suggest that the individual died in winter or spring. An indeterminate lower deciduous tooth of horse is unworn. Death in spring or early summer is most likely because modern comparative material suggests that the individual to whom this tooth belonged was younger than four months and no more than a month old, based on data provided by Levine (1979). Unfortunately, no other information on seasonality is available for this level. Importantly, EGPF is the only assemblage discussed in this section that lacks reindeer antlers. Additional information on seasonality should become available once the study of this level is completed.

---

[3] It is important to note that the interval given by Berger and Cunningham (1994) does not correspond to the most compressed period of births. Rather, the interval reflects the time elapsed from the *first* birth to 80% of the births. As a result, 40% of the births on each side of the mean birthing date may give an interval smaller than the 49.6 days time span provided here. However, because the distribution of births in a year tends to follow a lognormal distribution (Berger and Cummingham 1994), which results in most births being compressed into the first few weeks of the calving season with increasingly fewer births occurring later, this issue is probably minor.

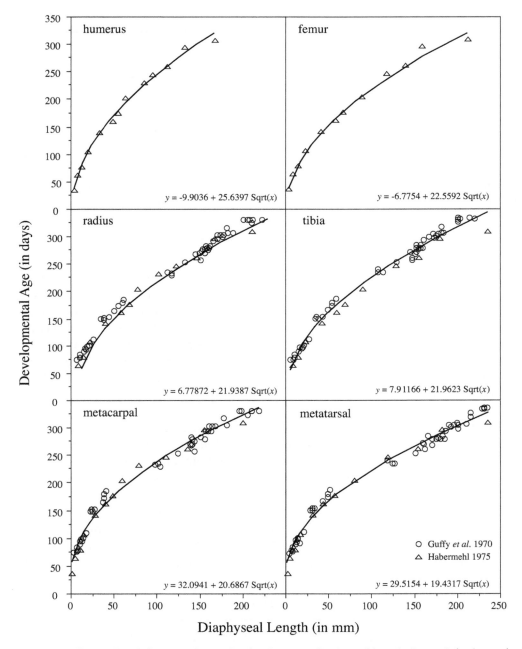

FIGURE 7.4. Regressions of ontogenic age (in days) versus diaphyseal length (in mm) for horse fetal bones. The data are from Guffy *et al.* (1970) and Habermehl (1975, as cited in Prummel 1989).

2. THE DENTICULATE MOUSTERIAN EJOP INF ASSEMBLAGE. More data on seasonality was gathered for this level. A d_2 and a d_3 or d_4, both of horse, are characterized by an absence of wear. It is unclear whether these teeth derive from the same individual. Using the age classification of Levine, these teeth are from a fetus or a foal that was less than two weeks old, which implies death in spring or early summer.

TABLE 7.3. *Percentages of shed and unshed antlers by level at Saint-Césaire*

	Unshed antlers		Shed antlers		Total	
	n	%	n	%	n	%
Evol Aurignacian (Ejj)	3	75.0	1	25.0	4	100.0
Evol Aurignacian (Ejm)	9	45.0	11	55.0	20	100.0
Middle Auri (Ejf)	47	67.1	23	32.9	70	100.0
Middle Auri (Ejo sup)	1	11.1	8	88.9	9	100.0
low density (Ejo inf)	2	25.0	6	75.0	8	100.0
EJO (inf or sup)	2	28.6	5	71	7	100.0
Moust/Châtel (Ejop sup)	3	13.0	20	87.0	23	100.0
Dent Mousterian (Ejop inf)	0	0.0	8	100.0	8	100.0
EJOP (inf or sup)	2	10.5	17	89	19	100.0
Total	69	41.1	99	58.9	168	100.0

In this and the following tables, the mixed EJOP and EJO samples are shown in italics.

Eight reindeer antler burrs are documented in this occupation. All are shed antlers from juveniles or adults (Table 7.3). Calves are not represented in this antler sample. Three of the antlers in Figure 7.5 are attributed to females and might have been obtained in the snow-free season. Although incomplete, a shed burr with a circumference larger than 115 mm is attributed to a male. This specimen was possibly collected in winter or in the snow-free season. A fetal bone from an unidentified mammal was found in this level (Table 7.4). Death in fall or winter can be suggested for this specimen, assuming that it is from an ungulate.

3. THE MOUSTERIAN/CHÂTELPERRONIAN (EJOP SUP) ASSEMBLAGE. An unworn d_3 or d_4 of horse was assigned to an individual that died at a very young age, well before four months, based on tooth wear from a modern individual of that age. According to Levine's classification, this tooth may indicate the presence of a fetus or neonate. Death in spring or early summer is probable in this case.

Three teeth can be used to identify seasons of reindeer procurement. Two teeth, a d_4 and a d_3, are from individuals that were in their first and second winter or spring, respectively, when they died (Table 7.5). The third individual is represented by a d_2 and was procured in summer or fall. Crown height comparisons with Verberie and

TABLE 7.4. *Distribution of fetal bones by species and level*

	Horse	Artiodactyl	Mammal	Total
	n	n	n	n
Evol Aurignacian (Ejj)	–	–	1	1
Evol Aurignacian (Ejm)	2	–	–	2
Middle Aurignacian (Ejf)	12	1	9	22
EJO (inf or sup)	2	–	1	3
Moust/Châtel (Ejop sup)	–	–	7	7
Dent Mousterian (Ejop inf)	–	–	1	1
EJOP (inf or sup)	–	–	3	3
Total	16	1	22	39

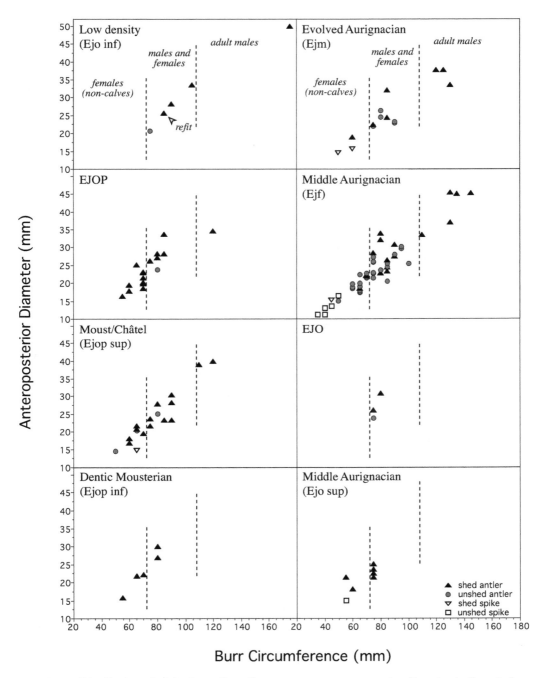

FIGURE 7.5. Distribution of antler burr circumference versus anteroposterior diameter in the reindeer assemblages of Saint-Césaire. Non-calf burr circumferences less than 71.9 mm (left dashed line in the diagrams) likely belonged to females, whereas those greater than 107.8 mm (right dashed line in the diagrams) are attributed to males (see text for details).

TABLE 7.5. *Distribution of reindeer teeth by age class for individuals younger than 24 months*

	Age Classes							
	I (fetus)	II (0–3)	III (3–5)	IV (5–12)	V (12–17)	VI (17–24)	V/VI (15–20)	total
Evol Auri (Ejj)					1		1	2
Evol Auri (Ejm)						2	1	3
Middle Auri (Ejf)				9		2	1	12
Middle Auri (Ejo sup)	1							1
EJO (inf or sup)				1				1
Moust/Chât (Ejop sup)				1	1	1		3
EJOP (inf or sup)				1[a]				1
Total	1			12	2	5	3	23

The age classes are those defined in Table 7.1 and are indicated along with the age interval (in months). The mixed EJOP and EJO samples are shown in italics.

[a] Most likely from the Mousterian/Châtelperronian (EJOP sup) level based on stratigraphic information.

Pincevent – two Magdalenian sites inferred to have been occupied in the fall season (discussed earlier) – are compatible with these estimates (Figure 7.6).

Several reindeer antlers are found in this level, the majority (87.0%) of which are shed antlers (Figure 7.7). A shed spike would have been collected in the snow-free season. At least six (one not shown in Figure 7.5) shed and two unshed antlers are from females, based on burr circumference. The shed antlers were possibly gathered sometime between spring and fall, the unshed ones between fall and spring. In addition, three shed antlers (one not shown in Figure 7.5) are assigned to males. These antlers were likely collected in the snow-free season.

Two isolated d_4, which may belong to the same individual, can be used for determining the seasons of bison procurement. These teeth are unworn and may have been erupting at the time of death. On the basis of the classifications of Reher and Frison, these teeth indicate acquisition in spring or summer. Two M_1 or M_2, visibly from two distinct individuals, do not show evidence of wear. According to Reher and Frison's data, these teeth are from calves or yearlings obtained in spring/summer.

Seven fetal bones are associated with this level. Unfortunately, none could be taxonomically identified. Assuming that these bones are from ungulates, their size is consistent with death in fall or winter.

The EJOP sup level contains three fish vertebrae from two species (salmon and an unidentified cyprinid). These three vertebrae correspond to two or three individuals. Because fish vertebrae grow incremental structures, the season of capture can sometimes be inferred by using the proportion of the last annulus that is present (Le Gall 2003). According to Le Gall (pers. comm., 2002), two of the fish vertebrae are associated with a fall and spring capture, respectively. The third vertebra is broken, but the last annulus is visible on the fragment. This individual died in winter. These results may imply that the fish were procured at different seasons of the year or may reflect the imperfect preservation of the external annulus on some or all of the remains. Given that these vertebrae were found together, the latter explanation is favored here. It is unknown whether these fish remains were brought to the site by humans or by other animals.

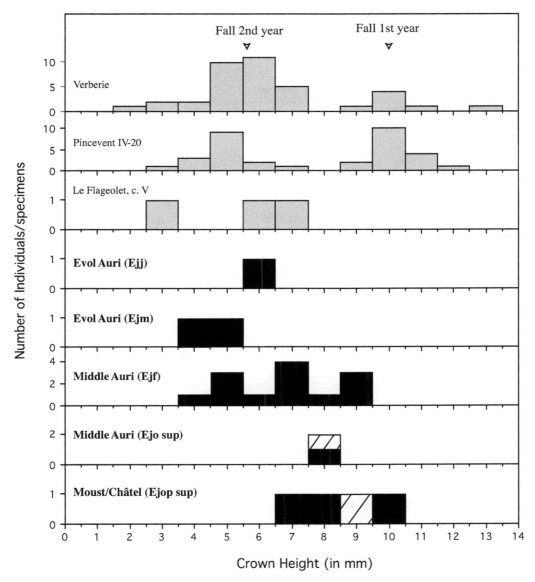

FIGURE 7.6. Crown height measurements for reindeer d4 and d3 from Saint-Césaire compared to Verberie (Magdalenian, Enloe 1997:98, figure 2), Pincevent IV-20 (Magdalenian, David and Enloe 1993:34, figure 2), and Le Flageolet, couche V (Gravettian, David and Enloe 1993:35, figure 3). Measurements were taken on the protoconid, except in two cases where the measurements were taken on the metaconid. The stippled specimen in the EJOP sup assemblage is from the EJOP sample, whereas the stippled specimen in the EJO sup assemblage is from the EJO sample. These specimens probably belong to the layers shown in the figure.

4. THE EJOP SAMPLE (EJOP INF OR EJOP SUP). A horse d_2 that shows little wear was attributed to a near-term fetus or a foal that was no more than 1 or 2 months old. This individual died in spring or early summer. Season of bison procurement can be investigated using three unworn teeth. Two are isolated d_4 that were possibly erupting

FIGURE 7.7. Shed antlers of reindeer from the Mousterian/Châtelperronian level of Saint-Césaire.

when the animals died, whereas the third is a M_2. Spring or summer is the probable season of death in these cases.

A reindeer d_4 is compatible with procurement in winter or spring. However, based on its stratigraphic position, there is little doubt that this specimen belonged to the Mousterian/Châtelperronian (EJOP sup) level. Several antlers have been identified in the EJOP assemblage. Eleven shed (one not shown in Figure 7.5) antlers are attributed to females and would have been collected during the snow-free season. An unshed antler from a male was possibly obtained sometime between fall and spring. In addition, three fetal bones were recovered from this level. These could not be identified to taxon but probably reflect death in fall or winter.

5. THE LOW DENSITY (EJO INF) ASSEMBLAGE. This small faunal assemblage contains several reindeer antlers, mostly shed. One unshed antler (not shown in Figure 7.5) from a female was presumably obtained sometime between fall and spring. One of the shed antlers, identified by an arrow in the figure, was refitted with its pedicle (Figure 7.8). This individual apparently died shortly before shedding its antlers. Procurement of this specimen probably took place in late winter or spring. Two shed antlers, including a very large burr from a prime-aged individual, are from males (only the larger specimen is shown in Figure 7.5). These antlers might have been collected in winter or in the snow-free season.

6. THE MIDDLE AURIGNACIAN EJO SUP ASSEMBLAGE. A reindeer d_3 indicates the presence of a near-term fetus or a neonate in this level. This individual died in winter or spring, a finding that is consistent with seasonality estimates for Pincevent and Verberie, which were based on crown height measurements. Reindeer antlers are present in this assemblage. Two antlers, which are probably shed, are from females. Collection of these

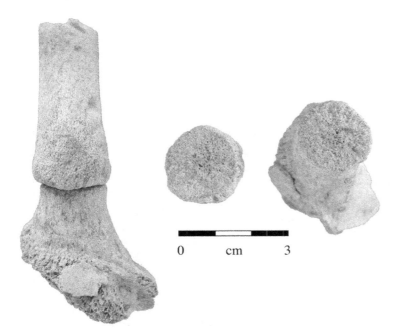

FIGURE 7.8. A reindeer antler from the low-density (EJO inf) assemblage refitted with its pedicle.

antlers might have occurred during the snow-free period. An unshed spike antler was probably obtained sometime during fall through spring.

7. THE EJO SAMPLE (EJO INF AND EJO SUP). Two horse fetal bones, a humerus and a metapodial, are present in the EJO sample (Table 7.6). The humerus comes from an approximately 150-day-old fetus that would have died sometime between early October and mid-December (Figure 7.9). The metapodial may belong to the same individual. One fetal remain from an unidentified mammal was also recovered. This last specimen indicates fall or winter death. Concerning reindeer, only three burrs, two shed and one unshed, could be measured. None of them could be sexed. Lastly, a reindeer d_3 indicates an individual killed in winter or spring.

8. THE MIDDLE AURIGNACIAN EJF ASSEMBLAGE. Information on seasonality is rich and varied for this assemblage. A horse deciduous incisor is attributed to a near-term fetus or a newborn foal less than 2 months old. On the basis of this estimate, this individual died in spring or early summer. A slightly worn d_3 or d_4 indicates the presence of a second foal approximately 2 to 3 months old (Figure 7.10). In this case, death would have occurred in summer. A horse radius has no attached ulna. This specimen provides additional evidence for spring or summer acquisition of horses.

Eleven juvenile reindeer (nine calves and two yearlings) appear to have been killed in winter/spring, as suggested by tooth wear patterns. However, two individuals lie near the upper (older) boundary of their respective age classes and are close to overlapping with the subsequent age class. These specimens indicate procurement sometime between late winter and early summer. An additional reindeer appears to have died in summer or fall.

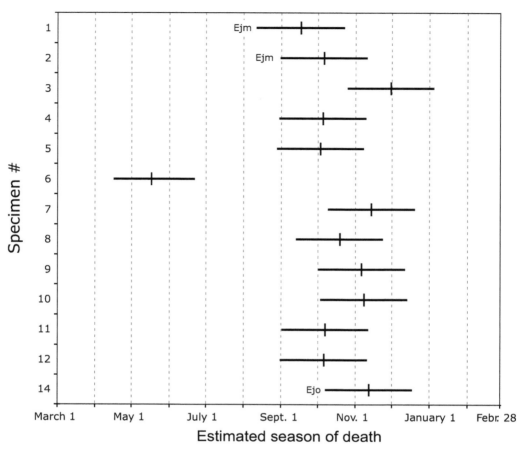

FIGURE 7.9. Estimated season of death for the horse fetal remains of Saint-Césaire. The vertical bar indicates the central date, whereas the horizontal bar shows the confidence interval associated with the central date. The data and specimen numbers are from Table 7.6. Specimens #3–12 are from the Middle Aurignacian EJF level.

FIGURE 7.10. A horse d3 or d4 (right) from the Middle Aurignacian EJF level of Saint-Césaire.

TABLE 7.6. *Estimation of season of death, including confidence intervals, for the fetal bones from Saint-Césaire*

Specimen #, level	Part	Length (mm)	Age at death (days)	Estimated date of death	Confidence interval
1. Evol Auri Ejm	Horse left femur	19.9	94	17 September	12 Aug–22 Oct
2. Evol Auri Ejm	Horse right humerus	23.1	113	6 October	1 Sept–10 Nov
3. Mid Auri Ejf	Horse right femur	60.0*	168	30 November	26 Oct–4 Jan
4. Mid Auri Ejf	"	27.8	112	5 October	31 Aug–9 Nov
5. Mid Auri Ejf	Horse right tibia	21.8	110	3 October	29 Aug–7 Nov
6. Mid Auri Ejf	Horse left metatarsal	255.0	336	17 May	13 April–21 June
7. Mid Auri Ejf	Horse metatarsal	40.0*	152	14 November	10 Oct–19 Dec
8. Mid Auri Ejf	Horse right humerus	28.0*	126	19 October	14 Sept–23 Nov
9. Mid Auri Ejf	Horse left radius	39.2	144	6 November	2 Oct–11 Dec
10. Mid Auri Ejf	Horse right radius	40.5	146	8 November	4 Oct–13 Dec
11. Mid Auri Ejf	Horse metacarpal	15.7	114	7 October	2 Sept–11 Nov
12. Mid Auri Ejf	Horse metapodial[a]	14.9	105–112	6 October	1 Sept–10 Nov
13. Mid Auri Ejf	Artiodactyl right radius[b]	30.0*	133	11 December	12 Nov–10 Jan
14. EJO (inf or sup)	Horse right femur	48.0*	150	12 November	8 Oct–17 Dec

Asterisks denote extrapolated measurements.
[a] Calculated for the metatarsal and metacarpal. The 80% confidence interval incorporates both age predictions.
[b] The developmental age of this specimen is calculated using the equation for bison. Unfortunately, no equation exists for the reindeer radius.

Focusing now on crown height in the EJF assemblage, three modes can be observed in Figure 7.6. It is unclear whether these modes testify to an intermittent occupation of the site or are simply statistical artifacts caused by the small size of the sample. Unlike Pincevent and Verberie, crown heights in the EJF assemblage suggest that juveniles were mostly obtained in the snow-covered season and in the early summer, as seems to be the case for at least some of the individuals from couche V at Le Flageolet (other individuals at this site seem to have been obtained in late summer/early fall). Overall, during the Middle Aurignacian EJF occupation at Saint-Césaire, wear patterns and crown height measurements imply that reindeer juveniles were mostly killed in the cold season and in the beginning of the snow-free season.

The EJF assemblage comprises a large sample of reindeer antlers. Unshed antlers are relatively abundant (67.1%) in this sample, in contrast to the older levels where they account for no more than 28.6% of the antler burrs (Figure 7.11). This increase is

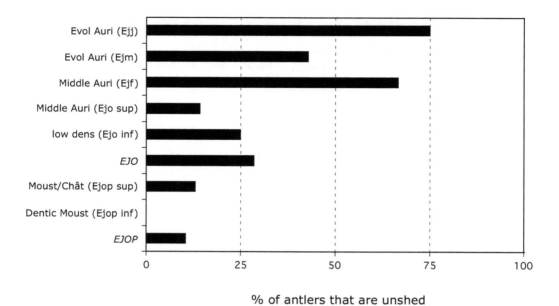

% of antlers that are unshed

FIGURE 7.11. Variation in the percentage of unshed antlers in the sequence of Saint-Césaire. Percentages are calculated relative to the sum of antler burrs. The data are from TABLE 7.3.

statistically significant ($t_s = 3.50$, $p < .001$, EJO sup vs. EJF, data from Table 7.3). This change in the proportions of unshed and shed antlers may signal a slight shift in the period of antler acquisition.

Some of the antlers from EJF could be sexed. A minimum of seventeen females are represented by fourteen unshed and three shed antlers. The unshed antlers were obtained sometime between fall and spring, whereas the shed specimens were most likely procured during the snow-free period. The five shed antlers attributed to males are suggestive of collection sometime between spring and fall. All but one of the six spike antlers identified are shed. The shed spike antlers were most likely acquired during the warm season, whereas the unshed one would have been obtained sometime from fall to spring.

Fetal bones are well represented in this level. Twelve specimens are attributed to horse, one is from an unidentified artiodactyl (most likely reindeer or bison), and nine could only be attributed to the mammal class. A minimum of seven individuals are represented in the sample of horse fetal bones (Figures 7.12 and 7.13). Ontogenic age estimates signal death in fall for all but one of the fetal horse specimens (Figure 7.9). The exception is a left metatarsal from a fetus that died in spring. The radius of an artiodactyl fetus may correspond to one of the two following periods of procurement, depending on the species to which it belongs. If the specimen is from a bison, death might have taken place in late fall or early winter, whereas if the specimen is from a reindeer, death would have occurred in winter (this last inference is based on visual estimation because no equation is available for reindeer radii). Diaphyseal lengths of the other, unidentified, fetal remains are compatible with a fall or winter occupation, assuming that these bones belong to one of the three most common taxa at Saint-Césaire.

FIGURE 7.12. Fetal horse radii from the Middle Aurignacian EJF level of Saint-Césaire.

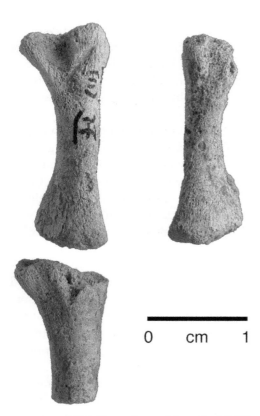

FIGURE 7.13. Fetal horse humeri from the Middle Aurignacian EJF (upper left) and the Evolved Aurignacian EJM (lower left) levels. The provenance of the right specimen is unknown.

FIGURE 7.14. A mandibular series of deciduous teeth of horse from the Evolved Aurignacian EJM layer.

9. THE EVOLVED AURIGNACIAN EJM ASSEMBLAGE. A slightly worn horse mandibular series of d_2-d_3-d_4 was identified in this assemblage (Figure 7.14). Wear patterns suggest that this mandible belonged to a foal less than 4 months old, which implies spring or summer acquisition. The diaphyseal length of two fetal horse specimens is indicative of procurement in the fall. Three reindeer teeth provide additional evidence that the site was occupied during the fall season. Another tooth, a d_4, suggests death sometime in late summer to early winter. Lastly, a nearly complete mandible and a d_4 are consistent with winter/spring kills. This last inference is supported by crown height comparisons with Pincevent and Verberie.

Shed antlers are well represented in this assemblage. Six (three not shown in Figure 7.5) antlers are attributed to adult males. Two of these are unshed, suggesting death in fall or early winter (Figure 7.15). These are the only two specimens of unshed male antlers identified at Saint-Césaire. The shed male antlers would have been collected in winter or anytime thereafter during the snow-free period. An additional shed antler is attributed to a female on the basis of its position in the scatter plot. This specimen was possibly collected sometime from spring through fall. Two shed spikes are compatible with procurement during the snow-free period.

10. THE EVOLVED AURIGNACIAN EJJ ASSEMBLAGE. A single fetal bone of an unidentified mammal was recorded in this level. Assuming that this bone is from reindeer, bison, or horse, death in fall or winter appears likely. Wear patterns on a reindeer d_4 and a M_1-M_2-M_3 mandibular series suggest that these parts were obtained sometime in late summer to early winter. An unworn bison d_4 comes from an animal killed in spring or summer.

The sample of reindeer antlers is small for this assemblage. The burr circumference could only be estimated on two incomplete specimens, both unshed. One of them can be assigned to a female. Procurement of this antler would have occurred sometime between fall and spring. A large, fragmented, shed burr is attributed to an adult male and might have been collected in winter.

0   cm   5

FIGURE 7.15. Two unshed antlers attributed to reindeer males from the Evolved Aurignacian EJM level of Saint-Césaire.

CONCLUSIONS ON SEASONALITY PATTERNS AT SAINT-CÉSAIRE

The first conclusion that emerges from this analysis is that Saint-Césaire was generally occupied during more than one season for all of the levels considered. However, the information is often "noisy," in large part because of small sample sizes and the imprecision of some of the methods that were used. Seasonal predictions based on shed antlers are usually less robust, given that these parts can, in theory, be collected throughout the year. For this reason, shed antlers are not included in Figure 7.16, which provides a summary of the seasonality data. It should be noted that the largest assemblages appear more multi-seasonal than the smaller ones, possibly because more data could be collected for these levels. Indeed, the larger sample sizes available for these assemblages likely increase the chance of identifying short and infrequent periods of occupation.

A second conclusion is that seasons of acquisition vary among reindeer, bison, and horse. In the sequence, the data suggest that reindeer was mostly hunted in winter and/or spring, and, to a lesser extent, in the fall. In contrast, summer was apparently not a significant period of reindeer procurement, despite the fact that some shed antlers might have been collected in this season. For horse, spring to early summer kills are documented in several occupations. Additionally, all but one of the horse fetal remains in the Aurignacian assemblages are consistent with fall deaths. Unlike reindeer, horse does not seem to have been frequently obtained in winter. Data are sparse for bison. Tooth wear patterns suggest a seasonal schedule similar to that documented for horse, although no support was found in the samples for a fall capture of bison.

A third conclusion is that the layers show robust patterning in the timing of the occupations, which suggests that the site was repeatedly occupied during the same seasons. Despite this relative stability, some changes in the periods of procurement are

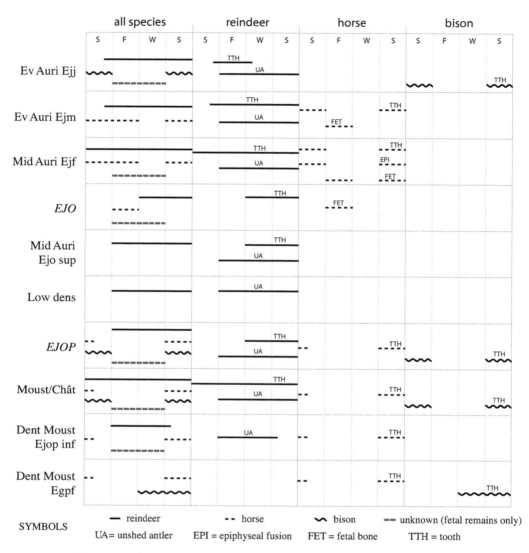

FIGURE 7.16. Summary of the seasonal evidence for the Saint-Césaire assemblages. The first column combines the information for all taxa. Fish are excluded. The specimens of unknown species are fetal remains that could only be attributed to the mammal class.

perceptible. For instance, the proportions of unshed antlers are considerably lower in the Denticulate Mousterian EJOP inf, Mousterian/Châtelperronian, and Middle Aurignacian EJO sup assemblages than in the Middle Aurignacian EJF and Evolved Aurignacian assemblages. This may attest to a slight shift in the period of reindeer acquisition, from mostly late winter through early summer to mostly mid-winter through late spring. In addition, the evidence for fall procurement of reindeer seems stronger in the more recent levels. The lack of antlers in the Denticulate Mousterian EGPF assemblage is intriguing because this part is present in significant numbers in all of the other occupations, including the overlying Denticulate Mousterian EJOP inf assemblage. Lastly, fall deaths of horse are only documented in the Aurignacian occupations.

In essence, procurement of ungulates in winter and spring – two seasons of low resource availability – is well documented in the assemblages. These seasons likely coincided with periods of resource stress for the human occupants of Saint-Césaire. Moreover, despite some evidence for changes, the sequence shows redundancy in the timing of the occupations, which decreases the probability that changes in diet breadth in the assemblages were caused by shifts in site function. Both sets of observations strengthen the relevance of Saint-Césaire for testing the early Upper Paleolithic intensification model.

8

TRANSPORT DECISIONS AND CURRENCY ANALYSIS

ARCHAEOLOGISTS FREQUENTLY ASSUME THAT NET ENERGY INTAKE IS AN APPROPRIATE proxy measure of fitness. However, this assumption may not always be warranted because the selection of a currency is influenced by the behavioral context, the gender and age group of the forager, and, of course, the type of question being asked (Danchin *et al.* 2005; Bird and O'Connell 2006). For instance, in certain contexts, the net acquisition rate of a specific macronutrient (e.g., fat) or the number of mates or children may constitute more appropriate proxy measures of fitness than overall energy intake. In this chapter, the focus is on the transport of skeletal elements, a dimension of foraging for which there is abundant information at Saint-Césaire. Because of the very nature of the data, only a small range of currencies – namely, marrow, grease, and overall food utility – is examined in this chapter. Despite this limitation, we will see that some of these currencies predict the transport of anatomical parts very well at Saint-Césaire.

Before assessing which currency best explains skeletal abundances in the assemblages, this chapter first considers whether transport goals *remained constant over time*. This issue, which has received little consideration in archaeozoological research, is significant because a change in transport goals in a sequence may require a corresponding change in the currency used to interpret that sequence. This problem is critical in the context of the Middle to Upper Paleolithic transition because some authors (e.g., Mellars 1996) have argued that archaic *sapiens* and early modern humans differed in terms of foraging strategies. At Saint-Césaire, this problem is, in part, addressed by comparing skeletal profiles in the assemblages through rank-order comparisons.

METHODOLOGICAL NOTES ON THE STUDY OF SKELETAL REPRESENTATION

Rank-order correlations of anatomical profiles were calculated between the largest assemblages from Saint-Césaire. These inter-assemblage correlations, which are successively presented for reindeer, bison, and horse, may yield critical information about change in foraging goals over time. To counter potential biases in specimen preservation, the samples used in the correlations only consider elements with similar bone density, with the exception of the second and third phalanges (Table 8.1). Despite their lower density, these last parts were included in the analysis to increase the sample of elements. It should be noted that although density values are available for bison (Kreutzer 1992), data derived for another bovid, the wildebeest (*Connochaetes taurinus*), were used instead because the latter values benefit from advances in density calculations (Lam *et al.* 1999).

TABLE 8.1. *Selected scan sites for wildebeest, horse, and reindeer presented in decreasing order of density (mineral density values, data from Lam* et al. *1999)*

Element	Wildebeest	Reindeer	Horse	Element	Wildebeest	Reindeer	Horse
Maxillary teeth	.	.	.	Innominate AC1	0.64	0.64	0.65
Mandibular teeth	.	.	.	Cubonavicular NC1	0.59	0.56	0.71
Femur shaft FE4	**1.16**	**1.15**	**1.09**	Lumbar vert. Lu1	0.58	0.49	0.48
Metacarpal sh. Mc3	**1.15**	**1.10**	**1.10**	Metacarpal dist. Mc5	0.56	0.48	0.56
Metatarsal sh. Mr3	**1.14**	**1.08**	**1.10**	**Phalanx 2 P2–2**	**0.56**	**0.72**	**0.59**
Tibia shaft TI3	**1.12**	**1.13**	**1.07**	Atlas AT1	0.55	0.47	0.51
Humerus shaft HU3	**1.10**	**1.12**	**1.10**	Metatarsal dist. Mr5	0.54	0.41	0.58
Radio-ulna sh. Ra3	**1.07**	**1.09**	**1.08**	**Phalanx 3 P3–1**	**0.53**	**0.48**	**0.57**
Scapula SP1	**1.02**	**1.01**	**1.03**	Cervical vert. Ce1	0.52	0.45	0.50
Phalanx 1 P1–2	**1.02**	**0.92**	**1.02**	Humerus distal HU5	0.51	0.48	0.36
Rib RI3	1.02	0.96	0.50	Radio-ulna prox RA1	0.51	0.53	0.37
Calcaneum CA2	0.92	0.94	0.69	Femur prox FE2	0.51	0.52	0.30
Metatarsal prox MR1	0.83	0.90	0.59	Tibia distal TI5	0.48	0.73	0.45
Greater cuneiform cun	0.79	0.71	0.60	Radio-ulna distal RA5	0.47	0.49	0.42
Hamatum HAM	0.77	0.72	0.67	Patella PA1	0.44	0.57	0.40
Scaphoid SCA	0.76	0.70	0.62	Tibia prox TI1	0.42	0.35	0.30
Fibula MAL/FIB	0.75	0.68	0.59	Axis AX2	0.41	0.42	0.37
Metacarpal prox MC1	0.72	0.92	0.55	Thoracic vert. Th1	0.38	0.38	0.32
Lunate LUN	0.70	0.67	0.57	Femur distal FE6	0.38	0.32	0.30
Magnum CAP	0.67	0.69	0.62	Sacrum SC1	0.35	0.37	0.36
Talus AS1	0.67	0.68	0.67	Humerus prox HU1	0.32	0.26	0.23

Skeletal parts used are shown in bold. Other parts were excluded because of differential fragmentation, their frequent use as fuel, and/or their low density.

As discussed in previous chapters, patterns of long bone representation can be reliably assessed based on shaft portions at Saint-Césaire because, unlike the epiphyses, they were rarely burned. In contrast, the initial abundances of innominates, vertebrae, malleoli, carpals, and tarsals are difficult to estimate with confidence, given that they were generally burned complete (see also Morin 2010). Likewise, evaluating the representation of ribs in the assemblages is complex because of moderate to intense fragmentation.

For these reasons, these elements were left out of the inter-assemblage analyses. The exclusion of these parts may affect the currency analysis because the sample is dominated by long bone elements. In particular, the possibility that a different currency underlay the transport of elements from the axial skeleton must be kept in mind while interpreting the results.

In the correlations, NISP counts were "normed" (hereafter NNISP) through a simple mathematical transformation in which the NISP value of an element is divided by the number of times the element is represented in a living animal (Grayson and Frey 2004; Grayson and Delpech 2008). This procedure facilitates comparisons with utility models, which are normally based on complete elements, which are analytically equivalent to MNE counts. NNISP is a useful unit because it avoids several of the shortcomings of MNE, such as the non-additivity of the samples and the nonlinear increase of values with increasing sample size.

For long bones, NNISP values were obtained by dividing the NISP counts by two, these elements having duplicates in the body of ungulates. The same logic prevailed for the other elements. Concerning the cranium and the mandible, NISP values were also divided by two because left and right teeth, by far the most frequent head parts in the samples, were rarely found in connection at Saint-Césaire. The presence of incisors and canines in the mandible of reindeer and bison may inflate the representation of this part relative to the maxilla. This bias is of minor importance here because incisors and canines are poorly represented in the tooth samples. Lastly, %MAU values were calculated as described in Chapter 4. However, for long bones, the highest MNE values – irrespective of the bone portion – were used in the comparisons, a procedure that should reduce sampling error. To avoid duplicating the information derived from the radius, counts for isolated ulnas were ignored in both NNISP and %MAU correlations.

We saw in Chapter 6 that variations in postdepositional damage and/or sample size may affect anatomical profiles generated using MNE counts. Consequently, patterns of correlations are only considered robust if confirmed by both NNISP-based and %MAU-based counts. Wherever required, aggregation of samples was limited to NNISP counts because MNE counts could not be recalculated for the merged samples.

RESULTS OF THE INTER-ASSEMBLAGE RANK-ORDER CORRELATIONS

The six largest reindeer assemblages were compared in the rank-order correlations. It is important to note that the NISP samples are moderate to fairly large in the Aurignacian occupations but are much smaller in the Denticulate Mousterian EGPF and the Mousterian/Châtelperronian occupations.

Based on NNISP, all fifteen rank-order correlations obtained between the six assemblages are strong, positive, and statistically significant (Table 8.2). Correlations are also significant but tend to be weaker, using %MAU. The correlations that involve the Mousterian/Châtelperronian sample are not as strong according to both count methods. These lower correlations may reflect sampling error or indicate a lesser fit with the other assemblages. When the comparisons are instead performed with a sample that merges EJOP sup with EJOP – thereby nearly doubling sample size for the Mousterian/Châtelperronian occupation – the correlation coefficients for the two cells both become >.850 (Table 8.2, NNISP only). This suggests that the Mousterian/Châtelperronian

TABLE 8.2. *Spearman's rho correlations (cells below the dashes) between reindeer assemblages at Saint-Césaire*

	Inter-Assemblage Correlations: Reindeer						
	Evol Auri (Ejj)	Evol Auri (Ejm)	Mid Auri (Ejf)	Mid Auri (Ejo sup)	M/Châtel (Ejop sup)	D Moust (Egpf)	Ejop sup+Ejop
NNISP-based							
Evol Auri (Ejj)	—	*<.01*	*<.01*	*<.01*	*<.01*	*<.01*	*<.01*
Evol Auri (Ejm)	.944	—	*<.01*	*<.01*	*<.01*	*<.01*	*<.01*
Mid Auri (Ejf)	.879	.963	—	*<.01*	*<.01*	*<.01*	*<.01*
Mid Auri (Ejo sup)	.942	.970	.965	—	*<.01*	*<.01*	*<.01*
M/Châtel (Ejop sup)	.918	.906	.808	.850	—	*<.02*	—
D Moust (Egpf)	.827	.911	.984	.928	.729	—	*<.01*
Ejop sup+Ejop	.955	.969	.920	.949	—	.851	—
%MAU-based							
Evol Auri (Ejj)	—	*<.01*	*<.03*	*<.01*	*<.02*	*<.03*	—
Evol Auri (Ejm)	.837	—	*<.01*	*<.01*	*<.02*	*<.01*	—
Mid Auri (Ejf)	.685	.853	—	*<.01*	<.08	*<.01*	—
Mid Auri (Ejo sup)	.792	.795	.937	—	<.06	*<.01*	—
M/Châtel (Ejop sup)	.773	.741	.544	.580	—	<.10	—
D Moust (Egpf)	.678	.892	.955	.869	.500	—	—

p values (cells above the dashes) are shown in bold when ≤ .05 and in bold italic when ≤ .01. Abundance of skeletal parts based on NNISP (upper rows) and %MAU (lower rows). Parts (*n* = 12) that are considered in the correlations include the cranium, mandible, and scapula; all six long bones; and all three types of phalanges. Concerning long bones, only shaft portions are considered. Isolated ulna fragments were excluded.

assemblage is in line with the other assemblages and that the differences were caused by small sample size.

For bison, the inter-assemblage comparisons focus on the four largest assemblages. Table 8.3 shows that all of the assemblages are highly, and significantly, correlated with

TABLE 8.3. *Spearman's rho correlations (cells below the dashes) between bison assemblages at Saint-Césaire*

	Inter-Assemblage Correlations: Bison				
	Middle Auri (Ejf)	M/Châtel (Ejop sup)	Dent Moust (Ejop inf)	Dent Moust (Egpf)	Ejop sup +Ejop
NNISP-based					
Middle Aurignacian (Ejf)	—	*<.01*	*≤.01*	*<.02*	*<.01*
Moust/Châtel (Ejop sup)	.808	—	*<.01*	*<.01*	—
Denticulate Moust (Ejop inf)	.776	.913	—	*<.01*	*<.01*
Denticulate Moust (Egpf)	.726	.892	.781	—	*<.01*
Ejop sup+Ejop	.813	—	.897	.892	—
%MAU-based					
Middle Aurignacian (Ejf)	—	*<.01*	*<.01*	*<.01*	—
Moust/Châtel (Ejop sup)	.911	—	*<.02*	*<.01*	—
Denticulate Moust (Ejop inf)	.788	.771	—	*<.01*	—
Denticulate Moust (Egpf)	.937	.914	.902	—	—

p values (cells above the dashes) are shown in bold when ≤ .05 and in bold italic when ≤ .01. Abundance of skeletal parts based on NNISP (upper rows) and %MAU (lower rows). Parts (*n* = 12) that are considered in the correlations include the cranium, mandible, and scapula; all six long bones; and all three types of phalanges. Concerning long bones, only shaft portions are considered. Isolated ulna fragments were excluded.

TABLE 8.4. *Spearman's rho correlations (cells below the dashes) between horse assemblages at Saint-Césaire*

	Inter-Assemblage Correlations: Horse					
	Evol Auri Ejm	Middle Auri Ejf	M/Châtel Ejop sup	Dent Moust Ejop inf	Dent Moust Egpf	Ejop sup +Ejop
NNISP-based						
Evolved Auri Ejm	–	**<.01**	**<.01**	**<.01**	**<.01**	**<.01**
Middle Auri Ejf	.911	–	**<.01**	**<.02**	**<.01**	**<.01**
Moust/Châtel Ejop sup	.879	.934	–	**<.03**	**<.01**	
Dent Moust Ejop inf	.818	.736	.701	–	**<.01**	**<.02**
Dent Moust Egpf	.878	.881	.815	.829	–	**<.01**
EJOP sup+Ejop	.881	.965	–	.745	.818	–
%MAU-based						
Evolved Auri Ejm	–	**<.05**	**<.04**	**<.01**	**<.01**	
Middle Auri Ejf	.607	–	**<.02**	**<.05**	<.23	
Moust/Châtel Ejop sup	.640	.752	–	**<.05**	<.07	
Dent Moust Ejop inf	.888	.603	.608	–	**<.02**	
Dent Moust Egpf	.876	.369	.559	.741	–	–

p values (cells above the dashes) are shown in bold when ≤ .05 and in bold italic when ≤ .01. Abundance of skeletal parts based on NNISP (upper rows) and %MAU (lower rows). Parts ($n = 12$) that are considered in the correlations include: the cranium, mandible, and scapula, all six long bones, and all three types of phalanges. Concerning long bones, only shaft portions are considered. Isolated ulna fragments were excluded.

each other, irrespective of the measure. These findings suggest that similar rank-order criteria mediated the transport of bison skeletal parts across the Saint-Césaire sequence.

The size of the horse assemblages is small to moderate at Saint-Césaire. Inter-assemblage correlations for the five largest samples are presented in Table 8.4. Again, all of the NNISP correlations are high and statistically significant. However, although significant, correlations based on %MAU tend to be weaker than those based on NNISP.

Overall, all of the reindeer, horse, and bison inter-assemblage correlations based on NNISP counts are statistically significant (*p* value ≤ .05). Only four out of thirty-one inter-assemblage correlations calculated using this measure did not have a *p* value ≤ .01. %MAU comparisons are in broad agreement with the results obtained with NNISP, although the correlations tend to be weaker. Despite these minor differences, the results suggest that transport strategies varied little across the Saint-Césaire sequence.

SELECTION OF A CURRENCY

The rank-order correlations suggest that the same currencies prevailed throughout the Saint-Césaire sequence, which points to stability in food procurement goals. Our next task is to identify these currencies and to assess whether they differed between reindeer, bison, and horse. In the following analysis, it will be assumed that a strong correlation with the overall food value of the parts indicates that foragers were concerned with maximizing energy procurement, whereas stronger correlations with marrow or bone grease utility models reflect a focus on fat procurement. Although both NNISP and %MAU data are used in the analysis, only %MAU data are shown in the utility diagrams. NNISP-based correlations are not displayed to avoid duplication of information.

TABLE 8.5. *Correlations between the abundance of reindeer skeletal parts in six assemblages from Saint-Césaire and two models: i) the Food Utility Index (FUI, Metcalfe and Jones 1988:492, table 2) and ii) the percentages of parts selected for grease rendering by two Nunamiut women ("spring" episode, Binford 1978:36, table 1.13, column 6)*

| | Food Utility Index (FUI) | | | | Nunamiut Grease Rendering Model | | | |
| | All elements | | All minus femur | | All elements | | All minus femur | |
	rho	p	rho	p	rho	p	rho	p
NNISP-based								
Evolved Auri (Ejj)	.427	<.16	.475	<.14	.752	**<.03**	.779	**<.03**
Evolved Auri (Ejm)	.594	**<.05**	.627	**<.05**	.703	**<.04**	.775	**<.03**
Middle Auri (Ejf)	.579	<.06	.670	**<.04**	.645	<.06	.762	**<.04**
Middle Auri (Ejo sup)	.470	<.12	.525	<.10	.694	**<.04**	.767	**<.04**
Moust/Chât (Ejop sup)	.462	<.13	.527	<.10	.736	**<.03**	.771	**<.03**
Dentic Moust (Egpf)	.568	<.06	.657	**<.04**	.630	<.06	.742	**<.04**
EJOP sup+EJOP	.451	<.14	.541	<.08	.703	**<.04**	.775	**<.03**
%MAU-based								
Evolved Auri (Ejj)	.336	<.27	.352	<.27	.900	***<.01***	.942	***<.01***
Evolved Auri (Ejm)	.743	**<.02**	.675	**<.04**	.945	***<.01***	.942	***<.01***
Middle Auri (Ejf)	.675	**<.03**	.741	**<.02**	.770	**<.03**	.933	***<.01***
Middle Auri (Ejo sup)	.493	<.11	.659	**<.04**	.755	**<.03**	.912	***<.01***
Moust/Chât (Ejop sup)	.568	<.06	.559	<.08	.836	**<.02**	.812	**<.03**
Dentic Moust (Egpf)	.717	**<.02**	.698	**<.03**	.824	**<.02**	.854	**<.02**

p values are shown in bold when ≤ .05 and in bold italic when ≤ .01. Abundance of skeletal parts based on NNISP (upper rows) and %MAU (lower rows). FUI values (in g) for the proximal and distal portions of the long bones were summed to obtain values for whole long bones. Conversely, because the Nunamiut grease rendering data are provided as percentages, values for the proximal and distal portions of the long bones were, this time, averaged for each long bone element. Parts ($n = 12$) that were considered in this table are: the cranium, mandible, scapula, all six long bones, and all three types of phalanges.

Transport Decisions in the Reindeer Assemblages

Decisions underlying the transport of reindeer skeletal parts can be evaluated by comparing the Saint-Césaire samples with the Food Utility Index (FUI) for caribou, a scale ranking caribou elements according to their combined meat, marrow, and bone grease utility (Metcalfe and Jones 1988). This model is a simpler derivation of Binford's (1978) Modified General Utility Index.

The reindeer assemblages from Saint-Césaire tend to correlate positively with the FUI (Table 8.5). Correlations are significant or close to reaching significance in four of the six %MAU-based and in three of the six NNISP-based samples. A look at Figure 8.1 shows that in most layers, the fit is reasonably good for most elements, except the femur, which tends to be under-represented relative to the FUI. Exclusion of the femur, which is probably under-identified at Saint-Césaire (see Chapter 6), increases the correlation coefficients – irrespective of the counting method – but has marginal effects on the *p*-values. Combining the EJOP sup and EJOP samples does not affect the results markedly. Although this utility model may account for the presence of some of the elements, the

FUI model does not optimally explain the frequencies of long bones in the samples, as many of the correlations are not significant.

Bone grease utility might also have affected bone transport decisions, given that many elements were presumably used as fuel at Saint-Césaire. Binford (1978) carried out a detailed study of skeletal fat utility in caribou and sheep, which led to the formulation of a Bone Grease Index for caribou. However, Chase (1985) criticized Binford's Bone Grease Index for being unnecessarily complex. Additionally, the values for one of the variables incorporated in Binford's formula, bone density, are now considered to be inaccurate (Lam and Pearson 2005). An alternative to using the Bone Grease Index is to compare the Saint-Césaire assemblages with ethnoarchaeological data on bone grease production.

Binford (1978) collected information on bone grease rendering on two occasions during his study of the Nunamiut. First, a woman was asked: "to save bones exactly as she would if planning the manufacture of white bone grease" (Binford 1978:35). This episode occurred in summer. Two women were invited to do the same in spring 1971. Although there were notable differences in the pool of parts available for selection in each of the episodes, Binford (1978:36–37) observed a very strong linear relationship[1] between the types and percentages of skeletal parts selected by these women. This result may imply that the ranking of skeletal elements relative to grease rendering varied little between seasons among the Nunamiut.

The Nunamiut data on grease rendering were compared with the abundances of reindeer skeletal parts in the Saint-Césaire assemblages. The Nunamiut values correspond to the percentage, by element, of specimens selected for grease rendering. Values from the spring episode (Binford 1978:36, table 1.13, column 6) were used in the correlations, as they are congruent with one of the main seasons of reindeer procurement at the site. At Saint-Césaire, it appears that skeletal parts were selected for fuel on the basis of grease utility (Morin 2010). Therefore, in this case the Nunamiut model of grease selection may also be conceived as a *Fuel Index*.

All of the reindeer assemblages from Saint-Césaire are or are almost, significantly correlated with the spring episode of part selection (Table 8.5 and Figure 8.1). This pattern is true for NNISP-based, and more particularly, for %MAU-based counts. Excluding the femur increases the correlation coefficients for most assemblages. In general, the Nunamiut model of bone grease production is much better at predicting reindeer element representation at Saint-Césaire than the FUI model.

The abundance of shaft fragments, percussion marks, and green-bone fractures and the strikingly low representation of whole long bones ($n = 6$, all layers, excluding fetal bones) provide overwhelming evidence for systematic marrow-cracking of ungulate limb elements in the occupations at Saint-Césaire. This food product may therefore explain the transport of marrow-yielding bones to the site.

Marrow utility in the reindeer samples is evaluated using the Unsaturated Marrow Index or UMI (Morin 2007). This utility model focuses on the total quantity of unsaturated fatty acids contained in caribou marrow. Unsaturated fatty acids are important because their lower melting point relative to saturated fatty acids (Pond 1998) increases

---

[1] The correlation is not provided by Binford, but was calculated to be $r_s = .92$, $p \leq .001$ (metacarpal excluded, as it was not initially present).

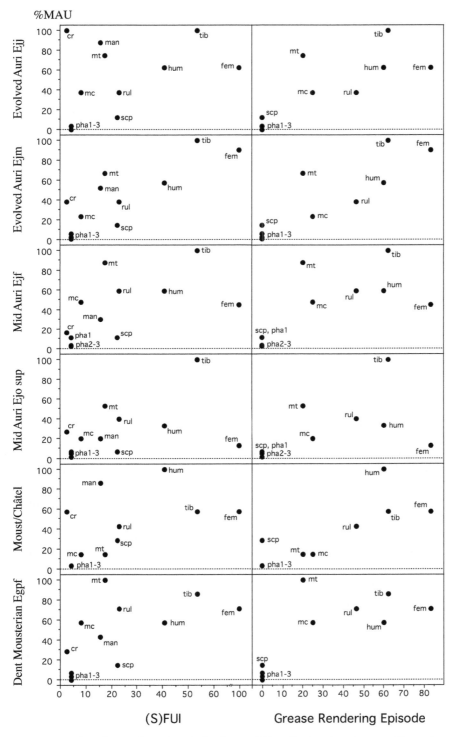

FIGURE 8.1. Abundance of reindeer skeletal parts (%MAU values) in six assemblages from Saint-Césaire versus the (S)FUI (Metcalfe and Jones 1988:4392, table 2) and the percentage of parts selected for grease rendering by two Nunamiut women ("spring" episode, Binford 1978:36, table 1.13, column 6).

TABLE 8.6. *Correlations between the abundance of skeletal parts in six reindeer assemblages from Saint-Césaire and the Unsaturated Marrow Index (UMI, Morin 2007:77, table 4)*

| | Unsaturated Marrow Index (UMI) | | | |
| | All parts | | All minus femur | |
	rho	*p*	rho	*p*
NNISP-based				
Evol Aurignacian (Ejj)	.975	*<.01*	.970	**<.02**
Evol Aurignacian (Ejm)	.933	*<.01*	.976	*<.01*
Middle Aurignacian (Ejf)	.879	**<.02**	.970	**<.02**
Middle Aurignacian (Ejo sup)	.933	**<.02**	.970	**<.02**
Moust/Chât (Ejop sup)	.879	**<.05**	.875	**<.03**
Dentic Mousterian (Egpf)	.867	*<.01*	.952	**<.02**
EJOP sup+EJOP	.917	*<.01*	.952	**<.02**
%MAU-based				
Evol Aurignacian (Ejj)	.954	*<.01*	.952	**<.02**
Evol Aurignacian (Ejm)	.967	*<.01*	.976	*<.01*
Middle Aurignacian (Ejf)	.896	**<.02**	.994	*<.01*
Middle Aurignacian (Ejo sup)	.883	**<.02**	.976	*<.01*
Moust/Chât (Ejop sup)	.725	**<.05**	.780	**<.04**
Dentic Mousterian (Egpf)	.975	*<.01*	.970	**<.02**

p values are shown in bold when $\leq .05$ and in bold italic when $\leq .01$. Abundance of skeletal parts based on NNISP (upper rows) and %MAU (lower rows). Parts ($n = 9$) that were considered in this table are all six long bones and all three types of phalanges.

fat softness and palatability. This issue is potentially significant, as the proportion of unsaturated fat has been shown to influence how certain foragers select bones in marrow procurement activities (Binford 1978; Morin 2007).

Correlations obtained between the assemblages and the UMI are exceptionally high, regardless of the quantitative unit considered (Table 8.6 and Figure 8.2). Both count methods indicate a slightly lesser fit with the Mousterian/Châtelperronian reindeer sample. However, the very high correlation obtained with the merged EJOP sup-EJOP sample suggests that the lower correlation observed with the Mousterian/Châtelperronian occupation is largely due to sampling error. These results indicate that reindeer limb elements were probably transported to Saint-Césaire as a function of their marrow utility, including during occupations marking the Middle to Upper Paleolithic boundary.

A few more words need to be added regarding the UMI. Because of a lack of data on unsaturated fatty acid composition, the UMI does not provide values for the scapula and the mandible, two bones with low marrow utility. Excluding these bones from the correlations may alter the patterns, although probably only slightly. Additional marrow data will be needed to test this possibility.

Transport Decisions in the Bison Assemblages

The abundance of bison elements in the assemblages is first compared with the (S)AVGFUI model for whole bones developed by Emerson (1993). This model, which measures the total amount of meat, marrow, and bone grease associated with an

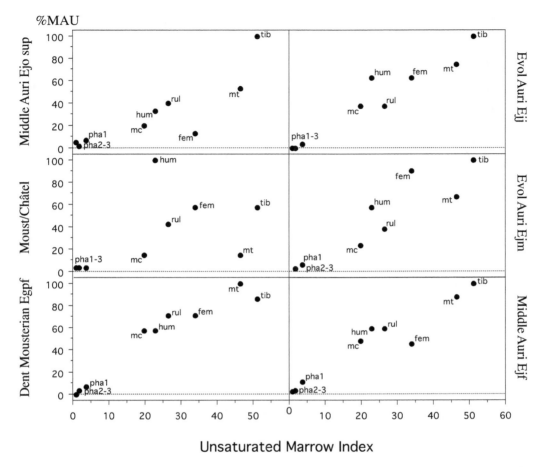

%MAU

FIGURE 8.2. Relationship between the abundance of skeletal parts (%MAU values) in six reindeer assemblages from Saint-Césaire and the Unsaturated Marrow Index (Morin 2007:77, table 4).

element, is an average (AVG in the acronym) of four bison of various age and sex classes. "S" means that the values have been standardized according to a scale ranging from 0 to 100%. Emerson's (S)AVGFUI model focuses on calories and was generated following the FUI protocol (Metcalfe and Jones 1988).

At Saint-Césaire, the NNISP of skeletal parts in the four largest bison assemblages show a poor fit with the (S)AVGFUI model (Figure 8.3). Two of the four %MAU-based correlations are statistically significant (Table 8.7). Removing the femur from the samples increases the correlation coefficients, sometimes considerably. However, differential identification alone seems an unlikely explanation for the very low percentages of femurs in the assemblages.

The Total Fat model ([S]MAVGTF), which is more narrowly defined than the FUI model, focuses only on skeletal, intramuscular, and dissectible fat utility of whole bones (excluding stomach and intestinal deposits). Like the FUI model, the Total Fat model was modified to account for the effects of riders (Emerson 1993). This last model is important because it measures a dimension that may be critical in the cold season in

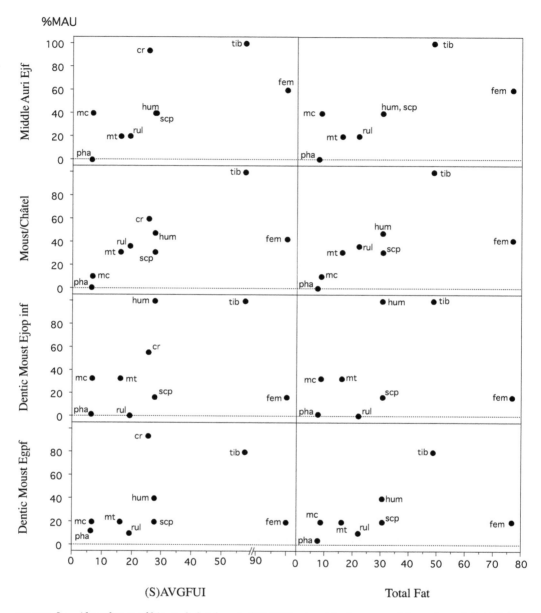

FIGURE 8.3. Abundance of bison skeletal parts (%MAU values) in four assemblages from Saint-Césaire versus the Food Utility ([S]AVGFUI, Emerson 1993:142, figure 8.2b and ii) and Total Fat ([S]MAVGTF, Emerson 1993:143, figure 8.3b) models.

mid- to high-latitude environments (Stefansson 1969; Speth and Spielmann 1983; Speth 1990).

Relationships between the abundances of bison skeletal parts and total fat utility are displayed in Figure 8.3. Skeletal elements correlate to some extent with total fat in the Saint-Césaire assemblages, although only one of the NNISP-based and two of the %MAU-based correlations are significant (Table 8.7). Excluding the femur increases

TABLE 8.7. *Abundance of bison skeletal parts in four assemblages from Saint-Césaire versus the Food Utility Index ([S]AVGFUI, Emerson 1993:142, figure 8.2b) and the Total Fat model ([S]MAVGTF, Emerson 1993:143, figure 8.3b)*

| | Food Utility Index ([S]AVGFUI) | | | | Total Fat Model ([S]MAVGTF) | | | |
| | All elements | | All minus femur | | All elements | | All minus femur | |
	rho	p	rho	p	rho	p	rho	p
NNISP-based								
Middle Auri (Ejf)	.642	<.07	.667	<.08	.750	**<.05**	.750	<.07
Moust/Chât (Ejop sup)	.454	<.20	.542	<.16	.530	<.17	.598	<.15
Dent Moust (Ejop inf)	.529	<.14	.649	<.09	.554	<.15	.634	<.13
Dent Moust (Egpf)	.504	<.16	.637	<.10	.601	<.12	.741	<.07
EJOP sup+EJOP	.537	<.13	.661	<.09	.649	<.09	.777	<.06
%MAU-based								
Middle Auri (Ejf)	.750	**<.04**	.762	**<.05**	.833	**<.03**	.786	<.06
Moust/Chât (Ejop sup)	.754	**<.04**	.827	**<.03**	.851	**<.03**	.902	**<.03**
Dent Moust (Ejop inf)	.367	<.30	.607	<.11	.321	<.40	.536	<.19
Dent Moust (Egpf)	.558	<.12	.696	<.07	.655	<.09	.795	<.06

p values $\leq$ .05 are shown in bold. Abundance of skeletal parts based on NNISP (upper rows) and %MAU (lower rows). Following Emerson, parts ($n = 9$) that were considered in this table are the skull, scapula, all six long bones, and the combined set of phalanges.

the correlations, several of them reaching or coming close to reaching, statistical significance.

Emerson (1993) also produced a (S)MAVGMAR index focusing on the caloric yield of bison marrow. Like the previous two indices, this index is also standardized and modified to account for the effect of riders. The Saint-Césaire bison assemblages correlate relatively well with Emerson's marrow index, although some inconsistencies are noted between the two count methods. Correlation coefficients are significant, or close to being significant, in three of the four %MAU-based comparisons but in only one (the merged EJOP sup-EJOP samples) of the five NNISP-based comparisons (Table 8.8). For both count methods, changes are minor when the femur is excluded.

The Saint-Césaire bison assemblages were compared with a fourth utility model, the (S)MAVGSKF index, which explores variation in skeletal fat content (Emerson 1993). Like the (S)MAVGMAR model, the skeletal fat model includes marrow in its formulation but differs from it by also considering the lipids enclosed in cancellous bones (e.g., long bone epiphyses). The skeletal fat model may help ascertain whether parts were selected for transport based on some combination of marrow and grease/fuel utility. At Saint-Césaire, comparisons with the skeletal fat model give correlation coefficients that are, on average, slightly lower than those obtained based on marrow alone (Table 8.8).

As a result of its focus on energy content, Emerson's Marrow Index does not consider how marrow fatty acid composition influences the process of bone selection. In this spirit, it might be productive to examine whether the bison assemblages correlate with the UMI (Morin 2007). Given that the UMI was derived for caribou, it may be not be a perfect model for bison. Nevertheless, the overall similarity of the two species in

TABLE 8.8. *Abundance of bison skeletal parts in four assemblages from Saint-Césaire versus the Marrow ([S]MAVGMAR, Emerson 1993:144, figure 8.5a), Skeletal Fat ([S]MAVGSKF, Emerson 1993:143, figure 8.4a), and Unsaturated Marrow Index (UMI, Morin 2007:77, table 4) models*

	Marrow				Skeletal Fat				UMI			
	All elements		Minus femur		All elements		Minus femur		All elements		Minus femur	
	rho	p	rho	p	rho	p	rho	p	rho	p	rho	p
NNISP-based												
Middle Auri Ejf	.542	<.16	.455	<.27	.601	<.12	.580	<.16	.771	**<.03**	.756	**<.05**
M/Chât Ejop sup	.619	<.11	.571	<.17	.476	<.21	.500	<.23	.800	**<.03**	.762	**<.05**
D Moust Ejop inf	.661	<.09	.634	<.13	.530	<.17	.580	<.16	.683	<.06	.619	<.11
D Moust Egpf	.613	<.11	.679	<.10	.506	<.19	.643	<.12	.817	**<.03**	.756	**<.05**
EJOP sup+EJOP	.786	**<.04**	.821	**<.05**	.643	<.09	.750	<.07	.950	***<.01***	.976	***<.01***
%MAU-based												
Middle Auri Ejf	.732	<.06	.598	<.15	.768	**<.05**	.688	<.10	.783	**<.03**	.774	**<.05**
M/Chât Ejop sup	.970	**<.02**	.991	**<.02**	.923	**<.02**	.991	**<.02**	.846	**<.02**	.899	**<.02**
D Moust Ejop inf	.446	<.24	.571	<.17	.304	<.43	.518	<.21	.575	<.11	.560	<.14
D Moust Egpf	.702	<.07	.750	<.07	.619	<.11	.750	<.07	.787	**<.03**	.810	**<.04**

p values are shown in bold when ≤ .05 and in bold italic when ≤ .01. Abundance of skeletal parts based on NNISP (upper rows) and %MAU (lower rows). Following Emerson, parts (*n* = 8) that were considered in the Marrow and Skeletal Fat models are the scapula, all six long bones, and the combined set of phalanges. For the UMI, the following parts (*n* = 9) were considered: all six long bones and all three types of phalanges. Note that the first, second, and third phalanges are considered separately in the UMI, but not in the other two models.

terms of physiology and bone morphology suggests that the caribou UMI should be a reasonable basis for interpreting bison assemblages. It must be pointed out that more bone categories can be compared with the UMI than with the (S)MAVGMAR model (Emerson's Marrow Index merges all phalange types into a single category, whereas the UMI considers them separately). This difference may result in higher *p* values with the UMI model.

Regardless of whether counts are based on NNISP or %MAU, the bison assemblages are all highly and significantly or nearly significantly, correlated with the UMI, with one exception (Table 8.8 and Figure 8.4). The relationship is particularly strong in the Mousterian/Châtelperronian and Middle Aurignacian EJF occupations but is slightly weaker in the Denticulate Mousterian EJOP inf occupation. Excluding the femur also results in high and mostly significant correlations.

Of the six utility models that have been examined for bison, the highest correlations were obtained with the UMI. This finding suggests that marrow procurement was the primary factor influencing the transport of bison skeletal elements to Saint-Césaire, at least for those parts that were considered in the analysis.

Transport Decisions in the Horse Assemblages

Two utility models, the first focusing on overall food utility, the second on marrow, have been published for horse (Outram and Rowley-Conwy 1998). Unfortunately, no index is available for bone grease. Moreover, it should be emphasized that because the horse

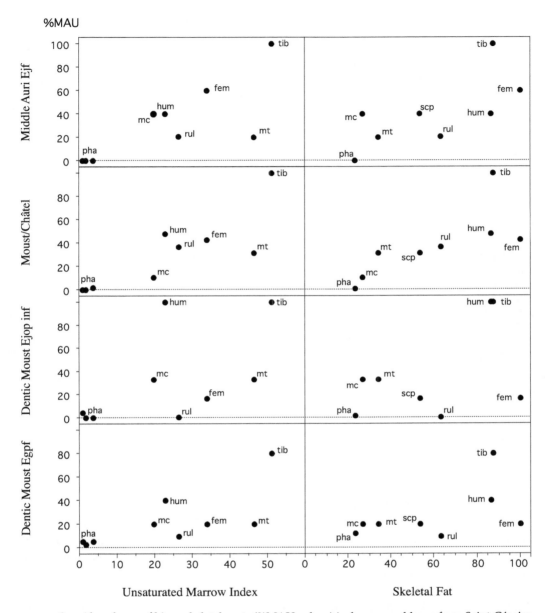

%MAU

FIGURE 8.4. Abundance of bison skeletal parts (%MAU values) in four assemblages from Saint-Césaire and the Unsaturated Marrow Index (UMI, Morin 2007:77, table 4) and Skeletal Fat ([S]MAVGSKF Emerson 1993:144, figure 8.4a) models.

assemblages at Saint-Césaire are fairly small, sampling error is more likely to affect the results than was the case for bison or reindeer. These problems limit the interpretation of transport decisions for the horse assemblages.

Like the caribou (S)FUI, the horse (S)FUI model (Outram and Rowley-Conwy 1998) incorporates all types of tissues and fat products by element, minus their associated dry bone weight. Because Outram and Rowley-Conwy (1998) provide values for long

TABLE 8.9. *Abundance of horse skeletal parts in five assemblages from Saint-Césaire and the FUI, Marrow (Outram and Rowley-Conwy 1998:845, table 6 and p. 842, table 3, respectively), and UMI models*

	FUI				Marrow				UMI			
	All elements		Minus femur		All elements		Minus femur		All elements		Minus femur	
	rho	p	rho	p	rho	p	rho	p	rho	p	rho	p
NNISP-based												
Evol Auri Ejm	.659	**<.03**	.630	**<.05**	.762	**<.04**	.780	**<.04**	.908	**<.02**	.917	**<.02**
Mid Auri Ejf	.755	**<.02**	.755	**<.02**	.662	<.07	.637	<.10	.783	**<.03**	.738	<.06
M/Chât Ejop sup	.346	<.26	.548	<.09	.242	<.50	.542	<.16	.363	<.31	.613	<.11
D Moust Ejop inf	.503	<.10	.693	**<.03**	.471	<.19	.756	**<.05**	.554	<.12	.786	**<.04**
D Moust Egpf	.572	<.06	.709	**<.03**	.688	<.06	.976	**<.01**	.767	**<.04**	.970	**<.02**
EJOP sup+EJOP	.624	**<.04**	.609	<.06	.683	<.06	.708	<.07	.812	**<.03**	.810	**<.04**
%MAU-based												
Evol Auri Ejm	.493	<.11	.575	<.07	.562	<.11	.738	**<.05**	.658	<.07	.768	**<.05**
Mid Auri Ejf	.657	**<.03**	.639	**<.05**	.367	<.30	.280	<.46	.671	<.06	.619	<.11
M/Chât Ejop sup	.715	**<.02**	.773	**<.02**	.629	<.08	.690	<.07	.808	**<.03**	.851	**<.03**
D Moust Ejop inf	.462	<.13	.689	**<.03**	.354	<.32	.673	<.08	.433	<.23	.702	<.07
D Moust Egpf	.538	<.08	.675	**<.04**	.479	<.18	.756	**<.05**	.654	<.07	.810	**<.04**

p values ≤ .05 are shown in bold. Abundance of skeletal parts based on NNISP (upper rows) and %MAU (lower rows). Parts ($n = 12$) that were considered in the FUI model include the cranium, mandible, scapula, all six long bones, and all three types of phalanges. The same sample of parts was used for the marrow model, except that the cranium was excluded. Parts ($n = 9$) that were considered in the UMI model include all six long bones and all three types of phalanges.

bone halves only, (S)FUI values for the proximal and distal parts were averaged in the comparisons.

Skeletal part abundance tends to correlate positively with the (S)FUI in the Saint-Césaire horse assemblages (Figure 8.5). However, the patterns are not easily interpreted because of discrepancies between NNISP-based and %MAU-based results. These discrepancies are most likely caused by small sample sizes. Correlations are significant or close to being significant, in three (four, if the mixed EJOP sup-EJOP sample is included) of the NNISP-based cells but in only two of the %MAU-based cells (Table 8.9). Correlation coefficients increase and become significant or almost significant in the majority of the assemblages when the femur is excluded, regardless of the counting method.

The horse samples from Saint-Césaire are also compared with a second model, the Marrow Index (Outram and Rowley-Conwy 1998), which is based on wet marrow weight. However, before proceeding further, it is necessary to emphasize a few points about this index. Outram and Rowley-Conwy (1998) noted considerable inter-individual fluctuation in marrow weight within their sample. Additionally, their marrow weight values are markedly higher than those published by Blumenschine and Madrigal (1993) for zebra, a closely related taxon. Because the source of this variation is not perfectly understood – species, sex, age, activity levels, health, and nutritional condition being likely contributing factors – the horse Marrow Index should be used with caution. Lastly, a minor modification to this index was made here. A value of 1 g (equal to the marrow weight for the first phalanx) was arbitrarily attributed to the scapula to account for the fact that this element tends to contain a small quantity of marrow.

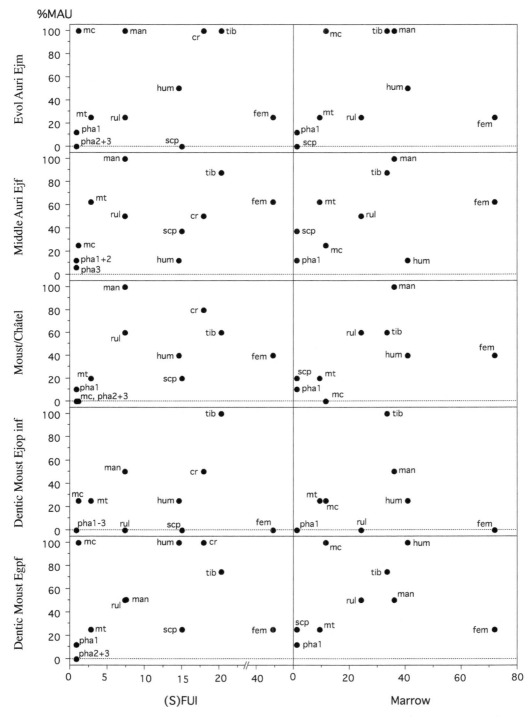

FIGURE 8.5. Abundance of horse skeletal parts (%MAU values) in five assemblages from Saint-Césaire and the (S)FUI and Marrow models (Outram and Rowley-Conwy 1998, p. 845, table 6 and p. 842, table 3, respectively).

TABLE 8.10. *The Unsaturated Marrow Index (UMI) as applied to horse*

Skeletal part	Horse marrow cavity volume (mL)	Proportion of unsaturated fatty acids in caribou	MCV × unsaturated (UMI)
Humerus	86.7	0.6007	52.1
Radius	50.5	0.7313	36.9
Carpals	1	0.8776	0.9
Metacarpal	16	0.9320	14.9
Femur	114	0.6546	74.6
Tibia	59.7	0.7986	47.7
Tarsals	1	0.8776	0.9
Talus	1	0.8776	0.9
Calcaneum	3	0.8776	2.6
Metatarsal	16.8	0.9123	15.3
Phalanx 1	3	0.9179	2.8
Phalanx 2	2	0.9184	1.8
Phalanx 3	1	0.9089	0.9

Horse marrow cavity volumes (MCV) are from Outram and Rowley-Conwy (1998:843, table 4, mean of three individuals). The unsaturated fatty acid data for caribou are from Meng and colleagues (1969:189, tables 1 and 2, double bond index column). Unsaturated fatty acid values for long bones are from the shaft portion. Unsaturated fatty acid values for phalanges correspond to the mean of both posterior and anterior phalanges. Carpals, tarsals, and talus were conferred the same unsaturated fatty acid values as the calcaneum. Following Jones and Metcalfe (1988), a marrow cavity of 1 mL was attributed to the carpals, tarsals, talus, and third phalanx.

The abundances of skeletal parts in the horse samples tend to correlate positively with the Marrow Index (Figure 8.5). As shown in Table 8.9, two (or three if the mixed EJOP sup-EJOP sample is considered) of the NNISP-based comparisons, but none of the %MAU-based comparisons, are significant or approach statistical significance. Removing the femur increases the correlation coefficients in most assemblages.

To further investigate correlations between horse skeletal abundances and marrow utility, comparisons were also performed with a variant of the caribou UMI. This model was modified because caribou bones, particularly the metapodials, differ in size and morphology from those of horse (Outram and Rowley-Conwy 1998). A UMI was created specifically for horse by multiplying the cavity volume of horse elements by the proportion of unsaturated fats observed in homologous bones in caribou (Table 8.10). The use of caribou fatty acid data is reasonable in the present case, given that trends in fatty acid composition in limb elements are very similar in mammals (Irving *et al.* 1957), with the exception of animals coping with extremely hot ground temperatures (e.g., bighorn sheep in desert environments, Turner 1979).

The horse assemblages from Saint-Césaire correlate well with the horse UMI. Three (or four if the mixed EJOP sup-EJOP sample is considered) of the NNISP-based and two of the %MAU-based correlations are statistically significant or close to reaching significance. The small Denticulate Mousterian EJOP inf assemblage shows a weaker fit according to both measures. On the basis of NNISP, the Mousterian/Châtelperronian assemblage also appears to correlate poorly with the UMI, although the pattern is reversed when the comparison is based on %MAU values. The fact that the aggregated EJOP sup-EJOP sample shows a strong correlation with the horse UMI suggests that the poor fit observed with the Mousterian/Châtelperronian NNISP-based values is due to sampling error. Lastly, most comparisons are statistically significant or close to reaching significance when the femur is excluded.

Of the three indices examined, the horse assemblages correlate most strongly with the horse UMI. It is interesting to note that four of the six complete ungulate long bones identified at Saint-Césaire are horse metapodials, including that of a juvenile. This pattern is possibly explained by the low marrow utility of these bones.

SUMMARY OF THE CURRENCY ANALYSIS

Marrow utility stands out as the most important factor structuring the transport of limb elements at Saint-Césaire. Correlations with the UMI are very strong and in agreement for all three species examined. These results suggest that foragers at Saint-Césaire were concerned with maximizing the net delivery rate of unsaturated fats when selecting reindeer, bison, and horse limb elements for transport. Thus, marrow procurement is considered in the remainder of this study as the most appropriate currency for assessing change in foraging patterns at Saint-Césaire. However, it must be reiterated that because the currency analyses are biased in favor of long bones, the possibility that other criteria (e.g., overall food value) influenced the transport of the axial skeleton cannot be excluded.

The next chapter builds on these findings and determines whether the Saint-Césaire assemblages are consistent with the dietary predictions of the intensification model.

9

TESTING THE HYPOTHESES

IN CHAPTER 3, SEVERAL SUBSISTENCE IMPLICATIONS OF THE EARLY UPPER Paleolithic intensification hypothesis were derived. This hypothesis, as proposed by O'Connell (2006), suggests that modern humans expanded their diet by increasing their use of costly resources. By permitting demographic growth, this broader diet would have allowed the replacement of archaic *sapiens* through competitive exclusion. In the region considered in this study, fast small-bodied taxa, particularly birds, leporids, and small carnivores, as well as small elements from large animals containing marginal amounts of marrow, such as the calcaneum and the phalanges, are the additional food resources that may have been more regularly included in the diet. The exploitation of fish and bone grease would also be compatible with the intensification hypothesis, given that these resources were mostly ignored during the Mousterian. In this model, it is assumed that Neandertals, in contrast to modern humans, exploited a narrow range of resources dominated by large ungulates and focused on elements with high marrow utility.

As discussed earlier, in the present context, it is not possible to corroborate O'Connell's intensification hypothesis but only to refute it. This is because cooler climatic conditions during the early Upper Paleolithic (Morin 2008) *could* also have prompted a diet breadth expansion, which creates a problem of equifinality. Because their test implications are similar, the foraging implications of these two hypotheses are explored in this chapter. The emphasis is first laid on the climatic deterioration hypothesis. Evidence for shifts in encounter rates with reindeer, bison, and, to a lesser extent, horse, is examined using data on taxonomic composition, age structure, and anatomical profiles. In Chapter 3, it was argued that these taxa would always have been pursued on encounter by hunters during the transition period. Consequently, climatic change was likely the principal factor mediating their archaeological representation at Saint-Césaire.

The second half of this chapter evaluates whether the data are consistent with the intensification hypothesis by focusing on low-ranked resources. As noted earlier, this part of the discussion is also relevant to the climatic deterioration hypothesis because the occupants of Saint-Césaire might have responded to a decline in environmental carrying capacity by increasing their use of low-return resources.

It should be noted that the samples used in this chapter are not always large enough to allow the calculation of true significance levels. This problem is particularly acute for bison. However, both the diagrams and the correlations suggest that for the majority of the analyses, the patterns would be statistically significant if larger samples were available. Additionally, because the Protoaurignacian and Early Aurignacian do not seem to be represented at Saint-Césaire – a finding that changes earlier assessments of the cultural sequence – the patterns examined here may not document the entire range of variation encountered during the Middle to Upper Paleolithic transition. Comparisons with other sites in Chapter 10 partly circumvent this problem by allowing a fuller examination of the transition period.

ENCOUNTER RATES WITH HIGH-RETURN PREY TAXA

At the center of the climatic deterioration hypothesis is the assertion that cooler climatic conditions decreased encounter rates with at least three high-ranked prey taxa – bison, horse, and red deer – during the Middle to Upper Paleolithic transition (Morin 2008). Two abundance indices, the *Bison Index* and the *Horse Index*, were created to evaluate this proposition. These abundance indices compare the representation of bison or horse relative to reindeer, a cold-adapted taxon that might have increased in relative frequency during the transition. Red deer was excluded from these analyses because of limited data.

Bison Availability

The Bison Index ($\sum$ NISP bison / [$\sum$ NISP bison + reindeer]) explores variation in the representation of bison relative to reindeer, two taxa that, based on their body size, were presumably part of the optimal diet during the Middle to Upper Paleolithic transition. For this reason, this index cannot inform us about shifts in diet breadth but may shed light on fluctuations in the availability of bison, which were likely the most profitable prey in the dry land patch. Trends in this index were analyzed using Cochran's test for linear trend (denoted χ^2_{trend}), a chi-square-based statistical method well suited for the detection of temporal patterns (Cannon 2001b). The data used to calculate this index are taken from Table 5.8.

Figure 9.1 shows values for the Bison Index across the Saint-Césaire sequence. The data suggest that bison decreased relative to reindeer between the Denticulate Mouste-rian EGPF occupation and the Middle Aurignacian EJO sup occupation. This temporal decline is highly significant ($\chi^2_{trend} = 217.4$, $p \leq .001$, bison versus reindeer NISP counts, antlers excluded). The trend is reversed in the later occupations, the Bison Index show-ing a weak but statistically significant increase in bison representation ($\chi^2_{trend} = 48.7$, $p \leq .001$; Middle Aurignacian EJO sup to Evolved Aurignacian EJJ). In sum, the Saint-Césaire sequence suggests a dramatic decline followed by a slight increase in the relative abundance of bison over time. Does the sequence show a similar pattern for horse?

Horse Availability

Values for the Horse Index ($\sum$ NISP horse / [$\sum$ NISP horse + reindeer]) are compared with the Bison Index in the lower panel of Figure 9.2. The two data sets show very similar patterns. As was the case for the Bison Index, the Horse Index reveals a decline in the representation of horse relative to reindeer between the Denticulate Mousterian EGPF and the Middle Aurignacian EJO sup layers ($\chi^2_{trend} = 231.3$, $p \leq .001$, horse and reindeer NISP counts, antlers excluded). During the Aurignacian, the Horse Index suggests a modest increase in the relative abundance of horse, again in agreement with

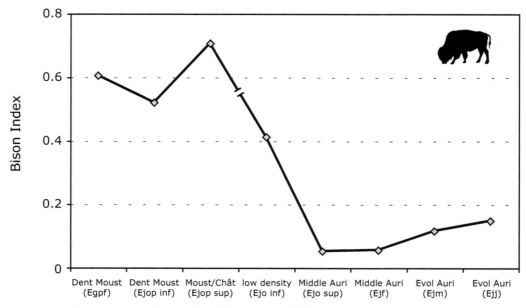

FIGURE 9.1. Variation in the Bison Index ($\sum$ NISP bison/[$\sum$ NISP bison + reindeer]) at Saint-Césaire. NISP data were taken from Table 5.8. Antlers were excluded.

the Bison Index. This trend is also statistically significant ($\chi^2_{trend} = 36.5, p \leq .001$; Middle Aurignacian EJO sup to Evolved Aurignacian EJJ).

The very close match observed between the two abundance indices may indicate that encounter rates with bison and horse severely declined between the Denticulate Mousterian EGPF and the Middle Aurignacian EJO sup before slightly rebounding in the later part of the sequence. Alternatively, these patterns may simply reflect fluctuating encounter rates with reindeer in a context of unchanging availability of bison and horse. As presented, the indices cannot discriminate between these two possibilities.

To solve this problem, we first need to determine whether the putative changes in encounter rates correlate in one way or another with other variables, such as climate change, that are known to affect the geographic ranges occupied by bison, horse, and reindeer. Micro-mammals are particularly useful in this regard, because these taxa tend to have very specific habitat requirements, which make them excellent climatic proxies (Chaline 1972; Tchernov 1998). In particular, the discussion builds on the trend for micro-mammal species diversity to decrease with latitude (Badgley and Fox 2000), the corollary being that, all else being equal, an assemblage with high micro-mammal diversity reflects a more favorable climatic regime than one associated with low diversity. This approach expands on a previous study of micro-mammal species diversity at Saint-Césaire (Morin 2008).

The upper panel of Figure 9.2 compares the micro-mammal diversity data presented in Figure 3.2 with the horse and bison indices. The fit between the diversity values and the two abundance indices is very good, although the minima are not attained in the same level (EJO inf for micro-mammals, Middle Aurignacian EJO sup for bison and horse). Despite these minor differences, these data suggest that climate was the driving force behind variations in the abundance indices, an issue that is explored further in

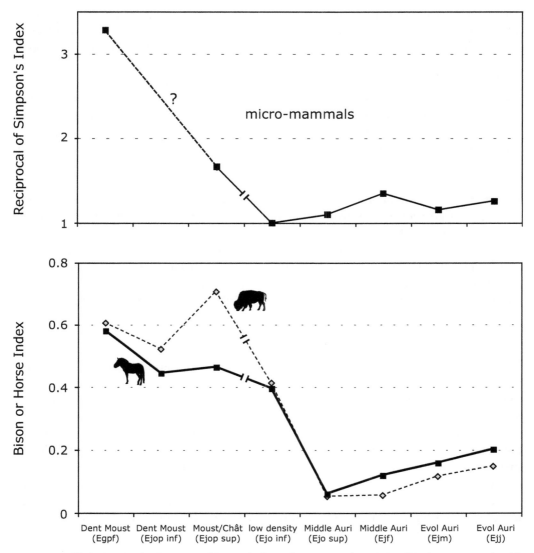

FIGURE 9.2. Variation in the Horse and Bison Indices (lower panel) at Saint-Césaire compared with patterns of micro-mammal diversity (upper panel). Low values in the upper panel indicate reduced species diversity and, presumably, cooler climatic conditions. Diversity values calculated using the Reciprocal of Simpson's Index (data from Morin 2008:51, table 2). The "?" symbol in the upper panel emphasizes the very small micro-mammal sample available for the EJOP inf level. NISP data for the two indices were taken from Table 5.8. Antlers were excluded.

Chapter 11. This relationship begs the question of whether bison, horse, and reindeer were equally affected by the climatic changes recorded at Saint-Césaire.

Ecological observations can be used to address this question. Historically, the geographic ranges of the Przewalski's horse (Bannikov 1958; Mohr 1971) and the steppe bison (Pucek *et al.* 2003) only partly overlapped with that of reindeer, which were mostly distributed north of the other two species (MacDonald and Barrett 2001). Differences in habitat requirements and in adaptation to cold weather largely account for this pattern because reindeer can subsist on a poorer, lichen-based diet and can better cope with adverse snow conditions than horse and bison, which prefer grasses and limited snow cover in winter (Telfer and Kelsall 1984; Berger 1986; Groves 1994; Pucek *et al.* 2003; Reynolds *et al.* 2003).

These contrasts in niche characteristics, which remain striking in contact zones (e.g., Fischer and Gates 2005), mean that a sensible increase in encounter rates with reindeer is unlikely to have occurred in the study region without a concomitant decline in encounter rates with bison or horse. This assumes a geographically small contact zone for these three species. However, Holocene contact zones might not be fully representative in this regard, given that Guthrie (1984:266) argued that a longer growing season in the Pleistocene permitted greater sympatric tolerance between ungulate species in mid- to high-latitude habitats. If this assertion is correct, more extensive contact zones during the transition might, from an archaeological point of view, have increased the odds of sampling changes in encounter rates with a single ungulate species, rather than changes in encounter rates with all three species. However, this possibility seems highly improbable given the dramatic fluctuations in bison and horse representation observed at Saint-Césaire. We will see in the following pages that other lines of evidence substantiate the argument for variations in encounter rates with all three ungulates.

AGE STRUCTURE ANALYSIS

In Chapter 3, it was hypothesized that reindeer juveniles and old adults mostly fell within the optimal diet because, with the exception of very young calves, they are larger than prime adults in small-bodied ungulates (e.g., roe deer) that are assumed to have always been pursued on encounter. Furthermore, it was argued that hunting pressure had only limited effects on population age structure because of the presumed migratory behavior of reindeer in the study area (Britton 2009). If accurate, the implication of these propositions is that archaeological changes in the representation of reindeer age classes at Saint-Césaire should reflect natural variations in availability rather than shifts in diet breadth or harvest pressure. The age data presented in the following paragraphs investigate these propositions. Small sample sizes prevented the study of age structure in bison and horse.

Juvenile and Old Adult Representation in the Reindeer Assemblages

The analysis of reindeer age structure focuses on three age classes derived from tooth data: juveniles, adults, and old adults. Using the tooth aging methods laid out in Chapter 7, specimens were classified as juveniles when they included one or more deciduous teeth. Erupting permanent premolars and molars were also attributed to this age category when from individuals less than 24 months old. Old adults correspond to individuals that were at least 123 months (10 years) old at the time of death. Adults were broadly defined and consist of all specimens intermediate in age between juveniles and old adults. The Denticulate Mousterian EGPF and EJOP inf occupations were excluded from this analysis because teeth were too infrequent in these assemblages. The EJOP and EJOP sup samples, as well as the EJO and EJO sup samples, were aggregated to increase the sample size for these occupations.

The results are presented as percentages of juvenile or old adult teeth relative to the total number of mandibular and maxillary teeth for which age estimates were assigned, including incisors and canines. Percentages for a given age class were then compared across the Saint-Césaire sequence using graphs. In these comparisons, NISP was favored over MNE because the former approach does not induce head overrepresentation in small samples (see Chapter 6). To control as much as possible for the effects of differential fragmentation, a second series of percentages – based exclusively on highly identifiable teeth (lower and upper D4s and lower and upper M3s) – was produced for juveniles (NISP = 57, irrespective of tooth type). This procedure could not be extended to old individuals because of their low representation (NISP = 11, irrespective of tooth type) at Saint-Césaire, which makes the analysis of temporal trends less secure for this age class. Extensive refitting and matching of tooth specimens should have reduced the possibility of repeated sampling of the same individuals. This problem could not be totally eliminated, however, despite these efforts.

Percentages of juvenile and old adult reindeer in the Saint-Césaire levels are shown in Figure 9.3, along with the Bison Index and data on the relative abundance of reindeer. The middle panel of Figure 9.3 reveals an initial decline followed by a continuous increase in juvenile representation during the Aurignacian. Despite small sample sizes, trends for D4s and M3s are in agreement with those for all teeth ($r_s = 1.00$, $p \leq .05$), which demonstrate that the trends are not caused by differential fragmentation. Both approaches indicate that variations in juvenile representation are highly and negatively correlated with the taxonomic representation of reindeer (all teeth: $r_s = -1.00$, $p \leq .05$; D4s and M3s only: $r_s = -1.00$, $p \leq .05$, reindeer representation based on %NISP).

Old adults also show similar variations in relative abundance (Figure 9.3, lower panel), although the minimum is reached in the Middle Aurignacian EJF rather than the Middle Aurignacian EJO sup level. It is not clear whether this slight difference in patterning is real or a statistical anomaly. The percentage of old adults is positively correlated with the percentage of juveniles ($r_s = .90$, $p \leq .08$) and negatively correlated with the taxonomic abundance of reindeer ($r_s = -.90$, $p \leq .08$, reindeer representation based on %NISP). However, these high correlations are not statistically significant, possibly because of the limited number ($n = 5$) of levels that could be considered in this analysis.

Conclusions about Reindeer Age Structure

A first conclusion that can be drawn from these data concerns the impact of the Saint-Césaire foragers on local populations of reindeer. We have seen that in certain species, particularly sedentary ones, a high predation rate may lower the probability of achieving old age in the prey population, resulting in an L-shaped (i.e., juvenile-dominated) age structure (Lyman 1987; Wolverton 2008). No such shift is recorded at Saint-Césaire. Instead, the relative abundances of juveniles and old adults decreased and increased in tandem, which indicates that hunting pressure on reindeer was either too light and/or that the mobility of this prey was such that it prevented a human-induced shift toward a juvenile-dominated age structure.

These data have further implications. It was argued that reindeer juveniles and old adults might have mostly fallen within, rather than outside, of the optimal diet, which implies that they would normally have been pursued on encounter. If this assumption is correct, the representation of juveniles and old adults is not expected to have changed over time, except if the availability of these age classes changed in the environment. The fact that juvenile and old adult representation did not increase, as one might predict from the intensification model, but rather decreased during the Middle to Upper Paleolithic transition, is consistent with this assumption or at least does not contradict it.

The foregoing statements assume captures of a single animal at a time. However, the presumed increase in reindeer densities with the advent of the early Upper Paleolithic may have led to more frequent kills of groups of reindeer composed of individuals of different age classes near the central place. According to the field-processing model of Barlow and Metcalfe (1996), rate-maximizing foragers are expected to make more trips with lower-utility loads as average transport distances decrease. In this context, therefore, we could expect that as encounter rates decrease, foragers would more frequently exclude juvenile and old adult parts. This is not the trend observed at Saint-Césaire, given that juvenile and old adult teeth are proportionally more abundant when reindeer is poorly, rather than highly, represented in the NISP samples. This finding has at least two possible implications: i) that multiple kills were infrequent during the site occupation or ii) that transport distance was less important than other factors in conditioning reindeer age structure at Saint-Césaire. Evidently, these options are not mutually exclusive.

Although precise predictions about changes in reindeer age structure could not be generated in the present case because of the difficulty of controlling for many of the variables that were possibly at work, certain alternatives can be excluded. The relative abundances of reindeer juveniles and old adults deposited at Saint-Césaire were probably mostly influenced by their availability in the environment rather than by changes in human harvest pressure or diet breadth. Today, the proportion of juveniles and old adults in *Rangifer* populations depends on the interplay of several factors. Foremost among them are *Rangifer* density, forage abundance, weather conditions, carnivore predation, and the frequency of disease outbreaks (Miller 2003). However, a lack of fine-grained data about how these and the previous factors (i.e., the frequency of single vs. multiple kills) interacted with climatic change during the transition limits our understanding of variations in age structure at Saint-Césaire.

TRANSPORT OF BISON AND REINDEER PARTS

The analysis of the taxonomic data suggested significant climatically-induced changes in encounter rates with reindeer, bison, and horse during the Middle to Upper Paleolithic transition. Trends in body part representation are now examined to ascertain whether patterns of body part representation in the Saint-Césaire assemblages are in agreement with this interpretation, the emphasis being on the relationship between transport distance and field processing decisions. Horse is excluded from this discussion because of sample size limitations.

Cranium Transport

Several actualistic studies of human foragers have observed biases against the transport of the heads of large ungulates (e.g., caribou, zebra, giraffe), particularly when the

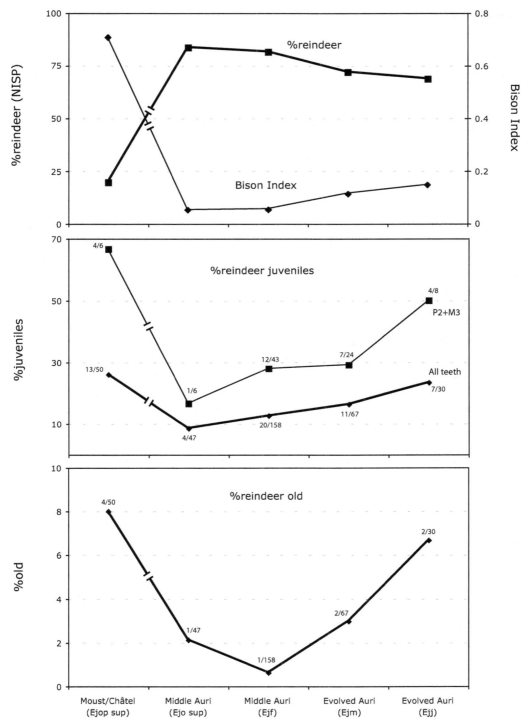

FIGURE 9.3. Percentages of juvenile (middle panel) and old adult (lower panel) teeth in five reindeer tooth samples compared with the taxonomic abundance of reindeer and the Bison Index (upper panel). Numbers next to data points give raw data for each sample. Specimens from individuals that were no more than 24 months old are considered juveniles, whereas the "old adult" category only includes specimens from individuals that were at least 123 months old at death. For juveniles, a second set of data based exclusively on highly identifiable teeth (lower and upper D4s and M3s) is also presented. All counts omit teeth that could not be attributed to an age class. To increase sample size, EJOP sup was combined with EJOP, and EJO sup with EJO, in this figure.

butchering station is far from the residential camp (Binford 1978; Bunn *et al.* 1988; O'Connell *et al.* 1988, 1990). This bias has generally been attributed to economic decisions, because the heads of these animals have a low food utility in addition to being heavy and bulky (Binford 1978; Speth 1983; Bunn 2007). Even though it consists of two sets of bones – the cranium and the mandible – the head is often treated as a unit with respect to discard and transport (Monahan 1998). This practice is best viewed as an effective adjustment to differences in processing costs: the head is easily severed from the body, in opposition to the mandible that is tightly maintained to the cranium by powerful masticatory muscles and ligaments.

Yet because it takes no more than a few minutes to disjoin these bones and because they have distinct economic properties, crania and mandibles may sometimes follow separate trajectories in the field. For instance, in *Rangifer*, the mandible is smaller, lighter and, with the tongue, contains more food than the cranium (Binford 1978). Consequently, we can expect reindeer crania to be discarded more frequently than mandibles at remote butchering locations, given that both food utility and portability favor the latter part. Comparable data are lacking for bison, but the very large weight of the cranium relative to the mandible (6.6 kg vs. 1.5 kg in an adult male, fresh bone weight, Emerson 1990:291) favors a similar conclusion for this species.

Building on these economic observations, the field processing implications of the central place forager prey choice model can be used to predict how the frequencies of crania should have varied relative to mandibles at Saint-Césaire. If the propositions made about changes in encounter rates with bison and reindeer are accurate, head completeness should correlate positively with the taxonomic abundance of the species of interest, considering the latter as an inverse proxy of mean transport distance. This relationship assumes that the Saint-Césaire foragers operated under constraints that limited head transport.

If the climatic deterioration hypothesis is correct, it is expected that proportionately fewer complete bison heads would have been transported to Saint-Césaire because this taxon declined in abundance during the early Upper Paleolithic. The logic behind this argument is that lower encounter rates with this species probably increased transport costs, because of an increased likelihood of the kill being located far from the central place, which should have resulted in more crania being left behind. Conversely, the proportion of crania is expected to have rebounded with the slight resurgence of bison in the later Aurignacian. The opposite predictions (an initial increase followed by a decrease in cranium transport) are made for reindeer, based on its patterns of taxonomic abundance.

As was the case for the examination of age structure, two quantitative methods were used in concert to investigate variations in cranium transport at Saint-Césaire. The first approach compares the sum of all maxillary teeth relative to the sum of all teeth (excluding tooth fragments and non-descript teeth). The second approach focuses exclusively on P2s and M3s because these highly diagnostic teeth should be less affected by problems of differential fragmentation. In this last approach, the sum of maxillary P2s and M3s was divided by the sum of all P2s and M3s (all counts based on NISP values). Regardless of which measure is examined, a value larger than 0.5 indicates that crania prevail in an assemblage, whereas a value lower than 0.5 points to a dominance of mandibles. The Evolved Aurignacian EJM and EJJ occupations

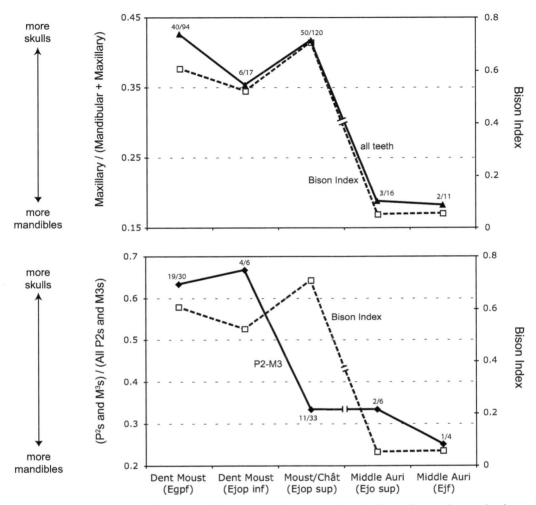

FIGURE 9.4. Proportions of bison mandibles compared with the Bison Index in five tooth samples from Saint-Césaire. Values were calculated as labeled on the y-axes. Tooth fragments and non-descript teeth (e.g., "indeterminate lower premolar") were excluded from the counts. Numbers next to data points give raw data for each sample. Tooth rows counted as a single specimen in the upper panel. In the lower panel, all P2s and M3s were counted regardless of whether they were found isolated or associated in tooth rows. The samples from EJOP sup and EJOP are aggregated in both panels.

were omitted from this analysis because bison teeth are poorly represented in these levels.

Figure 9.4 displays proportions of crania relative to teeth in the five largest bison tooth samples. In agreement with the argument raised earlier about utility and processing costs, crania tend to be less abundant than mandibles in the occupations. However, there are two possible exceptions to this generalization. P2-M3 values indicate a dominance of crania in the Denticulate Mousterian EGPF and EJOP inf occupations. In contrast, values for all teeth suggest a greater abundance of mandibles in the same levels. Yet the differences between the two sets of values are only significant in one case (all teeth vs. P2s–M3s: EGPF, $t_s = 1.99$, $p < .05$; EJOP inf, $t_s = 1.35$, $p < .18$). The source of the

189

discrepancies in the EGPF layer remains unclear, but taphonomic issues and sampling error are likely contributing factors.

Turning now to the temporal trends, the proportion of bison crania – as assessed using all of the teeth – show a very good match with the Bison Index (Figure 9.4, upper panel), although the results are not significant ($r_s = .88$, $p \leq .09$). The fit is not as satisfactory when the focus is placed on the much smaller P2-M3 samples ($r_s = .42$, $p \leq .40$, Figure 9.4, lower panel). Although the results are not statistically significant, the data suggest a positive relationship between the taxonomic abundance of bison and the proportion of bison crania. As predicted, crania are rare relative to mandibles when bison is poorly represented in the assemblages.

Similar data were gathered for reindeer, with one notable modification. The preceding analysis was essentially based on isolated teeth because bison tooth rows are rare in the samples (12/320 or 3.7% of all bison tooth entries, excluding EJOP and EJO). In contrast, tooth rows are far more frequent in the reindeer tooth samples (60/356 or 16.8%, $t_s = 5.94$, $p < .0001$), a pattern that may, in part, be explained by the rarity of bison remains in the best-preserved layers. Because both the preservation of mandibular tooth rows and the proportions of mandibles and crania vary between the reindeer assemblages, these patterns may, in combination, affect the study of cranium transport for this species. To counter this problem, the NISP counts for reindeer mandibles and crania were modified. Whereas in the previous analyses, a tooth row was tallied as a single specimen, all of the individual teeth – whether present in a tooth row or not – were considered in the study of reindeer cranium and mandible representation. For example, a P4-M1-M2 tooth row, which was counted as 1 specimen in the bison analysis, was tallied as three specimens in the analysis of reindeer head transport.

Figure 9.5 shows patterns of cranium representation in the six largest reindeer samples at Saint-Césaire. Values for all teeth, displayed in the upper panel, point to a weak correlation with the taxonomic representation of reindeer ($r_s = .26$, $p \leq .57$). In contrast, patterns for P2s and M3s (Figure 9.5, lower panel) indicate a very strong, and statistically significant, correlation between the same variables ($r_s = .93$, $p \leq .04$). Both panels suggest that the Middle Aurignacian EJF occupation contains fewer skulls than expected. Lastly, mandibles dominate in all of the occupations, independently of the approach. These results are globally in agreement with the prediction that the proportion of crania should correlate positively with the relative abundance of reindeer in the assemblages.

Digit Transport

The representation of low-utility parts in the assemblages may generate further insight into changes in encounter rates with high-return prey taxa. Digits, which include phalanges as well as proximal and distal sesamoids, are a notoriously poor source of food in large ungulates. Moreover, their weight can sometimes be significant. For example, bison digits may weigh more than a kilogram (Emerson 1990:292). Rate-maximizing foragers should reduce the transport of these low-utility parts as the distance to the point of delivery increases. Consequently, as was the case for crania, digit representation in the Saint-Césaire assemblages should correlate positively with the abundance of the species of interest.

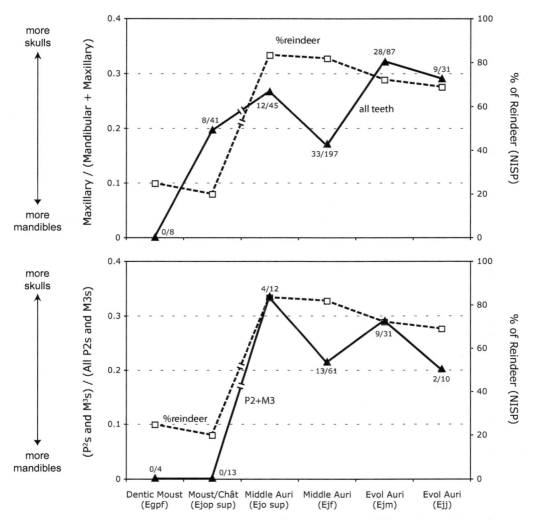

FIGURE 9.5. Proportions of reindeer mandibles compared with the taxonomic representation of reindeer in six tooth samples from Saint-Césaire. Values were calculated as labeled on the y-axes. Numbers next to data points give raw data for each sample. Tooth fragments and non-descript teeth (e.g., "indeterminate lower premolar") were excluded from the counts. Contrary to the bison analysis, all teeth in tooth rows were considered in the reindeer NISP counts (see text for explanation). The samples from EJOP sup and EJOP are aggregated in both panels.

To test this prediction, the relative abundance of digits in the bison assemblages was computed by dividing the total NNISP for the first phalanx, second phalanx, third phalanx, and sesamoids (proximal and distal) by the total NNISP for all long bones, phalanges, and sesamoids. Values were then multiplied by 100 to obtain percentages. However, because bison digits are poorly represented at Saint-Césaire (phalanges: $n = 18$; sesamoids: $n = 9$), the results may be subject to sampling error.

The relative abundance of bison digits in the occupations is plotted in the upper panel of Figure 9.6. Visually, variations in the percentages of digits show a relatively good match with the Bison Index. However, values for the Denticulate Mousterian EJOP inf and Mousterian/Châtelperronian occupations are depressed compared with the Bison Index (Figure 9.6, lower panel). These deviations may explain the low correlation obtained between the two sets of data ($r_s = .26, p \leq .57$).

For reindeer, larger samples of phalanges and sesamoids allowed the partitioning of the data according to element (i.e., first phalanx, second phalanx, third phalanx, sesamoids). This breakdown is instructive because it tests for consistency in decision making. Figure 9.7 compares the respective abundances of the four categories of digit elements across the Saint-Césaire sequence. A salient feature of this figure is that the patterns are largely redundant, which suggests that phalanges and sesamoids were usually transported or discarded together. A statistical analysis supports this conclusion; rank-order correlations between adjacent bones are significant or close to reaching significance, except for two pairs (first vs. second phalanx: $r_s = .76, p \leq .07$; first phalanx vs. sesamoids: $r_s = .92, p \leq .03$; second vs. third phalanx: $r_s = .49, p \leq .23$; second phalanx versus sesamoids $r_s = 0.83, p \leq .05$: third phalanx versus sesamoids: $r_s = .54, p \leq .19$). However, the possibility that digit elements occasionally went on separate paths cannot be excluded, given the generally higher representation of the first phalanx. Alternatively, this pattern may simply reflect differential preservation, the first phalanx being denser than the other digit elements (Lam *et al.* 1999).

Figure 9.8 synthesizes the data by comparing the percentages for all of the digit elements with the percentages of reindeer specimens in the occupations. In this figure, the percentage of digit bones shows a non-significant correlation with reindeer representation ($r_s = .14, p \leq .73$). However, the correlation becomes strong and almost significant if the Mousterian/Châtelperronian occupation is excluded ($r_s = .83, p \leq .07$). This last result is consistent with the argument that encounter rates with reindeer increased during the transition but decreased in the later Aurignacian. Yet because one occupation was excluded, more data will be needed to fully assess the relationship between these variables.

Long Bone Transport

The positive relationships observed between the relative abundance of crania in the bison and reindeer assemblages and the taxonomic representation of these species provide support for the climatic deterioration hypothesis because these relationships are consistent with presumed changes in encounter rates. The relative abundance of digits is also qualitatively in agreement with this hypothesis, although the relationships are not statistically significant, possibly because of sample size limitations. The following sections assess whether long bones fit these patterns.

From the perspective of the central place forager prey choice model, a rate-maximizing forager handling large prey taxa should increase field processing as the distance between the point of capture and the central place increases in order to reduce the number of trips. This means that at longer distances from the central place, the mean utility of the long bones composing the loads is expected to be higher due to the removal of low-utility elements. Loads transported over long distances will also be less diverse relative to loads transported over short distances. Consequently, a comparison of the diversity and the mean marrow utility of the long bone samples with patterns of taxonomic representation

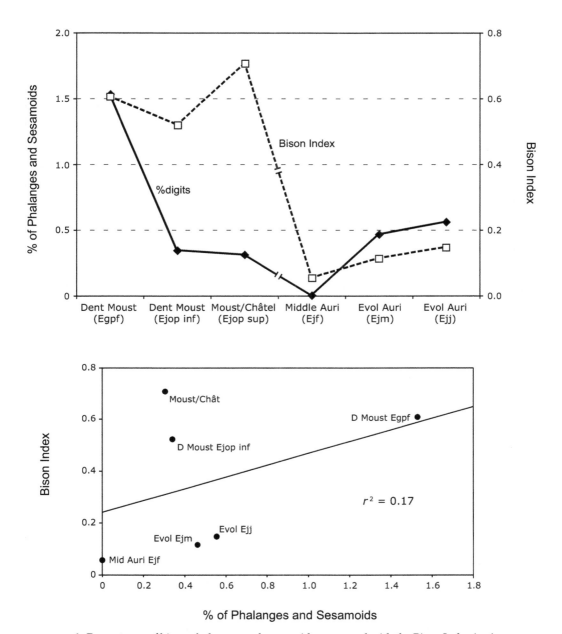

FIGURE 9.6. Percentages of bison phalanges and sesamoids compared with the Bison Index in six assemblages from Saint-Césaire (upper panel). The lower panel shows the goodness-of-fit between the percentages of digit elements and the Bison Index. Percentages of phalanges and sesamoids were calculated as follows: ($\sum$ NNISP of phalanges and sesamoids)/($\sum$ NNISP of long bones, scapulae, phalanges, and sesamoids) × 100. The samples from EJOP sup and EJOP are aggregated in both panels. Phalanx and sesamoid data were taken from Appendix 2. Only the proximal and distal sesamoids ($n = 24$ in a standard bison skeleton) were considered in the calculations.

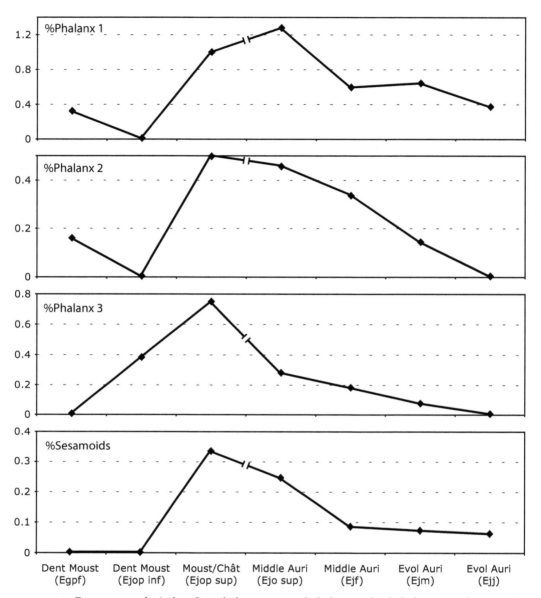

FIGURE 9.7. Percentages of reindeer first phalanges, second phalanges, third phalanges, and sesamoids across the Saint-Césaire occupations. Percentages were calculated as follows: $\sum$ NNISP of digit$_i$/ ($\sum$ NNISP of long bones, scapulae, and digit$_i$) $\times$ 100, where $_i$ represents a specific digit element. The samples from EJOP sup and EJOP, as well as from EJO sup and EJO, are aggregated in the panels. Phalanx and sesamoid data were taken from Appendix 2. Only the proximal and distal sesamoids ($n = 24$ in a standard reindeer skeleton) were considered in the calculations.

should help determine whether the reindeer and bison assemblages from Saint-Césaire meet these predictions.

CHANGE IN MEAN MARROW UTILITY. Using UMI as a proxy measure of marrow utility, mean marrow values were calculated for each long bone sample, following a variant of a

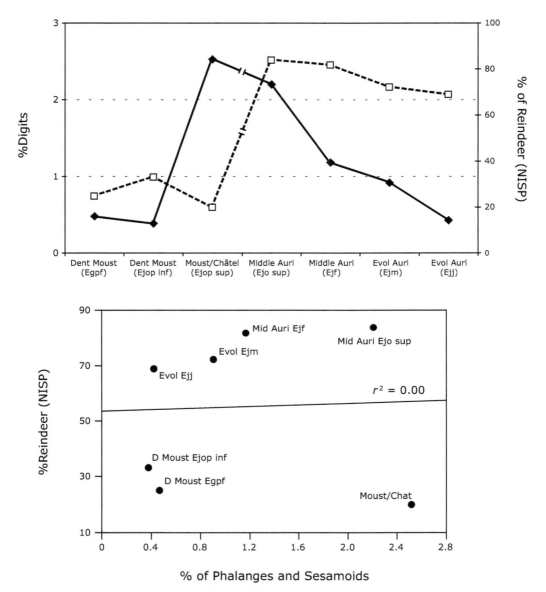

FIGURE 9.8. Percentages of digit bones and the taxonomic abundance of reindeer across the Saint-Césaire occupations (upper panel). The lower panel shows the goodness-of-fit between the percentages of digit elements and the relative abundance of reindeer. Percentages of digit bones were calculated as follows: $(\sum \text{NNISP of phalanges and sesamoids})/(\sum \text{NNISP of long bones, scapulae, phalanges, and sesamoids}) \times 100$. The samples from EJOP sup and EJOP, as well as from EJO sup and EJO, are aggregated in the panels. Phalanx and sesamoid data were taken from Appendix 2.

procedure presented by Broughton (1999). Specifically, mean UMI values were obtained for all of the long bones by multiplying the NNISP of a long bone by its associated unsaturated marrow value. The values obtained were then summed and divided by the long bone sample size. Finally, the resulting values were plotted on a diagram to visually assess change in transport behavior.

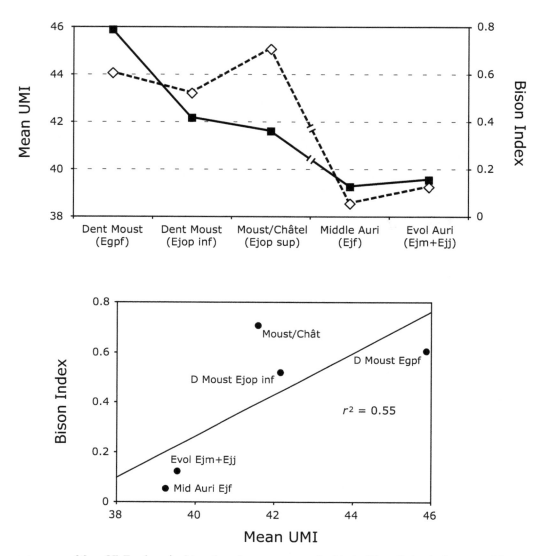

FIGURE 9.9. Mean UMI values for bison long bones compared with the Bison Index in five assemblages from Saint-Césaire (upper panel). The lower panel shows the goodness-of-fit between the UMI values and the Bison Index. Mean UMI values were calculated using the equation: $\sum(RSA_i \times UMI_i)/\sum RSA$, where RSA is the relative skeletal abundance and i represents specific long bone elements (Broughton 1999; Faith 2007). Only the six long bones were included in the samples. The two Evolved Aurignacian occupations (EJM and EJJ) were aggregated to increase sample size.

Mean UMI values computed for bison are compared with the Bison Index in the upper panel of Figure 9.9. In this figure, the two Evolved Aurignacian levels are aggregated to increase sample size. Contrary to the prediction, the data reveal a positive, although non-significant, relationship between the two data sets ($r_s = .70$, $p \leq .17$). The Mousterian/Châtelperronian occupation represents a minor deviation from this relationship (Figure 9.9, lower panel), as the value for this level is higher than expected based on the Bison Index.

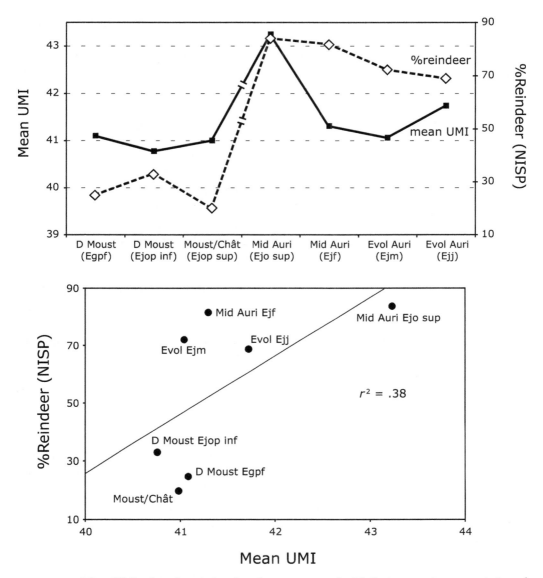

FIGURE 9.10. Mean UMI values for reindeer long bones compared with the taxonomic representation of reindeer in seven assemblages from Saint-Césaire (upper panel). The lower panel shows the goodness-of-fit between the UMI values and the taxonomic representation of reindeer. Mean UMI values were calculated according to the equation presented in FIGURE 9.9. Only the six long bones were included in the samples.

The results are more difficult to interpret for reindeer because of the small range of variation (40–43) in the mean UMI values. As for bison, the mean UMI values for reindeer long bones tend to correlate positively with changes in the taxonomic representation of reindeer. Once again, the relationship is not significant ($r_s = .68$, $p \leq .10$, Figure 9.10). This finding conflicts with the prediction of a negative relationship between the mean marrow utility of reindeer long bones and the relative abundance of this species.

It is possible to draw some preliminary conclusions on the basis of these results. Contrary to the initial predictions, mean UMI values for bison and reindeer long bones appear to correlate positively, rather than negatively, with the taxonomic representation of these taxa. This may suggest that the climatic deterioration hypothesis is inaccurate or that the occupants of Saint-Césaire did not behave according to the expectations of the central place forager prey choice model. In either case, the long bone patterns are difficult to reconcile with the patterns uncovered for crania and digits at first glance.

CHANGE IN LONG BONE DIVERSITY. As emphasized earlier, a reduction or an increase in mean transport distance may affect not only the types of elements that are included in loads that are carried back to the central place but also the diversity of elements included in these loads. In archaeology, diversity is often calculated using the Reciprocal of Simpson's Index or the Shannon Index (Grayson 1984; Lyman 2008). The former statistic is employed here because it is more responsive to dominance than to richness, in contrast to the Shannon index (Magurran 2004). This is often advantageous because the results are less likely to be affected by rare occurrences, which may not infrequently owe their presence in an assemblage to nonhuman activities and/or postdepositional processes. Moreover, the Reciprocal of Simpson's Index performs better with small sample sizes than the Shannon Index and is considered a more robust measure of diversity in general (Magurran 2004:101 and 115). To derive diversity values using this index, D was calculated as follows (Simpson 1949):

$$D = \frac{n(n-1)}{N(N-1)} \tag{2}$$

where n is the total number of identified remains for a particular long bone and N is the total number of identified remains for all long bones.

Diversity data for bison long bones are displayed in the upper panel of Figure 9.11. The diversity values tend to covary negatively with the Bison Index, although the relationship lacks statistical significance ($r_s = -.60, p \leq .24$). The Mousterian/Châtelperronian occupation seems to depart from the general pattern, based on the lower panel of Figure 9.11. These observations concur with the preceding results in suggesting that the Saint-Césaire foragers transported a wider variety of bison long bones with declining abundance of this taxon.

The same analysis was performed for reindeer long bone representation. As shown in Figure 9.12, the correlation between long bone diversity and the taxonomic representation of this species is strong, negative, and close to reaching statistical significance ($r_s = -.75, p \leq .07$). These results mean that assemblages with fewer reindeer specimens frequently contain a wider variety of reindeer long bones, and conversely.

Conclusions on Transport Strategies

The analysis of transport strategies yielded conflicting results. Patterns of cranium and, to a lesser extent, digit abundance provide support for the climatic deterioration hypothesis. Indeed, the representation of these low-utility parts varies more or less in tandem with the relative frequency of bison or reindeer, as predicted. In contrast, patterns of long bone representation indicate that elements with low marrow value were more frequently

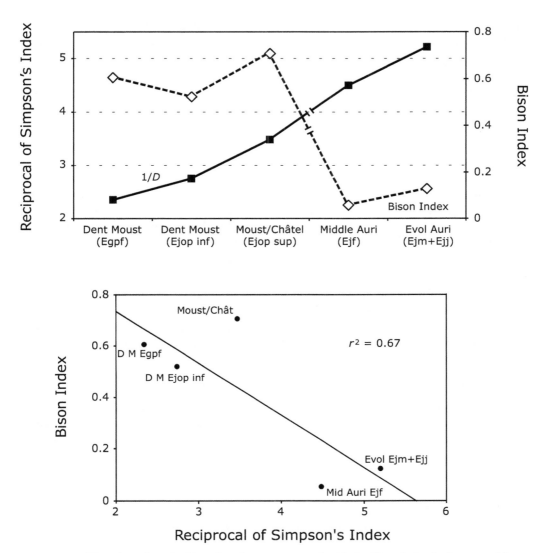

FIGURE 9.11. Diversity values for bison long bones compared with the Bison Index in five assemblages from Saint-Césaire (upper panel). The lower panel shows the goodness-of-fit between the diversity values and the Bison Index. The Reciprocal of Simpson's index was used to derive the diversity values (see text). Only the six long bones were included in the samples. The two Evolved Aurignacian occupations (EJM and EJJ) were aggregated to increase sample size.

transported when encounter rates with the species of interest were probably declining. This last observation does not match the prediction made using the central place forager prey choice model. The implication is that the Saint-Césaire foragers appear to have maximized the net delivery rate of crania and digits, but not the net delivery rate of long bone marrow. How can we explain these opposing trends?

One possibility is that the transport strategies documented at Saint-Césaire may reflect the existence of trade-offs between two opposing goals: maximizing the net delivery rate of overall food – as suggested by the patterns of head and digit representation – and intensifying the exploitation of long bone marrow, a strategy that may be adaptive in a context of declining carrying capacity. Unfortunately, in the absence of supplementary data, this last proposition remains speculative.

The remainder of this chapter turns to resources that were likely candidates for a diet breadth expansion. These resources include fast small-bodied prey species, low-utility marrow bones, and bone grease.

PREY CHOICE AT SAINT-CÉSAIRE

Central to the intensification hypothesis is the notion that modern humans exploited low-return resources, such as fast small-sized taxa, much more frequently than Neandertals who mostly ignored them. Three analytical patches (dry land, wetland, and freshwater) were defined in Chapter 3 to examine this hypothesis. As emphasized earlier, although an increased exploitation of low-return taxa in these patches during the early Upper Paleolithic may provide support for the intensification hypothesis (and/or for the climatic deterioration hypothesis), a lack of comparable evidence would clearly conflict with it. This problem is addressed in the remainder of this chapter. However, as discussed below (see also Chapter 6), fluctuations in the abundance of low-ranked taxa at Saint-Césaire must be interpreted carefully, as these species might have been accumulated by natural agents or for reasons other than food procurement.

Exploitation of Fast Small-Sized Taxa in the Dry Land Patch

In Chapter 3, taxa in the dry land patch were ranked along two distinct scales of profitability: a body weight scale and a fat weight scale. Both scales were in agreement in ascribing high rank positions to ungulates and low rank positions to leporids, birds, and small carnivores. On the basis of these rankings, two abundance indices were created for this patch:

Large Ungulate-Fox Index

$$= \Sigma NISP \text{ large ungulates (bison + horse + reindeer)}/(\Sigma NISP \text{ fox + large ungulates}) \quad (3)$$

Large Ungulate-Small Taxa Index

$$= \Sigma NISP \text{ large ung.}/(\Sigma NISP \text{ leporids + large birds + large ung.}) \quad (4)$$

The first of these abundance indices, the Large Ungulate-Fox Index, compares the representation of horse, bison, and reindeer across the Saint-Césaire levels relative to red and arctic fox. As noted earlier, complications may arise in the interpretation of this index because small prey taxa might have been procured for raw materials (e.g., fur, canines) rather than for food. This issue is important because it implies that a change in the indices may reflect *new technological or symbolic needs rather than a shift in diet breadth*. Therefore, this and the following chapter also consider the incidence and location of cutmarks on remains of small fast game to assess how they were exploited during the Middle to Upper Paleolithic transition. Incidentally, it is worth mentioning that a fox canine from the Middle Aurignacian EJF level, displayed in the Musée des Bujoliers near the village of Saint-Césaire, was modified into a pendant. This specimen was

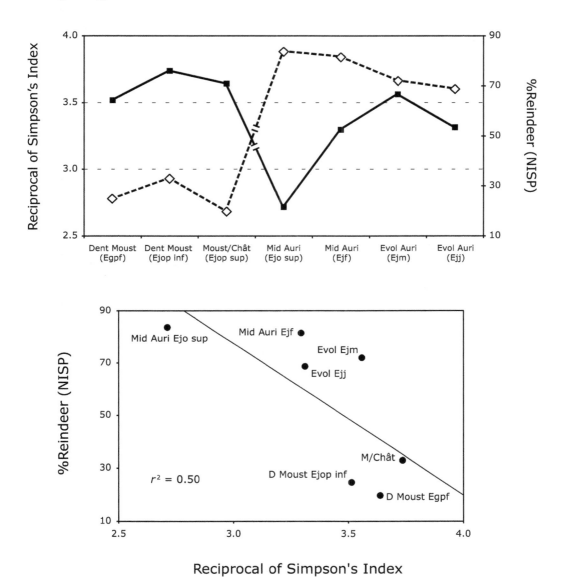

FIGURE 9.12. Diversity values for reindeer long bones compared with the taxonomic representation of reindeer in seven assemblages from Saint-Césaire (upper panel). The lower panel shows the goodness-of-fit between the diversity values and the taxonomic representation of reindeer. The Reciprocal of Simpson's index was used to derive the diversity values (see text). Only the six long bones were included in the samples.

excluded from the analysis. Furthermore, some of the fox remains from Saint-Césaire bear carnivore marks (Table 27), which may indicate that they were accumulated by non-human agents. Despite these ambiguities, the Large Ungulate-Fox Index is important for our discussion, given that fox remains from coeval sites sometimes show evidence of exploitation for food (e.g., Costamagno and Laroulandie 2004, see next chapter).

Variations in the Large Ungulate-Fox Index are presented in Figure 9.13 along with values for the Bison Index and micro-mammal species diversity data. These last two

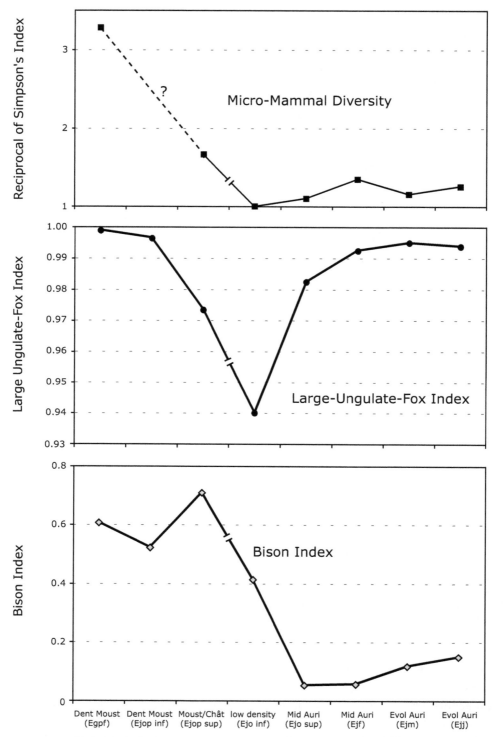

FIGURE 9.13. Variation in the Large Ungulate–Fox Index at Saint-Césaire (middle panel) compared with micro-mammal diversity (upper panel) and the Bison Index (lower panel). A low value indicates a greater proportion of foxes, whereas a value of "1.00" indicates that no fox remains were identified.

FIGURE 9.14. A fox calcaneum from the Middle Aurignacian EJF level showing a puncture mark presumably produced by a carnivore or raptor.

sets of data are helpful because they provide information on taxonomic shifts that were probably largely caused by climatic change. Values for the Large Ungulate-Fox Index suggest a short-lived decline in the relative abundance of large-bodied taxa in the lower half of the Saint-Césaire sequence followed by an increase during the Aurignacian. These results mean that foxes are better represented in the middle than at the two ends of the sequence. Although visually the values suggest a good match with trends in micro-mammal diversity, the correlation is not significant ($r_s = .50, p \leq .23$). Likewise, the correlation between the Large Ungulate-Fox Index and the Bison Index does not approach statistical significance ($r_s = .14, p \leq .71$).

These shifts in fox abundance may corroborate the intensification hypothesis because they may testify to an ephemeral increase in diet breadth. However, as mentioned earlier, human involvement in the fox accumulations is uncertain, given that cutmarks, burning, and percussion notches are completely absent in the fox sample ($n = 70$). In contrast, two of the fox specimens, one of which is shown in Figure 9.14, bear carnivore marks, for a percentage of 2.9%. This percentage is higher, but not significantly different, from the percentage of carnivore marks in the bison-horse-reindeer sample (44/8704 or 0.5%; $t_s = 1.67, p < .10$). Therefore, with the available data, the possibility that the fox remains were deposited by the Saint-Césaire occupants cannot be excluded.

Additional information about the fox accumulations can be gained by examining how carnivore taxa and specimens modified by carnivores are distributed across the Saint-Césaire stratigraphy. Figure 9.15 reveals broadly comparable temporal trends, with carnivore representation and the abundance of carnivore marks increasing and decreasing in concert. These two variables are strongly and significantly correlated ($r_s = .85, p \leq .03$). A plausible explanation for this relationship is that carnivores were present in greater numbers and scavenged the anthropic faunas more actively during the occupations in the middle of the Saint-Césaire sequence. Alternatively, these results might mean that humans increased scavenging of carcasses in tandem with an intensification of fox exploitation. If the latter suggestion is true, the relative abundance of fox should be unrelated to the incidence of burning in the assemblages.

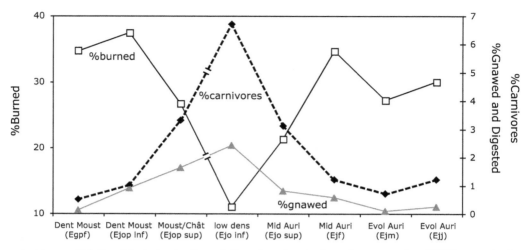

FIGURE 9.15. Relationship between the relative abundance of carnivore remains (NISP counts), the percentage of burned bones, and the percentage of specimens modified by carnivores in the Saint-Césaire sequence. Data are from Tables 5.6, 6.4, and 6.5.

As highlighted in Figure 9.15, the opposite is the case. The relative abundance of carnivores shows an inverse relationship with the percentage of burned bones at Saint-Césaire. Rank-order correlations between these two variables are moderately strong, but not significant, perhaps because of minor rank inversions ($r_s = -.68, p \leq .08$). If Pearson's product-moment correlation coefficient is used instead, the correlations become much stronger and significant (Pearson's $r = -.91, p \leq .01$). Correlations between percentages of carnivore-modified specimens and burning are low to moderately high, depending on the statistical method ($r_s = -.40, p \leq .30$, Pearson's $r = -.69, p \leq .06$). On the basis of these inverse relationships, it is possible to conclude that heavily burned assemblages were less attractive to carnivores. Together, these patterns suggest that humans rarely exploited foxes at Saint-Césaire.

The intensification hypothesis can be further tested using the Large Ungulate-Small Taxa Index, which monitors variations in the abundance of bison, horse, and reindeer relative to leporids and large birds. The birds included in this index are the Galliformes (ground-feeding birds such as pheasants) and raven (*Corvus corax*). Very small birds (< 200 g) were excluded from this index because they probably represent background accumulations. Similarly, the few bones that were attributed to Accipitriformes (eagles and vultures, $n = 7$) and Strigiformes (owls, $n = 2$) were not considered because they may indicate procurement for non-food-related activities (see examples in Laroulandie 2004a). The Large Ungulate-Small Taxa index is key because leporids and birds play central roles in debates about dietary change during the Upper Paleolithic (e.g., Hockett and Haws 2002; Stiner and Munro 2002; Cochard 2004; Costamagno and Laroulandie 2004; Manne *et al.* 2005; Brugal 2006; O'Connell 2006; Manne and Bicho 2009; Stiner 2009).

Figure 9.16 compares variations in the Large Ungulate-Small Taxa Index with the Bison Index and micro-mammal species diversity across the Saint-Césaire occupations. The data indicate that the relative abundance of large ungulates decreased and then increased in the middle assemblages, which points to a greater representation of leporids

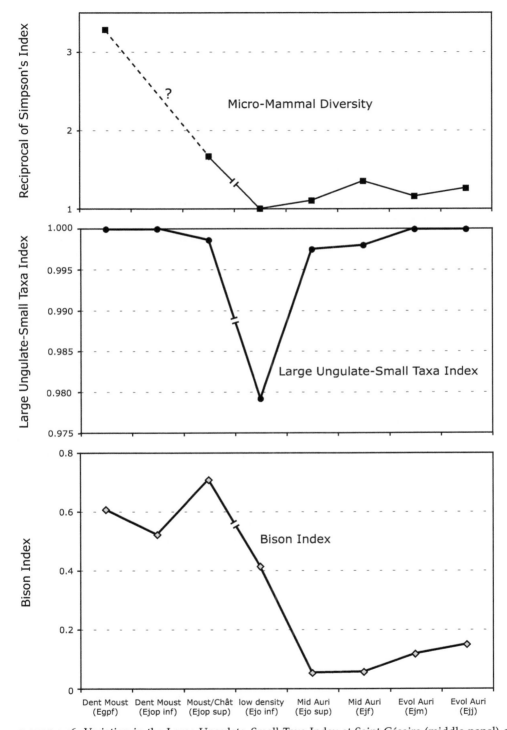

FIGURE 9.16. Variation in the Large Ungulate–Small Taxa Index at Saint-Césaire (middle panel) compared with micro-mammal diversity (upper panel) and the Bison Index (lower panel). Low values indicate greater proportions of leporids and birds, whereas a value of "1.000" means that no leporids or birds were identified.

and birds in this portion of the sequence. These patterns are very similar to those reported for the Large Ungulate-Fox Index, which is strongly correlated with the Large Ungulate-Small Taxa Index ($r_s = .87, p \leq .03$).

The trends observed in Figure 9.16 may signal successive episodes of expansion and contraction of diet breadth. However, as was the case for the fox remains, there is additional evidence that challenges this interpretation. Foremost among these is the fact that the total number of leporid ($n = 7$) and bird ($n = 3$) specimens included in the index sample is exceedingly small, as is the range of variation in the index (0.98–1.00). Additionally, there are reasons to suspect that nonhuman agents introduced at least some, perhaps most, of these small taxa into the site.

Two of the ten leporid specimens uncovered at Saint-Césaire bear carnivore marks, for a percentage of 20.0%. Despite the very small sample size, this percentage is significantly higher than the percentage of these marks on the combined reindeer, bison, and horse sample (44/8704 or 0.5%; $t_s = 2.48, p < .02$). No burning, cutmarks, or percussion cones were recorded on the leporid remains. However, a hare radius found in the Middle Aurignacian EJF level was modified into a tool. This bone was not considered in the analysis.

Bird species, such as willow grouse (*Lagopus lagopus*), snowy owl (*Bubo scandiacus*), and alpine chough (*Pyrrhocorax graculus*), which sometimes reach high frequencies in human-accumulated avifaunal assemblages dated to the Late Glacial (Vilette 1999; Laroulandie 2003, 2004a), have not been identified in the Saint-Césaire samples, with the possible exception of two indeterminate *Lagopus* remains. Moreover, none of the bird specimens present in the Saint-Césaire assemblages exhibit traces of human activity (Laroulandie 2004b). These observations suggest that the occupants consumed birds very infrequently, if at all. This last interpretation should be treated cautiously, however, because anthropic marks are rarely abundant on bird bones, even in assemblages of unequivocal human origin (Laroulandie 2000). The same observation applies to leporids (Cochard 2004).

In general, the very small number of remains and the lack of anthropic marks, along with indications of carnivore damage, point to a mostly natural accumulation or at least to a non-alimentary exploitation, of foxes, leporids, and birds at Saint-Césaire. However, no firm conclusion can be reached on this issue. The following section assesses patterns of dietary breadth in the wetland and freshwater patches.

Prey Choice in the Wetland and Freshwater Patches

A single abundance index, the Giant Deer Index ($\sum$ NISP giant deer/[$\sum$ NISP giant deer + Anseriformes]), was considered for the wetland patch. However, taxa associated with this patch are poorly represented and unevenly distributed in the assemblages. For instance, 7 of the 14 giant deer remains identified at Saint-Césaire derive from a single layer. For the Anseriformes (aquatic birds such as ducks and geese), two occupations provided 11 of the 13 specimens. Concerning these counts, it should be noted that five giant deer teeth from the Middle Aurignacian EJF level and six pintail bones from the Middle Aurignacian EJO sup level were counted as a single specimen in each case because anatomical refitting and contextual data suggest the presence of single individuals. No evidence of cultural or carnivore modification was detected on any of

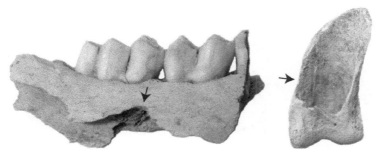

FIGURE 9.17. A marrow-cracked mandible (left) from the Evolved Aurignacian EJJ level and a marrow-cracked second phalanx (right) from the Middle Aurignacian EJO sup level. Both specimens are from reindeer. The point of impact is shown by an arrow on each specimen.

the wetland taxa (Laroulandie 2004b). These findings, combined with the absence of specimens in many of the layers, preclude analysis of the Giant Deer Index.

In France, inland sites provide little evidence for the exploitation of fish during the Mousterian (Le Gall 2000). At Saint-Césaire, the freshwater patch is represented by only three fish vertebrae (two trout and a cyprinid, see Chapters 5 and 7). These specimens, all from the Mousterian/Châtelperronian level, probably correspond to a single deposition event. Their mode of introduction is unknown. The small number of these remains suggests that the diet of the Saint-Césaire occupants rarely, if ever, included fish.

Overall, little support was found in any of the three patches for dietary use of fast small-bodied taxa in the early Upper Paleolithic. This conclusion contradicts the intensification hypothesis.

INTENSITY OF BONE PROCESSING

We saw in Chapter 3 that the investigation of change in the intensity of bone processing provides one of the simplest, and least controversial, approaches to the study of diet breadth. At Saint-Césaire, long bones were systematically fractured for marrow. Therefore, these elements cannot be used to document shifts in processing intensity because they present virtually no variation in the frequency of fragmentation. However, the picture may be different for bones with marginal amounts of marrow, such as the scapula, innominates, calcaneum, talus, mandible, and phalanges. Do these elements show temporal variation in processing behavior that is consistent with the intensification hypothesis?

At Saint-Césaire, limited sample sizes hinder the study of processing intensity for most of the low-utility marrow bones. The problem is different for the reindeer mandible. Despite adequate samples and evidence for marrow-cracking (Figure 9.17, left), this element could not be considered because of frequent postdepositional damage to the mandibular body. In the assemblages, only the first and second phalanges of reindeer allow a quantitative analysis of processing intensity. To increase sample sizes, both types of phalanges were combined. It should be noted that the thin walls of these bones complicated the identification of percussion notches (Figure 9.17, right). Therefore, although fracture patterns on broken phalanges are similar to those produced during

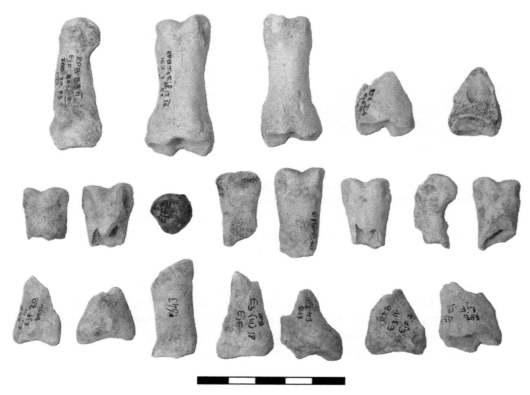

FIGURE 9.18. Reindeer first phalanges uncovered in the Middle Aurignacian EJF layer from Saint-Césaire. Only the largest specimens are shown. The majority of the fragmented phalanges in this figure appear to have been marrow-cracked.

marrow-cracking activities, the possibility that some of the fractures have a natural, as opposed to a cultural, origin cannot be excluded (Figure 9.18).

Percentages of broken reindeer phalanges are shown by stratigraphic unit in Figure 9.19. Although the samples are very small in some cases, the values indicate a steady increase in processing intensity over time. This trend is significantly correlated with the stratigraphic position of the assemblage ($r_s = .93$, $p \leq .04$) but, importantly, not with sample size ($r_s = .16$, $p \leq .73$). These results provide limited evidence for resource intensification at Saint-Césaire.

Other patterns are suggested by the data. The increase in phalanx processing between the Mousterian/Châtelperronian (5/6 or 83.3%) and the Middle Aurignacian EJO sup (18/20 or 90.0%) is *not* significant ($t_s = 0.43$, $p < .67$). Therefore, no threshold change in processing behavior between these two layers is apparent, although this may be an artifact of small sample size. In contrast, the increase in processing intensity between the Middle Aurignacian EJF (57/64 or 89.1%) and the aggregated EJM and EJJ samples (10/10 or 100%) *is* statistically significant ($t_s = 1.98$, $p < .05$). This last trend may indicate that the overall return rate continued to decline after the Middle to Upper Paleolithic transition (*sensu stricto*). However, these propositions should be regarded with caution, given the small sizes of the samples. Overall, the lack of threshold change in the intensity

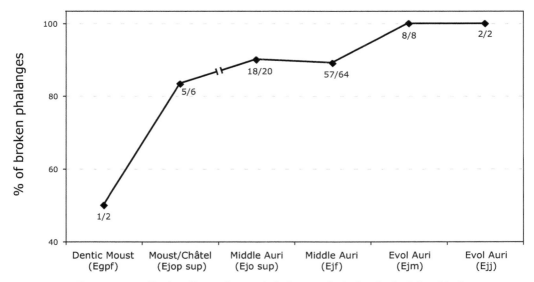

FIGURE 9.19. Percentages of broken first and second phalanges of reindeer in the Saint-Césaire sequence. Values in the figure refer to the number of fragmented phalanges relative to the total number of phalanges in the assemblage. Three complete phalanges, one from the Middle Aurignacian EJO sup level and two from the Middle Aurignacian EJF level, were identified at the Musée des Bujoliers in the village of Saint-Césaire. These phalanges are included in this figure. Other analyses and tables omit them.

of phalanx processing at Saint-Césaire seems to better fit the expectations of the climatic deterioration hypothesis than those of the intensification hypothesis.

BONE GREASE RENDERING

Bone grease is generally considered a low-ranked resource, given that it is associated with very high processing costs and low returns (Manne *et al.* 2005; Munro and Bar-Oz 2005; Stiner *et al.* 2008). These costs normally include wood and stone collecting, water fetching, arduous fragmentation of the skeletal elements, fire preparation, in-water replacement of cool stones by hot ones, and removal of the floating grease (Leechman 1951; Zierhut 1967; Vehik 1977; Binford 1978; Saint-Germain 1997; Church and Lyman 2003). Given that bone grease rendering is undocumented in the Mousterian in general (but see Costamagno 2010 for possible exceptions), evidence for grease rendering in the transitional occupations at Saint-Césaire could support the intensification hypothesis. However, there are several lines of evidence which suggest that this is not the case.

Four faunal patterns attest to the intentional exploitation of grease-rich elements and bone portions as fuel, rather than for food, at Saint-Césaire (see Chapter 6). First, burning is prevalent throughout the sequence, affecting between 21.6 and 37.8% of the specimens (excluding the low density EJO inf layer). Second, burning is not random: throughout the sequence, long bone epiphyses are frequently carbonized (40.6% on average), in marked contrast to long bone shafts (1.3% on average). In this regard, it should be noted that in the Middle Aurignacian EJF assemblage, a statistically significant relationship was observed between grease utility and the percentage of burned reindeer elements (Morin

2010). This result is consistent with experiments showing that grease-rich elements and bone portions burn well in open-air hearths (Costamagno *et al.* 1999; Théry-Parisot 2002; Théry-Parisot and Costamagno 2005). Third, the abundance of carbonized *spongiosa* fragments in the indeterminate samples, many of which appear to derive from epiphyses, confirm that grease-rich elements were selectively burned at Saint-Césaire. Fourth, the intensity of burning is not compatible with roasting or cooking because the specimens tend to be completely carbonized.

A last point concerns mark production. Efficient grease extraction requires significant fragmentation, which is usually achieved by pounding bones with a hammer over an anvil (Zierhut 1967; Vehik 1977; Church and Lyman 2003). Pounding and crushing marks on bone fragments are generally produced during this process. At Saint-Césaire, these marks are virtually absent on grease-rich bone portions. The scarcity of fire-cracked rocks, objects often associated with grease extraction (Vehik 1977; Brink and Dawe 2003; Church and Lyman 2003), may support this conclusion. However, this last line of evidence should be considered with caution, given that other techniques of grease extraction that have not been ethnographically documented might have existed in the past. Nevertheless, it seems reasonable to conclude that grease rendering was not regularly performed at Saint-Césaire.

SUMMARY AND DISCUSSION

This chapter examined the implications of two propositions, the climatic deterioration hypothesis and the intensification hypothesis. The results of the tests of these implications, which are briefly summarized here, deserve some comments.

The analysis of the Bison and Horse Indices pointed to significant changes in encounter rates with high-ranked prey taxa over time, an observation that is central to the climatic deterioration hypothesis. Using the central place forager prey choice model as a framework, it was suggested that these changes in encounter rates influenced the transport of skeletal elements. Specifically, it was inferred that, to maximize the net delivery rate of food to the central place, low-utility elements should have been less frequently transported when the species of interest was rare and, consequently, more likely captured further from the central place.

In the reindeer and bison samples, the negative relationships observed between the relative abundance of crania and digits – two low-utility elements – and the relative abundances of these species are in accord with the climatic deterioration hypothesis. However, long bone representation is at variance with this hypothesis because, contrary to the prediction, the diversity and mean utility of these elements decreased with lowered encounter rates with reindeer or bison. These contradictory results may reflect the existence of trade-offs between the need to maximize the net delivery rate of food and the need to increase marrow delivery in absolute terms. The argument for intensification of marrow delivery remains tentative, however, and calls for further testing.

The discussion then turned to the analysis of low-ranked resources, which are central to the test of O'Connell's intensification hypothesis. Resource exploitation was examined at various scales, from species to bone portions, to assess whether the diet breadth of Neandertals and early modern humans differed. Several pieces of evidence suggest that non-human agents were primarily responsible for the deposition of the small number of bird, leporid, and fox remains uncovered at Saint-Césaire. Yet the presence of a few tools and ornaments made from hare and fox parts indicates at least occasional exploitation of fast small-sized taxa by humans during the early Upper Paleolithic.

The analysis of bone processing yielded information relevant to the intensification hypothesis. Specifically, we saw that the reindeer samples suggest that the intensity of phalanx processing increased over time at Saint-Césaire. Interestingly, a statistically significant increase in processing intensity was observed between the Middle Aurignacian EJF and the Evolved Aurignacian occupations, but not between the Mousterian/Châtelperronian and Middle Aurignacian EJO sup occupations. In combination with the gradual nature of the trend, these results were inferred to better match the expectations of the climatic deterioration hypothesis than those of the intensification hypothesis.

Overall, the large ungulate data imply a marked climatically-induced decline in foraging efficiency during the Middle to Upper Paleolithic transition. Yet the foragers who occupied Saint-Césaire do not seem to have responded to this decline by widening their diet breadth, which they could have achieved, for instance, by beginning to consume fast small-sized taxa or bone grease. In fact, the Neandertals and modern humans at Saint-Césaire differed little in terms of foraging behavior because they apparently exploited the same range of resources. Both populations ignored low-ranked resources, with the exception of the phalanges of large ungulates, which were more frequently processed when foraging efficiency declined. Although the taphonomic data argue against it, the possibility that a dietary expansion was incipient in the middle of the Saint-Césaire sequence cannot be entirely ruled out. However, if it occurred, this dietary expansion was, from an evolutionary standpoint, a failed experiment because it was not continued during the Aurignacian. Comparisons with other assemblages from the same region will show that these results are not limited to Saint-Césaire.

10

DIET BREADTH AT THE REGIONAL LEVEL

LITTLE SUPPORT WAS FOUND FOR DIETARY USE OF LOW-RANKED RESOURCES BY THE occupants of Saint-Césaire. However, this evidence must be compared with that from other sequences to determine whether the results obtained for this site are of general significance. As noted earlier, the number of faunal sequences that span the Middle to Upper Paleolithic transition in France is low. Moreover, the assemblages from these sites are often affected by problems of selective recovery of the faunal remains (Grayson and Delpech 2002, 2008) and/or were extensively modified by carnivores (e.g., David 2004; Zilhão *et al.* 2007). Fortunately, a small number of sites are largely exempt from these problems.

One of these exceptions is Grotte du Renne at Arcy-sur-Cure, a Middle-to-Upper Pale-olithic sequence characterized by large anthropic assemblages (David 2002). Compar-isons with this site will permit an evaluation of whether the foraging patterns uncovered at Saint-Césaire are representative for the study area. For the Aurignacian, comparisons are also made with two occupations from Abri Pataud in the Dordogne region. These comparisons are important because they provide valuable data for cultural phases that are documented – or missing – at Saint-Césaire. To better inform the comparisons, this section begins with a brief presentation of the Grotte du Renne and Abri Pataud assem-blages and an investigation of transport decisions at these sites.

GROTTE DU RENNE (ARCY-SUR-CURE)

The Grotte du Renne at Arcy-sur-Cure belongs to a complex of caves located near the Cure River in Bourgogne (see Figure 2.1 for general location). Excavated between 1949 and 1963 by André Leroi-Gourhan, the sequence comprises fourteen levels ranging from the Mousterian through the Gravettian (Leroi-Gourhan and Leroi-Gourhan 1964). Five levels – XI (Denticulate Mousterian), X, IX, VIII (Châtelperronian), and VII (Early Aurignacian) – document the transition from the Middle to the Upper Paleolithic.

The faunal assemblages from these levels have been the focus of several publications (David and Poulain 1990, 2002; David 2002; David *et al.* 2005). In the next section, the com-parisons based on these assemblages exclude level VIII, the most recent Châtelperronian occupation, because during this period, the cave appears to have largely functioned as a bear nursery (David 2002; David *et al.* 2005). In addition, level IX is not considered because of a lack of data. It is important to note that recently published radiocarbon dates attest to occupation mixing at Grotte du Renne (Higham *et al.* 2010). This problem may undermine some of the trends reported here for this site.

The Faunal Assemblages

Reindeer (59.7%) and horse (24.6%) provide the majority of faunal remains in the Denticulate Mousterian (level XI) occupation of Grotte du Renne (NISP = 1436, David and Poulain 1990:320, figure 1). Other ungulates are poorly represented. Although carnivore remains (91/1436 or 6.3%), particularly those of cave bear ($n = 53$), are moderately abundant in the faunal sample, limited evidence for carnivore activity was found in this level. This pattern is probably explained by the low frequency of hyena ($n = 22$) and wolf ($n = 7$) specimens in the assemblage, two species notorious for inflicting damage on faunal remains. The abundance of cutmarks and burning in this and other assemblages from the site indicates that humans were the main depositional agents (David and Poulain 1990, 2002).

Reindeer (60.3%) and, to a lesser extent, horse (11.8%) dominate the overlying level X (subdivision Xc), which coincides with the earliest of three Châtelperronian occupations (NISP = 1808, David 2004:763, table 2). Mammoth (9.6%), cave bear (7.6%), bison/aurochs (3.6%), and hyena (3.4%) rank next in abundance. In comparison, horse (47.6%) is more frequent, and reindeer (34.4%) less frequent, in the Early Aurignacian level VII (NISP = 4481, David and Poulain 2002:51). Carnivores (15.1%), including cave bear (9.3%) and fox (6.0%), are relatively common. Lastly, seasonality data, which are unavailable for the previous occupations, suggest that horse was obtained in fall and winter during the Early Aurignacian, whereas reindeer was obtained in winter only.

Transport Decisions

A major foraging goal of the people at Saint-Césaire was to deliver marrow bones to the site. Were the foragers at Grotte du Renne motivated by a similar goal? This question is key because it may affect the analysis of diet breadth at this site.

To investigate variations in transport decisions between the two sequences, the abundances of reindeer skeletal parts in the Châtelperronian and the Early Aurignacian of Grotte du Renne were compared, through rank-order correlations, with six reindeer assemblages from Saint-Césaire. Correlations were also calculated for horse, but the comparisons were only performed with the Early Aurignacian level VII because of the small sample sizes. Correlations were calculated twice, once including parts that are frequently burned at Saint-Césaire (and, perhaps, at Grotte du Renne as well – discussed subsequently), and once excluding them to control for the effects of sample composition. These comparisons are strengthened by the fact that, despite some differences (summer acquisition of horse is documented at Saint-Césaire but not at Grotte du Renne), seasons of procurement appear to be roughly similar at these sites, at least as suggested by data for the Early Aurignacian level VII.

Concerning the Châtelperronian level Xc, the correlations between the two sites are strong for reindeer and horse and increase slightly when the comparisons include parts that are frequently burned (Table 10.1). The correlations remain high and significant,

TABLE 10.1. *Spearman's rho correlations between the skeletal profiles from Grotte du Renne and those from Saint-Césaire*

	Grotte du Renne					
	Châtelperronian		Early Aurignacian level VII			
	Reindeer		Reindeer		Horse	
	All minus burned[a]	All parts[b]	All minus burned	All parts	All minus burned	All parts
Saint-Césaire	rho $\quad$ p	rho $\quad$ p	rho $\quad$ p	rho $\quad$ p	rho $\quad$ p	rho $\quad$ p
Evol Auri Ejj	.911 $\quad$ <.01	.869 $\quad$ ≤.0001	.764 $\quad$ <.02	.791 $\quad$ <.001	— $\quad$ —	— $\quad$ —
Evol Auri Ejm	.829 $\quad$ <.01	.930 $\quad$ ≤.0001	.622 $\quad$ <.04	.843 $\quad$ ≤.001	.720 $\quad$ <.02	.682 $\quad$ <.01
Mid Auri Ejf	.794 $\quad$ <.01	.875 $\quad$ ≤.0001	.673 $\quad$ <.03	.908 $\quad$ <.0001	.607 $\quad$ <.05	.712 $\quad$ <.01
Mid Auri Ejo sup	.858 $\quad$ <.01	.908 $\quad$ <.0001	.760 $\quad$ <.02	.876 $\quad$ ≤.0001	— $\quad$ —	— $\quad$ —
Moust/Châtel	.802 $\quad$ <.01	.829 $\quad$ ≤.001	.790 $\quad$ <.01	.786 $\quad$ <.001	.937 $\quad$ <.001	.771 $\quad$ <.01
Dent Moust Egpf	.703 $\quad$ <.02	.888 $\quad$ <.0001	.589 $\quad$ <.06	.774 $\quad$ <.001	.668 $\quad$ <.03	.850 $\quad$ <.001

Data for Grotte du Renne levels Xc and VII are from David (2002:189, figure 5) and David and Poulain (2002:57, table IV and p. 68, table V). The Saint-Césaire data are from Appendix 2. Abundances of skeletal parts based on %MAU. Concerning Grotte du Renne, values for the reindeer cranium and mandible are those for "maxillaire supérieur" and "maxillaire inférieur," respectively. In the case of horse, values for the cranium and mandible are those for "dent jugale supérieure" and "dent jugale inférieure," respectively.

[a] Includes all six long bones, the cranium, the mandible, the scapula, and all three types of phalanges.

[b] Includes same as in note[a] plus all five types of vertebrae (atlas, axis, other cervical vertebrae, thoracic vertebrae, lumbar vertebrae), carpals, tarsals, ribs, and pelvis (innominates and sacrum combined).

although they are a bit weaker, when the comparisons involve the Early Aurignacian level VII. These observations indicate that the skeletal profiles for reindeer and horse are similar at Saint-Césaire and Grotte du Renne.

To identify the currency that best explains transport strategies at Grotte du Renne, the anatomical profiles for this site were compared with the same range of utility models considered in the analysis of Saint-Césaire. For reindeer, these models include the caribou UMI (Morin 2007), FUI (Metcalfe and Jones 1988), and Nunamiut data on bone grease production (Binford 1978). The horse samples were compared with the horse FUI (Outram and Rowley-Conwy 1998) and UMI (see Chapter 8). As emphasized earlier, no bone grease model is currently available for horse.

Table 10.2 shows that the abundance of reindeer parts correlates most strongly with the UMI and the bone grease model. Clearly, the fit is much poorer with the FUI. Likewise, the data for horse show a stronger correlation with the UMI than with the FUI. These patterns are consistent with those documented at Saint-Césaire and emphasize the importance of marrow procurement in the transport strategies of the Grotte du Renne foragers. Another important finding is that these transport strategies persisted throughout the early Upper Paleolithic, at least for reindeer. The next task is to determine whether the similarities noted between these sites extend to the exploitation of low-ranked resources.

Fast Small-Bodied Taxa

Fast small-sized mammals are uncommon in the Denticulate Mousterian (level XI) occupation of Grotte du Renne, given that they are only represented by nine fox and one

TABLE 10.2. *Spearman's rho correlations between the abundances of elements in the Châtelperronian and Aurignacian of Grotte du Renne and various utility models for reindeer*

| | Reindeer | | | | | | Horse | | | |
| | FUI | | Bone grease | | UMI | | FUI | | UMI | |
Grotte du Renne	rho	*p*	rho	*p*	rho	*p*	rho	*p*	rho	*p*
Aurignacian (VII)	.341	<.26	.691	<.04	.671	<.06	**.668**	**<.03**	**.842**	**<.02**
Châtelperronian (Xc)	.434	<.16	**.821**	**<.02**	**.862**	**<.02**	–	–	–	–

p ≤ 0.05 are shown in bold. Abundances of skeletal parts based on %MAU. Categories of parts are the same as in Table 10.1, note a. The Saint-Césaire data are from Appendix 2.

Note: The utility models that are used are: the caribou FUI (Metcalfe and Jones 1988:492, table 2), the percentages of parts selected for grease rendering (Binford 1978:36, table 1.13, column 6, spring episode), and the caribou UMI (Morin 2007:77, table 4); for horse, the FUI (Outram and Rowley-Conwy 1998:845, table 6) and horse UMI (see Chapter 8).

hare specimen. None of the fox remains seems to have been utilized by humans (David and Poulain 1990). Birds are also present, but information is lacking on species composition and patterns of representation (Mourer-Chauviré 2002). Likewise, no data on fish abundance are available for any of the Grotte du Renne occupations.

Fast small-bodied mammals, again represented by fox (*n* = 19) and hare (*n* = 7), are also rare in the Châtelperronian level Xc (David 2004). The anatomical profile for fox is dominated by teeth and phalanges, combined with the presence of cutmarks on the phalanges, which is possibly indicative of skin procurement (Leroi-Gourhan 1961; David and Poulain 1990). Human involvement in the accumulation of this species is further shown by the fact that at least four fox teeth from level X (irrespective of the subdivisions) were perforated or grooved, presumably for use as ornaments (Taborin 1990; d'Errico *et al.* 1998). Whether humans deposited the hare specimens remains to be more fully documented (David 2004). With respect to birds, one swan (*Cygnus cygnus*) bone tube from sub-level Xb has sawing traces. According to d'Errico and collaborators (1998:S10), fox and birds were not exploited for food during the Châtelperronian at Grotte du Renne but rather for technical and symbolic purposes.

The picture is slightly different for the Early Aurignacian. Fox, a moderately abundant species in this occupation (*n* = 223), shows both human- and carnivore-inflicted marks. Of particular importance is the presence of cutmarks on two vertebrae, which probably indicates human consumption (David and Poulain 2002:84). Moreover, an awl made from a fox-sized carnivore ulna was identified in this occupation by Julien *et al.* (2002). In contrast, no mention of cultural modification is made for any of the hare remains from this level (*n* = 39, Mourer-Chauviré 2002; David and Poulain 2002). However, a hare ulna was tooth-marked, possibly by a fox (David and Poulain 2002).

The Early Aurignacian is the only transitional level at Grotte du Renne for which quantitative information is available for birds. The small bird assemblage (*n* = 23) is dominated by raven (*Corvus corax, n* = 17) and golden eagle (*Aquila chrysaetos, n* = 3). Other species, such as willow grouse (*Lagopus lagopus*), alpine accentor (*Prunella collaris*), and crag martin (*Ptyonoprogne rupestris*), are each represented by a single specimen. Lastly, a tube made from a long bone attests to the technical exploitation of birds (Julien *et al.* 2002).

Overall, the Grotte du Renne sequence contains few remains of fast small-sized taxa. The available data for this site show that birds and hares are slightly outranked in terms of abundance by fox. The marginal occurrence of these taxa and the trend toward a greater representation of fox relative to birds and hare at Grotte du Renne are in good agreement with the patterns uncovered at Saint-Césaire. The recovery of a few objects and ornaments made from small animal parts is also in agreement with Saint-Césaire, despite minor differences in the species involved (fox and birds at Grotte du Renne, fox and hare at Saint-Césaire). However, in contrast to Saint-Césaire, a small number of fox remains from the Early Aurignacian level VII at Grotte du Renne suggest human consumption. This point raises the following question: is there any indication of a shift toward a broader diet at Grotte du Renne?

This question is addressed using two abundance indices. The first of these, the *Large Ungulate-Fox Index* was presented in the preceding chapter. The second, the *Large Ungulate-Hare Index*, was created specifically for Grotte du Renne. This index focuses on fluctuations in the abundance of hares relative to large ungulates and was calculated as follows:

$$\text{Large Ung.-Hare Index} = \frac{\Sigma \; NISP \; ungulates \; (reindeer + horse + bovines)/}{(\Sigma \; NISP \; Lepus \; sp. + large \; ungulates)} \tag{5}$$

These two indices are plotted in Figure 10.1. Unlike at Saint-Césaire, the values for the two indices decrease almost linearly across the Grotte du Renne sequence, which means that small taxa increased in abundance relative to large ungulates. These statistically significant trends (fox: $\chi^2_{trend} = 84.8$, $p \leq .001$; hare: $\chi^2_{trend} = 13.3$, $p \leq .001$; fox or hare NISP vs. the sum of reindeer, bison, and horse NISP) are qualitatively consistent with the intensification hypothesis.

However, two sets of observations undermine the significance of these trends. First, as emphasized earlier, the presence of several small taxa in the Châtelperronian level at Grotte du Renne has been attributed to raw material procurement rather than food acquisition (Leroi-Gourhan 1961; d'Errico *et al.* 1998). Thus, the modest increase in the representation of fast small-bodied species at Grotte du Renne might, in part, have been driven by changes unrelated to diet. Second, as was the case at Saint-Césaire, the range of variation in the indices is extremely small (0.94–0.99 and 0.99–1.00 for the fox and hare indices, respectively). As a result of these ambiguities, more data are needed to interpret the minor increase in small prey representation at Grotte du Renne.

Bone Processing

Information on the processing of low-utility marrow elements is scarce at Grotte du Renne. David and Poulain (1990) noted that reindeer phalanges are often broken in the Denticulate Mousterian and Châtelperronian (level Xc) occupations. However, the authors do not provide data on the intensity of the breakage or on the probable agent of fragmentation. In the Early Aurignacian occupation, slightly more than half of the reindeer first (13/20) and second (10/16) phalanges appear to have been marrow-cracked, although the possibility that these bones were fractured by carnivores cannot be excluded (David and Poulain 2002:69). Concerning horse, marrow-cracking was diagnosed on

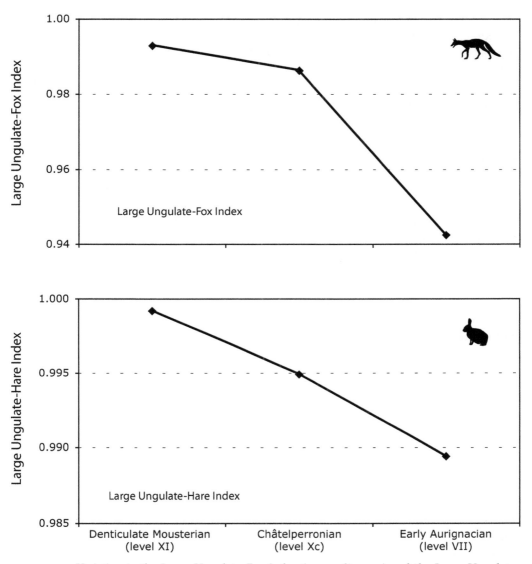

FIGURE 10.1. Variation in the Large Ungulate–Fox Index (upper diagram) and the Large Ungulate–Hare Index (lower diagram) at Grotte du Renne. For the Early Aurignacian level VII, the hare sample excludes possibly intrusive material. NISP data from David and Poulain (1990:320, figure 1 and 2002:51) and David (2004:763, table 2).

several first phalanges and on some second phalanges as well (David and Poulain 2002). Unfortunately, limited data preclude inter-level comparisons for these species.

With respect to bone grease manufacture, David and Poulain (1990:321) pointed out that the Denticulate Mousterian and Châtelperronian occupations contain large quantities of shaft fragments but few long bone epiphyses. These authors attributed this trend to the use of epiphyses as fuel. The fact that 40% of the fragments are burned in these levels (David and Poulain 1990:320) substantiates this view. In the Early Aurignacian, nearly half (47%) of the unidentified epiphyses are burned (David and Poulain 2002:51). Vertebrae, innominates, carpals, and tarsals are also frequently burned in the same occupation. These patterns, which are very similar to those observed at Saint-Césaire, argue against the practice of bone grease rendering at Grotte du Renne.

Comparisons with two Early Aurignacian occupations from Abri Pataud will show that these observations appear to be typical of the early Upper Paleolithic in the study area.

ABRI PATAUD

Abri Pataud is a rockshelter located in the village of Les Eyzies-de-Tayac (Dordogne) in western France. Hallam L. Movius uncovered an exceptional sequence of Aurignacian, Gravettian, and Magdalenian occupations at this site, which he excavated between 1953 and 1964 (Bricker 1995). This discussion focuses on the two large Early Aurignacian assemblages from levels 14 and 11. The two Evolved Aurignacian occupations (layers 8 and 7) from this sequence are not considered here because of a lack of anatomical information and sample size constraints.

The analysis of the Abri Pataud faunas sometimes presented problems because the NISP values for the Aurignacian assemblages are not always consistent between or even within publications, especially with regard to the abundance of non-reindeer remains. As a rule, the highest published values were used to estimate species abundance.

The Faunal Assemblages

The faunal assemblage from level 14, the basal occupation of the Abri Pataud sequence, has been studied by Bouchud (1975), Spiess (1979), and Sekhr (1998). According to Sekhr (1998:64), 98.4% of the specimens that were identified in this large assemblage (NISP = 1960, specimens only identified to body size class excluded) belong to reindeer. Humans deposited the vast majority of these remains, as evidenced by the abundance of burned bones, the frequent occurrence of cutmarks, and the low frequency of carnivore-inflicted marks. According to Spiess (1979), reindeer in this level were procured during the winter.

Level 14 is capped by four smaller assemblages, levels 13/14, 13, 12/13, and 12, and a much larger one, level 11 (NISP = 2916, Chiotti *et al.* 2003:163, specimens only identified to family or body size class excluded). Reindeer (46.9%) and horse (46.9%) are equally represented in this occupation. Like level 14, the assemblage from level 11 is unambiguously anthropogenic. The data for level 11 suggest acquisition of reindeer during the winter, whereas horse appears to have been obtained during the summer (Spiess 1979; Chiotti *et al.* 2003).

Transport Decisions

The assemblages from Abri Pataud were compared using rank-order correlations with assemblages from Saint-Césaire in order to assess whether these sites show similar patterns of skeletal representation. The comparisons were performed separately for the reindeer and horse assemblages. The fact that the seasons of procurement for these

TABLE 10.3. *Spearman's rho correlations between reindeer and horse assemblages from Abri Pataud and Saint-Césaire*

	Abri Pataud					
	Early Aurignacian level 14		Early Aurignacian level 11			
	Reindeer		Reindeer		Horse	
	All minus burned[a]	All parts[b]	All minus burned	All parts	All minus burned	All parts
Saint-Césaire	rho p	rho p	rho p	rho p	rho p	rho p
Evol Auri Ejj	.748 <.02	.754 <.01	.808 <.01	.806 <.01	— —	— —
Evol Auri Ejm	.825 <.01	.859 <.001	.846 <.01	.888 <.001	.795 <.01	.794 <.01
Mid Auri Ejf	.925 <.01	.918 <.001	.928 <.01	.940 <.001	.883 <.01	.811 <.01
Mid Auri Ejo sup	.869 <.01	.875 <.001	.897 <.01	.901 <.001	— —	— —
Moust/Châtel	.675 <.03	.790 <.01	.717 <.02	.819 <.01	.867 <.01	.884 <.001
Dent Moust Egpf	.946 <.01	.944 <.001	.949 <.01	.940 <.001	.829 <.01	.843 <.01

The data for Abri Pataud are from Sekhr (1998:305, 310–311). Abundances of skeletal parts based on NNISP. The Saint-Césaire data are from Appendix 2.

[a] Includes all six long bones, the cranium, mandible, scapula, and all three types of phalanges. Concerning Abri Pataud, for the cranium, counts combine values for "hémi-maxillaire" and "dents supérieures isolées." For the mandible, counts combine values for "hémi-mandibule" and "dents inférieures isolées." For the radius, counts combine values for the "radius" and "radius-ulna" but exclude values for the "ulna."

[b] Includes same as in note[a] plus the carpals, tarsals, ribs, and pelvis (sacrum and innominates combined). Vertebrae were excluded due to limited data.

species were similar at Abri Pataud and Saint-Césaire strengthens the comparisons. The comparisons for horse only involve level 11 because this species is poorly represented in level 14.

Table 10.3 presents the rank-order correlations for the reindeer and horse assemblages. As shown in this table, the correlations are very high and significant, irrespective of the species or level. Importantly, correlations are strong whether parts that were frequently burned are included or not. These results demonstrate that patterns of body part representation are very similar at these sites.

Factors that guided the transport of skeletal elements to Abri Pataud were examined by comparing levels 14 and 11 with the utility models considered in the analysis of Grotte du Renne and Saint-Césaire. The rank-order correlations obtained with these models, which are presented in Table 10.4, indicate strong and statistically significant relationships between the reindeer assemblages and the UMI. In comparison, the correlations are slightly weaker with the bone grease model and much weaker with the FUI. Likewise, the level 11 horse assemblage is highly correlated with the horse UMI, but shows a slightly weaker relationship with the FUI. These results are congruent with those obtained at Saint-Césaire and Grotte du Renne and suggest that unsaturated marrow utility influenced transport decisions at all three sites.

Fast Small-Bodied Taxa

Fast small-bodied taxa are rare at Abri Pataud. However, this may partly be the result of the excavation methods, given that sediment sieving was unsystematic

TABLE 10.4. *Spearman's rho correlations between the abundances of skeletal parts in the Early Aurignacian of Abri Pataud and various utility models for reindeer*

| | Reindeer | | | | | | Horse | | | |
| | FUI | | Bone Grease | | UMI | | FUI | | UMI | |
Abri Pataud	rho	p	rho	p	rho	p	rho	p	rho	p
Early Aurignacian 11	.476	<.12	.606	<.07	.783	<.03	.736	<.02	.854	<.02
Early Aurignacian 14	.434	<.16	.558	<.10	.700	<.05	–	–	–	–

$p \leq 0.05$ are shown in bold. Abundances of skeletal parts based on NNISP. Categories of parts are the same as in Table 10.3, note a. The Saint-Césaire data are from Appendix 2.

Note: The utility models that are used are: the caribou FUI (Metcalfe and Jones 1988:492, table 2), the percentages of parts selected by two Nunamiut women for grease rendering (Binford 1978:36, table 1.13, column 6, spring episode), and the caribou UMI (Morin 2007:77, table 4); for horse, the FUI (Outram and Rowley-Conwy 1998:845, table 6) and horse UMI (see Chapter 8).

(Chiotti *et al.* 2003). A minimum of six fox remains were found in level 14 (Sekhr 1998:64), including an ulna with disarticulation cutmarks, which may attest to human consumption (Vercoutère 2004:66). An additional fox specimen, a canine modified into a pendant, is reported for this level (Brooks 1995; Vercoutère 2004). The assemblage also contains a single leporid specimen (a radius) but no birds or fish (Bouchud 1975; Sekhr 1998). Vercoutère (2004) noted that a leporid radius from the same level was modified into an awl. It is unclear whether this specimen is the same hare radius identified by Bouchud in the faunal assemblage.

The sample of fox remains from level 11 is moderately large ($n = 127$, Chiotti *et al.* 2003:195). The presence of cutmarks on a humerus and phalanx of fox, as well as the identification of three items of personal adornment made from fox parts (a perforated canine, metacarpal, and humerus), suggests that humans were involved in the deposition of at least some of the fox remains. Specifically, the cutmarks on the humerus have been attributed to disarticulation and meat removal, and those on the phalanx to skinning (Chiotti *et al.* 2003:195). Other small taxa, such as hares ($n = 5$) and birds ($n = 1$, alpine chough, *Pyrrhocorax graculus*), occur at extremely low frequencies in this level (Bouchud 1975; Chiotti *et al.* 2003). The assemblage contains no fish remains.

Abundance indices for small taxa were not calculated for Abri Pataud because comparisons cannot be made with final Mousterian and/or Châtelperronian occupations at this site. However, if we compare fox representation between levels 14 and 11, a statistically significant increase[1] is observed ($\chi^2_{trend} = 72.9$, $p \leq .001$). In contrast, the same levels show no comparable change in hare representation ($\chi^2_{trend} = 1.5$, $p \leq .22$). Therefore, unlike Saint-Césaire, both Grotte du Renne and Abri Pataud suggest a modest increase in the relative abundance of fox during the Aurignacian.

[1] As was the case for Grotte du Renne, statistical tests for linear trends at Abri Pataud compare fox or hare NISP to the sum of reindeer, bison, and horse NISP. For level 14, the NISP counts used for fox, leporids, and large ungulates (reindeer, bison, and horse) are, respectively, 6, 1, and 1,937. In level 11, the values for the same taxa are: 127, 5, and 2,750. The NISP data for level 14 are from Sekhr (1998:64, table 17, fox and large ungulates) and Bouchud (1975:123, table 33, leporids) and for level 11 from Chiotti *et al.* (2003:163, table 1, fox, leporids, and large ungulates).

Bone Processing

There is little information on bone processing at Abri Pataud. The majority of the long bones in the assemblages seem to have been marrow-cracked. Sekhr (1998) noted that reindeer phalanges are often broken in levels 14 and 11, which may constitute evidence of marrow procurement, although the agent that broke these bones is not identified. With respect to grease rendering, the diagrams presented by Sekhr (1998) for levels 14 and 11 show a very low representation of long bone ends relative to shafts. The use of epiphyses as fuel may be responsible for this underrepresentation, given that there are numerous burned specimens at Abri Pataud, particularly within and around hearth structures (Théry-Parisot 2002; Chiotti *et al.* 2003; Vercoutère 2004). Unfortunately, the published data do not specify which elements or bone portions were frequently burned.

SUMMARY OF DIET BREADTH IN WESTERN FRANCE

Patterns of species composition and body part representation are very similar in the sequences of Saint-Césaire, Grotte du Renne, and Abri Pataud. This seems also to be true of patterns of burning and breakage, although the data on these issues are often sparse. Given these results, it is reasonable to conclude that the Saint-Césaire assemblages are globally representative of the variability observed in western France during the Middle to Upper Paleolithic transition.

The analyses indicated that low-ranked taxa are infrequently represented at all three sites. Yet in contrast to Saint-Césaire, fox was apparently occasionally eaten at Grotte du Renne and Abri Pataud. Cut-marked fox specimens found at Grotte des Hyènes (Brassempouy) and Le Tarté in southwestern France also imply human consumption of fox during the Aurignacian (Letourneux 2003; Costamagno and Laroulandie 2004). These findings may point to a marginal increase in diet breadth during the early Upper Paleolithic of France. The production of novel objects such as awls, tubes, and ornaments from small animal parts (Costamagno and Laroulandie 2004; Vanhaeren and d'Errico 2006) likely contributed to this trend.

DIET BREADTH IN OTHER REGIONS OF EUROPE AND SOUTHWEST ASIA

The following sections adopt a broader perspective by briefly discussing the evidence relevant to the early Upper Paleolithic intensification model in Europe and southwest Asia. The review focuses exclusively on the exploitation of low-ranked taxa because little information on bone processing is available. Importantly, slow and sessile small-sized taxa (e.g., tortoises, shellfish) are left out of this discussion because there are some ambiguities about their actual profitability. It is suggested that several taxa within this class of prey types – especially the larger ones (e.g., tortoises) – may have yielded higher returns than medium-sized or even large-sized prey taxa, including ungulates, given the relative ease with which they can be caught. The implication is that several slow small-sized taxa may, in fact, have belonged to the optimal diet during the Paleolithic.

Slow small-sized taxa definitely would have been among the highest-ranked resources that can be procured by human groups moving at low speed, such as parties of children or adults foraging in tandem with young children (Hawkes *et al.* 1995; Bird and Bliege Bird

2000; Lupo 2007). Therefore, because of uncertainties about how these species actually scaled in profitability relative to larger prey taxa and the impossibility of estimating variations in the composition of foraging parties in the past, increased representation of slow small-sized taxa in archaeological sequences may not be indicative of resource intensification. For these reasons, slow small-sized taxa are not considered further here.

In contrast, when non-food utilization can be ruled out or controlled for, an analysis of the abundance of small *swift* taxa (i.e., leporids, birds, small carnivores, fish) allows a less ambiguous assessment of diet breadth, because these taxa would have been low-ranked by most human foragers, irrespective of the age or sex of the forager. The preceding assumes that snaring and trapping of these species would have provided low returns throughout much of Europe and southwest Asia. Although reasonable in these regions, this assumption may be problematic in other regions where the animal communities are characterized by a narrower range of prey body sizes (e.g., Australia, South America), which may cause frequent violations of the body size rule (see Chapter 3). Mass collecting would probably have provided low returns in the regions considered in this review, given the opportunity costs associated with this method of procurement (Lupo 2007). However, because this point is disputed for rabbits (e.g., Jones 2004b, 2006, 2009; Ugan 2005), the potentially confounding effect of mass collecting is addressed in the conclusions.

These points naturally lead to the issue of biogeography. This factor certainly considerably influenced variations in small prey representation in Europe and southwest Asia. For instance, the rabbit (*Oryctolagus* sp.) was confined to the Iberian Peninsula and southern France until well into the Holocene (Callou 2003; Cochard 2004). For this reason, this taxon is not likely to be detected in the archaeological record of other regions, such as the northern plains or eastern Europe, where hare (*Lepus* sp.) is better represented. In the same vein, the lynx (*Lynx* sp.) seems to be more frequently represented in the paleontological record of Iberia than that of France. The implication of these trends is that the diversity of potential candidates for resource intensification probably varied sensibly depending on the specific region and time period under scrutiny. We will see that this issue is particularly important when interpreting patterns of small prey abundance.

The data examined in the next sections are those found in the literature. The review begins with transitional assemblages from the northeastern plains of Europe and then moves to those from the Mediterranean basin. In this last region, the discussion proceeds in a clockwise fashion starting with Iberia and ending with the Near East. Regarding these regions, an effort was made to include all of the sites dating to the Middle to Upper Paleolithic transition that contain well-studied and carefully excavated faunas. Primary publications were consulted whenever possible. This proved to be a challenge, given the diversity of languages and the difficulty of gaining access to poorly diffused publications. Faunal assemblages for which only a species list was provided were ignored. Similarly, assemblages affected by selective recovery of the specimens or that were mostly accumulated by natural agents were excluded, except where they clearly contained significant and reliable information on human procurement of small prey species. These data are used to ascertain whether faunal assemblages from Europe and southwest Asia conform to the expectations of the intensification model.

To fully capture geographic and temporal variations in diet breadth in these regions, assemblages that are mostly anthropogenic are discussed irrespective of whether they yield indications of dietary use of small prey taxa or not. This approach was favored for several reasons. First, human-inflicted marks are generally rare in assemblages of fast small-bodied taxa, even in contexts in which these remains were clearly deposited by humans (Laroulandie 2000; Hockett and Haws 2002; Cochard 2004). This means that it may be difficult to identify with confidence the agent(s) of accumulation in these assemblages, *even when a taphonomic analysis of the remains has been conducted*. As a result of this ambiguity, considering the full range of anthropogenic assemblages seems most appropriate. Second, only a fraction of the studies reviewed here contain relevant taphonomic information on small prey taxa. Omitting these studies would have unnecessarily narrowed the discussion.

The database presents other problems. One major limitation is that objects made from small animal parts are not always published or identified to species. As emphasized earlier, this issue is important because fast small-sized species might have been obtained for purposes other than food acquisition. As a result, changes in the representation of small swift taxa cannot be assumed to reflect an increase in consumption without concomitant taphonomic data. Moreover, as a result of incomplete reporting, the discussion is sometimes restricted to qualitative statements, although this applies only to a minority of cases. As a result of these limitations, the data must be interpreted with caution.

This review focuses on four categories of low-ranked species: leporids, birds, foxes, and fish. These prey taxa were selected because they are frequently observed in paleontological sequences from Eurasia – which imply that they would have been available in many, although not necessarily all, regions. In addition, these taxa are often cited as potential candidates for resource intensification. To assess variation in small prey representation in the assemblages, the relative abundance of a particular small swift taxon was estimated using one of the following four abundance indices:

$$Leporid\ Index = \Sigma\ NISP\ leporids/(\Sigma\ NISP\ ungulates + leporids) \qquad (6)$$

$$Bird\ Index = \Sigma\ NISP\ birds/(\Sigma\ NISP\ ungulates + birds) \qquad (7)$$

$$Fox\ Index = \Sigma\ NISP\ fox/(\Sigma\ NISP\ ungulates + fox) \qquad (8)$$

$$Fish\ Index = \Sigma\ NISP\ fish/(\Sigma\ NISP\ ungulates + fish) \qquad (9)$$

In these indices, the higher the value, the higher the proportion of the small prey category within the assemblage. Ungulate specimens identified only to body size class or family were excluded from the counts to avoid duplication of information and due to methodological differences between publications. In contrast, all avian specimens, regardless of the level of identification, were included in the Bird Index because counts were sometimes presented without taxonomic data. In Iberia, the Fox Index was modified into a *Fox-Lynx Index* to take into account the importance of lynx in this region:

$$Fox\text{-}Lynx\ Index = (\Sigma\ NISP\ fox + lynx)/(\Sigma\ NISP\ ungulates + fox + lynx) \qquad (10)$$

These abundance indices are useful because they compare in a simple way two sets of taxa (a small swift taxon vs. a set of large swift taxa) that are unlikely to have overlapped in net return rates, irrespective of the type of forager (e.g., children, adult males, etc.).

The Northeastern Plains

In the northeastern plains, information on the utilization of small swift prey taxa is mostly limited to southwestern Germany and Russia. Concerning the former region, faunal data are available for three sites: Vogelherd, Geissenklösterle, and Hohle Fels (Figure 10.2).

Vogelherd is a cave that was occupied during the Mousterian, Aurignacian, and Magdalenian (Niven 2006, 2007). The moderately large faunal assemblage (NISP = 519) from the Mousterian level VII, which is dominated by horse, is poorly preserved and presents clear symptoms of extensive ravaging by carnivores (Niven 2006). Although humans might have participated in the formation of the assemblage, no cutmarks were observed in the faunal sample. The other Mousterian levels at Vogelherd have very small sample sizes. Consequently, these occupations are omitted from the present discussion.

Preservation is good in the human-accumulated Aurignacian assemblage, which includes two distinct levels (V and IV) that were combined for analysis as a result of occupation mixing and sampling issues (Niven 2003, 2006). This assemblage contains a large sample of mammoth,[2] horse, and reindeer remains, whereas hare, fox, and bird specimens are poorly represented (60/3330 or 0.02, sum of all three taxa relative to the sum of ungulates, birds, foxes, and hares; data from Niven 2007:366, table 1). It is unclear whether the occupants of Vogelherd consumed these rare species or only occasionally used their bones and teeth to manufacture objects. Three hare and two bird (raven *Corvus corax* and swan *Cygnus* sp.) bones from this level present evidence of shape modification or intentional engraving (Niven 2006:177–179). In addition, one snowy owl (*Bubo scandiacus*) tarsometatarsus and the lingual side of one fox mandible bear cutmarks (Niven 2006: 178 and 184). These last marks may attest to feather and tongue removal, respectively.

A potential problem with these data is that selective recovery may have depressed the abundance of small taxa at Vogelherd (Niven 2006, 2007). Therefore, comparisons with modern excavations are necessary to validate the patterns that were uncovered at this site. As we will see, the recently excavated faunas from Geissenklösterle and Hohle Fels are consistent with the picture that emerges from Vogelherd. Both archaeological sequences comprise Mousterian, Aurignacian, Gravettian, and Magdalenian assemblages.

The Geissenklösterle sequence includes two Aurignacian assemblages separated from the Middle Paleolithic by a low-density layer (Conard *et al.* 2006). Cave bear, mammoth, reindeer, and horse dominate the fauna from these assemblages. Values for the Leporid Index suggest no change in the representation of hares between the Mousterian (8/126 or 0.06) and the lower Aurignacian (27/483 or 0.06). However, hares increase in

---

[2] Mammoth remains were excluded from the ungulate counts because they were possibly transported for reasons other than food procurement (Niven 2007). Specimens identified only to body size class were also excluded.

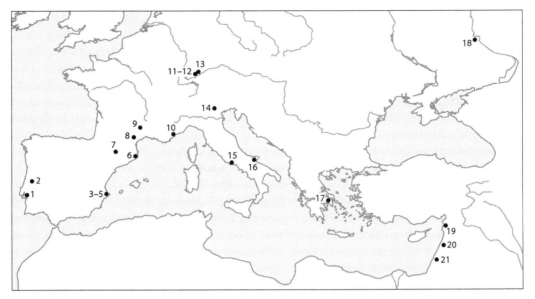

FIGURE 10.2. Location of sites mentioned in the text. Most of these sites show possible evidence for early dietary use of small swift animals. 1. Figueira Brava; 2. Caldeirão; 3–5. Cova Negra, Mallaetes, Cova Beneito; 6. L'Arbreda; 7. Gabasa 1; 8. Tournal; 9. Les Canalettes; 10. Riparo Mochi; 11. Hohle Fels; 12. Geissenklösterle; 13. Vogelherd; 14. Grotta di Fumane; 15. Grotta del Fossellone; 16. Grotta Paglicci; 17. Klissoura; 18. Kostenki; 19. Üçağızlı; 20. Ksar 'Akil; 21. Hayonim.

relative abundance[3] in the overlying upper Aurignacian (182/919 or 0.20) and Gravettian (240/596 or 0.40) occupations. This increase is highly significant ($\chi^2_{trend} = 188.3$, $p \leq .001$, lower Aurignacian to Gravettian). In contrast, no clear trend is seen in the representation of fox remains between the layers (Mousterian: 26/144 or 0.18; lower Aurignacian: 86/542 or 0.16; upper Aurignacian: 73/810 or 0.09; Gravettian: 109/465 or 0.23; $\chi^2_{trend} = 3.4, p \leq .07$). It is not possible to determine whether humans are responsible for the presence of small swift taxa at Geissenklösterle because no taphonomic analysis of these remains has been published to date. Nevertheless, bird bones, some of which were shaped into flutes, as well as perforated and dyed fish vertebrae, are documented in the upper Aurignacian (Münzel 2004:71–72). Lastly, three fox canines attributed to the lower Aurignacian were modified into ornaments (Conard and Bolus 2003).

Similar patterns characterize Hohle Fels, a cave located 2 km upstream from Geissenklösterle. The most frequent species in the Upper Paleolithic occupations from this site are cave bear, horse, and reindeer (Münzel and Conard 2004b). The Mousterian fauna is unpublished. Like Vogelherd and Geissenklösterle, the Hohle Fels sequence reveals a

---

3 All NISP data are from Münzel and Conard (2004a:228, table 1). Mammoth remains and specimens only assigned to a body size class were excluded from the ungulate counts, with the exception of specimens attributed to *Bos/Bison*. Mammoth was excluded because several fragments from this species appear to be related to object manufacture rather than subsistence (Münzel and Conard 2004a). If we include the cave bear – a large taxon associated with cutmarks at Geissenklösterle (Münzel 2004) – with the large swift taxa, the Leporid Index values for the lower Aurignacian, upper Aurignacian, and Gravettian become 0.02, 0.07, and 0.12, respectively. Including the cave bear dramatically decreases the relative abundance of hare but does not alter the pattern of increase, which remains significant ($\chi^2_{trend} = 157.4, p \leq .001$). Tests for linear trends compare *Lepus* or fox NISP with ungulate or ungulate-bear NISP.

significant increase[4] in leporid representation between the mostly anthropogenic Aurignacian level V–III (2/63 or 0.03), the Aurignacian/Gravettian level IId–e (11/72 or 0.15), and Gravettian level IIcf (155/284 or 0.55, $\chi^2_{\text{trend}} = 74.9$, $p \leq .001$). In contrast, these levels show no significant change in the Fox Index (Aurignacian V–III, 4/65 or 0.06; Aurignacian/Gravettian IId–e, 7/68 or 0.10; Gravettian IIcf, 14/143 or 0.10; $\chi^2_{\text{trend}} = 0.6$, $p \leq .46$). The Aurignacian of Hohle Fels also contains objects made from small animal parts, including perforated fox canines and a *Gyps fulvus* (griffon vulture) bone shaped into a flute (Conard *et al.* 2006; Conard 2009).

Information on faunal assemblages from the cold steppes of the Eastern European plains is limited. Hoffecker (2002, 2009) noted that small swift mammals are common at Kostenki, a complex of open-air sites overlooking the Don River in Russia. For instance, abundant specimens (>800) of Don hare (*Lepus tanaiticus*) were recovered from the early Upper Paleolithic layer II at Kostenki 14 (Hoffecker *et al.* 2010:1076), which is reflected in the moderately high Leporid Index value (≈800/2959 or ≈0.27, ungulate data from Hoffecker 2002:182, table 5.5) calculated for this mostly anthropogenic assemblage. This value should be considered a minimum estimate, given that the absence of sediment-sieving likely depressed the representation of small taxa in this occupation.

According to Hoffecker (2002, 2009), hares are even more abundant in Kostenki 8, layer II and in Kostenki 14, layer III–IV than in layer II at Kostenki 14. Remains of arctic fox (*Alopex lagopus*), some of which were modified into pendants (Sinitsyn 2003), are also argued to be frequent in some of the Kostenki layers (Hoffecker 2009). Importantly, cutmarks, including one on a hare tibia, were observed on both of these taxa at Kostenki 14, in a layer containing ash derived from the Campanian Ignimbrite Y5 eruption (Hoffecker 2009:94). This well-studied volcanic event slightly post-dated the earliest Protoaurignacian in Italy (Fedele *et al.* 2008). Unlike hares, birds and fish are uncommon at the Kostenki sites (Hoffecker 2009). Consequently, it remains uncertain whether aquatic resources were regularly consumed in this area during the early Upper Paleolithic, as stable isotope analyses have suggested (Richards *et al.* 2001; Richards 2009).

Iberia

Swift small-bodied taxa are generally far more common in the transitional occupations of Iberia than is the case in northwestern Europe. Specifically, there is abundant evidence for the consumption of rabbits (*Oryctolagus cuniculus*) during and after the Gravettian, as indicated by fracture patterns and frequent occurrences of cutmarks and burned specimens (Villaverde and Martínez Valle 1992; Villaverde *et al.* 1998; Pérez Ripoll and Martínez Valle 2001; Aura Tortosa *et al.* 2002; Davis 2002; Hockett and Haws 2002, 2009; Stiner 2003; Pérez Ripoll 2004, 2005/2006; Manne *et al.* 2005; Brugal 2006; Sanchis Serra and Fernández Peris 2008; Manne and Bicho 2009). For the late Mousterian, most of the information on small prey exploitation derives from four Spanish and two Portuguese

---

[4] NISP data are from Münzel and Conard (2004b:879, table 1). Mammoth and specimens only attributed to body size class were excluded from the ungulate NISP counts. Trends compare leporid or fox NISP with ungulate NISP.

sites: l'Arbreda and Gabasa 1 in the central and eastern Pyrenees, Cova Beneito and Cova Negra in the Valencia region, and Caldeirão and Figueira Brava in central Portugal.

Faunal data have been presented for l'Arbreda (Maroto *et al.* 1996, 2001; Lloveras *et al.* 2010). These results show that level I, attributed to the late Mousterian, is dominated by rabbits (≥87% of mammal NISP, Maroto *et al.* 1996:225), followed by the cave bear, the latter mostly represented by newborns and cubs. Small carnivores (Fox-Lynx Index: 13/289 or 0.04) are documented in this layer but possibly reflect natural deaths (Maroto *et al.* 1996, 2001). A recent study of a leporid sample (NISP = 2407) from squares A4, B3, C3, and D3 indicates that the specimens were probably mostly deposited by carnivores (Lloveras *et al.* 2010). This interpretation is substantiated by an absence of cutmarks and a high percentage of digested remains (32.4%) in the sample. However, as noted by Lloveras *et al.* (2010), the presence of a few burned specimens (0.5%) and long bone cylinders ($n = 12$) – a type of breakage common in anthropogenic rabbit assemblages (Hockett and Haws 2002) – may indicate that humans sporadically contributed specimens as well.

Rabbits are even more abundant (≈96% of mammal NISP, Maroto *et al.* 1996:232) in the overlying level H, which contains a Protoaurignacian industry (but see the subsequent discussion on issues concerning the stratigraphy at l'Arbreda). The fact that the rabbit sample from this level comprises some cutmarks, several burned specimens, and is dominated by adults suggested to Maroto *et al.* (1996) that humans were actively involved in the deposition of the specimens. Preliminary taphonomic data appear to support this interpretation (Maroto *et al.* 2010). However, it is unclear whether humans consumed the small carnivores present in level H (Fox-Lynx Index: 14/146 or 0.10, data from Maroto *et al.* 1996: 225, table III and p. 233, table V). Importantly, the increase in the Fox-Lynx Index observed between levels I and H is significant[5] ($t_s = 1.99, p < .05$).

Bird remains are relatively abundant at l'Arbreda. To estimate the relative abundance of these remains in the assemblages, the avian data collected by Garcia i Petit (1995:217, table 1) were compared using the Bird Index with counts of ungulates published by Maroto *et al.* (1996:225, table III and p. 233, table V). Values for this index suggest a statistically significant *decrease* in bird representation between levels I (395/671 or 0.59) and H (109/241 or 0.45, $t_s = 3.66, p < .001$). The Mousterian avian sample is dominated by corvids (NISP = 258/395 or 65.3%), with choughs (*Pyrrhocorax* spp.) being the best represented genus within this taxonomic group (156/202 or 77.2%, *Pyrrhocorax* spp. relative to all corvids, specimens identified at least to genus only, data from Garcia i Petit 1995:217, table 1). Other frequent bird taxa include pigeons (*Columba* spp., NISP = 35), partridges (*Alectoris* spp. and *Perdix perdix*, NISP = 20), the common quail (*Coturnix coturnix*, NISP = 6), and species of the duck, goose, and swan biological family (Anatidae, NISP = 4).

Corvids constitute the majority (62/109 or 56.9%) of the bird remains in the Protoaurignacian level H. This occupation also contains remains of pigeons (NISP = 8), Anatidae (NISP = 7), common quail (NISP = 3), and partridges (NISP = 1). Unfortunately, little

---

[5] In this review, abundance index values were converted into percentages (by multiplying them by 100) when statistically comparing assemblages using the arcsine transformation. Specimens assigned to "*Capreolus-Cervus*" and "*Mammuthus-Elephas*" were not included in the l'Arbreda abundance indices.

taphonomic information is available on the l'Arbreda bird samples. However, higher up in the sequence, in the Solutrean, many of the same birds are believed to reflect natural accumulations (Garcia i Petit 1997). By extension, the same interpretation may apply to levels I and H.

Fish specimens were recovered in small numbers at l'Arbreda. Values for the Fish Index increase slightly between levels I (18/294 or 0.06) and H (11/143 or 0.08, fish data from Muñoz and Casadevall 1997:114, table 1; ungulate data from Maroto *et al.* 1996:225, table III and p. 233, table V). However, this trend is not statistically significant ($t_s = 0.62$, $p < .54$). Both fish samples are dominated by the common eel (*Anguilla anguilla*, level I: 10/16 or 62.5%; level H: 6/8 or 75.0%, fragmented and indeterminate specimens excluded). Given these low frequencies, the l'Arbreda fish specimens have been interpreted as indicating marginal uses of aquatic environments by human or other biological agents (Muñoz and Casadevall 1997; Roselló Izquierdo and Morales Muñiz 2005).

Overall, small swift taxa, particularly rabbits and birds, are well represented at l'Arbreda. Preliminary data point to a greater use of leporids by humans in level H. However, the role played by humans in the deposition of birds and fish is unclear. It should be noted that there is some controversy regarding the integrity of the stratigraphy at l'Arbreda, which has been challenged on the basis of evidence for occupation mixing and post facto sorting of the archaeological assemblages (Zilhão and d'Errico 1999, 2003; Zilhão 2006, see reply by Soler Subils *et al.* 2008). Additional taphonomic studies of the lithic and faunal samples should improve our understanding of dietary change at l'Arbreda.

Gabasa 1 (also known as Los Moros de Gabasa 1) is a Mousterian cave located in the piedmont of the Pyrenees in northern Spain (Montes *et al.* 2001). Six faunal assemblages (*h*, *g*, *f*, *e*, *d*, and *c–a*, from oldest to most recent) from this site were studied by Blasco (1997). The faunal accumulations, which are dominated by ibex (*Capra pyrenaica*), horse, and red deer, have been attributed to the activities of both humans and natural agents (Blasco 1997; Steele 2004). Along with ungulates, the assemblages contain moderately low frequencies of wolf, hyena, lynx, and fox specimens, as well as hyena coprolites (Blasco 1997; González Sampériz *et al.* 2003). [14]C dates suggest that these remains were deposited during MIS (Marine Isotope Stage) 3. However, because the dates are infinite in all but one case, it is uncertain whether this sequence can be placed at the very end of the Mousterian (Montes *et al.* 2001; González Sampériz *et al.* 2003).

Relatively small quantities of bird remains were uncovered at Gabasa 1 (Bird Index: 0.03–0.06, data from Blasco 1997:181–182, tables 1–2). Unfortunately, information on the taxonomic composition of the avian samples is limited to a species list for layers *g–f* (Hernández Carrasquilla 2001; Sánchez Marco 2007). This list includes raptors (*Gyps/Aegypius*, *Gypaetus barbatus*, *Aquila chrysaetos*, *Falco tinnunculus*, *Bubo bubo*), partridges (*Alectoris rufa*), pigeons (*Columba* sp.), choughs (*Pyrrhocorax pyrrhocorax* and *P. graculus*), ravens (*Corvus corax*), and magpies (*Pica pica*). Small carnivore specimens do not present anthropic marks and are very rare throughout the Gabasa 1 sequence (Fox-Lynx Index: 0.00–0.04, data from Blasco 1997:182, table 2).

More information is available for leporids (all of which are rabbits with the exception of a distal humerus attributed to hare). Although the pattern is not strictly linear, the relative abundance of leporids increases steadily from 0.10 in level *h* to 0.52 in levels *c–a*

(Leporid Index, data from Blasco 1997:182, table 2). This pattern is statistically significant ($\chi^2_{trend} = 448.3$, $p \leq .0001$, leporid NISP vs. ungulate NISP). Of particular importance is the presence of cutmarks (0.1%) and carnivore damage (5.1%) on some of the rabbit remains (Blasco 1997:202). These results may indicate that humans more frequently exploited leporids in the later part of the Gabasa 1 sequence.

Although the cultural sequences of l'Arbreda and Gabasa 1 are consistent with the traditional chronocultural framework used in France, the one that prevails in central and southern Iberia is slightly different. Radiocarbon dates and lithic syntheses suggest that the Middle Paleolithic in that region ended later, possibly around *ca.* 30 ka, when it gave way to late Aurignacian or early Gravettian industries (Aubry *et al.* 2007). These observations have been viewed as supporting the argument for a longer persistence of Neandertals in Iberia (e.g., Hublin *et al.* 1995; Tzedakis *et al.* 2007).

In Valencia (central eastern Spain), several Late Pleistocene assemblages show a tendency toward leporid dominance, as illustrated by the high Leporid Index values for the Mousterian of Cova Negra (range: 0.49–0.95, levels VII–II) and Cova Beneito (range: 0.64–0.86, levels D4–D2, data from Villaverde and Martínez Valle 1992:79, table 1, level D1 excluded because of occupation mixing). As at l'Arbreda, these remains were presumably brought to the caves by carnivores and raptors, although a low number of specimens with cutmarks at Cova Negra attest to human exploitation as well (Pérez Ripoll and Martínez Valle 2001; Sanchis Serra and Fernández Peris 2008).

Bird specimens ($n = 420$), including *Pyrrhocorax* (choughs), *Alectoris* (partridges), and *Columba* (pigeons), were also identified at Cova Beneito. Importantly, one of these specimens, a carpometacarpus from a partridge found in the Mousterian layer D1, is cut-marked (Martínez Valle and Iturbe Polo 1993:38). However, because this level suffers from disturbance (Domènech Faus 2004; Zilhão 2006), the attribution of this specimen to the Mousterian is not secure.

Observations from Cova Beneito and Mallaetes suggested to Villaverde and Martínez Valle (1992, see also Pérez Ripoll 2004) that humans were more actively involved in the accumulation of leporids in the Aurignacian, based on fracture patterns and the abundance of their remains (Cova Beneito B9–B8, range: 0.90–0.93; Mallaetes: 55/66 or 0.83, Leporid Index, data from Villaverde and Martínez Valle 1992:86, table 5). However, this possible increase in anthropic exploitation remains to be confirmed because of stratigraphic (Domènech Faus 2004; Zilhão 2006) and taphonomic (calcareous concretions prevented the tallying of cutmarks) problems affecting Cova Beneito (Pérez Ripoll 2004) and the very small size of the Mallaetes faunal sample (Davidson 1989). Concerning carnivores, the Fox-Lynx Index at Cova Beneito increases significantly between the Mousterian layer D2 (1/95 or 0.01) and the Aurignacian layer B9 (6/51 or 0.12, $t_s = 2.83$, $p < .01$). Moreover, Soler-Major (2001) reported that one perforated lynx canine was found in the Aurignacian layers at this site.

In Portugal, rabbits are well represented in some Mousterian sites, such as Figueira Brava and Caldeirão (Mein and Antunes 2000; Davis 2002; Davis *et al.* 2007). At the latter site, taphonomic data suggest that non-human predators were largely responsible for the deposition of the rabbit remains during the Mousterian. However, human intervention cannot be entirely ruled out because burning has been identified on 1% of the rabbit specimens in this assemblage (Davis *et al.* 2007:219). Moreover, this value is possibly an underestimation because the Caldeirão specimens are often encrusted by calcite.

In the overlying early Upper Paleolithic occupation, 3% of the rabbit specimens show anthropic marks, all from burning (Davis *et al.* 2007:219). Although the temporal pattern is not significant ($t_s = 1.45, p < .15$), this may indicate that humans accumulated rabbits more frequently during this occupation. This interpretation finds support in a statistically significant increase in the representation[6] of rabbits (Leporid Index: 806/902 or 0.89 vs. 1553/1639 or 0.95, $t_s = 4.79, p < .0001$) and a significant decrease in the percentage of carnivore-digested rabbit bones (20 vs. 11%, $t_s = 2.46, p < .02$, data from Davis *et al.* 2007:219, table 5) between the levels. With respect to small carnivores, the Fox-Lynx Index at Caldeirão shows no significant change between the Mousterian (12/108 or 0.11) and the early Upper Paleolithic (5/91 or 0.05, $t_s = 1.45, p < .15$). The same is true for the Bird Index (Late Mousterian: 9/105 or 0.09, Evolved Aurignacian: 10/96 or 0.10, $t_s = 0.44, p < .66$).

In general, evidence for dietary use of rabbits in Portugal is much stronger during the Gravettian and onward (Brugal 2006; Manne and Bicho 2009). Yet change was not linear, given that rabbit exploitation seems to have fluctuated in importance throughout the Upper Paleolithic in certain sequences, such as that of Vale Boi (Manne and Bicho 2009). Lastly, birds are present in low numbers at Figueira Brava (Mourer-Chauviré and Antunes 2000) and Caldeirão (Davis 2002). As is the case for small carnivores and fish, it is unknown whether humans consumed birds at this site.

Mediterranean France

Mousterian and early Upper Paleolithic assemblages from Mediterranean France do not follow the Iberian pattern; leporids are rarely abundant in the former region. Tournal, a cave site with evidence of alternating human and carnivore occupations (Patou-Mathis 1994; Magniez 2010), illustrates this point. Indeed, the relative abundance[7] of leporids is very low (13/904 or 0.01) in the mixed carnivore/human assemblage from the Mousterian II_B level. Similarly, leporids are poorly represented in the mostly anthropic samples from the Aurignacian F_3 (2/97 or 0.02) and F_4 (7/120 or 0.06) levels. However, despite these low numbers, the data point to a statistically significant increase in the number of leporid specimens in these assemblages ($\chi^2_{trend} = 9.6, p \leq .01$, leporid NISP vs. ungulate NISP). Unlike leporids, no increase is observed in the relative abundance of fox, which is a rare taxon at Tournal ($II_B = 9/900$ or 0.01, $F_3 = 0/95$ or 0.00, $F_4 = 1/114$ or 0.01, $\chi^2_{trend} = 0.2, p \leq .66$). Combined with the previous observations on Saint-Césaire, Abri Pataud, and Grotte du Renne, the results for the Mediterranean zone make it clear that small swift taxa were rarely consumed in France before the Magdalenian. Concerning leporids, the dietary implications of the marginal increases observed at Tournal and Grotte du Renne are unclear.

---

[6] All of the NISP data were taken from Davis (2002:42, table 6). Specimens attributed to "Goat/Chamois/Sheep" were excluded.

[7] NISP data were taken from Patou-Mathis (1994, p. 33, table V for level II_B; p. 63, table LI for levels F_3 and F_4). Specimens only assigned to "Cervidae" or "bovines/equids" were excluded from the ungulate counts. For level F_3, the NISP count for leporids is given as "2?." This value is taken as correct here. The more recent data presented by Magniez (2010) for the Tournal assemblages could not be used here because, unlike Patou-Mathis's (1994) study, they do not include leporids. This is not consequential because both studies show similar patterns of taxonomic composition.

However, the *earlier* Mousterian of Mediterranean France contains several exceptions to this generalization (Cochard 2004). Les Canalettes, a stratified site in the Aveyron department dated to the interface between MIS 5 and 4, is particularly illuminating in this regard. Cochard (2004) identified numerous rabbit bones ($n = 1202$) in layer 4, an anthropic assemblage that also includes lower frequencies of red deer, horse, and bovine remains. The rarity of carnivore-inflicted marks ($n = 11$), the presence of cut-marked ($n = 9$) and burned ($n = 4$) specimens, along with a large number of bone cylinders ($n = 136$, ulna excluded), strongly suggest that the rabbits in this layer, which account for 67% of the identified specimens, were mostly accumulated by humans (Cochard 2004:185, 195–201). Likewise, a few cut-marked rabbit bones have been identified in MIS 4 contexts at Pié-Lombard and La Crouzade (Gerber 1972). These findings are puzzling given that they suggest a contraction, rather than an expansion, of diet breadth during the later Mousterian in Mediterranean France.

Italy

Small swift taxa, particularly birds, are sometimes well represented in Middle and early Upper Paleolithic sites from Italy (Cassoli and Tagliacozzo 1994, 1997; Alhaique and Tagliacozzo 2000; Stiner and Munro 2002; Fiore *et al.* 2004; Tagliacozzo and Gala 2005a; Peresani *et al.* 2011). Four of these sites – Riparo Mochi, Fumane, Grotta del Fossellone, and Grotta Paglicci – are briefly reviewed here because they contain the most information about shifts in human foraging behavior in this region.

Riparo Mochi is one of the Balzi Rossi (or Grimaldi) sites, a complex of Paleolithic caves in the Liguria region near the French border. This coastal site contains an important stratigraphic succession of Mousterian, Aurignacian, Gravettian, and Epigravettian occupations (Kuhn and Stiner 1992; Bietti *et al.* 2004). According to Alhaique (2000; Alhaique *et al.* 2004), humans deposited the bulk of the faunal debris in the early Upper Paleolithic occupations. Remains of red deer, roe deer, and other ungulates (suids, caprines, bovines) abound in these assemblages (Stiner and Munro 2002). Unfortunately, data are lacking for the late Mousterian, a period during which the site possibly functioned as a carnivore den (Alhaique *et al.* 2004).

Genus-level data provided by Stiner and Munro (2002:208, appendix B) indicate that small swift animals are present in appreciable numbers at Riparo Mochi. For instance, birds (38/318 or 0.12) and leporids (31/311 or 0.10) are abundant in the Early Aurignacian layer G. The overlying level F, attributed to the typical Aurignacian, contains a similar ($t_s = 1.46$, $p < .15$) proportion of birds (30/351 or 0.09) but a statistically *lower* ($t_s = 3.52$, $p < .001$) proportion of leporids (11/332 or 0.03). Most of the Upper Paleolithic bird specimens from Riparo Mochi are Grey partridges (*Perdix perdix*), common quails (*Coturnix coturnix*), and, to a lesser extent, rock doves (*Columbia livia*) and Anseriform birds (Stiner *et al.* 2000). Alhaique (2000) noted that calcite concretions and less than ideal bone surface preservation probably depressed cutmark identification, which may obscure the analysis of small prey use at Riparo Mochi.

Another issue is that because Stiner's and Munro's (2002) data for Riparo Mochi correspond to materials excavated between 1938 and 1959 (Kuhn and Stiner 1992, 1998), problems of selective recovery might have depressed the taxonomic representation of small prey taxa in the assemblages. Yet the small faunal samples presented by Alhaique

(2000:126, table 1) for the newer (1995 and later) excavations also point to a poor representation of leporids in the aggregated Early and Typical Aurignacian samples (layers G–F, 1/41 or 0.02). Therefore, selective recovery does not appear to explain the low occurrence of leporids at Riparo Mochi. Alhaique's (2000) study suggests that fox is comparably rare in the Aurignacian layers (layers G–F, 1/41 or 0.02).

Located in the Alpine piedmont, Grotta di Fumane is an inland site with a 10-m-thick sedimentary sequence that encompasses Mousterian, Uluzzian (an industry analogous to the Châtelperronian), Aurignacian, and Gravettian components (Peresani 2008). The fauna in these occupations are mainly present because of human activities and are dominated by cervid (especially red deer and roe deer), ibex, and chamois remains (Cassoli and Tagliacozzo 1994; Fiore *et al.* 2004). In this sequence, the relative abundance[8] of birds shows a significant increase between the pooled Mousterian layers A13–A4II (99/732 or 0.14) and the pooled Proto/Early Aurignacian layers A3–A1 (327/793 or 0.41, $t_s = 12.51$, $p < .0001$). However, bird representation does not vary significantly between the latter set of layers and the overlying Typical Aurignacian sample (layers D7–D1c: 387/992 or 0.39, $t_s = 0.94$, $p < .35$). The alpine chough (*Pyrrhocorax graculus*), black grouse (*Tetrao tetrix*), and corn crake (*Crex crex*) dominate all three sets of layers.

At least seven bird bones with cutmarks were found in the Mousterian of Fumane (Peresani *et al.* 2011). These marks were observed on the wing elements from bearded vulture (*Gypaetus barbatus*), black vulture (*Aegypius monachus*), red-footed falcon (*Falco vespertinus*), common wood pigeon (*Columba palumbus*), and alpine chough (*Pyrrhocorax graculus*) and on the talon from a golden eagle (*Aquila chrysaetos*). The anatomical position of the cutmarks suggests that these birds were exploited for their feathers or claws, which has been interpreted as a form of symbolic behavior (Fiore *et al.* 2004; Peresani *et al.* 2011). Consumption of birds is possibly attested by the presence of ripping (*arrachement*) marks on a black grouse (*Tetrao tetrix*) ulna and a probable cutmark on a willow grouse (*Lagopus* cf. *lagopus*) carpometacarpus. In contrast, bird bones from the larger, well-preserved Aurignacian samples from layers A3–A1 and D7–D1c do not bear any tool marks, although some of them are burned (Gala and Tagliacozzo 2005; Peresani *et al.* 2011). Puncture marks and gastric etching indicate that raptors and carnivores contributed, along with humans, to the accumulations of birds in these layers (Fiore *et al.* 2004; Gala and Tagliacozzo 2005; Peresani *et al.* 2011).

Small swift mammals were also identified in the Fumane assemblages. Foxes, which were possibly exploited for pelts (Fiore *et al.* 2004), increase gradually in relative abundance from the Mousterian (17/650 or 0.03) to the Proto/Early Aurignacian (24/490 or 0.05) and Typical Aurignacian (75/680 or 0.11). A similar pattern characterizes the slightly less common leporids (Mousterian: 1/634 or 0.00; Proto/Early Aurignacian: 4/470 or 0.01; Typical Aurignacian: 33/638 or 0.05). Both patterns of increase are significant (foxes: $\chi^2_{trend} = 39.7$, $p \leq .001$; leporids: $\chi^2_{trend} = 37.5$, $p \leq .001$, Mousterian to Typical Aurignacian, leporid or fox NISP versus ungulate NISP).

In coastal Latium, Grotta del Fossellone is a stratified site excavated during the 1940s and the early 1950s. The cave contains numerous Middle and Upper Paleolithic

---

[8] NISP data for Fumane are taken from Cassoli and Tagliacozzo (1994:358–359, table 2 for mammals and pp. 362–363, table 4 for birds). Although newer NISP counts have been published for birds (Peresani *et al.* 2011), these results were not used here because of a lack of comparatively recent data for the mammal assemblages.

occupations (Blanc and Segre 1953; Mussi 2001). Only two faunal samples from that sequence – the pooled Mousterian levels 27–23 and the single Aurignacian level 21 – are relevant to the present discussion. Red deer, aurochs, and/or wild ass prevail in these largely anthropogenic assemblages (Alhaique and Tagliacozzo 2000). As noted by Alhaique *et al.* (1998), selective recovery probably biased the representation of small taxa in the faunal assemblages.

At Grotta del Fossellone, birds are a minor component of the Mousterian levels 27–23 (23/346 or 0.07) but are significantly more abundant in the Aurignacian level 21 (449/3635 or 0.12, $t_s = 3.48$, $p < .001$, data from Alhaique *et al.* 1998:574, table 1). Partridges (*Perdix perdix* and *Alectoris* spp., 10/23 or 43.5%) are the most frequent bird in the Mousterian sample, followed by rock pigeon (*Columba livia*, 8/23 or 34.8%), and alpine chough (*Pyrrhocorax graculus*, 3/23 or 13.0%). In comparison, partridges are better represented in the Aurignacian level 21 (304/449 or 67.7%, $t_s = 2.30$, $p < .03$, Alhaique *et al.* 1998:574, table 1). With respect to fox and leporids, the data show that they are rare in both the Mousterian (4/327 or 0.01) and Aurignacian (23/3209 or 0.01, data from Alhaique *et al.* 1998:574, table 1, values correspond to the sum of fox and leporid NISP relative to the sum of ungulate, fox, and leporid NISP).

Bone surface preservation is poor in the Mousterian sample, which means that this level is unlikely to reveal much information regarding the agents of accumulation for the small prey taxa. In contrast, preservation is good in the Aurignacian level 21, which permitted the identification of cutmarks on two bird bones (humeri from a partridge and a snowy owl, *Bubo scandiacus*). In one of these cases, the marks may be ornamental (Alhaique *et al.* 1998:573). Taphonomic data are unavailable for fox and leporids. However, Blanc and Segre (1953) indicated the presence of a modified fox canine in the Aurignacian occupation.

The last site examined in this survey of Italy – Grotta Paglicci – is located at the western edge of the Gargano promontory in the region of Apulia, at approximately the same latitude as Grotta del Fossellone. The sequence of Grotta Paglicci encompasses occupations spanning the Aurignacian to the late Epigravettian (Palma di Cesnola 2006). Remains of wild ass dominate the small (NISP = 114) and poorly preserved mammal sample from layer 24, the only faunal assemblage assigned to the Aurignacian at this site (Boscato 1994). This assemblage, which consists of materials from several sub-levels (24b4–24a), also includes specimens attributed to ibex, horse, red deer, chamois, and aurochs. The occurrence of anthropic and carnivore marks in the faunal sample, as well as the presence of hyena coprolites in the sediments, suggest a complex depositional history for this assemblage (Boscato 1994, 2004; Cremaschi and Ferraro 2007). Despite the interpretive challenges posed by these taphonomic observations, Grotta Paglicci contains valuable information on small prey exploitation during the early Upper Paleolithic of Italy.

Birds are moderately abundant in the Aurignacian of Grotta Paglicci (43/151 or 0.28, avian data from Tagliacozzo and Gala 2005a:193, table 1; ungulate data from Boscato 1994:149, table 1). The alpine chough (*Pyrrhocorax graculus*, 23/43 or 53.5%) is the most common taxon in the avian sample. Other species include the mallard (*Anas platyrhynchos*, 4/43 or 9.3%), rock pigeon (*Columba livia*, 3/43 or 7.0%), and red-billed chough (*Pyrrhocorax pyrrhocorax*, 3/43 or 7.0%). Two of the avian specimens, both of alpine chough, show traces made by a stone tool (Tagliacozzo and Gala 2005a:196). However, nonhuman agents also modified the bird remains, given that at least three bones show marks made by carnivores and/or rodents (Tagliacozzo and Gala 2005b:74). No leporid remains were recorded in the Aurignacian assemblage. Yet the small leporid sample (NISP = 20) from layer 23 (early Gravettian) comprises a hare (*Lepus europaeus*) calcaneum with cutmarks. Lastly, none of the three fox specimens found in the Aurignacian faunal sample bear cutmarks (Boscato 1994).

The Eastern Mediterranean

Recent work in the eastern Mediterranean has greatly contributed to our understanding of diet breadth during the Middle to Upper Paleolithic transition. Most of this new information has arisen from three stratigraphic sequences containing early Upper Paleolithic components: Klissoura in Greece (Koumouzelis *et al.* 2001a, 2001b; Tomek and Bocheński 2002; Starkovich 2009; Bocheński and Tomek 2011), Üçağızlı Cave I in Turkey (Stiner *et al.* 2002; Kuhn *et al.* 2009; Stiner 2009), and Hayonim in Israel (Rabinovich *et al.* 1996; Rabinovich 1998, 2003; Bar-El and Tchernov 2001; Stiner 2005). The fact that the results for several of these sites are preliminary complicates the analysis for this region. Nevertheless, the available data allow some general conclusions to be drawn about dietary shifts in the eastern Mediterranean.

Klissoura Cave 1 belongs to a complex of karstic sites located in a gorge in the Peloponnese region of southern Greece. A Pleistocene sequence ranging from the Mousterian through the Epigravettian has been uncovered at this site since 1994, when systematic excavations were initiated (Koumouzelis *et al.* 2001a, 2001b). Capping fifteen Middle Paleolithic layers (XXg–VI) and a single Uluzzian level (layer V), the Aurignacian at Klissoura consists of four distinct assemblages (layers IV, IIIe–g, IIIb–d, and 6–7). However, the most recent of these Aurignacian occupations is isolated from the previous three by two "non-Aurignacian" (layers III″ and III′) assemblages (Sitlivy *et al.* 2007; Starkovich 2009).

According to Starkovich (2009), the European fallow deer (*Dama dama*) is the most common taxon in the large game assemblages from Klissoura. In general, the faunal samples show little indication of carnivore activities. Moreover, despite low frequencies of cutmarks – a phenomenon probably accentuated by the presence of solidified ash concretions on many remains – fracture patterns and damage due to burning suggest that humans were the primary accumulators of the faunal assemblages (Starkovich 2009; Bocheński and Tomek 2011).

The European hare (*Lepus europaeus*) is moderately abundant in the five lowermost Upper Paleolithic assemblages (range: ≈0.11–≈0.31) from Klissoura, including the Uluzzian (≈0.25) and the earliest Aurignacian (≈0.24, Leporid Index values[9] derived from Starkovich 2009:6, figure 3). The subsequent occupations, starting with layers III′ (non-Aurignacian, ≈0.46) and 6–7 (Late Aurignacian, ≈0.75), all show proportionately more remains of this taxon, which translates into dominance – or near dominance – of leporids over ungulates.

In contrast, avian specimens are rare (Bird Index ≈0.03 or less) in the three bottommost Upper Paleolithic occupations (i.e., layers V, IV, and IIIe–g). The Aurignacian

---

[9] The values presented for Klissoura are estimates based on histograms. NISP data for the recent excavations are not available yet.

occupation from layer IIIb–d marks an inflection point, given that birds are common (≈0.21) in this assemblage and remain abundant afterward, despite wide fluctuations (range ≈0.17–≈0.75). This observation excludes layer III″ (non-Aurignacian), an occupation with sparse bird specimens (≈0.01). The majority of the avian remains identified at Klissoura belong to rock partridge (*Alectoris graeca*) and great bustard (*Otis tarda*), other species being rare (Tomek and Bocheński 2002). Bocheński and Tomek (2011, figure 6) identified cutmarks on some of the Klissoura bird bones, including a crow (*Corvus corone*) tibiotarsus from the Late Aurignacian. Lastly, small carnivores occur in low numbers at Klissoura (Starkovich 2009). The ongoing analysis of these assemblages should shed light on the role played by humans in the deposition of these small taxa.

Üçağızlı Cave I is a collapsed karstic chamber in the Hatay province of Turkey comprising a sequence of, from earliest to latest, Initial Upper Paleolithic (layers I–F) and Ahmarian (layers C–B) occupations. The intermediate layers E and D are less diagnostic, but show stronger ties with the Ahmarian than with the earlier technocomplex (Kuhn 2004; Kuhn *et al.* 2009). All of these levels are radiocarbon-dated between roughly 41 and 29 ka (Kuhn *et al.* 2009). Epipaleolithic material has also been uncovered at Üçağızlı Cave I in a zone unconnected with the early Upper Paleolithic sequence (Kuhn 2004). The faunal assemblages are clearly anthropogenic and display good preservation (Stiner *et al.* 2002; Kuhn *et al.* 2009). Middle Paleolithic occupations are not documented in the cave but are recorded in an adjacent site called "Üçağızlı Cave II" (Stiner 2009). Used in combination, the faunas from these two sites enable us to compare diet breadth across the transition. However, it should be noted that a temporal gap of 10,000 years or more separates the two sequences (Stiner 2009).

Medium-sized ungulates, especially wild goat (*Capra aegagrus*), roe deer (*Capreolus capreolus*), and fallow deer (*Dama mesopotamica*) abound in the Initial Upper Paleolithic and Ahmarian faunas of Üçağızlı Cave I (Stiner *et al.* 2002; Kuhn *et al.* 2009). In contrast, small swift taxa are poorly represented, as values[10] for the Leporid, Fox, and Fish indices exceed 0.03 only in the Epipaleolithic sample (Leporid Index: 71/154 or 0.46; Fox Index: 12/95 or 0.13; Fish Index 7/90 or 0.08).

Birds show a different pattern. This taxonomic group is sporadically attested in the Initial Upper Paleolithic layers I–F (0.01 or less) but increases in proportion from the pre-Ahmarian layer E (2/311 or 0.01) to the pre-Ahmarian and Ahmarian layers D–C (31/632 or 0.05). The change between the last two samples is significant ($t_s = 4.21$, $p < .0001$). Relative to layers D–C, birds are slightly more common in the younger Ahmarian layers B1–3 (359/2756 or 0.13) and B (82/818 or 0.10) and are very frequent in the Epipaleolithic sample (61/144 or 0.42). Future studies should reveal whether the rise in bird representation in the Ahmarian and the Epipaleolithic was accompanied by a parallel increase in anthropic marks. However, such a pattern may be difficult to verify at Üçağızlı Cave I given the presence of calcite concretions on some of the specimens (Kuhn *et al.* 2009). Only a few specimens of fish, fox, birds, and leporids were found in the Middle Paleolithic of the adjacent Üçağızlı Cave II (Stiner 2009).

---

[10] NISP values for Üçağızlı Cave I are from Stiner (2009:16, appendix 1). Specimens identified only to family (e.g., "Cervidae") or body size class (e.g., "small mammals" or "large ungulates") were excluded.

Farther south, in Israel, an exceptionally rich sequence of Acheulo-Yabrudian, Mousterian, Aurignacian, Kebaran, and later occupations was brought to light at Hayonim cave. Of particular relevance here is Aurignacian layer D, which is most accurately dated to ≈27–29 ka (Bar-Yosef *et al.* 2005). This layer is separated from the underlying Mousterian (layer E) by erosional unconformities, resulting in a cultural hiatus of approximately 50–70 ka (Bar-Yosef *et al.* 2005:26). Another hiatus of approximately 6–10 ka separates the Aurignacian occupation from the more recent, but currently undated, Kebaran assemblage excavated in layer C (Bar-Yosef 1991). These stratigraphic gaps mean that the Hayonim sequence yields information pertinent only to the very end of the transition process, given that no late Mousterian, Initial Upper Paleolithic or Ahmarian occupations were encountered during the excavations. Additionally, it should be noted that the wide range of dates (≈20–29 ka) and the complex formation processes associated with layer D raise the issue of potential mixing with adjacent layers (Belfer-Cohen and Bar-Yosef 1981; Bar-Yosef 1991).

The Aurignacian from Hayonim, which consists of four sub-layers (D4–1), is associated with a rich mammal assemblage strongly dominated by gazelle (*Gazella gazella*), with fallow deer (*Dama mesopotamica*) being secondary in abundance. These remains show unambiguous evidence of human intervention, including cutmarks and burning (Rabinovich *et al.* 1996; Rabinovich 1998, 2003). Limited data are available on the representation and mode of introduction of small swift animals in this occupation. Bird remains, a large proportion of which are from large raptors, are moderately frequent[11] in layer D (NISP ≈878). One of these bones – an eagle tibia found in sub-layer D3 – was shaped into an object (Belfer-Cohen and Bar-Yosef 1981:31). Importantly, Rabinovich (2003:39) indicated that many bones of griffon vulture (*Gyps fulvus*) and other large birds from the Aurignacian levels show cutmarks, which attest to human procurement. Specimens of cape hare (*Lepus capensis*) and red fox (*Vulpes vulpes*) also occur in layer D but are uncommon (Leporid Index: 83/7695 or 0.01; Fox Index: 147/7759 or 0.02). No cutmarks were observed on the fox and hare specimens (Rabinovich *et al.* 1996; Rabinovich 1998; Bar-El and Tchernov 2001).

In sum, in the Levant, the patterns suggest only minor changes in the use of fast small-sized prey taxa across the Middle to Upper Paleolithic transition. However, recent studies have observed a decline in the exploitation of high-ranked species – particularly the aurochs – during the late Middle Paleolithic, presumably as a consequence of overhunting (Speth and Clark 2006). Large prey taxa do not show signs of recovery in this region during the Upper Paleolithic and the Epipaleolithic (Stiner 2005; Stutz et al. 2009).

DISCUSSION

This brief review highlights a number of significant spatial and temporal patterns regarding the consumption of small swift prey taxa in the Mediterranean region and the northern plains. With respect to leporids, the prevalence of rabbits in the early Upper Paleolithic of Iberia is potentially compatible with O'Connell's intensification model

---

[11] NISP data for birds, ungulates, and hares were taken, respectively, from Stiner (2005:256, appendix 12), Rabinovich (1998:52 table 1), and Bar-El and Tchernov (2001:98, figure 2). Specimens only identified as "Cervidae" were excluded. The NISP value for birds is an estimate as the analysis of the avian sample is ongoing. The fox data were taken from Rabinovich (1998:52 table 1).

TABLE 10.5. *Patterns of small prey representation in transitional sequences from Europe and southwest Asia*

Country/region	Site	Leporid index	Bird index	Fox index	Ornament/tool
Iberia	l'Arbreda	+	−	+	
	Cova Beneito	+		+	lynx
	Caldeirão	+	·	·	
France	Saint-Césaire	·	·	·	hare, fox
	Grotte du Renne	+		+	bird, fox
	Abri Pataud	· (EA)		+ (EA)	hare, fox
	Tournal	+		·	
Northern plains	Geissenklösterle	+ (UA)		·	bird, fox, fish
	Hohle Fels	+ (UA)		·	bird, fox
Italy	Riparo Mochi	− (TA)	· (TA)		
	Fumane	+	+	+	
	Fossellone	·	+	·	fox
Levant	Klissoura	+ (LA)	+ (n-A)		
	Üçağızlı	·	+ (Ah)	·	

A "·" sign means no change, a "−" sign means a statistically significant decline in the index, and a "+" sign means a statistically significant increase in the index. The "ornament/tool" column identifies the small swift species in the assemblage that was/were exploited for nonfood purposes. An empty cell indicates a lack of data. The index columns normally assess variation between late Mousterian and early Upper Paleolithic (generally Aurignacian) assemblages. Time periods in parentheses indicate that the pattern postdated the earliest Aurignacian. The Fox-Lynx Index was used at l'Arbreda, Cova Beneito, and Caldeirão, whereas the Fox Index was used at all of the other sites.

EA = Early Aurignacian; TA = Typical Aurignacian; LA = Late Aurignacian; n-A = non-Aurignacian; Ah = Ahmarian.

(Figure 10.3, left panel). Indeed, in this region, at least three sequences (l'Arbreda, Cova Beneito, Caldeirão) show a statistically significant increase in leporid representation between the Middle and the early Upper Paleolithic (Table 10.5). However, as noted by Villaverde *et al.* (1996) and Pérez Ripoll (2004), rabbits also frequently dominate Mousterian sequences with substantial indications of carnivore agency, such as those of Cova Negra and Cova Beneito. This pattern means that leporid representation per se is of limited diagnostic value in Iberia, which puts the burden of proof on patterns of bone fracture and surface modifications (Hockett and Haws 2002).

Although recent studies have contributed to fill the gap (e.g., Davis *et al.* 2007; Sanchis Serra and Fernández Peris 2008; Lloveras *et al.* 2010), few taphonomic analyses of Mousterian rabbit assemblages have been carried out in the Iberian Peninsula. Moreover, results are often limited by the presence of calcite concretions on the faunal specimens. An additional complication is that leporids were occasionally exploited for raw materials during the early Upper Paleolithic, which may obscure the interpretation of foraging patterns. For these reasons, it remains to be confirmed whether the main increase in the dietary importance of rabbits occurred during the early Upper Paleolithic or somewhat later – for instance, during the Gravettian. However, regardless of its exact timing, this dietary shift was not as abrupt as commonly alleged, given that several Iberian assemblages point toward minor human exploitation of rabbits during the final Mousterian, as evidenced by the presence of butchery marks. These assemblages include Cova Beneito levels D4, D2, and D1, Gabasa 1 (unspecified level[s]), and Cova Negra levels IV, IIIb, IIIa, and II (Table 10.6). Furthermore, evidence for rabbit consumption in this region during the Middle Pleistocene attests to the complexity of diet breadth patterns in the

TABLE 10.6. *Late Pleistocene Mousterian and Aurignacian assemblages from Europe and southwest Asia that contain specimens of fast small-bodied species with possible butchery marks*

Period, country, and assemblage	Species	No. of cut-marked specimens and part	Reference
Mousterian (MIS 6–4)			
France (MIS 5/4)			
Combe-Grenal, 24	hare	(1) ulna	Chase 1984; Personal observation
Jonzac	fox	(1?) tib	Jaubert *et al.* 2008:217
Pié Lombard	rabbit	(1) hum	Gerber 1972:86
La Crouzade	rabbit	(1 or 2?) fem, tib	Gerber 1972:205
Canalettes, 4	rabbit	(6 or 8?) 2 fem, 2 tib, 2 hum, 2 inn	Cochard 2004:195
Israel (MIS 6)			
Hayonim, 4b–1	fox	(1) scapula	Stiner 2005:104
Mousterian (MIS 3)			
Germany			
Salzgitter-Lebenstedt	swan	(1?) cpm	Gaudzinski and Niven 2009:101
	duck	(1) hum	Gaudzinski and Niven 2009:101
Italy			
Fumane, A6–A5	bird	(1?) cpm	Peresani *et al.* 2011:3892
Spain			
Cova Beneito, D4	rabbit	(1) fem	Sanchis Serra and Fern. Peris 2008:39
Cova Beneito, D2	rabbit	(2 or 3?) hum, inn, tib	Sanchis Serra and Fern. Peris 2008:39
Cova Negra, IV	rabbit	(1) fem	Sanchis Serra and Fern. Peris 2008:39
Cova Negra, IIIb	rabbit	(1 or 3?) fem, 2 tib	Sanchis Serra and Fern. Peris 2008:39
Cova Negra, IIIa	rabbit	(1) fem	Sanchis Serra and Fern. Peris 2008:39
Cova Negra, II	rabbit	(1?) tib	Sanchis Serra and Fern. Peris 2008:39
Gabasa 1	rabbit	(2 or 3?) fem, inn, tib	Blasco 1997:202
Mousterian?			
Spain			
Cova Beneito, D1	partridge	(1?) cpm	Martínez Valle and Iturbe Polo 1993:38
	rabbit	(1) hum	Sanchis Serra and Fern. Peris 2008:39
France			
La Ferrassie, L3a	bird	(2?) hum, tbt	Mourer-Chauviré 1984:102
Aurignacian (or like)			
France			
Grotte du Renne, VII	fox	(2) vertebrae	David and Poulain 2002:84
Abri Pataud, 11	fox	(1) hum	Chiotti *et al.* 2003:195
Abri Pataud, 14	fox	(1) ulna	Vercoutère 2004:66
Tournal, E1	fox	(1?) tib	Magniez 2010:573
Le Tarté	fox	(1) fem	Costamagno and Laroulandie 2004:407
Grotte des Hyènes, 2a	fox	(1) scapula	Letourneux 2003:261
Grotte des Hyènes, 2c	fox	(5) fem, ulna, 3 hum	Letourneux 2003:261
Germany			
Vogelherd, V/IV	fox	(1) mandible	Niven 2006:184
Greece			
Klissoura, upper Auri.	crow	(1) tibiotarsus	Bocheński and Tomek 2011: fig. 6
Italy			
Grotta del Fossellone	snowy owl	(1) hum	Alhaique *et al.* 1998:573
Grotta Paglicci	chough	(2) coracoid, hum	Tagliacozzo and Gala 2005a:196
Russia			
Kostenki 14, EUP	hare	(1?) tib	Hoffecker 2009:94

Cutmarks on presumably ornamental specimens (e.g., raptor phalanges) were excluded from this table, as well as those clearly related to skin procurement (e.g., metapodials and phalanges).

The "?" symbol means that the cutmark may indicate butchery or skin/feather procurement. fem = femur, tib = tibia, inn = innominate, hum = humerus, cpm = carpometacarpus, tbt = tibiotarsus.

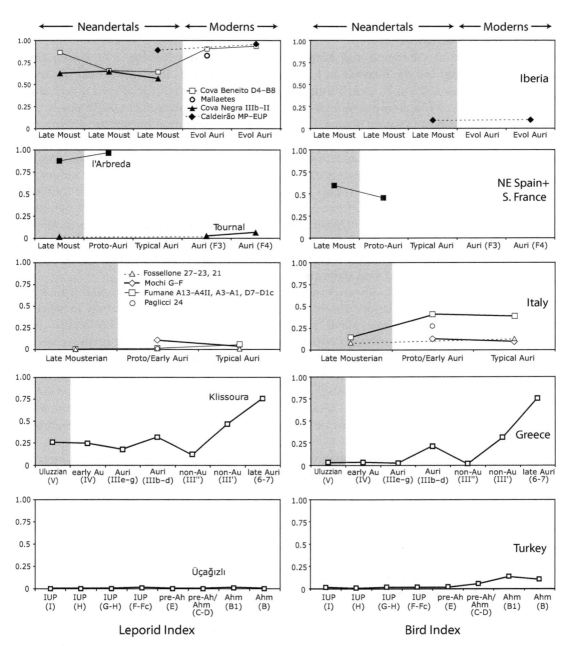

FIGURE 10.3. Relative abundances of small swift prey taxa in archaeological sequences from Eurasia. The left panels show variations in the Leporid Index, whereas the right panels show variations in the Bird Index. Shaded and unshaded areas indicate assemblages traditionally attributed to Neandertals and early modern humans, respectively. Values are from the text. The broken lines for Tournal, Caldeirão, and Grotta del Fossellone indicate a significant hiatus in the sequence or that intermediate assemblages were excluded due to evidence of extensive carnivore occupation. Lastly, the Bird Index values for Klissoura only include medium- and large-sized birds.

Iberian Paleolithic (Sanchis Serra and Fernández Peris 2008; Blasco and Fernández Peris 2009; Blasco *et al.* 2010).

Assuming that Villaverde and Martínez Valle (1992) and Maroto *et al.* (1996) are correct in attributing the increase in leporid representation in Iberian sites during the early Upper Paleolithic to human hunting, several explanations can be offered to account for this change. A first interpretation focuses on how long-term shifts in the intensity of human occupation of natural shelters affected the representation of rabbits in various types of sites. As suggested by a number of authors (Straus 1982; Villaverde *et al.* 1998; Aura Tortosa *et al.* 2002; Davis 2002; Pérez Ripoll 2005/2006; Hockett and Haws 2009), humans possibly occupied natural shelters only occasionally and for a narrow range of activities during the Mousterian. This intermittent use of caves might have led rabbits to be more commonly deposited in open-air sites. In contrast, intensive use of natural shelters by humans during the Upper Paleolithic might have increased opportunities for accumulating and processing rabbits in this type of deposit. This possibility calls for additional studies bearing on the relationship between site type (e.g., open-air vs. cave sites), occupation intensity, and patterns of rabbit representation.

A second, but not mutually exclusive, interpretation centers on methods of rabbit procurement. The early Upper Paleolithic increase in rabbit representation in Iberia may reflect a shift toward communal exploitation of warrens. Indeed, the exploitation of these structures – which generally consist of a set of interconnected rabbit burrows (Parer *et al.* 1987) – is argued by Jones (2004b, 2006) to have substantially raised the net return rates of rabbits, which might have moved them into the optimal diet. However, one should note that these return rates were probably quite variable, given that warren size and density fluctuate appreciably between habitats and depending on soil conditions, patterns of precipitation, and history of use, among other factors (Kolb 1985; Palomares 2001, 2003; Galvez *et al.* 2008).

Return rates from warrens probably varied over time as well. Assuming that larger warrens are more profitable than smaller ones, future research should investigate whether the globally more xeric conditions documented in Iberia during the Upper Paleolithic (d'Errico and Sánchez Goñi 2003) increased average warren size. This is because drier conditions may reduce overall rabbit densities but incidentally increase the average size of warrens (Palomares, pers. comm., 2010). Despite the complexity of the problem, the archaeological criteria proposed by Jones (2004b, 2006) for teasing apart single and mass captures should, in concert with a study of climatic trends, enable testing of these propositions.

East of southern France, hares (*Lepus* sp.) replace rabbits in the early Upper Paleolithic record. This difference is consequential because hares, unlike rabbits, tend to live alone or in small groups (Gibb 1990). However, there are notable exceptions. For instance, in favorable patches in open country, *Lepus timidus* may aggregate to form large groups of 50 to 300 hares (Angerbjörn and Flux 1995), which means that the problem of mass collecting may also occasionally apply to them. This behavioral characteristic must therefore be taken into account when interpreting patterns of hare representation.

After a review of faunal patterns in southern Germany, Conard *et al.* (2006) concluded that in this region, a similar spectrum of animal species was exploited throughout the Middle to Upper Paleolithic transition. Although the data are meager, the present study is consistent with this interpretation. However, a substantial and statistically significant increase in hare representation was observed at Geissenklösterle and Hohle Fels between the lower Aurignacian and the Gravettian (Table 10.5). As hinted at by Niven (2006), these findings point to diet widening in the northern plains during the later Aurignacian and the Gravettian. This interpretation finds support in a recent study suggesting consumption of birds in a Gravettian context in the Czech Republic (Bocheński *et al.* 2009).

Farther east, we saw that hares are well represented in the archaeological sequences of Klissoura (Greece) and Kostenki 14 (Russia). Because the imprint of nonhuman predators is slight in the Upper Paleolithic assemblages at both sites, Klissoura and Kostenki 14 may constitute particularly compelling cases of early broad-based diets, if mass collecting can be ruled out. Also of great significance in the Klissoura sequence are the similar Leporid Index values obtained for the Uluzzian (≈0.25) and the earliest Aurignacian (≈0.24). This similarity is particularly significant because these industries are generally ascribed to late Neandertals and early modern humans, respectively (Mussi 2001). The comparable representation of hares in the Klissoura assemblages suggests that there was little variation in diet breadth between these populations, at least in the Klissoura region. At Kostenki, the information is too sparse to assess changes across the transition.

Evidence for human procurement of birds during the shift from the Middle to the Upper Paleolithic is severely limited by a lack of data. Moreover, the fact that objects made of bird bones are not uncommon during the early Upper Paleolithic complicates the picture. In Iberia, information on bird exploitation is scarce. At Caldeirão in Portugal, bird representation changed little across the transition, although a possible hiatus in the sequence limits the utility of this observation (Figure 10.3, right panel). Moreover, the few bird bones identified at this site do not bear any sign of anthropogenic modification (Davis 2002). The faunal assemblages from l'Arbreda in northeastern Spain indicate a decrease in the relative abundance of birds from the late Mousterian to the Protoaurignacian. However, no taphonomic analysis is currently available for this site.

Given these results, one might conclude that birds in southwestern Europe were mostly ignored as prey items throughout the early Upper Paleolithic. Although reasonable, such a conclusion may be premature at the moment, in light of reports attesting to the consumption of birds (ducks *Aythya* sp., swan *Cygnus olor*) at Cova del Bolomor during the Middle Pleistocene (Blasco and Fernández Peris 2009; Blasco *et al.* 2010) and at Cova Beneito (partridge *Alectoris* sp.) during the transition (Table 10.6). It is hoped that new analyses will allow a better assessment of the role played by humans in the accumulation of birds in Late Pleistocene cave deposits of Spain and Portugal.

In Italy, the increase in bird representation observed in the transitional occupations from Grotta di Fumane and Grotta del Fossellone (Figure 10.3, right panel) is compatible with the intensification hypothesis. However, the fact that anthropic marks on bird specimens at Grotta di Fumane are more frequent in the late Mousterian than in the Early Aurignacian is at variance with this model (Peresani *et al.* 2011). Unfortunately, similar comparisons cannot be pursued at Grotta del Fossellone because of the poor preservation of the Mousterian sample (Alhaique and Tagliacozzo 2000).

In the eastern Mediterranean, the information on bird exploitation is uneven. At Klissoura, medium- and large-sized birds only become frequent starting in the middle of the Aurignacian sequence (Figure 10.3, right panel). Occurrences of cutmarks and burning in the avian samples suggest that humans were responsible for this increase (Bocheński and Tomek 2011). An earlier shift toward bird exploitation is possibly documented in the pre-Ahmarian at Üçağızlı in Turkey. Although taphonomic data are not yet available, Stiner (2009) noted that burning at this site is as frequent on the bird remains as on those from other vertebrate taxa. At Ksar 'Akil in Lebanon, burning was recorded on large bird specimens from both the Middle and Upper Paleolithic (Kersten 1991). No stone tool damage was observed on these specimens. In Israel, cutmarks were identified on large bird bones in the Aurignacian of Hayonim (Rabinovich 2003).

Concerning small carnivores, the sample of sites examined in this chapter confirms the weak representation of fox and lynx in the early Upper Paleolithic record. This poor representation may reflect the fact that these species typically occur at low densities in the environment. However, this explanation is not entirely satisfactory, given that certain assemblages dated to the later Pleistocene, such as Grotta Romanelli (Compagnoni *et al.* 1997) and Netiv Hagdud (Yeshurun *et al.* 2009), show substantial signs of human consumption of carnivore taxa. The lack of comparable evidence for the early Upper Paleolithic may imply that humans did not increase their consumption of small carnivores during this period.

However, this interpretation seems only partially accurate. Despite the overall low numbers of small carnivore specimens in the assemblages that were examined, several sites with relevant data (5 out of 12) show a statistically significant increase in the representation of these animals during the early Upper Paleolithic (Table 10.5). Importantly, these increases occur in both mostly anthropogenic (Grotte du Renne, Abri Pataud, Fumane) and more taphonomically complex sequences (l'Arbreda, Cova Beneito). The generality of the pattern indicates that the increases were not simply driven by a shift in the main agents of deposition.

As noted earlier, an increase in the abundance of small carnivore remains may signal the emergence of novel practices unrelated to food procurement, such as the need to make tools and ornaments from small animal parts. Yet by raising the utility of small carnivores, these needs may have concomitantly fueled a modest increase in fox and lynx consumption. This was possibly the case in France, as suggested by the more frequent occurrences of butchery marks on fox specimens during the Aurignacian than during the much longer Mousterian period (Table 10.6). However, additional samples will be necessary to establish whether small carnivore consumption marginally increased during the early Upper Paleolithic, as possibly evidenced by the French sites.

Lastly, the data indicate that fish are, with few exceptions (Le Gall 2000; Roselló Izquierdo and Morales Muñiz 2005), seldom represented in inland sites prior to the last glacial maximum. This conclusion is in agreement with previous faunal syntheses (Le Gall 1992; Villaverde *et al.* 1998; Aura Tortosa *et al.* 2002; Costamagno and Laroulandie 2004; Stiner 2005). Yet because fish specimens are often underreported, more work is needed to ensure that this trend is not, in part, the result of research bias.

CONCLUSIONS ON DIET BREADTH IN EUROPE AND WESTERN ASIA

The information presented in this chapter is summarized in Figure 10.4. This figure suggests a more complex picture of small swift prey exploitation during the Late Pleistocene than generally appreciated. In Iberia, there are ambiguities about the exact timing of the diet breadth expansion, as well as uncertainties concerning the influence of some critical

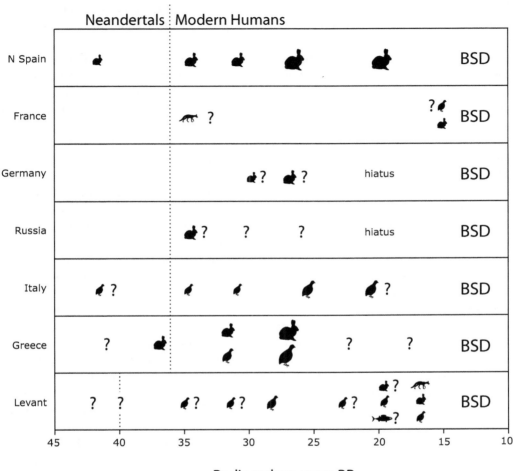

FIGURE 10.4. Trends toward diet widening in Europe and southwest Asia during MIS 3–1. The size of the animal symbol is a proxy for the importance that fox, birds, and/or leporids might have taken in the human diet, as determined based on a combination of taxonomic representation *and* butchery mark data. "BSD" stands for *broad-spectrum diet* and indicates the addition, and often the prevalence, of fish and other classes of small swift taxa in the diet. The data suggest that the emergence of broad-based diets was more or less synchronous across Europe and southwest Asia. The "?" next to the animal symbols indicates that either the increase in taxonomic representation or the butchery marks are poorly documented. "hiatus" means that the region would have been largely depopulated during the concerned time period. Note that the exact timing of the transition between Neandertals and early modern humans is unclear in the Levant. References used for constructing this figure are those cited in the text, completed by the following ones for the later Paleolithic: Simmons and Nadel (1998), Bar-Oz *et al.* (1999), Bar-Oz and Dayan (2002), Fontana (2004), Marom and Bar-Oz (2008), Munro (2009), and Stutz *et al.* (2009).

parameters (i.e., change in methods of procurement, warren profitability, and/or site function) on the representation of leporids in cave assemblages. The dietary role of birds during the transition is also unclear in Iberia. In Italy and the eastern Mediterranean, most sequences show embryonic signs of bird consumption in the early phases of the

Upper Paleolithic, although not always in synchrony with the inferred modern human dispersal. In the northern plains, diet widening might have taken place in the later Aurignacian.

More problematic than this complex picture, however, is the finding that numerous assemblages spread across the Mediterranean basin suggest a minor, and at least in one case frequent, consumption of small swift prey taxa by late Neandertals. This interpretation is corroborated by the presence of butchery marks on small swift taxa in several assemblages dated to the late or final Mousterian. This pattern undermines the intensification hypothesis because it suggests that, at least in Iberia, and perhaps Italy and Greece, the early Upper Paleolithic trend toward diet broadening *was rooted in the local Mousterian.*

The spatial distribution of the sites also reveals patterns that are incompatible with the intensification model. Eurasian sites with evidence suggesting that small swift game were exploited during the Middle to Upper Paleolithic transition are identified in Figure 10.5 by animal symbols. These symbols represent specific small swift species for which there is persuasive evidence of dietary use by humans, whereas the hatched zone indicates regions where these prey types were rarely exploited, with the possible exception of small carnivores. The map is instructive because it shows *a break of at least 400 km in the distribution of sites with evidence for early diet broadening*. This break, which largely coincides with the southern plains of France, is not likely due to sampling bias because the early Upper Paleolithic record of this region is one of the most intensively studied in the world. As emphasized by several authors (Le Gall 1992, 1999; Cochard 2004; Costamagno and Laroulandie 2004; Laroulandie 2004a; but see Richards 2009 for a possible exception to this rule), low-return resources did not form a measurable part of the human diet in France until relatively recently, presumably around 15 to 17 ka.

The implications of these patterns are far-reaching because they suggest that the trends for diet widening in Iberia on the one hand, and Italy and the eastern Mediterranean on the other, *were relatively independent phenomena*. Combined with indications for an emerging use of leporids in the late Mousterian of Iberia, this observation is difficult to reconcile with the proposition of a westward spread of small fast game exploitation from the eastern Mediterranean to southwestern Europe, which has been viewed as support for the modern human expansion model (O'Connell 2006). An additional complication with this hypothesis is that the earliest evidence for use of small fast game in the Levant (*ca.* 35 ka in layer D–C at Üçağızlı) is *no earlier, and possibly younger*, than the evidence in Iberia and perhaps Italy. How then can these patterns be explained?

Several issues need to be considered to answer this question. Foremost among these is the argument that diet breadth varied significantly among the Neandertal populations that participated in the Middle to Upper Paleolithic transition. In some regions, late Neandertals made initial steps toward a broad-based diet, whereas in others, the hunter's "search images" – in the language of foraging theory, the perceptual templates representing the target prey taxa (Adams-Hunt and Jacobs 2007) – remained essentially the same. In the western plains, adjustments to shifts in foraging efficiency during both the late Mousterian and early Upper Paleolithic appear to have been largely limited to changes in transport decisions and processing intensity, as suggested by the

FIGURE 10.5. Distribution of sites with early evidence for small swift prey exploitation. The hatched area includes sites that are indicative of narrow diets. The animals represented are rabbit (Iberia), partridge (Italy and Turkey), chough (Italy), great bustard (Greece), hare (Greece and Russia), and griffon vulture (Lebanon and Israel). A single species is shown for sites with evidence for use of several bird taxa. Two symbols are shown for Klissoura, because this site suggests exploitation of both leporids and birds. Large question marks means that dietary breadth is poorly documented in the represented area, and the small question marks mean that the specific bird species remains to be confirmed.

Saint-Césaire faunas. Given this regional variation, the dietary differences observed in the early Upper Paleolithic of Eurasia cannot be accounted for by the existence of a behavioral frontier separating early modern humans from late Neandertals, an assumption that underlies many socio-economic explanations for the Middle to Upper Paleolithic transition.

Among the sites that were reviewed, the faunal assemblages varied markedly in taxonomic composition and in the range of body sizes present. Because animal communities in Eurasia show strong regional patterning in taxonomic and body size distributions, this pattern may help explain some of the spatial variability observed in diet breadth during MIS 3. Generally, the ungulate taxa that thrived in the western plains (primarily moderate- to large-sized cervids, bovines, and perissodactyls) were more gregarious and considerably larger, on average, than those (i.e., gazelles, caprines, and smaller cervids) typically found in the Mediterranean basin, southern France excluded. Therefore, the gap in profitability separating ungulates from small swift game was presumably greater – according to the body size rule – in the former regions. Given these differences, the addition of small swift prey taxa into the diet probably involved smaller changes in overall foraging efficiency in the more rugged areas of the Mediterranean basin than in the western plains. These features possibly favored diet breadth expansions in the former areas.

In essence, the data reviewed here highlight significant variations in diet breadth among late Neandertal populations. Moreover, the patterns of change across the Middle to Upper Paleolithic transition vary from region to region, in ways that are not yet clearly understood. Notably, it was shown that several regions of the Mediterranean basin provide evidence for a minor, and in at least one case, frequent, use of small fast game in the late Mousterian and the Uluzzian. This includes Iberia, a region located at the westernmost end of the alleged point of expansion of early modern humans (i.e., southwest Asia) and separated from it by a zone characterized by narrow diet breadth (the western plains). Both of these results appear to invalidate the intensification hypothesis. An alternative interpretation of the Middle to Upper Paleolithic transition in the western plains is offered in the final section of this study.

11

AN ALTERNATIVE LOOK AT THE MIDDLE TO UPPER PALEOLITHIC TRANSITION

IN CHAPTER 9, FORAGING THEORY PROVIDED THE ANALYTICAL FRAMEWORK FOR investigating alleged differences in the resource exploitation strategies of late Neandertals and early modern humans in Europe and southwest Asia. The examination of eight stratified assemblages from Saint-Césaire showed no significant change in diet breadth, although the samples attest to increased food stress during the Aurignacian. The many similarities observed between the assemblages from Saint-Césaire and those from Grotte du Renne and Abri Pataud are concordant with this conclusion, although limited data at these last two sites may indicate a modest increase in fox consumption during the Early Aurignacian.

In Chapter 10, a review of the literature revealed that transitional occupations in southwestern Germany are also associated with narrow diets. Conversely, diet breadth expansions during the earliest Upper Paleolithic were documented in various regions of the Mediterranean basin, particularly in habitats where large ungulates are naturally poorly represented. This last pattern is in agreement with the intensification model. However, the fact that some of these regions are separated by areas where narrow diets persisted well after the transition is difficult to reconcile with the hypothesis of a westward diffusion of a broad-based foraging system. Likewise, evidence for incipient diet broadening among some late Neandertal groups from Iberia, and possibly, Greece and Italy, is inconsistent with this model.

Diet breadth changed little during the transition in the western plains of Europe, despite evidence for a dramatic reduction in environmental carrying capacity, as inferred from a decline in mammal species diversity (Morin 2008, see Chapter 3). Exploring the potential effects of these environmental changes on human demography is important, given that it may shed light on the origins of modern humans in Europe. Specifically, evidence presented in this chapter shows that human foragers became increasingly dependent on a very narrow range of highly cyclical resources – mainly reindeer – during the early Upper Paleolithic, a situation that would have negatively affected their population densities. However, before addressing the demographic implications of a narrow diet, we first need to investigate whether the inferred shift toward reindeer dominance was a general pattern in France.

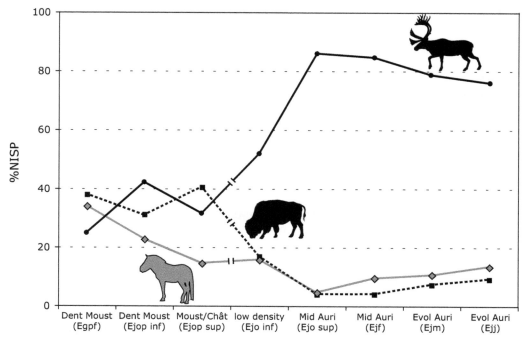

FIGURE 11.1. Taxonomic representation of reindeer, bison, and horse at Saint-Césaire. Data from Table 5.8.

HOW GENERAL WAS THE SHIFT TOWARD REINDEER DOMINANCE IN THE EARLY AURIGNACIAN?

In the plains of western France, final Mousterian and Châtelperronian assemblages generally contain a moderately wide range of ungulate taxa. With few exceptions, reindeer, bison, red deer, and horse account for the vast majority of the ungulate remains in these assemblages (Delpech 1983, 1996; Guadelli 1987; David and Poulain 1990; Mellars 1996, 1998; Armand in Debénath and Jelinek 1998; Grayson and Delpech 2002, 2008; Rendu 2007). A similar range of species is documented in comparably dated assemblages primarily accumulated by large carnivores (Guadelli *et al.* 1988; David 2004; Beauval and Morin 2010).

Patterns of taxonomic composition subsequently changed, as suggested by the strong dominance of reindeer in the Early Aurignacian assemblages of Abri Pataud (Bouchud 1975; Sekhr 1998) and Roc de Combe (Grayson and Delpech 2008). This strong dominance of reindeer is also manifest in the Middle Aurignacian occupations at Saint-Césaire (Figure 11.1). But was the shift toward reindeer dominance during the Early Aurignacian general in western France, or was it limited to a few sites? To address this question, faunal trends were investigated in a moderately large sample of well-controlled assemblages.

The study of reindeer dominance presented here is geographically limited to assemblages deposited in karstic contexts in southwestern France, the Pyrenees excluded. Each of the time periods considered – the final Mousterian (*ca.* 40–45 ka), the Châtelperronian, and the Proto/Early Aurignacian – cover relatively short time spans, which should

TABLE 11.1. *Faunal assemblages from western France used in the analysis of reindeer dominance*

Assemblage	Time period	NISP	References
Les Rochers de Villeneuve, J*	Final Mousterian	1724	Unpublished data
La Quina, layer 2b	Final Mousterian	436	Debénath and Jelinek 1998:56
Saint-Césaire, EJOP inf	Final Mousterian	278	This study
Saint-Césaire, EGPF	Final Mousterian	847	This study
Camiac*	Châtelperronian?	688	Guadelli *et al.* 1988:62
Saint-Césaire, EJOP sup	Moust/Châtel	734	This study
Roc de Combe,[a] layer 8	Châtelperronian	301	Grayson and Delpech 2008:343
Grotte XVI, layer B	Châtelperronian	422	Grayson and Delpech 2003:1636
Les Cottés, 04 inf	Protoaurignacian	205	Rendu 2009, pers. comm., 2011
Abri Pataud, layer 11	Early Aurignacian	2758	Chiotti *et al.* 2003:163
Abri Pataud, layer 12	Early Aurignacian	259	Sekhr 1998:64
Abri Pataud, layer 14	Early Aurignacian	1937	Sekhr 1998:64
Le Flageolet I, layer XI	Early Aurignacian	633	Grayson and Delpech 1998:1121
Castanet	Early Aurignacian	1486	Villa *et al.* 2004:712
Roc de Combe, layer 7	Early Aurignacian	1338	Grayson and Delpech 2008: 343

The NISP values only include red deer, bovines, horse, and reindeer. Assemblages with substantial evidence of carnivore occupation (bear excluded) are identified by an asterisk. These assemblages were included in the sample because they may yield information about climate change.
[a] Grayson's and Delpech's (2008) study excludes material derived from disturbed areas.

minimize temporal averaging. To reduce sampling error, the analysis only includes moderate- to large-sized assemblages (NISP > 200), irrespective of whether carnivores played a significant role in their accumulation or not. The fifteen assemblages that met all of these conditions are listed in Table 11.1. To simplify the analysis, the comparisons focused exclusively on red deer, bovines, reindeer, and horse. As indicated earlier, these four taxa largely dominate ungulate assemblages attributed to MIS 3 in the study region.

It should be noted that the transitional assemblages from Roc de Combe were included in the sample, despite the fact that they are affected by collection bias (Bordes 2003; Grayson and Delpech 2008). This issue should be of minor concern in the present case because the criteria that guided the retrieval of the specimens at this site are unlikely to have varied significantly between ungulate species. However, the possibility that certain classes of small elements (e.g., sesamoids, carpals, tarsals, deciduous teeth) were less frequently collected for small- than for large-bodied ungulates at Roc de Combe cannot be excluded. Lastly, the sample also includes assemblages principally deposited by carnivores, because these may yield information about climatic change.

The degree of reindeer dominance in the assemblages was evaluated using a ternary diagram. This approach was preferred over a simple comparison of reindeer percentages because it permits the simultaneous comparison of three variables of potential significance. Three ungulate groups (reindeer, horse, and bovines/red deer), one for each axis of the diagram, were created for this purpose. NISP values for red deer and bovines were pooled in this analysis because they occupied habitats that were, in general, more temperate than those in which thrived horse and reindeer (Delpech 1983, 1996; Guadelli 1987). This pooling is useful in the present case because it emphasizes climatic differences between the taxa, a variable central to the debate about reindeer dominance. The representation of ungulate groups in the ternary diagram was calculated according to the following equation:

$$\%NISP\ UG_i = \frac{NISP\ UG_i}{NISP\ UG_{total}} \times 100 \tag{11}$$

where UG_i is the ungulate group $_i$ and UG_{total} the sum of all three ungulate groups (reindeer, horse, and bovines/red deer).

RESULTS OF THE REINDEER DOMINANCE ANALYSIS

Figure 11.2 shows variations in the representation of reindeer, horse, and bison/red deer in the sample. There is a clear tendency in this figure for Proto/Early Aurignacian assemblages to be positioned near the apex and along the right boundary of the diagram. These areas, identified by light gray shading, are associated with reindeer dominance and reindeer-horse codominance, respectively. The absence of Proto/Early Aurignacian assemblages as one moves away from the right boundary of the diagram suggests that bovines and red deer were very rare during these time periods.

Conversely, final Mousterian and Châtelperronian assemblages tend to occupy the central part of the ternary diagram, regardless of the primary agent of deposition. This area, shown in dark gray in Figure 11.2, corresponds to assemblages with moderately high percentages of bovines and red deer. On the basis of these results, it can be concluded that the shift toward reindeer dominance during the Early Aurignacian at Grotte du Renne and Abri Pataud constitutes a reliable signal of a regional phenomenon. The next section assesses two hypotheses that have been put forward to explain these changes in taxonomic composition.

REVISITING MELLARS'S REINDEER SPECIALIZATION HYPOTHESIS

The shift toward reindeer dominance in the early phases of the Aurignacian has traditionally been attributed to climatic change (Bordes and Prat 1965; Beckouche 1981; Delpech 1983, 1996; Grayson and Delpech 2002, 2008; Morin 2008). However, a minority view challenges this interpretation, holding instead that this shift "reflects a deliberate economic and logistical strategy on the part of the Upper Palaeolithic groups to concentrate specifically on the exploitation of reindeer resources at particular times and places within the Perigord landscape" (Mellars 2004:615). According to Mellars, this highly "specialized" foraging pattern – which he distinguishes from the "generalized" or "broad-spectrum" strategy of resource exploitation of Neandertals – was aimed at reducing competition:

> If the Chatelperronian and Aurignacian groups were exploiting different resources then it is likely that they were utilizing to some extent different ranges within the same general territories. Thus the Aurignacians, for example, could have been exploiting predominantly seasonally migrating reindeer herds in the main river valleys of the Perigord (the Vézère, Dordogne, Isle, etc.) while the Chatelperronians were concentrating mainly on more widely dispersed and solitary species (e.g., horse or aurochs) on the intervening

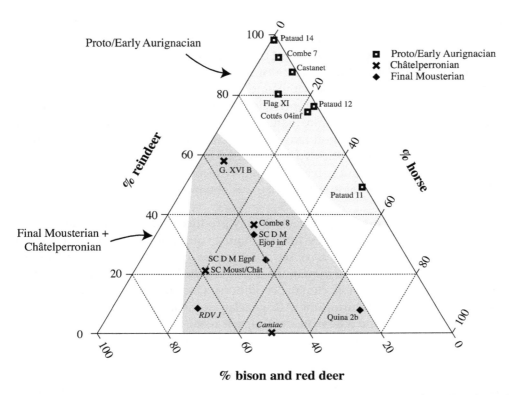

FIGURE 11.2. Ternary diagram showing variations in the relative abundances of reindeer, bison/red deer, and horse in final Mousterian, Châtelperronian, and Proto/Early Aurignacian assemblages from western France. Assemblages with substantial evidence of carnivore occupations are in italics. See Table 11.1 for data and references.

plateau and upland areas (Mellars 1989, 1992b). The same patterns could even be tied into more general seasonal contrasts in foraging patterns for these resources, which would have helped further to avoid any direct conflicts for the exploitation of specific resources at the same times and locations. (Mellars 1998:500)

It is essential to note that this view, which Mellars (1989, 1996, 2004) has reiterated in a number of publications, attributes to Neandertals and early modern humans foraging patterns that are inverse of those suggested by O'Connell (2006) and Kuhn and Stiner (2006).

Because Mellars's specialization hypothesis downplays the importance of climatic change as an explanation for shifts in the taxonomic representation of reindeer during the transition, his arguments can be tested using paleoenvironmental proxy data (Grayson and Delpech 2003, 2008; Morin 2008). However, discerning the respective influences of climatic and cultural factors on the composition of ungulate assemblages in the study region has been hindered by the difficulty of correlating anthropogenic faunal sequences with independent climatic data sets. Naturally accumulated micro-mammals can help resolve this issue because they are highly sensitive to variations in ecological conditions and often co-occur with ungulates in archaeological assemblages (Chaline 1970;

Marquet 1993). At Saint-Césaire, a previous study comparing micro- and macro-mammals found little support for the reindeer specialization hypothesis (Morin 2008).

To further explore this hypothesis, faunal trends at Saint-Césaire were compared with the Middle-to-Upper Paleolithic sequence of Roc de Combe in southwestern France. This site was selected because it is, with Saint-Césaire, one of the few sequences with a substantial data set on taxonomic representation of macro- *and* micro-mammals for the Middle to Upper Paleolithic transition. In addition, Roc de Combe provides data for the Early Aurignacian, a period that we now know to be unrepresented at Saint-Césaire. Comparisons between the two sites focused on three types of information: red deer/bovine representation and species diversity in micro- versus macro-mammals. The relevant faunal information for Roc de Combe was obtained from Grayson and Delpech (2008) and Marquet (1993).

Species diversity was examined because it may produce valuable information about climatic change, given the tendency for the number of mammal species to decrease toward the poles (Lomolino *et al.* 2006; see also Chapter 3). Red deer/bovine representation was considered because it may, in the context of the Middle to Upper Paleolithic transition, signal more favorable climatic conditions. One should note that the strong representation of reindeer during the Aurignacian automatically entails low species diversity for this time period (Grayson and Delpech 1998). However, the opposite is not necessarily true because reindeer-poor assemblages may also have low diversity if they are strongly dominated by another taxon, such as bovines or red deer.

The three variables of interest (i.e., micro-mammal species diversity, macro-mammal species diversity, red deer/bovine representation) show similar patterns of variation at Saint-Césaire and Roc de Combe, despite differences in the cultural composition of the two sequences (Figure 11.3). The Mousterian/Châtelperronian of Saint-Césaire deviates slightly from the trend, however, because this occupation contains fewer micro-mammal species than expected based on the abundance of macro-mammal species. Nonetheless, the data are consistent with the climatic hypothesis. Additional support for this hypothesis comes from Figure 11.4, which compares the relative abundances of two cold-adapted taxa: reindeer and the narrow-skulled vole, a control species accumulated by non-human agents. The two sequences are, again, in agreement, as they show comparable fluctuations in the representation of cold-adapted species. Overall, these results demonstrate that, during the transition, changes in the composition of ungulate assemblages were mostly, if not exclusively, driven by fluctuations in climatic conditions. These results appear to falsify the reindeer specialization hypothesis.

An observation of importance for the remainder of this chapter is that despite the many similarities observed between the sequences of Saint-Césaire and Roc de Combe, the narrow-skulled vole is always proportionally more abundant at the former site. For example, 93.0% (93/100, Morin 2008:51, table 2) of the micro-mammal remains identified in the Evolved Aurignacian EJM occupation at Saint-Césaire belong to this taxon, versus only 17.3% (9/52, Marquet 1993:73, table 17) in the (possibly more recent?) Evolved Aurignacian layer 6 at Roc de Combe. This highly significant difference ($t_s = 10.22$, $p < .0001$) contrasts with the similar percentages of reindeer in the same occupations (72.0% in EJM vs. 72.2% in layer 6, $t_s = 0.07$, $p < .95$). These results suggest the existence of cooler climatic conditions at Saint-Césaire, possibly as a result of its more northerly position ($\approx$180 km NW) relative to Roc de Combe. If real, this latitudinal effect was

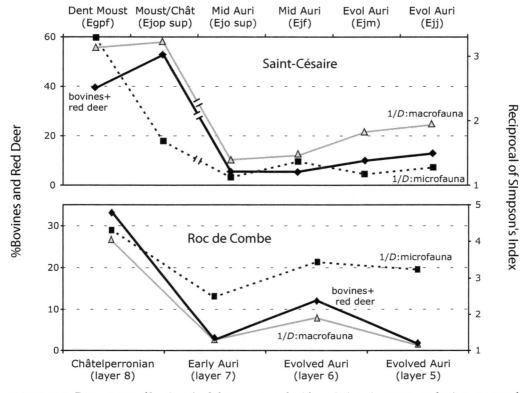

FIGURE 11.3. Percentages of bovines/red deer compared with variations in macro- and micro-mammal diversity at Saint-Césaire and Roc de Combe. Note the existence of a hiatus in the Saint-Césaire sequence. Species diversity is measured using the Reciprocal of Simpson's Index. Macro- and micro-mammal data for Roc de Combe are from Grayson and Delpech (2008:343–344, tables 2 and 3; carnivores included, mammoth tusk and indeterminate *Equus* specimens excluded) and Marquet (1993:73, table 17), respectively. Macro- and micro-mammal data for Saint-Césaire are from Tables 5.8 and 5.11. At this last site, antlers, fish, unspecified foxes and leporids, and the probably intrusive *Rattus* specimen were excluded.

apparently too weak to have affected the representation of the larger taxa in a significant way.

THE RELATIONSHIP BETWEEN HUMAN DENSITY AND MAMMAL SPECIES DIVERSITY

It is commonly assumed that human population densities increased in western Europe during the shift from the Middle to the Upper Paleolithic. This assertion is generally based on date or site/level counts. However, the reliability of this approach is controversial for the Paleolithic because it builds on a number of questionable assumptions about site production, residential mobility, sampling effort, the time span represented by the industries, their archaeological visibility, the accuracy of radiometric dates, the sedimentation rate, etc. A productive alternative is to focus on the relationship between hunter-gatherer density and mammal species diversity because these two variables appear to be linked in some direct or indirect way.

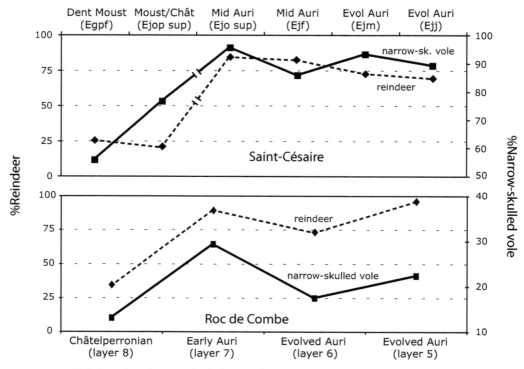

FIGURE 11.4. Relative abundances of reindeer and narrow-skulled vole at Saint-Césaire and Roc de Combe. Data are from the sources cited in Figure 11.3.

Morin (2008) found a moderately high and significant correlation ($r_s = 0.62$, $p < .002$) between mammal species diversity and the historical population density of 27 Plains, Subarctic, and Arctic hunter-gatherer groups from North America. These groups were all characterized by an economy primarily based on hunting (>45% of subsistence activities, using the classification[1] of Murdoch 1981). To increase comparability with Late Pleistocene inland foragers, ethnographic groups that were heavily reliant on fish (>45% of the diet) were excluded from this correlation. The relationship between mammal species diversity and hunter-gatherer density appears to be robust given that the correlation is virtually identical ($r_s = 0.62$, $p < .02$, $n = 18$) when the sample is restricted to groups with a diet that was more than 55% dependent on hunting (Figure 11.5). This result means that limiting the sample to groups with a greater reliance on hunting does not alter the relationship. However, at higher thresholds (e.g., 65%, 75%), the sample sizes are greatly reduced and, as a result, the correlations become non-significant.

A close inspection of Figure 11.5 shows that the data form not one but two linear relationships, as noted in a previous analysis (Morin 2008). Groups that belong to the upper cluster in this figure tend to occupy cold open-country environments, whereas

---

[1] Murdoch's (1981) classification of hunters-gatherers focuses on three subsistence activities: i) wild plant and small land fauna collecting, ii) hunting, including trapping and fowling, and iii) fishing and shellfish collection. The values for the groups that were not included in his study were derived from the group with the most similar diet.

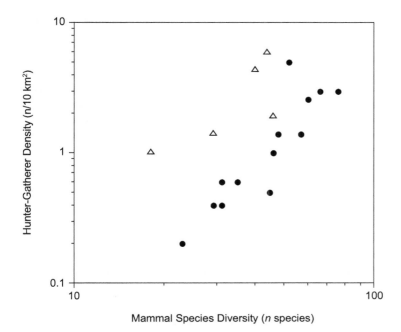

FIGURE 11.5. Relationship between current mammal species diversity and the historical population densities of 18 North American Arctic, Subarctic, and Plains forager groups. Triangles are cold open-country groups, whereas solid circles are northern forest and temperate grassland groups. Data shown are for the groups numbered 1, 2, 4, 5, 7, 11–13, 16, 19–27 in Morin (2008:49, table 1).

those associated with the lower cluster are found in temperate grasslands and northern forests. Both of these clusters show a very strong correlation between hunter-gatherer density and mammal species diversity, even though one of the relationships cannot be assessed properly because of its small sample size (upper cluster; $r_s = .70$, $p < .17$, $n = 5$; lower cluster: $r_s = .91$, $p < .002$, $n = 13$). The presence of two separate clusters in this figure means that species diversity does not explain all of the variation in the hunter-gatherer sample.

Yet given that the relationship remains strong when the two clusters are combined, it seems reasonable to conclude that, during the contact period in North America, areas with high species diversity supported, on average, greater densities of human foragers than regions with low numbers of species. Assuming that this relationship also held in the past, it might be possible to use mammal species diversity as a yardstick for predicting the *direction* (increasing or decreasing) of changes in human densities in Late Pleistocene Europe. However, before exploring its archaeological implications, we should consider an important question that this relationship raises: why do human foragers rarely thrive in environments with low mammal species diversity?

The most likely answer to this question is that low species diversity may not only decrease the overall long-term return rate of foraging but possibly also increase variation in game procurement. The fact that in ethnographic and historical accounts low productivity environments are more frequently associated with episodes of famines than high productivity environments – despite the very low human densities recorded in the former areas – brings support to this view (Keeley 1988). Variation in game procurement seems to have been particularly acute for foragers heavily dependent on *Rangifer* (Burch 1972), as the first Aurignacians presumably were. It is now well documented that caribou and reindeer herds experience dramatic cycles of abundance with fluctuations sometimes approaching ratios of 1:200 *within a few decades* (Meldgaard 1986; Boudreau *et al.* 2003; Gunn 2003; Valkenburg *et al.* 2003; Couturier *et al.* 2004). These fluctuations, which seem to occur independently of hunting pressure, have been attributed to the interaction of several phenomena. Among various possible causal factors, poor grazing and adverse snow conditions are the most frequently cited (Aanes *et al.* 2003; Gunn 2003).

In low-diversity environments, the impact of the demographic crash of a *Rangifer* herd on human populations was often buffered by enlisting help from neighboring groups or by moving into a contiguous territory to exploit another herd (Minc 1986; Whallon 2006). However, these strategies probably sporadically failed because *Rangifer* herds tend to crash synchronously at the regional level (Meldgaard 1986; Gunn 2003; Post and Forchhammer 2006; Morin 2008). A few decades ago, Burch (1972:356, original emphasis) emphasized the vulnerability of *Rangifer*-dependent economies to these abundance cycles:

> The more restricted the temporal scope and geographic scope under consideration, the greater the likelihood that fluctuations will occur, the more often they are likely to occur, and the more extreme the fluctuations are likely to be. It is at the level of the individual herd that the dependability of caribou as a human resource is most questionable. Major fluctuations at this level inevitably impose severe limitations on human numbers and distributions in every locality in which caribou are a major basis of human subsistence. Since the range of a given herd can cover anywhere from tens to hundreds of thousands of square kilometers, fluctuations in a single herd might well affect a number of human populations. Given the current state of knowledge, it is not unreasonable to assume that *human populations largely dependent upon caribou will be faced with a major resource crisis once at least every 2 or 3 generations.*

These comments have important demographic ramifications. If Burch is correct, it can be hypothesized that heavy dependence on reindeer during the Proto/Early Aurignacian would have *increased fluctuations of human densities in the western and northern plains.* In addition, the correlation between mammal species diversity and historical forager densities suggest that the spectacular shift toward strong reindeer dominance during the Protoaurignacian was also associated with *significant declines in human population densities, particularly in regions that lack substantial evidence for dietary intensification, such as France and Germany.* The fact that archaeological sequences in Germany tend to show an abrupt break between the Middle Paleolithic and the Early Aurignacian may testify to the intensity of these declines in human densities (Conard and Bolus 2003). If accurate, these propositions would contradict most interpretations of demographic change during the Middle to Upper Paleolithic transition.

The issue now is to determine whether these inferred changes in human population dynamics were exceptional or the rule during the Middle and Upper Paleolithic. Broadening the temporal scope of the analysis to the entire Late Pleistocene should aid in elucidating this problem.

ENVIRONMENTAL CARRYING CAPACITY IN LATE PLEISTOCENE FRANCE

To assess how change in environmental carrying capacity might have affected human densities over time, a composite time series spanning from the end of the Middle Pleistocene to the earliest stages of the Holocene (end of MIS 6–beginning of MIS 1) was assembled for southwestern France. The time series was created with the assistance of several lithic specialists using lithic assemblage composition to determine the chronological placement of the faunal sequences.[2] Three variables – the percentage of reindeer, the diversity of ungulate species (as measured by the Reciprocal of Simpson's Index), and the percentage of cold-adapted micro-mammals – were examined in this series to identify fluctuations in environmental carrying capacity.

This composite time series represents a compromise between several constraints. As much as possible, efforts were made to i) use well-documented anthropogenic assemblages accumulated over roughly comparable time spans (this implies that assemblages were combined if deposition occurred over short periods of time); ii) control for variation due to geography by focusing on sites from a single homogeneous area (the Dordogne, the northwestern margin of the Lot, and the Poitou-Charentes); iii) limit the number of sites composing the series to reduce mismatches in sequence correlations; iv) keep sample sizes at an acceptable level, while minimizing temporal averaging; and v) eliminate gaps within the series by intercalating chronologically relevant assemblages.

Twelve archaeological sequences form the backbone of the time series. These sequences all originate from cliff base deposits, rockshelters or caves. The series first builds on the remarkably long and detailed stratigraphy of Combe-Grenal, which covers the end of MIS 6 and the interval from MIS 5b to the first half of MIS 3 (Bordes and Prat 1965; Bordes *et al.* 1966; Laquay 1981; Mellars 1986, 1996; Guadelli 1987; Delpech and Prat 1995; Delpech 1996; this study). La Quina (station amont, Debénath and Jelinek 1998; Rendu 2007), Saint-Césaire, Les Cottés (Rendu 2009, pers. comm., 2011), Abri Pataud (Bouchud 1975; Cho 1998; Sekhr 1998), Roc de Combe (Grayson and Delpech 2008), and Le Flageolet I (Grayson and Delpech 1998) provided assemblages for the second half of MIS 3 and the beginning of MIS 2. These assemblages are associated with industries spanning from the late Mousterian to the Final Gravettian. Finally, the Late Glacial and early Holocene occupations from Laugerie Haute Est (Delpech 1983), Le Taillis des Coteaux (Griggo 2009, pers. comm., 2011), Le Flageolet II, La Madeleine (Delpech 1983), and Bois-Ragot (Griggo 1995, 2005) document faunal variation during the Solutrean, Badegoulian, Magdalenian, and Azilian periods. Appendix 15 summarizes the principal characteristics (cultural period, size of the faunal samples) of the ungulate and micro-mammal assemblages.

Geographic variation in the time series ($n = 96$ faunal assemblages) is limited given that most units (82/96 or 85.4%) are from sites found within a maximum distance of 50 km from each other. More distantly located sites include La Quina (max. dist. $\approx$120 km), Bois-Ragot (max. dist. $\approx$170 km), Saint-Césaire (max. dist. $\approx$170 km), le Taillis des Coteaux (max. dist. $\approx$180 km), and Les Cottés ($\approx$210 km). The Gironde, the Lot-et-Garonne, and the "Causses" region are omitted from the present analysis because they differ from the

---

[2] The help received from Alexandre Michel, Jean-Philippe Faivre, Damien Pesesse, Sylvain Ducasse, Catherine Cretin, André Morala, and Mathieu Langlais was invaluable in this respect.

Périgord and the Poitou-Charentes in terms of topography and/or the composition of ungulate communities. Importantly, the sequences were aligned relative to each other using only stratigraphic observations and the typo-technological characteristics of the lithic assemblages. This procedure should permit an objective assessment of patterns of faunal change during the Late Pleistocene.

Another point concerns the absolute chronology of the time series. TL dates were used in combination with lithic criteria to assess the age of the Mousterian occupations from La Quina (Debénath and Jelinek 1998) and Saint-Césaire (Mercier *et al.* 1993). The task is more complicated at Combe-Grenal because this site lacks reliable radiometric dates (Guibert *et al.* 2008). Despite this difficulty, the chronology of Combe-Grenal is relatively well understood thanks to sedimentologic, lithic, and paleontological correlations with other archaeological sequences (Bordes and Prat 1965; Bordes *et al.* 1966, 1972; Laquay 1981; Mellars 1986, 1996; Guadelli 1987; Delpech and Prat 1995; Delpech 1996; Turq 2000; Faivre 2008; Guibert *et al.* 2008). The chronology adopted here for this site differs only in minor details from these earlier studies, except for the earliest Late Pleistocene occupations (starting with layer 55), which are here placed in MIS 5b instead of MIS 5d/c, based on correlations with marine cores (discussed subsequently). However, because the chronology of Combe-Grenal cannot be anchored with absolute dates, the proposed correlations must be considered tentative.

The picture is very different for the Upper Paleolithic. In France, the age of the lithic industries attributed to this time period is particularly well constrained with hundreds of assemblages having been dated using the ^{14}C method. Widely accepted time limits, as presented in recent syntheses (e.g., Zilhão and d'Errico 1999; Zilhão *et al.* 1999; Langlais 2008; Pesesse 2008), are followed here. The earliest Aurignacian is assumed to date to ≈37 ka, the earliest Gravettian to ≈28.5 ka, the earliest Solutrean to ≈21 ka, the earliest Badegoulian to ≈19 ka, and the earliest Magdalenian to ≈18 ka (dates are uncalibrated). This chronology is considered robust enough to allow the positioning of millennial climatic events within a relatively narrow range of stratigraphic units.

As mentioned earlier, the Combe-Grenal sequence is marked by a hiatus largely coinciding with MIS 5e–c. The rest of the series is thought to be roughly continuous, although minor gaps and misalignments may affect certain stratigraphic units. A related issue is the temporal resolution of the assemblages. The average time span of the stratigraphic units for each of the MIS represented in the series is estimated in Table 11.2. The estimates suggest that the chronological grain is approximately constant across the sequence (range: 0.8–0.9 ka per unit).

The ungulate samples composing the series vary widely in size, with NISP values ranging from 13 to 23,392. The vast majority (86/96 or 89.6%) of the assemblages encompass a minimum of 30 specimens identified at least to the genus level, with more than two-thirds of the samples (61/96 or 63.5%) containing a minimum of 100 identified specimens. However, the small samples (i.e., NISP < 100) are not randomly distributed within the series; most of them (29/35 or 82.9%) are from Combe-Grenal. The latter samples were not aggregated with stratigraphically adjacent assemblages because this procedure would have substantially reduced the temporal resolution of the Combe-Grenal sequence. Consequently, sampling error is more likely to influence faunal patterns in this portion of the time series. Nevertheless, the overall trends are believed to be representative of taxonomic changes in ungulate assemblages during the Late Pleistocene.

TABLE 11.2. *Average time span for the 96 assemblages ("units") represented in the faunal series (see Appendix 15 for a description of the assemblages)*

Stratigraphic units	Number of units	Total time span (in ka)	Average time span (in ka per unit)
Combe-Grenal, layers 63–56 (end of MIS 6)	8	?	?
Hiatus (MIS 5e–c)	–	25	–
Combe-Grenal, layers 55–34 (MIS 5b–a)	18	15	0.8
Combe-Grenal, layers 33–17 (MIS 4)	17	13	0.8
Combe-Grenal, layers 16–1 to Le Flageolet I, layer VII (MIS 3)	35	31	0.9
Abri Pataud, layer 4 lower to Bois-Ragot, layers 6–5 (MIS 2)	16	14	0.9
Bois-Ragot, layers 4 and 3 (beginning of MIS 1)	2	?	?

The average time span of the stratigraphic units was calculated by dividing the estimated time span of the MIS by the number of corresponding stratigraphic units within the faunal series. The chronology for Combe-Grenal largely follows the arguments made by Delpech and Prat (1995), Delpech (1996), and Mellars (1986, 1996), except for the position of the earliest Late Pleistocene occupations from that site, which are here placed during MIS 5b rather than MIS 5d/c.

Species diversity and the percentage of reindeer were calculated relative to ungulates only. Carnivores were excluded from these calculations because of a general lack of data regarding the agents of accumulation for these taxa. Small-bodied animals (e.g., birds, leporids) were also ignored because they would have obscured comparisons between assemblages that pre- and postdated the Late Glacial shift toward broad diets. Moreover, selective recovery probably reduced the representation of these taxa at Combe-Grenal, Roc de Combe, and Laugerie Haute Est. As noted earlier, this problem is less significant for ungulates because their larger remains are more likely to have been collected, with the possible exception of small elements such as sesamoids and deciduous teeth. Lastly, because values for the Reciprocal of Simpson's Index can be affected by sample size (Magurran 2004), assemblages with less than ≈50 specimens were omitted from the calculation of species diversity.

To control for climate change, the percentage of cold-adapted micro-mammals (Male/root vole, narrow-skulled vole, and collared lemming) throughout the series was evaluated using data gathered by Marquet (1993) and Oppliger (2008). Unfortunately, only a limited number of stratigraphic units (17/96 or 17.7%) contain substantial samples (total MNI $\geq$ 10) of micro-mammal specimens. Furthermore, the size of these samples tends to be very small, given that approximately two-thirds of them comprise less than 30 individuals. It should be noted that the data set excludes the micro-mammal samples from Saint-Césaire and Bois-Ragot (Marquet 1993) because these "northern" sites tend to show consistently higher percentages of cold-adapted micro-mammals relative to coeval samples from the Dordogne and Lot region (see discussion above on Roc de Combe).

To enlarge the data set, 12 additional archaeological assemblages comprising larger micro-mammal samples (Roc de Combe layers 8, 7, 4, and 1; Le Flageolet I layers V and IV; Cassegros layers 10 and 9; Combe-Saunière layers IV1-IV10; Moulin du Roc couche brune; and Pont d'Ambon layers 3 and 2) were tentatively correlated with units of the time series using lithic criteria. These additional micro-mammal samples are presented in Appendix 15. Although helpful, adding these samples to the data set has the drawback of raising the issue of possible misalignments. Obviously, this issue must be kept in mind when drawing conclusions about variations in the relative abundance of cold-adapted micro-mammals.

The Time Series

The assembled time series is presented in Figure 11.6. A first observation is that episodes of strong reindeer dominance (>80% of ungulate NISP) were rare, although not entirely lacking (discussed later), during the approximately 95,000-year period separating the end of MIS 6 (Combe-Grenal, layers 63–56) from the Protoaurignacian. Reindeer is virtually absent in the earliest Late Pleistocene levels from Combe-Grenal, and it can be safely assumed that this was also the case for the warm substages 5e–c that are not represented in the series.

In comparison, reindeer is moderately common in the later Mousterian (MIS 4 and the first half of MIS 3) where it sometimes accounts for as much as 50 to 60% of the ungulate specimens. Reindeer representation peaked at least twice during this last period. A first set of peaks, analyzed by Delpech (1996), is recorded in the Quina occupations (layers 26–17) at Combe-Grenal. This set of peaks is distinct from a more recent peak in reindeer abundance recorded in layers 8–6, which are attributed to the Typical Mousterian.

Upper Paleolithic assemblages tend to depart from the Late Pleistocene Mousterian pattern, given that reindeer frequently comprises more than 80%, and sometimes 95%, of the ungulate remains. As noted by Mellars (1973, 1996, 2004) and Delpech (1983, 1999), this last trend is particularly apparent during MIS 2. In essence, in contrast to the Late Pleistocene Mousterian, episodes of strong reindeer dominance were common during the Upper Paleolithic and the norm during the Late Glacial. However, as shown later, these generalizations are of limited use because they sometimes mask considerable variation in reindeer abundance within these time periods.

One of the most striking features of Figure 11.6 is the amplitude of the faunal changes during the early Upper Paleolithic. Indeed, this time period is associated with several spectacular oscillations in the relative abundance of reindeer in ungulate assemblages (range: 10.3–98.7%). Despite their importance, these dramatic variations have received very little attention in the literature (but see Delpech *et al.* 2000 and Delpech and Texier 2007). Importantly, the early Upper Paleolithic is also characterized by marked fluctuations in species diversity, which suggests that, during this time period, assemblages that were strongly dominated by reindeer frequently gave way to assemblages containing a more even range of ungulate taxa, except for a short episode of red deer dominance during the Early Gravettian (Delpech and Texier 2007). However, additional samples will be needed to validate these inferences, given that some of the extreme fluctuations lie at the interface of separate sequences.

These temporal patterns characterize the time series. Yet because the grain of the series is relatively coarse, one cannot exclude the possibility that small gaps or time averaging muted the signal of certain events of short duration. Specifically, it is of interest to determine with greater certainty whether episodes of strong reindeer dominance (>80% of ungulate NISP) were rare during the Late Pleistocene Mousterian, as argued

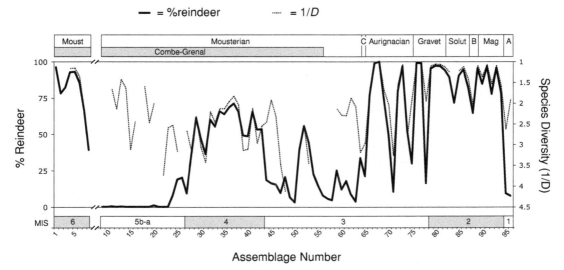

FIGURE 11.6. Composite series of faunal assemblages showing variations in the percentage of reindeer and in ungulate species diversity between the end of MIS 6 and the beginning of MIS 1. The numbers (from 1 to 96) in the time series correspond to the ungulate assemblages listed in Appendix 15. The diversity of ungulate species, shown here on an inverted scale, was assessed using the Reciprocal of Simpson's Index. A value of "1" on this scale means that all of the specimens belong to a single species. Conversely, a value of "5" means that species are all equally represented if the sample consists of five species. Note the hiatus between the MIS 6 and MIS 5 occupations. As discussed in the text, species diversity values are not provided for small assemblages, this statistic being particularly sensitive to sample size. NISP count for rhinocerotids, including *Dicerorhinos* and *Coelodonta*, were treated as a single taxon, as was respectively the case for *Capra* and bovine species. The taxa considered in the analysis of species diversity are: *Sus scrofa*, *Cervus elaphus*, *Megaloceros giganteus*, *Capreolus capreolus*, *Rangifer tarandus*, bovines, *Rupicapra rupicapra*, caprines, *Equus ferus caballus*, *Equus hydruntinus*, rhinocerotids, *Dama dama*, and *Saiga tatarica*.

earlier. The issue is important given its possible demographic implications for human populations.

A review of the literature indicates that few ungulate assemblages[3] are strongly dominated by reindeer during this otherwise well-documented period. These assemblages include Marillac layers 11–8 (80.0–90.9%, Costamagno *et al.* 2008:381), Grotte Vaufrey layer I (82.9%, Delpech 1988:267–8), Chez Pinaud layers 24–9 (76.9–95.2%, Beauval 2004:126; Jaubert *et al.* 2008:216), Pech de l'Azé IV layers I1–G (82.5–93.4%, Laquay 1981:70–71), and La Quina layer 8 (90.0%, Armand in Debénath and Jelinek 1998:56). Excluding this last occupation, these assemblages are all attributed to the Quina facies (Delpech 1996; Jaubert *et al.* 2008; Turq *et al.* 2008). Given this strong association, it is not unreasonable to conclude, as Delpech (1996) did based on a smaller sample, that the majority of these assemblages were roughly contemporary with the reindeer-dominated Quina occupations of Combe-Grenal (layers 26–17).

Among the assemblages just listed, the ungulate assemblage from La Quina layer 8 constitutes an exception because it is not associated with the Quina facies. Yet this

---

[3] Percentages were calculated using only ungulate remains. Elephantids, indeterminate cervids, and possible *Megaloceros* remains were excluded, as were samples with fewer than 30 specimens.

assemblage contains a high percentage of reindeer and presents many similarities with the reindeer peak documented in layers 8–6 at Combe-Grenal. One of these similarities relates to their stratigraphic relationships with well-described facies. In their respective sequences, only one or two layers separate the La Quina layer 8 and the Combe-Grenal layers 8–6 assemblages from an overlying series of Mousterian of Acheulean Tradition layers. Because this last facies is highly diagnostic and relatively well constrained in time (Delagnes *et al.* 2007; Guibert *et al.* 2008), these stratigraphic observations may imply that these assemblages were approximately coeval.

However, this argument is complicated by the fact that the Combe-Grenal[4] layers 7–6 have been ascribed to the Typical Mousterian (Bordes *et al.* 1966), while the La Quina layer 8 belongs to the Denticulate Mousterian (Park 2007). This inconsistency might be more apparent than real, given that both the Combe-Grenal layers 7–6 and the La Quina layer 8 occupations are rich in sidescrapers (Debénath and Jelinek 1998:47; Turq 2000:282), a feature central to the definition of the Typical Mousterian (Bordes 1981b). Moreover, the preferential use of Levallois blanks for making sidescrapers is documented in both sets of assemblages (Turq 2000:280–282; Park 2007:184). Further analysis of these levels is needed to establish whether these similarities are circumstantial or extend to other aspects of the lithic assemblages.

The time series indicates that episodes of strong reindeer dominance occurred with varying frequencies during the period corresponding to MIS 6–2. Can the emergence of these reindeer peaks be attributed mostly to climate change, as argued for the Middle to Upper Paleolithic transition? Despite the limitations of the samples, the micro-mammal data set assembled here suggests that climatic forcing was the principal mechanism influencing change in reindeer representation. This is demonstrated by a statistically significant correlation between the percentage of reindeer and the percentage of cold-adapted micro-mammals in the stratigraphic units in the time series ($r_s = .52$, $p < .01$, $n = 29$, micro-mammal samples with MNI ≥ 10). The correlation between these variables becomes exceptionally strong when the data set is limited to micro-mammal samples with MNI ≥ 50 ($r_s = .94$, $p < .002$, $n = 12$, Figure 11.7). The importance of climate as a causal factor driving taxonomic representation in the time series is further confirmed by a statistically significant relationship between species diversity values for ungulates and those for micro-mammals ($r_s = .66$, $p < .03$, $n = 12$, micro-mammal samples with MNI ≥ 50). These correlations are notable because they imply that, during the Late Pleistocene, humans transported ungulate taxa to shelters in a way that closely tracked variations in the natural abundance of these species.

In sum, the time series and data taken from the literature point to the existence of only two episodes of strong reindeer dominance during the Late Pleistocene Mousterian. A first episode – or set of episodes – is associated with the Quina facies. Several lines of evidence, including trends in reindeer body size, indicate that this or these event(s) took place during MIS 4 (Delpech 1996). A second, apparently short-lived, episode of strong reindeer dominance occurred during MIS 3 just before the emergence of the Mousterian of Acheulean Tradition facies. Factors that possibly affected the temporal spacing of these reindeer peaks are discussed subsequently.

---

[4] Few data are available on the composition of the lithic assemblage from layer 8 at Combe-Grenal.

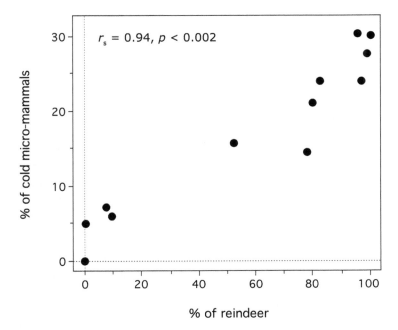

FIGURE 11.7. Correlation between the relative abundance of reindeer and the relative abundance of cold-adapted micro-mammals (Male/root vole, narrow-skulled vole, and the collared lemming) in the time series. Only the micro-mammal assemblages with MNI > 50 are shown in this graph. The data are from the sources cited in Appendix 15.

Reindeer Peaks and Millennial-Scale Climatic Events

The study of ice cores has led to the discovery of several climatic oscillations operating at the millennial scale during the last glacial period, including Dansgaard-Oeschger cycles (e.g., Dansgaard *et al.* 1993; Grootes and Stuiver 1997). Dansgaard-Oeschger cycles are marked by warm interstadial (GIS, Greenland interstadial) and cold stadial (GS, Greenland stadial) phases. Climatic oscillations have also been detected in deep-sea cores from the North Atlantic region (Bond *et al.* 1992, 1993; Broecker 1994; Bond and Lotti 1995; Chapman and Shackleton 1998; Voelker *et al.* 2002). Some of these oscillations, the so-called "Heinrich events," were extremely cold and were caused by episodes of massive iceberg discharges into the North Atlantic region (e.g., Bond and Lotti 1995; Hemming 2004).

The Heinrich events caused a reduction of sea-surface temperatures, which would have fueled a southward migration of the oceanic thermal front toward the mid-latitudes of the North Atlantic (Paillard and Labeyrie 1994; Cortijo *et al.* 1997; Naughton *et al.* 2009). Several climatic simulations have demonstrated that significant freshwater pulses into this region can decrease or stop thermohaline circulation (Hemming 2004; Timmermann *et al.* 2005). Changes in thermohaline circulation would have inhibited the diffusion of comparatively warm and humid atmospheric conditions from the equatorial zone to the high latitudes of the North Atlantic and therefore would have affected vegetation in Europe. Vegetative change associated with Heinrich events is attested in marine sequences from the eastern North Atlantic and the Mediterranean regions (e.g., Sánchez Goñi *et al.* 2000, 2008; Roucoux *et al.* 2005; Naughton *et al.* 2009; Fletcher *et al.* 2010).

The amplitude of these oscillations means that climatic variations have been significantly underestimated in previous reconstructions of continental environments. This problem has been attributed to insufficient chronological resolution, the use of a small number of indirect climatic proxies from often-distant geographic regions, and erroneous assumptions about the response of vegetation to rapid climatic change:

> Our record from Monticchio [a lacustrine sequence in Italy] demonstrates the capability of late Quaternary lake sediments to provide sensitive, high-resolution records of rapid (centennial-millennial) environmental fluctuations comparable to those obtained from ice cores. It also reveals that the biosphere was a full participant in these rapid fluctuations, contrary to widely held views that vegetation is unable to change with such rapidity. (Allen *et al.* 1999:743)

> While several periods of high primary productivity are seen at Les Echets between c. 36.2 and 28 kyr BP, only two interstadial events, Hengelo and Denekamp, have been recognized in pollen-stratigraphic records from central and northwest Europe for the same time interval (Behre 1989; Allen and Huntley 2000; Caspers and Freund 2001; Guiter *et al.* 2003; Müller *et al.* 2003; Preusser 2004). The high-resolution geochemical and chronological record for core EC1 indicates that these terrestrial interstadials were not individual events, but may contain several events with alternating interstadial and stadial conditions, partly explaining the discrepancies in the dating (Behre 1989; Caspers and Freund 2001) and environmental reconstructions (Guiter *et al.* 2003) for these events. (Veres *et al.* 2008:240)

In archaeology, similar problems have limited the accuracy of models assessing the impact of climate change on the composition of ungulate assemblages. The resolution of the present time series should allow an examination of correlations between the relative abundance of reindeer and climatic cycles at the millennial to orbital (glacial/interglacial) scale. At the millennial scale, Heinrich events are central to the discussion, given that they may have decreased global temperatures by several degrees Celsius (Broecker 1994; Chapman *et al.* 1998; Sachs and Anderson 2005; Maslin 2009). Because Heinrich events are considered to have had stronger effects on the eastern than on the western North Atlantic (Seidov 2009), these cold episodes might have been involved in the formation of the strong reindeer peaks documented in the time series.

This hypothesis was evaluated by comparing the time series with data derived from the DSDP-609 core in the North Atlantic (Bond *et al.* 1992, 1993; Bond and Lotti 1995; Allen *et al.* 1999) and the twin MD95–2042 and SU81–18 cores on the western Iberian margin (Sánchez Goñi *et al.* 2008). Three climatic proxies were considered in these comparisons: i) the relative abundance of *Neogloboquadrina pachyderma* (left coiling), a planktic (planktonic) foraminifer indicative of cold water conditions (Bond *et al.* 1992); ii) the concentration of ice-rafted debris, which reflects episodes of icebergs reaching the Iberian margin; and iii) planktic $\delta^{18}O$, an indirect indicator of sea-surface temperatures. These proxies were compared with the high-resolution GISP2 timescale from Greenland (Dansgaard *et al.* 1993; Blunier and Brook 2001), which is used here as a reference.

The sequences are compared in Figure 11.8. The general shape of the reindeer curve is very similar to that of the *N. pachyderma* and planktic $\delta^{18}O$ curves, which confirms that

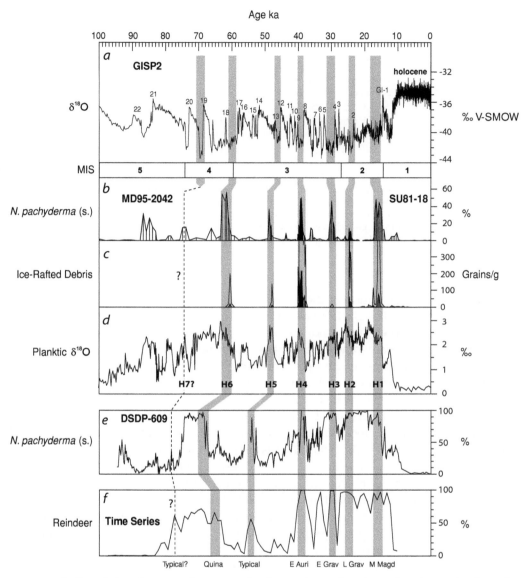

FIGURE 11.8. Correlations between the composite time series and various climatic proxies from the marine and glacial records: *a*) $\delta^{18}O$ in the GISP2 ice core; *b* and *e*) the relative abundance of *Neogloboquadrina pachyderma* (left coiling) in the DSDP-609 (*b*) and the MD95–2042 and SU81–18 (*e*) cores; *c*) concentration of ice-rafted debris (IRD) in the MD95–2042 and SU81–18 cores; *d*) planktic $\delta^{18}O$ in the MD95–2042 and SU81–18 marine cores; *f*) percentages of reindeer in the composite time series. H7–H1 are Heinrich events. Data for *a* are from Stuiver and Grootes (2000), as reported by Salgueiro *et al.* (2010:688, figure 7), those for *b–d* are from Sánchez Goñi *et al.* (2008:1142, figure 3). The data for *e* are those published by Bond *et al.* (1992) and Bond and Lotti (1995), as interpreted by Allen *et al.* (1999:742, figure 3), whereas the data for *f* are from Figure 11.6. In the GISP2 ice core (panel *a*), $\delta^{18}O$ values in the samples correspond to the relative difference, given as per mil, in the abundance ratios of $^{18}O/^{16}O$ with respect to a standard (V-SMOW, the Vienna Standard Mean Ocean Water). In panel *d*, $\delta^{18}O$ values were taken on *Globigerina bulloides*.

TABLE 11.3. *Marine and glacial dates for Heinrich events and coeval cultural periods in western France*

Heinrich event	Marine dates (in ka)	Corresponding cultural period
H1	14.4 ± 0.4 (AMS)	Middle Magdalenian
H2	21.0 ± 0.4 (AMS)	Late Gravettian
H3	26.9 ± 0.7 (AMS)	Early Gravettian (pre-Fontirobertian)
H4	34.8 ± 0.6 (AMS)	Proto/Early Aurignacian
H5	45.0 ± 1.5 (AMS)	Typical Mousterian
H6	≈60.0 (GRIP age)	Quina facies
H7	≈69.0? (GRIP age)	Typical Mousterian?

The ^{14}C (AMS) dates are average uncalibrated dates from marine cores provided by Chapman *et al.* (2000:17, table 3). These authors applied a reservoir correction of 400 years to the dates. The dates for H7 and H6 are calendar dates from the GISP2 core, as presented in Salgueiro *et al.* (2010:686, figure 4). The cultural periods were identified based on ^{14}C dates in the archaeological record and the patterns of reindeer dominance in Figure 11.8.

the taxonomic representation of the former taxon was strongly influenced by climatic oscillations during the last glacial period. Correlations with Heinrich events H7–H1 point to a relationship between the episodes of strong reindeer dominance and millennial-scale cycles. Although there are some uncertainties concerning the exact position of the earliest events – particularly H7 – the interpolations link the reindeer peak in the recent Quina occupations of Combe-Grenal with H6, whereas the peak in the Typical Mousterian layers 8–6 appears to have been coeval with H5.

The placement of H4–H1 is better constrained because these events fall within the effective range of the radiocarbon method. The correlations indicate that H4 occurred during the Proto/Early Aurignacian. This is congruent with the associated ^{14}C dates for this event (Table 11.3) and with the proposed stratigraphic position of the Laschamp excursion, an episode of change in the earth's magnetic field that slightly pre-dated H4, which has been documented in several archaeological sequences from Central and Eastern Europe (Fedele *et al.* 2008; Hoffecker *et al.* 2008). Lastly, the H3, H2, and H1 events would have been contemporary with the Early Gravettian, Late Gravettian, and Middle Magdalenian, respectively.

In general, correlations with marine and ice core data suggest that the relative frequency with which ungulate species were transported to cave sites in southwestern France was directly or indirectly influenced by climatic fluctuations operating at the millennial to orbital scale. Yet it should be noted that these observations, which reinforce conclusions made earlier using micro-mammal samples, do not mean that ungulate species were procured in proportions that exactly match their natural abundances in the landscape. As argued in Chapter 3, a perfect match with natural proportions seems unlikely because some taxa were probably more difficult to locate or obtain than others due to differences in speed, strength, social behavior, and other factors. In addition, certain aspects of the correlations will require further analysis. For instance, it will be important in future work to determine what caused the reindeer peak recorded in the time series between H4 and H3.

THE EARLY UPPER PALEOLITHIC "ANOMALY"

Correlations with several climatic proxies suggest that, in the study area, episodes of strong reindeer dominance were coeval with Heinrich events. This result is concordant with the current consensus in paleoclimatology that Heinrich events "coincided with the coldest periods of the last ice age" (Sachs and Anderson 2005:1118). However, for human populations, the short episodes of dramatic warming that generally terminated the Heinrich events may have been as important as the severe cooling episodes:

> Late Pleistocene Heinrich events... in the North Atlantic are identified by distinct ice-rafted-detritus (IRD) layers primarily derived from the Laurentide Ice Sheet... Eight such events coincided with the coldest, stadial phase of some Dansgaard-Oeschger (D/O) events in Greenland ice cores over the past ~65,000 years. D/O events typically start with an abrupt 9 to 15°C... warming over a few decades or less, followed by gradual cooling over several millennia. (Rashid and Boyle 2007:439)

> The climate of the last glacial period was characterised by strong atmospheric temperature oscillations. Over a few years high latitude air temperatures could increase with more than 12 °C. However, the warmings were short and immediately followed by a stepwise return to cold conditions. The fluctuations are recorded in the Greenland ice core records (Dansgaard *et al.*, 1993), and they are generally known as Dansgaard-Oeschger events. (Rasmussen and Thomsen 2004:101)

The impact of Dansgaard-Oeschger events has rarely been assessed in the archaeological record. In the time series, these warming events were probably involved in the sometimes strong resurgence of temperate species after Heinrich events (e.g., the, respectively, bovine- and red deer-dominated samples from stratigraphic units 71 and 78). Yet because the severity, duration, and pacing of Dansgaard-Oeschger and Heinrich events show some variation (Dansgaard *et al.* 1993; Hemming 2004; Ahn and Brook 2008), the impact of these oscillations on ungulate communities might have varied as well. This problem was evaluated within the time series by examining percent change in reindeer representation. These values were obtained by subtracting the percentage of reindeer in a layer from the corresponding percentage in the underlying layer (the numbers are presented as absolute values, that is, without regard to the direction of change). This can mathematically be expressed as follows:

$$|z| = x - y, \tag{12}$$

where x is a layer and y the layer that precedes it stratigraphically. The same equation was used to assess change in species diversity values between adjacent layers. As noted earlier, because diversity measures are particularly sensitive to sample size, assemblages with less than ≈50 specimens were excluded from the analysis. Unfortunately, this removes several data points from the Combe-Grenal sequence.

As shown in Figure 11.9, the extreme variations in reindeer representation and species diversity during the early Upper Paleolithic are somewhat anomalous and stand in sharp contrast to the more uniform values seen in the Mousterian and the later Upper Paleolithic. These trends suggest that the early Upper Paleolithic occupants of western France

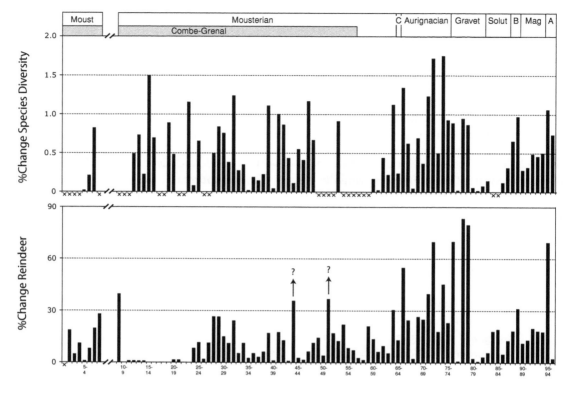

$|z|$ = value from layer x minus value from the underlying layer y

FIGURE 11.9. Absolute percent change in reindeer representation (lower diagram) and species diversity (upper diagram) between stratigraphically adjacent layers. The "×" symbols indicate that the data were unavailable due to small sample size or lack of underlying layer. Note the hiatus between the MIS 6 and MIS 5 occupations of Combe-Grenal. The arrows highlight the fact that other Mousterian assemblages suggest stronger reindeer dominance during these time periods than is indicated at Combe-Grenal.

faced unusually high-amplitude cycles of faunal change marked by shifts from cold and species-poor to temperate and species-rich ungulate communities. The demographic implications of these changes will now be considered.

DEMOGRAPHIC AND GENETIC IMPLICATIONS

Given the relationship between species diversity, economic dependence on reindeer, and historical hunter-gatherer densities (discussed earlier), the high-amplitude variations in ungulate communities observed during the early Upper Paleolithic likely had a marked impact on the demography of human populations. In western Europe, the Heinrich events probably substantially reduced environmental carrying capacity and caused concomitant declines in human densities. The effects of these cold episodes on human groups would have been particularly severe during H4 (Figure 11.10a), one of the harshest, if not the harshest, of the Heinrich events (Hemming 2004). The Dansgaard-Oeschger event that terminated this Heinrich event presumably had the opposite results: it would have increased environmental carrying capacity and coincidentally fostered marked

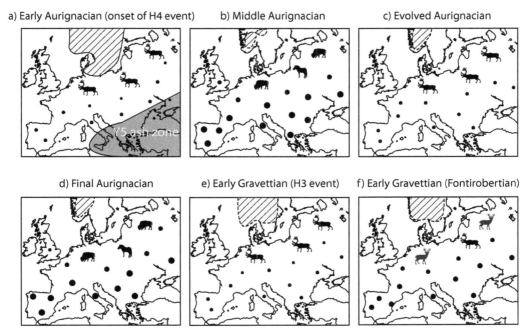

FIGURE 11.10. Demographic model for western Europe representing change in the distribution and density of human populations during the early Upper Paleolithic. Larger dots in the figure denote higher population densities. The shaded area indicates the ash zone associated with the Campanian Y5 Ignimbrite eruption. The dashed lines show the possible limits of glaciated zones (limits are extrapolated following Lambeck et al. 2010).

rebounds in human densities (Figure 11.10b). This demographic cycle would have been repeated at least three times during the early Upper Paleolithic, as suggested by the time series (Figure 11.10c–f).

Another phenomenon requires attention in this discussion. Approximately at the time of the onset of H4, a massive volcanic eruption occurred north of the Bay of Naples (Phlegrean Fields, southern Italy), spreading ashes across the northeastern Mediterranean, the Balkans, and much of Eastern Europe (Fedele *et al.* 2008). This event, named the Campanian Ignimbrite (Y5) eruption, is significant because it was one of the largest eruptions of the late Quaternary (Self 2006). As pointed out by Zilhão (2006) and Fedele *et al.* (2008), this volcanic episode likely affected the local populations, perhaps by decreasing human densities. Although its overall effects on human genetic diversity might have been relatively limited, this eruption probably temporarily enhanced population subdivisions in Eastern Europe during the early phase of H4.

The data collected for southwestern France imply that the early Upper Paleolithic was characterized by a rapid succession of bottlenecks in human populations. These conditions likely favored micro- and macro-evolutionary change among the last Neandertals. The bottleneck events possibly contributed to reduce genetic diversity, and the subsequent episodes of demographic growth might have facilitated the spread of new adaptive features via the recolonization of habitats, including the northern plains. These issues are of interest because it has been pointed out that genetic drift may explain why mtDNA sequences from modern humans lack evidence for gene flow with

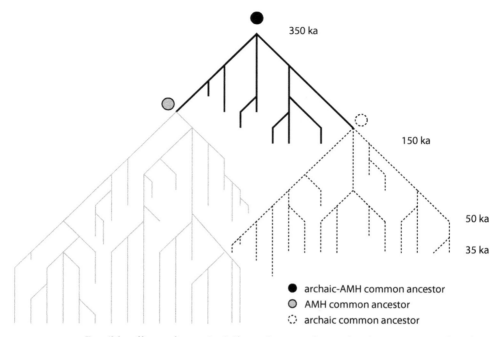

350 ka

150 ka

50 ka

35 ka

● archaic-AMH common ancestor
○ AMH common ancestor
◌ archaic common ancestor

FIGURE 11.11. Possible effects of genetic drift on the genealogy of archaic *sapiens* and early modern humans. In this figure, archaic *sapiens* ("archaic") and anatomically modern humans ("AMH") diverge early. The example shows that most of the archaic lineages become extinct by 35 ka, with the exception of a few lineages (one of the left-most archaic lineages) that persist somewhat longer.

Neandertals (Nordborg 1998; Cox and Hammer 2010). Indeed, appreciable admixture might have occurred between the two groups, but unless the Neandertal contribution was high, random loss through genetic drift might have eliminated any evidence for it (Figure 11.11).

Indirect support for these propositions comes from the mtDNA sequence of the ≈5,200 year-old Tyrolean "iceman," a naturally mummified corpse found on a glacier in the Alps near the Austro-Italian border. The analysis of this mummy led to the identification of a subhaplogroup (K1) that probably occurred in this population. Yet this subhaplogroup is unknown in current European populations, which may indicate that drift eliminated or nearly eliminated it (Ermini *et al.* 2008). These observations are consistent with other analyses that have concluded that the role of drift may be an important factor explaining genetic variation in ancient populations, including archaic *sapiens* (Orlando *et al.* 2006; Reich *et al.* 2010).

More generally, the severe contraction of the human niche in France during the beginning of the Aurignacian that has been argued for here conflicts with the conventional wisdom that early modern humans dispersed through western Europe during this period. This last view has received wide support from genetics, given that most molecular studies perceive a signal of an out-of-Africa population expansion around 50 ka (Tishkoff *et al.* 1996; Excoffier 2002; Serre *et al.* 2004; Ramachandran *et al.* 2005; Noonan *et al.* 2006; Tishkoff and Gonder 2007; Li *et al.* 2008; DeGiorgio *et al.* 2009; Shi *et al.* 2009; Xing *et al.* 2010). Although several anthropologists have interpreted this signal as indicating the replacement of one human species by another (e.g., Stringer and

Andrews 1988; Mellars 1998; Bar-Yosef 2002; Klein 2003, 2008), growing evidence for episodes of gene flow between archaic *sapiens* and early modern humans indicates that this scenario requires modifications (Harris and Hey 1999; Templeton 2002; Yu *et al.* 2002b; Zietkiewicz *et al.* 2003; Garrigan *et al.* 2005; Plagnol and Wall 2006; Wall *et al.* 2008; Cox *et al.* 2009; Green *et al.* 2010; Reich *et al.* 2010).

Overall, the faunal record of western Europe suggests that Neandertals and early modern humans shared a similar range of foraging behaviors. These similarities also seem to extend to the symbolic realm (Zilhão *et al.* 2010; Peresani *et al.* 2011). A major interpretive challenge in this context is to determine how archaic *sapiens* could have been partially replaced *across a wide range of habitats by an expanding population with whom they occasionally exchanged genes, and possibly, information*. Phrased otherwise, if genes or ideas were sometimes shared between these groups, then what prevented the spread of selectively advantageous traits between the same populations? Undoubtedly, considerable theoretical and empirical work will be required to solve this problem. What also becomes increasingly clear is that current replacement scenarios need to be substituted by more integrative models that address demographic and behavioral variation through time and across traditional taxonomic classifications of Late Pleistocene humans.

12

CONCLUDING THOUGHTS

IN THIS STUDY, PREDICTIONS ABOUT CHANGES IN ARCHAEOLOGICAL FAUNAL REMAINS during the Middle to Upper Paleolithic transition were generated on the basis of a recent proposition holding that modern humans diversified their diet as they dispersed into western Europe (O'Connell 2006). A test of these predictions at Saint-Césaire largely failed to find evidence for resource intensification, with the exception of the marrow contained in reindeer phalanges, which was exploited more frequently over time. Yet despite only weak evidence for intensification, foraging practices were not invariant. The occupants of Saint-Césaire adapted to natural changes in the relative abundances of ungulate taxa by modifying their transport strategies.

The exploitation of fast small-sized prey taxa did not increase significantly at Saint-Césaire during the early Upper Paleolithic, a period that coincided with a dramatic reduction in ungulate species diversity. However, other sites in western France indicate that small carnivores may constitute an exception to this general pattern, as implied by a marginal rise in the occurrence of butchery marks on fox parts in Early Aurignacian assemblages.

The lack of a significant shift in diet breadth during the early Upper Paleolithic may appear counter-intuitive in the context of deteriorating climatic conditions. However, O'Connell (2006) pointed out that the persistence of narrow diets may attest to a strong commitment among archaic *sapiens* males to activities, such as large game hunting, that favor mating opportunities and enhance social standing. These high-profile activities were possibly actively sought by Neandertal males, even in situations in which the exploitation of a broader range of resources would have constituted a more profitable dietary option. The information gathered here suggests that the same explanation may account for the foraging behavior of early modern humans in the western plains before the Magdalenian.

In contrast, certain faunal sequences from Iberia, the eastern plains, and the eastern Mediterranean yield clear indications of diet widening during the early Upper Paleolithic. This evidence generally involves varying percentages of leporid and/or bird specimens in the faunal assemblages and, more rarely, on the positive identification of anthropic marks on these taxa. Despite a relatively rich late Middle to early Upper Paleolithic record, the picture is unclear in Italy, largely because the data for this region suggest an infrequent exploitation of birds for mostly symbolic, as opposed to dietary, purposes (e.g., Fiore *et al.* 2004; Peresani *et al.* 2011). This last pattern is similar to the one observed in coeval assemblages from France and Germany.

Overall, sites from Europe and Southwest Asia attest to considerable regional variation in diet breadth during the Middle to Upper Paleolithic transition. Although there is some disagreement on the extent of this variation (Stiner 2005; Grayson and Delpech 2008; Morin 2008; Richards and Trinkaus 2009; Stiner and Kuhn 2009; Trinkaus *et al.* 2009), the fact that narrow diets dominate the early Upper Paleolithic record of the western plains conflicts with models reliant on a westward diffusion of broad-spectrum foraging strategies from the eastern Mediterranean to Iberia. Likewise, embryonic signs of diet broadening in the late Mousterian of Spain and in the Uluzzian of Greece suggest that changes in foraging practices were mostly the result of local processes rather than the testimony of a population expansion. Given these patterns, it seems reasonable to conclude that there was *as much, if not more, dietary variation between Neandertal populations than between these groups and early modern humans.*

The study of ungulate assemblages can also shed light on the relationship between diet breadth and human densities. The analysis of faunal sequences from Saint-Césaire and other similar sites showed that in western France, the early phases of the Aurignacian coincided with a sharp rise in the relative abundance of reindeer and a concomitant decline in species diversity. Micro-mammal samples indicate that climatic forcing was mostly, if not exclusively, responsible for these fluctuations. These results seem to invalidate Mellars's (1989, 1996, 1998, 2004) specialization hypothesis, which attributes the early Upper Paleolithic shift toward reindeer dominance to a logistical organization deliberately focused on *Rangifer*. Because low species diversity seems to depress, directly or indirectly, human forager densities, the human ecological niche in the western plains likely contracted considerably at the onset of the Aurignacian. The conclusions drawn here suggest that, before the Late Glacial, *forager densities in the western plains simply tracked climatically-induced fluctuations in environmental carrying capacity.*

Episodes of strong reindeer dominance were also examined at a broader temporal scale – from the end of MIS 6 to the beginning of MIS 1 – to ascertain change in their frequency and/or duration over time. The analysis of the composite time series presented in the preceding chapter led to the identification of several trends. Most striking among these are the dramatic fluctuations in reindeer representation observed in the early Upper Paleolithic, which imply significant shifts in environmental carrying capacity. Moreover, correlations with climatic proxies from marine and glacial records suggest that variations in reindeer representation in the time series were induced by millennial-scale oscillations (Heinrich and Dansgaard-Oeschger events). This last observation is particularly significant because this seems to be the first data set to find support for such a relationship in ungulate assemblages.

These results have wider implications for the debate on modern human origins. The relatively short period of time during which Neandertals and early African *Homo sapiens* are believed to have diverged (270–440 ka according to Green *et al.* 2010:718), as well as genetic evidence for gene flow (e.g., Evans *et al.* 2006; Green *et al.* 2010; Reich *et al.* 2010), weaken the argument for a speciation event between these populations, at least as this concept is commonly used by biologists. The archaeological record is compatible with the perspective of limited biological differences, given that a similar range of behaviors has been documented for both roughly contemporary Neandertals and early African modern humans. This includes, among other things, the capacity for symbolic use of objects such as shells, pigments, raptor claws, and feathers. This capacity has been used by many archaeologists as a proxy for behavioral complexity (Soressi and d'Errico 2007; Zilhão *et al.* 2010; Peresani *et al.* 2011). For these reasons, the standard classification of these populations as distinct species may need to be abandoned. However, this proposition does not preclude the possibility that Neandertals contributed only minimally to the genome of living humans.

The information gathered here suggests that the early Upper Paleolithic in Europe coincided with a short series of population bottlenecks. These bottlenecks likely favored micro- and macro-evolutionary changes among Neandertals by increasing genetic drift and by sporadically altering patterns of gene flow with other regional populations. From this perspective, the next challenge will be to reconcile data attesting to a human niche contraction in western Europe during the early phases of the Aurignacian with molecular evidence for an out-of-Africa expansion during the same period.

APPENDICES

APPENDIX 1. *Minimum number of individual (MNI) counts by species and level for mammal and fish remains*

A1.1. *Saint-Césaire: Minimum number of individual (MNI) counts by species and level for mammal and fish remains*

	Dent Moust (Egpf)		EJOP		Dent Moust (Ejop inf)		Moust/ Châtel (Ejop sup)		EJO		Low density (Ejo inf)	
	MNI	%	MNI	%	MNI	%	MNI	%	MNI	%	MNI	%
Artiodactyla												
reindeer	4	19.0	5	20.0	2	12.5	6	14.0	5	27.8	2	18.2
bison	6	28.6	6	24.0	4	25.0	12	27.9	4	22.2	1	9.1
red deer	1	4.8	1	4.0	1	6.3	4	9.3	1	5.6	1	9.1
giant deer	1	4.8	1	4.0	1	6.3	.	.	1	5.6	.	.
roe deer	.	.	.	.	.	.	1	2.3	.	.	.	.
wild boar	.	.	1	4.0	1	6.3	1	2.3	1	5.6	.	.
Perissodactyla												
horse	4	19.0	4	16.0	3	18.8	6	14.0	2	11.1	1	9.1
wooly rhino	1	4.8	1	4.0	1	6.3	1	2.3	1	5.6	1	9.1
European ass	.	.	1	4.0	.	.	1	2.3	.	.	.	.
Proboscidea												
mammoth	1	4.8	1	4.0	1	6.3	1	2.3	.	.	1	9.1
Carnivora												
spotted hyena	1	4.8	1	4.0	.	.	1	2.3	1	5.6	1	9.1
wolf	1	4.8	.	.	1	6.3	1	2.3	1	5.6	.	.
arctic fox	.	.	.	.	.	.	1	2.3	.	.	1	9.1
unspec. fox	1	4.8	1	4.0	1	6.3	2	4.7	1	5.6	1	9.1
bear	.	.	1	4.0	.	.	.	.	.	.	.	.
polecat	.	.	.	.	.	.	1	2.3	.	.	.	.
pine marten	.	.	.	.	.	.	.	.	.	.	.	.
lynx	.	.	.	.	.	.	.	.	.	.	.	.
badger	.	.	.	.	.	.	.	.	.	.	.	.
cave lion	.	.	.	.	.	.	1	2.3	.	.	.	.
Leporidae												
hare	.	.	.	.	.	.	.	.	.	.	.	.
unspec. lepor.	.	.	1	4.0	.	.	1	2.3	.	.	1	9.1
Fish												
cyprinid	.	.	.	.	.	.	1	2.3	.	.	.	.
brown trout	.	.	.	.	.	.	1	2.3	.	.	.	.
Total NISP	21	100.2	25	100.0	16	100.4	43	99.8	18	100.3	11	100.1
Total + antlers	21		37		19		52		19		16	–

(*continued*)

A1.1 *(continued). Saint-Césaire: Minimum number of individual (MNI) counts by species and level for mammal and fish remains*

	Middle Auri (Ejo sup)		Middle Auri (Ejf)		Evol Auri (Ejm)		Evol Auri (Ejj)		Total	
	MNI	%	MNI	%	MNI	%	MNI	%	MNI	%
Artiodactyla										
reindeer	9	40.9	42	58.3	12	50.0	7	43.8	94	35.1
bison	2	9.1	5	6.9	2	8.3	2	12.5	44	16.4
red deer	1	4.5	1	1.4	1	4.2	1	6.3	13	4.8
giant deer	.	.	1	1.4	.	.	.	.	5	1.9
roe deer	.	.	.	.	.	.	.	.	1	0.4
wild boar	.	.	1	1.4	.	.	.	.	5	1.9
Perissodactyla										
horse	1	4.5	8	11.1	4	16.7	2	12.5	35	13.1
wooly rhino	1	4.5	1	1.4	1	4.2	.	.	9	3.4
European ass	.	.	.	.	.	.	.	.	2	0.7
Proboscidea										
mammoth	1	4.5	1	1.4	1	4.2	1	6.3	9	3.4
Carnivora										
spotted hyena	.	.	1	1.4	.	.	1	6.3	7	2.6
wolf	1	4.5	2	2.8	1	4.2	1	6.3	9	3.4
arctic fox	1	4.5	1	1.4	.	.	.	.	4	1.5
unspec. fox	1	4.5	3	4.2	1	4.2	1	6.3	13	4.9
bear	.	.	.	.	.	.	.	.	1	0.4
polecat	1	4.5	1	1.4	.	.	.	.	3	1.1
pine marten	2	9.1	.	.	.	.	.	.	2	0.7
lynx	.	.	1	1.4	.	.	.	.	1	0.4
badger	.	.	1	1.4	1	4.2	.	.	2	0.7
cave lion	.	.	1	1.4	.	.	.	.	2	0.7
Leporidae										
hare	1	4.5	.	.	.	.	.	.	1	0.4
unspec. lepor.	.	.	1	1.4	.	.	.	.	4	1.5
Fish										
cyprinid	.	.	.	.	.	.	.	.	1	0.4
brown trout	.	.	.	.	.	.	.	.	1	0.4
Total MNI	22	99.6	72	100.1	24	100.2	16	100.3	268	100.2
Total + antlers	22		77		25		16		304	

Periods indicate that no remains were found. Antlers counted separately.

APPENDIX 2. *Number of identified specimen (NISP) and minimum number of element (MNE) counts for reindeer, bison, and horse elements*

A2.1. *Saint-Césaire: skeletal representation for reindeer, bison, and horse in the Denticulate Mousterian EGPF assemblage*

Body part	Reindeer		Horse		Bison	
	NISP	MNE	NISP	MNE	NISP	MNE
Antler						
Cranium/maxillary teeth	4	1	67 (2)	2	90 (2)	4
Mandible/lower teeth	10	3	77	2	86 (1)	10
Atlas						
Axis						
Other cervical vertebrae	1	1			1	1
Thoracic vertebrae	3	1			2	1
Lumbar vertebrae					1	1
Sacrum						
Rib	8	1	9	1	15	1
Sternum	5	1				
Scapula	2	1	1	1	7	2
Proximal humerus						
Shaft humerus	10	4	8	4	6	4
Distal humerus						
Proximal radius					1	1
Shaft radius	17	5	5	2	2	1
Distal radius						
Proximal ulna						
Shaft ulna	2	1			3	2
Distal ulna					1	1
Scaphoid						
Lunatum						
Triquetrum					1	1
Pisiform					2	2
Capitatum	1	1	1	1		
Hamatum	1	1			1	1
Proximal metacarpal	1	1	4	4	1	1
Shaft metacarpal	12	4	3	4		
Distal metacarpal			1	2	2	2
Innominates			2 (1)	1	2	1
Proximal femur			1	1		
Shaft femur	9	5	2	1	6	2
Distal femur			1	1		
Patella						
Proximal tibia			2	2		
Shaft tibia	36	6	6	3	46	8
Distal tibia					1	1

(continued)

A2.1 *(continued)*

Body part	Reindeer		Horse		Bison	
	NISP	MNE	NISP	MNE	NISP	MNE
Malleolar	1 (1)	1	3	3	2	1
Talus			1	1		
Calcaneum	1	1				
Cubonavicular/navicular			1	1		
Smaller cuneiform			1	1		
Greater cuneiform					1	1
Proximal metatarsal	3	3	1	1	1	1
Shaft metatarsal	73	7	2	1	13	2
Distal metatarsal					1	1
Proximal metapodial	1	1	1	1		
Shaft metapodial	5	1	3	1	4	1
Distal metapodial	1	1				
Vestigial metapodial			10	2		
Phalanx 1	2	2	1	1	2	2
Phalanx 2	1	1			2	1
Phalanx 3					3	2
Vestigial phalanges	2	1				
Sesamoid			1	1	8	
Tooth fragment	2		79 (8)		15	
Vertebra fragment			1			
Total	214 (1)	56	295 (11)	46	329 (3)	60

Values in parentheses give the number of specimens that are burned.

Abbreviations: MNE = minimum number of elements; NISP = number of identified specimens.

A2.2. *Saint-Césaire: skeletal representation for reindeer, bison, and horse in the Denticulate Mousterian EJOP inf assemblage*

Body part	Reindeer		Horse		Bison	
	NISP	MNE	NISP	MNE	NISP	MNE
Antler	45	2				
Cranium/maxillary teeth	2	1	8	1	8	2
Mandible/lower teeth	5	3	15	2	13	3
Atlas						
Axis						
Other cervical vertebrae					2	1
Thoracic vertebrae	1	1				
Lumbar vertebrae	1	1				
Sacrum					1	1
Rib	7	1	3	1	8	1
Sternum						
Scapula	3	2			2	1
Proximal humerus						
Shaft humerus	2	2	2	1	10	6
Distal humerus						
Proximal radius						
Shaft radius	5	2				
Distal radius						
Proximal ulna						
Shaft ulna						
Distal ulna					1	1
Scaphoid					1	1
Lunatum						
Triquetrum						
Pisiform						
Capitatum						
Hamatum						
Proximal metacarpal	1	1	1	1	1	1
Shaft metacarpal	8	1			2	2
Distal metacarpal						
Innominates			2	2	1	1
Proximal femur						
Shaft femur	5	1			3	1
Distal femur						
Patella						
Proximal tibia						
Shaft tibia	14	2	7	4	27	6
Distal tibia	1 (1)	1				
Malleolar						
Talus						
Calcaneum						
Cubonavicular/navicular	1	1				
Smaller cuneiform			1	1		
Greater cuneiform	1	1	1	1		

(continued)

A2.2 *(continued)*

Body part	Reindeer		Horse		Bison	
	NISP	MNE	NISP	MNE	NISP	MNE
Proximal metatarsal	1	1	1	1	1	1
Shaft metatarsal	29 (2)	2	1	1	5	2
Distal metatarsal						
Proximal metapodial	1	1				
Shaft metapodial	2	1	1	1	4	1
Distal metapodial	1	1			1	1
Vestigial metapodial						
Phalanx 1						
Phalanx 2						
Phalanx 3	1	1			1	1
Vestigial phalanges	2	1				
Sesamoid					1	1
Tooth fragment			30 (8)		9 (2)	
Vertebra fragment						
Mandible/maxillary			2			
Total	94 (3)	29	75 (8)	17	102 (2)	35

Values in parentheses give the number of specimens that are burned.
Abbreviations: MNE = minimum number of elements; NISP = number of identified specimens.

A2.3. *Saint-Césaire: skeletal representation for reindeer, bison, and horse in the Mousterian/Châtelperronian (EJOP sup) assemblage*

Body part	Reindeer		Horse		Bison	
	NISP	MNE	NISP	MNE	NISP	MNE
Antler	142	12				
Cranium/maxillary teeth	7	2	9	2	48	5
Mandible/lower teeth	22	6	35	5	71	12
Atlas						
Axis						
Other cervical vertebrae	1	1	1	1		
Thoracic vertebrae			4	1	3	1
Lumbar vertebrae						
Sacrum						
Rib	40	5	17	1	25	2
Sternum						
Scapula	2	2	1	1	15	6
Proximal humerus						
Shaft humerus	9	7	2	2	21	9
Distal humerus	1	1				
Proximal radius	3	3			3	2
Shaft radius	4	1	5	3	11	7
Distal radius					1	1
Proximal ulna						
Shaft ulna					5	4
Distal ulna						
Scaphoid						
Lunatum						
Triquetrum						
Pisiform						
Capitatum						
Hamatum	1	1				
Proximal metacarpal	1	1			2	1
Shaft metacarpal	2	1			5	2
Distal metacarpal						
Innominates	2	2	1	1	1	1
Proximal femur	3	3				
Shaft femur	5	4	4	2	18	8
Distal femur						
Patella	2	2				
Proximal tibia	1	1				
Shaft tibia	13	4	4	3	73	19
Distal tibia	2	2	1	1		
Malleolar						
Talus					1	1
Calcaneum					2	1
Cubonavicular/navicular	1	1				
Smaller cuneiform						
Greater cuneiform	1	1	1	1		

(*continued*)

A2.3 *(continued)*

Body part	Reindeer NISP	Reindeer MNE	Horse NISP	Horse MNE	Bison NISP	Bison MNE
Proximal metatarsal	1	1			11	6
Shaft metatarsal	18	1	1	1	26	6
Distal metatarsal			1	1		
Proximal metapodial						
Shaft metapodial	4	1			5	1
Distal metapodial			1	1	1	1
Vestigial metapodial			5	1		
Phalanx 1	1	1	2	1	3	1
Phalanx 2	1	1				
Phalanx 3	2	1				
Vestigial phalanges	1	1				
Sesamoid	3	2	1	1		
Tooth fragment	8		44 (2)		40	
Total	162	60	140 (2)	30	391	97

Antlers excluded from the total. Values in parentheses give the number of specimens that are burned.
Abbreviations: MNE = minimum number of elements; NISP = number of identified specimens.

A2.4. *Saint-Césaire: skeletal representation for reindeer, bison, and horse in the EJOP (EJOP inf or EJOP sup) assemblage*

Body part	Reindeer		Horse		Bison	
	NISP	MNE	NISP	MNE	NISP	MNE
Antler	93	14				
Cranium/maxillary teeth	3	1	13	1	11	3
Mandible/lower teeth	23	5	18	2	33	6
Atlas						
Axis						
Other cervical vertebrae	1	1				
Thoracic vertebrae	3	2	1	1		
Lumbar vertebrae						
Sacrum						
Rib	11	2	7	1	13	1
Sternum						
Scapula			1	1	4	1
Proximal humerus						
Shaft humerus	1	1	2	2	9	6
Distal humerus						
Proximal radius	1	1				
Shaft radius	7	3			1	1
Distal radius	1	1			1	1
Proximal ulna						
Shaft ulna	2	1				
Distal ulna						
Scaphoid					1	1
Lunatum						
Triquetrum						
Pisiform	1	1			1	1
Capitatum	1	1				
Hamatum	1	1				
Proximal metacarpal	2	2				
Shaft metacarpal	2	2			1	1
Distal metacarpal	1	1				
Innominates	3	2	1	1		
Proximal femur	1	1				
Shaft femur	1	1	1	1	6	2
Distal femur	1	1				
Patella						
Proximal tibia						
Shaft tibia	9	3	3	1	22	9
Distal tibia	1	1				

(continued)

A2.4 *(continued)*

Body part	Reindeer		Horse		Bison	
	NISP	MNE	NISP	MNE	NISP	MNE
Malleolar	1	1			1	1
Talus	2 (2)	1				
Calcaneum	2	2			2	2
Cubonavicular/navicular						
Smaller cuneiform						
Greater cuneiform	1	1				
Proximal metatarsal	1	1			1	1
Shaft metatarsal	27	3			6	2
Distal metatarsal						
Proximal metapodial						
Shaft metapodial	5	1	2	1	2	1
Distal metapodial						
Vestigial metapodial			1	1		
Phalanx 1	3	1			1	1
Phalanx 2	1	1			3	2
Phalanx 3	1	1			1	1
Vestigial phalanges	3	1				
Sesamoid	1	1				
Tooth fragment	4		27 (1)			
Mandible/maxillary			2		17	
Total	129 (2)	50	79 (1)	13	137	44

Antlers excluded from the total. Values in parentheses give the number of specimens that are burned.
Abbreviations: MNE = minimum number of elements; NISP = number of identified specimens.

A2.5. *Saint-Césaire: skeletal representation for reindeer, bison, and horse in the low-density (EJO inf) assemblage*

Body part	Reindeer		Horse		Bison	
	NISP	MNE	NISP	MNE	NISP	MNE
Antler	23	4				
Cranium/maxillary teeth	1	1	1	1	1	1
Mandible/lower teeth	8	1				
Atlas						
Axis						
Other cervical vertebrae						
Thoracic vertebrae						
Lumbar vertebrae						
Sacrum						
Caudal					1	
Rib	5	1	9	2	5	1
Sternum						
Scapula	1	1			1	1
Proximal humerus						
Shaft humerus	1	1				
Distal humerus						
Proximal radius					1	1
Shaft radius			1	1		
Distal radius						
Proximal ulna						
Shaft ulna					1	1
Distal ulna						
Scaphoid						
Lunatum						
Triquetrum	1	1				
Pisiform						
Capitatum						
Hamatum						
Proximal metacarpal						
Shaft metacarpal						
Distal metacarpal						
Innominates						
Proximal femur						
Shaft femur						
Distal femur						
Patella						
Proximal tibia	1	1				
Shaft tibia	1	1			3	2
Distal tibia						

(*continued*)

A2.5 *(continued)*

Body part	Reindeer		Horse		Bison	
	NISP	MNE	NISP	MNE	NISP	MNE
Malleolar						
Talus						
Calcaneum						
Cubonavicular/navicular						
Smaller cuneiform						
Greater cuneiform						
Proximal metatarsal			1	1		
Shaft metatarsal					1	1
Distal metatarsal						
Proximal metapodial						
Shaft metapodial						
Distal metapodial						
Vestigial metapodial						
Phalanx 1						
Phalanx 2						
Phalanx 3	1	1				
Vestigial phalanges						
Sesamoid						
Tooth fragment			1			
Total	20	9	13	5	14	8

Antlers excluded from the total.

A2.6. *Saint-Césaire: skeletal representation for reindeer, bison, and horse in the Middle Aurignacian EJO sup assemblage*

Body part	Reindeer		Horse		Bison	
	NISP	MNE	NISP	MNE	NISP	MNE
Antler	63	4				
Cranium/maxillary teeth	9 (1)	2	1	1	1	1
Mandible/lower teeth	23	3	2	1	6	2
Atlas			1	1		
Axis						
Other cervical vertebrae						
Thoracic vertebrae	1 (1)	1				
Lumbar vertebrae	3 (2)	1			1	1
Sacrum	1	1				
Rib	53	4	12	1	5	1
Sternum	2	1				
Scapula	1	1	1	1	1	1
Proximal humerus						
Shaft humerus	9	5				
Distal humerus						
Proximal radius						
Shaft radius	15 (1)	6			1	1
Distal radius	1	1				
Proximal ulna	1 (1)	1				
Shaft ulna	5	2				
Distal ulna						
Scaphoid	1 (1)	1				
Lunatum						
Triquetrum	1 (1)	1				
Pisiform	1	1				
Capitatum	1 (1)	1				
Hamatum	2	2				
Proximal metacarpal	2	2				
Shaft metacarpal	9	3				
Distal metacarpal	1	1				
Innominates	1	1	1	1		
Proximal femur	2 (1)	2				
Shaft femur	9	2				
Distal femur						
Patella						
Proximal tibia	2 (1)	2				
Shaft tibia	45	15	1	1	1	1
Distal tibia						
Malleolar						
Talus	4 (3)	3				
Calcaneum						
Cubonavicular/navicular	1	1				
Smaller cuneiform						
Greater cuneiform						

(*continued*)

A2.6 *(continued)*

Body part	Reindeer		Horse		Bison	
	NISP	MNE	NISP	MNE	NISP	MNE
Proximal metatarsal	7	6				
Shaft metatarsal	94 (1)	8			2	1
Distal metatarsal	1 (1)	1				
Proximal metapodial						
Shaft metapodial	13	1				
Distal metapodial	2	1				
Vestigial metapodial						
Phalanx 1	11	4				
Phalanx 2	4	1				
Phalanx 3	3	3				
Vestigial phalanges						
Sesamoid	5 (1)	3				
Tooth fragment	3		3		1	
Total	349 (17)	95	22	7	19	9

Antlers excluded from the total. Values in parentheses give the number of specimens that are burned.
Abbreviations: MNE = minimum number of elements; NISP = number of identified specimens.

A2.7. *Saint-Césaire: skeletal representation for reindeer, bison, and horse in the EJO (EJO inf or EJO sup) assemblage*

Body part	Reindeer		Horse		Bison	
	NISP	MNE	NISP	MNE	NISP	MNE
Antler	48	5				
Cranium/maxillary teeth	5	1	3	1	2	1
Mandible/lower teeth	22	5	3	1	8	3
Atlas						
Axis						
Other cervical vertebrae	1	1	3	1		
Thoracic vertebrae						
Lumbar vertebrae	1	1				
Sacrum						
Rib	17	2	7	1	12	1
Sternum						
Scapula	1	1	1	1	1	1
Proximal humerus						
Shaft humerus	1	1			1	1
Distal humerus						
Proximal radius	1	1			1	1
Shaft radius	6 (1)	3	1	1	1	1
Distal radius						
Proximal ulna						
Shaft ulna	1	1				
Distal ulna						
Scaphoid						
Lunatum	1	1				
Triquetrum						
Pisiform						
Capitatum						
Hamatum	1	1				
Proximal metacarpal					1	1
Shaft metacarpal	6	1				
Distal metacarpal						
Innominates	1 (1)	1				
Proximal femur						
Shaft femur	1	1	2	1		
Distal femur			1	1	1	1
Patella						
Proximal tibia						
Shaft tibia	21	4	1	1	4	2
Distal tibia	1	1	1	1		
Malleolar	1	1				
Talus						
Calcaneum	1 (1)	1				
Cubonavicular/navicular						
Smaller cuneiform						
Greater cuneiform						

(continued)

A2.7 *(continued)*

Body part	Reindeer		Horse		Bison	
	NISP	MNE	NISP	MNE	NISP	MNE
Proximal metatarsal	1	1			2	2
Shaft metatarsal	55 (1)	4				
Distal metatarsal						
Proximal metapodial						
Shaft metapodial	4	1				
Distal metapodial			1			
Vestigial metapodial						
Phalanx 1	3	1				
Phalanx 2	1	1				
Phalanx 3						
Vestigial phalanges						
Sesamoid	3	2				
Tooth fragment	5		8		3	
Total	162 (4)	39	32	10	37	15

Antlers excluded from the total. Values in parentheses give the number of specimens that are burned.
Abbreviations: MNE = minimum number of elements; NISP = number of identified specimens.

A2.8. *Saint-Césaire: skeletal representation for reindeer, bison, and horse in the Middle Aurignacian EJF assemblage*

Body part	Reindeer		Horse		Bison	
	NISP	MNE	NISP	MNE	NISP	MNE
Antler	643 (1)	47				
Cranium/maxillary teeth	63 (2)	6	32 (1)	2	6	2
Mandible/lower teeth	147	22	45	8	16	5
Atlas	3	2	1	1		
Axis	2 (1)	2				
Cervical vertebrae	7	4				
Thoracic vertebrae	3 (1)	2	7	4	8	4
Lumbar vertebrae	5 (4)	2	1	1	11	5
Sacrum					3	1
Rib	427 (9)	23	174	13	86	9
Sternum	1					
Scapula	20	8	5	3	7	2
Proximal humerus	1	1				
Shaft humerus	102 (1)	43	6	1	2	2
Distal humerus	5 (5)	4	1	1		
Proximal radius	29 (14)	11	4	1		
Shaft radius	205 (1)	43	7	4	1	1
Distal radius	4 (1)	4	2	2	1	1
Proximal ulna	3 (2)	2				
Shaft ulna	31 (4)	5			2 (1)	2
Distal ulna						
Scaphoid	9 (2)	8				
Lunatum	8 (1)	7				
Triquetrum	2	2				
Pisiform	3 (2)	3				
Capitatum	7	7				
Hamatum	1	1				
Proximal metacarpal	16	10	2	1		
Shaft metacarpal	102	35	3	1	3	2
Distal metacarpal	6	6	2	2		
Innominates	23 (10)	10	13 (2)	3		
Proximal femur	10 (4)	10	3	1		
Shaft femur	93 (1)	33	8	5	4	3
Distal femur	11 (4)	6	2 (1)	1		
Patella	6 (1)	6				
Proximal tibia	11 (8)	5			1 (1)	1
Shaft tibia	373 (11)	73	9	7	10	5
Distal tibia	8 (3)	5	7 (1)	5		
Malleolar	5 (4)	5				
Talus	18 (12)	12				
Calcaneum	11 (5)	6				
Cubonavicular/navicular	8 (5)	6	1 (1)	1	1	1
Smaller cuneiform	1	1				
Greater cuneiform	3 (1)	3				

(continued)

A2.8 *(continued)*

Body part	Reindeer		Horse		Bison	
	NISP	MNE	NISP	MNE	NISP	MNE
Proximal metatarsal	32 (1)	19	7	5		
Shaft metatarsal	806 (9)	64	3	5	1	1
Distal metatarsal	3	2	2	3		
Proximal metapodial	2	1	1			
Shaft metapodial	64 (1)	1		1		
Distal metapodial	9	4				
Vestigial metapodial	1		8	2		
Phalanx 1	40 (1)	32	4	2		
Phalanx 2	23 (2)	9	2	2		
Phalanx 3	12	8	1	1		
Vestigial phalanges	8 (1)	1				
Sesamoid	17	9	1	1		
Tooth fragment	7		21 (4)		1 (1)	
Vertebra fragment	6 (2)					
Total	2823 (137)	594	385 (10)	89	164 (3)	47

Antlers excluded from the total. Values in parentheses give the number of specimens that are burned.
Abbreviations: MNE = minimum number of elements; NISP = number of identified specimens.

A2.9. *Saint-Césaire: skeletal representation for reindeer, bison, and horse in the Evolved Aurignacian EJM assemblage*

Body part	Reindeer		Horse		Bison	
	NISP	MNE	NISP	MNE	NISP	MNE
Antler	250	10				
Cranium/maxillary teeth	21	4	10	2	2 (1)	1
Mandible/lower teeth	64	11	19	4	5	2
Atlas			1	1	1	1
Axis						
Other cervical vertebrae	1	1	1			
Thoracic vertebrae	1	1	3	2	3	2
Lumbar vertebrae						
Sacrum	1 (1)	1				
Rib	47	4	34	3	42	2
Sternum						
Scapula	9	3			3	2
Proximal humerus			1			
Shaft humerus	26 (1)	12	2	2	2	2
Distal humerus						
Proximal radius	2 (2)	2			1	1
Shaft radius	50	8	2	1	3	3
Distal radius	2	2	1	1		
Proximal ulna						
Shaft ulna	9 (3)	3			1	1
Distal ulna						
Scaphoid	1	1				
Lunatum						
Triquetrum						
Pisiform	1	1				
Capitatum	1	1			1	1
Hamatum	1	1				
Proximal metacarpal	5	5	4	4		
Shaft metacarpal	13	5	1	3	1	1
Distal metacarpal	2	2				
Innominates	5	2	4	2		
Proximal femur	1 (1)	1	1			
Shaft femur	22	19	3	1		
Distal femur	1 (1)	1				
Patella	2	2				
Proximal tibia	1	1	2	1		
Shaft tibia	80	21	4	4	8	2
Distal tibia			1	1		
Malleolar	1 (1)	1				
Talus	1 (1)	1				
Calcaneum	5 (3)	5	1	1		
Cubonavicular/navicular	3 (2)	3				
Smaller cuneiform						
Greater cuneiform	2 (1)	1				

(continued)

A2.9 *(continued)*

Body part	Reindeer		Horse		Bison	
	NISP	MNE	NISP	MNE	NISP	MNE
Proximal metatarsal	4 (1)	2	1	1	1	1
Shaft metatarsal	154 (3)	14	2	1	1	1
Distal metatarsal	2	2	1	1		
Proximal metapodial						
Shaft metapodial	41	1	1	1		
Distal metapodial	2	2	1	1		
Vestigial metapodial			5	1		
Phalanx 1	9	5	1	1	1	1
Phalanx 2	2	2				
Phalanx 3	1	1				
Vestigial phalanges	1					
Sesamoid	3	2				
Tooth fragment			4		2	
Mandible/maxillary			2			
Total	600 (21)	157	113	40	78 (1)	24

Antlers excluded from the total. Values in parentheses give the number of specimens that are burned.
Abbreviations: MNE = minimum number of elements; NISP = number of identified specimens.

A2.10. *Saint-Césaire: skeletal representation for reindeer, bison, and horse in the Evolved Aurignacian EJJ assemblage*

Body part	Reindeer		Horse		Bison	
	NISP	MNE	NISP	MNE	NISP	MNE
Antler	97	2				
Cranium/maxillary teeth	15	4	8	1	5	1
Mandible/lower teeth	22	7	15	2	4	1
Atlas			1	1	2	1
Axis						
Other cervical vertebrae	1	1				
Thoracic vertebrae	2	2	1	1		
Lumbar vertebrae						
Sacrum						
Rib	15 (2)	4	12	1	7	1
Sternum						
Scapula	1	1	3	2	2	1
Proximal humerus						
Shaft humerus	9	5	1	1	3	2
Distal humerus						
Proximal radius						
Shaft radius	11	3	1	1		
Distal radius			1 (1)	1		
Proximal ulna						
Shaft ulna	2 (1)	1				
Distal ulna						
Scaphoid	1	1				
Lunatum						
Triquetrum	1	1				
Pisiform						
Capitatum						
Hamatum						
Proximal metacarpal	2 (1)	2	1	1		
Shaft metacarpal	8	3			1	1
Distal metacarpal	1	1				
Innominates	2 (1)	1	1	1		
Proximal femur	1	1				
Shaft femur	11 (1)	5	1	1	1	1
Distal femur						
Patella						
Proximal tibia						
Shaft tibia	30	8	1	1	3	2
Distal tibia	2 (1)	2				
Malleolar						
Talus						
Calcaneum	3	2			1	1
Cubonavicular/navicular	1	1				
Smaller cuneiform						
Greater cuneiform	3 (1)	3				

(continued)

A2.10 *(continued)*

Body part	Reindeer		Horse		Bison	
	NISP	MNE	NISP	MNE	NISP	MNE
Proximal metatarsal	1	1			1	1
Shaft metatarsal	67	6			5	3
Distal metatarsal						
Proximal metapodial	1	1				
Shaft metapodial	7	1	1	1		
Distal metapodial						
Vestigial metapodial			4	1		
Phalanx 1	2 (1)	1	1	1	1	1
Phalanx 2						
Phalanx 3						
Vestigial phalanges						
Sesamoid	1	1				
Tooth fragment	3		4		3	
Total	226 (9)	70	57 (1)	18	39	17

Antlers excluded from the total. Values in parentheses give the number of specimens that are burned.
Abbreviations: MNE = minimum number of elements; NISP = number of identified specimens.

APPENDIX 3. *Distribution of faunal specimens by size class (in cm) in twelve décapages from Saint-Césaire*

	0–1		1–2		2–3		3–4		4–5		5–6		6 and +		Total	
	n	%	*n*	%	*n*	%	*n*	%	*n*	%	*n*	%	*n*	%	*n*	%
Burned	112	23.5	288	60.5	68	14.3	7	1.5	1	0.2	.	.	.	.	476	100
Unburned	151	17.2	352	40.1	229	26.1	93	10.6	24	2.7	19	2.2	9	1.0	877	100
Total	263	19.4	640	47.3	297	22.0	100	7.4	25	1.8	19	1.4	9	0.7	1353	100

The décapages are mostly from square E5 and include remains found in the Denticulate Mousterian EGPF, EJOP inf, and Evolved Aurignacian EJM and EJJ layers. The last size class is open and includes all fragments equal to or larger than 6 cm.

APPENDIX 4. *Mean fragment length of reindeer and bison bones in the stratigraphic sequence of Saint-Césaire*

	Reindeer									Bison		
	Tibia			Metatarsal			Rib			Tibia		
	n	Mean	σ	*n*	Mean	σ	*n*	Mean	σ	*n*	Mean	σ
Evol Auri Ejj	29	70.3	99.2	60	39.2	15.7	15	25.0	10.5	3	104.0	41.8
Evol Auri Ejm	75	55.3	19.4	156	43.9	20.4	41	37.1	13.0	8	94.3	36.2
Mid Auri Ejf	375	59.3	20.9	779	43.4	17.9	356	38.4	18.5	11	89.5	45.5
Mid Auri Ejo sup	43	52.5	17.3	96	38.4	17.8	45	39.5	18.2	1	55.3	–
Moust/Châtel	14	54.6	28.0	18	30.5	12.3	40	31.0	10.6	71	91.4	31.6
D Moust Ejop inf	14	46.2	20.4	27	32.3	14.1	7	30.8	5.6	26	92.7	27.7
D Moust Egpf	36	51.5	18.5	64	39.9	16.4	8	31.0	7.3	47	71.6	31.3
Total	586	57.9	29.4	1200	42.2	18.0	512	37.2	17.3	167	86.1	32.8

APPENDIX 5. *Bone surface preservation as a function of distance away from the cliff in a sample largely dominated by long bones*

	Distance away from the Cliff in Meters											
	2		3		4		5		6		Total	
	n	%	*n*	%	*n*	%	*n*	%	*n*	%	*n*	%
Evol Auri (Ejj)												
poorly preserved	2	25.0	2	3.9	3	12.0	10	10.0	6	6.7	23	8.4
damaged	1	12.5	25	49.0	14	56.0	70	70.0	62	69.7	172	63.0
slightly damaged	4	50.0	24	47.1	8	32.0	20	20.0	20	22.5	76	27.8
intact	1	12.5	0	0.0	0	0.0	0	0.0	1	1.1	2	0.7
total	8	100.0	51	100	25	100.0	100	100.0	89	100.0	273	99.9
Evol Auri (Ejm)												
poorly preserved	2	7.1	3	3.1	16	4.8	13	17.3	12	26.7	46	8.0
damaged	13	46.4	59	60.8	206	62.0	52	69.3	31	68.9	361	62.6
slightly damaged	13	46.4	35	36.1	109	32.8	10	13.3	2	4.4	169	29.3
intact	0	0.0	0	0.0	1	0.3	0	0.0	0	0.0	1	0.2
total	28	99.9	97	100.0	332	99.9	75	99.9	45	100.0	577	100.1
Middle Auri Ejf												
poorly preserved	1	0.2	4	0.9	6	2.6	4	8.0	5	10.2	20	1.4
damaged	254	38.4	145	32.7	118	50.4	37	74.0	39	79.6	593	41.2
slightly damaged	401	60.6	284	64.0	109	46.6	9	18.0	5	10.2	808	56.2
intact	6	0.9	11	2.5	1	0.4	0	0.0	0	0.0	18	1.3
total	662	100.1	444	100.1	234	100.0	50	100.0	49	100.0	1439	100.1
Middle Auri Ejo sup												
poorly preserved	1	0.5	3	2.5	2	5.7		0.0	1	6.7	7	2.0
damaged	100	54.6	32	26.9	17	48.6	4	66.7	11	73.3	164	45.8
slightly damaged	82	44.8	83	69.7	16	45.7	2	33.3	3	20.0	186	52.0
intact	0	0.0	1	0.8	0	0.0	0	0.0	0	0.0	1	0.3
total	183	99.9	119	99.9	35	100.0	6	100.0	15	100.0	358	100.1
M/Châtel (Ejop sup)												
poorly preserved	1	4.0	1	2.7	9	5.6	9	7.0	1	2.5	21	5.4
damaged	10	40.0	27	73.0	91	56.9	64	50.0	25	62.5	217	55.6
slightly damaged	13	52.0	9	24.3	59	36.9	54	42.2	13	32.5	148	37.9
intact	1	4.0	0	0.0	1	0.6	1	0.8	1	2.5	4	1.0
total	25	100.0	37	100.0	160	146	128	100.0	40	100.0	390	99.9
D Moust Ejop inf												
poorly preserved	0	0.0	3	8.1	0	0.0	0	0.0	4	11.4	7	4.0
damaged	11	19.3	10	27.0	17	60.7	8	40.0	17	48.6	63	35.6
slightly damaged	40	70.2	24	64.9	11	39.3	12	60.0	14	40.0	101	57.1
intact	6	10.5	0	0.0	0	0.0	0	0.0	0	0.0	6	3.4
total	57	100.0	37	100.0	28	100.0	20	100.0	35	100.0	177	100.1
D Moust Egpf												
poorly preserved	1	1.6	2	1.5	3	2.9	0	0.0	1	1.4	7	1.6
damaged	22	36.1	43	31.6	37	35.6	43	57.3	35	50.0	180	40.4
slightly damaged	37	60.7	91	66.9	63	60.6	30	40.0	34	48.6	255	57.2
intact	1	1.6	0	0.0	1	1.0	2	2.7	0	0.0	4	0.9
total	61	100.0	136	100.0	104	100.1	75	100.0	70	100.0	446	100.1

APPENDIX 6. *Incidence of cutmarks on long bone specimens by level and as a function of the degree of bone surface preservation*

	Poorly Preserved			Somewhat Damaged			Slightly Damaged			Intact		
	ncut	*n*	%	ncut	*n*	%	ncut	*n*	%	ncut	*n*	%
Evol Auri, Ejj	0	15	0.0	6	111	5.4	11	48	22.9	0	2	0.0
Evol Auri, Ejm	1	39	2.6	15	209	7.2	19	104	18.3	0	1	0.0
Mid Auri Ejf	0	20	0.0	42	375	11.2	104	472	22.0	2	8	25.0
Mid Auri Ejo sup	0	4	0.0	4	109	3.7	10	113	8.8	0	1	0.0
Low density	0	0	0.0	0	7	0.0	2	4	50.0	0	0	0.0
Moust/Châtel	1	23	4.3	12	154	7.8	39	127	30.7	2	6	33.3
D Moust Ejop inf	0	5	0.0	4	53	7.5	16	82	19.5	3	5	60.0
D Moust Egpf	1	5	20.0	15	94	16.0	52	197	26.4	1	3	33.3
Total	3	111	2.7	98	1112	8.8	253	1147	22.1	8	26	30.8

All of the species are included, excepting birds and microfauna.
Abbreviations: ncut = the number of cut-marked specimens; *n* = the total number of specimens considered.

APPENDIX 7. *Percentages of cutmarks on reindeer long bones as a function of the degree of bone surface preservation at Saint-Césaire*

	Reindeer: Hindleg								
	Femur			Tibia			Metatarsal		
	ncut	Total	%	ncut	Total	%	ncut	Total	%
Poorly preserved	0	8	0.0	0	23	0.0	0	5	0.0
Damaged	14	95	14.7	39	220	17.7	8	226	3.5
Slightly damaged	21	82	25.6	63	188	33.5	24	293	8.2
Intact	0	1	0.0	0	2	0.0	0	0	0.0
Total	35	186	18.8	102	433	23.6	32	524	6.1

	Reindeer: Foreleg								
	Humerus			Radio-ulna			Metacarpal		
	ncut	Total	%	ncut	Total	%	ncut	Total	%
Poorly preserved	0	6	0.0	0	11	0.0	0	2	0.0
Damaged	7	57	12.3	7	155	4.5	7	61	11.5
Slightly damaged	35	101	34.7	28	142	19.7	24	78	30.8
Intact	0	0	0.0	0	0	0.0	1	1	100.0
Total	42	164	25.6	35	308	11.4	32	142	22.5

Abbreviations: ncut = the number of cut-marked specimens.

APPENDIX 8. *Percentages of cutmarks on bison elements as a function of the degree of bone surface preservation at Saint-Césaire*

	Bison					
	Tibia			Humerus		
	ncut	Total	%	ncut	Total	%
Poorly preserved	0	6	0.0	0	1	0.0
Damaged	7	78	9.0	3	13	23.1
Slightly damaged	24	113	21.2	7	26	26.9
Intact	1	2	50.0	5	14	35.7
Total	32	199	16.1	15	54	27.8

Abbreviations: ncut = number of cut-marked specimens.

APPENDIX 9. *Distribution of taxonomically identified bones by level and as a function of distance away from the cliff at Saint-Césaire*

	Distance away from the Cliff in Meters											
	2		3		4		5		6		Total	
	n	%	n	%	n	%	n	%	n	%	n	%
Evol Auri, Ejj	14	3.3	70	16.5	45	10.6	148	34.9	147	34.7	424	100.0
Evol Auri, Ejm	45	4.2	146	13.7	653	61.4	133	12.5	86	8.1	1063	99.9
Mid Auri Ejf	1633	46.9	987	28.3	606	17.4	140	4.0	116	3.3	3482	99.9
Mid Auri Ejo sup	212	44.6	161	33.9	67	14.1	18	3.8	17	3.6	475	100.0
Moust/Châtel	70	9.5	106	14.5	272	37.1	213	29.1	72	9.8	733	100.0
D Moust Ejop inf	65	25.9	61	24.3	36	14.3	30	12.0	59	23.5	251	100.0
D Moust Egpf	119	14.2	270	32.2	197	23.5	127	15.1	126	15.0	839	100.0
Total	2158	29.7	1801	24.8	1876	25.8	809	11.1	623	8.6	7267	100.0

APPENDIX 10. *Change in skeletal representation in relation to the degree of identification at Saint-Césaire*

	NISP		NSUTS		
	n	%	*n*	%	%Difference
Antler	*1406*	*15.4*	*0*	*0.0*	*15.4*
Horncore	30	0.3	0	0.0	0.3
Cranial	**90**	**1.0**	**189**	**5.3**	**−4.3**
Mandible/maxillary	**256**	**2.8**	**226**	**6.3**	**−3.5**
Tooth	**1476**	**16.2**	**725**	**20.3**	**−4.1**
Hyoid	7	0.1	5	0.1	0.0
Atlas	11	0.1	0	0.0	0.1
Axis	3	0.0	0	0.0	0.0
Cervical	25	0.3	19	0.5	−0.2
Thoracic	**49**	**0.5**	**57**	**1.6**	**−1.1**
Lumbar	26	0.3	10	0.3	0.0
Sacrum	6	0.1	4	0.1	0.0
Caudal	1	0.0	7	0.2	−0.2
Vertebrae	**10**	**0.1**	**131**	**3.7**	**−3.6**
Ribs	**1161**	**12.7**	**2008**	**56.1**	**−43.4**
Sternum	8	0.1	1	0.0	0.1
Scapula	102	1.1	60	1.7	−0.6
Humerus	*271*	*3.0*	*18*	*0.5*	*2.5*
Radius/radio-ulna	*525*	*5.5*	*13*	*0.4*	*5.4*
Scaphoid	14	0.2	0	0.0	0.2
Lunatum	9	0.1	0	0.0	0.1
Hamatum	9	0.1	0	0.0	0.1
Capitatum	13	0.1	0	0.0	0.1
Pisiform	9	0.1	0	0.0	0.1
Triquetrum	6	0.1	0	0.0	0.1
Metacarpal	*250*	*2.7*	*0*	*0.0*	*2.7*
Innominates	71	0.8	12	0.3	0.5
Femur	*259*	*2.8*	*23*	*0.6*	*2.2*
Patella	10	0.1	1	0.0	0.1
Tibia	*915*	*10.0*	*59*	*1.6*	*8.4*
Malleolus/fibula	19	0.2	0	0.0	0.2
Talus	28	0.3	0	0.0	0.3
Calcaneum	34	0.4	0	0.0	0.4
Greater cuneiform	14	0.2	0	0.0	0.2
Smaller cuneiform	3	0.0	0	0.0	0.0
Cubonavicular/navicular	19	0.2	0	0.0	0.2
Metatarsal	*1498*	*16.4*	*0*	*0.0*	*16.4*
Metapodial	*195*	*2.1*	*3*	*0.1*	*2.0*
Vestigial metapodial	42	0.5	0	0.0	0.5
Phalanges	*172*	*1.9*	*8*	*0.2*	*1.7*
Vestigial phalanges	17	0.2	0	0.0	0.2
Sesamoids	45	0.5	0	0.0	0.5
Total	9114	100.0	3579	100.0	0.0

All of the taxa and levels are combined. The last column was calculated by subtracting %NSUTS from %NISP. Values in bold are elements that are over-represented (by at least −1.0%) in the NSUTS sample, whereas values in italics are elements that are over-represented (by at least 1.0%) in the NISP sample.

Abbreviations: NISP = number of identified specimens; NSUTS = number of specimens of uncertain taxonomic status.

APPENDIX 11. *Percentages of refitted fragments of reindeer long bones by size class (in mm²) at Saint-Césaire, irrespective of stratigraphic provenience*

| | Percentages of Refitted Long Bone Fragments by Size Class in Reindeer | | | | | | | | | | | |
| | 0–500 | | | 500–1000 | | | 1000–1500 | | | Total | | |
	Refit	n	%	Refit	n	%	Refit	n	%	Refit	n	%
Metatarsal	146	671	21.8	123	589	20.9	21	127	16.5	311	1553	20.0
Radio-ulna	17	98	17.3	20	146	13.7	16	83	19.3	64	400	16.0
Metacarpal	10	40	25.0	11	102	10.8	4	39	10.3	27	218	12.4
Tibia	13	58	22.4	22	192	11.5	19	213	8.9	71	693	10.2
Humerus	2	9	22.2	6	63	9.5	8	66	12.1	18	186	9.7
Femur	2	19	10.5	6	78	7.7	3	44	6.8	18	196	9.2
Total	190	895	21.2	188	1170	16.1	71	572	12.4	509	3246	15.7

The "Total" column comprises all of the fragments, including those that are ≥ 1500 mm². Percentages of refits were calculated by subtracting the number of specimens refitted from the pre-refit NISP counts. Abbreviations: MNE = minimum number of elements; NISP = number of identified specimens.

APPENDIX 12. *Minimum number of elements (MNE)-based counts of proximal epiphyses, distal epiphyses, and shafts at Saint-Césaire. Counts for reindeer, bison, and horse were combined. Specimens that were only identified as "metapodials" were excluded, as were isolated ulna fragments*

| | Total MNE Proximal | | Total MNE Shafts | | Total MNE Distal | | Total MNE | |
	n	%	n	%	n	%	n	%
Evol Auri, Ejj	6	11.3	43	81.1	4	7.5	53	99.9
Evol Auri, Ejm	19	14.7	100	77.5	10	7.8	129	100.0
Mid Auri Ejf	65	14.9	328	75.4	42	9.7	435	100.0
Mid Auri Ejo sup	12	20.7	43	74.1	3	5.2	58	100.0
Moust/Chât	18	17.3	80	76.9	6	5.8	104	100.0
D Moust Ejop inf	6	15.0	33	82.5	1	2.5	40	100.0
D Moust Egpf	15	17.6	63	74.1	7	8.2	85	99.9
Total	141	15.6	690	76.3	73	8.1	904	100.0

APPENDIX 13. *Fetal age in days and corresponding diaphyseal length in the horse foreleg*

Humerus			Radius			Metacarpal		
Age in days	Diaphyseal length	Reference	Age in days	Diaphyseal length	Reference	Age in days	Diaphyseal length	Reference
35	3.8	H	74.9	6.1	G	74.9	2.8	G
63	7.5	H	79.8	9.9	G	76.8	6.1	G
77	12.5	H	85.6	9.9	G	79.8	6.9	G
105	19.0	H	89.7	14.1	G	85.6	6.3	G
140	33.0	H	94.7	17.4	G	89.7	9.4	G
161	48.0	H	96.1	16.3	G	95.0	12.1	G
175	55.0	H	98.8	18.8	G	96.1	9.9	G
203	63.0	H	100.7	21.0	G	98.8	11.3	G
231	85.0	H	112.0	25.9	G	100.7	13.0	G
245	95.0	H	149.7	37.5	G	111.2	16.8	G
259	112.0	H	150.2	34.5	G	149.9	21.8	G
294	132.0	H	153.8	37.2	G	149.7	24.6	G
308	167.0	H	154.1	43.6	G	153.5	23.4	G
			166.7	50.2	G	153.8	26.8	G
			174.4	54.3	G	166.4	35.9	G
			180.2	59.0	G	173.8	37.2	G
			186.5	60.7	G	180.2	37.2	G
			229.6	116.1	G	186.5	40.6	G
			234.3	116.4	G	229.6	102.9	G
			234.9	111.2	G	234.6	96.8	G
			253.5	131.9	G	234.9	101.2	G
			257.4	150.6	G	253.3	123.6	G
			269.5	144.0	G	257.4	142.6	G
			271.1	148.7	G	269.8	139.3	G
			271.1	155.9	G	271.4	141.0	G
			274.4	151.2	G	271.7	138.2	G
			276.6	158.9	G	277.2	143.2	G
			277.7	155.0	G	279.4	141.0	G
			278.8	153.1	G	280.5	155.6	G

(*continued*)

APPENDIX 13 *(continued). Fetal age in days and corresponding diaphyseal length in the horse foreleg*

Radius			Metacarpal		
Age in days	Diaphyseal length	Reference	Age in days	Diaphyseal length	Reference
279.1	158.3	G	284.1	140.1	G
279.4	160.8	G	284.3	150.1	G
284.1	156.1	G	294.5	156.1	G
284.1	161.1	G	294.0	159.2	G
293.7	165.5	G	294.0	162.2	G
296.2	170.2	G	303.6	160.6	G
300.0	175.4	G	303.8	164.1	G
303.6	169.9	G	304.1	166.9	G
303.6	173.8	G	305.2	180.4	G
303.8	177.4	G	318.1	177.7	G
307.4	182.1	G	325.0	205.2	G
307.7	187.9	G	331.6	195.0	G
317.6	180.4	G	331.6	198.1	G
325.3	210.5	G	331.6	209.4	G
331.3	200.3	G	331.9	218.8	G
331.3	205.0	G	35	1.8	H
331.6	207.4	G	63	5.0	H
331.6	211.3	G	77	10.5	H
331.9	222.1	G	105	14.2	H
63	8.1	H	140	28.0	H
77	15.0	H	161	40.0	H
105	22.0	H	175	48.5	H
140	40.0	H	203	60.0	H
161	58.0	H	231	79.0	H
175	67.5	H	245	111.0	H
203	78.0	H	259	136.0	H
231	102.0	H	294	155.0	H
245	122.0	H	308	200.0	H
259	147.0	H			
294	168.0	H			
308	211.0	H			

Data from Habermehl (1975, as cited in Prummel 1989:75, table 3) and Guffy *et al.* (1970:368, figure 7).
Abbreviations: G = Guffy *et al.* 1970, H = Habermehl 1975.

APPENDIX 14. *Fetal age in days and corresponding diaphyseal length in the horse hindleg*

Femur			Tibia			Metatarsal		
Age in days	Diaphyseal length	Reference	Age in days	Diaphyseal length	Reference	Age in days	Diaphyseal length	Reference
35	4.2	H	74.9	5.2	G	74.6	3.6	G
63	8.3	H	75.7	8.8	G	76.6	6.9	G
77	15.0	H	79.3	9.9	G	79.6	6.6	G
105	23.0	H	85.6	9.9	G	85.4	7.2	G
140	41.5	H	89.8	14.3	G	89.5	10.5	G
161	58.0	H	95.3	17.7	G	92.5	15.2	G
175	67.0	H	96.9	16.0	G	94.7	12.4	G
203	89.0	H	98.3	19.3	G	97.2	11.0	G
245	118.0	H	101.9	21.0	G	98.8	13.2	G
259	140.0	H	112.3	27.0	G	101.9	13.2	G
294	159.0	H	150.9	34.5	G	112.1	21.2	G
308	212.0	H	150.6	37.2	G	150.9	28.1	G
			155.0	35.3	G	150.9	30.9	G
			154.7	41.9	G	154.7	30.6	G
			167.6	48.0	G	154.7	33.1	G
			175.1	53.2	G	167.6	42.1	G
			180.8	53.2	G	175.1	48.5	G
			188.3	58.2	G	181.1	49.0	G
			235.6	107.3	G	187.5	51.0	G
			235.9	112.3	G	235.9	123.7	G
			241.1	107.3	G	235.9	126.7	G
			254.6	128.8	G	240.8	118.2	G
			257.9	146.5	G	254.6	149.9	G
			262.3	147.0	G	262.3	162.0	G
			268.6	150.1	G	270.6	160.6	G
			272.2	144.0	G	269.7	170.5	G
			272.2	151.4	G	272.8	158.7	G
			278.8	154.5	G	280.5	170.2	G
			280.2	152.0	G	280.7	174.4	G
			280.7	156.1	G	281.0	177.1	G

(continued)

APPENDIX 14 *(continued)*. *Fetal age in days and corresponding diaphyseal length in the horse foreleg*

Tibia			Metatarsal		
Age in days	Diaphyseal length	Reference	Age in days	Diaphyseal length	Reference
280.5	158.9	G	280.7	180.2	G
285.1	151.7	G	280.7	184.8	G
285.1	156.7	G	285.4	165.0	G
295.3	160.8	G	285.7	182.6	G
298.6	171.9	G	295.6	186.2	G
300.3	166.3	G	298.3	199.7	G
301.7	175.2	G	302.2	191.2	G
305.0	171.3	G	305.5	189.8	G
305.2	176.6	G	305.5	195.0	G
307.2	181.2	G	305.5	200.0	G
308.5	183.4	G	307.4	210.2	G
319.5	180.4	G	308.8	198.6	G
327.2	199.7	G	320.6	214.3	G
331.6	200.3	G	327.2	214.3	G
333.3	202.8	G	335.5	228.7	G
334.1	219.9	G	335.5	231.1	G
334.9	200.0	G	337.4	233.9	G
334.9	213.2	G	337.7	230.0	G
63	8.3	H	35	2.1	H
77	15.0	H	63	5.0	H
105	23.0	H	77	11.5	H
140	42.0	H	105	17.0	H
161	59.0	H	140	32.0	H
175	69.0	H	161	44.0	H
203	90.0	H	175	57.0	H
245	129.0	H	203	80.0	H
259	155.0	H	245	119.0	H
294	180.0	H	259	154.0	H
308	235.0	H	294	182.0	H
			308	236.0	H

Data from Habermehl (1975, as cited in Prummel 1989:75, table 3) and Guffy *et al.* (1970:369, figure 8).
Abbreviations: G = Guffy *et al.* 1970, H = Habermehl 1975.

APPENDIX 15. *Assemblages composing the time series, from earliest to latest*

#	Site, layer	Cultural period	Sample sizes: ungulates, rodents	%reindeer, %cold microfauna	References: ungulates, rodents
1	Combe-Grenal, 63	Middle Paleolithic[a]	25	96.0	D&P 95:135
2	Combe-Grenal, 62	"	50	78.0	"
3	Combe-Grenal, 61	"	28	82.1	"
4	Combe-Grenal, 60	"	382	92.7	"
5	Combe-Grenal, 59	"	1138	93.0	"
6	Combe-Grenal, 58	"	554	85.6	"
7	Combe-Grenal, 57	"	131, 20	66.4, 45.0	", M 93:67
8	Combe-Grenal, 56 hiatus	"	41	39.0	"
9	Combe-Grenal, 55–54	Layer 55: unknown; Layer 54: Typical Moust.	282	0.0	L 81:93–103
10	Combe-Grenal, 53	Mousterian	41, 24	0.0, 66.7	", M 93:67
11	Combe-Grenal, 52	Typical Mousterian	854	0.4	"
12	Combe-Grenal, 51	Mousterian	73, 22	0.0, 0.0	", M 93:67
13	Combe-Grenal, 50	Typical Mousterian	818	0.2	"
14	Combe-Grenal, 50a	"	342, 77	0.0, 5.2	", M 93:67
15	Combe-Grenal, 49–48	Mousterian	60	0.0	"
16	Combe-Grenal, 47	Typical Mousterian	63	0.0	"
17	Combe-Grenal, 46–44	Mousterian	39, 125	0.0, 0.0	", M 93:67
18	Combe-Grenal, 43–42	Typical Mousterian	149	0.0	"
19	Combe-Grenal, 41	"	59, 37	0.0, 0.0	", M 93:67
20	Combe-Grenal, 40	"	108	0.9	"
21	Combe-Grenal, 39	Mousterian	18	0.0	"
22	Combe-Grenal, 38	Denticulate Mousterian	80	0.0	"
23	Combe-Grenal, 37	Typical Mousterian	56	0.0	"
24	Combe-Grenal, 36	"	78	7.7	"
25	Combe-Grenal, 35	Ferrassie Mousterian	331	18.7	G 87:377–392
26	Combe-Grenal, 34	Ferrassie Mousterian?	20	20.0	"
27	Combe-Grenal, 33	Ferrassie Mousterian	54	9.3	"
28	Combe-Grenal, 32	"	153	35.3	"
29	Combe-Grenal, 31	Typical Mousterian?	85	61.2	"
30	Combe-Grenal, 30	Typical Mousterian	77	46.8	"
31	Combe-Grenal, 29	"	224	36.2	"
32	Combe-Grenal, 28	"	122	59.8	"
33	Combe-Grenal, 27	Ferrassie Mousterian	296	55.1	"
34	Combe-Grenal, 26	Quina Mousterian	105, 25	65.7, 0.0	", M 93:67
35	Combe-Grenal, 25	"	284, 16	63.7, 6.3	", "
36	Combe-Grenal, 24	"	285, 16	68.4, 0.0	", "
37	Combe-Grenal, 23	"	1101	71.0	"
38	Combe-Grenal, 22	"	982	65.4	"
39	Combe-Grenal, 21	"	270	48.9	"
40	Combe-Grenal, 20	"	190, 10	48.4, 10.0	", M 93:66
41	Combe-Grenal, 19	"	104	65.4	"
42	Combe-Grenal, 18	"	49, 12	53.1, 8.3	", M 93:66
43	Combe-Grenal, 17	"	148, 11	53.4, 0.0	", "
44	Combe-Grenal, 16–15	Denticulate Mousterian	93, 15	18.3, 6.7	", "

(continued)

APPENDIX 15 *(continued)*

#	Site, layer	Cultural period	Sample sizes: ungulates, rodents	%reindeer, %cold microfauna	References: ungulates, rodents
45	Combe-Grenal, 14	"	537	16.2	"
46	Combe-Grenal, 13	"	171	15.2	"
47	Combe-Grenal, 12	"	85	9.4	"
48	Combe-Grenal, 11	"	158	20.3	"
49	Combe-Grenal, 10	Typical Mousterian?	31	6.5	"
50	Combe-Grenal, 9	Mousterian	34	2.9	"
51	Combe-Grenal, 8	"	23	39.1	"
52	Combe-Grenal, 7	Typical Mousterian	54	55.6	"
53	Combe-Grenal, 6	"	55	43.6	"
54	Combe-Grenal, 5–4	Layer 5: Mousterian; Layer 4: MAT	27	22.2	"
55	Combe-Grenal, 3	MAT	14	14.3	"
56	Combe-Grenal, 2–1	Layer 2: Mousterian; Layer 1: MAT	13	7.7	"
57	La Quina, 6c	Denticulate Mousterian	271	5.5	A 98:56
58	La Quina, 6b	"	22	4.5	"
59	La Quina, 6a	"	972	25.0	"
60	La Quina, 4b	"	885	11.9	"
61	La Quina, 4a	"	74	17.6	"
62	La Quina, 2b	"	437	8.5	"
63	La Quina, 2a	"	56	3.6	"
64	Saint-Césaire, EGPF	"	281	33.5	this study
65	Saint-Césaire, EJOP sup; *Roc de Combe, 8*	Moust/Châtelperronian, *Châtelperronian*	772, 31	21.0, 12.9	", M 93:73
66	Les Cottés, 04 inf	Protoaurignacian	205	75.1	R09
67	Abri Pataud, 14	Early Aurignacian	1954	98.7	S 98:64
68	Abri Pataud, 13; *Roc de Combe, 7*	"	226, 295	100.0, 30.2	", M 93:73
69	Abri Pataud, 12	"	269	74.0	"
70	Abri Pataud, 11	"	2763	49.5	C 03:163
71	Abri Pataud, 8	Middle Aurignacian	87	10.3	S 98:64
72	Roc de Combe, 6	Evolved Aurignacian (with nosed and busked burins)	297, 52	79.5, 21.2	G&D 08:343, M 93:73
73	Roc de Combe, 5	Evolved Aurignacian ("busqué déstructuré")	1520, 54	96.7, 24.1	", "
74	Le Flageolet I, VIII	Evolved Aurignacian (with Vachons burins)	461, 70	52.1, 15.7	G&D 98:1121, M 93:81
75	Abri Pataud, 6	Final Aurignacian	81	29.6	S 98:64
76	Abri Pataud, 5 extension+inférieur	Early Gravettian	9126	99.0	B 75:120
77	Abri Pataud, 5 moyen+supérieur; *Roc de Combe, 4*	"	11841, 148	98.7, 27.7	", M 93:73
78	Le Flageolet I, VII	Gravettian (Fontirobertian)[b]	1768	16.0	G&D 98:1121
79	Abri Pataud, 4 lower; *Le Flageolet I, V*	Middle Gravettian (Noaillian)	7769, 13	95.1, 7.7	C 98:194, M 93:81

#	Site, layer	Cultural period	Sample sizes: ungulates, rodents	%reindeer, %cold microfauna	References: ungulates, rodents
80	Abri Pataud, 4 middle	Middle Gravettian	11972	96.9	"
81	Abri Pataud, 4 upper; *Le Flageolet I, IV*	Middle Gravettian (Rayssian)	23392, 22	96.8, 36.4	", M 93:81
82	Abri Pataud, 3; *Roc de Combe, 1*	Late Gravettian	9320, 25	94.1, 8.0	C 98:37, M 93:73
83	Abri Pataud, 2	Final Gravettian ("Proto-Magdalenian")	3253	89.0	"
84	Laugerie Haute Est, 34+33	Proto-Solutrean	21	71.4	D 83:360
85	Laugerie Haute Est, 31	Early Solutrean	354	90.1	"
86	Laugerie Haute Est, 30–29	Middle Solutrean	272	94.5	"
87	Laugerie Haute Est, 23–22 +Solutréen supérieur; *Combe Saunière, IV1–IV10*	Late Solutrean	209, 1623	82.3, 24.1	", M 93:91
88	Laugerie Haute Est, 20+18; *Cassegros, 10*	Badegoulian without raclettes	400, 47	64.5, 53.2	", M 93:111
89	Laugerie Haute Est, 16+14+12+10; *Cassegros, 9*	Badegoulian with raclettes	1247, 119	95.3, 30.3	", "
90	Taillis des Coteaux, Ensemble III	Early Magdalenian	1942	84.5	G 09:95
91	Le Flageolet II, IX	Middle Magdalenian	1908, 27	97.0, 18.5	D 94:14, M 93:84
92	La Madeleine, 15–14	Late Middle Magdalenian	971	77.5	D 83:363
93	La Madeleine, 13–12	Late Magdalenian	2188	95.6	"
94	Bois-Ragot, 6–5; *Moulin du Roc, c. brune*	Final Magdalenian	1561, 177	78.0, 14.7	G 95:290, O 08:30
95	Bois-Ragot, 4; *Pont d'Ambon, 3a+3b+3*	Azilian	728, 578	9.1, 6.1	", M 93:88
96	Bois-Ragot, 3; *Pont d'Ambon, 2*	"	205, 96	7.3, 7.3	G 84, M 93:88

The "#" column identifies the assemblages ("stratigraphic units") shown in Figure 11.6. Sample sizes correspond to number of identified specimen (NISP) counts for ungulates and to minimum number of individuals (MNI) counts for micromammals. "%cold microfauna" is the percentage of cold-adapted species (Male/root vole, narrow-skulled vole, and the collared lemming) in micromammal samples. Assemblages in italic designate micromammal assemblages considered approximately coeval with the ungulate assemblages with which they are associated. Mammoth and indeterminate cervids and equids were excluded from the ungulate NISP counts, as were the few specimens attributed to *Ovibos* by Bouchud (1975). These last specimens were possibly misidentified. MNI counts for rodents only include remains identified to species, save for specimens attributed to *Microtus malei/oeconomus*.

[a] The attribution of layers 63–56 to the Acheulean is no longer accepted (Mourre and Colonge 2007). Therefore, these assemblages are simply identified as belonging to the Middle Paleolithic. The other attributions for Combe-Grenal follow Bordes *et al.* (1966) and Faivre (2008).

[b] There is some ambiguity concerning the chronological placement of the Fontirobertian. The tentative chronology proposed by Pesesse (2008) is followed here.

Abbreviations: A 98 = Armand in Debénath and Jelinek 1998; B 75 = Bouchud 1975; C 98 = Cho 1998; C 03 = Chiotti *et al.* 2003; D 83 = Delpech 1983; D 94 = Deplano 1994; D&P 95 = Delpech and Prat 1995; G 84 = Gilbert 84, as cited in Cochard 2004:206; G 87 = Guadelli 1987; G 95 = Griggo 1995; G 09 = Griggo in Primault 2009, pers. comm., 2010; G&D 98 = Grayson and Delpech 1998; G&D 08 = Grayson and Delpech 2008; L 81 = Laquay 1981; M 93 = Marquet 1993; MAT = Mousterian of Acheulean Tradition; O 08 = Oppliger 2008; R 09 = Rendu 2009, pers. comm., 2011; S 98 = Sekhr 1998.

REFERENCES

Aanes, R., B. E. Saether, E. J. Solberg, S. Aanes, O. Strand, and N. A. Øritsland. 2003. Synchrony in Svalbard reindeer population dynamics. *Canadian Journal of Zoology* 81:103–110.

Adams, D. C., and J. O. Church. 2007. Amphibians do not follow Bergmann's rule. *Evolution* 62:413–420.

Adams-Hunt, M. M., and L. F. Jacobs. 2007. "Cognition for foraging," in *Foraging: Behavior and Ecology*. Edited by D. W. Stephens, J. S. Brown, and R. C. Ydenberg. Chicago: University of Chicago Press, pp. 105–138.

Adler, D. S., G. Bar-Oz, A. Belfer-Cohen, and O. Bar-Yosef. 2006. Ahead of the game: Middle and Upper Palaeolithic hunting behaviors in the southern Caucasus. *Current Anthropology* 47:89–118.

Ahn, J., and E. J. Brook. 2008. Atmospheric CO_2 and climate on millennial time scales during the last glacial period. *Science* 322:83–85.

Airvaux, J., A. L. Berthet, and J.-C. Castel. 2003. Le gisement Aurignacien de Chez-Pinaud 2, à Jonzac, Charente-Maritime. *Préhistoire du Sud-Ouest* 10:25–75.

Alhaique, F. 2000. "Analisi preliminare dei reperti faunistici rivenuti nei livelli del Paleolitico superiore di Riparo Mochi (Balzi Rossi): Scavi 1995–1996," in *Atti del 2° Convegno Nazionale di Archeozoologia*. Edited by G. Malerba, C. Cilli, and G. Giacobini. Forlí: ABACO, pp. 125–130.

Alhaique, F., S. V. Biondi, P. F. Cassoli, A. Recchi, and A. Tagliacozzo. 1998. "Modifications in the exploitation of animal resources between the Middle Paleolithic and the Aurignacian at Grotta del Fossellone (Monte Circeo, Italy)," in *Atti del XIII° Congresso dell'Unione Internazionale di Scienze Preistoriche e Protostoriche*. Edited by R. Grifoni Cremonesi, C. Tozzi, A. Vigliardi, and C. Peretto. Forlí: ABACO, pp. 571–576.

Alhaique, F., M. Bisconti, E. Castiglioni, C. Cilli, L. Fasani, G. Giacobini, R. Grifoni, A. Guerreschi, A. Iacopini, G. Malerba, C. Peretto, A. Recchi, A. Rocci Ris, A. Ronchitelli, M. Rottoli, U. Thun-Hohenstein, C. Tozzi, P. Visentini, and B. Wilkens. 2004. Animal resources and subsistence strategies. *Collegium Antropologicum* 28:23–40.

Alhaique, F., and A. Tagliacozzo. 2000. "L'interpretazione dei dati faunistici nella ricostruzione delle strategie di sussitenza del Paleolitico Medio: L'esempio del Lazio," in *Atti del 2° Convegno Nazionale di Archeozoologia*. Forlí: ABACO, pp. 111–124.

Allen, J. R. M., U. Brandt, A. Brauer, H.-W. Hubberten, B. Huntley, J. Keller, M. Kraml, A. Mackensen, J. Mingram, J. F. W. Negendank, N. R. Nowaczyk, H. Oberhänsli, W. A. Watts, S. Wulf, and B. Zolitschka. 1999. Rapid environmental changes in southern Europe during the last glacial period. *Nature* 400:740–743.

Alvard, M. 1993. Testing the "ecologically noble savage" hypothesis: Interspecific prey choice by Piro hunters of Amazonian Peru. *Human Ecology* 21:355–387.

————. 1995. Intraspecific prey choice by Amazonian hunters. *Current Anthropology* 35:789–818.

Angerbjörn, A., and J. E. C. Flux. 1995. *Lepus timidus*. *Mammal Species* 495:1–11.

Arensburg, B., and A. Belfer-Cohen. 1998. "*Sapiens* and Neandertals. Rethinking the Levantine Middle Palaeolithic hominids," in *Neandertals and modern humans in Western Asia*. Edited by T. Akazawa, K. Aoki, and O. Bar-Yosef. New York: Plenum Press, pp. 311–322.

Armand, D., and A. Delagnes. 1998. "Les retouchoirs en os d'Artenac (couche 6c): Perspectives archéozoologiques, taphonomiques et expérimentales," in *Économie préhistorique: Les comportements de subsistance au Paléolithique. XVIIIe rencontres internationales d'archéologie et d'histoire d'Antibes*. Edited by J.-P. Brugal, L. Meignen, and M. Patou-Mathis. Sophia-Antipolis: Éditions APDCA, pp. 205–214.

Armand, D., E. Pubert, and M. Soressi. 2001. Organisation saisonnière des comportements de prédation des Moustériens de Pech-de-l'Azé I. Premiers résultats. *Paléo* 13:19–28.

Asa, C. S. 2002. "Equid reproductive biology," in *Equids: zebras, asses, and horses. Status survey and conservation action plan*. Edited by P. D. Moehlman. Cambridge: IUCN Publication Services Unit, pp. 113–117.

Ashton, K. G. 2002. Patterns of within-species body size variation of birds: Strong evidence for Bergmann's rule. *Global Ecology and Biogeography* 11:505–523.

————. 2004. Sensitivity of intraspecific latitudinal clines of body size for tetrapods to sampling, latitude and body size. *Integrative and Comparative Biology* 44:403–412.

Ashton, K. G., and C. R. Feldman. 2003. Bergmann's rule in nonavian reptiles: Turtles follow it, lizards and snakes reverse it. *Evolution* 57:1151–1163.

Ashton, K. G., M. C. Tracy, and A. de Queiroz. 2000. Is Bergmann's rule valid for mammals? *The American Naturalist* 156:390–415.

Aubry, T., J. Zilhão, and F. Almeida. 2007. À propos de la variabilité technique et culturelle de l'entité gravettienne au Portugal: Bilan des dernières découvertes et perspectives de recherche. *Paléo* 19:53–72.

Aura Tortosa, J. E., V. Villaverde Bonilla, M. Pérez Ripoll, R. Martínez Valle, and P. Guillem Calatayud. 2002. Big game and small prey: Paleolithic and Epipaleolithic economy from Valencia (Spain). *Journal of Archaeological Method and Theory* 9:215–267.

Backer, A. M. 1993. "Spatial distribution at la Roche à Pierrot, Saint-Césaire: Changing uses of a rockshelter," in *Context of a late Neandertal: Implications of multidisciplinary research for the transition to Upper Paleolithic adaptations at Saint-Césaire*. Edited by F. Lévêque, A. M. Backer, and M. Guilbaud. Madison: Prehistory Press, pp. 105–127.

————. 1994. Site structure of Saint-Césaire: Changing uses of a Paleolithic rockshelter. Unpublished Ph.D. dissertation, University of New Mexico.

Badgley, C., and D. L. Fox. 2000. Ecological biogeography of North American mammals: Species density and ecological structure in relation to environmental gradients. *Journal of Biogeography* 27:1437–1467.

Bailey, S. E., and J.-J. Hublin. 2005. Who made the Early Aurignacian? A reconsideration of the Brassempouy dental remains. *Bulletins et Mémoires de la Société d'Anthropologie de Paris* 17:115–121.

Bailey, S. E., T. D. Weaver, and J.-J. Hublin. 2009. Who made the Aurignacian and other early Upper Paleolithic industries? *Journal of Human Evolution* 57:11–26.

Ballesio, R. 1979. Le gisement pléistocène supérieur de la grotte de Jaurens à Nespouls, Corrèze, France: Les carnivores (Mammalia, Carnivora). I. Canidae et Hyaenidae. *Nouvelles Archives du Musée d'Histoire Naturelle de Lyon* 17:25–55.

Balter, V., A. Person, N. Labourdette, D. Drucker, M. Renard, and B. Vandermeersch. 2001. Les Néandertaliens étaient-ils essentiellement carnivores? Résultats préliminaires sur les teneurs en Sr et Ba de la palébiocénose mammalienne de Saint-Césaire. *Comptes Rendus de l'Académie des Sciences de Paris. Sciences de la Terre et des Planètes* 332:59–65.

Balter, V., and L. Simon. 2006. Diet and behavior of the Saint-Césaire Neanderthal inferred from biogeochemical data inversion. *Journal of Human Evolution* 51:329–338.

Banfield, A. W. F. 1951. *The barren-ground caribou*. Ottawa: Ministry of Resources and Development.

Bannikov, A. G. 1958. Distribution géographique et biologie du cheval sauvage et du chameau de Mongolie (*Equus przewalski* et *Camelus bactrianus*). *Mammalia* 22:152–160.

Bar-El, T., and E. Tchernov. 2001. Lagomorph remains at prehistoric sites in Israel and southern Sinai. *Paléorient* 26:93–109.

Bar-Oz, G., and D. S. Adler. 2005. The taphonomic history of the Middle and Upper Palaeolithic faunal assemblages from Ortvale Klde, Georgian Republic. *Journal of Taphonomy* 3:185–211.

Bar-Oz, G., and T. Dayan. 2002. "After 20 years": A taphonomic re-evaluation of Nahal Hadera V, an Epipalaeolithic site on the Israeli coastal plain. *Journal of Archaeological Science* 29:145–156.

Bar-Oz, G., T. Dayan, and D. Kaufman. 1999. The Epipalaeolithic faunal sequence in Israel: A view from Neve David. *Journal of Archaeological Science* 26:67–82.

Bar-Yosef, O. 1991. "The archaeology of the Natufian layer at Hayonim Cave," in *The Natufian culture in the Levant*. Edited by O. Bar-Yosef and F. Valla. Ann Arbor: International Monographs in Prehistory, pp. 81–93.

———. 1994. "The contributions of southwest Asia to the study of the origin of modern humans," in *Origins of anatomically modern humans*. Edited by M. H. Nitecki and D. V. Nitecki. New York: Plenum Press, pp. 23–66.

———. 2002. The Upper Paleolithic revolution. *Annual Review of Anthropology* 31:363–393.

Bar-Yosef, O., A. Belfer-Cohen, P. Goldberg, S. L. Kuhn, L. Meignen, B. Vandermeersch, and S. Weiner. 2005. "Archaeological background to Hayonim Cave and Meged rockshelter," in *A 200,000 year record of Paleolithic diet, demography and society*. Edited by M. C. Stiner. American School of Prehistoric Research Bulletin 48. Cambridge, MA: Peabody Museum of Archaeology and Ethnology, pp. 17–38.

Bar-Yosef, O., and J.-G. Bordes. 2010. Who were the makers of the Châtelperronian culture? *Journal of Human Evolution* 59:586–593.

Barlow, R. K., and D. Metcalfe. 1996. Plant utility indices: Two Great Basin examples. *Journal of Archaeological Science* 23:351–371.

Barone, R. 1999. *Anatomie comparée des mammifères domestiques. Volume 1: Ostéologie*. Paris: Vigot.

Barreiro, L. B., E. Patin, O. Neyrolles, H. M. Cann, B. Gicquel, and L. Quintana-Murci. 2005. The heritage of pathogen pressures and ancient demography in the human innate-immunity *CD209/CD209L* region. *American Journal of Human Genetics* 77:869–886.

Barrette, C., and D. Vandal. 1990. Sparring and access to food in female caribou in the winter. *Animal Behaviour* 40:1183–1185.

Barron, E., T. H. van Andel, and D. Pollard. 2003. "Glacial environments II. Reconstructing the climate of Europe in the last glaciation," in *Neanderthals and modern humans in the European landscape during the last glaciation. Archaeological results of the Stage 3 Project*. Edited by T. H. van Andel and W. D. Davies. Cambridge: The McDonald Institute for Archaeological Research, pp. 57–78.

Bartram, L. E. 1993. "Perspectives on skeletal part profiles and utility curves from eastern Kalahari ethnoarchaeology," in *From bones to behavior: Ethnoarchaeological and experimental contributions to the interpretation of faunal remains*. Edited by J. Hudson. Carbondale: Center for Archaeological Investigation, Southern Illinois University, pp. 115–155.

Bartram, L. E., and C. W. Marean. 1999. Explaining the "Klasies pattern": Kua ethnoarchaeology, the Die Kelders Middle Stone Age archaeofauna, long bone fragmentation and carnivore ravaging. *Journal of Archaeological Science* 26:9–29.

Bayham, F. E. 1979. Factors influencing the Archaic pattern of animal exploitation. *The Kiva* 44:219–235.

Beauval, C. 2003. "*Vulpes/ Alopex* à Saint-Césaire." Manuscript on file.

———. 2004. "La faune des niveaux moustériens de "Chez Pinaud" (Jonzac, Charente-Maritime). Première analyse," in *Le site paléolithique de Chez-Pinaud à Jonzac, Charente-Maritime. Premiers résultats: Études sur la coupe gauche*. Edited by J. Airvaux. Préhistoire du Sud-Ouest Supplément 8, pp. 125–156.

Beauval, C., F. Lacrampe-Cuyaubère, B. Maureille, and E. Trinkaus. 2006. Direct radiocarbon dating and stable isotopes of the Neandertal femur from Les Rochers-de-Villeneuve (Lussac-les-Châteaux, Vienne). *Bulletins et Mémoires de la Société d'Anthropologie de Paris* 18:35–42.

Beauval, C., and E. Morin. 2010. "Les repaires d'hyènes du Lussacois (Lussac-les-Châteaux, Vienne, France). Apport des sites des Plumettes et des Rochers-de-Villeneuve," in *Préhistoire entre Vienne et Charente: Hommes et sociétés du Paléolithique*. Edited by J. Buisson-Catil and J. Primault. Chauvigny: Association des Publications Chauvinoises, pp. 175–189.

Beckouche, S. 1981. "Les grands mammifères du Paléolithique supérieur du Piage (Lot)," in *Le Piage. Site Préhistorique du Lot*. Edited by F. Champagne and R. Espitalié. Paris: Éditions du CNRS, pp. 165–192.

Behrensmeyer, A. K. 1978. Taphonomic and ecologic information from bone weathering. *Paleobiology* 4:150–162.

Belfer-Cohen, A., and O. Bar-Yosef. 1981. The Aurignacian at Hayonim cave. *Paléorient* 7:19–42.

Belfer-Cohen, A., and E. Hovers. 2010. Modernity, enhanced working memory, and the Middle to Upper Paleolithic record in the Levant. *Current Anthropology* 51:S167–S175.

Belk, M. C., and D. D. Houston. 2002. Bergmann's rule in ectotherms: A test using freshwater fishes. *The American Naturalist* 160:803–808.

Berger, J. 1986. *Wild horses of the Great Basin: Social competition and population size*. Chicago: University of Chicago Press.

Berger, J., and C. Cunningham. 1994. *Bison: Mating and conservation in small populations*. New York: Columbia University Press.

Bergerud, A. T. 1976. The annual antler cycle in Newfoundland caribou. *The Canadian Field-Naturalist* 90:449–463.

———. 1996. Evolving perspectives on caribou population dynamics, have we got it right yet? *Rangifer Special Issue* 9:95–116.

Bergerud, A. T., S. N. Luttich, and L. Camps. 2008. *The return of caribou to Ungava*. Montreal: McGill-Queen's University Press.

Bettinger, R. L. 1991. *Hunter-gatherers: Archaeological and evolutionary theory*. New York: Plenum Press.

Bettinger, R. L., R. Malhi, and H. McCarthy. 1997. Central place models of acorn and mussel processing. *Journal of Archaeological Science* 24:887–899.

Bietti, A., G. Boschian, G. M. Crisci, E. Danese, A. M. de Francesco, M. Dini, F. Fontana, A. Giampetri, R. Grifoni, A. Guerreschi, J. Liagre, F. Negrino, G. Radi, C. Tozzi, and R. Tykot. 2004. Inorganic raw materials economy and provenance of chipped industry in some stone age sites of northern and central Italy. *Collegium Antropologicum* 28:42–51.

Biewener, A. A. 1989. Mammalian terrestrial locomotion and size: Mechanical design principles define limits. *Bioscience* 39:776–783.

———. 2005. Biomechanical consequences of scaling. *The Journal of Experimental Biology* 208:1665–1676.

Binford, L. R. 1962. Archaeology as anthropology. *American Antiquity* 28:217–225.

———. 1968. "Post-Pleistocene adaptations," in *New perspectives in archaeology*. Edited by S. Binford and L. Binford. Chicago: Aldine, pp. 313–341.

———. 1978. *Nunamiut ethnoarchaeology*. New York: Academic Press.

———. 1980. Willow smoke and dogs' tails: Hunter-gatherer settlement systems and archaeological site formation. *American Antiquity* 45:4–20.

———. 1981. *Bones: Ancient men and modern myths*. New York: Academic Press.

———. 1982. Comment on R. White "Rethinking the Middle/Upper Paleolithic transition." *Current Anthropology* 23:177–181.

———. 1984. *Faunal remains from Klasies River Mouth*. Orlando: Academic Press.

Bird, D. W. 1997. Behavioral ecology and the archaeological consequences of central place foraging among the Meriam. *Archaeological Papers of the American Anthropological Association* 7:291–306.

Bird, D. W., and R. Bliege Bird. 1997. Contemporary shellfish gathering strategies among the Meriam of the Torres Strait islands, Australia: Testing predictions of a central place foraging model. *Journal of Archaeological Science* 24:39–63.

———. 2000. The ethnoarchaeology of juvenile foragers: Shellfishing strategies among Meriam children. *Journal of Anthropological Archaeology* 19:461–476.

Bird, D. W., R. Bliege Bird, and B. F. Codding. 2009. In pursuit of mobile prey: Martu hunting strategies and archaeofaunal interpretation. *American Antiquity* 74:3–29.

Bird, D. W., and J. F. O'Connell. 2006. Behavioral ecology and archaeology. *Journal of Archaeological Research* 14:143–188.

Blackburn, T. M., and K. J. Gaston. 1996. Spatial patterns in the body sizes of bird species in the New World. *Oikos* 77:436–446.

Blackburn, T. M., K. J. Gaston, and N. Loder. 1999. Geographic gradients in body size: A clarification of Bergmann's rule. *Diversity and Distributions* 5:165–174.

Blackburn, T. M., and B. A. Hawkins. 2004. Bergmann's rule and the mammal fauna of northern North America. *Ecography* 27:715–724.

Blake, J. E., J. E. Rowell, and J. M. Suttie. 1998. Characteristics of first-antler growth in reindeer and their association with seasonal fluctuations in steroid and insulin-like growth factor 1 levels. *Canadian Journal of Zoology* 76:2096–2102.

Blanc, A. C., and A. G. Segre. 1953. "Le Quaternaire du Mont Circé. Livret-Guide 'Excursion au Mont Circé'," in IVth International Meeting INQUA.

Blasco, M. F. 1997. In the pursuit of game: The Mousterian cave site of Gabasa 1 in the Spanish Pyrenees. *Journal of Anthropological Research* 53:177–217.

Blasco, R., and J. Fernández Peris. 2009. Middle Pleistocene bird consumption at level XI of Bolomor Cave (Valencia, Spain). *Journal of Archaeological Science* 36:2213–2223.

Blasco, R., J. Fernández Peris, and J. Rosell. 2010. Several different strategies for obtaining animal resources in the late Middle Pleistocene: The case of level XII at Bolomor Cave (Valencia, Spain). *Comptes Rendus Palevolution* 9:171–184.

Bliege Bird, R., and D. W. Bird. 2008. Why women hunt: Risk and contemporary foraging in a Western Desert aboriginal community. *Current Anthropology* 49:655–693.

Blumenschine, R. J. 1995. Percussion marks, tooth marks, and experimental determinations of the timing of hominid and carnivore access to long bones at FLK Zinjanthropus, Olduvai Gorge, Tanzania. *Journal of Human Evolution* 29:21–51.

Blumenschine, R. J., and T. C. Madrigal. 1993. Variability in long bone marrow yields of east African ungulates and its zooarchaeological implications. *Journal of Archaeological Science* 20:555–587.

Blumenschine, R. J., C. W. Marean, and S. D. Capaldo. 1996. Blind test of inter-analyst correspondence and accuracy in the identification of cut marks, percussion marks, and carnivore tooth marks on bone surfaces. *Journal of Archaeological Science* 23:493–507.

Blunier, T., and E. J. Brook. 2001. Timing of millennial-scale climate change in Antarctica and Greenland during the last glacial period. *Science* 291:109–112.

Bocheński, Z. M., and T. Tomek. 2011. The birds of Klissoura Cave 1: A window into the Upper Palaeolithic of Greece. Eurasian Prehistory, in press.

Bocheński, Z. M., T. Tomek, J. Wilczynski, K. Wertz, and P. Wojtal. 2009. Fowling during the Gravettian: the avifauna of Pavlov I, the Czech Republic. *Journal of Archaeological Science* 36:2655–2665.

Bocherens, H., and D. Drucker. 2003. "Reconstructing Neandertal diet from 120,000 to 30,000 BP using carbon and nitrogen isotopic abundances," in *Le rôle de l'environnement dans les comportements des chasseurs-cueilleurs préhistoriques*, vol. 1105. Edited by M. Patou-Mathis. Oxford: BAR International Series, pp. 1–7.

Bocherens, H., D. Drucker, D. Billiou, M. Patou-Mathis, and B. Vandermeersch. 2005. Isotopic evidence for diet and subsistence pattern of the Saint-Césaire I Neanderthal: Review and use of a multi-source mixing model. *Journal of Human Evolution* 49:71–87.

Bon, F. 2002. *L'Aurignacien entre mer et océan. Réflexion sur l'unité des phases anciennes de l'Aurignacien dans le sud de la France*. Paris: Mémoires de la Société Préhistorique Française 29.

Bond, G., W. Broecker, S. Johnsen, J. McManus, L. Labeyrie, J. Jouzel, and G. Bonani. 1993. Correlations between climate records from North Atlantic sediments and Greenland ice. *Nature* 365:143–147.

Bond, G., H. Heinrich, W. Broecker, L. Labeyrie, J. McManus, J. Andrews, S. Huon, R. Jantschik, S. Clasen, C. Simet, K. Tedesco, M. Klas, G. Bonani, and S. Ivy. 1992. Evidence for massive discharges of icebergs into the North Atlantic ocean during the last glacial period. *Nature* 360:245–249.

Bond, G., and R. Lotti. 1995. Iceberg discharges into the North Atlantic on millennial time scales during the last glaciation. *Science* 267:1005–1010.

Bordes, F. 1961. Mousterian cultures in France. *Science* 134:803–810.

———. 1972a. "Allocution du Professeur F. Bordes," in *Origine de l'homme moderne*. Edited by F. Bordes. Paris: UNESCO, pp. 295–296.

———. 1972b. "Du Paléolithique moyen au Paléolithique supérieur, continuité ou discontinuité?" in *Origine de l'homme moderne*. Edited by F. Bordes. Paris: UNESCO, pp. 211–217.

———. 1981a. Un Néandertalien encombrant. *La Recherche* 122:644–645.

————. 1981b. Vingt-cinq ans après: Le complexe moustérien revisité. *Bulletin de la Société Préhistorique Française* 78:77–87.

————. 1984. *Leçons sur le Paléolithique: Le Paléolithique en Europe*. Paris: Éditions du CNRS.

Bordes, F., and J. Labrot. 1967. La stratigraphie du gisement de Roc de Combe et ses implications. *Bulletin de la Société Préhistorique Française* 64, Études et Travaux:15–28.

Bordes, F., H. Laville, H. de Lumley, J. C. Miskovsky, M. M. Paquereau, B. Pillard, F. Prat, J. Renault-Miskovsky, J. Chaline, C. Mourer-Chauviré, R. Jullien, and J. L. Vernet. 1972. Le Würmien II. Tentative de corrélations entre le Languedoc méditerranéen (l'Hortus) et le Périgord (Combe-Grenal). *Études Quaternaires Mémoire* 1:353–362.

Bordes, F., H. Laville, and M. M. Paquereau. 1966. Observations sur le Pleistocène supérieur du gisement de Combe-Grenal (Dordogne). *Actes de la Société Linnéenne de Bordeaux* 103, Série B, 10:3–19.

Bordes, F., and F. Prat. 1965. Observations sur les faunes du Riss et du Würm I en Dordogne. *L'Anthropologie* 69:32–45.

Bordes, J.-G. 2002. Les interstratifications Châtelperronien/Aurignacien du Roc-de-Combe et du Piage (Lot, France). Analyse taphonomique des industries lithiques, implications archéologiques. Unpublished Ph.D. dissertation, Université de Bordeaux I.

Bordes, J.-G. 2003. "Lithic taphonomy of the Châtelperronian/Aurignacian interstratifications in Roc de Combe and Le Piage (Lot, France)," in *The chronology of the Aurignacian and of the transitional technocomplexes: Dating, stratigraphies, cultural implications*. Edited by J. Zilhão and F. d'Errico. Oxford: Oxbow Books, pp. 223–244.

Boscato, P. 1994. Grotta Paglicci: La fauna a grandi mammiferi degli strati 22–24 (Gravettiano antico – Aurignaziano). *Rivista di Scienze Preistoriche* 46:145–176.

————. 2004. "I macromammiferi dell'Aurignaziano e del Gravettiano antico di Grotta Paglicci," in *Paglicci – L'Aurignaziano e il Gravettiano antico*. Edited by A. Palma di Cesnola. Foggia: Claudio Grenzi, pp. 49–62.

Boskey, A. H. 2006. "Mineralization, structure, and function of bone," in *Dynamics of bone and cartilage metabolism*. Edited by M. J. Seibel, S. P. Robins, and J. P. Bilezikian. Toronto: Academic Press, pp. 201–212.

Bouchud, J. 1962. "Nouvelles recherches sur le renne quaternaire en France," in *Problèmes actuels de paléontologie*. Edited by G. G. Simpson. Paris: Éditions du CNRS, pp. 417–432.

————. 1966. *Essai sur le renne et la climatologie du Paléolithique moyen et supérieur*. Périgueux: Magne.

————. 1975. "Étude de la faune de l'Abri Pataud," in *Excavation of the Abri Pataud, Les Eyzies (Dordogne)*. Edited by H. L. Movius. Cambridge, MA: Peabody Museum of Archaeology and Ethnology, pp. 69–153.

Boudreau, S., S. Payette, C. Morneau, and S. Couturier. 2003. Recent decline of the George River caribou herd as revealed by tree-ring analysis. *Arctic, Antarctic and Alpine Research* 35:187–195.

Boule, M. 1908. L'Homme fossile de La Chapelle-aux-Saints (Corrèze). *L'Anthropologie* 19:517–525.

————. 1923. *Les hommes fossiles: Éléments de paléontologie humaine*. Paris: Masson et Cie.

Boulet, M., S. Couturier, S. D. Côté, R. D. Otto, and L. Bernatchez. 2007. Integrative use of spatial, genetic, and demographic analyses for investigating genetic connectivity between migratory, montane, and sedentary caribou herds. *Molecular Ecology* 16:4223–4240.

Bouman, I., J. Bouman, and L. Boyd. 1994. "Reintroduction," in *Przewalski's horse: The history and biology of an endangered species*. Edited by L. Boyd and K. A. Houpt. Albany: State University of New York Press, pp. 255–263.

Brace, C. L. 1964. The fate of the "Classic" Neanderthals: A consideration of hominid catastrophism. *Current Anthropology* 5:3–43.

Braüer, G. 1981. New evidence on the transitional period between Neanderthal and modern man. *Journal of Human Evolution* 10:467–474.

Braüer, G., M. Collard, and C. Stringer. 2004. On the reliability of recent tests of the Out of Africa hypothesis for modern human origins. *The Anatomical Record, Part A* 279A:701–707.

Breuil, H., and R. Lantier. 1951. *Les hommes de la pierre ancienne (Paléolithique et Mésolithique)*. Paris: Payot.

Bricker, H. M. Editor. 1995. *Le Paléolithique supérieur de l'Abri Pataud (Dordogne): Les fouilles de H. L. Movius Jr.* Documents d'Archéologie Française 50. Paris: Éditions de la Maison des Sciences de l'Homme.

Brink, J. W., and B. Dawe. 2003. Hot rocks as scarce resources: The use, re-use and abandonment of heating stones at Head-Smashed-In Buffalo Jump. *Plains Anthropologist* 48:85–104.

Britton, K. H. 2009. Multi-isotope analysis and the reconstruction of prey species palaeomigrations and palaeoecology. Unpublished Ph.D. dissertation, Durham University.

Broecker, W. S. 1994. Massive iceberg discharges as triggers for global climate change. *Nature* 372:421–424.

Brooks, A. S. 1995. "L'Aurignacien de l'Abri Pataud, niveaux 6 à 14," in *Le Paléolithique supérieur de l'abri Pataud (Dordogne): Les fouilles de H. L. Movius, Jr.* Edited by H. M. Bricker. Documents d'Archéologie Française 50. Paris: Éditions de la Maison des Sciences de l'Homme, pp. 167–222.

Brose, D. S., and M. H. Wolpoff. 1971. Early Upper Paleolithic man and late Middle Paleolithic tools. *American Anthropologist* 73:1156–1194.

Broughton, J. M. 1994. Declines in mammalian foraging efficiency during the Late Holocene, San Francisco Bay, California. *Journal of Anthropological Archaeology* 13:371–401.

———. 1999. *Resource depression and intensification during the late Holocene, San Francisco Bay: Evidence from the Emeryville shellmound vertebrate fauna.* University of California Anthropological Records 32. Berkeley and Los Angeles: University of California Press.

———. 2002. Prey spatial structure and behavior affect archaeological tests of optimal foraging models: Examples from the Emeryville shellmound vertebrate fauna. *World Archaeology* 34:6–83.

Brown, W. M. 1980. Polymorphism in mitochondrial DNA of humans as revealed by restriction endonuclease analysis. *Proceedings of the National Academy of Sciences* 77:3605–3609.

Brugal, J.-P. 1983. Applications des analyses multidimensionnelles à l'étude du squelette des membres des grands bovidés pléistocènes (Grotte de Lunel-Viel, Hérault): Perpectives évolutives. Unpublished Ph.D. dissertation, Université Aix-Marseille I.

———. 1999. "Étude de populations de grands bovidés européens: Intérêt pour la connaissance des comportements humains au Paléolithique," in *Le bison: Gibier et moyen de subsistance des hommes du Paléolithique aux Paléoindiens des Grandes Plaines.* Edited by J.-P. Brugal, F. David, J. G. Enloe, and J. Jaubert. Antibes: ADPCA, pp. 85–103.

———. 2006. Petit gibier et fonction de sites au Paléolithique supérieur: Les ensembles fauniques de la grotte d'Anecrial (Porto de Mos, Estremadure, Portugal). *Paléo* 18:45–68.

Brugal, J.-P., F. David, and C. Farizy. 1994. Quantification d'un assemblage osseux: Paramètres et tableaux. *Outillage peu élaboré en os et en bois de cervidés IV: Taphonomie/Bone Modification* 9:143–153.

Brugal, J.-P., P. Fosse, and J.-L. Guadelli. 1997. "Comparative study of bone assemblages made by recent and Pleistocene hyenids," in *Proceedings of the 1993 bone modification conference, Hot Springs,*

South Dakota. Edited by L. A. Hannus, L. Rossum, and R. P. Winham. Sioux Falls, SD: Occasional Publications No. 1. Archaeology Laboratory, Augustana College, pp. 158–187.

Bubenik, G. A., R. G. White, and L. Bartos. 2000. Antler growth in male and female reindeer and its relationship to seasonal blood levels of alkaline phosphatase. *Folia Zoologica* 49:161–166.

Bunn, H. T. 2007. "Butchering backstraps and bearing backbones: Insights from Hadza foragers and implications for Paleolithic archaeology," in *Breathing life into fossils: Taphonomic studies in honour of C.K. (Bob) Brain*. Edited by T. R. Pickering, K. Schick, and N. Toth. Gosport, IN: Stone Age Institute Press, pp. 269–279.

Bunn, H. T., L. E. Bartram, and E. M. Kroll. 1988. Variability in bone assemblage formation from Hadza hunting, scavenging, and carcass processing. *Journal of Anthropological Archaeology* 7:412–457.

Bunn, H. T., and E. M. Kroll. 1986. Systematic butchery by Plio/Pleistocene hominids at Olduvai Gorge, Tanzania. *Current Anthropology* 27:431–452.

Burch, E. 1972. The caribou/wild reindeer as a human resource. *American Antiquity* 37:339–368.

Burger, O., M. J. Hamilton, and R. Walker. 2005. The prey as patch model: Optimal handling of resources with diminishing returns. *Journal of Archaeological Science* 32:1147–1158.

Burke, A. 1995. *Prey movements and settlement patterns during the Upper Paleolithic in southern France*. British Archaeological Reports, International Series S619. Oxford: Tempus Reparatum Press.

———. 2000. Hunting in the Middle Palaeolithic. *International Journal of Osteoarchaeology* 10:281–285.

———. 2004. The ecology of Neanderthals: Preface. *International Journal of Osteoarchaeology* 14:155–161.

Burke, A., and J. Castanet. 1995. Histological observations of cementum growth in horse teeth and their application to archaeology. *Journal of Archaeological Science* 22:479–493.

Byers, D. A., and A. Ugan. 2005. Should we expect large game specialization in the late Pleistocene? An optimal foraging perspective on early Paleoindian prey choice. *Journal of Archaeological Science* 32:1624–1640.

Callou, C. 2003. *De la garenne au clapier: Étude archéozoologique du lapin en Europe occidentale*. Paris: Mémoires du Muséum National d'Histoire Naturelle.

Cann, R., M. Stoneking, and A. C. Wilson. 1987. Mitochondrial DNA and human evolution. *Nature* 325:31–36.

Cannon, M. D. 2000. Large mammal relative abundance in Pithouse and Pueblo period archaeofaunas from southwestern New Mexico: Resource depression among the Mimbres-Mogollon? *Journal of Anthropological Archaeology* 19:317–347.

———. 2001a. Large mammal resource depression and agricultural intensification: An empirical test in the Mimbres Valley, New Mexico. Unpublished Ph.D. dissertation, University of Washington.

———. 2001b. Archaeofaunal relative abundance, sample size and statistical methods. *Journal of Archaeological Science* 28:185–195.

———. 2003. A model of central place forager prey choice and an application to faunal remains from the Mimbres Valley, New Mexico. *Journal of Anthropological Archaeology* 22:1–25.

Capaldo, S. D., and R. J. Blumenschine. 1994. A quantitative diagnosis of notches made by hammerstone percussion and carnivore gnawing on bovid long bones. *American Antiquity* 59:724–748.

Cardillo, M. 2002. Body size and latitudinal gradients in regional diversity of New World birds. *Global Ecology and Biogeography* 11:59–65.

Caro, T. M. 2005. *Antipredator defenses in birds and mammals.* Chicago: University of Chicago Press.

Cassoli, P. F., and A. Tagliacozzo. 1994. Considerazioni paleontologiche, paleoecologiche e archeo-zoologiche sui micromammiferi egli uccelli dei livelli del Pleistocene superiore del Riparo di Fumane (VR) (Scavi 1988–91). *Bollettino del Museo Civico di Storia Naturale di Verona* 18:349–445.

———. 1997. Butchering and cooking of birds in the Palaeolithic site of Grotta Romanelli. *International Journal of Osteoarchaeology* 7:303–320.

Castel, J.-C. 1999. Comportements de subsistance au Solutréen et au Badegoulien d'après les faunes de Combe-Saunière (Dordogne) et du Cuzoul de Vers (Lot). Unpublished Ph.D. dissertation, Université de Bordeaux I.

Chaline, J. 1970. La signification des rongeurs dans les dépôts quaternaires. *Bulletin de l'Assocation Française pour l'Étude du Quaternaire* 7:229–241.

———. 1972. *Les rongeurs du Pléistocène moyen et supérieur de la France. Cahiers de Paléontologie.* Paris: Éditions CNRS.

Champagne, F., and R. Espitalié. 1967. La stratigraphie du Piage: Note préliminaire. *Bulletin de la Société Préhistorique Française, Études et Travaux* 64:29–34.

Chapman, M. R., and N. J. Shackleton. 1998. Millennial-scale fluctuations in North Atlantic heat flux during the last 150,000 years. *Earth and Planetary Science Letters* 159:57–70.

Chapman, M. R., N. J. Shackleton, and J.-C. Duplessy. 2000. Sea surface temperature variability during the last glacial-interglacial cycle: Assessing the magnitude and pattern of climate change in the North Atlantic. *Palaeogeography, Palaeoclimatology, Palaeoecology* 157:1–25.

Charnov, E. L. 1976. Optimal foraging, the marginal value theorem. *Theoretical Population Biology* 9:129–136.

Charnov, E. L., G. H. Orians, and K. Hyatt. 1976. Ecological implications of resource depression. *The American Naturalist* 110:247–259.

Chase, P. G. 1985. On the use of Binford's utility indices in the analysis of archaeological sites. *PACT* 11:287–302.

———. 1990. Tool-making tools and Middle Paleolithic behavior. *Current Anthropology* 31:443–447.

———. 1999. "Bison in the context of complex utilization of faunal resources: A preliminary report on the Mousterian zooarchaeology of La Quina (Charente, France)," in *Le bison: Gibier et moyen de subsistance des hommes du Paléolithique aux Paléoindiens des Grandes Plaines.* Edited by J.-P. Brugal, F. David, J. G. Enloe, and J. Jaubert. Antibes: ADPCA, pp. 159–184.

Chiotti, L., M. Patou-Mathis, and C. Vercoutère. 2003. Comportements techniques et de subsistance à l'Aurignacien ancien. La couche 11 de l'Abri Pataud (Dordogne). *Gallia Préhistoire* 45:157–203.

Cho, T.-S. 1998. Étude archéozoologique de la faune du Périgordien supérieur (couches 2, 3 et 4) de l'abri Pataud (Les Eyzies, Dordogne): Paléoécologie, taphonomie, paléoéconomie. Unpublished Ph.D. dissertation, Muséum National d'Histoire Naturelle, Paris, France.

Church, R. R., and R. L. Lyman. 2003. Small fragments make small differences in efficiency when rendering grease from fractured artiodactyl bones by boiling. *Journal of Archaeological Science* 30:1077–1084.

Churchill, S., and F. H. Smith. 2000. Makers of the early Aurignacian of Europe. *Yearbook of Physical Anthropology* 43:61–115.

Clark, G. A. 1992. "Continuity or replacement? Putting modern human origin in an evolutionary context," in *The Middle Palaeolithic: Adaptation, behaviour and variability.* Edited by H. L. Dibble and P. Mellars. Philadelphia: University Museum Monograph 72, University of Pennsylvania, pp. 183–207.

Cochard, D. 2004. Les léporidés dans la subsistance Paléolithique du sud de la France. Unpublished Ph.D. dissertation, Université de Bordeaux I.

Compagnoni, B., A. Curci, and A. Tagliacozzo. 1997. Exploitation of the fox in the Epigravettian levels of Grotta Romanelli (Apulia, Italy). *Anthropozoologica* 25–26:319–328.

Conard, N. J., and M. Bolus. 2003. Radiocarbon dating the appearance of modern humans and timing of cultural innovations in Europe: New results and new challenges. *Journal of Human Evolution* 44:331–371.

Conard, N. J., M. Bolus, P. Goldberg, and S. C. Münzel. 2006. "The last Neanderthals and first modern humans in the Swabian Jura," in *When Neanderthals and modern humans met*. Edited by N. J. Conard. Tübingen: Kerns Verlag, pp. 305–341.

Conard, N. J., M. Malina, and S. C. Münzel. 2009. New flutes document the earliest musical tradition in southwestern Germany. *Nature* 460:737–740.

Cortijo, E., L. Labeyrie, L. Vidal, M. Vautravers, M. Chapman, J.-C. Duplessy, M. Elliot, M. Arnold, J.-L. Turon, and G. Auffret. 1997. Changes in sea surface hydrology associated with Heinrich event 4 in the North Atlantic Ocean between 40° and 60°N. *Earth and Planetary Science Letters* 146:29–45.

Cossette, E. 2000. *Prélude à l'agriculture dans le nord-est américain. Le site Hector Trudel et les stratégies de subsistance entre 500 et 1000 de notre ère dans la vallée du Saint-Laurent, Québec, Canada*. Oxford: British Archaeological Reports, International Series 884.

Costamagno, S. 1999. Stratégies de chasse et fonction des sites au Magdalénien dans le sud de la France. Unpublished Ph.D. dissertation, Université de Bordeaux I.

———. 2010. "Processing techniques for bone grease rendering in Mousterian context," in *ICAZ 2010. 11th International Conference of Archaeozoology. Paris, 23–28 August 2010*. Paris: Muséum Nationale d'Histoire Naturelle, p. 115.

Costamagno, S., C. Beauval, B. Lange-Badré, B. Vandermeersch, A. Mann, and B. Maureille. 2008. Homme ou carnivore? Protocole d'étude d'ensembles osseux mixtes: L'exemple du gisement moustérien des Pradelles (Marillac-le-Franc, Charente). *Palethnologie* 1:372–400.

Costamagno, S., C. Griggo, and V. Mourre. 1999. Approche expérimentale d'un problème taphonomique: Utilisation de combustible osseux au Paléolithique. *Préhistoire Européenne* 13:167–194.

Costamagno, S., and V. Laroulandie. 2004. "L'exploitation des petits vertébrés dans les Pyrénées françaises du Paléolithique au Mésolithique: Un inventaire taphonomique et archéozoologique," in *Petits animaux et sociétés humaines. Du complément alimentaire aux ressources utilitaires*. Edited by J.-P. Brugal and J. Desse. Antibes: Éditions APDCA, pp. 403–416.

Couturier, S., D. Jean, R. Otto, and S. Rivard. 2004. *Demography of the migratory tundra caribou (Rangifer tarandus) of the Nord-du-Québec region and Labrador*. Québec: Ministère des Ressources naturelles, de la Faune et des Parcs. Direction de l'aménagement de la faune du Nord-du-Québec and Direction de la recherche sur la faune.

Cox, M. P., and M. F. Hammer. 2010. A question of scale: Human migrations writ large and small. *BMC Biology* 8:98.

Cox, M. P., D. A. Morales, A. E. Woerner, J. Sozanski, J. D. Wall, and J. D. Hammer. 2009. Autosomal resequence data reveal late stone age signals of population expansion in sub-Saharan African foraging and farming populations. *PLoS ONE* 4:6366.

Cremaschi, M., and F. Ferraro. 2007. The Upper Pleistocene in the Paglicci Cave (Gargano, southern Italy): Loess and tephra in the anthropogenic sequence. *Atti della Societa Toscana di Scienze Naturale, Memorie, Serie A* 112:153–163.

Crèvecoeur, I. 2002. Étude biométrique et morphologique des restes de mains de la couche castelperronienne du gisement de Saint-Césaire (Charente-Maritime). Unpublished DEA thesis, Université de Bordeaux I.

d'Errico, F., and M. F. Sánchez Goñi. 2003. Neandertal extinction and the millennial scale climatic variability of OIS 3. *Quaternary Science Reviews* 22:769–788.

d'Errico, F., J. Zilhao, D. Baffier, M. Julien, and J. Pelegrin. 1998. Neanderthal acculturation in Western Europe? A critical review of the evidence and its interpretation. *Current Anthropology* 39:S1–S44.

Dale, B. W., L. G. Adams, and R. T. Bowyer. 1994. Functional response of wolves preying on barren-ground caribou in a multiple-prey ecosystem. *Journal of Animal Ecology* 63:644–652.

Danchin, É., L.-A. Giraldeau, and F. Cézilly. 2005. *Écologie comportementale.* Paris: Dunod.

Dansgaard, W., S. J. Johnsen, H. B. Clausen, D. Dahl-Jensen, N. S. Gundestrup, C. U. Hammer, C. S. Hvidberg, J. P. Steffensen, A. E. Sveinbjörnsdottir, J. Jouzel, and G. Bond. 1993. Evidence for general instability of past climate from a 250-kyr ice-core record. *Nature* 364:218–220.

Dauphiné, T. C. 1976. *Biology of the Kaminuriak population of barren-ground caribou, Part 4: Growth, reproduction and energy reserves.* Canadian Wildlife Service Report Series 38. Ottawa: Environment Canada, Wildlife Service.

David, F. 2002. "Les ours du Châtelperronien de la grotte du Renne à Arcy-sur-Cure (Yonne)," in *L'Ours et l'Homme.* Edited by T. Tillet and L. R. Binford. Liège: ERAUL vol. 100, pp. 185–192.

———. 2004. Note sur l'hyène des cavernes (*Crocuta spelaea* G.) dans trois secteurs de la Grotte du Renne à Arcy-sur-Cure (Yonne): Moustérien de la galerie Schoepflin et de la Rotonde, Châtelperronien du Xc. *Revue de Paléobiologie* 23:761–769.

David, F., N. Connet, M. Girard, J.-C. Miskovsky, C. Mourer-Chauviré, and A. Roblin-Jouve. 2005. Les niveaux du Paléolithique supérieur à la grotte du Bison (Arcy-sure-Cure, Yonne): Couches a à d. *Revue Archéologique de l'Est* 54:5–50.

David, F., and J. G. Enloe. 1993. "L'exploitation des animaux sauvages de la fin du Paléolithique moyen au Magdalénien," in *Exploitation des animaux sauvages à travers le temps.* Edited by J. Desse and F. Audouin. Juan-les-Pins: Éditions APDCA, pp. 29–47.

David, F., and T. Poulain. 1990. "La faune des grands mammifères des niveaux XI et Xc de la Grotte du Renne à Arcy-sur-Cure (Yonne)," in *Paléolithique moyen récent et Paléolithique supérieur ancien en Europe.* Edited by C. Farizy. Nemours: Mémoire du Musée de Préhistoire d'Ile de France 3, pp. 319–323.

———. 2002. "Les mammifères (herbivores, carnivores, petits mammifères)," in *L'Aurignacien de la Grotte du Renne. Les fouilles d'André Leroi-Gourhan à Arcy-sur-Cure (Yonne).* Gallia Préhistoire 34. Edited by B. Schmider. Paris: Éditions CNRS, pp. 49–95.

Davidson, I. 1989. *La economía del final del Paleolítico en la España oriental.* Serie de Trabajos Varios, Servicio de Investigación Prehistórica 85.

Davis, S. J. M. 2002. The mammals and birds from the Gruta do Caldeirão, Portugal. *Arqueologia* 5:29–98.

Davis, S. J. M., I. Robert, and J. Zilhão. 2007. Caldeirão Cave (central Portugal) – whose home? Hyaena, man, bearded vulture. *Courier Forschungsinstitut Senckenberg* 259:213–226.

Debénath, A., and A. J. Jelinek. 1998. Nouvelles fouilles à La Quina (Charente): Résultats préliminaires. *Gallia Préhistoire* 40:29–74.

DeGiorgio, M., M. Jakobsson, and N. A. Rosenberg. 2009. Explaining worldwide patterns of human genetic variation using a coalescent-based serial founder model of migration outward from Africa. *Proceedings of the National Academy of Sciences* 106:16057–16062.

Del Prête, A., and B. Vandermeersch. 2001. La diaphyse fémorale droite du squelette néandertalien de Saint-Césaire. *Comptes Rendus de l'Académie des Sciences de Paris. Sciences de la Terre et des Planètes* 333:149–154.

Delagnes, A., J. Jaubert, and L. Meignen. 2007. "Les techno-complexes du Paléolithique moyen en Europe occidentale dans leur cadre diachronique et géographique," in *Les Néandertaliens. Biologie et cultures.* Edited by B. Vandermeersch and B. Maureille. Paris: Ed. du CTHS vol. 23, pp. 213–229.

Delpech, F. 1983. *Les faunes du Paléolithique supérieur dans le sud-ouest de la France.* Bordeaux: Éditions du CNRS, Cahiers du Quaternaire 6.

———. 1988. "Les grands mammifères de la grotte Vaufrey à l'exception des Ursidés," in *La Grotte Vaufrey à Cénac et Saint-Julien (Dordogne): Paléoenvironnements, chronologie et activités humaines, Mémoires de la Société Préhistorique Française* 19. Edited by J.-P. Rigaud, pp. 213–290.

———. 1996. L'environnement animal des Moustériens Quina du Périgord. *Paléo* 8:31–46.

———. 1999. Biomasse d'ongulés au Paléolithique et inférences sur la démographie. *Paléo* 11:19–42.

Delpech, F., D. K. Grayson, and J.-P. Rigaud. 2000. Biostratigraphie et paléoenvironnements du début du Würm récent d'après les grands mammifères de l'abri du Flageolet I (Dordogne, France). *Paléo* 12:97–126.

Delpech, F., and F. Prat. 1995. Nouvelles observations sur les faunes acheuléennes de Combe Grenal (Domme, Dordogne). *Paléo* 7:123–137.

Delpech, F., and J.-P. Texier. 2007. Approche stratigraphique des temps gravettiens: L'éclairage aquitain. *Paléo* 19:15–29.

Demars, P. Y., and J.-J. Hublin. 1989. "La transition néandertaliens/hommes de type moderne en Europe occidentale: Aspects paléontologiques et culturels," in *L'Homme de Néandertal*, vol. 7: *L'Extinction.* Edited by M. Otte. Liège: ERAUL 34, pp. 23–37.

Deplano, S. 1994. Étude de la faune de la couche IX de l'abri du Flageolet II (Dordogne): Approche taphonomique et palethnographique. Unpublished master's thesis, Université de Paris I.

Discamps, E. 2008. Identification d'épisodes de recrudescence de l'hyène des cavernes. Unpublished master II thesis, Université de Bordeaux I.

Discamps, E., M.-C. Soulier, F. Bachellerie, J.-G. Bordes, J.-C. Castel, and E. Morin. 2010. Quelles interactions entre changements environnementaux et culturels à la fin du Paléolithique moyen et au début du Paleolithique supérieur? Paper presented at the 27th Congrès Préhistorique de France, Bordeaux.

Djawdan, M., and T. Garland Jr. 1988. Maximal running speeds of bipedal and quadrupedal rodents. *Journal of Mammalogy* 69:765–772.

Domènech Faus, E. M. 2004. "Le Paléolithique moyen et supérieur dans le Levant Espagnol: La séquence de la Cova Beneito (Muro, Alicante, Espagne)," in *Acts of the XIVth UISPP Congress, University of Liège, Belgium, 2001, Section 6: Le Paléolithique supérieur/The Upper Palaeolithic, BAR International Series 1240.* Oxford: Archaeopress, pp. 1–5.

Drucker, D., H. Bocherens, A. Mariotti, F. Lévêque, B. Vandermeersch, and J.-L. Guadelli. 1999. Conservation des signatures isotopiques du collagène d'os et de dents du Pléistocène supérieur (Saint-Césaire, France): Implications pour les reconstitutions des régimes alimentaires des Néandertaliens. *Bulletins et Mémoires de la Société d'Anthropologie de Paris* 11:289–305.

Duarte, C., J. Maurício, P. B. Pettitt, P. Souto, E. Trinkaus, H. van der Plicht, and J. Zilhão. 1999. The early Upper Paleolithic human skeleton from the Abrigo do Lagar Velho (Portugal) and modern human emergence in Iberia. *Proceedings of the National Academy of Sciences* 96:7604–7609.

Eloranta, E., and M. Nieminen. 1986. The effects of maternal age and body weight on reindeer calf birth-weight and survival. *Rangifer* 1, appendix: 105.

Emerson, A. E. 1990. Archaeological implications of variability in the economic anatomy of *Bison bison*. Unpublished Ph.D. dissertation, Washington State University.

———. 1993. "The role of body part utility in small-scale hunting under two strategies of carcass recovery," in *From bones to behavior: Ethnoarchaeological and experimental contributions to the interpretation of faunal remains*. Edited by J. Hudson. Carbondale: Center for Archaeological Investigation, Southern Illinois University at Carbondale, pp. 138–155.

Emlen, J. M. 1966. The role of time and energy in food preference. *The American Naturalist* 100:611–617.

Enloe, J. G. 1991. Subsistence organization in the Upper Paleolithic: Carcass refitting and food sharing at Pincevent. Unpublished Ph.D. dissertation, University of New Mexico.

———. 1993. "Subsistence organization in the early Upper Paleolithic: Reindeer hunters of the Abri du Flageolet, Couche V," in *Before Lascaux: The complex record of the early Upper Paleolithic*. Edited by H. Knecht, A. Pike-Tay, and R. White. Ann Arbor: CRC Press, pp. 101–115.

———. 1997. Seasonality and age structure in remains of *Rangifer tarandus*: Magdalenian hunting strategy at Verberie. *Anthropozoologica* 25–26:95–102.

Enloe, J. G., and F. David. 1997. "Rangifer herd behavior: Seasonality of hunting in the Magdalenian of the Paris Basin," in *Caribou and reindeer hunters in the Northern Hemisphere*. Edited by L. J. Jackson and P. T. Thacker. Aldershot: Avebury Press, pp. 52–68.

Ermini, L., C. Olivieri, E. Rizzi, G. Corti, R. Bonnal, P. Soares, S. Luciani, I. Marota, G. de Bellis, M. B. Richards, and F. Rollo. 2008. Complete mitochondrial genome sequence of the Tyrolean iceman. *Current Biology* 18:1–7.

Erwin, R. M. 1989. Predator-prey interactions, resource depression and patch revisitation. *Behavioural Processes* 18:1–16.

Espmark, Y. 1971. Antler shedding in relation to parturition in females reindeer. *Journal of Wildlife Management* 35:175–177.

Eswaran, V. 2002. A diffusion wave out of Africa. *Current Anthropology* 43:749–774.

Eswaran, V., H. Harpending, and A. R. Rogers. 2005. Genomics refutes an exclusively African origin of humans. *Journal of Human Evolution* 49:1–18.

Evans, P. D., S. L. Gilbert, N. Mekel-Bobrov, E. J. Vallender, J. R. Anderson, L. M. Vaez-Azizi, S. A. Tishkoff, R. R. Hudson, and B. T. Lahn. 2005. *Microcephalin*, a gene regulating brain size, continues to evolve adaptively in humans. *Science* 309:1717–1720.

Evans, P. D., N. Mekel-Bobrov, E. J. Vallender, R. R. Hudson, and B. T. Lahn. 2006. Evidence that the adaptive allele of the brain size gene *microcephalin* introgressed into *Homo sapiens* from an archaic *Homo* lineage. *Proceedings of the National Academy of Sciences* 103:18178–18183.

Excoffier, L. 2002. Human demographic history: Refining the recent African origin model. *Current Opinion in Genetics and Development* 12:1–8.

Faith, J. T. 2007. Changes in reindeer body part representation at Grotte XVI, Dordogne, France. *Journal of Archaeological Science* 34:2003–2011.

Faivre, J. P. 2008. Organisation techno-économique des systèmes de production dans le Paléolithique moyen récent du Nord-est aquitain: Combe-Grenal et les Fieux. Unpublished Ph.D. dissertation, Université de Bordeaux I.

Farizy, C. 1994. "Behavioural and cultural changes at the Middle to Upper Palaeolithic transition in Western Europe," in *Origins of anatomically modern humans*. Edited by M. H. Nitecki and D. D. Nitecki. New York: Plenum Press, pp. 93–100.

Fedele, F. G., B. Giaccio, and I. Hajdas. 2008. Timescales and cultural process at 40,000 BP in the light of the Campanian Ignimbrite eruption, Western Eurasia. *Journal of Human Evolution* 55:834–837.

Ferrié, J.-G. 2001. La faune des niveaux Paléolithique moyen de Saint-Césaire. Paléontologie et observations archéozoologiques. Unpublished DEA thesis, Université de Bordeaux I.

Finstad, G. L., and A. K. Pritchard. 2000. Growth and body weight of free-range reindeer in western Alaska. *Rangifer* 20:221–227.

Fiore, I., M. Gala, and A. Tagliacozzo. 2004. Ecology and subsistence strategies in the eastern Italian Alps during the Middle Palaeolithic. *International Journal of Osteoarchaeology* 14:273–286.

Fischer, L. A., and C. C. Gates. 2005. Competition potential between sympatric woodland caribou and wood bison in southwestern Yukon, Canada. *Canadian Journal of Zoology* 83:1162–1173.

Flannery, K. V. 1969. "Origins and ecological effects of early domestication in Iran and the Near East," in *The domestication and exploitation of plants and animals*. Edited by P. J. Ucko and G. W. Dimbleby. Chicago: Aldine, pp. 73–100.

Fleming, T. H. 1973. Numbers of mammal species in North and Central American forest communities. *Ecology* 54:555–563.

Fletcher, W. J., M. F. Sánchez Goñi, J. R. M. Allen, R. Cheddadi, N. Combourieu-Nebout, B. Huntley, I. Lawson, L. Londeix, D. Magri, V. Margari, U. C. Muller, F. Naughton, E. Novenko, K. Roucoux, and P. C. Tzedakis. 2010. Millennial-scale variability during the last glacial in vegetation records from Europe. *Quaternary Science Reviews* 29:2839–2964.

Fontana, L. 2000. La chasse au renne au Paléolithique supérieur dans le sud-ouest de la France: Nouvelles hypothèses de travail. *Paléo* 12:141–164.

———. 2004. "Le statut du Lièvre variable (*Lepus timidus*) en Europe occidentale au Magdalénien: Premier bilan et perspectives," in *Petits animaux et sociétés humaines. Du complément alimentaire aux ressources utilitaires*. Edited by J.-P. Brugal and J. Desse. Antibes: Éditions APDCA, pp. 297–312.

Fosse, P. 1995. Le rôle de l'hyène dans la formation des associations osseuses: 150 ans de controverses. *Paléo* 7:49–84.

———. 1997. Variabilité des assemblages osseux créés par l'Hyène des cavernes. *Paléo* 9:15–54.

Franzmann, A. W., R. E. LeResche, R. A. Rausch, and J. L. Oldemeyer. 1978. Alaskan moose measurements and weights and measurement-weight relationships. *Canadian Journal of Zoology* 56:298–306.

Freckleton, R. P., P. H. Harvey, and M. Pagel. 2003. Bergmann's rule and body size in mammals. *The American Naturalist* 161:821–825.

Frison, G. C., and C. A. Reher. 1970. "Appendix I: Age determination of buffalo by tooth eruption and wear," in *The Glenrock Buffalo Jump, 48Co304: Late prehistoric period buffalo procurement and butchering in the Northwest Plains*. Memoir 7. Topeka: Plains Anthropologist, pp. 46–50.

Fritz, H., and A. Loison. 2006. "Large herbivores across biomes," in *Large herbivore ecology, ecosystem dynamics and conservation*. Edited by K. Danell, R. Bergstrom, P. Duncan, and J. Paster. Cambridge: Cambridge University Press, pp. 19–49.

Fryxell, J. M., J. Greever, and A. R. E. Sinclair. 1988. Why are migratory ungulates so abundant? *The American Naturalist* 131:781–798.

Fuller, W. A. 1959. The horns and teeth as indicators of age in bison. *Journal of Wildlife Management* 23:342–344.

Gagnon, L., and C. Barrette. 1992. Antler casting and parturition in wild female caribou. *Journal of Mammalogy* 73:440–442.

Gala, M., and A. Tagliacozzo. 2005. L'avifauna dei livelli aurignaziani di Grotta di Fumane (VR). Risultati preliminari dello studio tafonomico. *Atti del 4° Convegno Nazionale di Archeozoologia, Quaderni del Museo Archeologico del Friuli Occidentale* 6:53–57.

Gálvez, L., A. López-Pintor, J. M. de Miguel, G. Alonso, M. Rueda, S. Rebolla, and A. Gómez-Sal. 2008. "Ecosystem engineering effects of European rabbits in a Mediterranean habitat," in *Lagomorph biology: Evolution, ecology, and conservation*. Edited by P. C. Alves, N. Ferrand, and K. Hackländer. Berlin: Springer-Verlag, pp. 125–139.

Gamble, C. 1999. *The Palaeolithic societies of Europe*. Cambridge: Cambridge University Press.

Garcia i Petit, L. 1995. Preliminary study of Upper Pleistocene bird bone remains from L'Arbreda Cave (Catalonia). *Courier Forschungsinstitut Senckenberg* 181:215–227.

———. 1997. "Les restes d'oiseaux des sites de Serinyà (Pays Catalans)," in *El món mediterrani després del Pleniglacial (18.000–12.000 BP)*. Edited by J. M. Fullola and N. Soler. Sèrie Monogràfica 17. Girona: Museu d'Arqueologia de Catalunya-Girona, pp. 329–344.

Garland, T., Jr. 1983. The relation between maximal running speed and body mass in terrestrial mammals. *Journal of Zoology* 199:157–170.

Garland, T., Jr., F. Geiser, and R. V. Baudinette. 1988. Comparative locomotor performance of marsupial and placental mammals. *Journal of Zoology* 215:505–522.

Garland, T., Jr., and C. M. Janis. 1993. Does metatarsal/femur ratio predict maximal running speed on cursorial mammals? *Journal of Zoology* 229:133–151.

Garrigan, D., and M. F. Hammer. 2006. Reconstructing human origins in the genomic era. *Nature Reviews Genetics* 7:669–680.

Garrigan, D., Z. Mobasher, S. B. Kigan, J. A. Wilder, and M. F. Hammer. 2005. Deep haplotype divergence and long-range linkage disequilibrium at Xp21.1 provide evidence that humans descend from a structured ancestral population. *Genetics* 170:1849–1856.

Garrigan, D., Z. Mobasher, T. Severson, J. A. Wilder, and M. F. Hammer. 2005. Evidence for archaic Asian ancestry on the human X chromosome. *Molecular Biology and Evolution* 22:189–192.

Garrod, D. 1938. The Upper Palaeolithic in the light of recent discovery. *The Prehistoric Society* 1:1–26.

Garrott, R. A. 1991. Bias in aging feral horses. *Journal of Range Management* 44:611–613.

Gaston, K. J., S. L. Chown, and K. L. Evans. 2008. Ecogeographical rules: Elements of a synthesis. *Journal of Biogeography* 35:483–500.

Gaudzinski, S., and L. Niven. 2009. "Hominin subsistence patterns during the Middle and Late Paleolithic in Northwestern Europe," in *The evolution of hominin diets: Integrating approaches to the study of Palaeolithic subsistence*. Edited by J.-J. Hublin and M. P. Richards. Berlin: Springer, pp. 99–111.

Geist, V. 1991. Phantom subspecies: The wood bison *Bison bison "athabascae"* Rhoads 1897 is not a valid taxon, but an ecotype. *Arctic* 44:283–300.

———. 1998. *Deer of the world. Their evolution, behaviour, and ecology*. Mechanicsburg, PA: Stackpole Books.

Gende, S. M., T. P. Quinn, and M. F. Willson. 2001. Consumption choice by bears feeding on salmon. *Oecologia* 1278:372–382.

Gerber, J.-P. 1972. La faune de grands mammifères du Würm ancien dans le sud-est de la France. Unpublished Ph.D. dissertation, Université de Provence.

Gibb, J. A. 1990. "The European rabbit *Oryctolagus cuniculus*," in *Rabbits, hares and pikas: Status survey and conservation action plan*. Edited by J. A. Chapman and J. E. C. Flux. Oxford: IUCN, pp. 116–120.

Gifford-Gonzalez, D. 1991. Bones are not enough: Analogues, knowledge, and interpretive strategies in zooarchaeology. *Journal of Anthropological Archaeology* 10:215–254.

Giraldeau, L.-A. 2005. "Stratégies d'approvisionnement solitaire," in *Écologie comportementale*. Edited by É. Danchin, L. A. Giraldeau, and F. Cézilly. Paris: Dunod, pp. 129–148.

González Sampériz, P., L. Montes, and P. Utrilla. 2003. Pollen in hyena coprolites from Gabasa Cave (northern Spain). *Review of Palaeobotany and Palynology* 126:7–15.

Gordon, B. C. 1988. *Of men and reindeer herds in French Magdalenian prehistory*. International Series 390. Oxford: British Archaeological Reports.

Gravina, B., P. Mellars, and C. Bronk Ramsey. 2005. Radiocarbon dating of interstratified Neanderthal and early modern human occupations at the Chatelperronian type-site. *Nature* 438:51–56.

Grayson, D. K. 1983. *The establishment of human antiquity*. New York: Academic Press.

———. 1984. *Quantitative zooarchaeology. Topics in the analysis of archaeological faunas*. New York: Academic Press.

———. 1989. Bone transport, bone destruction, and reverse utility curves. *Journal of Archaeological Science* 16:643–652.

Grayson, D. K., and M. D. Cannon. 1999. "Human paleoecology and foraging theory in the Great Basin," in *Models for the millennium: Great Basin anthropology today*. Edited by C. Beck. Salt Lake City: University of Utah Press, pp. 141–151.

Grayson, D. K., and F. Delpech. 1998. Changing diet breadth in the early Upper Palaeolithic of southwestern France. *Journal of Archaeological Science* 25:1119–1129.

———. 2002. Specialized early Upper Palaeolithic hunters in southwestern France? *Journal of Archaeological Science* 29:1439–1449.

———. 2003. Ungulates and the Middle-to-Upper Paleolithic transition at Grotte XVI (Dordogne, France). *Journal of Archaeological Science* 30:1633–1648.

———. 2008. The large mammals of Roc de Combe (Lot, France): The Châtelperronian and Aurignacian assemblages. *Journal of Anthropological Archaeology* 27:338–362.

Grayson, D. K., F. Delpech, J.-P. Rigaud, and J. Simek. 2001. Explaining the development of dietary dominance by a single ungulate taxon at Grotte XVI, Dordogne, France. *Journal of Archaeological Science* 28:115–125.

Grayson, D. K., and C. J. Frey. 2004. Measuring skeletal part representation in archaeological faunas. *Journal of Taphonomy* 2:27–42.

Green, R. E., J. Krause, A. W. Briggs, T. Maricic, U. Stenzel, M. Kircher, N. Patterson, H. Li, W. Zhai, M. H.-Y. Fritz, N. F. Hansen, E. Y. Durand, A.-S. Malaspinas, J. D. Jensen, T. Marques-Bonet, C. Alkan, K. Prüfer, M. Meyer, H. A. Burbano, J. M. Good, R. Schultz, A. Aximu-Petri, A. Butthof, B. Höber, B. Höffner, M. Siegemund, A. Weihmann, C. Nusbaum, E. S. Lander, C. Russ, N. Novod, J. Affourtit, M. Egholm, C. Verna, P. Rudan, D. Brajkovic, Z. Kucan, I. Gusic, V. B. Doronichev, L. V. Golovanova, C. Lalueza-Fox, M. de la Rasilla, J. Fortea, A. Rosas, R. W. Schmitz, P. L. F. Johnson, E. E. Eichler, D. Falush, E. Birney, J. C. Mullikin, M. Slatkin, R. Nielsen, J. Kelso, M. Lachmann, D. Reich, and S. Pääbo. 2010. A draft sequence of the Neandertal genome. *Science* 328:710–722.

Griggo, C. 1995. Significations paléoenvironnementales des communautés animales pléistocènes reconnues dans l'abri Suard (Charente) et la grotte de Bois-Ragot (Vienne): Essai de quantification de variables climatiques. Unpublished Ph.D. dissertation, Université de Bordeaux I.

———. 2005. "Les grands Mammifères de la grotte du Bois-Ragot," in *La grotte du Bois-Ragot à Gouex (Vienne) – Magdalénien et Azilien – Essai sur les hommes et leur environnements*. Edited by A. Chollet and V. Dujardin. Paris: Société Préhistorique Française Mémoire XXXVIII, pp. 289–317.

————. 2009. "Archéozoologie des grands mammifères," in La grotte du Taillis des Coteaux, Antigny (Vienne). Rapport intermédaire de la fouille programmée pluri-annuelle 2009–2011. Edited by J. Primault. 2009. Report for the Service régional de l'archéologie. Ministère de la culture et de la communication, Préfecture de la région Poitou-Charentes, Direction régionale des affaires culturelles, pp. 94–104.

Grootes, P. M., and M. Stuiver. 1997. Oxygen 18/16 variability in Greenland snow and ice with 10^{-3}- to 10^5-year time resolution. *Journal of Geophysical Research* 102:26455–26470.

Groves, C. P. 1994. "Morphology, habitat, and taxonomy," in *Przewalski's horse: The history and biology of an endangered species*. Edited by L. Boyd and K. A. Houpt. Albany: State University of New York Press, pp. 39–59.

————. 2002. "Taxonomy of living equidae," in *Equids: Zebras, asses, and horses. Status survey and conservation action plan*. Edited by P. D. Moehlman. Cambridge: IUCN Publication Services Unit, pp. 94–107.

Guadelli, J.-L. 1987. Contribution à l'étude des zoocoenoses préhistoriques en Aquitaine (Würm ancien et interstade würmien). Unpublished Ph.D. dissertation, Université de Bordeaux I.

————. 1998. Détermination de l'âge des chevaux fossiles et établissement des classes d'âge. *Paléo* 10:87–93.

————. 1999. "Quelques clés de détermination des portions pétreuses de temporal de(s) bison(s). Comparaisons avec les rochers de *Bos*," in *Le bison: Gibier et moyen de subsistance des hommes du Paléolithique aux Paléoindiens des Grandes Plaines*. Edited by J.-P. Brugal, F. David, J. G. Enloe, and J. Jaubert. Antibes: ADPCA, pp. 51–62.

Guadelli, J. L., M. Lenoir, L. Marambat, and M. M. Paquereau. 1988. "Un gisement de l'interstade würmien en Gironde: Le gisement de Camiac à Camiac-et-Saint-Denis," in *L'Homme de Néandertal*, vol. 4: La Technique. Edited by M. Otte. Liège: ERAUL, pp. 59–69.

Guerra, R. F., and C. Ades. 2002. An analysis of travel costs on transport of load and nest building in golden hamster. *Behavioural Processes* 57:7–28.

Guffy, M. M., W. C. Bergin, and H. T. Gier. 1970. Radiographic fetometry of the horse. *The Cornell Veterinarian* 39:359–371.

Guibert, P., F. Bechtel, L. Bourguignon, M. Brenet, I. Couchoud, A. Delagnes, F. Delpech, L. Detrain, M. Duttine, M. Folgado, J. Jaubert, C. Lahaye, M. Lenoir, B. Maureille, J.-P. Texier, A. Turq, E. Vieillevigne, and G. Villeneuve. 2008. "Une base de données pour la chronologie du Paléolithique moyen dans le Sud-Ouest de la France," in *Les sociétés du Paléolithique dans un grand Sud-Ouest de la France: Nouveaux gisements, nouveaux résultats, nouvelles méthodes*. Edited by J. Jaubert, J.-G. Bordes, and I. Ortega. Paris: Société Préhistorique Française Mémoire XLVII, pp. 19–40.

Guilbaud, M. 1993. "Debitage from the Upper Castelperronian level at Saint-Césaire: Methodological approach and implications for the transition from the Middle to Upper Paleolithic," in *Context of a late Neandertal: Implications of multidisciplinary research for the transition to Upper Paleolithic adaptations at Saint-Césaire*. Monographs in World Archaeology 16. Edited by F. Lévêque, A. M. Backer, and M. Guilbaud. Madison: Prehistory Press, pp. 37–58.

Guiot, J. 1990. Methodology of the last climatic cycle reconstruction in France from pollen data. *Palaeogeography, Palaeoclimatology, Palaeoecology* 80:49–69.

Guiot, J., and R. Cheddadi. 2004. Variabilité des écosystèmes terrestres et du climat sur un cycle glaciaire-interglaciaire. *Comptes Rendus Geoscience* 336:667–675.

Gunn, A. 2003. Voles, lemmings and caribou – population cycles revisited? *Rangifer Special Issue* 14:105–111.

Guthrie, R. D. 1984. "Mosaics, allelochemics and nutrients: An ecological theory of Late Pleistocene megafaunal extinctions," in *Quaternary extinctions: A prehistoric revolution*. Edited by P. S. Martin and R. G. Klein. Tucson: University of Arizona Press, pp. 259–298.

Hames, R. B. 1992. "Time allocation," in *Evolutionary ecology and human behavior*. Edited by E. A. Smith and B. Winterhalder. New York: Aldine, pp. 203–236.

Hames, R. B., and W. T. Vickers. 1982. Optimal diet breath theory as a model to explain variability in Amazonian hunting. *American Ethnologist* 9:358–378.

Hardy, J., A. Pittman, A. Myers, K. Gwinn-Hardy, H. C. Fung, R. de Silva, M. Hutton, and J. Duckworth. 2005. Evidence suggesting that *Homo neanderthalensis* contributed the H2 MAPT haplotype to *Homo sapiens*. *Biochemical Society Transactions* 33:582–585.

Harris, E. E., and J. Hey. 1999. X chromosome evidence for ancient human histories. *Proceedings of the National Academy of Sciences of USA* 96:3320–3324.

Harrold, F. B. 1981. New perspectives on the Châtelperronian. *Ampurias* 43:1–51.

Hawkes, K., and R. Bliege Bird. 2002. Showing off, handicap signaling, and the evolution of men's work. *Evolutionary Anthropology* 11:58–67.

Hawkes, K., K. Hill, and J. F. O'Connell. 1982. Why hunters gather: Optimal foraging and the Ache of eastern Paraguay. *American Ethnologist* 9:379–398.

Hawkes, K., and J. F. O'Connell. 1992. On optimal foraging models and subsistence transitions. *Current Anthropology* 33:63–66.

Hawkes, K., J. F. O'Connell, and N. G. Blurton Jones. 1995. Hadza children's foraging: Juvenile dependency, social arrangements, and mobility among hunter-gatherers. *Current Anthropology* 36:688–700.

———. 2001. Hadza meat sharing. *Evolution and Human Behavior* 22:113–142.

Hawkes, K., J. F. O'Connell, and J. E. Coxworth. 2010. Family provisioning is not the only reason men hunt: A comment on Gurven and Hill. *Current Anthropology* 51:259–264.

Hawks, J., K. Hunley, S.-H. Lee, and M. H. Wolpoff. 2000. Population bottlenecks and Pleistocene human evolution. *Molecular Biology and Evolution* 17:2–22.

Hayakawa, T., I. Aki, A. Varki, Y. Satta, and N. Takahata. 2006. Fixation of the human-specific CMP- N-Acetylneuraminic acid hydroxylase pseudogene and implications of haplotype diversity for human evolution. *Genetics* 172:1139–1146.

Haynes, G. 1983. Frequencies of spiral and green-bone fractures on ungulate limb bones in modern surface assemblages. *American Antiquity* 48:102–114.

———. 1984. Tooth wear rate in northern bison. *Journal of Mammalogy* 65:487–491.

Helle, T. 1980. "Sex segregation during calving and summer period in wild forest reindeer (*Rangifer tarandus fennicus* Lönn.) in eastern Finland with special reference to habitat requirements and dietary preferences," in *Proceedings of the second international reindeer/caribou symposium*. Edited by E. Reimers, E. Gaare, and S. Skjenneberg. Trondheim, Norway: Direktoratet for Vilt og Ferskvannsfisk, pp. 508–518.

Hemming, S. R. 2004. Heinrich Events: Massive Late Pleistocene detritus layers of the North Atlantic and their global climate imprint. *Review of Geophysics* 42:1–43.

Henri-Martin, L. 1907. *Recherches sur l'évolution du Moustérien dans le gisement de La Quina (Charente) – Premier fascicule: Industrie osseuse*. Paris: Schleicher Frères.

Henry-Gambier, D., B. Maureille, and R. White. 2004. Vestiges humains des niveaux de l'Aurignacian ancien du site de Brassempouy (Landes). *Bulletins et Mémoires de la Société d'Anthropologie de Paris* 16:49–87.

Henry-Gambier, D., and D. Sacchi. 2008. La Crouzade V-VI (Aude, France): Un des plus anciens fossiles d'anatomie moderne en Europe occidentale. *Bulletins et Mémoires de la Société d'Anthropologie de Paris* 20:79–104.

Henshilwood, C. S., and C. W. Marean. 2003. The origin of modern human behaviour: Critique of the models and their test implications. *Current Anthropology* 44:627–651.

Hernández Carrasquilla, F. 2001. A new species of vulture (Aves, Aegypiinae) from the Upper Pleistocene of Spain. *Ardeola* 48:47–53.

Higham, T., R. Jacobi, M. Julien, F. David, L. Basell, R. Wood, W. Davies, and C. B. Ramsey. 2010. Chronology of the Grotte du Renne (France) and implications for the context of ornaments and human remains within the Châtelperronian. *Proceedings of the National Academy of Sciences* 107:20234–20239.

Higham, T., C. B. Ramsey, I. Karanavic, F. H. Smith, and E. Trinkaus. 2006. Revised direct radiocarbon dating of the Vindija G1 Upper Paleolithic Neandertals. *Proceedings of the National Academy of Sciences* 103:553–557.

Hill, K. 1988. Macronutrient modifications of optimal foraging theory: An approach using indifference curves applied to some modern foragers. *Human Ecology* 16:157–197.

Hill, K., K. Hawkes, M. Hurtado, and H. Kaplan. 1984. Seasonal variance in the diet of Ache hunter-gatherers in Eastern Paraguay. *Human Ecology* 12:101–135.

Hill, K., K. Hawkes, H. Kaplan, and A. M. Hurtado. 1987. Foraging decisions among Ache hunter-gatherers: New data and implications for optimal foraging models. *Ethology and Sociobiology* 8:1–36.

Hockett, B. S., and J. A. Haws. 2002. Taphonomic and methodological perspectives of leporid hunting during the Upper Paleolithic of the western Mediterranean Basin. *Journal of Archaeological Method and Theory* 9:269–302.

————. 2009. Continuity in animal resource diversity in the Late Pleistocene human diet of Central Portugal. *Before Farming* 2009/2, article 2:1–14.

Hoffecker, J. F. 2002. *Desolate landscapes: Ice-age settlement in Eastern Europe*. Piscataway, NJ: Rutgers University Press.

————. 2009. "Neanderthal and modern human diet in Eastern Europe," in *The evolution of hominin diet: Integrating approaches to the study of Palaeolithic subsistence*. Edited by J.-J. Hublin and M. P. Richards. Berlin: Springer, pp. 87–98.

Hoffecker, J. F., V. T. Holliday, M. V. Anikovich, A. A. Sinitsyn, V. V. Popov, S. N. Lisitsyn, G. M. Levkovskaya, G. A. Pospelova, S. L. Forman, and B. Giaccio. 2008. From the Bay of Naples to the River Don: The Campanian Ignimbrite eruption and the Middle to Upper Paleolithic transition in Eastern Europe. *Journal of Human Evolution* 55:858–870.

Hoffecker, J. F., I. E. Kuz'mina, E. V. Syromyatnikova, M. V. Anikovich, A. A. Sinitsyn, V. V. Popov, and V. T. Holliday. 2010. Evidence for kill-butchery events of early Upper Paleolithic age at Kostenki, Russia. *Journal of Archaeological Science* 37:1073–1089.

Holand, Ø., H. Gjøstein, A. Losvar, J. Kumpula, M. E. Smith, K. H. Roed, M. Nieminen, and R. B. Weladji. 2004. Social rank in female reindeer (*Rangifer tarandus*): Effects of body mass, antler size and age. *Journal of Zoology* 263:365–372.

Holthe, V. 1975. "Calving season in different populations of wild reindeer in south Norway," in *Proceedings of the first international reindeer and caribou symposium*. Edited by J. R. Luick, P. C. Lent, D. R. Klein, and R. G. White. Fairbanks: Biological Papers of the University of Alaska, pp. 194–198.

Howells, W. W. 1976. Explaining modern man: Evolutionists versus migrationists. *Journal of Human Evolution* 5:477–495.

Høymork, A., and E. Reimers. 2002. Antler development in reindeer in relation to age and sex. *Rangifer* 22:75–82.

Hrdlicka, A. 1927. The Neanderthal phase of man. *Journal of the Royal Anthropological Institute* 67:249–269.

Hublin, J.-J., C. B. Ruiz, P. M. Lara, M. Fontugne, and J. L. Reyss. 1995. The Mousterian site of Zafarraya (Andalucia, Spain): Dating and implications on the Palaeolithic peopling processes of Western Europe. *Comptes Rendus de l'Académie des Sciences de Paris* 321, série IIa:931–937.

Hufthammer, A. K. 1995. Age determination of reindeer (*Rangifer tarandus* L.). *Archaeozoologia* 7:33–42.

Hunley, K. L., M. E. Healy, and J. C. Long. 2009. The global pattern of gene identity variation reveals a history of long-range migrations, bottlenecks, and local mate exchange: Implications for biological race. *American Journal of Physical Anthropology* 139:35–46.

Hurtado, A. M., and K. Hill. 1990. Seasonality in a foraging society: Variation in diet, work effort, fertility, and sexual division of labor among the Hiwi of Venezuela. *Journal of Anthropological Research* 46:293–346.

International Human Genome Sequencing Consortium. 2010. A map of human genome variation from population-scale sequencing. *Nature* 467:1062–1073.

Iriarte-Díaz, J. 2002. Differential scaling of locomotor performance in small and large terrestrial mammals. *The Journal of Experimental Biology* 205:2897–2908.

Irving, L., K. Schmidt-Nielsen, and S. B. Abrahamsen. 1957. On the melting points of animal fats in cold climates. *Physiological Zoölogy* 30:93–105.

Jacobi, R. M., T. F. G. Higham, and C. B. Ramsey. 2006. AMS radiocarbon dating of Middle and Upper Palaeolithic bone in the British Isles: Improved reliability using ultrafiltration. *Journal of Quaternary Science* 21:557–573.

Jaubert, J., J.-J. Hublin, S. P. McPherron, M. Soressi, J.-G. Bordes, É. Claud, D. Cochard, A. Delagnes, J.-B. Mallye, A. Michel, M. Niclot, L. Niven, S.-J. Park, W. Rendu, M. Richards, D. Richter, M. Roussel, T. E. Steele, J.-P. Texier, and C. Thiébaut. 2008. "Paléolithique moyen récent et Paléolithique supérieur ancien à Jonzac (Charente-Maritime): Premiers résultats des campagnes 2004–2006," in *Les sociétés du Paléolithique dans un grand Sud-Ouest de la France: Nouveaux gisements, nouveaux résultats, nouvelles méthodes.* Edited by J. Jaubert, J.-G. Bordes, and I. Ortega. Paris: Société Préhistorique Française Mémoire XLVII, pp. 203–243.

Jenkins, S. H. 1980. A size-distance relation in food selection by beavers. *Ecology* 61:740–746.

Jones, E. L. 2004a. Dietary evenness, prey choice, and human-environment interactions. *Journal of Archaeological Science* 31:307–317.

———. 2004b. "The European rabbit (*Oryctolagus cuniculus*) and the development of broad-spectrum diets in south-western France: Data from the Dordogne Valley," in *Petits animaux et sociétés humaines. Du complément alimentaire aux ressources utilitaires.* Edited by J.-P. Brugal and J. Desse. Antibes: Éditions APDCA, pp. 223–234.

———. 2006. Prey choice, mass collecting, and the wild European rabbit (*Oryctolagus cuniculus*). *Journal of Anthropological Archaeology* 25:275–289.

———. 2009. Climate change, patch choice, and intensification at Pont d'Ambon (Dordogne, France) during the Younger Dryas. *Quaternary Research* 72:371–376.

Jones, K. T., and D. B. Madsen. 1989. Calculating the cost of resource transportation: A Great Basin example. *Current Anthropology* 30:529–534.

Jones, K. T., and D. Metcalfe. 1988. Bare bones archaeology: Bone marrow indices and efficiency. *Journal of Archaeological Science* 15:415–423.

Julien, M., D. Baffier, D. Liolios, and B. Schmider. 2002. "L'outillage en matières dures animales," in *L'Aurignacien de la Grotte du Renne. Les fouilles d'André Leroi-Gourhan à Arcy-sur-Cure (Yonne).* Gallia Préhistoire 34. Edited by B. Schmider. Paris: CNRS Éditions, pp. 217–250.

Kaplan, H., and K. Hill. 1992. "The evolutionary ecology of food acquisition," in *Evolutionary ecology and human behaviour.* Edited by E. A. Smith and B. Winterhalder. New York: Aldine de Gruyter, pp. 167–201.

Kaplan, H., K. Hill, J. Lancaster, and A. M. Hurtado. 2000. A theory of human life history evolution: Diet, intelligence, and longevity. *Evolutionary Anthropology* 9:156–185.

Keegan, W. F. 1986. The optimal foraging analysis of horticultural production. *American Anthropologist* 88:92–107.

Keeley, L. H. 1988. Hunter-gatherer economic complexity and "population pressure": A cross-cultural analysis. *Journal of Anthropological Anthropology* 7:373–411.

Kelly, R. L. 1995. *The foraging spectrum.* Washington, DC: Smithsonian Institution Press.

Kelsall, J. P. 1968. *The migratory barren-ground caribou of Canada.* Ottawa: Queen's Printer.

Kersten, A. M. P. 1991. Birds from the Palaeolithic rock shelter of Ksar 'Akil, Lebanon. *Paléorient* 17:99–116.

King, S. R. B., and J. Gurnell. 2005. Habitat use and spatial dynamics of takhi introduced to Hustai National Park, Mongolia. *Biological Conservation* 124:277–290.

———. 2007. Scent-marking behaviour by stallions: An assessment of function in a reintroduced population of Przewalski horses (*Equus ferus przewalskii*). *Journal of Zoology* 272:30–36.

Klein, R. G. 1989. Why does skeletal part representation differ between smaller and larger bovids at Klasies River Mouth and other archaeological sites? *Journal of Archaeological Science* 6:363–381.

———. 2003. Whither the Neanderthals? *Science* 299:1525–1527.

———. 2008. Out of Africa and the evolution of human behavior. *Evolutionary Anthropology* 17:267–281.

Klein, R. G., and K. Cruz-Uribe. 1983. The computation of ungulate age (mortality) profiles from dental crown heights. *Paleobiology* 9:70–78.

———. 1984. *The analysis of animal bones from archaeological sites.* Chicago: University of Chicago Press.

Kojola, I., T. Helle, E. Huhta, and A. Niva. 1998. Foraging conditions, tooth wear and herbivore body reserves: A study of female reindeer. *Oecologia* 117:26–30.

Kolb, H. H. 1985. The burrow structure of the European rabbit (*Oryctolagus cuniculus* L.). *Journal of Zoology* 206.

Koster, J. M. 2008a. Hunting with dogs in Nicaragua: An optimal foraging approach. *Current Anthropology* 49:935–944.

———. 2008b. The impact of hunting with dogs on wildlife harvests in the Bosawas Reserve, Nicaragua. *Environmental Conservation* 35:221–220.

Koumouzelis, M., B. Ginter, J. K. Kozlowski, M. Pawlikowski, O. Bar-Yosef, R. M. Albert, M. Litynska-Zajac, E. Stworzewicz, P. Wojtal, G. Lipecki, T. Tomek, Z. M. Bochenski, and A. Pazdur. 2001a. The Early Upper Palaeolithic in Greece: The excavations in Klisoura Cave. *Journal of Archaeological Science* 28:515–539.

Koumouzelis, M., J. K. Kozlowski, C. Escutenaire, V. Sitlivy, K. Sobczyk, H. Valladas, N. Tisnerat-Laborde, P. Wojtal, and B. Ginter. 2001b. La fin du Paléolithique moyen et le début du Paléolithique supérieur en Grèce: La séquence de la Grotte 1 de Klissoura. *L'Anthropologie* 105:469–504.

Krasinska, M., K. Cabon-Raczynska, and Z. A. Krasinski. 1987. Strategy of habitat utilization by European bison in the Bialowieza forest. *Acta Theriologica* 32:147–202.

Kreutzer, L. A. 1992. Bison and deer bone mineral densities: Comparisons and implications for the interpretation of archaeological faunas. *Journal of Archaeological Science* 19:271–294.

Krings, M., C. Capelli, F. Tschentscher, H. Geisert, S. Meyer, A. Von Haeseler, K. Grossschmidt, G. Possnert, M. Paunovic, and S. Pääbo. 2000. A view of Neandertal genetic diversity. *Nature Genetics* 26:144–146.

Krings, M., A. Stone, R. W. Schmitz, H. Krainitzid, M. Stoneking, and S. Pääbo. 1997. Neandertal DNA sequences and the origin of modern humans. *Cell* 90:19–30.

Kuhn, S. L. 2004. Upper Paleolithic raw material economies at Üçağızlı cave, Turkey. *Journal of Anthropological Archaeology* 23:431–448.

Kuhn, S. L., and M. C. Stiner. 1992. New research on Riparo Mochi, Balzi Rossi (Liguria): Preliminary results. *Quaternaria Nova* 2:77–90.

———. 1998. The earliest Aurignacian of Riparo Mochi (Liguria, Italy). *Current Anthropology* 39:S175–S189.

———. 2006. What's a mother to do? The division of labor among Neandertals and modern humans in Eurasia. *Current Anthropology* 47:953–980.

Kuhn, S. L., M. C. Stiner, E. Güleç, I. Özer, H. Yilmaz, I. Baykara, A. Açikkol, P. Goldberg, K. Martínez Molina, E. Ünay, and F. Suata-Alpaslan. 2009. The early Upper Paleolithic occupations at Üçağızlı Cave (Hatay, Turkey). *Journal of Human Evolution* 56:87–113.

Kumpula, J., K. Kumpula, and M. Nieminen. 1992. Dominance relationships among female semi-domesticated reindeer: The function of antlers. *Rangifer* 12:173–174.

Lalueza, C., A. Pérez-Pérez, and D. Turbón. 1996. Dietary inferences through buccal microwear analysis of Middle and Upper Pleistocene human fossils. *American Journal of Physical Anthropology* 100:367–387.

Lam, Y. M., X. Chen, and O. M. Pearson. 1999. Intertaxonomic variability in patterns of bone density and the differential representation of bovid, cervid, and equid elements in the archaeological record. *American Antiquity* 64:343–362.

Lam, Y. M., and O. M. Pearson. 2005. Bone density studies and the interpretation of the faunal record. *Evolutionary Anthropology* 14:99–108.

Lambeck, K., A. Purcell J. Zhao, and N.-O. Svensson. 2010. The Scandinavian Ice Sheet: From MIS 4 to the end of the Last Glacial Maximum. *Boreas* 39:410–435.

Langlais, M. 2008. Chronologie et territoires au Magdalénien entre le Rhône et l'Èbre: L'exemple des armatures lithiques. *Palethnologie* 1:220–249.

Laquay, G. 1981. Recherches sur les faunes du Würm I en Périgord. Unpublished Ph.D. dissertation, Université de Bordeaux I.

Laroulandie, V. 2000. Taphonomie et archéozoologie des oiseaux en grotte: Applications aux sites paléolithiques du Bois-Ragot (Vienne), de Combe Saunière (Dordogne) et de la Vache (Ariège). Unpublished Ph.D. dissertation, Université de Bordeaux I.

———. 2003. "Exploitation des oiseaux au Magdalénien en France: État des lieux," in *Mode de vie au Magdalénien: Apports de l'archéozoologie*. Edited by S. Costamagno and V. Laroulandie. British Archaeological Reports, International Series 1144. Oxford: Archaeopress, pp. 129–138.

————. 2004a. "Exploitation des ressources aviaires durant le Paléolithique en France: Bilan critique et perspectives," in *Petits animaux et sociétés humaines. Du complément alimentaire aux ressources utilitaires*. Edited by J.-P. Brugal and J. Desse. Antibes: Éditions APDCA, pp. 163–172.

————. 2004b. "Les oiseaux de Saint-Césaire," in Late Pleistocene population interaction in western Europe and modern human origins: New insights based on the faunal remains from Saint-Césaire, southwestern France. Edited by E. Morin. Unpublished Ph.D. dissertation, University of Michigan, pp. 390–394.

Lau, A. N., L. Peng, H. Goto, L. Chemnick, O. A. Ryder, and K. D. Makova. 2009. Horse domestication and conservation genetics of Przewalski's horse inferred from sex chromosomal and autosomal sequences. *Molecular Biology and Evolution* 26:199–208.

Lavaud-Girard, F. 1987. "Les gisements castelperroniens de Quinçay et de St-Césaire. Quelques comparaisons préliminaires – les faunes," in *Préhistoire de Poitou-Charente: Problèmes actuels*. Edited by F. Lavaud-Girard. Paris: Éditions du Comité des Travaux Historiques et Scientifiques, pp. 115–123.

————. 1993. "Macrofauna from Castelperronian levels at Saint-Césaire," in *Context of a late Neandertal: Implications of multidisciplinary research for the transition to Upper Paleolithic adaptations at Saint-Césaire*. Monographs in World Archaeology 16. Edited by F. Lévêque, A. M. Backer, and M. Guilbaud. Madison: Prehistory Press, pp. 71–77.

Le Gall, O. 1992. Poissons et pêches au Paléolithique (Quelques données de l'Europe occidentale). *L' Anthropologie* 96:121–134.

————. 1999. "Éléments de réflexion sur la pêche dans le bassin méditerranéen nord-occidental pendant le développement des faciès leptolithiques," in *Les faciès leptolithiques du nord-ouest méditerranéen: Milieux naturels et culturels*. Edited by D. Sacchi. Paris: Société Préhistorique Française, pp. 251–265.

————. 2000. Les Moustériens étaient-ils pêcheurs? *Bulletin de la Société d'Anthropologie du Sud-Ouest* 34:3–11.

————. 2003. La squelettochronologie appliquée aux poissons. Une méthode de reconnaissance des saisons de capture. *Bulletin de Préhistoire du Sud-Ouest* 10:9–24.

Lee, R. B., and I. DeVore. 1968. *Man the hunter*. New York: Aldine.

Lee-Thorp, J. A. 2008. On isotopes and old bones. *Archaeometry* 50:925–950.

Lee-Thorp, J. A., and M. Sponheimer. 2006. Contribution of biogeochemistry to understanding hominin dietary ecology. *Yearbook of Physical Anthropology* 49:131–148.

Leechman, D. 1951. Bone grease. *American Antiquity* 16:355–356.

Leroi-Gourhan, A. 1961. Les fouilles d'Arcy-sur-Cure (Yonne). *Gallia Préhistoire* 4:3–16.

————. 1984. La place du Néandertalien de St-Césaire dans la chronologie würmienne. *Bulletin de la Société Préhistorique Française* 81:196–198.

Leroi-Gourhan, A., and A. Leroi-Gourhan. 1964. Chronologie des grottes d'Arcy-sur-Cure. *Gallia Préhistoire* 7:1–64.

Leroyer, C. 1988. "Des occupations castelperroniennes et aurignaciennes dans leur cadre chrono-climatique," in *L'Homme de Neanderthal*, vol. 8: La Mutation. Edited by M. Otte. Liège: ERAUL, pp. 103–108.

Leroyer, C., and A. Leroi-Gourhan. 1993. "Pollen analysis at Saint-Césaire," in *Context of a late Neandertal: Implications of multidisciplinary research for the transition to Upper Paleolithic adaptations at Saint-Césaire*. Monographs in World Archaeology 16. Edited by F. Lévêque, A. M. Backer, and M. Guilbaud. Madison: Prehistory Press, pp. 59–70.

Letourneux, C. 2003. Devinez qui est venu dîner à Brassempouy? Approche taphonomique pour une interprétation archéozoologique des vestiges osseux de l'Aurignacien ancien de la grotte des Hyènes (Brassempouy, Landes). Unpublished Ph.D. dissertation, Université de Paris I – Panthéon Sorbonne.

Lévêque, F. 1987. "Les gisements castelperroniens de Quinçay et de St-Césaire: Quelques comparaisons préliminaires. Stratigraphie et industries," in *Préhistoire de Poitou-Charente: Problèmes actuels*. Edited by F. Lavaud-Girard. Paris: Editions du Comité des Travaux Historiques et Scientifiques, pp. 91–98.

―――. 1989. "L'homme de Saint-Césaire: Sa place dans le Castelperronien de Poitou-Charentes," in *L'Homme de Néandertal*, vol. 7: L'Extinction. Edited by M. Otte. Liège: ERAUL, pp. 99–108.

―――. 1993a. "Introduction to Saint-Césaire," in *Context of a late Neandertal: Implications of multidisciplinary research for the transition to Upper Paleolithic adaptations at Saint-Césaire, Monographs in World Archaeology 16*. Edited by F. Lévêque, A. M. Backer, and M. Guilbaud. Madison: Prehistory Press, pp. 1–6.

―――. 1993b. "The Castelperronian industry of Saint-Césaire: The upper level," in *Context of a late Neandertal: Implications of multidisciplinary research for the transition to Upper Paleolithic adaptations at Saint-Césaire, Monographs in World Archaeology 16*. Edited by F. Lévêque, A. M. Backer, and M. Guilbaud. Madison: Prehistory Press, pp. 23–35.

―――. 1997. Le passage du Paléolithique moyen au Paléolithique supérieur: Données stratigraphiques de quelques gisements sous-grotte du sud-ouest. *Quaternaria* 8:279–287.

―――. 2002. "Méthodes de fouilles," in *Géologie de la préhistoire: Méthodes, techniques, applications*. Edited by J.-C. Miskovsky. Paris: Géopré, pp. 415–423.

Lévêque, F., A. M. Backer, and M. Guilbaud. Editors. 1993. *Context of a late Neandertal: Implications of multidisciplinary research for the transition to Upper Paleolithic adaptations at Saint-Césaire*. Madison: Monographs in World Archaeology 16, Prehistory Press.

Lévêque, F., and J.-C. Miskovsky. 1983. Le Castelperronien dans son environnement géologique. Essai de synthèse à partir de l'étude lithostratigraphique du remplissage de la grotte de la grande Roche de la Plématrie (Quincay, Vienne) et d'autres dépôts actuellement mis au jour. *L'Anthropologie* 87:369–391.

Lévêque, F., and B. Vandermeersch. 1980. Découverte de restes humains dans un horizon castelperronien de Saint-Césaire (Charente-Maritime). *Bulletin de la Société Préhistorique Française* 77:35.

Levine, M. A. 1979. Archaeozoological analysis of some Upper Pleistocene horse bone assemblages in Western Europe. Unpublished Ph.D. dissertation, Cambridge University.

Li, J. Z., D. M. Absher, H. Tang, A. M. Southwick, A. M. Casto, S. Ramachandran, H. M. Cann, G. S. Barsh, M. Feldman, L. L. Cavalli-Sforza, and R. M. Myers. 2008. Worldwide human relationships inferred from genome-wide patterns of variation. *Science* 319:1100–1104.

Lieberman, D. E., and J. J. Shea. 1994. Behavioural differences between archaic and modern humans in the Levantine Mousterian. *American Anthropologist* 96:300–322.

Lima, S. L. 1993. Ecological and evolutionary perspectives on escape from predatory attack: A survey of North American birds. *Wilson Bulletin* 105:1–47.

Lindsey, C. C. 1966. Body sizes of poikilotherm vertebrates at different latitudes. *Evolution* 20:456–465.

Liolios, D. 1999. Variabilité et caractéristiques du travail des matières osseuses au début de l'Aurignacien: Approche technologique et économique. Unpublished Ph.D. dissertation, Université Paris X – Nanterre.

Lloveras, L., M. Moreno-García, J. Nadal, J. Maroto, J. Soler, and N. Soler. 2010. The application of actualistic studies to assess the taphonomic origin of Mousterian rabbit accumulations from Arbreda Cave (North-East Iberia). *Archaeofauna* 19:99–119.

Lomolino, M. V., B. R. Riddle, and J. H. Brown. 2006. *Biogeography*, 3rd edition. Sunderland, MA: Sinauer Associates.

Lupo, K. D. 2006. What explains the carcass field processing and transport decisions of contemporary hunter-gatherers? Measures of economic anatomy and zooarchaeological skeletal part representation. *Journal of Archaeological Method and Theory* 13:19–66.

———. 2007. Evolutionary foraging models in zooarchaeological analysis: Recent applications and future challenges. *Journal of Archaeological Research* 15:143–189.

Lupo, K. D., and D. N. Schmitt. 2002. Upper Paleolithic net-hunting, small prey exploitation, and women's work effort: A view from the ethnographic and ethnoarchaeological record of the Congo Basin. *Journal of Archaeological Method and Theory* 9:147–178.

———. 2005. Small prey hunting technology and zooarchaeological measures of taxonomic diversity and abundance: Ethnoarchaeological evidence from Central African forest foragers. *Journal of Anthropological Archaeology* 24:335–353.

Lyman, R. L. 1987. On the analysis of vertebrate mortality profiles: Sample size, mortality, type, and hunting pressure. *American Antiquity* 52:125–142.

———. 1994. *Vertebrate taphonomy*. Cambridge: Cambridge University Press.

———. 2003. Pinniped behavior, foraging theory, and the development of metapopulations and nondepression of a local population on the southern Northwest Coast of North America. *Journal of Anthropological Archaeology* 22:376–388.

———. 2008. *Quantitative paleozoology*. Cambridge: Cambridge University Press.

Lyman, R. L., and M. J. O'Brien. 1987. Plow-zone zooarchaeology: Fragmentation and identifiability. *Journal of Field Archaeology* 14:493–498.

MacArthur, R. H., and E. R. Pianka. 1966. On optimal use of a patchy environment. *The American Naturalist* 100:603–609.

MacDonald, D., and P. Barrett. 2001. *Mammals of Europe*. Princeton: Princeton University Press.

Madsen, D. B., and D. N. Schmitt. 1998. Mass collecting and the diet breadth model: A Great Basin example. *Journal of Archaeological Science* 25:445–455.

Magniez, P. 2010. Étude paléontologique des artiodactyles de la grotte Tournal (Bize-Minervois, Aude, France). Étude taphonomique, archéozoologique et paléoécologique des grands mammifères dans leur cadre biostratigraphique et paléoenvironnemental. Unpublished Ph.D. dissertation, Université de Perpignan.

Magurran, A. E. 2004. *Measuring biological diversity*. Oxford: Blackwell Publishing.

Mahoney, S. P., and J. A. Schaefer. 2002. Long-term changes in demography and migration of Newfoundland caribou. *Journal of Mammalogy* 83:957–963.

Maitland, P. S. 2000. *Guide to freshwater fish of Britain and Europe*. London: Hamlyn.

Manne, T. H., and N. F. Bicho. 2009. Vale Boi: Rendering new understanding of resource intensification and diversification in southwestern Iberia. *Before Farming* 2009/2, article 1:1–21.

Manne, T. H., M. C. Stiner, and N. F. Bicho. 2005. "Evidence for bone grease rendering during the Upper Paleolithic at Vale Boi (Algarve, Portugal)," in *Animais na pré-história e arqueologia da península Ibérica. Actas do I Congresso de Arqueología Peninsular. Promontorio monográfica*. Edited by N. F. Bicho. Faro: Universidade do Algarve, pp. 145–158.

Marean, C. W., and S. Y. Kim. 1998. Mousterian large-mammal remains from Kobeh Cave: Behavioral implications for Neanderthals and early modern humans. *Current Anthropology* 39:S79–S113.

Marom, N., and G. Bar-Oz. 2008. "Measure for measure": A taphonomic reconsideration of the Kebaran site of Ein Gev I, Israel. *Journal of Archaeological Science* 35:214–227.

Maroto, J., S. Ramió, and A. Solés. 2001. The *Ursus spelaeus* disappearance archaeologically registered in the Northeast of Catalonia. *Cadernos do Laboratorio Xeolóxico de Laxe* 26:407–414.

Maroto, J., J. Rosell, L. Lloveras, R. Blasco, C. Fernández-Laso, J. Gabucio, L. Garcia, J. Soler, N. Soler, and E. Carbonell. 2010. "Changements dans les stratégies de subsistance entre les derniers Néandertaliens et les premiers hommes modernes en Catalonie," in *Paper presented at the 11th International Conference of Archaeozoology, Paris, France, 23–28 August 2010*. Paris, France, p. 182.

Maroto, J., N. Soler, and J. M. Fullola. 1996. "Cultural change between Middle and Upper Palaeolithic in Catalonia," in *The last Neandertals, the first anatomically modern humans. Cultural change and human evolution: The crisis at 40 ka BP*. Edited by E. Carbonell and M. Vaquero. Barcelona: Igualada, pp. 219–250.

Marquet, J.-C. 1988. "L'homme de Neandertal et son environnement dans la moitié ouest de la France d'après les rongeurs," in *L'homme de Néandertal, Volume 2: L'Environnement*. Edited by M. Otte. Liège: ERAUL, pp. 105–110.

———. 1993. *Paléoenvironnement et chronologie des sites du domaine atlantique français d'âge Pléistocène moyen et supérieur d'après l'étude des rongeurs*. Tours: Les Cahiers de la Claise, Supplément 2.

Marshall, F., and T. Pilgram. 1993. NISP vs. MNI in quantification of body-part representation. *American Antiquity* 58:261–269.

Martin, H. 2004. "Analyse cémentochronologique des restes dentaires recueillis sur deux sites quercynois," in *Le Paléolithique supérieur/The Upper Paleolithic*. Edited by M. Dewez, P. Noiret, and E. Teheux. Oxford: British Archaeological Reports, International Series 1240, pp. 131–134.

Martínez Valle, R., and G. Iturbe Polo. 1993. "La fauna de Cova Beneito," in *Cova Beneito (Muro, Alicante): Una perspectiva interdisciplinar*. Edited by G. Iturbe, M. P. Fumanal, J. S. Carrion, E. Cortell, R. Martinez, P. M. Guillem, M. D. Garralda, and B. Vandermeersch. *Recerques del Museu d'Alcoi* 2:35–38.

Maslin, M. 2009. "Quaternary climate transitions and cycles," in *Encyclopedia of paleoclimatology and ancient environments*. Edited by V. Gornitz. Dordrecht: Springer, pp. 841–855.

Meagher, M. M. 1973. *The bison of Yellowstone National Park*. Scientific Monograph Series 1. Washington, D.C.: National Park Service.

Mein, P., and M. T. Antunes. 2000. "Gruta da Figueira Brava: Petits mammifères – Insectivora, Chiroptera, Lagomorpha," in *Últimos Neandertais em Portugal – Evidência, odontológica e outra*. Edited by M. T. Antunes. Lisbon: Academia das Ciêncas de Lisboa, pp. 163–177.

Meiri, S., and T. Dayan. 2003. On the validity of Bergmann's rule. *Journal of Biogeography* 30:331–351.

Meiri, S., and Gavin H. Thomas. 2007. The geography of body size – challenges of the interspecific approach. *Global Ecology and Biogeography* 16:689–693.

Meiri, S., Y. Yom-Tov, and E. Geffen. 2007. What determines conformity to Bergmann's rule? *Global Ecology and Biogeography* 16:788–794.

Meldgaard, M. 1986. The Greenland caribou – zoogeography, taxonomy and population dynamics. *Meddelelser om Grønland Bioscience* 20:1–88.

Mellars, P. 1973. "The character of the Middle-Upper Palaeolithic transition in south-west France," in *The explanation of culture change*. Edited by C. Renfrew. London: Duckworth, pp. 255–276.

———. 1986. A new chronology for the French Mousterian period. *Nature* 322:410–411.

———. 1989. Major issues in the emergence of modern humans. *Current Anthropology* 30:349–385.

———. 1996. *The Neanderthal legacy: An archaeological perspective from Western Europe.* Princeton: Princeton University Press.

———. 1998. "The impact of climatic changes on the demography of late Neandertal and early anatomically modern populations in Europe," in *Neandertals and modern humans in Western Asia.* Edited by T. Akazawa, K. Aoki, and O. Bar-Yosef. New York: Plenum Press, pp. 493–507.

———. 2004. Reindeer specialization in the early Upper Palaeolithic: The evidence from south west France. *Journal of Archaeological Science* 31:613–617.

Mellars, P., M. Otte, L. G. Straus, J. Zilhão, and F. d'Errico. 1999. The Neanderthal problem continued. *Current Anthropology* 40:341–364.

Meng, M. S., G. C. West, and L. Irving. 1969. Fatty acid composition of caribou bone marrow. *Comparative Biochemistry and Physiology* 30:187–191.

Mercier, N., H. Valladas, J. L. Joron, and J. L. Reyss. 1993. "Thermoluminescence dating of the prehistoric site of la Roche à Pierrot, Saint-Césaire," in *Context of a late Neandertal: Implications of multidisciplinary research for the transition to Upper Paleolithic adaptations at Saint-Césaire.* Monographs in World Archaeology 16. Edited by F. Lévêque, A. M. Backer, and M. Guilbaud. Madison: Prehistory Press, pp. 15–21.

Metcalfe, D., and K. R. Barlow. 1992. A model for exploring the optimal trade-off between field processing and transport. *American Anthropologist* 94:340–356.

Metcalfe, D., and K. T. Jones. 1988. A reconsideration of animal body-part utility indices. *American Antiquity* 53:486–504.

Miller, F. L. 1974. *Biology of the Kaminuriak population of barren-ground caribou. Part 2: Dentition as an indicator of age and sex; composition and social organization of the population.* Ottawa: Environment Canada, Wildlife Service Report Series 31.

———. 1982. "Caribou," in *Wild mammals of North America: Biology, management, and economics.* Edited by J. A. Chapman and G. A. Feldhammer. Baltimore: Johns Hopkins University Press, pp. 923–959.

———. 2003. "Caribou," in *Wild mammals of North America: Biology, management, and conservation,* 2nd edition. Edited by G. A. Feldhamer, B. C. Thompson, and J. A. Chapman. Baltimore: Johns Hopkins University Press, pp. 965–997.

Millien, V., S. K. Lyons, L. Olson, F. A. Smith, A. B. Wilson, and Y. Yom-Tov. 2006. Ecotypic variation in the context of global climate change: Revisiting the rules. *Ecology Letters* 9:853–869.

Mills, L. S. 2007. *Conservation of wildlife populations: Demography, genetics, and management.* Malden, MA: Blackwell.

Milo, R. G., and D. Quiatt. 1993. Glottogenesis and anatomically modern *Homo sapiens*: The evidence for and implications of a late origin of vocal language. *Current Anthropology* 34:569–598.

Minc, L. D. 1986. Scarcity and survival: The role of oral tradition in mediating subsistence crises. *Journal of Anthropological Archaeology* 5:39–113.

Miskovsky, J.-C., and F. Lévêque. 1993. "The sediments and stratigraphy of Saint-Césaire: Contributions to the paleoclimatology of the site," in *Context of a late Neandertal: Implications of multidisciplinary research for the transition to Upper Paleolithic adaptations at Saint-Césaire.* Monographs in World Archaeology 16. Edited by F. Lévêque, A. M. Backer, and M. Guilbaud. Madison: Prehistory Press, pp. 7–14.

Mitchell, J. A., and C. C. Gates. 2002. *Status of the wood bison* (Bison bison athabascae) *in Alberta*. Wildlife Status Report No. 38. Edmonton: Alberta Sustainable Resource Development, Fish and Wildlife Division, and Alberta Conservation Association.

Mohr, E. 1971. *The Asiatic wild horse*. London: J. A. Allen and Co.

Monahan, C. M. 1998. The Hadza carcass transport debate revisited and its archaeological implications. *Journal of Archaeological Science* 25:405–424.

Montes, L., P. Utrilla, and R. Hedges. 2001. "Le passage Paléolithique moyen-Paléolithique supérieur dans la Vallée de l'Ebre (Espagne). Datation radiométriques des grottes de Peña Miel et Gabasa," in *Les premiers hommes modernes de la péninsule ibérique, Actes du colloque de la commission VIII de L'UISPP*. Lisbon: Trabalhos de Arqueologia 17, pp. 87–102.

Montfort, S. L., N. P. Arthur, and D. E. Wildt. 1994. "Reproduction in the Przewalski's horse," in *Przewalski's horse: The history and biology of an endangered species*. Edited by L. Boyd and K. A. Houpt. Albany: State University of New York Press, pp. 173–193.

Morin, E. 2004. Late Pleistocene population interaction in Western Europe and modern human origins: New insights based on the faunal remains from Saint-Césaire, southwestern France. Unpublished Ph.D. dissertation, University of Michigan.

———. 2007. Fat composition and Nunamiut decision-making: A new look at the marrow and bone grease indices. *Journal of Archaeological Science* 34:69–82.

———. 2008. Evidence for declines in human population densities during the early Upper Paleolithic in Western Europe. *Proceedings of the National Academy of Sciences* 105:48–53.

———. 2010. Taphonomic implications of the use of bone as fuel. *Palethnologie* 2:209–217.

Morin, E., and D. Liolios. 2008. "Bone tool technology and animal food procurement at Saint-Césaire: Some thoughts about site function and settlement patterns during the Middle to Upper Paleolithic transition." Paper presented at the Society for American Archaeology annual meeting, Vancouver, Canada.

Morin, E., T. Tsanova, N. Sirakov, W. Rendu, J.-B. Mallye, and F. Lévêque. 2005. Bone refits in stratified deposits: Testing the chronological grain at Saint-Césaire. *Journal of Archaeological Science* 32:1083–1098.

Morlan, R. E. 1994. Bison bone fragmentation and survivorship: A comparative method. *Journal of Archaeological Science* 21:797–807.

Mourer-Chauviré, C. 1984. "Les oiseaux du grand abri de La Ferrassie," in *Le grand abri de la Ferrassie, Fouilles 1968–1976, dirigé par H. Delporte*. Etudes Quaternaires 7, pp. 99–103.

———. 2002. "Les oiseaux," in *L'Aurignacien de la Grotte du Renne. Les fouilles d'André Leroi-Gourhan à Arcy-sur-Cure (Yonne)*. Gallia Préhistoire 34. Edited by B. Schmider. Paris: Éditions CNRS, pp. 103–105.

Mourer-Chauviré, C., and M. T. Antunes. 2000. "L'avifaune pléistocène et holocène de Gruta da Figueira Brava (Arrábida, Portugal)," in *Colóquio. Últimos Neandertais em Portugal. Evidência, odontológica e outra*. Edited by M. T. Antunes. Lisboa: Memórias da Academia das Ciências, Tomo XXXVIII, pp. 129–161.

Mourre, V., and D. Colonge. 2007. "Et si l'Acheuléen méridional n'était pas là où on l'attendait?" in *Congrès du centenaire de la Société Préhistorique Française: Un siècle de construction du discours scientifique en préhistoire*. Volume 3. Edited by J. Évin. Paris: Éditions de la Société Préhistorique Française, pp. 63–78.

Muñoz, M., and M. Casadevall. 1997. Fish remains from Arbreda Cave (Serinyà, Girona), northeast Spain, and their palaeoecological significance. *Journal of Quaternary Science* 12:111–115.

Munro, N. D. 2004. Zooarchaeological measures of hunting pressure and occupation intensity in the Natufian: Implications for agricultural origins. *Current Anthropology* 45:S5–S33.

———. 2009. "Epipaleolithic subsistence intensification in the southern Levant: The faunal evidence," in *The evolution of hominin diets: Integrating approaches to the study of Palaeolithic subsistence.* Edited by J.-J. Hublin and M. P. Richards. Berlin: Springer, pp. 141–155.

Munro, N. D., and L. Atici. 2009. Human subsistence change in the Late Pleistocene Mediterranean basin: The status of research on faunal intensification, diversification, and specialization. *Before Farming* 2009/1, article 1:1–6.

Munro, N. D., and G. Bar-Oz. 2005. Gazelle bone fat processing in the Levantine Epipalaeolithic. *Journal of Archaeological Science* 32:223–239.

Münzel, S. C. 2004. "Subsistence patterns in the Gravettian of the Ach valley, a former tributary of the Danube on the Swabian Jura," in *The Gravettian along the Danube.* Proceedings of the Mikulov Conference, 20–21 November 2002. Dolní Vestonice Studies 11. Edited by J. Svoboda and L. Sedláčková. Brno: Institute of Archaeology and Academy of Sciences of Czech Republic, pp. 71–85.

Münzel, S. C., and N. J. Conard. 2004a. Change and continuity in subsistence during the Middle and Upper Palaeolithic in the Ach Valley of Swabia (south-west Germany). *International Journal of Osteoarchaeology* 14:225–243.

———. 2004b. Cave bear hunting in Hohle Fels Cave in the Ach Valley of the Swabian Jura. *Revue de Paléobiologie, Genève* 23:877–885.

Murdoch, G. P. 1981. *Atlas of World Cultures.* Pittsburgh: University of Pittsburgh Press.

Mussi, M. 2001. *Earliest Italy: An overview of the Italian Paleolithic and Mesolithic.* New York: Kluwer Academic.

Nagaoka, L. 2005. Declining foraging efficiency and moa carcass exploitation in southern New Zealand. *Journal of Archaeological Science* 32:1328–1338.

———. 2006. Prehistoric seal carcass exploitation at the Shag Mouth site, New Zealand. *Journal of Archaeological Science* 33:1474–1481.

Naughton, F., M. F. Sánchez Goñi, M. Kageyama, E. Bard, J. Duprat, E. Cortijo, S. Desprat, B. Malaizé, C. Joly, F. Rostek, and J.-L. Turon. 2009. Wet to dry climatic trend in north-western Iberia within Heinrich events. *Earth and Planetary Science Letters* 284:329–342.

Niven, L. 2003. "Patterns of subsistence and settlement during the Aurignacian of the Swabian Jura, Germany," in *The chronology of the Aurignacian and of the transitional technocomplexes: Dating, stratigraphies, cultural implications.* Trabalhos de Arqueologia 33. Edited by J. Zilhão and F. d'Errico. Lisbon: Instituto Português de Arqueologia pp. 199–211.

———. 2006. *The Palaeolithic occupation of Vogelherd Cave: Implications for the subsistence behavior of late Neanderthals and early modern humans.* Tübingen: Kerns Verlag.

———. 2007. From carcass to cave: Large mammal exploitation during the Aurignacian at Vogelherd, Germany. *Journal of Human Evolution* 53:362–382.

Nonacs, P. 2001. State dependent behavior and the marginal value theorem. *Behavioral Ecology* 12:71–83.

Noonan, J. P., G. Coop, S. Kudaravalli, D. Smith, J. Krause, J. Alessi, F. Chen, D. Platt, S. Pääbo, J. K. Pritchard, and E. M. Rubin. 2006. Sequencing and analysis of Neanderthal genomic DNA. *Science* 314:1113–1118.

Nordborg, M. 1998. On the probability of Neanderthal ancestry. *American Journal of Human Genetics* 63:1237–1240.

Normand, C., S. A. de Beaune, S. Costamagno, M.-F. Diot, D. Henry-Gambier, N. Goutas, V. Laroulandie, A. Lenoble, M. O'Farrell, W. Rendu, J. Rios Garaizar, C. Schwab, A. Tarriño Vinagre, J.-P. Texier, and R. White. 2007. "Nouvelles données sur la séquence aurignacienne de la Grotte d'Isturitz (communes d'Isturitz et de Saint-Martin-d'Arberoue, Pyrénées-Atlantiques)," in *Congrès du centenaire de la Société Préhistorique Française: Un siècle de construction du discours scientifique en préhistoire.* Edited by J. Évin. Paris: Société Préhistorique Française, pp. 277–293.

O'Connell, J. F. 2000. "An emu hunt," in *Australian archaeologist: Collected papers in honor of Jim Allen.* Edited by A. Anderson and T. Murray. Canberra: Coombs Academic Publishing, The Australian National University, pp. 172–181.

———. 2006. "How did modern humans displace Neanderthals? Insights from hunter-gatherer ethnography and archaeology," in *When Neanderthals and modern humans met.* Edited by N. J. Conard. Tübingen: Kerns Verlag, pp. 43–64.

O'Connell, J. F., K. Hawkes, and N. Blurton Jones. 1988. Hadza scavenging: Implications for Plio/Pleistocene hominid subsistence. *Current Anthropology* 29:356–363.

———. 1990. Reanalysis of large mammal body part transport among the Hadza. *Journal of Archaeological Science* 17:301–316.

Olalla-Tárraga, M. Á., and M. Á. Rodríguez. 2007. Energy and interspecific body size patterns of amphibian faunas in Europe and North America: Anurans follow Bergmann's rule, urodeles its converse. *Global Ecology and Biogeography* 16:606–617.

Olalla-Tárraga, M. Á., M. Á. Rodríguez, and B. A. Hawkins. 2006. Broad-scale patterns of body size in squamate reptiles of Europe and North America. *Journal of Biogeography* 33:781–793.

Olifiers, N., M. V. Vieira, and C. E. V. Grelle. 2004. Geographic range and body size in Neotropical marsupials. *Global Ecology and Biogeography* 13:439–444.

Oliver, J. S. 1993. "Carcass processing by the Hadza: Bone breakage from butchery to consumption," in *From bones to behavior: Ethnoarchaeological and experimental contributions to the interpretation of faunal remains.* Edited by J. Hudson. Carbondale: Center for Archaeological Investigation, Southern Illinois University, pp. 200–227.

Olsen, S. L. 1989. Solutré: A theoretical approach to the reconstitution of Upper Palaeolithic hunting strategies. *Journal of Human Evolution* 18:295–327.

Oppliger, J. 2008. Les micromammifères (Chiroptera, Insectivora et Rodentia) comme indicateurs de l'environnement au Tardiglaciaire et à l'Holocène: Le cas du Moulin du Roc (Saint-Chamassy, Dordogne, France). Unpublished Mémoire de Diplôme, Université de Genève.

Orians, G. H., and N. E. Pearson. 1979. "On the theory of central place foraging," in *Analysis of ecological systems.* Edited by D. J. Horn, R. D. Mitchell, and G. R. Stairs. Columbus: Ohio State University Press, pp. 155–177.

Orlando, L., P. Darlu, M. Toussaint, D. Bonjean, M. Otte, and C. Hänni. 2006. Revisiting Neandertal diversity with a 100,000 year old mtDNA sequence. *Current Biology* 16:R400–R402.

O'Rourke, D. H. 2007. "Ancient DNA and its application to the reconstruction of human evolution and population history," in *Anthropological genetics: Theory, methods and applications.* Edited by M. H. Crawford. Cambridge: Cambridge University Press, pp. 210–231.

Otte, M. 1990. "Les processus de transition du Paléolithique moyen au supérieur," in *Paléolithique moyen récent et Paléolithique supérieur ancien en Europe.* Edited by C. Farizy. Nemours: Mémoire du Musée de Préhistoire d'Ile de France 3, pp. 145–149.

Outram, A. K. 2001. The scapula representation could be the key: A further contribution to the "Klasies pattern" debate. *Journal of Archaeological Science* 28:1259–1263.

Outram, A. K., and P. Rowley-Conwy. 1998. Meat and marrow utility indices for horse (*Equus*). *Journal of Archaeological Science* 25:839–849.

Paillard, D., and L. Labeyrie. 1994. Role of the thermohaline circulation in the abrupt warming after Heinrich events. *Nature* 372:162–164.

Palma di Cesnola, A. 2006. L'Aurignacien et le Gravettien ancien de la grotte Paglicci au Mont Gargano. *L' Anthropologie* 110:355–370.

Palomares, F. 2001. Comparison of 3 methods to estimate rabbit abundance in a Mediterranean environment. *Wildlife Society Bulletin* 29:578–585.

———. 2003. Warren building by European rabbits (*Oryctolagus cuniculus*) in relation to cover availability in a sandy area. *Journal of Zoology* 259:63–67.

Parer, I., P. J. Fullagar, and K. W. Malafant. 1987. The history and structure of a large warren of the rabbit, *Oryctolagus cuniculus*, at Canberra, A.C.T. *Australian Wildlife Research* 14:505–513.

Park, S.-J. 2007. Systèmes de production lithique et circulation des matières premières au Paléolithique moyen récent et final. Une approche techno-économique à partir de l'étude des industries lithiques de La Quina (Charente). Unpublished Ph.D. dissertation, Université de Paris X.

Parker, G. R. 1972. *Biology of the Kaminuriak population of barren-ground caribou, Part 1: Total numbers, mortality, recruitment, and seasonal distribution*. Canadian Wildlife Service Report Series 20. Ottawa: Environment Canada, Wildlife Service.

Pate, D. 1986. The effects of drought on Ngatatjara plant use: An evaluation of optimal foraging theory. *Human Ecology* 14:95–115.

Patou-Mathis, M. 1993. "A taphonomic and paleoethnographic study of the fauna associated with the Neandertal of Saint-Césaire," in *Context of a late Neandertal: Implications of multidisciplinary research for the transition to Upper Paleolithic adaptations at Saint-Césaire*. Monographs in World Archaeology 16. Edited by F. Lévêque, A. M. Backer, and M. Guilbaud. Madison: Prehistory Press, pp. 79–102.

———. 1994. Archéozoologie des niveaux moustériens et aurignaciens de la grotte Tournal à Bize (Aude). *Gallia Préhistoire* 36:1–64.

Patou-Mathis, M., and C. Schwab. 2002. "Fiche générale," in *Retouchoirs, compresseurs, percuteurs . . . Os à impressions et éraillures*. Fiches de la Commission de Nomenclature sur l'Industrie de l'Os Préhistorique, Cahier X. Paris: Editions Société Préhistorique Française, pp. 11–19.

Payne, S. 1972. "Partial recovery and sample bias: The results of some sieving experiments," in *Papers in economic prehistory*. Edited by E. S. Higgs. Cambridge: Cambridge University Press, pp. 49–64.

Peresani, M. 2008. A new cultural frontier for the last Neanderthals: The Uluzzian in northern Italy. *Current Anthropology* 49:725–731.

Peresani, M., I. Fiore, M. Gala, M. Romandini, and A. Tagliacozzo. 2011. Late Neandertals and the intentional removal of feathers as evidenced from bird bone taphomony at Fumane Cave 44 ky B.P., Italy. *Proceedings of the National Academy of Sciences* 108:3888–3893.

Pérez Ripoll, M. 2004. "La consommation humaine des lapins pendant le Paléolithique dans la région de Valencia (Espagne) et l'étude des niveaux gravettiens de la Cova de les Cendres (Alicante)," in *Petits animaux et sociétés humaines. Du complément alimentaire aux ressources utilitaires*. Edited by J.-P. Brugal and J. Desse. Antibes: Éditions ADPCA, pp. 191–206.

———. 2005/2006. Caracterización de las fracturas antrópicas y sus tipologías en huesos de conejo procedentes de los niveles gravetienses de la Cova de les Cendres (Alicante). *Munibe* 57:239–254.

Pérez Ripoll, M., and R. Martínez Valle. 2001. "La Caza, el aprovechamiento de las presas y el comportomiento de las comunidades cazadoras prehistóricas," in *De Neandertales a Cromañones. EL inicio del poblamiento humano en las tierras valencianas.* Edited by V. Villaverde. València: Universitat de València, pp. 73–98.

Pesesse, D. 2008. Les premières sociétés gravettiennes. Analyse comparée des systèmes lithiques de la fin de l'Aurignacien aux débuts du Gravettien. Unpublished Ph.D. dissertation, Université de Provence.

Peters, R. H. 1983. *The ecological implications of body size.* Cambridge: Cambridge University Press.

Petersson, C. J., and B. Danell. 1993. Causes of variation in growth rate of reindeer calves. *Rangifer* 13:105–116.

Peyrony, D. 1933. Les industries 'aurignaciennes' dans le bassin de la Vézère. *Bulletin de la Société Préhistorique Française* 30:543–559.

———. 1934. La Ferrassie: Moustérien, Périgordien, Aurignacien. *Préhistoire* 3:1–92.

Pickering, T. R., and C. P. Egeland. 2006. Experimental patterns of hammerstone percussion damage on bones: implications for inferences of carcass processing by humans. *Journal of Archaeological Science* 33:459–469.

Pickering, T. R., C. W. Marean, and M. Domínguez-Rodrigo. 2003. Importance of limb bone shaft fragments in zooarchaeology: A response to "On *in situ* attrition and vertebrate body part profiles" (2002), by M.C. Stiner. *Journal of Archaeological Science* 30:1469–1482.

Pike-Tay, A. 1995. Variability and synchrony of seasonal indicators in dental cementum microstructure of the Kaminuriak *Rangifer* population. *Archaeofauna* 4:273–284.

Pike-Tay, A., C. A. Morcomb, and M. O'Farrell. 2000. Reconsidering the quadratic crown height method of age estimation for *Rangifer* from archaeological sites. *Archaeozoologia* 11:145–174.

Plagnol, V., and J. D. Wall. 2006. Possible ancestral structure in human populations. *PLoS Genetics* 2: 972–979.

Pond, C. M. 1998. *The fats of life.* Cambridge: Cambridge University Press.

Pond, C. M., and C. A. Mattacks. 1985a. Body mass and natural diet as determinants of the number and volume of adipocytes in eutherian mammals. *Journal of Morphology* 185:183–193.

———. 1985b. Cellular structure of adipose tissue in birds. *Journal of Morphology* 185:185–202.

Pond, C. M., C. A. Mattacks, R. H. Colby, and N. J. C. Tyler. 1993. The anatomy, chemical composition and maximum glycolytic capacity of adipose tissue in wild Svalbard reindeer (*Rangifer tarandus platyrhynchus*) in winter. *Journal of Zoology* 229:17–40.

Pond, C. M., C. A. Mattacks, and P. Prestrud. 1995. Variability in the distribution and composition of adipose tissue in wild arctic foxes (*Alopex lagopus*) on Svalbard. *Journal of Zoology* 236:593–610.

Poplin, F. 1976. *Les grands vertébrés de Gönnersdorf, fouilles 1968.* Wiesbaden: Franz Steiner.

Pösö, A. R. 2005. Seasonal changes in reindeer physiology. *Rangifer* 25:31–38.

Post, E., P. S. Bøving, C. Pedersen, and M. A. MacArthur. 2003. Synchrony between caribou calving and plant phenology in depredated and non-depredated populations. *Canadian Journal of Zoology* 81:1709–1714.

Post, E., and M. C. Forchhammer. 2004. Spatial synchrony of local populations has increased in association with the recent northern hemisphere climate trend. *Proceedings of the National Academy of Sciences* 101:9286–9290.

———. 2006. Spatially synchronous population dynamics: An indicator of Pleistocene faunal response to large-scale environmental change in the Holocene. *Quaternary International* 151:99–105.

Prat, F. n.d. *Quelques mammifères pléistocènes. Odontologie-ostéologie*. Bordeaux: Université de Bordeaux I.

Prummel, W. 1987a. Atlas for identification of foetal skeletal elements of cattle, horse, sheep and pig. Part 1. *Archaeozoologia* 1:23–30.

————. 1987b. Atlas for identification of foetal skeletal remains of cattle, horse, sheep and pig. Part 2. *Archaeozoologia* 1:11–52.

————. 1988. Atlas for identification of foetal skeletal elements of cattle, horse, sheep and pig. Part 3. *Archaeozoologia* 2:13–26.

————. 1989. Appendix to atlas for identification of foetal skeletal remains of cattle, horse, sheep and pig. *Archaeozoologia* 3:71–78.

Prusak, B., G. Grzybowski, and G. Zieba. 2004. Taxonomic position of *Bison bison* (Linnaeus 1758) and *Bison bonasus* (Linnaeus 1758) as determined by means of cytb gene sequence. *Animal Science Papers and Reports* 22:27–35.

Pucek, Z., I. P. Belousova, Z. A. Krasinki, M. Krasinska, and W. Olech. 2003. "European bison (*Bison bonasus*). Current state of the species and an action plan for its conservation." Strasbourg: Convention of the Conservation of European Wildlife and Natural Habitats.

Pulliam, H. R. 1974. On the theory of optimal diets. *The American Naturalist* 108:59–74.

Pushkina, D., and P. Raia. 2008. Human influence on distribution and extinctions of the late Pleistocene Eurasian megafauna. *Journal of Human Evolution* 54:769–782.

Pyke, G. H., H. R. Pulliman, and E. L. Charnov. 1977. Optimal foraging: a selective review of theory and tests. *The Quarterly Review of Biology* 52:137–154.

Rabinovich, R. 1998. "Drowning in numbers" – Gazelles dominance and body size groups in the archaeozoological record," in *Archaeozoology of the Near East III. Proceedings of the third international symposium on the archaeozoology of southwestern Asia and adjacent areas*. Edited by H. Buitenhuis, L. Bartosiewicz, and A. M. Choyke. ARC Publicaties 18. Groningen: Centre for Archaeological Research and Consistency, pp. 45–71.

————. 2003. "The Levantine Upper Palaeolithic faunal record," in *More than meets the eye: Studies on Upper Palaeolithic diversity in the Near East*. Edited by A. Belfer-Cohen and N. Goring-Morris. Oxford: Oxbow Books, pp. 33–48.

Rabinovich, R., O. Bar-Yosef, and E. Tchernov. 1996. "How many ways to skin a gazelle" – butchery patterns from an Upper Palaeolithic site, Hayonim Cave, Israel. *Archaeozoologia* 8:11–52.

Ramachandran, S., O. Deshpande, C. C. Roseman, N. A. Rosenberg, M. W. Feldman, and L. L. Cavalli-Sforza. 2005. Support from the relationship of genetic and geographic distance in human populations for a serial founder effect origination in Africa. *Proceedings of the National Academy of Sciences* 102:15942–15947.

Ramirez, L., J. A. Felizola Diniz-Felho, and B. A. Hawkins. 2008. Partitioning phylogenetic and adaptive components of the geographical body-size pattern of New World birds. *Global Ecology and Biogeography* 17:100–110.

Ramirez Rozzi, F. V., F. d'Errico, M. Vanhaeren, P. M. Grootes, B. Kerautret, and V. Dujardin. 2009. Cutmarked human remains bearing Neandertal features and modern human remains associated with the Aurignacian at Les Rois. *Journal of Anthropological Sciences* 87:153–185.

Rands, S. A., A. I. Houston, and C. E. Gasson. 2000. Prey processing in central place foragers. *Journal of Theoretical Biology* 202:161–174.

Rashid, H., and E. A. Boyle. 2007. Mixed-layer deepening during Heinrich events: A multi-planktonic foraminiferal $\partial^{18}O$ approach. *Science* 318:439–441.

Rasmussen, T. L., and E. Thomsen. 2004. The role of the North Atlantic Drift in the millenial timescale glacial climate fluctuations. *Palaeogeography, Palaeoclimatology, Palaeoecology* 210:101–116.

Reher, C. C., and G. C. Frison. 1980. *The Vore Site, 48CK302, a stratified buffalo jump in the Wyoming Black Hills*. Memoir 16. Topeka: Plains Anthropologist.

Reich, D., R. E. Green, M. Kircher, J. Krause, N. Patterson, E. Y. Durand, B. Viola, A. W. Briggs, U. Stenzel, P. L. F. Johnson, T. Maricic, J. M. Good, T. Marques-Bonet, C. Alkan, Q. Fu, S. Mallick, H. Li, M. Meyer, E. E. Eichler, M. Stoneking, M. Richards, S. Talamo, M. V. Shunkov, A. P. Derevianko, J.-J. Hublin, J. Kelso, M. Slatkin, and S. Paabo. 2010. Genetic history of an archaic hominin group from Denisova Cave in Siberia. *Nature* 468:1053–1060.

Reimers, E. 1979. "Activity pattern: The major determinant for growth and fattening in *Rangifer*?," in *Proceedings of the second international reindeer/caribou symposium*. Edited by E. Reimers, E. Gaare, and S. Skjenneberg. Røros: Direktoratet for Vilt og Ferskvannsfisk, pp. 466–474.

———. 1983. Growth rate and body size differences in *Rangifer*, a study of causes and effects. *Rangifer* 3:3–15.

———. 1984. Body composition and population regulation of Svalbard reindeer. *Rangifer* 4:16–21.

———. 1993. Antlerless females among reindeer and caribou. *Canadian Journal of Zoology* 71:1319–1325.

———. 2002. Calving time and foetus growth among wild reindeer in Norway. *Rangifer* 22:61–66.

Relethford, J. H. 2001. *Genetics and the search for modern human origins*. New York: Wiley.

Rendu, W. 2007. Planification des activités de subsistance au sein du territoire des derniers Moustériens. Cémentochronologie et approche archéozoologique de gisements du Paléolithique moyen (Pech-de-l'Azé I, La Quina, Mauran) et Paléolithique supérieur ancien (Isturitz). Unpublished Ph.D. dissertation, Université de Bordeaux I.

———. 2009. "Études taphonomiques et archéozoologiques," in Les Cottés (Vienne). Rapport de fouille programmée 2009. Edited by M. Soressi. Report for the Service Régional de l'Archéologie de Poitou-Charentes, pp. 191–217.

Reynolds, H. W., C. C. Gates, and R. D. Glaholt. 2003. "Bison," in *Wild mammals of North America: Biology, management, and conservation*, 2nd edition. Edited by G. A. Feldhamer, B. C. Thompson, and J. A. Chapman. Baltimore: Johns Hopkins University Press, pp. 1009–1060.

Reynolds, H. W., R. D. Glaholt, and A. W. L. Hawley. 1982. "Bison," in *Wild mammals of North America: Biology, management, and economy*. Edited by J. A. Chapman and G. A. Feldhammer. Baltimore: Johns Hopkins University Press, pp. 972–1007.

Reynolds, J. D., and C. A. Peres. 2005. "Overexploitation," in *Principles of conservation biology*, 3rd edition. Edited by M. Groom, G. Meffe, and R. Carroll. Sunderland, MA: Sinauer, pp. 249–287.

Richards, M. P. 2009. "Stable isotope evidence for European Upper Paleolithic human diets," in *The evolution of hominin diets: Integrating approaches to the study of Palaeolithic subsistence*. Edited by J.-J. Hublin and M. P. Richards. Berlin: Springer, pp. 251–257.

Richards, M. P., P. B. Pettitt, M. C. Stiner, and E. Trinkaus. 2001. Stable isotope evidence for increasing dietary breadth in the European mid-Upper Paleolithic. *Proceedings of the National Academy of Sciences* 98:6528–6532.

Richards, M. P., P. B. Pettitt, E. Trinkaus, F. H. Smith, M. Paunovic, and I. Karavanic. 2000. Neanderthal diet at Vindija and Neanderthal predation: The evidence from stable isotopes. *Proceedings of the National Academy of Sciences* 97:7663–7666.

Richards, M. P., and E. Trinkaus. 2009. Isotopic evidence for the diets of European Neanderthals and early modern humans. *Proceedings of the National Academy of Sciences* 106:16034–16039.

Ritchie, M. E. 1998. Scale-dependent foraging and patch choice in fractal environments. *Evolutionary Ecology* 12:309–330.

Rodríguez, M. Á., I. L. López-Sañudo, and B. A. Hawkins. 2006. The geographic distribution of mammal body size in Europe. *Global Ecology and Biogeography* 15:173–181.

Rodríguez, M. Á., M. Á. Olalla-Tárraga, and B. A. Hawkins. 2008. Bergmann's rule and the geography of mammal body size in the Western Hemisphere. *Global Ecology and Biogeography* 17:274–283.

Rogers, A. R. 2000. On the value of soft bones in faunal analysis. *Journal of Archaeological Science* 27:635–639.

Roselló Izquierdo, E., and A. Morales Muñiz. 2005. Ictiofaunas musterienses de la Península Ibérica: ¿Evidencias de pesca Neandertal? *Munibe* 57:183–195.

Roucoux, K. H., L. de Abreu, N. J. Shackleton, and P. C. Tzedakis. 2005. The response of NW Iberian vegetation to North Atlantic climate oscillations during the last 65 kyr. *Quaternary Science Reviews* 24:1637–1653.

Rougier, H., S. Milota, R. Rodrigo, M. Gherase, L. Sarcina, O. Moldovan, J. Zilhão, S. Constantin, R. G. Franciscus, P. E. Z. Christoph, M. Ponce de León, and E. Trinkaus. 2007. Pestera cu Oase 2 and the cranial morphology of early modern Europeans. *Proceedings of the National Academy of Sciences* 104:1165–1170.

Rubicz, R., P. Melton, and M. H. Crawford. 2007. "Molecular markers in anthropological genetic studies," in *Anthropological genetics: Theory, methods and applications.* Edited by M. H. Crawford. Cambridge: Cambridge University Press, pp. 141–186.

Rudolph, S. G., and C. Loudon. 1986. Load size selection by foraging leaf-cutter ants. *Ecological Entomology* 11:401–410.

Ryder, O. A. 1994. "Genetic studies of Przewalski's horses and their impact on conservation," in *Przewalski's horse: The history and biology of an endangered species.* Edited by L. Boyd and K. A. Houpt. Albany: State University of New York Press, pp. 75–92.

Sachs, J. P., and R. F. Anderson. 2005. Increased productivity in the subantarctic ocean during the Heinrich events. *Nature* 434:1118–1121.

Sahlins, M. D. 1972. *Stone Age economics.* Chicago: Aldine-Atherton.

Saint-Germain, C. 1997. The production of bone broth: A study in nutritional exploitation. *Anthropozoologica* 25–26:153–156.

Salgueiro, E., A. H. L. Voelker, L. de Abreu, F. Abrantes, H. Meggers, and G. Wefer. 2010. Temperature and productivity changes off the western Iberian margin during the last 150 kyr. *Quaternary Science Reviews* 29:680–695.

Sánchez Goñi, M. F. 1994. The identification of European Upper Palaeolithic interstadials from cave sequences. *American Association of Stratigraphic Palynologists Contributions Series* 29:161–182.

Sánchez Goñi, M. F., A. Landais, W. J. Fletcher, F. Naughton, S. Desprat, and J. Duprat. 2008. Contrasting impacts of Dangaard-Oeschger events over a western European latitudinal transect modulated by orbital parameters. *Quaternary Science Reviews* 27:1136–1151.

Sánchez Goñi, M. F., J.-L. Turon, F. Eynaud, and S. Gendreau. 2000. European climatic response to millenial-scale changes in the atmosphere-ocean system during the Last Glacial period. *Quaternary Research* 54:394–403.

Sánchez Marco, A. 2007. New occurrences of the extinct vulture *Gyps melitensis* (Falconiformes, Aves) and a reappraisal of the paleospecies. *Journal of Vertebrate Paleontology* 27:1057–1061.

Sanchis Serra, A., and J. Fernández Peris. 2008. Procesado y consumo antrópico de conejo en la Cova del Bolomor (Tavernes de la Valldigna, Valencia). El nivel XVIIc (*ca* 350 ka). *Complutum* 19:25–46.

Schaefer, J. A., and S. P. Mahoney. 2001. Antlers on female caribou: Biogeographical bones of contention. *Ecology* 82:3556–3560.

Schiegl, S., P. Goldberg, H. U. Pfretzschner, and N. J. Conard. 2003. Paleolithic burnt bone horizons from the Swabian Jura: Distinguishing between in situ fireplaces and dumping areas. *Geoarchaeology* 18:541–565.

Schoener, T. W. 1971. Theory of feeding strategies. *Annual Review of Ecology and Systematics* 2:369–404.

————. 1979. Generality of the size-distance relation in models of optimal feeding. *The American Naturalist* 114:902–914.

Seidov, D. 2009. "Heat transport, oceanic and atmospheric," in *Encyclopedia of paleoclimatology and ancient environments*. Edited by V. Gornitz. Dordrecht: Springer, pp. 407–409.

Seip, D. R. 1991. Predation and caribou populations. *Rangifer* Special Issue 7:46–52.

————. 1992. Factors limiting woodland caribou populations and their interrelationships with wolves and moose in southeastern British Columbia. *Canadian Journal of Zoology* 70:1494–1503.

Sekhr, A. 1998. Étude archéozoologique des niveaux aurignaciens (couches 14 à 6) et de la base des niveaux gravettiens (niveaux X à T4) de l'Abri Pataud (Les Eyzies, Dordogne). Unpublished Ph.D. dissertation, Muséum National d'Histoire Naturelle, Paris, France.

Self, S. 2006. The effects and consequences of very large explosive volcanic eruptions. *Philosophical Transactions of the Royal Society of London A* 364:2073–2097.

Serre, D., A. Langaney, M. Chech, M. Teschler-Nicola, M. Paunovic, P. Mennecier, M. Hofreiter, G. Possnert, and S. Pääbo. 2004. No evidence of Neandertal mtDNA contribution to early modern humans. *PloS Biology* 2:313–317.

Shi, W., Q. Ayub, M. Vermeulen, R. Shao, S. Zuniga, K. van der Gaag, P. de Knijff, M. Kayser, Y. Xue, and C. Tyler-Smith. 2009. A worldwide survey of human male demographic history based on Y-SNP and Y-STR data from the HGDP-CEPH populations. *Molecular Biology and Evolution* 27:385–393.

Shipman, P., G. Foster, and M. Schoeninger. 1984. Burnt bones and teeth: An experimental study of color, morphology, crystal structure and shrinkage. *Journal of Archaeological Science* 11:307–325.

Sih, A., and B. Christensen. 2001. Optimal diet theory: When does it work, and when and why does it fail? *Animal Behaviour* 61:379–390.

Simmons, T., and D. Nadel. 1998. The avifauna of the Early Epipalaeolithic site of Ohalo II (19,400 B.P.), Israel: Species diversity, habitat and seasonality. *International Journal of Osteoarchaeology* 8:79–96.

Simms, S. R. 1987. *Behavioral ecology and hunter-gatherer foraging: An example from the Great Basin*. International Series 381. Oxford: British Archaeological Reports.

Simpson, E. H. 1949. Measurement of diversity. *Nature* 163:688.

Sinclair, A. R. E., J. M. Fryxell, and G. Caughley. 2006. *Wildlife ecology, conservation, and management*, 2nd edition. Malden, MA: Blackwell.

Sinitsyn, A. A. 2003. A Paleolithic "Pompeii" at Kostenki, Russia. *Antiquity* 77:9–14.

Sitlivy, V., K. Sobczyk, P. Karkanas, and M. Koumouzelis. 2007. Middle Palaeolithic lithic assemblages of the Klissoura Cave, Peloponnesus, Greece: A comparative analysis. *Archaeology, Ethnology and Anthropology of Eurasia* 3:2–15.

Skogland, T. 1986. Density dependent food limitation and maximal production in wild reindeer herds. *Journal of Wildlife Management* 50:314–319.

———. 1988. Tooth wear by food limitation and its life history consequences in wild reindeer. *Oikos* 51:238–242.

Skoog, R. O. 1968. Ecology of the caribou in Alaska. Unpublished Ph.D. dissertation, University of California.

Slade, L. M., and E. B. Godfrey. 1982. "Wild horses (*Equus caballus* and allies)," in *Wild mammals of North America*. Edited by J. A. Chapman and G. A. Feldhamer. Baltimore: The Johns Hopkins University Press, pp. 1089–1098.

Slott-Moller, R. 1988. Contribution à l'étude paléontologique d'un gisement préhistorique: L'exemple du Roc de Marcamps (Gironde). Unpublished DESS thesis, Université de Bordeaux I.

———. 1990. "La faune," in *Les chasseurs d'aurochs de la Borde, un site du Paléolithique moyen (Livernon, Lot)*. Edited by J. Jaubert, M. Lorblanchet, H. Laville, A. Turq, and J.-P. Brugal. Paris: Documents d'Archéologie Française 27, pp. 33–68.

Smith, E. A. 1991. *Inujjuamiut foraging strategies. Evolutionary ecology of an Arctic hunting economy*. New York: Aldine de Gruyter.

Smith, E. A., R. Bliege Bird, and D. Bird. 2003. The benefits of costly signaling: Meriam turtle hunters. *Behavioral Ecology* 14:116–126.

Smith, F. H. 1982. Upper Pleistocene hominid evolution in south central Europe: A review of the evidence and analysis of trends. *Current Anthropology* 23:667–703.

Smith, F. H., A. B. Falsetti, and S. M. Donnelly. 1989. Modern human origins. *Yearbook of Physical Anthropology* 32:35–68.

Soficaru, A., A. Dobos, and E. Trinkaus. 2006. Early modern humans from the Pestera Muierii, Baia de Fier, Romania. *Proceedings of the National Academy of Sciences* 103:17196–17201.

Soficaru, A., C. Petrea, A. Dobos, and E. Trinkaus. 2007. The human cranium from the Pestera Cioclovina Uscata, Romania. *Current Anthropology* 48:611–619.

Sokal, R. R., and F. J. Rohlf. 1969. *Biometry: The principles and practice of statistics in biological research*. San Francisco: W. H. Freeman.

Soler-Mayor, N. 2001. "Adornen, imagen y comunicacion," in *De Neandertales a Cromañones. EL inicio del poblamiento humano en las tierras valencianas*. Edited by V. Villaverde. Valencia: Universita de Valencia, pp. 367–376.

Soler Subils, J., N. Soler Masferrer, and J. Maroto. 2008. L'Arbreda's archaic Aurignacian dates clarified. *Eurasian Prehistory* 5:45–55.

Sollas, W. J. 1911. *Ancient hunters and their modern representatives*. London: MacMillan and Co.

Sonneville-Bordes, D. de 1960. *Le Paléolithique supérieur en Périgord*. Bordeaux: Delmas.

———. 1989. Préface. *Bulletin de la Société Préhistorique de l'Ariège* 44:5–17.

Soressi, M. 2010. "La Roche-à-Pierrot à Saint-Césaire (Charente-Maritime). Nouvelles données sur l'industrie lithique du Châtelperronien," in *Préhistoire entre Vienne et Charente. Hommes et sociétés du Paléolithique*. Edited by J. Buisson-Catil and J. Primault: Mémoire XXXVIII, Ministère de la Culture et de la Communication, France.

Soressi, M., and F. d'Errico. 2007. "Pigments, gravures, parures: Les comportements symboliques controversés des Néandertaliens," in *Les Néandertaliens. Biologie et cultures*. Edited by B. Vandermeersch and B. Maureille. Paris: Éditions du CTHS, Documents Préhistoriques 23, pp. 297–309.

Speth, J. D. 1983. *Bison kills and bone counts*. Chicago: Chicago University Press.

———. 1990. Seasonality, resource stress, and food sharing in so-called "egalitarian" foraging societies. *Journal of Anthropological Archaeology* 9:148–188.

———. 2004a. News flash: Negative evidence convicts Neanderthals of gross mental incompetence. *World Archaeology* 36:519–526.

———. 2004b. "Hunting pressure, subsistence intensification, and demographic change in the Levantine late Middle Paleolithic," in *Human Paleoecology in the Levantine Corridor*. Edited by N. Goren-Inbar and J. D. Speth. Oxford: Oxbow Press, pp. 149–166.

Speth, J. D., and J. L. Clark. 2006. Hunting and overhunting in the Levantine Middle Palaeolithic. *Before Farming* 3:1–42.

Speth, J. D., and K. A. Spielmann. 1983. Energy source, protein metabolism, and hunter-gatherer subsistence strategies. *Journal of Anthropological Archaeology* 2:1–31.

Speth, J. D., and E. Tchernov. 2001. "Neandertal hunting and meat-processing in the Near East: Evidence from Kebara cave (Israel)," in *Meat-eating and human evolution*. Edited by C. B. Stanford and H. T. Bunn. Oxford: Oxford University Press, pp. 52–72.

Spiess, A. E. 1979. *Reindeer and caribou hunters: An archaeological study*. New York: Academic Press.

Starkovich, B. 2009. Dietary changes during the Upper Palaeolithic at Klissoura Cave 1 (Prosymnni), Peloponnese, Greece. *Before Farming* 2009/3, article 4:1–14.

Steele, T. E. 2004. Variation in mortality profiles of red deer (*Cervus elaphus*) in Middle Palaeolithic assemblages from Western Europe. *International Journal of Osteoarchaeology* 14:307–320.

Stefansson, V. 1969. *The friendly Arctic. The story of five years in polar regions*. New York: Greenwood Press.

Stephens, D. W., J. S. Brown, and R. C. Ydenberg. Editors. 2007. *Foraging: Behavior and ecology*. Chicago: University of Chicago Press.

Stephens, D. W., and J. R. Krebs. 1986. *Foraging theory*. Princeton: Princeton University Press.

Stiner, M. C. 1994. *Honor among thieves*. Princeton: Princeton University Press.

———. 2002. On *in situ* attrition and vertebrate body part profiles. *Journal of Archaeological Science* 29:979–991.

———. 2003. Zooarchaeological evidence for resource intensification in Algarve, southern Portugal. *Promontoria* 1:26–61.

———. 2005. *The faunas of Hayonim Cave: a 200,000-year record of Paleolithic diet, demography, and society*. American School of Prehistoric Research Bulletin 48. Cambridge, MA: Peabody Museum of Archaeology and Ethnology.

———. 2009. Prey choice, site occupation intensity and economic diversity in the Middle-early Upper Palaeolithic at the Üçagizli Caves, Turkey. *Before Farming* 2009/3, article 3:1–20.

Stiner, M. C., J. Beaver, N. D. Munro, and T. A. Surovell. 2008. "Modeling Paleolithic predator-prey dynamics and the effects of hunting pressure on prey choice," in *Recent advances in paleodemography: Data, techniques and patterns*. Edited by J. P. Bocquet-Appel. Dordrecht: Springer-Verlag, pp. 143–178.

Stiner, M. C., and S. L. Kuhn. 2009. "Paleolithic diet and the division of labor in Mediterranean Eurasia," in *The evolution of hominin diets: Integrating approaches to the study of Palaeolithic subsistence*. Edited by J.-J. Hublin and M. P. Richards. Springer, pp. 157–169.

Stiner, M. C., S. L. Kuhn, S. Weiner, and O. Bar-Yosef. 1995. Differential burning, recrystallization, and fragmentation of archaeological bone. *Journal of Archaeological Science* 22:223–237.

Stiner, M. C., and N. D. Munro. 2002. Approaches to prehistoric diet breadth, demography, and prey ranking systems in time and space. *Journal of Archaeological Method and Theory* 9:181–214.

Stiner, M. C., N. D. Munro, and T. A. Surovell. 2000. The tortoise and the hare: Small-game use, the broad-spectrum revolution and Paleolithic demography. *Current Anthropology* 41:39–73.

Stiner, M. C., N. D. Munro, T. A. Surovell, E. Tchernov, and O. Bar-Yosef. 1999. Paleolithic population growth pulses evidenced by small animal exploitation. *Science* 283:190–194.

Stiner, M. C., C. Pehlevan, M. Sagir, and I. Özer. 2002. Zooarchaeological studies at Üçağızlı Cave: Preliminary results on Paleolithic subsistence and shell ornaments. *Arasterma Sonuçlari Toplantisi, Ankara* 17:26–36.

Straus, L. G. 1982. Carnivores and cave sites in Cantabrian Spain. *Journal of Anthropological Research* 38:75–96.

———. 1997. "The Iberian situation between 40,000 and 30,000 B.P. in light of European models of migration and convergence," in *Conceptual issues in modern human origins research*. Edited by G. A. Clark and C. Willermet. New York: Aldine de Gruyter, pp. 235–252.

Stringer, C. B. 1974. Population relationship of the later Pleistocene hominids: A multivariate study of available crania. *Journal of Archaeological Science* 1:317–342.

———. 2003. Out of Ethiopia. *Nature* 423:692–694.

Stringer, C. B., and P. Andrews. 1988. Genetic and fossil evidence for the origin of modern humans. *Science* 239:1263–1268.

Stringer, C. B., and C. Gamble. 1993. *In search of the Neanderthals*. London: Thames and Hudson.

Struever, S. 1968. Flotation techniques for the recovery of small-scale archaeological remains. *American Antiquity* 33:353–362.

Stuiver, M., and P. M. Grootes. 2000. GISP2 oxygen isotope ratios. *Quaternary Research* 53:277–284.

Stutz, A. J. 2002. Polarizing microscopy identification of chemical diagenesis in archaeological cementum. *Journal of Archaeological Science* 29:1327–1347.

Stutz, A. J., N. D. Munro, and G. Bar-Oz. 2009. Increasing the resolution of the Broad Spectrum Revolution in the southern Levantine Epipaleolithic (19–12 ka). *Journal of Human Evolution* 56:294–306.

Syroechkovskii, E. E. 1995. *Wild Reindeer*. Washington, DC: Smithsonian Institution Libraries.

Taborin, Y. 1990. "Les prémices de la parure," in *Paléolithique moyen récent et Paléolithique supérieur ancien en Europe*. Edited by C. Farizy. Nemours: Mémoire du Musée de Préhistoire d'Ile de France 3, pp. 335–344.

Tagliacozzo, A., and M. Gala. 2005a. "L'avifauna dei livelli 24–22 (Aurignaziano e Gravettiano antico) di Grotta Paglicci: L'aspetto ambientale e quello economico," in *Paglicci. L'Aurignaziano e il Gravettiano antico*. Edited by A. Palma di Cesnola. Foggia: Grenzi, pp. 71–90.

———. 2005b. "Lo sfruttamento dell'avifauna nei livelli 24–22 (Aurignaziano e Gravettiano antico) di Grotta Paglicci (Rignano Garganico, Foggia)," in *Atti del 3° Convegno Nazionale di Archeozoologia*. Edited by I. Fiore, G. Malerba, and S. Chilardi. Roma: Istituto Poligrafico e Zecca dello Stato, pp. 191–204.

Tambling, C. J., and J. T. Du Toit. 2005. Modelling wildebeest population dynamics: Implications of predation and harvesting in a closed system. *Journal of Applied Ecology* 42:431–441.

Tappen, M. 1994. Bone weathering in the tropical rain forest. *Journal of Archaeological Science* 21:667–673.

Tchernov, E. 1998. "The faunal sequence of the southwest Asian Middle Paleolithic in relation to hominid dispersal events," in *Neandertals and Modern Humans in Western Asia*. Edited by T. Akazawa, K. Aoki, and O. Bar-Yosef. New York: Plenum Press, pp. 77–90.

Telfer, E. S., and J. P. Kelsall. 1984. Adaptation of some large North American mammals for survival in snow. *Ecology* 65:1828–1834.

Templeton, A. R. 2002. Out of Africa again and again. *Nature* 416:45–51.

Teplitsky, C., J. A. Mills, J. S. Alho, J. W. Yarrall, and J. Merila. 2008. Bergmann's rule and climate change revisited: Disentangling environmental and genetic responses in a wild bird population. *Proceedings of the National Academy of Sciences* 105:13492–13496.

Teyssandier, N., F. Bon, and J.-G. Bordes. 2010. Within projectile range. Some thoughts on the appearance of the Aurignacian in Europe. *Journal of Anthropological Research* 66:209–229.

Théry-Parisot, I. 2002. Fuel management (bone and wood) during the lower Aurignacian in the Pataud rock shelter (Lower Paleolithic, Les Eyzies de Tayac, Dordogne, France). Contribution of experimentation. *Journal of Archaeological Science* 29:1415–1421.

Théry-Parisot, I., and S. Costamagno. 2005. Propriétés combustibles des ossements. Données expérimentales et réflexions archéologiques sur leur emploi dans les sites paléolithiques. *Gallia Préhistoire* 47:235–254.

Thiébault, C. 2005. Le Moustérien à denticulés: Variabilité ou diversité techno-économique? Unpublished Ph.D. dissertation, Université d'Aix-en-Provence I.

Thomas, D. H. 1969. Great Basin hunting patterns: A quantitative method for treating faunal remains. *American Antiquity* 34:392–401.

———. 1971. On distinguishing natural from cultural bone in archaeological sites. *American Antiquity* 36:366–371.

———. 2008. *Native American landscapes of St. Catherines Island, Georgia.* Anthropological Papers of the American Museum of Natural History 88. New York: American Museum of Natural History.

Thorne, A. 1981. "The centre and the edge: The significance of Australia to African paleoanthropology," in *Proceedings of the 8th Panafrican Congress of Prehistory and Quaternary Studies.* Edited by R. E. Leakey and B. A. Ogot. Nairobi: Tillmiap, pp. 180–181.

Thorne, A., and M. H. Wolpoff. 1981. Regional continuity in Australasian Pleistocene hominid evolution. *American Journal of Physical Anthropology* 55:337–349.

Timmermann, A., S.-I. An, U. Krebs, and H. Goosse. 2005. ENSO suppression due to weakening of the North Atlantic thermohaline circulation. *Journal of Climate* 18:3122–3139.

Tishkoff, S. A., E. Dietzsch, W. Speed, A. J. Pakstis, J. R. Kidd, K. Cheung, B. Bonné-Tamir, A. S. Santachiara-Benerecetti, P. Moral, M. Krings, S. Pääbo, E. Watson, N. Ritsch, T. Jenkins, and K. K. Kidd. 1996. Global patterning of linkage disequilibrium at the CD4 locus of modern human origins. *Science* 271:1380–1387.

Tishkoff, S. A., and M. K. Gonder. 2007. "Human origins within and out of Africa," in *Anthropological genetics: Theory, methods and applications.* Edited by M. H. Crawford. Cambridge: Cambridge University Press, pp. 337–379.

Todd, L. C., and D. J. Rapson. 1988. Long bone fragmentation and interpretation of faunal assemblages: Approaches to comparative analysis. *Journal of Archaeological Science* 15:307–325.

Tomek, T., and Z. M. Bocheński. 2002. Bird scraps from a Greek table: The case of Klisoura Cave. *Acta Zoologica Cracoviensa* 45:133–138.

Trigger, B. G. 1989. *A history of archaeological thought.* Cambridge: Cambridge University Press.

Trinkaus, E. 2005. Early modern humans. *Annual Review of Anthropology* 34:207–230.

———. 2007. European early modern humans and the fate of the Neandertals. *Proceedings of the National Academy of Sciences* 104:7367–7372.

Trinkaus, E., O. Moldovan, S. Milota, A. Bilgar, L. Sarcina, S. Athreya, S. E. Bailey, R. Rodrigo, G. Mircea, T. Higham, C. B. Ramsey, and J. van der Plicht. 2003. An early modern human from the Pestera cu Oase, Romania. *Proceedings of the National Academy of Sciences* 100:11231–11236.

Trinkaus, E., C. Ruff, S. E. Churchill, and B. Vandermeersch. 1998. Locomotion and body proportions of the Saint-Césaire 1 Châtelperronian Neandertal. *Proceedings of the National Academy of Sciences* 95:5836–5840.

Trinkaus, E., and P. Shipman. 1993. *The Neandertal: Changing the image of mankind.* New York: Alfred A. Knopf.

Trinkaus, E., A. Soficaru, A. Dobos, S. Constantin, J. Zilhão, and M. Richards. 2009. Stable isotope evidence for early modern human diet in southeastern Europe: Pestera cu Oase, Pestera Muierii and Pestera Cioclovina Uscata. *Materiale si Cercetari Arheologice* 5:5–14.

Tsanova, T., and J.-G. Bordes. 2003. "Contribution au débat sur l'origine de l'Aurignacien: Principaux résultats d'une étude technologique de l'industrie lithique de la couche 11 de Bacho Kiro," in *The humanized mineral world: Towards social and symbolic evaluation of prehistoric technologies in South Eastern Europe*, vol. 103. Edited by T. Tsonev and E. Montagnari Kokelej. Liège: ERAUL, pp. 41–50.

Turner, A. 1989. Sample selection, schlepp effects and scavenging: The implications of partial recovery for interpretations of the terrestrial mammal assemblage from Klasies River Mouth. *Journal of Archaeological Science* 16:1–11.

———. 2009. The evolution of the guild of large Carnivora of the British Isles during the Middle and Late Pleistocene. *Journal of Quaternary Science* 24:991–1005.

Turner, J. C. 1979. Adaptive strategies of selective fatty acid deposition in the bone marrow of desert bighorn sheep. *Comparative Biochemistry and Physiology Part A: Physiology* 62:599–604.

Turq, A. 2000. *Le Paléolithique inférieur et moyen entre Dordogne et Lot.* Paléo supplément 2.

Turq, A., H. Dibble, J.-P. Faivre, P. Goldberg, S. J. P. McPherron, and D. Sandgathe. 2008. "Le Moustérien du Périgord Noir: Quoi de neuf?" in *Les sociétés du Paléolithique dans un grand Sud-Ouest de la France: Nouveaux gisements, nouveaux résultats, nouvelles méthodes, Mémoire XLVII de la Société Préhistorique Française.* Edited by J. Jaubert, J.-G. Bordes, and I. Ortega. Paris: Société Préhistorique Française, pp. 83–93.

Tzedakis, P. C., K. A. Hughen, I. Cacho, and K. Harvati. 2007. Placing late Neanderthals in a climatic context. *Nature* 449:206–208.

Ugan, A. 2005. Does size matter? Body size, mass collection, and their implications for understanding prehistoric foraging behaviour. *American Antiquity* 70:75–89.

Ugan, A., and J. Bright. 2001. Measuring foraging efficiency with archaeological faunas: The relationship between relative abundance and foraging returns. *Journal of Archaeological Science* 28:1309–1321.

Underhill, P. A., P. Shen, A. Lin, L. Jin, G. Passarino, W. H. Yang, E. Kauffman, B. Bonné-Tamir, J. Bertranpetit, P. Francalacci, M. Ibrahim, T. Jenkins, J. R. Kidd, S. Q. Mehdi, M. T. Seielstad, R. Spencer Wells, A. Piazza, R. W. Davis, M. W. Feldman, L. L. Cavalli-Sforza, and P. J. Oefner. 2000. Y chromosome sequence variation and the history of human populations. *Nature Genetics* 26:358–361.

Valkenburg, P., R. A. Sellers, R. C. Squibb, J. D. Woolington, A. R. Aderman, and B. W. Dale. 2003. Population dynamics of caribou herds in southwestern Alaska. *Rangifer* Special Issue 14:131–142.

Valladas, H., J. L. Reyss, J. L. Joron, G. Valladas, O. Bar-Yosef, and B. Vandermeersch. 1988. Thermoluminescence dates for the Mousterian Proto-Cro-Magnons from Qafzeh cave (Israel). *Nature* 331:614–616.

Vallois, H. 1949. The Fontéchevade fossil men. *American Journal of Physical Anthropology* 7:339–362.

Vandermeersch, B. 1984. À propos de la découverte du squelette néandertalien de Saint-Césaire. *Bulletins et Mémoires de la Société d'Anthropologie de Paris* 14:191–196.

———. 1993. "Appendix. Was the Saint-Césaire discovery a burial?," in *Context of a late Neandertal: Implications of multidisciplinary research for the transition to Upper Paleolithic adaptations at Saint-Césaire.* Monographs in World Archaeology 16. Edited by F. Lévêque, A. M. Backer, and M. Guilbaud. Madison: Prehistory Press, pp. 129–131.

Vandermeersch, B., and A. E. Mann. 2001. The dentition of Saint-Césaire I, a partial skeleton from the Châtelperronian levels of la Roche à Pierrot (Charente-Maritime). *American Journal of Physical Anthropology* 32:154–155.

Vanhaeren, M., and F. d'Errico. 2006. Aurignacian ethno-linguistic geography of Europe revealed by personal ornaments. *Journal of Archaeological Science* 33:1105–1128.

Vehik, S. C. 1977. Bone fragments and bone grease manufacturing: A review of their archaeological use and potential. *Plains Anthropologist* 22:169–182.

Vercoutère, C. 2004. Utilisation de l'animal comme ressource de matières premières non-alimentaires: Industrie osseuse et parure. Exemple de l'Abri Pataud (Dordogne, France). Unpublished Ph.D. dissertation, Muséum National d'Histoire Naturelle Paris, France.

Veres, D., E. Lallier-Vergès, B. Wohlfarth, T. Lacourse, D. Kéravis, S. Björck, F. Preusser, V. Andrieu-Ponel, and L. Ampel. 2008. Climate-driven changes in lake conditions during late MIS 3 and MIS 2: A high resolution geochemical record from Les Echets, France. *Boreas* 38:230–243.

Verneau, R. 1913. "L'anthropologie des Grottes de Grimaldi." *XIIIème Congrès d'Anthropologie et d'Archéologie Préhistoriques*, 1913, pp. 114–134.

Vilette, P. 1999. "Bilan provisoire sur la chasse aux oiseaux pendant le leptolithique dans le sud de la France," in *Les faciès leptolithiques du nord-ouest méditerranéen: Milieux naturels et culturels.* Edited by D. Sacchi. Paris: Société Préhistorique Française, pp. 267–276.

Villa, P., F. Bon, and J.-C. Castel. 2002. Fuel, fire and fireplaces in the Palaeolithic of Western Europe. *The Review of Archaeology* 23:33–42.

Villa, P., J.-C. Castel, C. Beauval, V. Bourdillat, and P. Goldberg. 2004. Human and carnivore sites in the European Middle and Upper Palaeolithic: Similarities and differences in bone modification and fragmentation. *Revue de Paléobiologie* 23:705–730.

Villa, P., and E. Mahieu. 1991. Breakage patterns of human long bones. *Journal of Human Evolution* 21:27–48.

Villaverde, V., J. E. Aura, and C. M. Barton. 1998. The Upper Paleolithic in Mediterranean Spain: A review of current evidence. *Journal of World Prehistory* 12:121–198.

Villaverde, V., and R. Martínez Valle. 1992. "Economía y aprovechamiento del medio en el Paleolítico de la región central del mediterráneo español," in *Elefantes, ciervos y ovicaprinos: Economía y aprovechamiento del medio en la Prehistoria de España y Portugal.* Edited by J. A. Moure Romanillo. Santander: Universidad de Cantabria, pp. 77–95.

Villaverde, V., R. Martínez Valle, P. Guillem, and M. P. Fumanal. 1996. "Mobility and the role of small game in the Middle Paleolithic of the Central Region of the Spanish Mediterranean: A comparison of Cova Negra with other Paleolithic deposits," in *The Last Neandertals, the First Anatomically Modern Humans. Cultural Change and Human Evolution: The Crisis at 40 ka BP.* Edited by E. Carbonell and M. Vaquero. Barcelona: Igualada, pp. 267–288.

Voelker, A. H. L. 2002. Global distribution of centennial-scale records for Marine Isotope Stage (MIS) 3: A database. *Quaternary Science Reviews* 21:1185–1212.

Wall, J. D. 2000. Detecting ancient admixture in humans using sequence polymorphism data. *Genetics* 154:1271–1279.

Wall, J. D., M. P. Cox, F. L. Mendez, A. Woerner, T. Severson, and M. F. Hammer. 2008. A novel DNA sequence database for analyzing human demographic history. *Genome Research* 18:1354–1361.

Wall, J. D., and S. K. Kim. 2007. Inconsistencies in Neanderthal genomic DNA sequences. *PLoS Genetics* 3:1862–1866.

Washburn, S. L. 1951. The new physical anthropology. *Transactions of the New York Academy of Sciences, Series II* 13:298–304.

Wasilewski, W. 1967. Differences in the wear of incisors in the European bison living under natural and reserve conditions. *Acta Theriologica* 12:459–479.

Weaver, T. D., and C. C. Roseman. 2008. New developments in the genetic evidence for modern human origins. *Evolutionary Anthropology* 17:80.

Weidenreich, F. 1947. Facts and speculations concerning the origin of *Homo sapiens*. *American Anthropologist* 49:187–203.

Weinstock, J. 2000. Osteometry as a source of refined demographic information: Sex-ratios of reindeer, hunting strategies, and herd control in the Late Glacial site of Stellmoor, northern Germany. *Journal of Archaeological Science* 27:1187–1195.

Wetterer, J. K. 1989. Central place foraging theory: When load size affects travel time. *Theoretical Population Biology* 36:267–280.

Whallon, R. 1989. "Elements of cultural change in the later Paleolithic," in *The human revolution. Behavioural and biological perspectives on the origins of modern humans*. Edited by P. Mellars and C. Stringer. Princeton: Princeton University Press, pp. 433–454.

———. 2006. Social networks and information: Non-"utilitarian" mobility among hunter-gatherers. *Journal of Anthropological Archaeology* 25:259–270.

White, R. 1982. Rethinking the Middle/Upper Paleolithic transition. *Current Anthropology* 23:169–192.

White, T. D., B. Asfaw, D. DeGusta, H. Gilbert, G. D. Richards, G. Suwa, and F. C. Howell. 2003. Pleistocene *Homo sapiens* from Middle Awash, Ethiopia. *Nature* 423:742–747.

Whittaker, W. E., and J. G. Enloe. 2000. Bison dentition studies revisited: Resolving ambiguity between archaeological and modern control samples. *Archaeozoologia* 11:113–120.

Whitten, K. R. 1995. Antler loss and udder distention in relation to parturition in caribou. *Journal of Wildlife Management* 59:273–277.

Wild, E. M., M. Teschler-Nicola, W. Kutschera, P. Steier, E. Trinkaus, and W. Wanek. 2005. Direct dating of early Upper Palaeolithic human remains from Mladec. *Nature* 435:332–335.

Wilson, D. E., and D. A. Reeder, editors. 2005. *Mammal species of the world: A taxonomic and geographic reference*, 3rd edition. Baltimore: Johns Hopkins University Press.

Winterhalder, B. 1981. "Foraging strategies in the boreal forest: An analysis of Cree hunting and gathering," in *Hunter-gatherer foraging strategies: Ethnographic and archaeological analyses*. Edited by B. Winterhalder and E. A. Smith. Chicago: University of Chicago Press, pp. 66–95.

Winterhalder, B., and D. J. Kennett. Editors. 2006. *Behavioral ecology and the transition to agriculture*. Berkeley: University of California Press.

Winterhalder, B., and E. A. Smith. 2000. Analyzing adaptive strategies: Human behavioural ecology at twenty-five. *Evolutionary Anthropology* 9:51–72.

Wolpoff, M. H. 1999. *Paleoanthropology*. Boston: McGraw-Hill.

Wolpoff, M. H., X. Wu, and A. G. Thorne. 1984. "Modern *Homo sapiens* origins: A general theory of hominid evolution involving the fossil evidence from East Asia," in *The origins of modern humans: A world survey of the fossil evidence*. Edited by F. H. Smith and F. Spencer. New York: Alan R. Liss, pp. 411–483.

Wolverton, S. 2008. Harvest pressure and environmental carrying capacity: An ordinal-scale model of effects on ungulate prey. *American Antiquity* 73:179–199.

Woodward, J. C., and P. Goldberg. 2001. The sedimentary records in Mediterranean rockshelters and caves: Archives of environmental change. *Geoarchaeology* 16:327–354.

Xing, J., W. S. Watkins, A. Shlien, E. Walker, C. D. Huff, D. J. Witherspoon, Y. Zhang, T. S. Simonson, R. B. Weiss, J. D. Schiffman, D. Malkin, S. R. Woodward, and L. B. Jorde. 2010. Toward a more uniform sampling of human genetic diversity: A survey of worldwide populations by high-density genotyping. *Genomics* 96:199–210.

Ydenberg, R. C. 2007. "Provisioning," in *Foraging: Behavior and ecology*. Edited by D. W. Stephens, J. S. Brown, and R. C. Ydenberg. Chicago: University of Chicago Press, pp. 273–303.

Ydenberg, R. C., J. S. Brown, and D. W. Stephens. 2007. "Foraging: An overview," in *Foraging: Behavior and ecology*. Edited by D. W. Stephens, J. S. Brown, and R. C. Ydenberg. Chicago: University of Chicago Press, pp. 1–28.

Yeshurun, R., G. Bar-Oz, and M. Weinstein-Evron. 2009. The role of foxes in the Natufian economy: A view from Mount Carmel, Israel. *Before Farming* 2009/1, article 3:1–15.

Yu, N., F. C. Chen, S. Ota, L. B. Jorde, P. Pamilo, L. Patthy, M. Ramsay, T. Jenkins, S. K. Shyue, and W. H. Li. 2002a. Larger genetic differences within Africans than between Africans and Eurasians. *Genetics* 161:269–274.

Yu, N., Y.-X. Fu, and W.-H. Li. 2002b. DNA polymorphism in a worldwide sample of human X chromosomes. *Molecular Biology and Evolution* 19:2131–2141.

Zeanah, D. W. 2004. Sexual division of labor and central place foraging: A model for the Carson Desert of western Nevada. *Journal of Anthropological Archaeology* 23:1–32.

Zeleznik, W., and I. Bennett. 1991. Assumption validity in human optimal foraging: The Barí hunters of Venezuela as a test case. *Human Ecology* 19:499–508.

Zierhut, N. W. 1967. Bone breaking activities of the Calling Lake Cree. *Alberta Anthropologist* 1:33–36.

Zietkiewicz, E., V. Yotova, D. Gehl, T. Wambach, I. Arrieta, M. Batzer, D. E. C. Cole, P. Hechtmann, F. Kaplan, D. Modiano, J. P. Moisan, R. Michalski, and D. Labuda. 2003. Haplotypes in the dystrophin DNA segment point to a mosaic origin of modern human diversity. *American Journal of Human Genetics* 73:994–1015.

Zilhão, J. 2006. Chronostratigraphy of the Middle-to-Upper Paleolithic transition in the Iberian Peninsula. *Pyrenae* 37:7–84.

———. 2007. The emergence of ornaments and art: An archaeological perspective on the origins of "behavioral modernity." *Journal of Archaeological Research* 15:1–54.

Zilhão, J., D. E. Angelucci, E. Badal-García, F. d'Errico, F. Daniel, L. Dayet, K. Douka, T. F. G. Higham, M. J. Martínez-Sánchez, R. Montes-Bernárdez, S. Murcia-Mascarós, C. Pérez-Sirvent, C. Roldán-García, M. Vanhaeren, V. Villaverde, R. Wood, and J. Zapata. 2010. Symbolic use of marine shells and mineral pigments by Iberian Neandertals. *Proceedings of the National Academy of Sciences* 107:1023–1028.

Zilhão, J., T. Aubry, and F. Almeida. 1999. "Un modèle technologique pour le passage du Gravettien au Solutréen dans le sud-ouest de l'Europe," in *Les faciès leptolithiques du nord-ouest méditerranéen:*

Milieux naturels et culturels. Edited by D. Sacchi. Paris: Société Préhistorique Française pp. 165–183.

Zilhão, J., and F. d'Errico. 1999. The chronology and taphonomy of the earliest Aurignacian and its implications for the understanding of Neandertal extinction. *Journal of World Prehistory* 13:1–68.

Zilhão, J., and F. d'Errico. 2003. "The chronology of the Aurignacian and transitional technocomplexes. Where do we stand?" in *The chronology of the Aurignacian and of the transitional complexes: Dating, stratigraphies, cultural implications.* Edited by J. Zilhao and F. d'Errico. Lisbon: Trabalhos de Arqueologia 33, pp. 313–349.

Zilhão, J., F. d'Errico, J.-G. Bordes, A. Lenoble, J.-P. Texier, and J.-P. Rigaud. 2007. La grotte des fées (Châtelperron, Allier) ou une interstratification "Châtelperronien-Aurignacien" illusoire. Histoire des fouilles, stratigraphie et datations. *Paléo* 19:391–432.

Zollikofer, C. P. E., M. S. Ponce de León, B. Vandermeersch, and F. Lévêque. 2002. Evidence for interpersonal violence in the St. Césaire Neanderthal. *Proceedings of the National Academy of Sciences* 99:6444–6448.

INDEX

www.ingramcontent.com/pod-product-compliance
Ingram Content Group UK Ltd.
Pitfield, Milton Keynes, MK11 3LW, UK
UKHW050416190625
45964\7UK0003\B/2809

For EU product safety concerns, contact us at Calle de José Abascal, 56–1º,
28003 Madrid, Spain or eugpsr@cambridge.org.